World's Largest Countries By Population

Rank	Country	Millions
1	China	1 330
2	India	1 173
3	United States	310
4	Indonesia	243
5	Brazil	201
6	Pakistan	184
7	Bangladesh	156
8	Nigeria	152
9	Russia	139
10	Japan	127

Source: CIA—World Factbook 2011.

World's Most Expensive Cities

Rank	City	Country
1	Tokyo	Japan
2	Osaka Kobe	Japan
3	Paris	France
4	Copenhagen	Denmark
5	Oslo	Norway
6	Zurich	Switzerland
7	Frankfurt	Germany
8	Helsinki	Finland
9	Geneva	Switzerland
10	Singapore	Singapore

Source: The Economist January 2011

World's Highest Unemployment Rates

Rank	Country	Unemployment Rate (%)
1	Zimbabwe	95
2	Nauru	90
3	Liberia	85
4	Burkina Faso	77
5	Turkmenistan	60
6	Cocos (Keeling) Islands	60
7	Djibouti	59
8	Namibia	51
9	Zambia	50
10	Senegal	48

Source: CIA—World Factbook 2011.

 ## STUDENTS...

Want to get **better grades**? *(Who doesn't?)*

Prefer to do your **homework online**? *(After all, you're online anyway...)*

Need **a better way** to **study** before the big test? *(A little peace of mind is a good thing...)*

With **McGraw-Hill's** *Connect,*™

STUDENTS GET:

- **Easy online access** to homework, tests, and quizzes assigned by your instructor.

- **Immediate feedback** on how you're doing. (No more wishing you could call your instructor at 1 a.m.)

- **Quick access** to lectures, practice materials, eBook, and more. (All the material you need to be successful is right at your fingertips.)

- A Self-Quiz and Study tool that **assesses your knowledge** and **recommends** specific readings, supplemental study materials, and additional practice work.

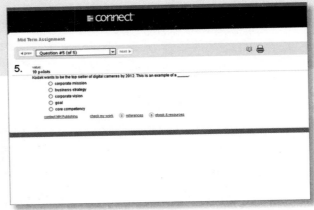

Less managing. More teaching. Greater learning.

 INSTRUCTORS...

Would you like your **students** to show up for class **more prepared**?
(Let's face it, class is much more fun if everyone is engaged and prepared...)

Want an **easy way to assign** homework online and track student **progress**?
(Less time grading means more time teaching...)

Want an **instant view** of student or class performance?
(No more wondering if students understand...)

Need to **collect data and generate reports** required for administration or accreditation?
(Say goodbye to manually tracking student learning outcomes...)

Want to **record and post your lectures** for students to view online?
(The more students can see, hear, and experience class resources, the better they learn...)

 With **McGraw-Hill's *Connect*,™**

INSTRUCTORS GET:

- Simple **assignment management**, allowing you to spend more time teaching.
- **Auto-graded** assignments, quizzes, and tests.
- **Detailed visual reporting** where student and section results can be viewed and analyzed.
- Sophisticated **online testing** capability.
- A **filtering and reporting** function that allows you to easily assign and report on materials that are correlated to learning objectives and Bloom's taxonomy.
- An easy-to-use **lecture capture** tool.
- The option to **upload course documents** for student access.

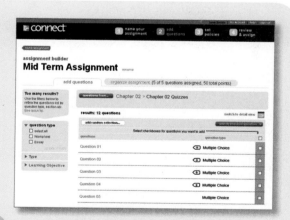

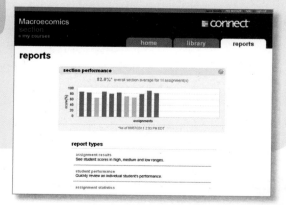

SEVENTH EDITION

PRINCIPLES OF
MACROECONOMICS

JOHN E. SAYRE

ALAN J. MORRIS
Capilano University

McGraw-Hill
Ryerson
Connect. Learn. Succeed.

The McGraw·Hill Companies

McGraw-Hill Ryerson
Connect. Learn. Succeed.

PRINCIPLES OF MACROECONOMICS
Seventh Edition

Copyright © 2012, 2009, 2006, 2004, 2001, 1999, 1996 by McGraw-Hill Ryerson Limited, a Subsidiary of The McGraw-Hill Companies. All rights reserved. No part of this publication may be reproduced or transmitted in any form or by any means, or stored in a data base or retrieval system, without the prior written permission of McGraw-Hill Ryerson Limited, or in the case of photocopying or other reprographic copying, a licence from The Canadian Copyright Licensing Agency (Access Copyright). For an Access Copyright licence, visit www.accesscopyright.ca or call toll free to 1-800-893-5777.

Statistics Canada information is used with the permission of Statistics Canada. Users are forbidden to copy this material and/or redisseminate the data, in an original or modified form, for commercial purposes, without the expressed permission of Statistics Canada. Information on the availability of the wide range of data from Statistics Canada can be obtained from Statistics Canada's Regional Offices, its World Wide Web site at http://www.statcan.ca and its toll-free access number 1-800-263-1136.

ISBN 13: 978-0-07-040098-6
ISBN 10: 0-07-040098-9

1 2 3 4 5 6 7 8 9 10 QDB 1 9 8 7 6 5 4 3 2

Printed and bound in the United States of America.

Care has been taken to trace ownership of copyright material contained in this text; however, the publisher will welcome any information that enables them to rectify any reference or credit for subsequent editions.

SPONSORING EDITOR: James Booty
MARKETING MANAGER: Jeremy Guimond
SENIOR DEVELOPMENTAL EDITOR: Maria Chu
EDITORIAL ASSOCIATE: Erin Catto
FREELANCE PERMISSIONS EDITOR: Lynn McIntyre
SUPERVISING EDITORS: Joanne Limebeer, Katie McHale
COPY EDITOR: Judy Sturrup
PROOFREADER: Rohini Herbert
PRODUCTION COORDINATOR: Sheryl MacAdam
INTERIOR DESIGN: Sarah Orr/ArtPlus
COMPOSITION: Heather Brunton/ArtPlus Limited
COVER DESIGN: Sarah Orr/ArtPlus Limited
COVER PHOTO: © Maria Wachala | Dreamstime.com
PRINTER: Quad/Graphics Dubuque (U.S.)

Library and Archives Canada Cataloguing in Publication Data

Sayre, John E., 1942–
    Principles of macroeconomics / John E. Sayre, Alan J. Morris.—7th ed.

Includes index.
ISBN 978-0-07-040098-6

1. Macroeconomics—Textbooks. I. Morris, Alan J. (Alan James) II. Title.

HB172.5.S29 2012   339   C2011-906472-3

To Daria: may the

blessings be

(JES)

———————— A N D ————————

To the ones I love:

Brian Trevor and Jean

(AJM)

ABOUT THE AUTHORS

John E. Sayre earned a BSBA at the University of Denver and an MA from Boston University. He began teaching principles of economics while in the Peace Corps in Malawi. He came to Vancouver to do PhD studies at Simon Fraser University and ended up teaching at Capilano University for the next thirty-nine years. Now retired from Capilano, John is an avid golfer who also enjoys walking with his dog and listening to a wide range of music.

Alan Morris, though loath to admit it, first worked as an accountant in England, where he became an Associate of the Chartered Institute of Secretaries and obtained his first degree in 1971 in Manchester, U.K. He subsequently obtained his Master's degree at Simon Fraser University, B.C., in 1973. He worked on his doctorate at Leicester University, U.K., and returned to work in business in Vancouver, B.C., until his appointment at Capilano University in 1988. He currently lives in North Vancouver with his wife and one of his two sons, and is an avid devotee of classical music, birding, soccer, and beer. To his knowledge, he has never been an adviser to the Canadian government.

BRIEF CONTENTS

CONTENTS

To the Students

So, you may well ask, why take a course in economics? For many of you, the obvious answer to this question is: "Because it is a requirement for the program or educational goal that I have chosen." Fair enough. But there are other reasons. It is a simple truth that if you want to understand the world around you, then you have to understand some basic economics. Much of what goes on in the world today is driven by economic considerations, and those who know nothing of economics often simply cannot understand why things are the way they are. In this age of globalization, we are all citizens of the world and we need to function effectively in the midst of the enormous changes that are sweeping across almost every aspect of the social/political/economic landscape. You can either be part of this, and all the opportunities that come with it, or not be part of it because you cannot make any sense of it.

It is quite possible that you feel a little apprehensive because you have heard that economics is a difficult subject. Though there may be a grain of truth in this, we are convinced that almost any student can succeed in economics. But it will require some real work and effort on your part. Here are some tips on the general approach to this course that you might find helpful. First, read the **Economics Toolkit** that appears at the beginning of the book. The section titled "Canadian Reality" offers basic information on Canada and its economic picture. "Graphing Reality" gives a quick lesson on graphs, which are an essential part of economics. These two sections will give you a solid foundation on which to build your knowledge of economics.

Second, before each lecture, quickly look over the chapter that will be covered. In this preliminary survey, you do not need to worry about the glossary boxes, the self-test questions, or the integrated Study Guide. Third, take notes as much as you can during the lecture because the process of forcing yourself to express ideas *in your own words* is a crucial stage in the learning process. Fourth, re-read the chapter, again taking notes and using your own words (do not just copy everything word for word from the text). While doing this, refer to your classroom notes and try to integrate them into your reading notes. After you finish this, you will be ready to take on the Study Guide. As painful as it may be for you to hear this, we want to say loud and clear that you should do *all* of the answered questions and problems in the Study Guide. You may be slow at first, but you will be surprised at how much faster you become in later chapters. This is a natural aspect of the learning process. It might be helpful for you to get together with one or two other students and form a study group that meets once or twice a week to do economics Study Guide questions. You will be amazed at how explaining an answer to a fellow student is one of the most effective learning techniques. If you ever come across a question that you simply cannot understand, this is a sure sign that you need to approach your instructor (or teaching assistant) for help. Do not get discouraged when this happens, and realize that it will probably happen more at the beginning of your process of learning economics than later on in the term. We are convinced that if you follow this process consistently, beginning in the very first week of class, you will succeed in the course—and not only succeed, but most likely do well. All it takes is effort, good time management, and consistent organization.

Finally, an enormous part of becoming educated involves gaining self-confidence and a sense of accomplishment. Getting an A in a "tough" economics course can be a great step in this direction. We wish you all the best.

To the Instructors

GENERAL PHILOSOPHY

Over the years, we have become increasingly convinced that most economics textbooks are written to impress other economists rather than to enlighten beginning students. Such books tend to be encyclopedic in scope and intimidating in appearance. Small wonder, then, that students often emerge from an economics course feeling that the discipline really is daunting and unapproachable. We agree that the study of economics is challenging, but our experience is that students can also see it as intriguing and enjoyable if the right approach is taken. It is our belief that this right approach starts with a really good textbook that is concise without sacrificing either clarity or accepted standards of rigour.

In writing this text, we attempted to stay focused on four guiding principles. The first is to achieve a well-written text. We have tried to write as clearly as possible, to avoid unnecessary jargon, to speak directly to the student, and to avoid unnecessary abstraction and repetition.

Of equal importance, our second principle is a focused emphasis on student learning. Many years of teaching the principles courses have convinced us that students *learn* economics by *doing* economics. To this end, self-test questions are positioned throughout each chapter. This encourages students to apply what they have just read and gives them continuous feedback on their comprehension of the material being presented. Further, we feel that we offer the most comprehensive and carefully crafted Study Guide on the market, which has evolved over the years as a result of continued use in our own classes. In addition, each chapter's Study Guide contains a Chapter Summary as well as Study Tips for the students.

Our third principle has been to avoid an encyclopedic text. It seems that in an effort to please everyone, textbook authors sometimes include bits and pieces of almost everything. The result is that students are often overwhelmed and find it difficult to sort out the more important material from what is less important.

The fourth principle is to avoid problems of discontinuity that can occur when different groups of authors do separate parts of a total package. To this end, we are the sole authors of the text, the instructor's manual, and the integrated Study Guide. We also carefully supervise the development of the test bank. We have tried to ensure that as much care and attention goes into the ancillary materials as goes into the writing of the text.

Few things are more satisfying than witnessing a student's zest for learning. We hope that this textbook adds a little to this process.

SEVENTH EDITION CHANGES

We have made major organizational revisions in this edition. First, we have moved the discussion of fiscal policy forward to Chapter 7 so that this application-type discussion now directly follows the presentation of the AD/AS model for the economy in Chapter 5 and (for those who use it) the Chapter 6 discussion of aggregate expenditure.

Second, we have moved the presentation of monetary policy forward to Chapter 9 (following the Chapter 8 discussion of money). These two moves enables instructors to open the discussion of real-life policy earlier in their courses.

Chapters 10 and 11 introduce and discuss the international market and thereby set up Chapter 12, Macro Policy Revisited, in which both fiscal and monetary policy are reviewed in context of the open economy.

Chapter 13 includes a section on the fascinating question of what caused the financial meltdown in 2007–2010 and why Canada suffered far less from the ensuing recession than did the United States and most other countries.

Also, note that the Unanswered Questions in each chapter's Study Guide have been removed and placed online in Connect as well as in the Instructor's Manual along with the answers to these questions.

The more specific changes to each particular chapter are largely a result of feedback provided by our many users and reviewers. The more important changes to the individual chapters are as follows:

- In **Chapter 1**, we eliminated the section on underlying values and replaced it with a new section titled "The Importance of Efficiency" in which the ideas of productive and allocative efficiency are explained. We brought forward the discussion of factors of production to the section on scarcity. Controversy Three on organ donations was replaced with one on road pricing and we sharpened the definition of positive and normative statements while placing emphasis on the difference between these two terms. We added a new section on shifts in the production possibilities curve and added new problems on deriving PP tables and graphing the results.

- In **Chapter 2**, we improved the economic conversation about demand and supply, and formally defined the terms "shortage" and "surplus." We re-wrote the AD box entitled "The Famous Scissors Analogy" and improved the graph in the next AD, "Sales Always Equal Purchases." We extended the discussion of both the benefits and costs of economic growth and then consolidated all material on growth in **Chapter 3** (it had been spread through Chapters 3, 4, and 5 previously). We removed discussion of loanable funds from the circular flow presentation. We simplified and reduced the discussion of measuring GDP and, following the trend set by the World Bank, added the concept of **GNI**.

- **Chapter 4** now has only two points of focus—unemployment and inflation—since all of the discussion of economic growth has been moved to Chapter 3. We added data on unemployment rates by gender and wrote a new section on how the consumer price index is derived using a simple example of a representative student's spending. We elaborated on the Rule of 70 discussion.

- New self-test and study questions on the calculation of potential GDP have been added in **Chapter 5**. We explain why we use the term "potential GDP" rather than "long-run aggregate supply."

- In **Chapter 6**, we introduce a new graphic to show exactly why an extra $100 of production in Canada led to an increase in spending of only $39 on Canadian goods and services. We algebraically clarified the difference between MPC and MPC_D. The section on the Keynesian Revolution was moved from this chapter to the next one. We added a Self Test question in support of Figure 6.1 and two new Study Guide questions on consumption and savings.

- **Chapter 7** on fiscal policy is, to a large extent, the Chapter 11 of the previous edition (with references to exchange rates and the crowding-out effect removed). We added two new AD boxes—one comparing long-term growth in government spending in Canada and the United States, and the other on Sylvia Ostry. We linked the use of fiscal policy to a discussion of the goals of an economy found in Chapter 1. We added a historical discussion of the Keynesian revolution in the 1930s as an introduction to the section on countercyclical fiscal policy. We added emphasis to the distinction between the effects of tax changes and government spending changes.

- In **Chapter 8**, we moved the section on the functions of the Bank of Canada forward from the previous edition's Chapter 12 on monetary policy.

- **Chapter 9** is now a combination of the former Chapter 8 (the money market) and most of Chapter 12 (monetary policy). We sharpened the distinction between the older theories (Keynesian and monetarists) that targeted the money supply, and the new anti-inflationary policy of the Bank of Canada that uses interest-rate targeting. We added a section on the transmission process in the context of contractionary monetary policy, and a graph to illustrate the Bank of Canada's targeting the interest rate. We elaborated on the use of the overnight lending rate and eliminated mention of SRAs and SPRAs.

- In **Chapter 10**, we updated the AD box on "Canada, the Great Trader." We also added a discussion about how low wages do not necessarily imply an advantage to the exporter, and material on the softwood lumber dispute.

- A table that clearly lays out why the Canadian dollar either appreciates or depreciates has been added to **Chapter 11**. We changed the presentation of all balance-of-payments tables to indicate whether it is the demand or supply of Canadian dollars that is affected.

- **Chapter 12** revisits fiscal and monetary policies in the context of an open economy. As a result, discussion of the crowding-out effect, and a new AD box on whether this effect was present in the recent financial crisis, are included. A new section entitled "Monetary Policy in an Open Economy" was added. We expand the discussion of how deflation can affect an economy. The material on the Phillips Curve and of supply side economies has been moved into this chapter from Chapter 13. A new section entitled "Exchange Rates Revisited" was added.

- In **Chapter 13**, we revised the section called "The Great Depression" to better highlight the work of Keynes. We tied the discussion on the stagflation of the 1970s to supply-side economics. Two new section were added: "The Financial Crisis of 2007–2010" and "From the Financial Crisis to Economic Recession."

LEARNING OBJECTIVES

At the end of this chapter, you should be able to...

LO1 understand the circular flow of national income.

LO2 explain the concept of equilibrium and why national income can rise and fall.

LO3 understand the components of GDP accounting and be aware of some of the problems in determining official statistics.

LO4 know how to measure economic growth and appreciate the benefits of economic growth.

LO5 understand the importance of productivity in encouraging growth and some of the problems of unchecked growth.

Textbook Features

As an initial review, and an ongoing resource, the book opens with the **Economics Toolkit**. The first section, "Canadian Reality," offers basic information on Canada and its economy. The second section, "Graphing Reality," provides the student with a primer on how to interpret and create tables and graphs. We have provided a number of features to help the student come to grips with the subject matter.

Learning Objectives, listed at the beginning of each chapter, form a learning framework throughout the text, with each learning objective repeated in the margin at the appropriate place in the main body of the chapter. Each chapter opens with a vignette that provides context and an overview.

Glossary terms indicate the first use of any term that is part of the language of economics. The term itself is in bold print and the definition is provided in the margin. The page number where the definition appears is supplied at the end of the chapter for quick and easy reference, and a complete glossary of terms appears at the end of the book.

Self-Test question boxes appear at important points throughout the main body of each chapter. They give students immediate feedback on how well they understand the more abstract concept(s) discussed. In doing this, we have tried to establish what we believe to be a minimum standard of comprehension that all students should strive to achieve. Students can check their own progress by comparing their answers with those in the Student Answer Key, which is available for download at Connect.

✓ SELF-TEST

1. If the economy is in disequilibrium because total income exceeds aggregate expenditure, what must be happening to inventories?

2. Does the term "consumption" refer to spending by households on domestically produced goods and services only? Does the term "investment" include the purchase of stocks and bonds?

Added Dimension boxes identify material that is either general information or supplementary material that we hope adds a little colour to the student's reading.

▶ ADDED DIMENSION   Adam Smith: The Father of Economics

Adam Smith (1723–90) is generally regarded as the founding father of economics. In his brilliant work, *The Wealth of Nations*, Smith posed so many interesting questions and provided such illuminating answers that later economists often felt that they were merely picking at the scraps he left behind. Smith was born and brought up in Scotland and educated at Glasgow and Oxford. He held the Chair of Moral Philosophy at Glasgow College for many years. He was a lifelong bachelor and had a kind but absent-minded disposition.

Smith was the first scholar to analyze the business of "getting and spending" in a detailed and systematic manner. In doing this, he gave useful social dignity to the professions of business and trading. Besides introducing the important idea of the *invisible hand*, which was his way of describing the coordinating mechanism of capitalism, he examined the division of labour, the role of government, the function of money, the advantages and disadvantages of free trade, what constitutes good and bad taxation, and a host of other ideas. For Smith, economic life was not merely a peripheral adventure for people but their central motivating force.

Highlighted Concepts are important ideas that are pulled out and presented in a separate box— signalling to students that this material is particularly relevant and crucial to their understanding.

An increase in price will lead to an *increase in the quantity supplied* and is illustrated as a movement up the supply curve.

A decrease in price will cause a *decrease in the quantity supplied* and is illustrated as a movement down the supply curve.

Simple, clear, and uncomplicated **visuals** are found throughout the text. These are supported by captions that thoroughly explain the concepts involved.

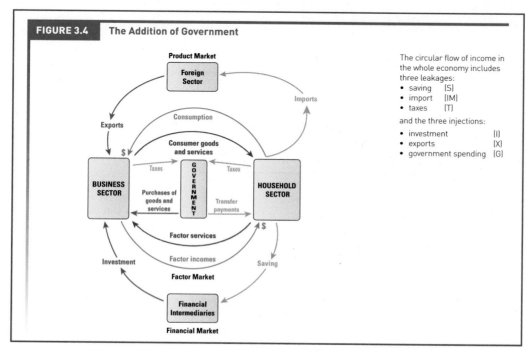

FIGURE 3.4   The Addition of Government

The circular flow of income in the whole economy includes three leakages:
- saving (S)
- import (IM)
- taxes (T)

and the three injections:
- investment (I)
- exports (X)
- government spending (G)

Integrated Study Guide Features

As expressed earlier, we believe that answering questions and doing problems should be an *active part of the students' learning process*. For this reason, we chose to integrate a complete Study Guide within the covers of this text. A **Study Guide** section, with pages screened in colour, immediately follows each chapter. We were careful to write the questions in the Study Guide to cover all the material, but only the material, found in the text itself. We have chosen a colourful, user-friendly design that we hope will encourage significant student participation.

The **Study Guide** has been reorganized into two main sections: a *Review* and a set of *Answered Questions and Problems*.

The Review section contains the *Chapter Summary*, *New Glossary Terms*, and *Key Equations*, as well as *Study Tips*, which are suggestions to help students manage the material in the chapter.

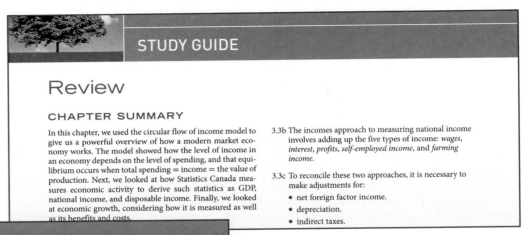

STUDY GUIDE

Review

CHAPTER SUMMARY

In this chapter, we used the circular flow of income model to give us a powerful overview of how a modern market economy works. The model showed how the level of income in an economy depends on the level of spending, and that equilibrium occurs when total spending = income = the value of production. Next, we looked at how Statistics Canada measures economic activity to derive such statistics as GDP, national income, and disposable income. Finally, we looked at economic growth, considering how it is measured as well as its benefits and costs.

3.3b The incomes approach to measuring national income involves adding up the five types of income: *wages, interest, profits, self-employed income,* and *farming income.*

3.3c To reconcile these two approaches, it is necessary to make adjustments for:
- net foreign factor income.
- depreciation.
- indirect taxes.

The **Answered Questions and Problems** sections include true/false and multiple-choice questions. The multiple-choice questions have been grouped into three learning levels: basic, intermediate, and advanced. In addition, there are a set of problems, each of which has a twin in the Unanswered Parallel Problems section available in Connect (with answers to instructors in the Instructors Manual).

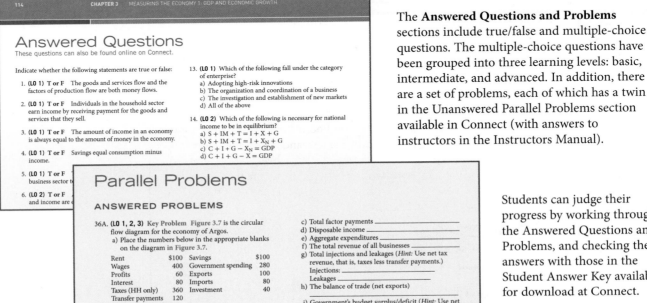

Answered Questions

These questions can also be found online on Connect.

Indicate whether the following statements are true or false:

1. **(LO 1) T or F**   The goods and services flow and the factors of production flow are both money flows.

2. **(LO 1) T or F**   Individuals in the household sector earn income by receiving payment for the goods and services that they sell.

3. **(LO 1) T or F**   The amount of income in an economy is always equal to the amount of money in the economy.

4. **(LO 1) T or F**   Savings equal consumption minus income.

5. **(LO 1) T or F**   business sector t

6. **(LO 2) T or F**   and income are

13. **(LO 1)** Which of the following fall under the category of enterprise?
a) Adopting high-risk innovations
b) The organization and coordination of a business
c) The investigation and establishment of new markets
d) All of the above

14. **(LO 2)** Which of the following is necessary for national income to be in equilibrium?
a) $S + IM + T = I + X + G$
b) $S + IM + T = I + X_N + G$
c) $C + I + G - X_N = GDP$
d) $C + I + G - X = GDP$

Parallel Problems

ANSWERED PROBLEMS

36A. **(LO 1, 2, 3)** Key Problem Figure 3.7 is the circular flow diagram for the economy of Argos.
a) Place the numbers below in the appropriate blanks on the diagram in Figure 3.7.

Rent	$100	Savings	$100
Wages	400	Government spending	280
Profits	60	Exports	100
Interest	80	Imports	80
Taxes (HH only)	360	Investment	40
Transfer payments	120		

What are the values of the following?
b) The costs of production _____

c) Total factor payments _____
d) Disposable income _____
e) Aggregate expenditures _____
f) The total revenue of all businesses _____
g) Total injections and leakages (*Hint:* Use net tax revenue, that is, taxes less transfer payments.)
Injections: _____
Leakages: _____
h) The balance of trade (net exports) _____

i) Government's budget surplus/deficit (*Hint:* Use net tax revenue.) _____

Students can judge their progress by working through the Answered Questions and Problems, and checking their answers with those in the Student Answer Key available for download at Connect.

Comprehensive Teaching and Learning Package

CONNECT

McGraw-Hill Connect™ is a web-based assignment and assessment platform that gives students the means to better connect with their coursework, with their instructors, and with the important concepts that they will need to know for success now and in the future.

With Connect, instructors can deliver assignments, quizzes, and tests online. Nearly all the questions from the text are presented in an auto-gradeable format and tied to the text's learning objectives. Instructors can edit existing questions and author entirely new problems. Track individual student performance—by question, assignment, or in relation to the class overall—with detailed grade reports. Integrate grade reports easily with Learning Management Systems (LMS) such as WebCT and Blackboard. And much more.

By choosing Connect, instructors are providing their students with a powerful tool for improving academic performance and truly mastering course material. Connect allows students to practice important skills at their own pace and on their own schedule. Importantly, students' assessment results and instructors' feedback are all saved online—so students can continually review their progress and plot their course to success.

Connect also provides 24/7 online access to an eBook—an online edition of the text—to aid them in successfully completing their work, wherever and whenever they choose.

CONNECT FOR STUDENTS

Connect provides students with a powerful tool for improving academic performance and truly mastering course material, plus 24/7 online access to an interactive and searchable eBook. Connect allows students to practice important skills at their own pace and on their own schedule. Importantly, students' assessment results and instructors' feedback are all saved online—so students can continually review their progress and plot their course to success. Answered Questions from the text Study Guide are also available in Connect for student self study.

INSTRUCTOR'S RESOURCES

INSTRUCTOR'S MANUAL

There are three parts to each chapter of the Instructor's Manual. First is a brief overview of the chapter, with some rationale for the topics included. Second is a description of how we think the material found in the chapter could be presented. Between them, this book's two authors have taught the introduction to macroeconomic principles over two hundred times, and we pass on helpful hints gained from this extensive experience to instructors who may not have been at it so long. More experienced instructors who have found a comfortable groove will simply ignore these suggestions.

The third part contains the answers to the Chapter Self-Test questions and all of the questions and problems in the Study Guide section of the text.

COMPUTERIZED TEST BANK

Prepared by Barbara Gardner of Southern Alberta Institute of Technology, much effort went into writing the Computerized Test Bank in order to ensure that the questions cover all topics in the textbook, but only those topics. The Computerized Test Bank is available through EZ Test Online, a flexible and easy-to-use electronic testing program that allows instructors to create tests from book-specific items. EZ Test accommodates a wide range of question types and allows instructors to add their own questions. Test items are also available in Word (Rich text format).

For secure online testing, exams created in EZ Test can be exported to WebCT and Blackboard. EZ Test Online is supported at **www.mhhe.com/eztest** where users can download a Quick Start Guide, access FAQs, or log a ticket for help with specific issues.

POWERPOINT® PRESENTATIONS

Prepared by Alanna Holowinsky of Red River College, this package includes dynamic slides of the important illustrations in the textbook, along with detailed, chapter-by-chapter reviews of the important ideas presented in the text.

lyryx

LYRYX ASSESSMENT FOR ECONOMICS [LAECON]

Based on *Principles of Macroeconomics* by Sayre and Morris, Lyryx Assessment for Economics is a leading-edge online assessment system, designed to support both students and instructors.

The assessment takes the form of a homework assignment called a *lab*. The assessments are algorithmically generated and automatically graded so that students get instant grades and feedback. New labs are randomly generated constantly, providing the student with unlimited opportunities to try a type of each question. After they submit a lab for marking, students receive extensive feedback on their work, thus promoting their learning experience. Text author Alan Morris collaborated with Lyryx Learning on the sixth-edition version of Lyryx to ensure the fullest integration possible between the text and Lyryx lab materials.

FOR THE INSTRUCTOR

The goal of Lyryx is to enable you to use these labs to generate course marks instead of having to create and mark your own labs. The content, marking, and feedback have been developed and implemented with the help of experienced instructors in economics. After registering your courses with us, you can then use LAECON content to create your own unique labs by selecting problems from our bank of questions and setting deadlines for each one of these labs. You have access to all your students' marks and can view their best labs. At any time, you can download the class grades for your own programs.

FOR THE STUDENT

LAECON offers algorithmically generated and automatically graded assignments. Students get instant grades and instant feedback—no need to wait until the next class to find out how well they did! Grades are instantly recorded in a grade book that the student can view.

Students are motivated to do their labs for two reasons. First, because their results can be tied to assessment, and second, because they can try the lab as many times as they wish prior to the due date and have only their best grade recorded.

Instructors know from experience that if students who do their economics homework will be successful in the course. Recent research regarding the use of Lyryx has shown that when labs are tied to assessment, even if worth only a small percentage of the total grade for the course, students WILL do their homework—and MORE THAN ONCE!!

Please contact your iLearning Sales Specialist for additional information on the Lyryx Assessment Economics system.

Visit http://laecon.lyryx.com

Other Services and Support

COURSE MANAGEMENT

CourseSmart brings together thousands of textbooks across hundreds of courses in an eTextbook format providing unique benefits to students and faculty. By purchasing an eTextbook, students can save up to 50 percent off the cost of a print textbook, reduce their impact on the environment, and gain access to powerful Web tools for learning—including full text search, notes and highlighting, and e-mail tools for sharing notes between classmates. For faculty, CourseSmart provides instant access to review and compare textbooks and course materials in their discipline area without the time, cost, and environmental impact of mailing print exam copies. For further details contact your *i*Learning Sales Specialist or go to www.coursesmart.com.

McGraw-Hill Ryerson offers a range of flexible integration solutions for Blackboard, WebCT, Desire2Learn, Moodle and other leading learning management platforms. Please contact your local McGraw-Hill Ryerson *i*Learning Sales Specialist for details.

CREATE ONLINE

McGraw-Hill's **Create Online** gives you access to the most abundant resource at your fingertips— literally. With a few mouse clicks, you can create customized learning tools simply and affordably. McGraw-Hill Ryerson has included many of our market-leading textbooks within Create Online for e-book and print customization as well as many licensed readings and cases. For more information, go to www.mcgrawhillcreate.ca.

Your **Integrated Learning Sales Specialist** is a McGraw-Hill Ryerson representative who has the experience, product knowledge, training, and support to help you assess and integrate any of the above-noted products, technology, and services into your course for optimum teaching and learning performance. Whether it's using our test bank software, helping your students improve their grades, or putting your entire course online, your *i*Learning Sales Specialist is there to help you do it. Contact your local *i*Learning Sales Specialist to learn how to maximize all of McGraw-Hill Ryerson's resources.

iLearning Services Program McGraw-Hill Ryerson offers a unique iServices package designed for Canadian faculty. Our mission is to equip providers of higher education with superior tools and resources required for excellence in teaching. For additional information, please visit www. mcgrawhill.ca/highereducation/iservices.

Teaching, Learning & Technology Conference Series
The educational environment continually changes, and McGraw-Hill Ryerson is committed to helping instructors acquire the skills they need to succeed in this new milieu. Our innovative Teaching, Learning & Technology Conference Series brings faculty together from across Canada with 3M Teaching Excellence award winners to share teaching and learning best practices in a collaborative and stimulating environment. Pre-conference workshops on general topics, such as teaching large classes and technology integration, are also offered. McGraw-Hill Ryerson will also work with instructors at their institution to customize workshops that best suit the needs of faculty.

Acknowledgments

We wish to thank the following economists who participated in the formal review process of the sixth edition:

Khyati Antani, Humber College Institute of Technology & Advanced Learning
Rauf A. Azhar, University of Guelph-Humber/Business
Terry Beange, Cambrian College
Ron Bianchi, Vanier College
Menouar Boulahfa, Dawson College
Sergio Buonocore, Lakehead University
Alison Coffin, Memorial University
Daria Crisan, Mount Royal University
Bruno Fullone, George Brown College
Pierre-Pascal Gendron, Humber College Institute of Technology & Advanced Learning
Alana Holowinsk , Red River College
Alfred Hong, Simon Fraser University
Rashid Khan, McMaster University
Ehsan Latif, Thompson Rivers University
Martin Moy, Cape Breton University
Geoffrey Prince, Centennial College
Harry A. Sackey, Vancouver Island University
Dr. John Saba, Champlain Regional College
Jim Sentance, University of Prince Edward Island
Peter Stasiuk, Durham College
Chieko Tanimura, Capilano University
Vitaly Terekhov, Marianopolis College
Angela Trimarchi, University of Waterloo
Sandra Wellman, Seneca College
Andrew Wong, University of Alberta

A very special thank you must be given to Stephanie Powers, Red Deer College, for her vigilant efforts as the technical reviewer for the text and answers.

We would like to acknowledge our colleagues in the Economics Department of Capilano University—Nigel Amon, Ken Moak, Mahak Yaseri, C.S. Lum, Chieko Tanimura, and Camlon Chau—for their encouragement and vigilance in spotting errors and omissions in earlier editions. Numerous colleagues in other departments also gave us encouragement, and sometimes praise, which is greatly appreciated.

We would also like to thank our many students, past and present, for their helpful comments (and occasional criticism). Most particularly, we wish to acknowledge the continued help and support of James Booty, our Sponsoring Editor. James continues to take an active interest in the book, and his desire to make it better is always apparent.

We would like to acknowledge Judy Sturrup's editing and Rohini Herbert's proofing while Maria Chu, Joanne Limebeer, and Katie McHale at McGraw-Hill Ryerson offered excellent professional skills, which are greatly appreciated.

In the end, of course, whatever errors or confusions remain are our responsibility.

Finally, we wish to acknowledge the continued love and support of our families and those close to us.

ECONOMICS TOOLKIT

Some students take economics because it is a requirement for a program they have chosen or degree that they are working toward. Some are interested in a career in business, and taking economics seems like a natural choice. Some even take it because they think that they might like it. Whatever your reasons for taking economics, we are glad you did and hope you will not be disappointed. Economics is a challenging discipline to learn, but it is also one of the most rewarding courses you will ever take. The logic and analysis used in economics is very powerful, and successfully working your way through the principles of economics over the next term will do for your mind what a serious jogging program will do for your body. Bon voyage!

THE CANADIAN REALITY

The Land

Canada is a huge country—in fact, it is the second-largest country on this planet. It contains seven percent of the world's land mass. It stretches 5600 kilometres from the Atlantic to the Pacific Ocean and encompasses six time zones. Ontario alone, which is the second-largest province (after Quebec), is larger than Pakistan, Turkey, Chile, France, or the United Kingdom. Canada's ten provinces range in size from tiny Prince Edward Island to Quebec, which is nearly 240 times as large. In addition, its three territories—the Northwest Territories, Yukon, and Nunavut—demand that we describe this country's reach as being from sea to sea *to sea*.

Within Canada, there are at least six major mountain ranges: the Torngats, Appalachians, and Laurentians in the east, and the Mackenzie, Rocky, and Coast ranges in the west. Any one of these rivals the European Alps in size and grandeur. In addition, Canada has vast quantities of fresh water—nine percent of the world's total—in tens of thousands of lakes and numerous rivers, of which the St. Lawrence and the Mackenzie are the largest.

Canada is richly endowed with natural resources, including gas, oil, gold, silver, copper, iron, nickel, potash, uranium, zinc, fish, timber, and as mentioned above, water—lots of fresh water. The conclusion is inescapable: Canada is a big, beautiful, and rich country.

The People

The word *Canada* comes from a Huron–Iroquois word meaning *village*. In a sense, this is very appropriate because, big as the nation is geographically, it is small in terms of population. Its 34 million people make up only 0.5 percent of the world's population. In fact, there are more people in California or in greater Tokyo than there are in the whole of Canada. Interestingly, Canada's population growth rate, at 1.2 percent, is the highest among G8 countries, primarily because of Canada's high rate of immigration. Thirty-nine percent of Canadians live in the province of Ontario and 23 percent in

Quebec. On the other hand, Prince Edward Island has a population of only 141 000, less than that of the cities of Sherbrooke, Quebec, or North Vancouver, B.C.

Despite the popular images of small Maritime fishing villages, lonely Prairie grain farmers, or remote B.C. loggers, Canada is, in fact, an urban nation. Over 80 per cent of Canadians live in what Statistics Canada calls "urban" areas. There are six Canadian metropolitan areas with populations of over 1 million: Toronto, with 5.6 million; Montreal, 3.8 million; Vancouver, 2.3 million; Calgary and Edmonton, each with 1.2 million and Ottawa–Gatineau, 1.2 million. It is also true that the vast majority of the 33 million Canadians live in a narrow band stretching along the border with the United States, which, incidentally, is the longest unguarded border in the world.

Approximately half of the Canadian population of 34 million is active in the labour force. The labour-force participation rate is 72 percent for males and 63 percent for females.

Multiculturalism

Within this vast, thinly populated country there is a truly diverse, multicultural mix of people. This reality was officially recognized in 1988 when Parliament passed the *Multiculturalism Act*.

There are two official languages in Canada, yet 18 percent of Canadians speak a language other than English or French. In fact, at least 60 languages are spoken in this country. In each year of the 1990s, more than 200 000 new immigrants arrived in Canada. Over 18 percent of all Canadians are first-generation immigrants. In both Toronto and Vancouver, over half the students in the public school system are from non–English-speaking homes. There are over 100 minority language publications in Toronto, and Vancouver has three daily Chinese-language newspapers.

Canada's First Nations people number 1.1 million (3.8 percent of the total population), and a quarter of them live in Ontario.

Government

Canada is a constitutional monarchy with a democratic parliament made up of the House of Commons, with 308 elected members, and the Senate, with 105 appointed members. In addition to Parliament, the other two decision-making divisions of the federal government are the cabinet, composed of the prime minister and 25 (or so) ministers and their departments, and the judiciary, which includes the Supreme Court as well as the federal and tax courts.

Just as there are two official languages in this country, Canada has two systems of civil law—one uncodified and based on common law in English Canada, and the other as codified civil law in Quebec. Canada's constitution, the first part of which is the *Canadian Charter of Rights and Freedoms*, came into being in 1982, a full 115 years after Confederation created the country in 1867.

The fact that Canada is a confederation means the federal government shares responsibilities with the provinces. For example, while the federal government has jurisdiction in national defence, international trade, immigration, banking, criminal law, fisheries, transportation, and communications, the provinces have responsibility for education, property rights, health, and natural resources. Inevitably, issues arise from time to time that do not fit neatly into any one of these categories, with the result that federal–provincial disputes are a continuous part of the Canadian reality.

Canada the Good

Most Canadians are well aware that they live in a good country. But perhaps many do not realize just how good. The average family after-tax income is currently over $74 000, which puts the Canadian living standard among the highest in the world.

The United Nations maintains a Human Development Index that considers factors in addition to average income levels, including life spans and literacy rates. In 2009, this index ranked Canada as the number four nation in the world in which to live. One reason for this high ranking is that Canadian governments spend over 10 percent of the country's gross domestic product (GDP) on health care.

More than 70 percent of Canadians own their homes, well over 90 percent are literate, and over 80 percent of all Canadians have access to the Internet. All three of these statistics are among the highest in the world.

Canada the Odd

Canada is a good country in which to live; however, it does have its oddities. In 1965—98 years after Confederation—it was decided that Canada really should have a national flag. A parliamentary selection committee was set up to choose one, and received no less than two thousand designs. The flag debate was acrimonious, to say the least, although today most Canadians seem quite comfortable with the Maple Leaf. The English-language lyrics of Canada's national anthem, *O Canada*, were formally approved only in 1975. Canada adopted the metric system of measurement in the 1970s, but the imperial system is still in wide use; for example, Statistics Canada still reports the breadth of this country in miles, we sell sizes of wood in inches (such as 2 × 4s), and football fields are 110 yards long.

In this bilingual country, it is odd to note that there are more Manitobans who speak Cree than British Columbians who speak French. In this affluent country of ours, it also interesting to note that 4 percent of Canadian homes are heated exclusively by burning wood. Canada's official animal is—the beaver.

On a more serious note, it is a sad fact that the trade of many goods, and even some services, between any one province and the United States is freer than trade between provinces. There is an interesting history concerning trade patterns in North America. At the time of Confederation, trade patterns on this continent were mostly north–south. The Maritimes traded with the New England states, Quebec with New York, Ontario with the Great Lakes states to its south, and the West Coast traded with California. Canada's first prime minister, John A. Macdonald, was also elected as its third. During his second administration, he implemented his party's National Policy, which resulted in 1) the building of a railway to the West Coast, which encouraged British Columbia to join Canada; 2) offering free land to new immigrants on the prairies in order to settle this area; and 3) forcing trade patterns into an east–west mode by erecting a tariff wall against American imports. British Columbia did join Confederation; people were enticed to settle in Manitoba, Saskatchewan, and Alberta; and the pattern of trade did become more east–west.

So, was the National Policy a success? Some would argue yes, pointing out that it built a nation and that Canada as we know it might not exist today without it. Others are not so sure and would argue that it set back Canada's development by encouraging and protecting new, less efficient industries through the creation of a branch-plant economy. This occurred because American firms that had previously exported to Canada simply jumped over the tariff walls and established Canadian branch plants. Some believe that the National Policy also promoted Canadian regionalism and aggravated relations between regions because both the West and the Maritimes felt that most of its economic benefits favoured central Canada.

In any case, as a result of the North American Free Trade Agreement (NAFTA) of 1992, trade with the United States (and Mexico) is now mostly without tariffs and north–south trade patterns are re-emerging. Historically, Canadian policy has come full circle. However, the trade barriers between provinces, which were built piece by piece over a century, remain.

The Economy

Canada is among the ten largest economies in the world, despite its small population. In 2008, Canada's GDP was $1600 billion. This figure can be broken down as illustrated in **Table T.1**.

TABLE T.1

Category	Amount ($ billion)
Personal expenditures	891
Investment spending	319
Government spending	365
Exports	564
Less imports	(539)
Total GDP	1 600

Source: Adapted from the Statistics Canada CANSIM database <http://cansim2.statcan.ca>, Table 380-0017, 11 January 2011.

The provincial breakdown of the 2008 GDP figure of $1600 billion is shown in **Table T.2**.

TABLE T.2

Province	Population (millions)	GDP ($ billions)	GDP per capita ($ thousands)
Newfoundland (and Labrador)	0.51	29.2	61.8
Prince Edward Island	0.14	4.5	33.2
Nova Scotia	0.94	32.9	36.5
New Brunswick	0.75	27.0	36.6
Quebec	7.8	297.4	39.0
Ontario	12.9	585.7	45.4
Manitoba	1.2	48.7	42.1
Saskatchewan	1.0	50.8	62.7
Alberta	3.6	256.9	81.0
British Columbia	4.4	191.6	45.2
Yukon	0.3	1.7	57.4
Northwest Territories (pre-Nunavut)	0.4	4.6	116.7
Nunavut	0.3	1.4	50.7

Source: Adapted from the Statistics Canada CANSIM database <http://cansim2.statcan.ca>, Tables 384-0002 and 051-0001, 11 January 2011.

This table illustrates the wide disparity in average incomes between provinces, from a low of $33 200 per person in Prince Edward Island to a high of $81 000 in Alberta (and even higher in the Northwest Territories).

In most years the economy grows and the GDP figure rises. To accurately compare growth in GDP, however, we need to use a common set of prices so that a simple rise in prices is not confused with an actual increase in the output of goods and services. Using *real* GDP figures, which correct for inflation, accomplishes this. **Table T.3** looks at some recent real GDP figures, using 2002 prices.

TABLE T.3

Year	Real GDP ($ billion)	Increase/Decrease ($ billion)	% Increase
2005	1248	—	—
2006	1281	+33	+2.6
2007	1307	+26	+2.0
2008	1304	−3	−0.2
2009	1279	−25	−1.9

Source: Adapted from the Statistics Canada CANSIM database <http://cansim2.statcan.ca>, Table 380-0017, 12 January 2011.

Next, let us look at a breakdown of Canada's GDP by industry in **Table T.4**, presented in order of importance.

TABLE T.4

Industry	Percentage of GDP
Finance	21.0
Manufacturing	12.6
Trade (wholesale & retail)	11.7
Professional & technical	7.6
Health	6.8
Public administration	6.1
Construction	5.8
Education	5.1
Transportation	4.7
Mining/Oil	4.3
Information & cultural	3.8
Other Services	2.7
Utilities	2.5
Accomodation & Food	2.2
Agriculture, fishing & forestry	2.2
Arts & entertainment	0.9

Source: Adapted from the Statistics Canada CANSIM database <http://cansim2.statcan.ca>, Table 379-0027, 12 January 2011.

This information is helpful in many ways. For example, it is certainly time to put to rest the idea that Canada is a resource-based economy and that Canadians are simply "hewers of wood and drawers of water," as many of us were taught in school. In fact, agriculture/fishing/forestry and mining/oil make up less than 7 percent of our economy's GDP. Only 4 percent of working Canadians are employed in primary industries, down dramatically from 13 percent a quarter of a century ago.

In contrast, one can marshal the argument that Canada is quite a sophisticated and technologically advanced economy. For example, it is not generally recognized that Canada was the world's third nation to go into space, with the Alouette I satellite in 1962. Canadian industries pioneered long-distance pipeline technology, and Canada is a world leader in several areas of aviation, including turboprop, turbofan, and firefighting aircraft, not to mention the well-known Canadarm used on space shuttles. Canada is also a world leader in commercial submarine technology, and routinely maintains one of the world's longest and most efficient railway systems.

One can also point to many outstanding Canadian companies that are truly world leaders in technology and performance, including Bombardier in transportation equipment, Ballard Power in fuel cell technology, SNC Lavalin in aluminum plant design, Rio Tinto in mining, Trizec Hahn in real estate development, and Magna International in automobile parts manufacturing.

Exports: The Engine that Drives the Economy

Exports are a fundamental part of the Canadian economy. Almost 40 percent of its GDP is exported, which makes Canada one of the world's greatest trading nations. Exports to the United States alone directly support over 1.5 million Canadian jobs, and a $1 billion increase in exports translates into 11 000 new jobs. Again, contrary to historical wisdom, only 20 percent of Canadian exports are resources—the figure was 40 percent a quarter of a century ago.

Table T.5 breaks down the $439 billion worth of goods Canada exported in 2009 into nine categories in order of size.

TABLE T.5	
Export Category	**Percentage of Total Exports**
Machinery & equipment	18.6
Energy products	18.4
Industrial goods	18.3
Services	15.9
Automotive products	10.1
Agricultural & fishing products	8.6
Forestry products	4.5
Other consumer goods	4.1
Special transactions trade	1.5

Source: Adapted from the Statistics Canada CANSIM database <http://cansim2.statcan.ca>, Tables 228-0043 and 380-0027, 11 January 2011.

A Mixed Economy

At the start of the twenty-first century, the market system dominates most of the world's economies, and Canada is no exception to this. Yet, government also plays a big role in our economy. For example, in 2009, the three levels of government collected $586 billion in tax revenue, which represented over 38 percent of Canada's 2009 GDP. **Table T.6** shows the sources and the use of this revenue.

The largest single source of the government's tax revenue, 32 percent, was personal income taxes. Consumption taxes include, most significantly, the GST (goods and services tax) and the PST (provincial sales tax) as well as gasoline, alcohol, and tobacco taxes, customs taxes, and gaming income. These indirect (consumption) taxes accounted for 18 percent of total revenue. Thus, we can see that the majority of the government's tax revenue comes from individual Canadians in the form of direct income taxes or consumption taxes.

And how does government spend these billions of dollars of tax revenue? The right column of **Table T.6** shows us.

TABLE T.6

Government Revenues	% of Total	Government Expenditures	% of Total
Personal income taxes	32.3	Social services	25.6
Consumption taxes	18.3	Health	20.5
Property taxes	9.4	Education	16.1
Investment income	9.2	Protection of persons & property	8.5
Sales of goods & services	9.2	Debt charges	7.6
Corporate incomes taxes	8.5	Environment	6.3
Social security premiums	6.0	Transportation	5.4
Other taxes	5.3	Government services	3.8

Source: Adapted from the Statistics Canada CANSIM database <http://cansim2.statcan.ca>, Table 385-0001, 12 January 2011.

Here, we see that government's largest single category of spending, 26 percent, was on social service payments to individuals. The lion's share of this expenditure, (approximately two-thirds), was social services (pensions, unemployment benefits, and welfare) payments. Thus, we see that a large percentage of spending by government is an attempt to direct income to poorer Canadians. Since all Canadians pay for most of these expenditures, we can see that government is actively involved in *transferring* income from higher-income to lower-income families and individuals. This income distribution role is seen by many Canadians as an important function of government.

On the other hand, some Canadians take the view that government has gone too far in its interventionist role and yearn for less governmental involvement in the economy. They often point to the United States as an example of an economy in which both welfare, unemployment, and pension payments to individuals and direct government aid to poor regions of the country are lower. The difference in the general approach of the two governments may well lie in historical differences in the attitudes of Canadians and Americans toward government. Over the years, Canadians, by and large, have trusted governments to act in their best interests and have been more tolerant of government attempts at income redistribution. Americans, on the other hand, have a history of being suspicious of big government and have repeatedly rejected attempts to expand its role. The recent controversy in the United States over attempts to implement a national health care policy is an example. Another is the Canadian government's direct aid to cultural endeavours, including the funding of national television and radio networks, while no such efforts exist in the United States.

The next two largest categories of spending are on two essentials, health and education. In 2009, the Canadian government allocated 21 and 16 percent of spending in these two areas. The fourth category, protection of persons and property, includes expenditures on the military, police, fire departments, the court system, and prisons. Interest on the national debt was the fifth biggest item of spending at just under 8 percent. The amount spent in this area has steadily declined in the last few years as Canada has started to get government budget deficits under control. (As recently as 1998, servicing the national debt amounted to as much as 30 percent of total spending). The other categories include a host of such items as culture (the Canada Council), housing, foreign affairs, immigration, labour, and research.

This completes our brief look at the Canadian economic reality. We hope that it has helped fill in some gaps in your knowledge of the country. We are confident that you will come to know your country much better after a thorough grounding in the principles of economics, for, in a very real sense, economics is about understanding and improving on what we already know.

Graphing Reality

Let us face it: a lot of students hate graphs. For them a picture is not worth a thousand words. It may even be true that they seem to understand some economic concepts just fine until the instructor draws a graph on the board. All of a sudden, they lose confidence and start to question what they previously thought they knew. For these students, graphs are not the solution but the problem. This section is designed to help those students overcome this difficulty. For those other, more fortunate, students who can handle graphs and know that they are used to illustrate concepts, a quick reading of this section will help reinforce their understanding.

It is probably true that if an idea can be expressed clearly and precisely with words, then graphs become an unnecessary luxury. The trouble is that, from time to time, economists find themselves at a loss for words and see no way of getting a certain point across except with the use of a graph. On the other hand, by themselves, graphs cannot explain everything; they need to be accompanied by a verbal explanation. In other words, graphs are not a substitute for words but a complement. The words accompanied by a picture can often give us a much richer understanding of economic concepts and happenings.

Graphing a Single Variable

The graphing of a single variable is reasonably straightforward. Often, economists want to concentrate on a single economic variable, such as Canada's exports, or consumers' incomes, or the production of wine in Canada. In some cases, they want to look at the composition of that variable, say, different categories of exports. In other cases, they are interested in seeing how one variable changed over a period of time, such as total exports for each of the years 2005 through 2009. In the first instance, we would be looking at a cross-section; in the second instance, we are looking at a *time series*.

Cross-Sectional Graphs

One popular way of showing cross-sectional data is in the form of a pie chart. **Figure T.1**, for instance, shows the composition of Canada's exports for 2009 in terms of the type of goods or services that Canada sells abroad. (This is the same data as presented in **Table T.1**. Which presentation format—table or graph—do you prefer? Which do you find easier to read and understand?)

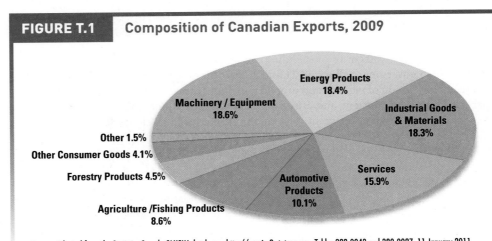

FIGURE T.1   **Composition of Canadian Exports, 2009**

Source: Adapted from the Statistics Canada CANSIM database <http://cansim2.statcan.ca>, Tables 228-0043 and 380-0027, 11 January 2011.

The size of each slice indicates the relative size of each category of exports. But the picture by itself is not always enough. We have added the percentage of total exports that each type represents. Note, however, that there are no dollar amounts for the categories.

Alternatively, the same information could be presented in the form of a bar graph, as in **Figure T.2.**

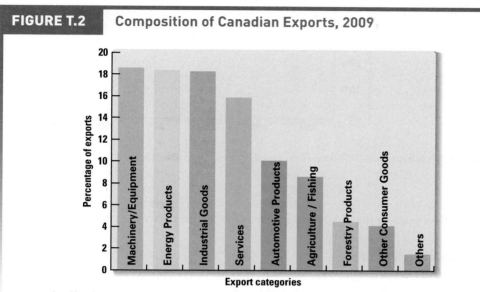

FIGURE T.2   **Composition of Canadian Exports, 2009**

Source: Adapted from the Statistics Canada CANSIM database <http://cansim2.statcan.ca>, Tables 228-0043 and 380-0027, 11 January 2011.

Unlike the pie chart, the bar graph allows us to more easily compare the relative sizes of each category since they are now placed side by side.

Time-Series Graphs

Time-series data can also be presented in the form of a bar graph. **Figure T.3** is a bar graph showing how the number of digital cameras owned by Canadian households has changed over a five-year period.

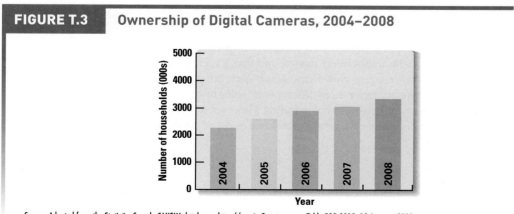

FIGURE T.3   **Ownership of Digital Cameras, 2004–2008**

Source: Adapted from the Statistics Canada CANSIM database <http://cansim2.statcan.ca>, Table 203-0010, 12 January 2011.

The same information can be presented in a line graph, as is done in **Figure T.4**.

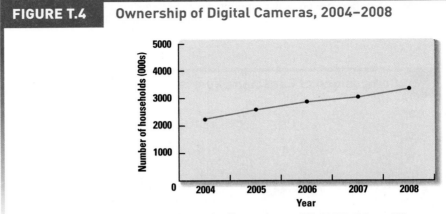

FIGURE T.4   Ownership of Digital Cameras, 2004–2008

Source: Adapted from the Statistics Canada CANSIM database <http://cansim2.statcan.ca>, Table 203-0010, 12 January 2011.

Note that in both cases, the years (time) are shown on the horizontal axis; early years are on the left and later years on the right. This is because graphs are always read from left to right.

Graphing Two Variables

Things get a little trickier when we want to deal with two variables at the same time. For instance, suppose we want to relate Canada's disposable income, which is the total take-home pay of all Canadians, and the amount spent on consumer goods (these numbers are in billions and are hypothetical). One obvious way to do this is with a table, as is done in **Table T.7**.

TABLE T.7

Year	Disposable Income	Spending on Consumer Goods
1	$100	$ 80
2	120	98
3	150	125
4	160	134
5	200	170

A time-series graph, using the same data, is presented in **Figure T.5**. You can see that the two lines in **Figure T.5** seem to be closely related, and that is useful information. To more clearly bring out the relationship, we could plot them against each other. But if you look again at **Table T.7**, you will see that there are really three different variables involved: the time (five years), the values of disposable income, and the values of spending. However, it is very difficult to plot three variables, all three against each other, on a two-dimensional sheet of paper.

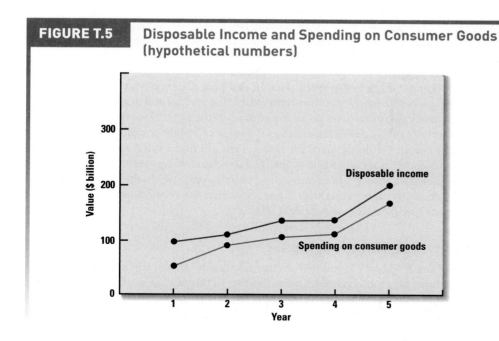

FIGURE T.5 Disposable Income and Spending on Consumer Goods (hypothetical numbers)

Instead, in **Figure T.6**, we will put disposable income on the horizontal axis (also called the *x*-axis), and consumer spending on the vertical axis (also called the *y*-axis) and indicate time with written notation. There is a rule about which variable goes on which axis, but we will leave that for later chapters.

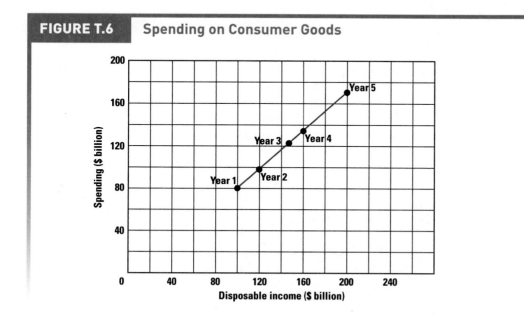

FIGURE T.6 Spending on Consumer Goods

Next, we need to decide on a scale for each of the two axes. There is no particular rule about doing this, but just a little experience will enable you to develop good judgment about selecting these values. We have chosen to give each square on the axes the value of $20. This can be seen in **Figure T.6**.

We started plotting our line using Year 1 data. In that year, disposable income was $100 and consumer spending was $80. Starting at the origin (where the vertical and horizontal axes meet), which has an assigned value of zero, we move five squares to the right. Now, from this income of $100, we move up vertically four squares, arriving at a value of $80 for consumer spending. This is our first plot (or point). We do the same for Year 2. First, we find a value of $120 on the horizontal (disposable income) axis and a value of $98 (just less than five squares) on the vertical axis. The place where these two meet gives us our second point to plot. We do the same for the three next years, and join up the five points with a line. Note that the relationship between income levels and consumer spending plots as a straight line.

Direct and Inverse Relationships

Next, if you look back at **Table T.7**, you will see that disposable income and consumer spending rise together over time. When two variables move together in this way, we say that there is a *direct* relationship between them. Such a direct relationship appears as an upward-sloping line. On the other hand, when two variables move in opposite directions so that one variable increases as the other variable decreases, we say there is an *inverse* relationship between them. In that case, plotting the two variables together would result in a downward-sloping line. (When we talk about upward-sloping and downward-sloping, remember that we are reading the graphs from left to right.)

One last point: the income–consumer-spending line in **Figure T.6** is a straight line. There is no reason that this has to always be the case. Some data might plot as a straight line, and other data might be nonlinear when plotted (as in **Figure T.5**). Either, of course, could still be downward or upward sloping.

Measuring the Slope of a Straight Line

As you proceed with this course, you will find that you need to go a bit further than merely being able to plot a curve—in economics, by the way, all lines are described as curves, whether they are linear or nonlinear. You will also need to know just how steep or how shallow the line is that you have plotted. In other words, you will need to measure the slope of the curve. What the slope shows, in effect, is how much one variable changes in relation to the other variable as we move along a curve. In graphic terms, this means measuring the change in the variable shown on the vertical axis (known as the *rise*), divided by the change in the variable shown on the horizontal axis (known as the *run*). The rise and the run are illustrated, using our disposable income/consumer-spending example, in **Figure T.7**.

Note that as we move from point *a* to point *b*, consumer spending increases by 80 (from 80 to 160). This is the amount of the rise. Looking along the horizontal axis, we see that disposable income increases by 100 (from 100 to 200). This is the amount of the run. In general, we can say:

$$\text{Slope} = \frac{\text{Rise}}{\text{Run}} = \frac{\text{Change in the value on the vertical axis}}{\text{Change in the value on the horizontal axis}}$$

Specifically, the slope of our line is, therefore, equal to:

$$\frac{+80}{+100} = +0.8$$

FIGURE T.7   Rise over Run

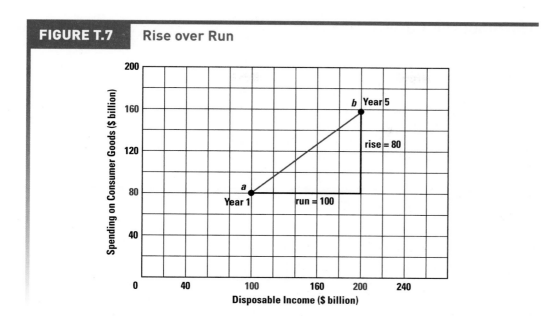

Figure T.8 shows four other curves, two upward-sloping and two downward-sloping, with an indication for each as to how to calculate the various slopes. In each case, we measure the slope by moving from point *a* to point *b*.

FIGURE T.8   Four Different Slopes

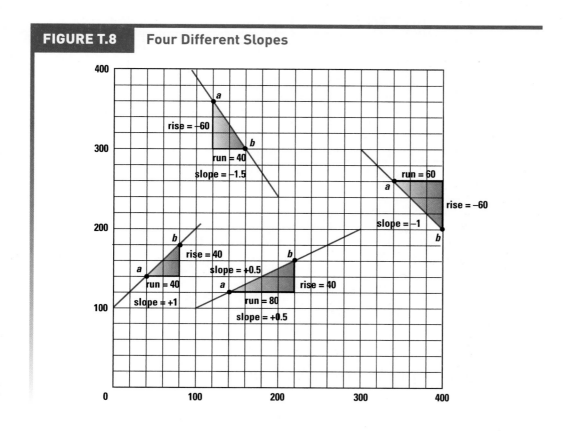

The Slopes of Curves

If a line is straight, it does not matter where on the line we choose to measure its slope; the slope is constant throughout its length. But this is not true of a curve. The slope of a curve will have different values at every point along its length. However, it is possible to measure the slope at any point by drawing a straight line that touches the curve at that point. Such a line is called a *tangent to the curve.* **Figure T.9**, for instance, shows a curve that, at various points, has a positive slope (the upward-sloping portion), a zero slope (the top of the curve), and a negative slope (the downward-sloping portion). We have drawn in three tangents at different positions along the curve. From these straight-line tangents we can calculate the value of the slope at each of these points.

FIGURE T.9   The Slope of a Curve

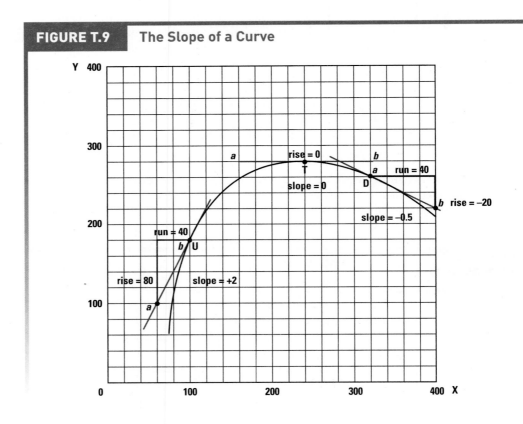

At point U, for example, the curve rises quite steeply. So, what is its slope? Well, its slope at this point is the same as the value of the slope of the straight-line tangent. As we already know the slope of astraight line is:

$$\frac{\text{Rise}}{\text{Run}}$$

At point U, this is equal to:

$$\frac{+80}{+40} = +2$$

This is also the value of the slope of the curve at point U.

At point T, the tangent is a horizontal line, which, by definition, does not rise or fall. The rise/run at this point, therefore, is equal to zero. Finally, at point D, both the curve and the tangent are downward-sloping, indicating a negative slope. Its value is calculated, as before, as rise/run, which equals $-20/40$ or -0.5.

Equations for a Straight Line

In economics, graphs are a very important and useful way to present information. Thus, you will find the pages of most economics books liberally sprinkled with graphs. But there are other, equally useful, ways of presenting the same data. One of these is an algebraic equation. You will often find it very useful to be able to translate a graph into algebra. In this short section, we will show you how to do this. To keep things simple, we will restrict our attention to straight-line graphs.

In order to find the equation for any straight line, you need only two pieces of information: the slope of the line and the value of the Y-intercept. You already know how to calculate the value of the slope. The value of the Y-intercept is simply the value at which the line crosses the vertical axis. In general, the algebraic expression for a straight line is given as

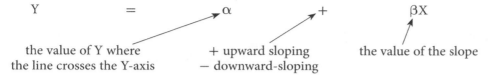

$$Y \qquad = \qquad \alpha \qquad + \qquad \beta X$$

the value of Y where   + upward sloping   the value of the slope
the line crosses the Y-axis   − downward-sloping

For instance, in **Figure T.10**, line 1 has a slope of $+1$ (the line is upward-sloping and therefore has a positive slope and rises by 10 units for every run of 10 units). The line crosses the y-axis at a value of 50. The equation for line 1, therefore, is:

$$Y = 50 + (1)X$$

FIGURE T.10   **Equations for Straight Lines**

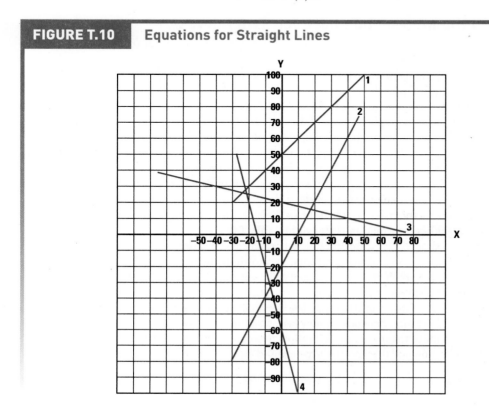

Armed with this equation, we could figure out the value of Y for any value of X. For example, when X (along the horizontal axis) has a value of 40, Y must be equal to:

$$Y = 50 + 40 = 90$$

You can verify this in **Figure T.10**. In addition, we can work out values of X and Y that are not shown on the graph. For example, when X equals 200, Y equals $50 + 200 = 250$.

Let us work out the equations for the other lines shown in **Figure T.10**. Line 2 is also upward-sloping, but it is steeper than line 1 and has a slope of $+2$ (it rises by 20 for every run of 10).

Its intercept, however, is in the negative area of the *y*-axis and crosses at the value of -20. The equation for line 2, then, is:

$$Y = -20 + 2X$$

Again, you can check that this is correct by putting in a value for X, finding the corresponding value of Y, and looking on the graph to see if it is correct. For instance, when X has a value of 40, the equation tells us that:

$$Y = -20 + 2(40) = 60$$

You can confirm in **Figure T.10** that this is, indeed, the case.

In contrast, line 3 has a negative slope of 0.25 and a Y-intercept at 20. Its equation, therefore, is:

$$Y = 20 - 0.25X$$

Finally, line 4 has the equation:

$$Y = -60 - 4X$$

Finding the Intersection between Two Curves

A good deal of economics is concerned with investigating two variables that are related to a common factor. As we shall see in Chapter 2, the quantities of a product that consumers want to buy and the amount that producers wish to sell (demand and supply) are both related to the price of that product. Similarly, the number of employees who are willing to work and the number of people whom employers are willing to hire are both related to the wage that is offered. You will, therefore, often need to be able to graph two sets of data and find where they coincide. Let us illustrate the process with a non-economics example. Suppose one early morning Jo is sitting at the bottom of a 2500-metre mountain. At the same time, Ed is sitting at the top of the same mountain. Assuming that they start off at the same time (say, 8 a.m.) with Jo climbing up at a rate of 400 metres per hour and Ed climbing down at 600 metres per hour, let us see if we can work out where on the mountain and at what time they will meet.

First, we need to transfer this data into a table showing where each individual climber will be at what time. This information is shown in **Table T.8**.

We can also show their ascent and descent graphically. In **Figure T.11**, we will use the vertical axis to show the elevation and the horizontal axis to show the time elapsed.

According to the graph, it seems that they will meet after exactly 2½ hours, that is, at 10:30 a.m. at an elevation of 1000 metres.

We can confirm this result if we translate these data into an algebraic expression. Let us look at Jo's ascent. Her elevation depends on how fast she climbs and how long she climbs. We know she starts at the bottom of the mountain (elevation zero) and climbs at a rate of 400 metres per hour. If we let the elevation equal Y and the time elapsed equal X, then her ascent can be shown as:

Jo's elevation: $\qquad\qquad\qquad Y = 0 + 400X$

TABLE T.8

Jo's Ascent			Ed's Descent		
Elapsed/Time		Elevation (metres)	Elapsed/Time		Elevation (metres)
0	(8 a.m.)	0	0	(8 a.m.)	2500
1	(9 a.m.)	400	1	(9 a.m.)	1900
2	(10 a.m.)	800	2	(10 a.m.)	1300
3	(11 a.m.)	1200	3	(11 a.m.)	700
4	(12 noon)	1600	4	(12 noon)	100
5	(1 p.m.)	2000	4:10	(12:10 p.m.)	0
6	(2 p.m.)	2400			
6:15	(2:15 p.m.)	2500			

FIGURE T.11

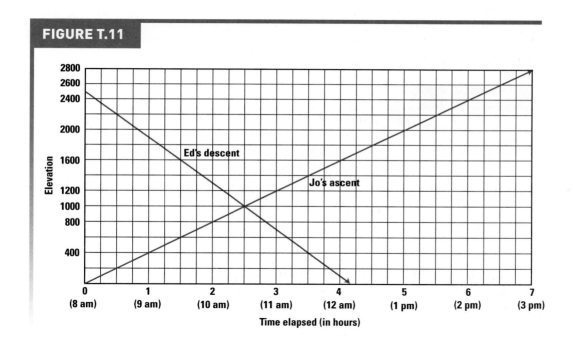

In contrast, Ed starts at an elevation of 2500 metres and his elevation falls as he climbs down. His descent can, therefore, be shown as:

Ed's elevation: $Y = 2500 - 600X$

To find out when and where they will meet is to recognize that whatever this point is, it occurs on the mountain is the same point for the two of them. In other words, Jo and Ed's elevation will be the same. Algebraically, we make the two equations equal and solve. Thus:

$$400X = 2500 - 600X$$

$$1000X = 2500$$

$$X = 2.5$$

So, they will meet after 2.5 hours (2 hours and 30 minutes), or at 10:30 a.m. To find out where they will meet, simply replace X with 2.5 in Jo's and/or Ed's elevation equation:

Jo: $400(2.5) = 1000$ (metres)

Ed: $2400 - 600(2.5) = 1000$

Graphs and Logic

Now, let us look at some potential problems in illustrating data with graphs. For example, the relationship between income and consumer spending in **Table T.7** is hypothetical, since we created it so that it would plot well on a graph. However, any real-world relationship between two variables may not be as neat and simple as this. Data does not always plot into a nice straight line.

Even more seriously, we can never be totally certain of the nature of the relationship between the variables being graphed. There is often a great danger of implying something that is not there. You, therefore, need to be on guard against logical fallacies. Suppose, for instance, that you were doing a survey of women's clothing stores across the country. Reviewing the data you have collected, you notice that there seems to be a close relationship between two particular sets of numbers: the rent paid by the owners of the store and the average price of wool jackets sold. These data are shown in **Table T.9**.

TABLE T.9

Monthly Rent (per 100 m²)	Average Jacket Price
$1500	$80
1600	90
1700	100
1800	110
1900	120
2000	130

The higher the monthly rent, the higher is the price of jackets charged in that store. It seems clear, therefore, that the higher rent is the cause of the higher price, and the higher price is the effect of the higher rent. After all, the store owner must recoup these higher rent costs by charging her customers a higher price. If you think this, then you are guilty of the logical fallacy of *reverse causality*. As you will learn in economics, although rent and product prices are, indeed, related, the causality is in fact the other way around. This is because stores in certain areas can charge higher product prices because of their trendy location, and landlords charge those stores higher rents for the same reason—it is a desirable location. Higher prices, therefore, are the cause and high rents the effect. This is not obvious and illustrates how using raw economic data without sound economic theory can lead to serious error.

A second logical fallacy is that of the *omitted variable*, which can also lead to confusion over cause and effect. **Table T.10** highlights this error. Here, we see hypothetical data on rates of alcoholism and the annual income levels of individuals.

There certainly seems to be a very close relationship between these two variables. Presented in this form, without any commentary, one is left to wonder if low income causes alcoholism or if alcoholism is the cause of low income. Perhaps some people with low incomes drink in order to try to escape the effects of poverty. Or perhaps instead it implies that people who drink to excess have great difficulty in finding or keeping a good job. In truth, it is possible that neither of

TABLE T.10

Average Income Levels ($)	Alcoholism (per thousand of population)
5 000	40
15 000	35
25 000	30
35 000	25
45 000	20
55 000	15

these views is true. Simply because two sets of data seem closely related does not necessarily mean that one is the cause of the other. In fact, it may well be that both are caused by an omitted variable. In the above example, it is possible, for instance, that both high alcoholism and low income levels are the result of low educational attainment.

A third fallacy can occur when people see a cause and effect relationship that does not really exist. This is known as the fallacy of *post hoc, ergo propter hoc*, which literally means "after this, therefore because of this." That is to say, it is a fallacy to believe that just because one thing follows another, that one is the result of the other. For example, just because my favourite soccer team always loses whenever I go to see them, that does not mean I am the cause of their losing!

There is a final fallacy you should guard against, a fallacy, unfortunately, that even the best economists commit from time to time. This is the *fallacy of composition*, which is the belief that because something is true for a part, it is true for the whole. You may have noticed, for instance, that fights occasionally break out in hockey games. These fights often occur in the corners of the rink, which makes them difficult to see. The best way for individuals to get a better view is by standing, and, of course, when everybody stands, then most people cannot see. Thus, what is true for a single fan—standing up to see better—is not true for the whole crowd. Similarly, a teacher who suggests that in order to get good grades students should sit at the front of the class is guilty of the same kind of logical fallacy!

We hope that this little primer on Canada and on graphing has been helpful. It is now time to move on to the study of economics.

Answered Questions

Indicate whether the following statements are true or false:

1. **T or F** Canada is the world's largest country in area and has 1 percent of the world's population.

2. **T or F** Ontario has the largest provincial economy, and the largest provincial population, and it is Canada's largest province in area.

3. **T or F** Over 50 percent of Canada's exports are resources.

4. **T or F** The largest single source of government tax revenue is personal income taxes.

5. **T or F** Spending on social services is the largest category of spending by (all) governments in Canada.

6. **T or F** Three popular types of graphs are pie charts, bar graphs, and line graphs.

7. **T or F** Since disposable income and consumer spending both rise together over time, there is a direct relationship between the two.

8. **T or F** The slope of a straight line is measured by dividing the run by the rise.

9. **T or F** If the equation $Y = 5 + 2X$ were plotted, the slope of the line would be equal to 1/2.

10. **T or F** The logic fallacy, *post hoc, ergo propter hoc* means "after this, therefore because of this."

Simple Calculations

11. **Table T.11** shows the dollar value of commercial sea fishing in Canada for 2002.
    a) From these data, construct a bar chart.
    b) Construct a pie chart showing the percentage of the total that each species represents.

TABLE T.11

	$ millions
Groundfish (including cod, halibut, etc.)	288
Pelagic Fish (including salmon and herring)	185
Lobster	594
Crab	505
Shrimps	294
Other shellfish	254
Total Value	**2 120**

12. Complete the following schedules, and plot the following equations:
    a) $Y = -200 + 2X$

Y	X
	0
	100
	200
	300
	400

b) $Y = 500 - 4X$

Y	X
	0
	100
	200
	300
	400

13. Given the lines shown in **Figure T.12**, complete the following tables, and calculate the equations for the lines:

a)

Y	X
	0
	20
	40
	60
	80
	100

b)

Y	X
	0
	20
	40
	60
	80
	100

FIGURE T.12

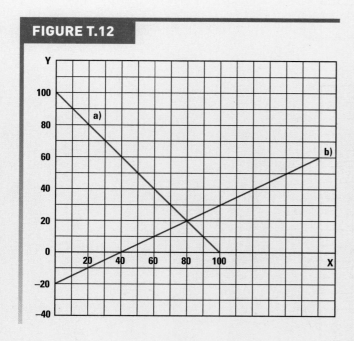

14. The data in **Table T.12** show the results of market research done on the latest Guns' n' Butter album. The numbers indicate the total quantity of albums that fans would purchase at the various prices.

TABLE T.12

Price per CD ($s)	Quantity (hundreds of thousands)
$20	20
19	30
18	40
17	50
16	60
15	70
14	80

a) Graph the table with the price on the vertical (y) axis and the quantity on the horizontal (x) axis.
b) What is the slope of the line?
c) What is the value of the Y-intercept?
d) What is the equation for this line?

15. What are the values of the slopes of the four lines shown in **Figure T.13**?

16. What are the equations that correspond to the four lines shown in **Figure T.14**?

17. Graph the following equations on a single graph, using the same scale for each axis, with the horizontal axis to 120 and the vertical axis to 200, both in squares of 10.
a) $Y = \frac{1}{2}X$
b) $Y = 40 + X$
c) $Y = 160 - \frac{1}{2}X$
d) $Y = -10 + 2X$

FIGURE T.13

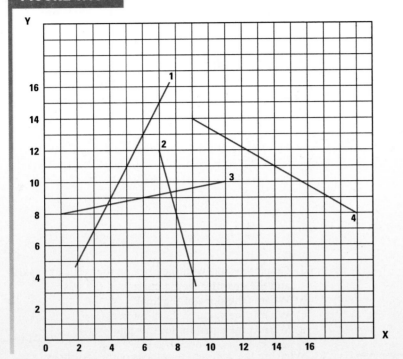

FIGURE T.14

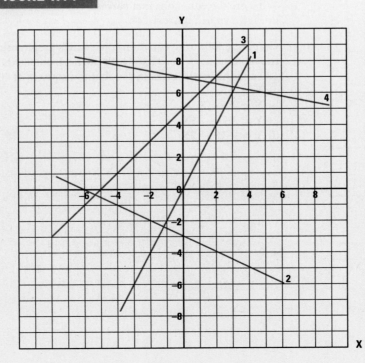

CHAPTER 1

THE ECONOMIC PROBLEM

LEARNING OBJECTIVES

At the end of this chapter, you should be able to...

LO1 understand why economics is a very relevant discipline and why so many of the controversies in our society have a distinct economic flavour.

LO2 define economics, make a distinction between microeconomics and macroeconomics, and understand the importance of the scientific method within the discipline.

LO3 realize that scarcity, choice, and opportunity cost are at the heart of economics and that efficiency, both productive and allocative, provides a major cornerstone.

LO4 understand why greater trade results in more productive economies.

LO5 explain the three fundamental questions that all societies must address and understand the four different ways that economic societies can be organized.

LO6 use the model of the production possibilities as a way to illustrate choice and opportunity cost, and efficiency and unemployment.

LO7 list the economic goals of society and understand why they are often difficult to achieve.

WHAT'S AHEAD...

In this first chapter, we introduce you to the study of economics and hope to arouse your curiosity about this fascinating discipline. First, we present six controversial statements to illustrate how relevant economics really is. Next, we discuss the nature of the discipline. From this, we derive a formal definition of economics. Then, we examine what efficiency means and why it is so important. Following this, we look at three of the fundamental questions that all societies face and see how four different types of economies address them. Next, we introduce the model of production possibilities which enables us to illustrate many of these concepts. Finally, we discuss seven important macroeconomic goals and briefly look at the policy tools used to achieve them.

A Question of Relevance...

Jon and Ashok are both avid soccer fans and play for local teams. They both like old movies, chess, and *Star Trek*. They are both 17 years of age, neither has a steady girlfriend, and both are vegetarians. The other thing they have in common is that their fathers are in banking. Jon's father is the executive vice president of customer relations for the Royal Bank of Canada in Toronto. Ashok's father is a night janitor at a branch of the Bank of India in the dock area of Bombay. All of these points are relevant in forming a mental picture of a person, but you will probably agree that a person's economic circumstances are the most relevant of all. In truth, economics is one of the most relevant subjects you will study.

What might you expect from a course in economics? Well, it will probably not help you balance your chequebook and may not be directly helpful in your choice of the right shares to buy. But the study of economics will give you a broad understanding of how a modern market economy operates and what relationships are important within it. If you see yourself as a budding businessperson, the study of economics can offer some general insights that will be helpful. However, you will not find specific tools or instructions here. Economics is an academic discipline, not a self-help or how-to course. The common conception that economics is about money is only partly true. Economists do study money, but more in the sense of what it is and the effects of different central-bank money policies than in the sense of how to make it. The study of economics may not help you function better in the world, but it will help you understand better how the world functions.

1.1   THE RELEVANCE OF ECONOMICS

LO1 ▶ Understand why economics is a very relevant discipline and why so many of the controversies in our society have a distinct economic flavour.

Furthermore, both of your authors believe that an introductory course in economics will be one of the most important and relevant courses that you will take in your college/university career. Unfortunately, economics has acquired the reputation of being both dull and overly theoretical. Nothing could be further from the truth. In fact, it is at the centre of some of the most vital controversies that engage us all. One of the most effective ways of demonstrating this is to look at six examples of important issues that provoke public opinion today and create debate within the discipline.

Controversy One

- **Economic growth is something that we should applaud and always strive to achieve.**

PRO: In real terms (removing the effects of inflation), the economic well-being of the average Canadian has more than doubled in the last two generations. This has meant a huge improvement in people's lives and has come about not because the world has become fairer but because of economic growth. As a result of this growth, the individual choices available to Canadians—ranging from education and career choices to lifestyle choices—have increased significantly. In addition, economic growth contributes a great deal to social and political stability simply because finding ways to divide up a growing pie is much easier than trying to divide one that is shrinking, or even one that is stable. Over just the last few generations, economic growth has accompanied a falling birth rate, which has meant lower population growth rates. This provides some welcome relief from threats to the environment.

CON: Continued economic growth simply means buying more of the same things but bigger, such as bigger houses, bigger cars, and holidays to more distant places, all of which adds little to human happiness. Economic growth also means greater environmental damage at a time when it is crucial we become more careful about the way we treat Mother Earth. It has also led to more daily stress in our lives because of things like increased traffic and living congestion. Growth puts too much focus on material things at the expense of things that are far more important for our overall well-being, such as greater contentment with our lives, more job satisfaction, and a stronger sense of community.

Controversy Two

- **Government should use its income redistribution tools—such as Employment Insurance, welfare payments, and pensions—to channel more income from the rich to the poor.**

PRO: There is too much poverty in this country, and the gap between the rich and poor is growing. In 2000, 53 percent of Canadians earned less than $20 000, and 9.6 percent earned more than $75 000; in 2004, 57 percent of Canadians were low-income earners, and 13.5 percent were high-income earners. The economic pie should be more evenly divided. Failure to do so is a recipe for social unrest and disharmony.

CON: The solution to the problem of poverty is not higher taxes paid by the affluent for the benefit of the less fortunate. Higher taxes are a disincentive to work hard and to take on the risks of more investment. Instead, polices that stimulate more growth will ultimately benefit all Canadians. This means lower, not higher, taxes. The answer is to have the same proportionately sized slice of a *larger* pie. Income distribution patterns of the rich countries of the world compared with the poor ones show that income is more evenly distributed in the rich countries.

Controversy Three

- The time has come to introduce road pricing in congested Canadian cities to reduce traffic during peak "rush hours."

PRO: Economists know that people respond to financial incentives and charging drivers more for using highways and bridges (which are very expensive to build) during rush hours and less for off-peak times will spread out road usage and thereby reduce congestion. This would also raise needed revenue for more road construction and save lives through reduced accident rates.

CON: Our system of unrestricted and free road usage has worked for generations, and road pricing would simply be another government tax grab and an unfair burden on Canadian drivers. It would also mean that low-income drivers would be paying proportionately more of their incomes than high-income drivers.

Controversy Four

- Globalization benefits large multinational corporations, not ordinary people.

PRO: Globalization leads to large corporations moving jobs from the rich countries to the poor countries. This creates a race to the bottom among poor countries that are willing to weaken environmental- and labour-standard regulations to appease the corporation. This lowers the cost of production for the corporation at the expense of ordinary people.

CON: Globalization means increased world trade, and economic theory clearly demonstrates that more trade means more benefits to those who trade. In fact, UN statistics demonstrate that, within the last fifteen years, 750 million people in the world have been pulled up out of the category of "abject poverty" (less than $1 a day income) into higher-income categories. Much of this is the direct result of increased trade. While this reduction in the amount of world poverty is encouraging, the causes of poverty are complex, and much remains to be done.

Controversy Five

- Canadians must insist that free-market elements are never allowed to creep into our health care system.

PRO: An egalitarian society cannot allow the rich to buy access to better and quicker health care than that which is available to all. The only fair way to allocate limited health care resources is our current system of first come, first served. Proponents of private, fee-paying medical services suggest that this system will reduce waiting lists in the public health care sector. What is forgotten is that it will also shift resources (doctors, nurses, and medical equipment) from the public to the private sector.

CON: Our health care system already has free-market elements—witness the family doctor's private practice. In addition, the rich are currently able to "jump the queue" by simply flying out of the country to buy medical services privately in another country. Several other systems in the world—France being a classic example—demonstrate that a judicious mixture of public and private health care can be quite effective. This option needs to be explored because wait lists in Canada are too long.

Controversy Six

> • The most effective way of dealing with the serious problem of global warming is by establishing a carbon trading system.

PRO: Since the electricity generation industry is the largest single source of carbon emissions, which is the main cause of global warming, let us put our focus there. In a carbon trading system, the government passes the necessary laws and regulations to put a maximum "cap" on the total amount of *net* carbon emissions that each electricity generation firm will be allowed and also creates a carbon trading market. A carbon trading system would provide an economic incentive for entrepreneurial firms to start growing trees on a large scale—much like wheat or oats are now grown. Regulations would provide a mechanism for these tree-growing firms to earn "carbon credits," which recognize the fact that the trees continually suck carbon out of the atmosphere as they grow. These credits would then be sold to the carbon-polluting companies, which must get their *net* emissions (the amount of carbon dumped into the air less the number of credits they have purchased) down to the capped level imposed by government.

CON: Global warming is just one more example of the very serious damage the market system does to our environment. To suggest that the same market system be used to solve the problem misses the mark. The solution should be higher taxes on the use of dirty fuels used to generate electricity, along with government subsidies to firms that use "green" fuels such as wind power. In addition, stricter government regulations to limit the amount of carbon emissions allowed is the most direct and effective way of reducing those emissions.

We have put these sample controversies right up front, not because economists have the right answers to any of them but to demonstrate that almost any issue that faces us today as a society—and thus also as individuals—has an economic dimension. In short, economics is one of the most relevant courses you will ever take. We sincerely hope that this text will help you understand your world a little bit better.

L02 Define economics, make a distinction between microeconomics and macroeconomics, and understand the importance of the scientific method within the discipline.

1.2   WHAT IS ECONOMICS?

From our discussion of controversies, are we to conclude that a person's position on these issues is just a matter of opinion? No, we do not believe that. Economics, as you will discover, provides a unique way of approaching controversies like these, thereby helping each of us reach reasoned positions on all issues. Generally in the social sciences, including economics, theories are absolutely vital in order to make sense of the world.

All of us ask questions to try to make sense of our existence: what? when? where? The answers to these questions are reasonably straightforward because they involve questions of fact. But the most important question of all, and often the most difficult to answer, is: why? "Why" always involves cause and effect, and it addresses the relationship between facts. Few people believe that things occur randomly in our world; we recognize that actions are related. A road is covered in ice, and a car crashes; a person smokes heavily for 40 years and dies of lung cancer; an army of beetles bores into a tree trunk, and the tree falls. Explaining why these things happen is a matter of uncovering the links between phenomena. That is what theory is all about: explaining *why* things happen.

But in order to begin an explanation, we first need to know *what* happened. In other words, theory must be based on solid facts. Theory is NOT just a matter of opinion; it is built on the solid foundation of facts, or what are termed **positive statements**. Positive statements are assertions about the world that can be verified by using empirical data. "Alexander Ovechkin scored 30 goals last year" or "The unemployment rate in Canada is presently 6.2 percent" are both positive statements because their truth can be verified by finding the appropriate data. But "Alexander Ovechkin should score more goals" or "The unemployment rate in Canada is far too high" are both what are termed **normative statements** because they are based on a person's beliefs or value systems and, as such, cannot be verified by appealing to facts. Note also that positive statements may not always be easily or readily verified. For instance, the statement: "It will rain tomorrow" is a positive statement despite the fact that it cannot be verified until tomorrow.

Economic theory is an attempt to relate positive statements. For instance, the price of apples decreases; people buy more apples. Economic theory looks at how the two things are related. In order to build a theory about, say, apple prices and apple purchases, we need to set up a simple *hypothesis*: for example, the lower the price of a product, the greater will be the quantity sold. But along with the hypothesis, we need to define the terms involved. For instance, what types of apples are we talking about—Granny Smiths, Galas, or all apples? And what price are we considering—wholesale? retail? Vancouver prices? Ottawa prices? Besides this, we need to spell out the assumptions (conditions) under which the hypothesis is true: people will buy more apples when the price falls, as long as the economy does not hit a recession or *as long as the prices of other fruits remain the same*, and so on. The hypothesis is now ready for testing by gathering actual data and, as a result, accepting, rejecting, or possibly modifying the theory.

This is what is termed the *scientific method*. It implies, among other things, that the results that the theory predicts should be valid regardless of who does the testing and that different people should be able to repeat the tests and obtain the same results.

However, some people say that there is no way that economics can ever be considered a true science, even though the discipline does use the scientific method. In some sense, this is true. Economics can never approach the pure sciences in terms of universality. For instance, it can never predict how every (or any one) consumer will react to the drop in the price of apples. But it can predict how the average consumer will react; that is, it deals in *generalities*. It is also true that the lag (delay) between the cause and the effect is often far longer in the social sciences than it is in the pure sciences, which makes the job of theorizing a lot more difficult. But to criticize economics because it is too abstract and unrealistic is not really fair. In fact, it could be suggested that the more realistic economic theory becomes, the less valuable it is. For example, no one would expect a map to be "realistic" because if it were, then every tree, house, and road would have to be drawn to scale. And what would the scale be? 1:1! So, while a map can capture a great deal of reality, trying to make it even more realistic can also make it useless.

At some point in the past, you may have heard jokes about economists, such as, "What do you get when you put five economists in the same room? Six opinions." Economists do often disagree with one another as is easily seen in the popular media. This is a natural by-product of a discipline that is part science and part art. An important reason for such disagreement is that every economist, just like all other people, have a particular set of values that they have

positive statement: a statement of fact that can be verified.

normative statement: a statement of opinion or belief that cannot be verified.

ADDED DIMENSION

To illustrate the point that there is a great deal of agreement among economists, here are five sample issues and the percentage of economists who agree with the statement:

1. A ceiling on rents reduces the quantity and quality of housing available. (93%)
2. Tariffs and quotas generally reduce economic welfare. (93%)
3. A tax cut or an increase in government expenditure has a stimulative effect on a less than fully employed economy. (90%)
4. Government should restructure the social assistance system along the lines of a negative income tax. (79%)
5. Effluent taxes and marketable pollution permits represent a better approach to pollution control than the imposition of pollution ceilings. (78%)

Source: Richard M. Alston, J. R. Kearl, and Michael B. Vaughn, "Is There Consensus among Economists in the 1990s?" *American Economic Review,* May 1992, 230–239.

accumulated over a lifetime, and these values vary, sometimes radically, from person to person. Nonetheless, if each of us uses the scientific method in developing our arguments, then lively debate can be fruitful despite the different value systems with which we started.

It is also true, however, that there is wide agreement among economists on many questions, and this is remarkable given that economists ask a wide variety of questions, many of which do not get asked in other disciplines. For example, why do firms produce some goods internally and buy others in the market? Why do nations sometimes both export and import similar goods? Why does society provide some things to children without charge (education) but not other things (food)?

Trying to understand economic theory can be challenging and certainly does not come easily, but the rewards, in terms of a better understanding of the world we live in, are great. Economics is the study of ideas, and in a very real way this is the most important thing that you can study. One of the most famous of twentieth-century economists, John Maynard Keynes, said: "The ideas of economists, both when they are right and when they are wrong, are more powerful than is commonly understood. Sooner or later, it is ideas, not vested interests, which are dangerous, for good or evil."[1]

There are any number of definitions of economics but most of them agree that it is about how best to use the resources we have available. For instance:

> Economics studies the ways that humans and societies organize themselves to make choices about the use of scarce resources, which are used to produce the goods and services necessary to satisfy human wants and needs.

This gives us the essence of the discipline. We need, then, to understand how societies attempt to satisfy seemingly unlimited human wants in the face of limited resources. As we shall see in the next section, it means that we humans are faced with some very difficult choices.

Finally, we need to make the distinction between macroeconomics and microeconomics. **Macroeconomics** is the study of how the major components of the economy—such as consumer spending, investment spending, government policies, and exports—interact. It includes most of the topics a beginning student would expect to find in an economics course: unemployment, inflation, interest rates, taxation and spending policies of governments, and national income determination.

macroeconomics: the study of how the major components of an economy interact; it considers unemployment, inflation, interest rate policy, and the spending and taxation policies of government.

---

[1] John Maynard Keynes, *The General Theory* (1936).

Microeconomics studies the outcomes of decisions made by people and firms and includes such topics as supply and demand, the study of costs, and the nature of market structures. This distinction can be described metaphorically as a comparison between the use of the wide-angle lens and the telephoto lens of a camera. In the first instance (macroeconomics), we see the big picture. In the second instance (microeconomics), a very small part of that big picture appears in much more detail. Many colleges and universities offer a separate course for each of these fields of study, but this is not always the case.

microeconomics: the study of the outcomes of decisions by people and firms; it focuses on the supply and demand of goods, the costs of production, and market structures.

 SELF-TEST

1. Identify each of the following statements as either positive (P) or normative (N).

   a) The federal government's budget this year is the largest in history.

   b) The national debt is at a manageable level and therefore is nothing to worry about.

   c) The price of gasoline is higher than it needs to be.

   d) Rising Canadian exports are creating many new jobs in the country.

2. Identify which of the following topics would likely appear in a microeconomics course (Mi) and which in a macroeconomics course (Ma).

   a) The price of iPods

   b) Unemployment rates

   c) The presence of monopolies

   d) The rate of economic growth

1.3 SCARCITY, CHOICE, COST, AND THE IMPORTANCE OF EFFICIENCY

L03 Realize that scarcity, choice, and opportunity cost are at the heart of economics and that efficiency, both productive and allocative, provides a major cornerstone.

Economists put a great deal of emphasis on scarcity and the need to economize. Individual households face income limitations and therefore must allocate income among alternative uses. Most individuals also face a scarcity of time and must somehow decide where to spend time and where to conserve it. In the same sense, an economy as a whole has limited resources and must allocate those resources among competing uses.

Thus, economists see **resources** (the **factors of production** or **inputs**) as *scarce* in the sense that no economy has sufficient resources to be able to produce all the goods and services everyone wants. Even though there may be some people who say they have all they want, there are millions of people who possess a seemingly endless list of wants, with millions more like them waiting to be born. Since the economy cannot produce all that everyone wants, the resources available for production are scarce.

And exactly what constitutes a resource? Well, of the myriad different resources that are or have been used to produce goods and services, economists are generally agreed that there are, in fact, four categories: labour, capital, land, and enterprise. **Labour** refers to a broad spectrum of human effort, ranging from the work of a skilled physician to that of a construction labourer. **Capital** is made up of the tools, equipment, factories, and buildings used in the production process and is not to be confused with financial capital, such as money, stocks, or bonds. **Land** is defined as any natural resource, such as fertile soil, forests, fishing grounds, or minerals in the ground. Finally, **enterprise** (some economists prefer the term *entrepreneurship*) is that very special human talent that is able to apply abstract ideas in a practical way. Entrepreneurs are innovators who invent new products or devise new forms of organization and are willing to take the risks to see such projects through to successful completion.

resources (or **factors of production** or **inputs**): physical or virtual entities that can be used to produce goods and services.

labour: human physical and mental effort that can be used to produce goods and services.

capital: the human-made resource that is used to produce other products.

land: any natural resource that can be used to produce goods and services.

enterprise: the human resource that innovates and takes risks.

wages: the payment made and the income received for the use of labour.

interest: the payment made and the income received for the use of capital.

rent: the payment made and the income received for the use of land.

profit: the income received from the activity of enterprise.

In a market economy, incomes are earned through the payment of wages, interest, rent, and profits to the private owners of the factors of production: labour, capital, land, and enterprise. The general term **wages** includes all forms of payment to the various kinds of labour services such as salaries, stock bonuses, gratuities, commissions, and various employee benefits. **Interest** means payments to the factor of real capital. **Rent** is the income received for the use of the factor of land such as royalty payments for a stand of timber. Finally, **profit** is the return to entrepreneurial effort.

Now, the way that these four factors of production are combined is what economists mean by a **technology**. A technology does not necessarily imply the use of machines or computers; it simply means a method of production. However, whatever technology we use to produce goods and services, the fact remains that we are simply not capable of producing everything that people want.

Therefore, some kind of mechanism must be put into place to choose what will be produced and, by implication, what will not be produced. This is why economics is sometimes called the *science of choice*.

In short:

> In the face of people's unlimited wants and society's limited productive resources, choice becomes a forced necessity. Because of these choices, the decision to produce one thing means that some other thing will not be produced.

technology: a method of production; the way in which resources are combined to produce goods and services.

opportunity cost: the value of the next-best alternative that is given up as a result of making a particular choice.

This last point is so fundamental that economists have coined a special term to identify it: **opportunity cost**. For instance, suppose that government is considering the purchase of new military aircraft with a price tag of $5 billion. In the conventional sense, that is their cost. However, economists would argue that it is more revealing to measure the cost of the helicopters in terms of, say, ten hospitals that will not be built because purchasing the helicopters was chosen instead. Opportunity costs can thus be defined as what must be given up as a result of making a particular choice: in this case, the hospitals are given up for the aircraft. In addition, we should recognize that the $5 billion could be spent on other things besides hospitals—say, schools, roads, or mass-transit systems. At this point, society would have to choose what it considers to be its next-best alternative: hospitals, schools, roads, or mass transit. Understanding this concept allows us to make a formal definition of opportunity cost: the next-best alternative that is given up as a result of making a particular choice. In conclusion, the making of any decision always involves a trade-off with the next-best alternative that is sacrificed.

consumer goods and services: products that are used by consumers to satisfy their wants and needs.

A classic example of this trade-off in economics is sacrificing consumer goods to produce more capital goods. Nations that wish to grow more quickly can achieve this if they produce more factories, tools, and equipment—more capital goods—that are used to make other goods. But, of course, an increase in capital goods production necessarily means a reduction in the output of **consumer goods and services**, which are defined as products that are used by consumers to satisfy their wants and needs.

Why is it better to think of cost in terms of opportunity cost rather than simply as money payments? Economists argue that using the concept of opportunity costs captures the true measure of any decision. If we use money payments as the measure, then we have seemingly unlimited means to produce goods, since governments can always print more money. But no matter what any government might wish, any society has only a limited amount of resources. When we understand this, we begin to realize that nothing in life is truly "free"—any decision (to produce military aircraft, for example) necessarily involves the use of scarce resources which could have been used alternatively to produce something else (hospitals).

Recognizing that there are opportunity costs involved also forces us to rethink our idea of what we mean by "free." Simply because money does not change hands does not mean that a product is free. The concept of opportunity cost can be applied not only at the level of the overall society, as we just saw, but also at the individual level. For the individual, the constraint is not the limited quantity of resources but, instead, a limited amount of income and time. For example, you could think of the cost of going to two movies on the weekend as the sacrifice of a haircut. If you want to think of both these choices (two movies or one haircut) as each costing about $20, that is fine. But thinking of the one as costing the other is often more effective. In general, your income will not allow you to have everything you may want, and so you are forced to make choices about what you buy. And the cost of these choices can be measured in terms of what must be given up as a result of making the choice.

Another application of opportunity costs is the one that many students face in choosing between taking more courses at college or continuing to work in a part-time job. If a student is presently taking three courses and working twenty hours a week and feels that this is a full-time load, then taking five courses next semester may well mean giving up the job. Thus, the opportunity cost of the two extra courses is the income that is sacrificed as a result of no longer working at the part-time job. We should also point out that there must be some benefit to be gained from the alternative that you do choose. For instance, returning to our example above, if you chose the two movies, the benefit from that choice, in your view, exceed (or at least equal) the opportunity cost of the haircut. In the same sense, a society faces a similar set of choices imposed not by limited income but by a constraint on the quantity and quality of the factors of production available.

SELF-TEST

3. Below is a list of economic goods. Decide whether each is a consumer good (C), a capital good (K), or possibly both (B), depending on the context in which it is used.

a) A jackhammer B

b) A carton of cigarettes C

c) An office building B K

d) A tooth-brush C

e) A hammer B

f) A farm tractor K

4. Below is a list of resources. Indicate whether the resource in question is labour (L), capital (K), land (N), or enterprise (E):

a) A bar-code scanner in a supermarket K

b) Fresh drinking water N

c) Copper deposits in a mine N

d) The work of a systems analyst L

e) The first application of e-technology to an economics textbook E

f) An office building K

The Importance of Efficiency

Perhaps not surprisingly, economists, like any other group of people, do not agree on the most important economic goals that an economy should pursue. Nor are they necessarily in agreement on the best methods to achieve those goals. However, they are generally in agreement on the importance of *efficiency*. In fact, this term crops up with great regularity in economic literature. As a result, it is important to have some initial understanding of what the term means and why economists attach so much importance to it.

One of the simplest ways of expressing efficiency is to suggest that it implies getting the most for the least. For example, a technology that requires the use of 10 units of inputs in order to produce an output of 100 units of goods and services would be preferable to one that uses 20 units of inputs to produce those same 100 units of output. Similarly, that same technology that uses 10 inputs to produce 100 units of output would be considered inferior to another technology that uses those same inputs but could produce an output of 150 units. In other words, economists define **productive efficiency** in terms of the ratio of outputs produced to inputs used. Those technologies that produce at a lower ratio will result in lower costs of production.

productive efficiency: the production of an output at the lowest possible average cost.

When you hear the term "productivity" used in the popular press it is usually referring to productive efficiency and is often measured in terms of the amount of output per hour of labour (or machine) input. If we want to be careful in our use of resources, then it is of great importance that every one of us try to be efficient. However, productive efficiency does not take us far enough. It is all right to produce things at low cost, but it is of little use if people simply are not interested in buying those products. For instance, what would be the point of producing big-screen TVs at $50 each if they could only broadcast in black and white? In other words, it is just as important to be efficient in what we produce as how we produce it. Societies therefore need to ensure that the right type of products are produced, those that match the demands of the public. This is what economists mean by **allocative efficiency**.

allocative efficiency: the production of the combination of products that best satisfies consumers' demands.

Allocative efficiency then puts the emphasis on the production of the right type of products. However, since all of us have different tastes, what might be the right products for you may not be the right products for me. So, it is important that products are allocated efficiently among people. In *Filthy Lucre*, Joseph Heath gives an amusing example illustrating this idea.

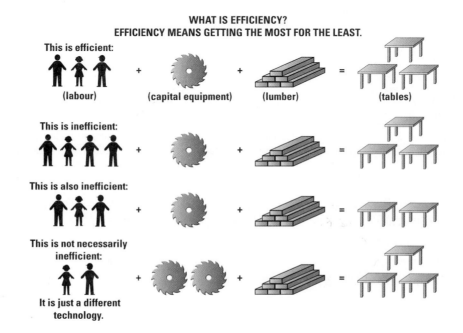

WHAT IS EFFICIENCY?
EFFICIENCY MEANS GETTING THE MOST FOR THE LEAST.

This is efficient:
(labour) + (capital equipment) + (lumber) = (tables)

This is inefficient:

This is also inefficient:

This is not necessarily inefficient:
It is just a different technology.

Imagine that you have been given the task of allocating candies to a group of children at a birthday party. Trying to be fair, you count out the different types of candies so that each child gets an equal number of each. But you discover that some of the kids are not too happy. One child is most upset because he has been given a peanut brittle, and the poor boy is allergic to peanuts! One girl positively detests raisins; some of them hate dark chocolate, while others detest milk chocolate. You can see that without increasing the overall quantity of candies, you could increase the general happiness of these children just by redistributing the candies. The kids might easily handle this allocation themselves by trading, something that children tend to do quite naturally.

1.4   THE POWER OF TRADE

The final quarter of the twentieth century revealed something very significant: economies that put an emphasis on the market system and international trade—Canada, South Korea, and Ireland, for example—continued to enjoy economic growth and a rising standard of living for their citizens, while economies that rely more on centrally controlled systems and self-sufficiency—the former USSR or today's Kirghizia and Myanmar, for example—faltered.

L04 Understand why greater trade results in more productive economies.

Adam Smith, the father of economics, gave us a simple but elegant idea that goes a long way toward explaining why, throughout history, some economies have prospered, while others have not. This is the recognition that *voluntary trade* always benefits both parties to the trade. If two peasants voluntarily trade a sack of rice for two bags of carrots, then we can assume that they both must feel that they have benefited, as otherwise they would not have done it. If you buy a slice of pizza and a pop for lunch for $3.50, then we must assume that you feel you have gained by giving up the money and receiving the lunch—otherwise, why did you do it? Likewise, the owner of the business that sold you the lunch must feel that she gained, or she would not have been willing to offer the lunch for sale. There is a gain to both parties engaged in voluntary trade.

It then follows that *the more trade there is, the greater are the overall benefits that accrue to those engaged in the trade.* It comes as a surprise to many people that the same principle that applies to individuals in this regard also applies to nations. We can demonstrate that this is true by using the concept of opportunity costs to construct a simple example of two hypothetical countries—Athens and Sparta—each of which produces only two goods: bread (a consumer good) and plows (a capital good).

Suppose that the maximum quantities that can be produced of each product are (in thousands of units):

Athens	20 bread	or	10 plows
Sparta	10 bread	or	20 plows

If each country is self-sufficient (no trade between them) and each devotes half its resources to producing the two products, the output in each country would be:

Athens	10 bread	and	5 plows
Sparta	5 bread	and	10 plows

Clearly, the combined output of the two economies is 15 units of bread and 15 plows. It is also clear that Athens is far better at producing bread and Sparta is much better at producing plows. Thus, if the two countries could overcome their sense of rivalry and if Athens concentrated on producing bread and Sparta on producing plows, then the total combined production of the two countries would be:

Athens	20 bread	(no plows)
Sparta	20 plows	(no bread)

With specialization, the two countries can produce a combined total that is five more of each product (20 units of bread and 20 plows) than when each was self-sufficient. This illustrates why specialization is so important—countries enjoy more output when they do what they do best (produce only the products with the lowest opportunity cost) rather than trying to produce both products. For Athens, the opportunity cost of producing plows is a large sacrifice in bread production, while in Sparta, the opportunity cost of producing bread is a large sacrifice in plow production. However, when they both specialize in what they do best, big benefits can be gained. But to reap the benefits of specialization, trade becomes imperative unless, of course, the countries are happy just consuming one product (which is most unlikely). In our example, if Athens were to trade 10 bread for 10 plows from Sparta, then both countries would finish up with 10 units of bread and 10 plows—an improvement for them both.

Returning to our original point about market economies versus planned economies, we know that specialization and trade are maximized when markets are used extensively. This simple illustration helps us understand that every economy faces important choices about what to produce. Let us expand on this point by turning to the three fundamental economic questions faced by every economy.

1.5 THREE FUNDAMENTAL QUESTIONS AND FOUR TYPES OF ECONOMIES

L05 Explain the three fundamental questions that all societies must address and understand the four different ways that economic societies can be organized.

A broad perspective on the discipline of economics can be obtained by focusing on the three fundamental questions of economics: *what? how?* and *for whom?* That is, economics is about what and how much gets produced, how it is produced, and who gets it.

What to Produce?

As we have just seen, underlying the question of *what* should be produced is the reality of scarcity. Any society has only a fixed amount of resources at its disposal. Therefore, it must have a system in place to make an endless number of decisions about production: from big decisions—such as should the government buy more military aircraft or build more hospitals?—down to more mundane decisions such as how many brands of breakfast cereal should be produced.

If we decide to produce hospitals, should we produce ten without research facilities for the study of genetics or eight without and one with such facilities? Should society exploit natural resources faster to create more jobs and more tax revenue or slower to conserve these resources for the future? Should our resources be directed toward more preschool day-care facilities so that parents are not so tied to the home? Or should those same resources be directed toward increasing the number of graduate students studying science and technology so that the Canadian economy can win the competitive international race in the twenty-first century?

Let us once again emphasize that no economist would claim to have the *right* answer to any of these questions. That is no more the role of an economist than it is of any other member of society. What the economist can do, however, is identify and measure both the benefits and the costs of any one answer—of any one choice.

How to Produce?

Let us move on to the second fundamental economic question that every society must somehow answer: what is the most appropriate technology to employ? We could reword this question by asking *how* we should produce what we choose to produce.

For example, there are many ways to produce ten kilometres of highway. At one extreme, a labour-intensive method of production could be used involving rock crushed with hammers, roadbed carved from the landscape with shovels, and material moved in wheelbarrows.

The capital equipment used in this method is minimal. The labour used is enormous, and the time it will take is considerable. At the other extreme, a capital-intensive method could be used involving large earthmoving and tarmac-laying machines, surveying equipment, and relatively little but highly skilled labour. In between these two extremes is a large variety of capital–labour mixes that could also produce the new highway.

The answer to the question of how best to build the highway involves, among other things, knowing the costs of the various resources that might be used. Remember that technology means the way the various factors of production are combined to obtain output. The most appropriate technology for a society to use (the best way to combine resources) depends, in general, on the opportunity costs of these resources. Thus, in the example above, the best way to build a highway depends on the opportunity costs of labour and of capital as well as the productivity of each factor.

Capital intensive technologies using heavy equipment are the most appropriate methods in most countries because they are the cheapest.

For Whom?

We are now ready to move to the third fundamental economic question that every society must somehow answer: *for whom?* Here, we are asking how the total output of a society should be shared among its citizens. In the end, we are really asking how the total income in a society should be distributed. Should it involve an equal share for all, or should it, perhaps, be based on people's needs? Alternatively, should it be based on the contribution of each member of society? If so, how should this contribution be measured—in numbers of hours, in skill level, or in some other way? Further, how should we define what constitutes an important skill and which ones are less important?

Wrapped up in all this is the question of the ownership of resources and whether it is better that certain resources (such as land and capital) be owned by society as a whole or by private individuals. In short, the *for whom* question (as well as the *what* and *how* questions) cannot be adequately addressed unless we look at society's attitude toward the private ownership of resources and the question of who has the power to make crucial decisions.

You can see that in addressing the *for whom* question, other questions about the fairness of income distribution, incentives, and the ownership of resources all come into play. John Stuart Mill pointed out, nearly 150 years ago, that once an economy's goods are produced and the initial market distribution of income has occurred, society can intervene in any fashion it wishes in order to redistribute such income; that is, there are no laws of distribution other than the ones that society wants to impose. Whether this observation by Mill gives enough consideration to the incentive for productive effort remains an open question to this day.

 ADDED DIMENSION

John Stuart Mill (1806–73) is considered the last great economist of the classical school. His *Principles of Political Economy*, first published in England in 1848, was the leading textbook in economics for 40 years. Raised by a strict disciplinarian father (James), John Stuart began to learn Greek at the age of three, authored a history of Roman government by 11, and studied calculus at 12—but did not take up economics until age 13.

Not surprisingly, this unusual childhood later led to a mental crisis. Mill credited his decision to put his analytical pursuits on hold and take up an appreciation of poetry as the primary reason for his recovery. He was a true humanitarian, who held a great faith in human progress, had a love of liberty, and was an advocate of extended rights for women.

How these fundamental questions actually get answered depends, to a large extent, on the way that different societies organize themselves. Let us now look at the four types of economic organization.

Four Types of Economies: The Four Cs

Societies have, throughout history, developed systems to co-ordinate their economies in order to answer the fundamental questions of what to produce, how, and for whom. Each of the numerous systems possible have used some blend of the four Cs: cooperation, command, custom, and competition. Whatever blend was used, it was a reflection of who owns and who controls the important resources of that economy.

In the foraging societies of pre-history, the few tools, weapons, and cooking items they possessed were commonly owned: belonging to the band as a whole and not to any one individual. Since these bands were nomadic, they did not preserve or store food, since carrying it around was difficult and undesirable. They lived very much a hand-to-mouth existence. This meant that these societies did not produce a surplus above subsistence that could be used to support non-producers. Consequently, they had no armies, no leaders, no priests, and no ruling hierarchy. The result was a society where decision making was democratic and egalitarian. In short, the members of foraging bands relied on *co-operation* with one another in order to survive the dual threats of starvation and predators.

As we shift our focus to the later command economies of ancient Egypt and Rome, we see that the most important resource was slaves, and whoever owned slaves was almost, by definition, rich and powerful. Decisions were made, and laws were ruthlessly enforced, by an elite group headed by a pharaoh or emperor. The fundamental questions were answered by using *command*.

In the age of feudalism in Europe, which filled the vacuum left by the fall of the Roman Empire, we see power centred on the ownership of land. The landowners—royalty, the aristocracy, and the Church—were very powerful, and everyone else knew his or her place within this rigidly hierarchical system. This was the age of *custom*, which dictated who performed which task—sons followed the work of their fathers, and daughters followed the roles of their mothers—and traditional technology was superior to new ways of doing things, since it had been tried and tested and could therefore be trusted. Above all, custom required that serfs turn over a portion of their produce to the feudal lords.

Then, beginning in Britain toward the end of the eighteenth century, the Industrial Revolution effectively brought feudalism to an end and ushered in the machine age. It is here that capital, in the form of factories, machines, and railroads became the economy's most important resource, and the industrial capitalists became very rich and powerful, while the ordinary people, the land less, capital-less working class, were left with nothing but their labour to sell. This marks the birth of the market system with its emphasis on *competition* as the coordinating mechanism and the private ownership of resources as a main characteristic. Many people are surprised to learn how modern an invention this form of economic organization really is. What today we call the market economy did not begin to emerge until approximately 250 years ago. although, of course, *markets* have existed for thousands of years.

So what do we see today as we look at the world in which we live? Well, custom is very much alive in a number of Islamic Republics such as Iran, where traditional values, enforced by religion, dominate most aspects of people's lives. But we also see that custom has a part to play in our own society. For instance, movie theatres provide expensive washrooms free of charge

Tradition plays a big role in the lives of many people in Muslim countries.

while charging for popcorn and soft drinks rather than the reverse. A much more significant example is the custom in our market economy of allowing people to pass wealth on to their children in the form of inheritance so that the income of the future generation is often based less on what they contribute to the economy and more on who their parents were.

As far as co-operation is concerned, it is impossible to find an example of a country where the economic decisions are made co-operatively by all the citizens. However, we can find many examples of small, self-contained communes where there is an emphasis on common ownership and concensus decision making. Included would be the kibbutzim of Israel or religious communities such as the Hutterites in the Canadian Prairies or the Doukhobors of British Columbia. Even the internal decision making process in today's large corporations that stresses the use of team play and group consensus is a form of co-operative behaviour. This same point can be made in reference to most family units within our society. Further, what, if not co-operation, would one call the fact that nearly half of all adults in our society engage (at some point in their lives) in voluntary unpaid activities such as coaching soccer or helping out at a local hospital or community centre?

To find examples of command economies in the modern world, we need look no further than the brutal totalitarian regimes of the twentieth century: fascism in Italy, Nazism in Germany, and communism in the Soviet Union. In all three examples, the complete command of the economy was in the hands of the leaders who also controlled most aspects of life and dictated what would be produced, how it would be produced, and who earned what.

Finally, competition is the main feature of today's capitalistic, or market, economies. Here, the forces of demand and supply determine most of what is produced, as well as what technology is used and how much people earn. In a pure market economy, government plays no role whatsoever. This means, for instance, that corporations would be totally unregulated, schools and hospitals would all charge fees, and those unable to work would simply receive no income or support from government at all.

It is clear that in our modern age, there are no examples of countries organized using only a single one of the Four Cs. Instead, all modern economies use a combination of all four, with competition and command being the dominant ones. Perhaps this is due to the rise in the importance of knowledge as the most important resource in today's fast-changing world; it is difficult to monopolize ownership of this particular resource. At the same time, today, we see only a single example of purely command economy: North Korea. Even "communist" China and Cuba have opened up their economies to private ownership and enterprise.

This blend of competition and command includes the large role played by governments through the provision of, for example, health care and education, leaving the private sector to provide the majority of consumer goods for personal use. The role of government in our economy represents the command function in the sense that the taxes needed to finance government activities are not voluntary, and in the same sense, the various laws governing human conduct and behaviour must be adhered to. This recognition of the roles of both market and government in our society is what we mean by the term *a mixed economy*. On the one hand, few of us would wish to live in a pure market economy where, for example, young children from dysfunctional families with no income would be left to starve or where there was no standardization of weights and measures and no "rules of the game" concerning the way business is conducted. On the other hand, few of us would want to live in a society where every decision about our lives was made by government. Some blend of the market, and the efficiencies achieved from its use, combined with the order and fairness imposed by government does seem to be the right way to go. However, exactly what constitutes the right amount of government intervention imposed upon the market is, of course, an issue of endless debate.

You have no doubt heard the terms "capitalism" and "socialism" used in the media and in conversation. Just what do these terms mean to an economist? Basically, they distinguish different degrees in the competition–command mix used by society to organize its economic affairs and answer the three fundamental questions. In "socialist" Sweden, for example, the state (government) plays a much larger role in the economy than in the "capitalist" United States. While Sweden does not have central planning as found in the former Soviet Union and does have private property, it also has high taxes and high levels of social spending. Eighty percent of the work force is unionized; everyone receives a generous number of paid vacation days per year and generous sick leave benefits at nearly full pay. Sweden has a wide-ranging unemployment insurance plan, which also includes mandatory retraining for those laid off from their jobs. Until very recently, the Swedish government mandated an investment fund requiring that corporations give a percentage of their profits to the central bank, which would then release these funds back to the companies in times of recession, with stipulations on how they were to be spent. By contrast, the United States has almost none of this and relies, instead, on a policy of *laissez-faire*, which minimizes the role of government and emphasizes the role of the market in the economy. Canada, France, and the United Kingdom lie somewhere between these extremes.

1.6   PRODUCTION POSSIBILITIES

L06 Use the model of the production possibilities as a way to illustrate choice and opportunity cost, and efficiency and unemployment.

Economists often use economic models when trying to explain the world in which we live. Let us explain what we mean by a "model" and look at one example. Imagine walking into the sales office of a condominium project under construction. Part of the sales presentation is a model of the entire project sitting on a table. You would have no trouble recognizing the model as an abstraction, a representation, of what the building will eventually look like. This is true despite the fact that many of the details such as the elevators, furniture, and appliances are absent from the model.

So, too, in making their models, do economists abstract from reality only the features that are relevant, ignoring extraneous material. Clearly, economists cannot construct a physical model of the economic world. Instead, the level of abstraction is greater in that the model is all on paper and often in the form of numbers, equations, and graphs. But for all that, the aim is not to make the simple and straightforward seem unnecessarily complicated. Just the opposite: the goal is to make the complexities of reality as clear and simple as possible.

Let us now construct a very simple model of a country's production possibilities. This allows us to return to a point that we made earlier: that every economy is faced with the constraint of limited resources. Imagine a society that produces only two products—cars and wheat. Let us then figure out what this economy is capable of producing if it works at maximum potential. This would mean that the society is making use of all of its resources: the labour force is fully employed, and all of its factories, machines, and farms are fully operational. But it means more than this. It also means that it is making use of the best technology and, as a result, overall efficiency is being achieved. Given all of this, and since it can produce either cars or wheat, the exact output of each depends on how much of its resources it devotes to the production of cars and wheat. **Table 1.1** shows six possible output combinations, as well as the percentage of the economy's resources used in producing each combination. These possible outputs are labelled A through F.

The finite resources available to this economy allow it to produce up to a maximum of 20 tonnes of wheat per year if 100 percent of its resources are used in wheat production. Note that this can be done only if no cars are produced (combination A). At the other extreme, a maximum of 30 cars per year can be produced if all available resources are used in car production. This, of course, would mean that no wheat is produced (combination F). There are many other possible combinations in between these two extremes, and **Table 1.1** identifies four of these (B, C, D, and E).

Since we want to focus on what is produced (the outputs) rather than on what resources are used to produce them (the inputs), we can present **Table 1.1** in the form of a production possibilities table, as is shown in **Table 1.2**:

TABLE 1.1   Production of Cars and Tonnes of Wheat (millions of units)

Possible Outputs	CARS % of Resources Used	CARS Output	WHEAT % of Resources Used	WHEAT Output
A	0	0	100	20
B	20	10	80	19
C	40	18	60	17
D	60	24	40	13
E	80	28	20	8
F	100	30	0	0

TABLE 1.2   Production Possibilities for Cars and Wheat

	A	B	C	D	E	F
Cars	0	10	18	24	28	30
Wheat	20	19	17	13	8	0

production possibilities curve: a graphical representation of the various combinations of maximum output that can be produced from the available resources and technology.

Further, we can take the data from **Table 1.2** and use it to graph what is called a **production possibilities curve**, which is a visual representation of the various outputs that can be produced. What appears in **Figure 1.1** is simply another way of presenting the data in **Table 1.2**.

FIGURE 1.1   Production Possibilities Curve I

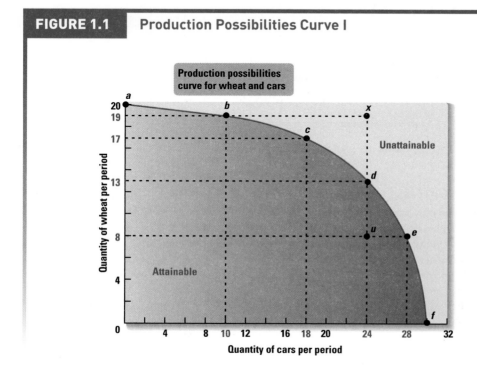

Production possibilities curve for wheat and cars

This society's limited resources allow for the production of a maximum of 20 tonnes of wheat if no cars are produced, as represented by point *a*. Moving down the curve from point *a*, we find other combinations of fewer tonnes of wheat and more cars until we reach point *f*, where 30 cars and no wheat are produced. Point *u* indicates either the underemployment of resources, inefficiency in resource use, or the use of inappropriate technology. Point *x* is unattainable.

Now, recall that:

> The three assumptions that lie behind the production possibilities curve are: full employment, the use of the best technology, and productive efficiency.

On the one hand, if any one of these three assumptions does not hold, then the economy will be operating somewhere inside the production possibilities curve, as illustrated by point *u*, which is 24 cars and 8 tonnes of wheat. On the other hand, point *x* represents an output of 24 cars and 19 tonnes of wheat, which, given this economy's current resources and technology, is unobtainable.

The Law of Increasing Costs

Next, let us consider the actual shape of the curve. Why is it bowed out this way? We need to understand the implication of this particular shape. **Figure 1.2** will help.

FIGURE 1.2   **Production Possibilities Curve II**

At point *b*, 19 tonnes of wheat and 10 cars are being produced. If this society decided that it wanted 8 more cars (point *c*), then 2 tonnes of wheat would have to be sacrificed. Thus, 1 more car would cost 0.25 tonnes of wheat. Moving from point *c* to *d* would increase car production by 6 (18 to 24) at a sacrifice of 4 tonnes of wheat (from 17 to 13). In this instance, 1 more car costs 0.67 tonnes of wheat. Moving from point *d* to *e* would increase car production by only 4 (from 24 to 28), while wheat production would drop by 5 (from 13 to 8). Thus, the cost of 1 more car rises to 1.25 tonnes of wheat.

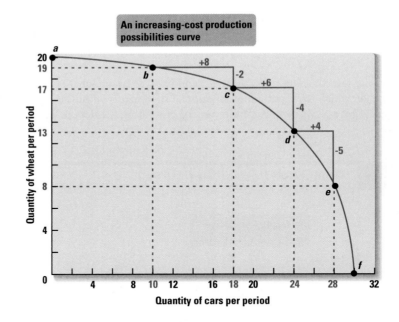

Assume that our hypothetical economy is currently producing 19 tonnes of wheat and 10 cars, as illustrated by point *b* on the production possibilities curve. Then, assume that production decisions are made to re-allocate 20 percent of the productive resources (labour, machines, materials) from wheat production to car production. This new output is illustrated by point *c*. Note that the opportunity cost of producing the additional 8 cars is *not* the additional 20 percent of resources that must be allocated to their production *but* the decreased output of wheat that these resources could have produced. That is to say, the additional 8 cars could only be obtained by reducing the output of wheat from 19 tonnes to 17 tonnes. Thus, 8 more cars cost 2 tonnes of wheat. This can be restated as: 1 more car costs 0.25 tonnes of wheat (2 divided by 8). This seems clear enough, but we are not done.

Next, assume that society, still at point *c*, decides to produce even more cars, as illustrated by moving to point *d* (24 cars and 13 tonnes of wheat). This time an additional 20 percent of the resources produces only 6 more cars (18 to 24) at a cost of 4 units of wheat (17 to 13). This can be restated as: 0.67 tonnes of wheat for every additional car. This is considerably more than the previous cost of 0.25 units of wheat per car. Another shift of 20 percent of resources would move the economy from point *d* to *e*, with the result of an addition of only 4 more cars at a cost of 5 tonnes of wheat. Now, each additional car costs 1.25 (5 divided by 4) units of wheat. **Table 1.3** summarizes all the figures above.

TABLE 1.3	Opportunity Cost per Car		
Graphical Movement	Gain in Cars	Opportunity Costs in Wheat	Opportunity Cost per Car
a to b	10	1	0.10
b to c	8	2	0.25
c to d	6	4	0.67
d to e	4	5	1.25
e to f	2	8	4.00

We have just identified what economists call the **law of increasing costs**. This law states that as the production of any single item increases, the per-unit cost of producing additional units of that item will rise. Note that this law is developed in the context of a whole economy and, as we will see in later chapters, need not apply to the situation of an individual firm.

law of increasing costs: as an economy's production level of any particular item increases, its *per-unit* cost of production rises.

Thus, you can see that as the total production of cars is increased, the rising per-unit cost of cars gives the production possibilities curve its bowed-out shape.

But why does the per-unit cost of cars increase—what is the reason behind the law of increasing costs? The answer is that not all resources are equally suitable for the production of different products. Our hypothetical society has a fixed amount of resources that are used to produce different combinations of both wheat and cars. However, some of these resources would be better suited to producing cars, whereas others would be better suited to producing wheat. An increase in the production of cars requires that some of the resources currently producing wheat would need to be re-allocated to the production of cars. It is only reasonable to assume that the resources that are re-allocated first are the ones that are relatively well suited to the production of cars, whereas those resources less well suited to the production of cars would continue to produce wheat. (Perhaps some of the farm workers are immigrants and have manufacturing experience in the old country, or maybe some of them are allergic to working in the sun.) After all this has taken place, if even *more* cars are to be produced, the only resources left to re-allocate will be ones that are not very well suited for the production of cars. Therefore, a larger quantity of less well suited resources will have to be re-allocated to obtain the desired increase in car production. This will increase the per-unit cost of cars because a larger sacrifice of wheat production will be required.

SELF-TEST

5. Given the accompanying figure:

   a) If society produces 1000 units of butter, what is the maximum number of guns it can produce?

   b) Suppose that society produces the combination shown as point *b* on the production possibilities curve; what is the cost of 1000 additional units of butter?

   c) Would the opportunity cost of 1000 additional units of butter be greater, the same, or smaller as society moves from point *c* to *d*, compared with a move from point *b* to *c*?

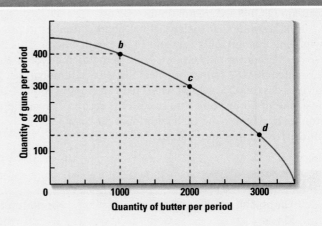

Shifts in the Production Possibilities Curve: The Causes of Economic Growth

A production possibility curve is like a snapshot of an economy: it shows in one quick diagram what an economy is capable of producing at a particular moment. But economies change from year to year, usually—although not always—for the better. The sources of economic growth have been debated for centuries, but our simple model is able to explain some of the important aspects of growth. **Figure 1.3**, for instance, illustrates what economic growth looks like diagrammatically. Here, we see that the maximums of both wheat and car production have increased; the PP curve has shifted out along both axes. Previously, the maximum amount of wheat the country could produce was 80. This has now increased to 100. Similarly, before the change, it could produce a maximum of 80 cars; now it is capable of producing 100 cars.

FIGURE 1.3   **The Effect of Economic Growth**

The production possibilities curve has shifted from PP1 to PP2, which shows that this economy is now capable of producing more cars *and* more wheat.

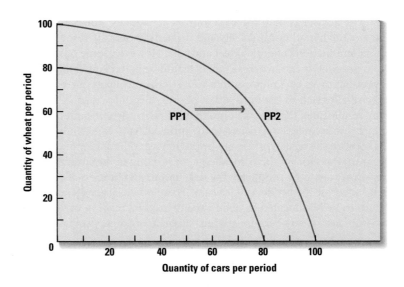

We have to be careful about how we interpret this shift. Remember that a production possibilities curve shows us what an economy is capable of producing; it does not show us what it is actually producing. The rightward shift from PP1 to PP2, then, does not say that this is economy is now producing more goods and services; it simply shows that it is capable of producing more products. In other words, its potential has now improved. And what could have brought about this change? The conditions under which we constructed the production possibilities curve provide a clue.

We assumed that the economy was operating at maximum efficiency: that is to say, it is fully employing its resources and using the best technology. An improvement in either of those last two factors will therefore shift the production possibilities curve to the right. So, here, we have the major causes of economic growth: an improvement in a country's resources or an improvement in its technology. An improvement in its resources could mean either an increase in the amount of available resources (increased population, discovery of new oil fields, improved infrastructure, perhaps) or, just as importantly, an increase in the quality of its resources (a better educated or trained work force, smarter machines, rather than simply more machines, and so on).

The other factor that has wrought significant change over the last few centuries is technological improvement. To illustrate the effects of technological change, imagine a society that produces capital goods and consumer goods and services. You will recall that consumer goods and services are those products used by consumers to satisfy their wants and needs. In contrast, capital goods such as machines and factories do not directly satisfy wants and needs but do help produce consumer goods and services.

Let us start, in **Figure 1.4**, with the economy operating efficiently on the production possibilities curve. PP1, at point *a*. Now, let us assume that a new technology becomes available that has application *only* in the consumer goods and services industry. This is represented by a shift outward in the curve, with the new production possibilities curve becoming PP2. There are

FIGURE 1.4   The Effect of Technological Change on the Production Possibilities Curve

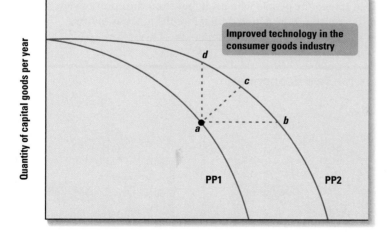

Quantity of consumer goods per year

Start at point *a*, which is a point of efficient production on PP1. An improvement in technology in the consumer goods and services industry shifts the production possibilities curve to PP2. This creates three possible results. First, the same quantity of capital goods and services, and more consumer goods and services can now be produced, as represented by point *b*. Alternatively, more of consumer goods and services *as well as* capital goods and services can be produced, as represented by point *c*. Point *d* represents the third possible result, which is more capital goods and services as well as the same quantity of consumer goods and services *despite* the fact that the technological change was in the consumer goods and services industry.

three possible results. First, the same quantity of capital goods but more consumer goods and services can be produced as represented by *b*. Second, more of *both* goods can also be produced, as represented by point *c*. And third, this economy could now increase the production of capital goods if the same number of consumer goods and services were produced (point *d*) *despite* the fact that this new technology could only be applied to the consumer goods and services industry.

This emphasizes the important role of technological change. It widens the choices (that word again!) available to society and is often seen in a positive light. Alas, technological change also has costs, and this is a subject that will receive our attention later.

Now, look at **Figure 1.4** and ask yourself the following question: which of the three new possible combinations is preferable? If the choice had been between two consumer goods and services, such as wheat and cars, then we could not give a definitive answer to this question without knowing something about the preferences of the country's consumers. But the choices illustrated in this figure are between capital goods and consumer goods and services, and choosing combination *d*—more capital goods—leads to significantly different effects from those of choosing combination *b*.

This point is illustrated in **Figure 1.5**, in which we show two different economies. Atlantis places greater emphasis on the production of capital goods than Mu does. This can be seen by comparing point a_1 (40 units of capital goods) with point b_1 (20 units of capital goods). This emphasis on capital goods production also means a lower production of consumer goods (30 units in Atlantis compared with 50 in Mu). The emphasis on capital goods production in Atlantis means that it will experience more economic growth in the future. This faster growth is illustrated by the production possibilities curve shifting, over time, more to the right in the case of Atlantis than in Mu. After the increase in production possibilities, Atlantis can continue producing 40 units of capital goods but now can produce 70 units of consumer goods (a_2). Mu, by contrast, can produce only 60 units of consumer goods and services while maintaining capital goods production at the original 20 units (b_2). All of this is a result of a different emphasis on the output choices by the two economies.

A sage of some bygone age said that there is no such thing as a free lunch. We can now make some sense out of this idea. Producing more of anything—a lunch, for example, since it involves the use of scarce resources—necessarily means producing less of something else. The lunch might be provided free to the people who eat it, but from the point of view of society as a whole, it took scarce resources to produce it, and therefore the lunch is *not* free.

FIGURE 1.5   Different Growth Rates for Two Economies

We begin with Atlantis and Mu being the same size, as indicated by the same PP1 curves. However, since Atlantis chooses to emphasize the production of capital goods (point a_1), while Mu emphasizes the production of consumer goods and services (point b_1), Atlantis will grow faster. The result of this faster growth is that over time PP2 shifts out further in the case of Atlantis than it does in the case of Mu.

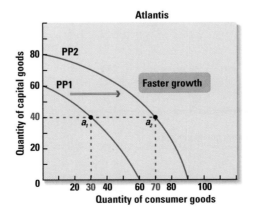

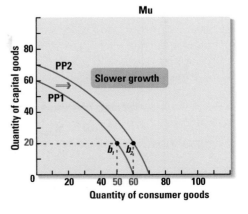

SELF-TEST

6. Assume that the economy of Finhorn faces the following production possibilities:

	Quantities per Year			
	A	B	C	D
Grain	0	25	40	50
Tools	12	8	4	0

a) Draw a production possibilities curve (PP1) with *Tools* on the horizontal axis and *Grain* on the vertical axis. Now, assume that a new technology that can be used only if the tool industry is developed, which increases tool output by 50 percent.

b) Draw a new production possibilities curve (PP2) that reflects this new technology.

c) If Finhorn produced 12 units of tools per year, how many units of grain could be produced after the introduction of the new technology?

1.7　MACROECONOMIC GOALS

The production possibilities model highlights important economic issues, including the costs of unemployment and the benefits of growth. But, more importantly, it graphically illustrates the important concepts of choice and cost. The dilemma facing policy makers in all governments is the same dilemma that faces all of us on a daily basis: how to satisfy conflicting goals. We know we cannot have everything in life, and so we have to make choices. You have six hours available; you want to go for a walk, you want to visit friends, you want to study economics. What do you do? You could abandon two of your goals and wisely decide to study for the whole six hours. More probably, you might decide to divide up your time among the three activities. But do you allocate two hours to each activity or rank them in importance and spend more time on things you consider of greater importance? These considerations also face policy makers who have to decide among a number of competing goals.

This raises the important question:

L07 List the economic goals of society and understand why they are often difficult to achieve.

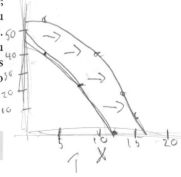

> **What are the typical economic goals of a modern market economy such as Canada's?**

Improved Standard of Living

An important goal for many of us is achieving and maintaining a decent standard of living. Each generation wants to improve on what the previous generation had and to leave the next generation even better off. Our standard of living is mostly determined by our income levels, and Canada has been successful in producing comparatively high incomes for its citizens, as **Figure 1.6** illustrates.

In Canada, each decade has seen an improvement in real incomes (eliminating the effects of inflation), from an average of just under $6000 in the 1930s to almost $38 000 per person in recent years. But higher incomes do not simply translate into bigger houses or more cars. A richer country has the power to enrich the lives of its people in terms of better health and education. It can also allow citizens to enjoy a clean environment, open parklands, and access to cultural pursuits. It is in this broad sense that people define the standard of living, rather than simply in terms of the quantity of goods produced. **Table 1.4** confirms what most Canadians realize: that they live in one of the richest countries in the world. (The incomes are shown in U.S. dollars in terms of purchasing power. We have omitted a few smaller countries such as the Bahamas and Cayman Islands from the rankings.) Of the G8 countries (the world's biggest and most economically advanced nations), Canada is second behind the United States and has an average income over three times the world average.

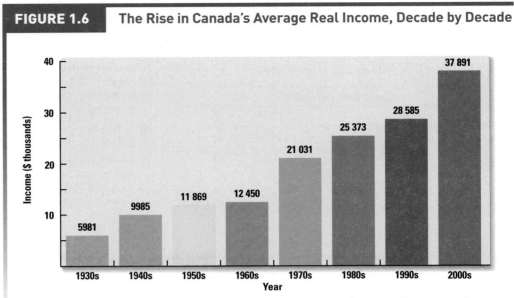

| FIGURE 1.6 | The Rise in Canada's Average Real Income, Decade by Decade |

Adapted from the Statistics Canada publication "Historical Statistics of Canada", 1983, Catalogue 11-516, July 29, 1999 and from Statistics Canada CANSIM database <http://cansim2.statcan.ca>, Tables 380-0002 and 051-0001, January 25, 2011.

TABLE 1.4	Average Incomes for G8 and Selected Countries in 2009		
	Average (Mean) Income	World Rank	G8 Rank
Luxembourg	59 550	1	
U.S.	45 640	5	1
Canada	**37 410**	**11**	**2**
U.K.	37 230	12	3
Germany	36 780	13	4
France	33 930	16	5
Japan	33 740	19	6
Italy	31 360	21	7
Russia	18 350	35	8
China	6890	80	
Average of 181 nations	10 604		

Source: International Bank for Reconstruction and Development / The World Bank: *World Development Indicators*, 2010.

If a country has a high national income, it does not necessarily guarantee that all of its citizens will enjoy a high standard of living. And it is equally true that not all citizens of poor countries are doomed to low standards of living. A high and growing national income, though, is a necessary condition for a high standard of living for most citizens. This brings us to the second goal: achieving economic growth.

Economic Growth

Canada's present high standard of living is as much the result of actions in the past as it is the result of actions in the present. Past actions have provided a social and economic climate that encourages productivity and inventiveness. The growth of production (or real GDP, as it is termed) is necessary in order to improve our standard of living and is essential in order to keep pace with the growth in Canada's population. As **Figure 1.7** shows, just a small change in growth rates can have a big impact on incomes and the standard of living.

FIGURE 1.7   **The Growth of Canada's Average Income**

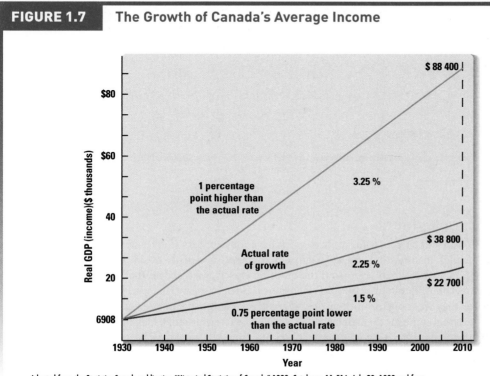

Adapted from the Statistics Canada publication "Historical Statistics of Canada" 1983, Catalogue 11-516, July 29, 1999 and from Statistics Canada CANSIM database <http://cansim2.statcan.ca>, Tables 380-0017 and 051-0001, January 25, 2011.

Over the past 80 years, the average income of Canadians has grown at a rate of 2.25 percent per year. While this may not sound impressive, it resulted in a quadrupling of incomes over this period. And an improvement of just 1 percent on our actual performance would have created an average income per person of over $88 000, more than double our present average. (By the same token, a slightly lower rate of 1.5 percent per annum would have left the average Canadian with an income today of just under $23 000.)

High growth rates do, indeed, increase our prosperity, but keep in mind that economic growth can be a double-edged sword: it can improve our standard of living, but unless the growth is handled sensibly, it can also have exactly the opposite result. This is because economic growth can often cause high rates of pollution, traffic congestion, noise, and stress. It can also lead to resource depletion and pressure on our natural environment, all of which can lower our quality of life despite leaving us with higher incomes. **Table 1.5** gives data on Canada's performance compared with the rest of the world. We can see here the significant impact of the world recession of 2008–10, which hit industrial countries far more than it did less developed countries and resulted in negative growth rates over much of this period. We will look at the financial crisis and the ensuing recession in detail in Chapter 13.

TABLE 1.5	Growth Rates for G8 and Selected Countries 2007–09		
	Growth Rate	**World Rank**	**G8 Rank**
Qatar	20.3	1	
Russia	1.2	134	1
Canada	**0.9**	**160**	**2**
France	–0.1	179	3
U.S.	–0.2	181	4
Germany	–0.4	183	5
U.K.	–0.6	191	6
Japan	–1.4	197	7
Italy	–1.6	201	8
China	11.0	6	
India	7.5	19	
Average of 208 nations	3.7		

Source: International Bank for Reconstruction and Development / The World Bank: *World Development Indicators*, 2010.

Full Employment

Ensuring that all citizens who want to work have jobs appears to be a straightforward goal. Since most people's incomes are derived from employment, few of us could survive for long without working. However, when we look at the question closely, we discover that the goal of full employment may be difficult to achieve. For instance, does it mean that everyone should have a job (whether they want one or not), or does it apply only to those who are willing and able to work? If we believe that it means the latter, should our goal be to ensure that such people have jobs, any jobs or that they have jobs that are satisfying or stimulating, jobs they have been trained or educated for, or jobs that are highly paid? If we grant that the goal of absolute full employment for all citizens all the time may be an impossibility, then what level of unemployment is acceptable: two percent? five percent? ten percent? As **Figure 1.8A** demonstrates, Canada's record on employment is a bit mixed. Although unemployment dropped steadily during the 1990s, it has barely gone below 6 percent in the last 30 years. Canada's unemployment record can be regarded as average at best. **Table 1.6** shows that it came in fourth among the G8 countries and thirty-ninth in the world.

Stable Prices

High rates of inflation can cause a great deal of damage to an economy and its people. But before we jump to the conclusion that a zero rate of inflation (no change in the overall price level) is desirable, remember that we are looking at things from a macroeconomic perspective. Thus, while higher prices may be viewed with alarm by buyers, they may be greatly welcomed by sellers. Perhaps some increase in prices is desirable. But how much—1, 3, or 5 percent per year? Furthermore, is inflation such a bad thing if wages can be increased by the same amount? As we shall see in Chapter 4, the major problem is not so much inflation itself—though it does cause a great deal of suffering for a number of groups in society—but the fact that its unpredictability can be ruinous for an economy.

Figure 1.8B shows Canada's experience with inflation since the 1930s. Looked at in combination with the unemployment rates, some interesting features become apparent. We can see that the 1930s was a period of high unemployment and low inflation (in fact, a period of falling prices,

FIGURE 1.8	**Unemployment and Inflation Rates in Canada**

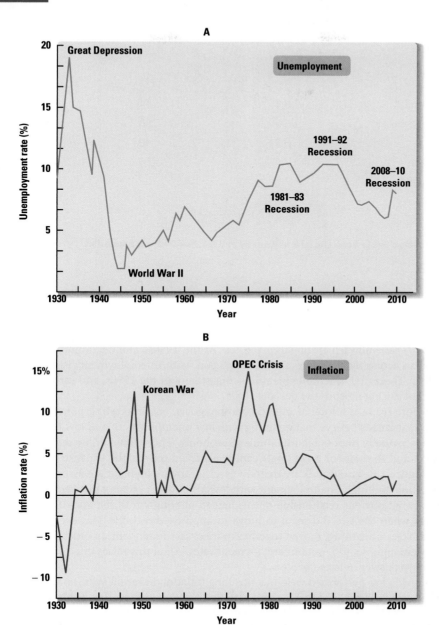

Adapted from the Statistics Canada publication "Historical Statistics of Canada", 1983, Catalogue 11-516, July 29, 1999 and from Statistics Canada CANSIM database <http://cansim2.statcan.ca>, Tables 109-5304 and 326-0021, March 15, 2011.

or deflation, until 1933). The decade of the 1930s was the period of the Great Depression. World War II brought about an economic recovery, which saw unemployment rates dipping below 5 percent for the first time in over a decade, along with rising inflation. The 1950s and 1960s were periods of low unemployment and generally low inflation rates, although prices did take a sharp turn upward during the Korean War in the early 1950s. The mid-1960s to the mid-1980s

TABLE 1.6	Unemployment Rates for G8 and Selected Countries in 2008		
	Unemployment Rate	**World Rank**	**G8 Rank**
Thailand	1.4	1	
Japan	4.0	16	1
U.K.	5.6	27	2
U.S.	5.8	30	3
Canada	**6.1**	**34**	**4**
Russia	6.2	36	5
Italy	6.7	40	6
France	7.4	50	7
Germany	7.5	52	8
China	4.2	19	
Macedonia	33.4	75	

Source: International Bank for Reconstruction and Development / The World Bank: *World Development Indicators*, 2010.

saw both unemployment and inflation starting to rise, with an extra jump in the unemployment rate during the recession of the early 1980s. Following this recession, unemployment, along with inflation, generally fell throughout the rest of the 1980s. The beginning of the 1990s saw the Canadian economy head into another recession, with unemployment rising to over 11 percent by 1992. Thereafter, unemployment fell consistently in the 1990s, and inflation was kept under 2 percent during most of the decade.

Before we take a look at other economic goals, one interesting point must be mentioned. Many economists believe that attaining *both* low unemployment and low inflation rates concurrently is virtually impossible in a modern economy. They would argue that the two goals are in conflict and that one of these goals can be achieved only at the expense of the other. If this is true, **Figure 1.8** should indicate that low levels of unemployment are associated with high levels of inflation and high unemployment with low inflation. A cursory glance at the two curves does not show an obvious relationship of this nature, although until the mid-1960s, there were a few periods when the two did seem to move in opposite directions. However, since 1967, the two curves have, if anything, moved together more or less in tandem. In other words, when inflation rates were high, so, too, were unemployment rates. All of this raises interesting questions that we will try to answer in later chapters.

Canada has performed well in controlling inflation in recent years and has one of the lowest rates in the world, as **Table 1.7** demonstrates. Another feature that **Table 1.7** shows is that for many countries—especially the industrialized ones—the possibility of *deflation* is as likely as that of inflation.

Viable Balance of International Trade

Canada is truly one of the world's greatest trading nations, and many would suggest that our high standard of living is a result of this. Economists would tend to agree that international trade is beneficial for all nations, since it encourages specialization and promotes competition. It is better for a nation to concentrate its resources on producing the goods and services that it can produce more efficiently and cheaply than can others. Then, with the proceeds, it is able to buy those

TABLE 1.7	Inflation Rates for G8 and Selected Countries (2009)		
	Inflation Rate	**World Rank**	**G8 Rank**
Afganistan	−13.3	1	
Japan	−1.4	9	1
U.K.	−0.6	18	2
U.S.	−0.4	34	3
France	0.1	33	4
Canada	**0.3**	**34**	**5**
Germany	0.3	38	5
Italy	0.8	42	7
Russia	11.7	156	8
China	−0.7	15	
Venezuela	31.8	168	
Average of 168 nations	3.7		

Source: International Bank for Reconstruction and Development / The World Bank: *World Development Indicators,* 2010.

things that others can produce more cheaply. The difference between what a nation exports and what it imports is known as the *balance of trade*. It may not be possible to have a trade surplus (when a country exports more than it imports) every year, but a country will also experience a number of economic problems if it consistently has trade deficits. **Figure 1.9** shows the Canadian experience for the last seven decades or so.

FIGURE 1.9	Canada's Balance of Trade 1930–2010

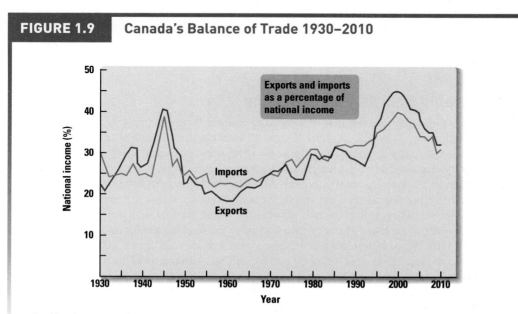

Adapted from the Statistics Canada publication "Historical Statistics of Canada", 1983, Catalogue 11-516, July 29, 1999 and from Statistics Canada CANSIM database <http://cansim2.statcan.ca>, Table 376-0001 and 380-0017, March 15, 2011.

As the graph illustrates, the 1990s saw a dramatic upswing in international trade for Canada, mainly as a result of the North American Free Trade Agreement (NAFTA). In the past decade, Canada has exported and imported as much as 45 percent of its national income, though in recent years that figure has declined to just over 30 percent. But we should add a note of caution: it is not enough for a country to sell abroad as much or more than it buys. The types of things a country sells can make a difference to its long-term welfare. For example, is a country selling manufactured and processed goods or selling off its raw materials? Is it selling goods and services or selling off its assets? These are important questions.

Interestingly, we could add that, except Russia and China, the world's top seven trading nations are also among the world's top ranked GDP nations (**Table 1.8**).

TABLE 1.8	Exports for G8 and Selected Countries 2009		
	Exports ($ billions)	World Rank	G8 Rank	% National Income
U.S.	1571	1	1	11.2
Germany	1377	2	2	40.8
Japan	674	4	3	12.5
France	617	5	4	23.0
U.K.	589	6	5	27.7
Italy	510	7	6	24.0
Canada	**384**	**8**	**7**	**28.7**
Russia	345	15	8	27.7
China	1333	3		36.9
Netherlands	518	9		

Source: International Bank for Reconstruction and Development / The World Bank: *World Development Indicators,* 2010.

An Equitable Distribution of Income

Someone once said that the true test of a civilized country is how it treats its poorest members. After all, from a social and moral point of view, an increase in a nation's prosperity is not much use unless all of its citizens, rather than just a select few, get to enjoy and share in it. Large disparities in incomes can lead to social unrest and high crime rates, so it is important that a country have a system in place to ensure that nobody literally dies for want of food or adequate medical services. But just how equal incomes should be is a vexing question. If everyone were guaranteed the same income regardless of their efforts, this would conflict with our desire to promote economic growth, since there would be little incentive for working harder or being innovative.

Figure 1.10 shows how Canada's economic pie was divided up in 2008. (It has hardly changed over the last 35 years.) The lowest quintile of Canadian families (the poorest 20 percent) received just over 4 percent of the national pie, whereas the top 20 percent received nearly one-half. Clearly, Canada's income is far from evenly distributed.

As **Table 1.9** shows, Japan is one of the most equitable of nations when it comes to the distribution of income: the top 20 percent of its income earners receive 3.4 times as much as the lowest 20 percent. (The numbers used in this table are a little different from those used by

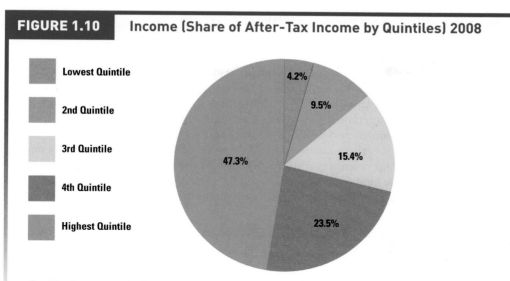

FIGURE 1.10   Income (Share of After-Tax Income by Quintiles) 2008

- Lowest Quintile
- 2nd Quintile
- 3rd Quintile
- 4th Quintile
- Highest Quintile

4.2%
9.5%
15.4%
47.3%
23.5%

Adapted from the Statistics Canada publication "Income distributions by size in Canada", 1997, Catalogue 13-207, April 14, 1999 and from Statistics Canada CANSIM database <http://cansim2.statcan.ca>, Table 202-0405, March 16, 2011.

TABLE 1.9   Income Distribution for G8 and Selected Countries 2007

	Income Distribution	World Rank	G8 Rank
Azerbaijan	2.3	1	
Japan	3.4	2	1
Germany	4.3	15	2
Canada	**5.5**	**34**	**3**
France	5.6	35	4
Italy	6.5	53	5
U.K.	7.2	68	6
U.S.	8.5	86	7
Russia	9.0	94	8
China	8.4	85	
Namibia	52.2	145	

Source: International Bank for Reconstruction and Development / The World Bank: *World Development Indicators*, 2010.

Statistics Canada because a slightly different methodology was used to obtain them.) Contrast this with the United States, where the top 20 percent earn 8.5 times as much as the lowest 20 percent. Compared with the other G8 countries, Canada's performance is quite good at 5.5 but is distinctly average in world rankings, coming in thirty-fourth. However, since the world average is 10.3, Canada's income distribution is more equitable than in most countries.

A Manageable Government Debt and Deficit

Most economists (unlike some politicians) believe that there is nothing intrinsically wrong with a government spending more than it earns in any one year—in other words, with running a budget deficit. It really depends on the state of the economy at any given time. But if a government runs deficits regardless of the state of the economy or runs deficits year in and year out, it is certainly going to cause grief for the nation and create a higher public debt. It would be prudent, then, for a government to exercise a certain degree of fiscal responsibility. A look at **Figure 1.11** shows how the Canadian government has performed in the fiscal stakes over the past 75 years. As we shall see in later chapters, it is perhaps unavoidable that a government might overspend in a depression (because of falling tax revenues) or during wartime (with rising expenditures), but it would be difficult to justify the high deficits that Canada experienced in the 1980s and early 1990s. It is only in recent years that the Canadian government seems to have put its fiscal house in order.

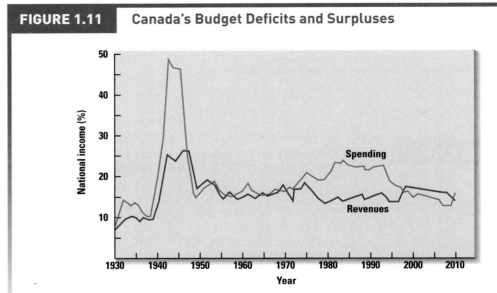

FIGURE 1.11   **Canada's Budget Deficits and Surpluses**

Adapted from the Statistics Canada publication "Historical Statistics of Canada" 1983, Catalogue 11-516, Series H18 and H19-34, July 29, 1999; Data regarding Budget Expenses and Revenues from the Department of Finance Canada, Fiscal Reference Tables, October 2010. Reproduced with the permission of the Minister of Public Works and Government Services, 2011.

Table 1.10 points out two important ideas. Firstly, it shows that countries suffering a recession tend to run up budget deficits as government tax revenues drop. The recession of 2008–10 resulted in a drop in national income for most countries, as well as an increase in budget deficits. Secondly, the table shows that Canada has outperformed most countries in managing its deficits. In fact, until the recession hit Canada, it had produced budget surpluses every year since the mid-1990s. Canada has ranked first among G8 countries in managing its budget over the past five years. (The figures are depicted in terms of the country's budget surplus or deficit as a percentage of its national income.)

We will discuss some theories about recessions and budget deficits in Chapter 7 and the realities in Chapter 13.

Finally, few people would disagree with the economic goals that we have briefly described, though they might argue about their order of importance. It is also clear that trying to achieve all seven goals simultaneously and consistently might be impossible. While some of these goals such as economic growth and full employment are complementary, others are likely to be in conflict.

TABLE 1.10	Government Surpluses/Deficits as % of GDP for G8 and Selected Countries		
	Surplus/Deficit % (% of GDP) Average 2006–08	Surplus/Deficit % (% of GDP) Average 2009–10	G8 Rank 2006–10
Canada	+1.1	−4.3	1
Germany	−0.5	−4.2	2
Italy	−2.5	−5.2	3
Japan	−2.0	−7.4	4
France	−2.8	−7.7	5
U.K.	−3.4	−11.4	6
U.S.	−3.8	−10.8	7
Ireland	−1.4	−13.0	
Greece	−5.6	59	

Source: Based on data from *Economic Outlook No 87—June 2010* under OECD Economic Outlook under *Economic Projections* from OECD Stat Extracts, http://stats.oecd.org accessed on May 3, 2011.

We have already mentioned how trying to achieve full employment and stable prices at the same time may be very difficult. The same may also be true if we try to stimulate economic growth by providing tax incentives for corporations and high-income groups. While this may increase growth, it may also lead to an increase in the government's budget deficit and also adversely affect equitable distribution of income.

One of the major tasks of government, then, is to try to balance these goals in a way that secures the long-term well-being of all its citizens. To accomplish this difficult task, government has a number of tools at its disposal.

Tools for Achieving Macroeconomic Goals

Governments around the world pursue what economists call fiscal and monetary policies in an attempt to achieve the macroeconomic goals that they have decided are most important, particularly full employment, stable prices, and economic growth. The term *fiscal policy* refers to government's taxation and spending policies, which we will study in detail in Chapter 7. Decreases in taxes or increases in spending will stimulate the economy toward more growth and lower unemployment.

Conversely, increased taxes and less spending tends to reduce growth and increase unemployment—but may well reduce inflation. *Monetary policy*, however, refers to the policies of the country's central bank regarding interest rates and the money supply. We will look at this in detail in Chapter 12. Lower interest rates have a stimulative effect on the economy, while higher rates are often used to control inflation.

There is also a category of policies that we call *direct controls*, which run the gamut from tariffs and quotas on imports, to minimum-wage laws, to anti-pollution regulations. These are used to address more specific macroeconomic goals and will also be discussed in more detail in Chapter 9.

We have discussed a number of issues in this chapter and have introduced a number of terms, some of which may be unfamiliar to you. It is not vital for you to understand everything all at once, and for that reason, we have avoided giving too many precise definitions at this stage. The topics discussed here, after all, are the subject matter of the whole book, and we will be returning to them throughout. It is hoped, however, that you can now at least taste the flavour of the various issues and debates.

Review

CHAPTER SUMMARY

In this introductory chapter, you gained an insight into the scope and depth of economics. You learned that economists are very focused on choices—and the related costs that individuals, corporations, and governments face when making decisions. In the discussion on macroeconomic goals, you got a taste of how government's emphasis on any particular set of goals can have a profound effect on the performance of the economy.

1.1 Topical controversies can easily be used to illustrate the relevance of economics.

1.2a Distinguishing between positive and normative statements is part of the scientific method that is used extensively by economists in their attempt to better understand the world.

1.2b The discipline of economics is subdivided into:

- microeconomics, which studies the decisions made by people and firms and their outcomes; and

- macroeconomics, which studies how the major components of the whole economy interact and how well an economy achieves economic goals such as full employment and economic growth.

1.3a Scarcity forces choice (for society, government, and the individual), and choice involves an (opportunity) cost.

1.3b Efficiency implies that economies make the best use of their resources and technology. There are two major types of efficiency: productive efficiency and allocative efficiency, and both are important.

1.4 Greater specialization and trade can make economies more productive.

1.5a The three fundamental questions that all societies must somehow answer are:

- *What* is the right combination of consumer goods to produce, and what is the right balance between consumer goods and capital goods?

- *How* should these various goods be produced?

- Who is to receive what share of these goods once they are produced?

1.5b There are four fundamental ways to organize society: co-operation, command, custom, and competition.

1.6 The production possibilities model is an abstraction and simplification that helps illustrate:

- the necessity of choice in deciding what to produce,

- the opportunity cost involved in making a choice,

- inefficient production and the consequences of unemployed resources, and

- economic growth.

1.7a The overall performance of an economy is measured by how well it achieves the seven economic goals:

- improving the standard of living

- maintaining economic growth

- full employment

- stable prices

- a viable balance of payments

- an equitable distribution of income

- maintaining a manageable government debt and budget deficit

1.7b The three tools that policy makers use to achieve economic goals are:

- fiscal policy

- monetary policy

- direct controls

NEW GLOSSARY TERMS

allocative efficiency   10

capital   7

consumer goods and services   8

enterprise   7

factors of production   7

inputs   7

interest   8

labour   7

land   7

law of increasing costs   19

macroeconomics   6

normative statements   5

microeconomics   7

opportunity cost   8

positive statements   5

production possibilities curve   17

productive efficiency   10

profit   8

rent   8

resources   7

technology   8

wages   8

STUDY TIPS

1. Since this is the first chapter, do not be concerned if the new terminology seems overwhelming. Mastering the principles of economics requires that you first learn the language of economics; the best way to do this is to use it over and over. Let this Study Guide help you do this. Conscientiously work through all of the answered questions before proceeding to the next chapter.

2. Developing a knack for inventing useful acronyms for yourself can be helpful. For example, wages, interest, rents, and profits could be remembered as "WIRP."

3. Opportunity cost is one of the most important concepts in economics. As a start, make sure that you understand the basic idea that cost are not just measured in dollars and cents but also in what has to be given up as a result of making a particular decision.

4. This chapter introduces you to the use of graphs with the production possibilities curve. If you have any difficulty understanding graphs, you might review the Tool Kit at the beginning of the book.

5. For many of you, economics will be one of the more difficult courses that you will encounter in your undergraduate studies. Yet it can be mastered, and doing so can be very rewarding. You will probably be much more successful if you work a little on economics several times a week rather than have one long session a week. This way, you will gain mastery over the language more quickly through repetition and thereby gain confidence. You might consider buying a pack of 3" × 5" index cards and writing two or three definitions or simple ideas on each card. Carry several cards around with you so that you can glance at them several times a day. The authors found this technique helpful when (oh, so many years ago) they started to learn the discipline.

Answered Questions

These questions can also be found online on Connect.

Indicate whether the following statements are true or false:

1. **(LO 3)** T or F̲   An economy as a whole faces scarcity because of limited national income.

2. **(LO 5)** T̲ or F   The three fundamental questions in economics are what, how, and how many.

3. **(LO 3)** T̲ or F   Opportunity cost is the value of the next-best alternative that is given up as a result of making a particular choice.

4. **(LO 5)** T or F̲   There are only three Cs that humankind has used to coordinate its economies: co-operation, custom, and competition.

Mc Graw Hill connect™

Practise and learn online with Connect, where you can find the Answered Questions and the Unanswered Problems for all chapters of this textbook's Study Guide section.

5. **(LO 3) T or F**   Wages, interest, rent, and profits are the four factors of production.

6. **(LO 6) T or F**   A production possibility curve is a graphical representation of the various combinations of output that are wanted.

7. **(LO 2) T or F**   Macroeconomics focuses on the outcomes of decisions by people and firms, whereas microeconomics is a study of how the major components of an economy interact.

8. **(LO 6) T or F**   Technological improvement can be illustrated graphically by a rightward shift in the production possibilities curve.

9. **(LO 7) T or F**   Tax policy, tariff policy, budget policy, monetary policy, and exchange rate policy are all examples of economic policies.

10. **(LO 7) T or F**   Canada's highest unemployment rates were recorded in the 1930s.

Basic (Questions 11–23)

11. **(LO 3)** All of the following statements, *except one*, are valid examples of the way economists use the term scarcity. Which is the exception?
    a) Households face a scarcity of income.
    b) Individuals face a scarcity of time.
    c) Economies face a scarcity of resources.
    d) The world faces a scarcity of ideas.

12. **(LO 3)** What is the definition of opportunity cost?
    a) The amount of money spent on a good.
    b) The value of the next best alternative that is given up as a result of making a particular decision.
    c) The value of all the alternatives given up as a result of making a particular decision.
    d) The cost incurred in producing a good.

13. **(LO 3)** Meridith had only $16 to spend this last weekend. She was, at first, uncertain about whether to go to two movies she had been wanting to see or to buy a new CD she had recently heard. In the end, she went to the movies. Which of the following statements is correct?
    a) The choice of the two movies and not the CD is an example of increasing costs.
    b) The opportunity cost of the two movies is one CD.
    c) The opportunity cost of the two movies is $16.
    d) The choice of two movies rather than one CD was a bad one.

14. **(LO 4)** In reference to voluntary trade, what was Adam Smith the first to recognize?
    a) It does not happen very often.
    b) It may or may not benefit one or both of the parties to the trade.

c) It benefits one party to the trade but only at the expense of the other.
    d) It benefits both parties to the trade.

15. **(LO 5)** What are the three fundamental questions in economics?
    a) What to produce, how to produce it, and for whom to produce it.
    b) Is it necessary, is it right, and is it valuable?
    c) Who should produce, what is the right way to produce, and how should we decide?
    d) What to produce, how to produce it, and who should produce it.

16. **(LO 5)** What are the four basic ways that society can organize its economic affairs?
    a) With consumer goods, capital goods, models, and positive statements
    b) Using co-operation, command, custom, or competition
    c) Using plentiful resources, opportunity costs, technology, and specialization
    d) Using capitalism, communism, enterprise, and technology

17. **(LO 3)** "Resources" is a term that can be used interchangeably with:
    a) Models
    b) Consumer goods
    c) Either factors of production or inputs
    d) Technologies

18. **(LO 3)** What are the factors of production?
    a) Land, labour, money, and enterprise
    b) Land, labour, money, and capital
    c) Land, labour, capital, and enterprise
    d) Competition, command, custom, and co-operation

19. **(LO 3)** What are the names of the factor payments?
    a) Consumption spending and investment spending
    b) Wages and profits
    c) Wages, interest, and profits
    d) Wages, interest, rent, and profits

20. **(LO 2, 6)** What is an example of an economic model?
    a) Opportunity costs and comparative advantage
    b) Scarcity of resources and unlimited wants
    c) Positive statements and normative statements
    d) The production possibilities curve

21. **(LO 3)** All of the following, *except one*, are capital goods. Which is the exception?
    a) An office building
    b) A boiler in a pulp mill
    c) A householder's garden shed
    d) An airport runway

22. **(LO 7)** Which of the following is not a macroeconomic goal?
    a) Improvements in the standard of living
    b) Ensuring that the true needs of all people are met
    c) Full employment
    d) Stable prices

23. **(LO 7)** All of the following, *except one*, are tools of macroeconomic policy. Which is the exception?
    a) Direct controls
    b) Fiscal policy
    c) Destabilization policy
    d) Monetary policy

Intermediate (Questions 24–30)

24. **(LO 5)** Which of the following refers to the concept of specialization?
    a) Different individuals value goods differently.
    b) Some individuals are richer than others.
    c) Different nations have different opportunity costs of producing goods.
    d) Some nations are richer than others.

25. **(LO 6)** All of the following, *except one*, are causes of economic growth. Which is the exception?
    a) The discovery of new oilfields
    b) Unemployed workers find jobs
    c) A number of new effective training schemes for young people are introduced
    d) An improved fuel-cell is invented

26. **(LO 7)** Which of the following is most valid with respect to macroeconomic goals?
    a) They tend to complement each other.
    b) They are always in conflict with each other.
    c) Some are complementary, and some are in conflict.
    d) The educational background of economists varies enormously.

27. **(LO 2)** What is the distinction between a positive statement and a normative statement?
    a) Positive statements are assertions that can be tested with data, whereas normative statements are based on a value system of beliefs.
    b) Normative statements are assertions that can be tested with data, whereas positive statements are based on a value system of beliefs.
    c) The distinction depends on the context in which each statement is used.
    d) Positive statements are correct statements of fact, whereas normative statements are incorrect.

Figure 1.12 shows Mendork's production possibility curve for the only two goods that it produces—guns and butter. Refer to this figure to answer questions 28–33.

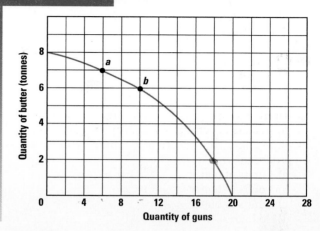

FIGURE 1.12

28. **(LO 6)** If Mendork's production is currently indicated by point *a*, what is the cost of producing four more guns?
    a) 1 tonne of butter
    b) 2 tonnes of butter
    c) 6 tonnes of butter
    d) 10 tonnes of butter

29. **(LO 6)** What is the opportunity cost of one more tonne of butter as output changes from point *b* to *a*?
    a) 2 guns
    b) 4 guns
    c) 10 guns
    d) 6 guns

30. **(LO 6)** Which of the following statements is correct if Mendork is currently producing 5 tonnes of butter and 8 guns?
    a) This society is using competition to coordinate its economic activities.
    b) This society is experiencing either unemployment or inefficiency.
    c) This economy is experiencing full employment.
    d) This society is not adequately answering the "for whom" question.
    e) This economy is growing quickly.

Advanced (Questions 31–35)

31. **(LO 6)** What is the opportunity cost of producing 2 tonnes of butter?
    a) 2 guns
    b) 18 guns
    c) 20 guns
    d) The answer cannot be determined from the information given

32. **(LO 6)** If new technology increased the output of guns by 50 percent, how many guns could be produced if 6 tonnes of butter were produced?
 a) 18 guns
 b) 20 guns
 c) 15 guns
 d) 10 guns
 e) 0 guns

33. **(LO 6)** If a depletion of resources reduces the production possibilities of butter production by one half, how much butter could be produced if 10 units of guns were produced?
 a) 4 units of butter
 b) 3 units of butter
 c) 2 units of butter
 d) No butter

34. **(LO 6)** Which of the following statements describes the law of increasing costs as it relates to the whole economy?
 a) As the quantity produced of any particular item decreases, its per-unit cost of production rises.

b) As the quantity produced of any particular item increases, its per-unit cost of production rises.
 c) The prices of consumer goods and services always rise and never fall.
 d) If you wait to make a purchase, you will pay a higher price.
 e) The total cost of production rises as output goes up.

35. **(LO 6)** Which of the following statements is correct for a society that emphasizes the production of capital goods over that of consumer goods?
 a) The society could enjoy the same quantity of capital goods and a larger quantity of consumer goods in the future.
 b) The society will have to save more now than a society that did not emphasize the production of capital goods.
 c) The society could enjoy the same quantity of consumer goods and a larger quantity of capital goods in the future.
 d) The society will grow faster than a society that emphasizes the production of consumer goods.
 e) All of the above are correct.

Parallel Problems

ANSWERED PROBLEMS

36A. **(LO 6)** **Key Problem Table 1.11** contains the production possibilities data for capital goods and consumer goods in the economy of New Harmony.

TABLE 1.11

	A	B	C	D	E
Capital goods	0	8	14	18	20
Consumer goods	30	27	21	12	0

 a) Use the grid in **Figure 1.13** to draw the production possibilities curve for New Harmony, and label it PPI. Label each of the five output combinations with the letters *a* through *e*.
 b) Assume that the people of New Harmony have decided to produce 12 units of consumer goods. How many units of capital goods could be produced?
 Answer: _____

FIGURE 1.13

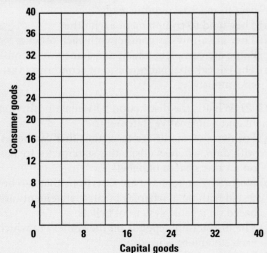

Consumer goods (vertical axis: 0, 4, 8, 12, 16, 20, 24, 28, 32, 36, 40)

Capital goods (horizontal axis: 0, 8, 16, 24, 32, 40)

c) Assume that the people of New Harmony have decided to produce 11 units of capital goods. Approximately, how many units of consumer goods could be produced?

Answer: _____

d) What is the total cost of (the first) 14 capital goods produced?

Answer: _____

e) Assuming the economy is producing combination C, what is the total cost of 6 additional consumer goods?

Answer: _____

f) Assuming the economy is producing combination B, what is the approximate per-unit cost of an additional capital good?

Answer: _____

g) Assuming the economy is producing combination C, what is the approximate per-unit cost of an additional capital good?

Answer: _____

h) What law is illustrated in your answers to f) and g)?

i) Fill in **Table 1.12** assuming that, 10 years later, the output potential of capital goods has increased by 50 percent, while the output potential for consumer goods has risen by 6 units for each combination A through D in **Table 1.11**.

TABLE 1.12

	V	W	X	Y	Z
Capital goods	___	___	___	___	___
Consumer goods and services	___	___	___	___	___

j) Using the data from this table, draw in PP2 in **Figure 1.13**.

k) As a result of the economic growth, can New Harmony now produce 24 capital goods and 26 consumer goods?

Answer: _____

l) What are three possible reasons that would explain the shift from PP1 to PP2?

Answer: _____

Basic (Problems 37A–45A)

37A. **(LO 7)** Match the letters on the left with the numbers on the right. Place the correct letter in the blank. (Data refer to Canada.)

a) $30 000 per person

b) 2.25 percent per year

c) above 6 percent for last 20 years

d) below 3 percent for last 20 years

1. inflation _____

2. unemployment _____

3. economic growth _____

4. standard of living _____

38A. **(LO 2)** Identify each of the following statements as positive or normative:

a) Canada is the best country in the world to live in. _____

b) Canada's national income has risen for the last five years. _____

c) If the world price of wheat rises, Canada will export less wheat. _____

d) Unemployment is a more serious problem than inflation. _____

39A. **(LO 6)** Answer the questions below based on **Figure 1.14** which is for the country of Quantz.

How much tea is gained and what is the cost in coffee:

a) in moving from U to V _____ tea is gained at the cost of _____.

b) in moving from V to W _____ tea is gained at the cost of _____.

FIGURE 1.14

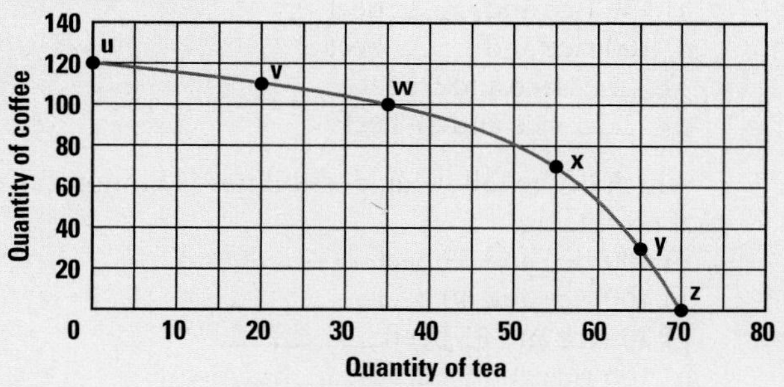

c) in moving from W to X _____ tea is gained at the cost of _____.

d) in moving from X to Y _____ tea is gained at the cost of _____.

e) in moving from Y to Z _____ tea is gained at the cost of _____.

40A. **(LO 3)** Below is a list of resources. Indicate whether each is labour (L), capital (K), land (N), or enterprise (E).
   a) An irrigation ditch in Manitoba _____
   b) The work done by Jim Plum, a labourer who helped dig the irrigation ditch _____
   c) A lake _____
   d) The air we breath _____
   e) The efforts of the founder and primary innovator of a successful new software company _____

41A. **(LO 3)** Below is a list of economic goods. You are to decide whether each is a consumer good (C), a capital good (K), or possibly both (B), depending on the context in which it is used.
   a) A pair of socks _____
   b) A golf course _____
   c) A Big Mac hamburger _____
   d) A wheelbarrow _____

42A. **(LO 6)** Table 1.13 shows the production possibilities for the country of Emilon.

TABLE 1.13

	A	B	C	D	E
Rice	0	50	90	120	140
Beef	50	45	35	20	0

Complete the following (approximate) possibilities for Emilon: _____
   a) 130 rice and _____ beef
   b) 100 rice and _____ beef
   c) _____ rice and 5 beef
   d) _____ rice and 47 beef

Which of the following possibilities is Emilon capable of producing?
   e) 100 rice and 35 beef _____
   f) 100 rice and 40 beef _____
   g) 70 rice and 35 beef _____
   h) 100 rice and 5 beef _____

43A. **(LO 6)** Table 1.14 shows the production possibilities for the country of Emilon.

TABLE 1.14

	A	B	C	D	E
Rice	0	50	90	120	140
Beef	50	45	35	20	0

   a) What is the total cost of producing 90 rice?
   Answer: _____ beef
   b) What is the total cost of producing 45 beef?
   Answer: _____ rice
   c) What is the total cost of going from possibility C to possibility D?
   Answer: _____ (rice/beef)
   d) What is the approximate per-unit cost of going from possibility C to possibility D?
   Answer: _____ (rice/beef)
   e) What is the total cost of going from possibility D to possibility C?
   Answer: _____ (rice/beef)
   f) What is the approximate per unit cost of going from possibility D to possibility C?
   Answer: _____ (rice/beef)

44A. **(LO 2)** Explain why the discipline of economics is sometimes called the *science of choice*.

45A. **(LO 5)** Identify and explain the four factors of production and the names given to payments received by each.

Intermediate (Problems 46A–52A)

46A. **(LO 6)** Utopia produces only two products: cheese and wine. The production levels are shown in **Table 1.15**.

TABLE 1.15

CHEESE		WINE	
% inputs	output	% inputs	output
0	0	0	0
20	30	20	40
40	50	40	70
60	65	60	95
80	75	80	105
100	80	100	110

From these data, complete Utopia's production possibilities table in **Table 1.16**.

TABLE 1.16

Possibility	A	B	C	D	E	F
Cheese	0	___	___	___	___	___
Wine	___	___	___	___	___	___

a) Can Utopia produce 65 cheese and 95 wine?
Answer: _____

b) Can Utopia produce 75 cheese and 40 wine?
Answer: _____

c) If Utopia is at D, what is the total cost of 10 more cheese?
Answer: _____

d) If Utopia is at D, what is the total cost of 25 more wine?
Answer: _____

47A. (LO 6) Table 1.17 shows Lanark's production possibilities:

TABLE 1.17

	A	B	C	D	E	F
Wheat	0	20	35	45	50	52
Cars	21	20	18	14	8	0

a) If Lanark is producing 16 cars, approximately how much wheat can it produce?
Answer: _____

b) If Lanark is currently producing combination C, what is the cost of 10 more wheat?
Answer: _____

c) If Lanark is currently producing combination C, what is the cost of 2 more cars?
Answer: _____

d) If Lanark is currently producing combination D, what is the approximate unit cost of an additional car?
Answer: _____

e) If Lanark is currently producing combination D, what is the approximate unit cost of an additional wheat?
Answer: _____

48A. (LO 6) Shangri-La produces only two goods: bats and balls. Each worker comes with a fixed quantity of material and capital, and the economy's labour force is fixed at 50 workers. **Table 1.18** indicates the amounts of bats and balls that can be produced daily with various quantities of labour.

TABLE 1.18

Number of Workers	Daily Production of Balls	Number of Workers	Daily Production of Bats
0	0	0	0
10	150	10	20
20	250	20	36
30	325	30	46
40	375	40	52
50	400	50	55

a) What is the opportunity cost of increasing the output of bats from 46 to 52 units per day? _____

b) What is the opportunity cost of increasing the output of balls from 325 to 375 units per day? _____

c) Suppose that a central planning office dictates an output of 250 balls and 61 bats per day. Is this output combination possible? _____

d) Now, assume that a new technology is introduced in the production of bats so that each worker can produce half a bat more per day. Can the planning office's goal of 250 balls and 61 bats now be met? _____

49A. (LO 5) The data below show the total production (in millions) of the only two goods produced in Kitchener and Waterloo, two small planets in deep space: **Kitchener:** 16 kiwis or 12 trucks; **Waterloo:** 8 kiwis or 14 trucks.

a) What is the opportunity cost of a kiwi in Kitchener? _____

b) What is the opportunity cost of a kiwi in Waterloo? _____

c) What is the opportunity cost of a truck in Kitchener? _____

d) What is the opportunity cost of a truck in Waterloo? _____

e) Which planet is best at producing kiwis?
_____

f) Which planet is best at producing trucks?
_____

g) If, before trade, each planet was devoting half its resources to producing each product, what is the total amount produced by both?
_____

h) If the two planets were to specialize in producing the product they do best, what would be the total amount they could produce?
_____

i) What are the total gains as a result of specialization? _____

50A. **(LO 2, 6)** Write down a normative statement that relates to economics. Next, change your statement to make it a positive one.

51A. **(LO 6)** Illustrate economic growth using a production possibilities curve (remember to label the axes). What are two possible causes of economic growth?

52A. **(LO 6)** Suppose the country of Catalona produces leather shirts and leather moccasins, and the production of each requires the same amount of leather and the same tools. Also, workers in Catalona are equally capable of producing either product. Draw a production possibilities curve for Catalona, and comment on its shape.

Advanced (Problems 53A–60A)

53A. **(LO 2)** Explain the analogy between the use of theory and the use of a map.

54A. **(LO 6)** The data in **Table 1.19** are for the small country of Xanadu. Assume that the economy is originally producing combination C, but technological change occurs that enables it to produce 60 percent more capital goods.

TABLE 1.19

	A	B	C	D	E	F
Capital goods	0	25	40	50	55	58
Consumer goods	50	40	30	20	10	0

a) If the economy wants to continue with the same quantity of consumer goods, how many more capital goods can it now have as a result of the technological improvement? _____

b) If the economy wants to continue with the same quantity of capital goods, how many more consumer goods can it now have as a result of the technological improvement? _____

c) Before the technological change, what was the opportunity cost of the first 40 consumer goods? _____

d) After the technological change, what was the opportunity cost of the first 40 consumer goods? _____

55A. **(LO 6)** Jennifer is planning how to spend a particularly rainy Sunday, and the choice is between watching video movies (each lasting two hours) or studying her economics textbook. She has 10 hours available to her. If she decides to study, she could read the following number of pages at the rate as shown in **Table 1.20**.

TABLE 1.20

Hours	Pages
2	80
4	130
6	160
8	175
10	180

a) Given this information, draw Jennifer's production possibilities curve between movies watched and pages studied on the grid in **Figure 1.15**.

FIGURE 1.15

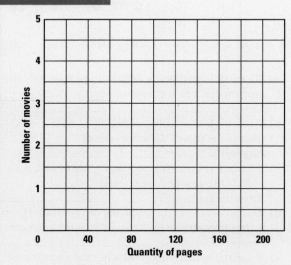

b) What is the opportunity cost of watching two movies? _____

c) Could Jennifer watch three movies and study 150 pages of her textbook? _____

d) If Jennifer has already watched four movies, what is the opportunity cost of watching the fifth movie? _____

56A. **(LO 5)** To what extent is the organization of family based on the four Cs? Give examples of how each of the four Cs is used to assign household chores to its members. What blend of the four Cs do you think is preferable, and why?

57A. **(LO 3)** Kant Skatte is a professional player in the National Hockey League. Because he loved the game so much, Kant dropped out of high school and worked very hard to develop his physical strength and overcome his limitations. Eventually, he made it to the NHL. What data are needed to estimate Kant's annual opportunity costs, in dollars, of continuing to play in the NHL?

58A. **(LO 6)** Assume that an economy can produce either 300 tonnes of coffee and no rubber, or 100 tonnes of rubber and no coffee. You may further assume that this coffee-rubber ratio of 3:1 is constant. Draw a production possibilities curve for this economy with coffee on the vertical axis. Next, indicate with the letters *a* and *b* an increase in rubber production. Finally, illustrate with a triangle the cost of this additional rubber.

59A. **(LO 7)** Does a high income level mean a higher standard of living? Why, or why not?

60A. **(LO 7)** Can an economy grow too fast? What might be some of the problems of high growth?

CHAPTER 2

DEMAND AND SUPPLY: AN INTRODUCTION

LEARNING OBJECTIVES

At the end of this chapter, you should be able to...

LO1 explain the concept of demand.

LO2 explain the concept of supply.

LO3 explain the term *market*.

LO4 understand the concept of (price and quantity) equilibrium.

LO5 understand the causes and effects of a change in demand.

LO6 understand the causes and effects of a change in supply.

LO7 understand why demand and supply determine price and the quantity traded and not the reverse.

WHAT'S AHEAD...

This chapter introduces you to the fundamental economic ideas of demand and supply. It explains the distinction between individual and market demands and looks at the various reasons that the demand for products changes from time to time. We then take a look at things from the producers' point of view and explain what determines the amounts that they put on the market. Next, we explain how markets are able to reconcile the wishes of the two groups and we introduce the concept of equilibrium. Finally, we look at how the market price and the quantity traded adjust to changes in demand or supply.

A Question of Relevance...

Have you ever wondered why the prices of some products, such as computers or DVD players tend to fall over time, while the prices of other products such as cars or auto insurance tend to rise? Or perhaps you wonder how the price of a house can fluctuate tens of thousands of dollars from year to year. Why does a poor orange harvest in Florida cause the price of apple juice made in Ontario to rise? And why do sales of fax machines continue to fall despite their lower prices? This chapter will give you insights into questions such as these.

If the average person were to think about the subject matter of economics, it is unlikely that she would immediately think of choice or opportunity costs, which was a principal topic of Chapter 1. More likely, she would think in terms of money or interest rates and almost certainly demand and supply. Most people realize, without studying the topic, that demand and supply are central to economics. In our own ways, and as a result of our experiences in life, most of us feel that we know quite a lot about the subject. After all, who are better experts on the reaction of consumers to changes in the market than consumers themselves? However, as we will see shortly, the way that economists define and use the terms "demand" and "supply" differs from the everyday usage of these terms. To make matters worse, there does not seem to be a consensus among non-economists about the meaning of either of these two words: there is a range of meanings. This is often the case with language, but it does lead to a great deal of confusion, which can be illustrated in the following exchange between two observers of the consumer electronic goods market:

Justine: "Have you noticed that the price of big-screen TVs has dropped quite a bit recently?"

Eric: "Well, yes, but that is just supply and demand."

Justine: Are you saying that the supply has gone up?"

Eric: "Sure, must have."

Justine: "But why would supply go up if the price is going down?"

Eric: "Well, I don't know—maybe it is because demand has gone up as well."

There is much confusion here. While Eric's belief that the price has fallen because supply went up is probably correct in this context, we see that price will also fall if demand decreases. Justine's second question about why supply would go up if the price goes down reveals a common confusion over cause and effect. And Eric's final response is confused because he is not aware that demand and supply factors are separate and not interrelated.

We hope to soon clarify all of this type of confusion. It is probably clear to you already that economists are very fussy about defining and using economic terms correctly, and this is particularly true in a discussion about demand and supply. As we shall see in this chapter, demand does not simply mean what people want to buy, nor is supply just the amount being produced.

Another source of confusion in the above discussion is a misunderstanding of cause and effect: is the change in TV prices the effect of changing demand, or is it the cause? This chapter will clear up some of the confusion and give us a basis upon which to analyze and clarify some real, practical problems. First, let us take a look at the concept of demand.

2.1 DEMAND

Individual Demand

L01 Explain the concept of demand.

There are several dimensions to **demand**. First, economists use the word in the sense of wanting something, not in the sense of commanding or ordering. However, this "want" also involves the ability to buy. In other words, demand refers to both the *desire* and the *ability* to purchase a good or service. This means that although I may well have a desire for a new top-of-the-line BMW, I unfortunately do not have the ability to buy one at current prices, and therefore my quantity demanded is zero. Similarly, I might have the income to buy only expensive, upmarket wines but no desire to do so.

demand: the quantities that consumers are willing and able to buy per period of time at various prices.

Second, even though many factors determine what products and what quantities a consumer purchases, economists would suggest that price is usually the most important. For this reason, they look at how consumers might react to a change in the price, assuming that all other factors remain unchanged. The Latin phrase for this perspective is **ceteris paribus**, which literally means "other things being equal." However, it is usually interpreted by economists to mean "other things remaining the same." In other words, demand is the relationship between the price of a product and the quantities demanded, *ceteris paribus*.

ceteris paribus: other things being equal, or other things remaining the same.

Third, demand is a hypothetical construct that expresses this desire and ability to purchase, not at a single price, but over a *range of* hypothetical prices. Finally, demand is also a flow concept in that it measures quantities over a period of time. In summary, demand:

- involves both the desire and the ability of consumers to purchase,
- assumes that other things are held constant,
- refers to a range of prices, and
- measures quantities over time.

demand schedule: a table showing the various quantities demanded per period of time at different prices.

All of these aspects of demand are captured in **Table 2.1**, which shows the **demand schedule** for an enthusiastic beer drinker named Tomiko.

TABLE 2.1	Individual Demand
Price per Case	**Quantity Demanded (Number of Cases per Month)**
$17	7
18	6
19	5
20	4
21	3
22	2

Once again, what we mean by demand is the entire relationship between the various prices and the quantities that people are willing and able to purchase. This relationship can be laid out in the form of a demand schedule. The above schedule shows the amounts per week that Tomiko is willing and able to purchase at the various prices shown. Note that there is an inverse relationship between price and quantity. This simply means that at higher prices, Tomiko would not be willing to buy as much as at lower prices. In other words:

> The higher the price, the lower will be the quantity demanded; and the lower the price, the higher will be the quantity demanded.

Another less obvious statement of this law of demand is to say that in order to induce Tomiko to buy a greater quantity of beer, the price must be lower. Tomiko's demand schedule is graphed in **Figure 2.1**.

In **Figure 2.1**, at a price of $21 per case, the quantity demanded by Tomiko is 3 cases per month, while at a lower price of $18 per case, she would be willing to buy 6 cases. The demand is therefore plotted as a downward-sloping curve by connecting these two price/quantity coordinates and then extending a straight line. (To economists, curves include straight lines!) Once again, note that when we say "demand," "demand schedule," or "demand curve," we are referring to a whole array of different prices and quantities.

It is very important for you to note that since the price of any product is part of what we call the "demand" for that product, a change in the price cannot change the demand. It can, however, affect the amounts we are willing to purchase, and we express this by saying that:

change in the quantity demanded: the change in quantity that results from a price change. It is illustrated by a movement along a demand curve.

> A change in the price of a product results in a **change in the quantity demanded** for that product.

FIGURE 2.1	Individual Demand Curve

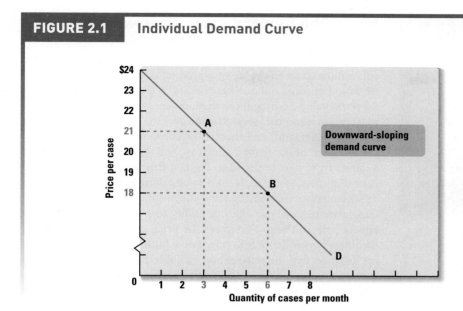

At a price of $18 per case, Tomiko is willing and able to buy 6 cases per month (point B). At a higher price, $21 per case, the amount she is willing and able to buy falls to 3 cases (point A). The higher the price, then, the lower is the quantity demanded. (Note that the vertical axis contains a "broken" portion. In general, an axis is often broken in this manner whenever the information about, say, low prices, is unavailable or unimportant.)

In other words, point A in **Figure 2.1** represents a price of $21 and a quantity demanded of 3 cases. Point B shows another possible combination: at a price of $18, the quantity demanded is 6 cases. The *quantity demanded*, then, is a single point on the demand curve, whereas the *demand* is the entire collection of points.

This is illustrated in **Figure 2.2**. Graphically, as we move the demand curve, from $18 to $17, the quantity demanded increases from 6 to 7 cases; as we move up the demand curve from $21 to $22, the quantity demanded decreases from 3 cases to 2 cases.

FIGURE 2.2	Changes in the Quantity Demanded

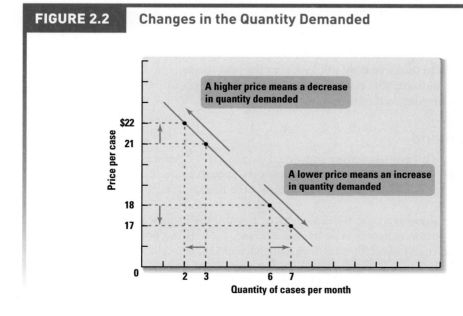

Whenever the price changes, there is a movement along the demand curve. An increase in the price from, say, $21 to $22, causes a decrease in the quantity demanded from 3 to 2. A decrease in the price from $18 to $17 leads to an increase in the quantity demanded from 6 to 7. Neither the demand nor the demand curve, however, changes.

A SALE sign is often all it takes to attract consumers.

Why Is the Demand Curve Downward Sloping?

People tend to buy more at lower prices rather than at higher prices. Most of us can confirm from our own experiences that a lower price will induce us to buy more of a product or to buy something that we would or could not purchase before. Witness the big crowds that are attracted to nothing more than a sign saying SALE. In addition, most microeconomic research done over the years tends to confirm this law of demand, and theories of consumer behaviour (such as the marginal utility theory, which we will study in Chapter 5) lend additional support to the idea. But is it that simple? Let us explore the question of why people tend to buy more at lower prices.

Remember that our demand for products is a combination of our desire to purchase and our ability to purchase. A lower price affects both of these. The lower the price of a product, the more income a person has left to purchase additional products. Assume, for instance, that the price of beer in **Table 2.1** was $20 and Tomiko was buying 4 cases per month for a total expenditure of $80 per month. If the price decreases to $18, Tomiko could buy the same quantity for an outlay of $72, thus saving a total of $8. It is almost as if Tomiko had received a pay raise of $8. In fact, in terms of its effect on Tomiko's pocketbook, it is exactly the same. Or, as economists would express it, her **real income** has increased. A decrease in price means that people can afford to buy more of a product (or more of other products) if they wish. This is referred to as the **income effect** of a price change, and it affects people's *ability* to purchase. This is because a lower price means a higher real income, so people will tend to buy more of a product. (Conversely, an increase in the price effectively reduces a person's real income.)

In addition to this, a price change also affects people's *desire* to purchase. We are naturally driven to buy the cheaper of competing products, and a drop in the price of one of them increases our desire to substitute it for a relatively more expensive product. If the price of wine were to drop (or if the price of beer were to increase), then some beer drinkers might well switch to what they regard as a cheaper substitute. In general, there are substitutes for most products, and people will tend to substitute a relatively cheap product for a more expensive one. This is called the **substitution effect**. A higher price, however, tends to make the product less attractive to us than its substitutes, and so we buy less of it.

When the price of a product drops, we buy more of it because we are *more able* (the income effect) and because we are *more willing* (the substitution effect). Conversely, a price increase means we are less able and less willing to buy the product, and therefore we buy less. (There is a possible exception to this, which we will look at in the next chapter.)

The close relationship that exists between price and the quantity demanded is so pervasive that it is often referred to as the *law of demand*.

real income: income measured in terms of the amount of goods and services that it will buy. Real income will increase if either actual income increases or prices fall.

income effect: the effect that a price change has on real income and therefore on the quantity demanded of a product.

substitution effect: the substitution of one product for another as a result of a change in their relative prices.

Market Demand

Up to this point, we have focused on individual demand. Now, we want to move to **market demand** (or total demand). Conceptually, this is easy enough to do. By summing every individual's demand for a product, we are able to obtain the market demand. **Table 2.2** provides a simple example.

Let us say we know not only Tomiko's demand but also the demands of three other friends in a small, four-person economy. The market demand, then, is the horizontal summation of individual demands, so to find the quantities demanded at $18, we add the quantities demanded by each individual: $6 + 3 + 4 + 9 = 22$. The same would be done for each price level. This particular market demand is graphed in **Figure 2.3**. Note that this demand curve, which is the

market demand: the total demand for a product by all consumers.

PhotoLink/Getty Images

TABLE 2.2	Deriving the Market Demand				
	NUMBER OF CASES PER MONTH				
Price per Case	Tomiko's Quantity Demanded	Meridith's Quantity Demanded	Abdi's Quantity Demanded	Jan's Quantity Demanded	Market Quantity Demanded
$18	6	3	4	9	22
19	5	2	4	7	18
20	4	2	4	6	16
21	3	0	3	3	9
22	2	0	3	1	6

FIGURE 2.3	The Market Demand Curve

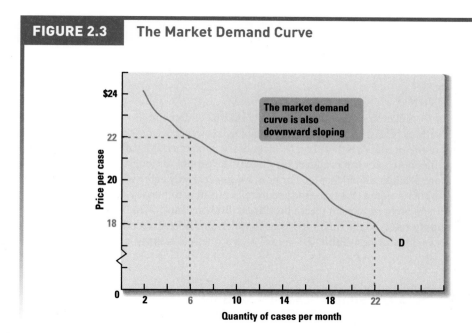

The market demand curve is also downward sloping

At a price of $18, the total or market quantity demanded equals 22 cases. As with individual demand, when the price increases to $22, the quantity demanded will drop, in this case to 6. This is because at a higher price, each individual buys less, and there are fewer people who can afford to or are willing to buy any at all. (Meridith has dropped out of the market.)

summation of the specific numbers of the four people in **Table 2.2**, is not a straight line. Yet it is still downward sloping and so conforms to the law of demand. For the most part, we will work with straight-line demand curves, although there is no reason to assume that all real-life demand curves plot as straight lines.

Note that, as with the individual demand curve, the market demand curve also slopes downward. This is because people buy more as the price drops—and more people buy. In our example, Meredith is not willing to buy any beer at a price of $22. Only if the price is $20 or lower will all four people buy beer.

Finally, before we look at the supply side of the market, note again that our demand schedule tells us only what people *might* buy; it tells us nothing about what they are actually buying. To know this, we also need to know the actual price. And to find out what the price of beer should be, we need to know…yes, the supply.

SELF-TEST

1. The data in the table indicate the weekly demand for litres of soy milk by Al, Bo, and Cole (the only three people in a very small market).

   a) Fill in the blanks in the table.

   b) What is the basic shape of the demand curve in this market?

   c) What is the highest price at which all three will buy at least one litre of milk?

Price	Quantity Demanded: Al	Quantity Demanded: Bo	Quantity Demanded: Cole	Total (market) Quantity Demanded:
$4.00	1	0	0	_____
3.50	1	1	0	_____
3.00	1	1	1	_____
2.50	2	1	1	_____
2.00	2	2	1	_____

2.2 SUPPLY

 LO2 Explain the concept of supply.

Individual Supply

In many ways, the formulation of supply is very similar to that of demand. Both measure hypothetical quantities at various prices, and both are flow concepts. However, we now need to look at things through the eyes of the producer rather than the eyes of the consumer. We will assume for the time being that the prime motive for the producer is to maximize profits, although we will examine this assumption in more detail in a later chapter. For now, we can certainly agree with Adam Smith who, in *The Wealth of Nations*, noted that few producers are in business to please consumers. Neither, of course, do consumers buy products to please producers. Both are motivated by self-interest.

supply: the quantities that producers are willing and able to sell per period of time at various prices.

The term **supply** refers to the quantities that suppliers are *willing* and *able* to make available to the market at various prices. **Table 2.3** shows a hypothetical **supply schedule** for Bobbie the brewer.

supply schedule: a table showing the various quantities supplied per period of time at different prices.

TABLE 2.3	The Supply Schedule for Bobbie the Brewer
Price per Case	**Quantity Supplied (Number of Cases per Month)**
$18	2
19	3
20	4
21	5
22	6

Note that there is a *direct* relationship between price and the quantity supplied, which means that a higher price will induce Bobbie to produce more. Remember that Bobbie's reason for being in business is to make as much profit as possible. How much would Bobbie, hypothetically, be prepared to supply if the beer could be sold at $18 per case? Knowing what her costs are likely to be, she figures that she could make the most profit if she produces two cases. At a higher price, there is a likelihood of greater profits, and therefore she is willing to produce more. Also, as we shall see in Chapter 6, when firms produce more, the cost per unit tends to rise. Therefore, a

ADDED DIMENSION   Adam Smith: The Father of Economics

Adam Smith (1723–90) is generally regarded as the founding father of economics. In his brilliant work, *The Wealth of Nations*, Smith posed so many interesting questions and provided such illuminating answers that later economists often felt that they were merely picking at the scraps he left behind. Smith was born and brought up in Scotland and educated at Glasgow and Oxford. He held the Chair of Moral Philosophy at Glasgow College for many years. He was a lifelong bachelor and had a kind but absent-minded disposition.

Smith was the first scholar to analyze the business of "getting and spending" in a detailed and systematic manner. In doing this, he gave useful social dignity to the professions of business and trading. Besides introducing the important idea of the *invisible hand*, which was his way of describing the coordinating mechanism of capitalism, he examined the division of labour, the role of government, the function of money, the advantages and disadvantages of free trade, what constitutes good and bad taxation, and a host of other ideas. For Smith, economic life was not merely a peripheral adventure for people but their central motivating force.

producer needs the incentive of a higher price *in order to* increase production. For the time being, however, we can rely on the proposition that a higher price means higher profits and therefore will lead to higher quantities produced. This is illustrated in **Figure 2.4**.

Joining the individual points from the supply schedule in **Table 2.3** gives us the upward-sloping supply curve shown in **Figure 2.4**. Again, we emphasize the fact that as with the term "demand," the term "supply" does not refer to a single price and quantity but to the whole array of hypothetical price and quantity combinations contained in the supply schedule and illustrated by the supply curve.

Since price is part of what we mean by the term *supply*, a change in the price level cannot change the supply. A change in price does, of course, lead to a change in the quantity that a producer is willing and able to make available. Thus, the effect of a change in price we call a **change in the quantity supplied**. This is illustrated in **Figure 2.5**.

change in the quantity supplied: the change in the amounts that will be produced as a result of a price change. This is shown as a movement along a supply curve.

| **FIGURE 2.4** | **Individual Supply Curve** |

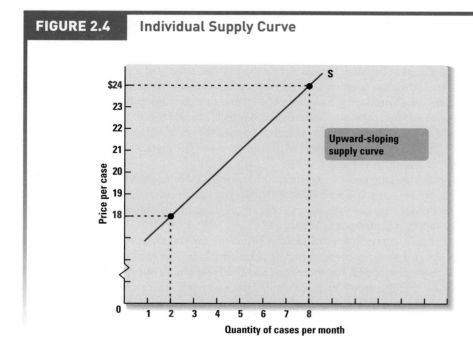

At a low price of $18, the most profitable output for Bobbie is 2 cases. If the price increased, she would be willing and able to produce more, since she would be able to make greater profits. At $24, for instance, the quantity she would produce increases to 8 cases.

FIGURE 2.5   **Changes in the Quantity Supplied**

A price change will lead to a movement along the supply curve. An increase in the price from, say, P_1 to P_2 will cause an increase in the quantity supplied from Q_1 to Q_2. A decrease in the price from P_3 to P_4 will lead to a decrease in the quantity supplied from Q_3 to Q_4. The supply curve itself, however, does not change.

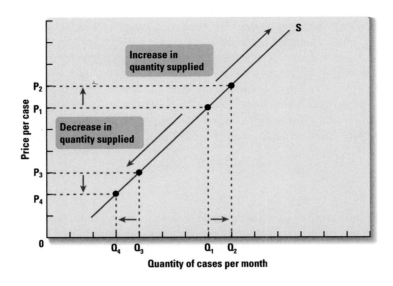

To summarize:

> An increase in price will lead to an *increase in the quantity supplied* and is illustrated as a movement up the supply curve.

> A decrease in price will cause a *decrease in the quantity supplied* and is illustrated as a movement down the supply curve.

Market Supply

market supply: the total supply of a product offered by all producers.

As we did with the market demand, we can derive the **market supply** of a product by summing the supply of every individual supplier. A word of caution, however. We must make the assumption that producers are all producing a similar product and that consumers have no preference as to which supplier or product they use. Given this, it is possible to add together the individual supplies to derive the market supply. In our example, suppose that Bobbie the brewer is competing with three other brewers of similar size and with similar costs. The market supply of beer in this market would be as shown in **Table 2.4**.

The total quantities supplied by the three other brewers are equal to the quantities that Bobbie would supply at each price, multiplied by three. The fourth column, market supply, is the addition of every brewer's supply—the second column plus the third column.

The market supply is illustrated in **Figure 2.6**.

The *market* supply curve is upward sloping primarily for the same reason the *individual* supply curve is upward sloping: because higher prices imply higher profits and will therefore induce a greater quantity supplied. But there is an additional reason. In our example, we assumed, for simplicity's sake, that the suppliers are of similar size and have similar costs. In reality, that is unlikely; costs and size probably differ, so a price that generates a profit for one firm may mean a loss for another. As the price of a product increases, however, some firms that were previously

TABLE 2.4	Deriving the Market Supply		
NUMBER OF CASES PER MONTH			
Price per Case	Bobbie the Brewer's Quantity Supplied	Quantity Supplied of Other Brewers	Market Quantity Supplied
$18	2	6	8
19	3	9	12
20	4	12	16
21	5	15	20
22	6	18	24

FIGURE 2.6	The Market Supply

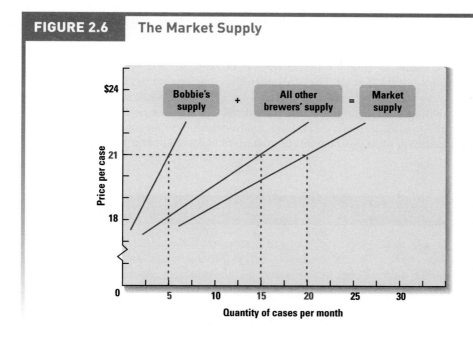

The market supply is the horizontal summation of each individual producer's supply curve. For instance, at a price of $21, Bobbie would supply 5 cases; the other brewers combined would supply 15 cases. The market quantity supplied, therefore, is the total quantity supplied of 20 cases. In short, to derive the market supply curve, we add the totals of each supplier at each price level.

unable to produce will now find that they can successfully operate at a profit. Thus, as the price of the product increases, currently operating firms will produce more, and other firms not previously producing will enter the market and start to produce.

In summary, a higher price, which deters consumers from buying more, is an incentive for suppliers to produce more. Conversely, a lower price induces consumers to buy more but is a reason for suppliers to cut back their output.

The motives of consumers and producers are very different: consumers wish to obtain the lowest price possible, and producers want to sell at the highest. How can their wishes converge? How is trade possible at all in these circumstances? Certainly, it is not possible for *all* prospective consumers and suppliers to be satisfied. But it is almost always possible for *some* of these people to be satisfied. Of course, this will require that they be able, in some sense, to meet and get together. A market enables them to do just that.

2.3 THE MARKET

market: a mechanism that brings buyers and sellers together and assists them in negotiating the exchange of products.

Most people are able to understand the terms *market price* and *market demand*, but many are not clear as to what constitutes a **market**. Certainly, the term includes places that have a physical location such as a local produce or fish market. But in broader terms, a market really refers to any exchange mechanism that brings buyers and sellers of a product together. There may be times when we need to inspect or get further on-the-spot information about a product before we buy it, and this is the purpose of the retail market. But there are other times when we possess sufficient information about a product or a producer, and it is not necessary to actually see either of them before we purchase. This applies, for instance, if you wish to buy stocks and bonds or make a purchase on the Internet. Increasingly, in these days of higher costs of personal service and greater availability of electronic communication, markets are becoming both wider and more accessible. The market for commodities such as copper, gold, and rubber, for instance, is both worldwide and anonymous in that the buyers and sellers seldom meet in person.

By a market, then, we mean any relatively open environment in which buyers and sellers can communicate and that operates without preference. When we talk of the market price, then, we mean the price available to *all* buyers and sellers of a product. By market demand, we mean the total quantities demanded. And market supply refers to the quantity made available by all suppliers at each possible price.

Later, you will encounter several different types of markets, some of which work very well and others that work poorly, if at all. The analysis in this chapter assumes that the market we are looking at is very (economists call it "perfectly") competitive. We will devote the whole of Chapter 8 to examining this type of market in more detail. For now, we need to mention that a perfectly competitive market is, among other things, one in which there are many small producers, each selling an identical product. Keeping this caution in mind, let us see how this market works.

⏵ ADDED DIMENSION Re-inventing the Market

Modern capitalism first emerged and began to spread about 250 years ago, as commerce moved out of the village markets of Europe into the age of factory-centred manufacturing, which was later combined with widespread systems of wholesale and retail. However, this transformation also introduced a less predictable chain of supply and demand. While the seller in the village market was in direct contact with the buyer, the evolution of capitalism's mass markets and mass production techniques imposed vast gulfs in time and space between buyer and seller. Producers became much less sure of what the demand for their product was, and buyers were never sure there wasn't a better deal somewhere else. In response to this, sellers used the blunt tool of a fixed price list and adjusted output accordingly, while buyers just did the best they could. The phenomenon of the Internet is re-inventing commerce as the seller's market horizon expands, buyers have more information, real-time sales become routine, and the need to stockpile inventory diminishes. In short, supply-chain bottlenecks are being eradicated. What is emerging is far *more efficient markets* and the rise of dynamic pricing based on constantly fluctuating demand and supply.

2.4 MARKET EQUILIBRIUM

We now examine the point at which the wishes of buyers and sellers coincide by combining the market demand and supply for beer in **Table 2.5**.

L04 Understand the concept of (price and quantity) equilibrium.

TABLE 2.5	Market Supply and Demand		
NUMBER OF CASES PER MONTH			
Price per Case	**Market Quantity Demanded**	**Market Quantity Supplied**	**Surplus (+)/ Shortage (−)**
$18	22	8	−14
19	18	12	−6
20	**16**	**16**	**0**
21	9	20	+11
22	6	24	+18

You can see from this table that there is only one price, $20, at which the wishes of consumers and producers coincide. Only if the price is $20 will the quantity demanded and the quantity supplied be equal. This price level is referred to as the **equilibrium price**. Equilibrium, in general, means that there is balance between opposing forces; here, those opposing forces are demand and supply. The word *equilibrium* also implies a condition of stability. If this stability is disturbed, there will be a tendency to automatically find a new equilibrium.

To understand this point, refer to **Table 2.5** and note that if the price were, say, $18, then the amount being demanded, 22, would exceed the amount being supplied, which is 8. At this price, there is an excess demand, or more simply, a shortage of beer, to the tune of 14 cases. This amount is shown in the last column and marked with a minus sign. In this situation, there would be a lot of unhappy beer drinkers. Faced with the prospect of going beer-less, many of them will be prepared to pay a higher price for their suds and will therefore bid the price up. As the price of beer starts to rise, the reaction of consumers and producers will differ. Some beer drinkers will not be able to afford the higher prices so the quantity demanded will drop. On the supply side, producers will be delighted with the higher price and will start to produce more—and the quantity supplied will increase. Both these tendencies will combine to reduce the shortage as the price goes up. Eventually, when the price has reached the equilibrium price of $20, the shortage will have disappeared, and the price will no longer increase. Part of the law of demand suggests, then, that:

equilibrium price: the price at which the quantity demanded equals the quantity supplied such that there is neither a surplus nor a shortage.

> Shortages cause prices to rise.

This is illustrated in **Figure 2.7**.

Now, again using **Table 2.5**, let us see what will happen if the price happens to be above equilibrium, at $22 a case. At this price, the quantity demanded is 6 cases, and the quantity supplied is 24 cases. There is insufficient demand from the producers' point of view, or more simply, there is a surplus (or excess supply) of 18 cases. This is shown in the last column of **Table 2.5** as +18. This is not a stable situation because firms cannot continue producing a product that they cannot sell. They will be forced to lower the price in an attempt to sell more. As the price starts to drop, two things happen concurrently. Consumers will be happy to consume more, or to use economic terms, there will be an increase in the quantity demanded.

FIGURE 2.7   How the Market Reacts to a Shortage

At a price of $18, the quantity supplied of 8 is far below the quantity demanded of 22. The horizontal distance between the two shows the amount of the shortage, which is 14. As a result of the shortage, price bidding between consumers will force up the price. As the price increases, the quantity demanded will drop, but the quantity supplied will rise until these two are equal at a quantity of 16.

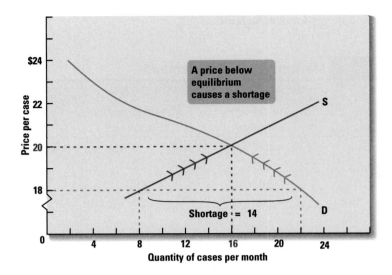

In **Figure 2.8**, note that as the price falls, the quantity demanded increases, and this increase is depicted as a movement down the demand curve. At the same time, faced with a falling price, producers will be forced to cut back production—decreasing the quantity supplied. In the same figure, this is shown as a movement along (down) the supply curve. The net result of this will be the eventual elimination of the surplus as the price moves toward equilibrium. In other words:

Surpluses cause prices to fall.

FIGURE 2.8   How the Market Reacts to a Surplus

A price above equilibrium will produce a surplus. At $22, the quantity supplied of 24 exceeds the quantity demanded of 6. The horizontal distance of 18 represents the amount of the surplus. The surplus will result in producers dropping the price in an attempt to increase sales. As the price drops, the quantity demanded increases, while the quantity supplied falls. The equilibrium quantity is 16.

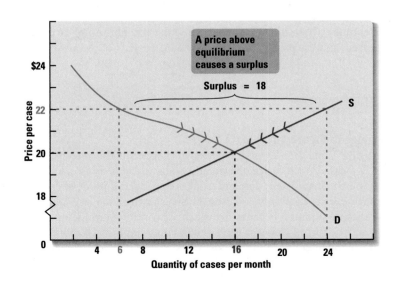

Only if the price is $14 will there be no surplus or shortage, and the quantity produced will be equal to the quantity demanded. This is the equilibrium price. The quantity prevailing at the equilibrium price is known as the **equilibrium quantity**, in this case 16 cases. This equilibrium quantity is the quantity both demanded and supplied (since they are equal).

equilibrium quantity: the quantity that prevails at the equilibrium price.

 SELF-TEST

2. What effect does a surplus have on the price of a product? What about a shortage?

3. The following table shows the demand and supply of eggs (in hundreds of thousands per day).

a) What are the equilibrium price and the equilibrium quantity?

b) Complete the surplus/shortage column. Using this column, explain why your answer to question A must be correct.

c) What would be the surplus/shortage at a price of $2.50? What would happen to the price and the quantity traded?

d) What would be the surplus/shortage at a price of $4? What would happen to the price and the quantity traded?

Price	Quantity Demanded	Quantity Supplied	Surplus/ Shortage
$2.00	60	30	_____
2.50	56	36	_____
3.00	52	42	_____
3.50	48	48	_____
4.00	44	54	_____

2.5 CHANGE IN DEMAND

Recall from the definition of demand that the concept refers to the *relationship* between various prices and quantities. In other words, both price and quantity make up what is known as demand. Thus, a change in price cannot cause a change in demand but does cause a change in the quantity demanded. That said, we must now ask: what are the other determinants, besides price, that influence how much of any particular product consumers will buy? Or once equilibrium price and quantity have been established, what might disturb that equilibrium? One general answer to this question is a **change in demand**. Table 2.6 shows such a change in the demand for beer.

Here, we will introduce new figures for demand in order to revert to straight-line demand curves. Let us say that D_1 is the demand for beer that existed last month and D_2 is the demand this month. Demand has increased by 6 cases per week at each price, so whatever the price, consumers are willing and able to consume an additional 6 cases. Thus, there has been an increase in demand. Figure 2.9 graphically illustrates an increase in demand.

L05 Understand the causes and effects of a change in demand.

change in demand: a change in the quantities demanded at every price, caused by a change in the determinants of demand.

TABLE 2.6	An Increase in Demand	
NUMBER OF CASES PER MONTH		
Price per Case of Beer	Quantity Demanded 1	Quantity Demanded 2
$18	16	22
19	15	21
20	14	20
21	13	19
22	12	18

FIGURE 2.9 **An Increase in Demand**

At each price, the quantities demanded have increased. In this example, the increase is by a constant amount of 6, thus producing a parallel shift in the demand curve. For example, at $20 the quantity demanded has increased from 14 to 20 (by 6).

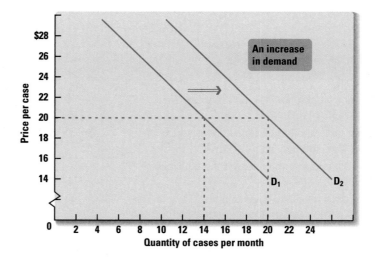

An increase in demand, then, means an increase in the quantities demanded *at each price,* that is, a total increase in the demand schedule, which is illustrated by a rightward shift in the demand curve. Similarly, a decrease in demand means a reduction in the quantities demanded at each price—a decrease in the demand schedule—and this is illustrated by a leftward shift in the demand curve.

Determinants of a Change in Demand

Now that we know what an increase in demand looks like, we need to look at the factors that could bring about such a change. Some of these determinants of demand affect people's willingness to purchase, others affect their ability to purchase, and still others affect both.

The first factor that affects our willingness to purchase a product is our own *preference.* An increase in demand as shown in **Table 2.6** could simply have been caused by a change in consumer preferences: consumers now prefer more beer.

But many things could affect our preferences. Tastes change over time and are influenced by the weather, advertising, articles and reports in books and magazines, opinions of friends, special events, and much more. Specific examples would include decreased demand for steak as the summer barbeque season passes, increased demand for a book that has won a prestigious literary award, or the increase in demand for hotel rooms in the host city of the Olympics.

The second factor affecting the demand for a product is the *income* of consumers. This affects their ability to consume. Generally speaking, you would expect that an increase in income leads most people to increase their purchases of most products and that a decrease in income generally causes a drop in demand—that is, there is a direct relationship between income and demand. This is true for most products that we buy, and these products are called **normal products** such as sushi, soda pop, cars, and movies.

But it is certainly not true for all people and all products. For instance, as the incomes of most people increase, these consumers tend to buy less of such things as low-quality hamburger meats, boxes of macaroni and cheese, cheap toilet paper, and so on. Instead, they start to substitute higher-quality and higher-priced articles that they could not previously afford. When income is low, we buy lower-quality staple products that economists call **inferior products**. There is an inverse relationship between income and the demand for inferior products: as income

normal products: products for which demand will increase as a result of an increase in income and decrease as a result of a decrease in income.

inferior products: products for which demand will decrease as a result of an increase in income and increase as a result of a decrease in income.

levels go up, the demand goes down. It also means that as incomes fall, demand for these inferior products will rise. In our beer example from **Table 2.6**, the increase in market demand could have been caused by an increase in incomes because beer is a normal product.

A third important determinant of demand is the *prices of related products*. A change in the price of related products will affect people's willingness and ability to purchase a particular good. Products are related if a change in the price of one causes a change in the demand for the other. For instance, if the price of Pepsi were to increase, a number of Pepsi drinkers might well switch over to Coke.

There are, in fact, two ways in which products may be related. They may be related as substitutes, or they may be related as complements. **Substitute products** (also known as *competitive products*) are those that are so similar in the eyes of most consumers that price is the main distinguishing feature. Pepsi and Coke, therefore, are substitute products because an increase in the price of one will cause an increase in the demand for the other. The relationship between the price of a product and the demand for its substitute is therefore a direct one. It also means that if the price of a product falls, then the demand for its substitute will also fall, since many consumers are now buying a cheaper product.

Complementary products tend to be purchased together, and their demands are interrelated. Skis and ski boots are complementary products as are cars and gasoline or beer and pretzels. If the price of one product increases, causing a decrease in the quantity demanded, then people will also purchase less of the complement. If the price of greens fees were to increase so that people were buying fewer rounds of golf, then we would also expect a decrease in the demand for complementary products such as golf balls and golf tees.

There is, in this case, an inverse relationship between the price of a product and the demand for its complement: an increase in price of one product leads to a decline in the demand for the complementary product. Similarly, a decrease in the price of a product will lead to an increase in the demand for a complement.

A fourth determinant of demand is consumers' *expectations of the future*. There are many ways that our feelings about the future influence our present behaviour. Future expected prices and incomes can affect our present demand for a product as can the prospect of a shortage. If consumers think that the price of their favourite beverage is likely to increase in the near future, they may well stock up, just in case. The present demand for the product will therefore increase. Conversely, expected future price declines cause people to hold off their current purchases while awaiting the hoped-for lower prices.

An anticipated pay increase may cause some people to spend more now as they adjust to their expected higher standard of living. People who fear a layoff or other cause of a loss of income may cut down spending in advance of the fateful date. Finally, the possibility of future shortages such as those caused by an impending strike may cause a frantic rush to the stores by anxious customers trying to stock up in advance.

These four determinants of demand—preferences, income, prices of related products, and future expectations—affect individual demand to varying degrees. If we shift our attention to market demand, these four factors still apply. In addition, a few other factors need to be mentioned. The *size of the market population* will affect the demand for all products. An increase in the size of the population, for example, leads to an increase in the demand for everything from houses and cars to sports equipment and credit cards. In addition, a *change in the distribution of incomes* leads to an increase in the demand for some products and a decrease in the demand for others. For example, if the percentage of total income earned by those over 65 years of age rises, while the percentage going to those under the age of 24 falls, then we would expect to see an increase in the demand for holiday cruises and a decrease in the demand for entry into popular night clubs.

The same will also be true for the *age composition of the population*. An aging population increases the demand for products that largely appeal to older people (Anne Murray recordings) and decrease the demand for those that appeal only to the young (Justin Bieber recordings).

substitute products: any products for which demand varies directly in relation to a change in the price of a similar product.

complementary products: products that tend to be purchased jointly and for which demand is therefore related.

Statistics Canada reports that annual per-capita beer sales fell to 84.7 litres in 2002 from 92 litres a decade earlier. The decline in beer drinking is probably due to an aging population, lifestyle changes, and higher taxes.

Note that one factor is *not* included on this list of determinants of demand, and that is supply. Economists are scrupulous in their attempts to separate the forces of demand and supply. Remember that the demand formulation is a hypothetical construct based on the quantities that consumers are willing and able to purchase at various prices. There is an implied assumption that the consumer will be able to obtain these quantities, otherwise the demand schedule itself would not be relevant. In other words, when specifying demand, we assume that the supply will be available, just as when formulating supply, we make the assumption that there will be sufficient demand.

In summary, the determinants of demand are as follows:

- consumer preferences
- consumer incomes
- prices of related goods
- expectations of future prices, incomes, or availability
- population size, or income and age distribution

✓ SELF-TEST

4. The accompanying table shows the initial weekly demand (D_1) and the new demand (D_2) for packets of pretzels (a bar snack).

To explain the change in demand from D_1 to D_2, what might have happened to the price of a complementary product such as beer? Alternatively, what might have happened to the price of a substitute product such as nuts?

Price	Quantity Demanded (D_1)	Quantity Demanded (D_2)
$2.00	10 000	11 000
3.00	9 600	10 600
4.00	9 200	10 200

The Effects of an Increase in Demand

We have just seen that the demand for any product is affected by many different factors. A change in any of these factors will cause a change in demand, which, as we shall see, leads to a change in price and production levels. Let us first consider the effects of an *increase* in the demand for a product. Any one of the following could cause such an increase in the market demand:

- a change in preferences toward the product
- an increase in incomes if the product is a normal product or a decrease in incomes if the product is an inferior product
- an increase in the price of a substitute product
- a decrease in the price of a complementary product
- the expectation that future prices or incomes will be higher or that there will be a future shortage of the product
- an increase in the population or a change in its income or age distribution

Any of these changes could cause people to buy more of a product, regardless of its price. As an example, let us combine supply and demand data in **Table 2.7**.

You can see that at the old demand (Demand 1) and supply, the equilibrium price was $20 and the quantity traded was 14 cases. Assume now that the demand for beer increases (Demand 2). Since consumers do not usually signal their intentions to producers in advance, producers are not aware that the demand has changed until they have evidence. The evidence will probably take

TABLE 2.7	The Effects of an Increase in Demand on the Market		
NUMBER OF CASES PER MONTH			
Price per Case	Quantity Supplied	Quantity Demanded 1	Quantity Demanded 2
$18	10	16	22
19	12	15	21
20	14	14	20
21	16	13	19
22	18	12	18

the form of unsatisfied customers. At a price of $20 a case, the producers in total have produced 14 cases. At this price, the new quantity demanded is 20 cases. There is a **shortage** of 6 cases, and some customers will go home disappointed because there is not sufficient beer, at a price of $20, to satisfy all customers. Will these brewers now increase production to satisfy the higher demand? The surprising answer is no—at least not at the present price. Brewers are not in the business of satisfying customers, they are in the business of making profits. As Adam Smith wrote over 200 years ago:

shortage: at the prevailing price, the quantity supplied is smaller than the quantity demanded.

> It is not from the benevolence of the butcher, the brewer, or the baker that we expect our dinner but from regard to their own self-interest.[1]

You may say that unless firms are responsive to the demands of customers, they will soon go out of business. And you are right. But a firm that is *solely* responsive to its customers will go out of business even faster. Look again at the supply schedule in **Table 2.7**. At a price of $20, the brewers are prepared to produce 14 cases. They are not prepared to produce 20 cases, the amount that consumers now want. Why is that? It may be because they can make more profits from producing 14 cases than from producing 20 cases; otherwise, they would have produced 20 in the first place. In fact, it may well be that if they produced 20 cases at the current price of $20, they would end up incurring a loss. Does this mean that the shortage of beer will persist? No. As we saw earlier, *shortages drive prices up* until the shortage disappears and the new quantity demanded is equal to the quantity supplied. This will occur at a price of $22, where the quantity demanded and the quantity supplied are equal at the equilibrium quantity of 18. This adjustment process can be seen in **Figure 2.10**.

You can see in the graph that at the old price of $20, the new quantity demanded exceeds the quantity supplied. This shortage causes the price to rise. As it does so, the quantity of beer that producers make also rises; that is, there will be an increase *in the quantity supplied*. Producers will produce more, not because there is a shortage but because the shortage causes a rise in price. Note also that the increase in price causes some customers to reduce their purchases of beer; that is, there is a decrease *in the quantity demanded*. The price of beer will continue to increase as long as there is a shortage and will stop as soon as the shortage disappears. This occurs when the price has increased to $22. At the new equilibrium price, the quantity demanded will again equal the quantity supplied but at a higher quantity traded of 18 cases.

An increase in demand causes an increase in both price and the quantity traded.

[1] Adam Smith, *Wealth of Nations* (Edwin Cannan edition, 1877), pp. 26–27.

FIGURE 2.10   Adjustment to an Increase in Demand

The increase in demand from D_1 to D_2 creates an immediate shortage of 6. This will cause an increase in the price of beer. The increase affects both producers, who will now increase the quantity supplied, and consumers, who will reduce the quantity demanded. Eventually, the price will reach a new equilibrium at $22, where the equilibrium quantity is 18, and there is no longer a shortage.

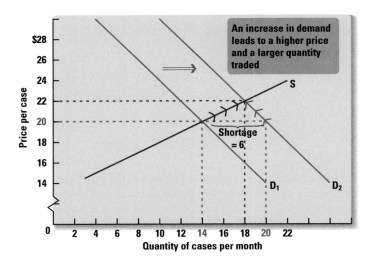

The Effects of a Decrease in Demand

Now, let us see what happens when there is a decrease in demand. Remember that a decrease in demand cannot be caused by an increase in price but is caused by a change in any of the nonprice determinants, including:

- a decrease in preferences for the product
- a decrease in incomes if the product is a normal product, or an increase in incomes if the product is an inferior product
- a decrease in the price of a substitute product
- an increase in the price of a complementary product
- the expectation that future prices or incomes will be lower
- a decrease in the population or a change in its income or age distribution

A decrease in demand is shown in **Table 2.8** and illustrated in **Figure 2.11**.

The initial equilibrium price is $14, and the quantity traded is 14. Assume that the demand now decreases to Demand 3 in the table and D3 in **Figure 2.11**. At a price of $14, producers will continue to produce 14 cases, yet consumers now wish to purchase only 8 cases. A **surplus** is immediately created in the market. Mounting unsold inventories and more intensive competition between suppliers will eventually push down the price. Note in **Figure 2.11** that as the price

surplus: at the prevailing price, the quantity demanded is smaller than the quantity supplied.

TABLE 2.8   The Effects on the Market of a Decrease in Demand

	NUMBER OF CASES PER MONTH		
Price per Case	Quantity Supplied	Quantity Demanded 1	Quantity Demanded 3
$18	10	16	10
19	12	15	9
20	14	14	8
21	16	13	7
22	18	12	6

| FIGURE 2.11 | **Adjustment to a Decrease in Demand** |

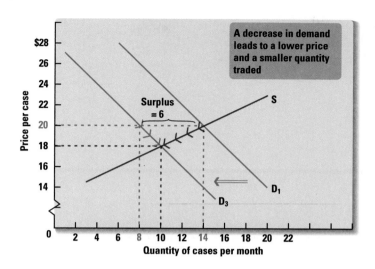

The drop in demand from D_1 to D_3 will cause an immediate surplus of 6, since the quantity supplied remains at 14 but the quantity demanded drops to 8. This surplus will cause the price to fall, and as it does, the quantity demanded will increase, while the quantity supplied will fall. This process will continue until the surplus is eliminated. This occurs at a new equilibrium price of $18 and an equilibrium quantity of 10.

decreases, the quantity supplied also starts to decrease, and the quantity demanded begins to increase. Both these factors will cause the surplus to disappear. The price will eventually drop to a new equilibrium of $18, where the quantity demanded and the quantity supplied are equal at 10 cases. In short:

A decrease in demand will cause both price and the quantity traded to fall.

 SELF-TEST

5. What effect will the following changes have on (i) the demand for, (ii) the price of, and (iii) the quantity traded of commercially brewed beer?

   a) A new medical report affirming the beneficial health effects of drinking beer (in moderation, of course)

   b) A big decrease in the price of home-brewing kits

   c) A rapid increase in population

   d) Talk of a strike by brewery workers

   e) A possible future recession

2.6   CHANGE IN SUPPLY

Let us reiterate what we mean by supply: it is the relationship between the price of the product and the quantities producers are willing and able to supply. Price is *part* of what economists call supply. In other words, supply does not mean a single quantity. We now need to address what could cause a **change in supply**. What factors will cause producers to offer a different quantity on the market, even though the price has not changed—what will cause a change in supply? We begin with **Table 2.9**, where an increase in supply is illustrated. For reasons we will soon investigate, suppliers are now willing to supply an extra 6 cases of beer at every possible price. This is illustrated in **Figure 2.12**.

L06 Understand the causes and effects of a change in supply.

change in supply: a change in the quantities supplied at every price, caused by a change in the determinants of supply.

TABLE 2.9	An Increase in Supply	
	NUMBER OF CASES PER MONTH	
Price per Case of Beer	**Quantity Supplied 1**	**Quantity Supplied 2**
$18	10	16
19	12	18
20	14	20
21	16	22
22	18	24

FIGURE 2.12   An Increase in Supply

At each price, the quantities supplied have now increased, that is, the supply curve has shifted right, from S_1 to S_2. For example, at a price of $20, the original quantity was 14 and has now increased to 20. Similarly, at a price of $16, the quantity supplied has increased from 6 to 12. In this example, the quantities supplied have increased by 6 units at every price level, thus causing a parallel shift in the supply curve.

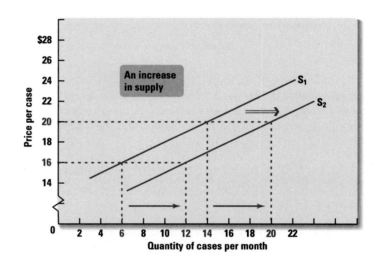

An increase in supply causes the whole supply curve to shift right. (Do not be tempted to describe it as a downward shift because then you would be saying that as the supply goes up, the supply curve goes down, which could make things very confusing! It would be better to talk about a rightward shift.) This means that at each and every price, producers are now willing to produce more.

Determinants of a Change in Supply

What could have happened in the brewers' world to make them wish to produce more, even though the price is unchanged? Since we are assuming that the prime motivation for the supplier is profit, then something must have happened to make brewing more profitable, which is inducing a higher supply. Profit is the difference between revenue and cost, and since the price (and therefore revenue) is unchanged, then something must have affected the cost of producing beer.

First, we will look at the *price of resources*. For brewers, this includes the price of yeast, hops, malt, and other ingredients, as well as the cost of brewing vats, bottles, and so on. If any of these should drop in price, then the cost for the brewers will fall, and profits will rise. Under these circumstances, since they are now making a bigger profit on each case of beer, they will be very willing to produce more. A fall in the price of resources will lead to an increase in supply. Conversely, an increase in the price of resources will cause a decrease in supply.

Another way of looking at the increase in supply, as shown in **Figure 2.12**, is to say that rather than firms being willing to produce more at a given price, they are willing to accept lower prices to produce any given quantity. For instance, previously, in order to induce the brewers to supply a total of 20 cases per week, the price needed to be $17. Now that the costs of production have dropped, these same brewers are able to make the same profits by producing the 20 cases at a lower price of $14: the brewers are now willing to produce the same quantities as before at lower prices. Again, this would produce a rightward shift in the supply curve.

A poor grape harvest is likely to cause the price of grapes to rise.

It is often suggested that the availability of resources is a major determinant of the supply of a product. A poor grape harvest—grapes being the key input in the making of wine—will obviously have an impact on the supply of wine. However, it is not really the difficulty in obtaining grapes that causes a decrease in the wine supply, since most things can be obtained *at a price*. But there's the rub. A poor grape harvest will cause the price of grapes to increase, and this increase will reduce the profitability and production of wine producers.

A second major determinant of supply is the *business taxes* levied by the various levels of government. They are similar to the other costs of doing business, and a decrease in them (or an increase in a subsidy) will lead firms to make higher profits and encourage them to increase supply. An increase in business taxes, conversely, will cause a decrease in supply.

A third determinant of supply is the *technology* used in production. An improvement in technology means nothing more than an improvement in the method of production. This will enable a firm to produce more with the same quantity of resources (or to produce the same output with fewer resources). An improvement in technology will not affect the actual price of the resources, but because more can now be done with less, it will lead to a fall in the per-unit cost of production. This means that an improvement in technology will lead to an increase in supply.

The price of related products also affects supply, just as it affected demand. But we must be careful, since we are looking at things from a producer's point of view and not a consumer's. What a producer regards as related will usually differ from what a consumer regards as related. A fourth determinant of supply, then, is the *price of substitutes in production*. To a wheat farmer, the price of other grains such as rye and barley will be of great interest because the production of all grain crops are related in terms of production methods and equipment. A significant increase in the price of rye may well tempt the wheat farmer to grow rye in the future instead of wheat. In other words, an increase in the price of one product will cause a drop in the supply of products that are substitutes in production. A decrease will have the opposite effect.

A fifth determinant of supply is the *future expectations of producers*. This is also analogous to the demand side of the market, but with a difference. While consumers eagerly look forward to a drop in the price of products, producers view the same prospect with great anxiety. Producers who feel that the market is going to be depressed in the future and that prices are likely to be lower may be inclined to change production now, before the anticipated collapse. Lower expected future prices therefore tend to increase the present supply of a product. Anticipating higher prices has the opposite effect; producers hold off selling all of their present production hoping to make greater profits from the future higher prices, assuming the product is something like oil, which is not perishable.

Finally, market supply will also be affected by the *number of suppliers*. An increase in the number of suppliers will cause an increase in market supply, whereas a decrease in the number of suppliers will reduce overall market supply.

Again, note that one thing omitted from this list of supply determinants is any mention of demand. At the risk of repetition, firms are not in business to satisfy demand but to make profits. Increased demand for a product does not mean that producers will immediately increase production to satisfy the higher demand. However, the higher demand will cause the price to increase, and this increase induces firms to supply more. But this is an increase in the quantity supplied and *does not* imply an increase in supply—the supply curve remains unchanged.

Michael Busselle/CORBIS

In summary, the determinants of market supply are as follows:

- prices of resources
- business taxes
- technology
- prices of substitutes in production
- future expectations of suppliers
- number of suppliers

The Effects of an Increase in Supply

We have just discussed six different factors that could affect the supply of a product. Let us be more specific and look at what can cause an *increase* in supply:

- a decrease in the price of resources
- a decrease in business taxes (or increase in subsidies)
- an improvement in technology
- a decrease in the price of a productively related product
- the expectation of a decline in the future price of the product
- an increase in the number of suppliers

Let us see the effects of an increase in supply using the original demand for beer and the increase in supply in **Table 2.10**.

TABLE 2.10	The Effect of an Increase in Supply on the Market		
	NUMBER OF CASES PER MONTH		
Price per Case of Beer	**Demand 1**	**Supply 1**	**Supply 2**
$18	16	10	16
19	15	12	18
20	14	14	20
21	13	16	22
22	12	18	24

At the original demand (Demand 1) and supply (Supply 1), the equilibrium price was $20 per case, and the quantity traded was 14 cases. Assume that the supply now increases to Supply 2. At the present price of $20, there will be an immediate surplus of 6 cases.

Before we look at the implications of this surplus, we ought to address a couple of possible qualms that some students might have. The first is this: won't customers take up this excess of beer? It is easy to see that at this price, consumers have already given their response. They want to buy 14 cases, not 20 cases, or any other number. In other words, consumers are buying beer to satisfy their own tastes, not to satisfy the brewers. A second question is this: why would producers produce 20 cases, knowing that the demand at this price is only 14 cases? The answer is that they do not know. Producers knows the circumstances in their own breweries and know that until now, they have been able to sell everything they have produced. With the prospect of higher profits coming from, say, a decrease in costs, a brewer wants to produce more. If all producers do the same, there will be a surplus of beer. **Figure 2.13** shows what happens as a result of this surplus.

Faced with a surplus of beer, market price will be forced down. As price falls, the quantity demanded increases, and the quantity supplied falls. Production increased initially but is now dropping slightly because of the resulting drop in price. The price will continue to drop until it reaches $18. **Table 2.10** shows that at this price, the quantity demanded and the quantity supplied are now equal at 16 cases. The effect of the increase in supply, then, is a lower price and a higher quantity traded.

We leave it to you to verify that a decrease in supply will cause a shortage that will eventually raise the price of the product. (The factors that cause such a decrease in supply are exactly the same as those mentioned above that cause an increase—except they move in the opposite direction.) The net result will be a higher price but a lower quantity traded.

FIGURE 2.13   **Adjustment to an Increase in Supply**

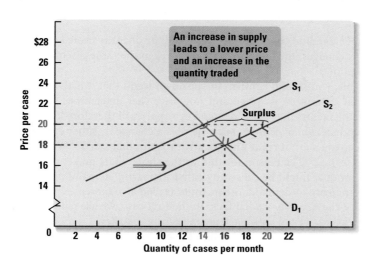

The increase in the supply has the immediate effect of causing a surplus because the demand has remained unchanged. In this figure, at a price of $20, the quantity supplied has increased from 14 to 20, causing a surplus of 6. This will cause the price to drop, and as it does, the quantity demanded increases, and the quantity supplied decreases, until a new equilibrium is reached at a new equilibrium price of $18 and quantity of 16.

 SELF-TEST

6. Suppose that the demand and supply for strawberries in Corona are as follows (the quantities are in thousands of kilos per week):

	QUANTITY		
Price	Demanded	Supplied 1	Supplied 2
$4.00	140	60	_____
4.50	120	80	_____
5.00	100	100	_____
5.50	80	120	_____

a) What are the present equilibrium price and equilibrium quantity? Graph the demand and supply curves, labelling them D_1 and S_1, and indicate equilibrium.

b) Suppose that the supply of strawberries were to increase by 50 percent. Show the new quantities in the Supply 2 column. What will be the new equilibrium price and quantity? Draw in S_2 on your graph, and indicate the new equilibrium.

7. What effect will the following changes have on the supply, price, and quantity traded of wine?

a) A poor harvest in the grape industry results in a big decrease in the supply of grapes.

b) The number of wineries increases.

c) The sales tax on wine increases.

d) The introduction of a new fermentation method reduces the time needed for the wine to ferment.

e) Government introduces a subsidy for each bottle of wine produced domestically.

f) Government introduces a quota limiting the amount of foreign-made wine entering Canada.

g) There is a big increase in wages for the workers in the wine industry.

h) A big increase occurs in the prices of wine coolers (an industry that is similar in technology to the wine industry).

2.7   FINAL WORDS

L07 Understand why demand and supply determine price and the quantity traded and not the reverse.

To complete this introduction to demand and supply, let us use the following chart as a summary:

↑ Demand	→	shortage	→	↑ P	and	↑ Q traded
↓ Supply	→	shortage	→	↑ P	and	↓ Q traded
↓ Demand	→	surplus	→	↓ P	and	↓ Q traded
↑ Supply	→	surplus	→	↓ P	and	↑ Q traded

Note that when demand changes, both price and the quantity traded move in the same direction; when supply changes, the quantity traded moves in the same direction, but price moves in the opposite direction.

From this table, you should confirm in your own mind that it is the supply of and demand for a product that determine its price and not price that determines supply and demand. A change in any of the factors that affect demand or supply will therefore lead to a change in price. The price of a product *cannot* change *unless* there is a change in either demand or supply. It follows therefore that you cannot really analyze any problem that starts: "What happens if the price increases (decreases)…?" The reason for this, as the above chart makes clear, is that an increase in the price of a product might be caused by either increasing demand or decreasing supply. But in the case of an increase in demand, the quantity traded also increases, whereas in the case of a decrease in supply, the quantity traded falls. In the first case, we are talking about an expanding industry; in the second, we are looking at a contracting industry.

Finally, make sure you understand clearly the distinction between changes in the quantities demanded and supplied and changes in demand and supply as illustrated in **Figure 2.14**.

To close this chapter, let us ponder a simple example and make some final observations. Looking back over the past decade or so, what has happened to the prices of laptops? Generally speaking, even allowing for inflation, prices have decreased. And what about the quantity of laptops that are bought and sold now compared with the situation a decade ago? Definitely, the quantity has increased. So, according to our chart above, what could have produced this result in the marketplace? Well, there is only one thing that could lead to a decrease in price and an increase in the quantity traded, and that is an increase in supply. And what in the computer world over the past years could have caused an increase in supply? At first glance, we might credit an improvement in technology that has significantly reduced the costs of producing computers as well as the continuously falling price of silicon chips used in computer hard drives. However, we should mention a number of themes that we will take up in Chapter 8. In the modern world, competitive markets are few and far between, since many markets are dominated by big corporations, big trade unions, and consumer associations and are affected by government intervention. In addition, even when they are competitive, markets do not provide any guarantee that there will not be future periods of recession or inflation. Further, competitive markets cannot ensure that the type of products produced meet external standards such as being environmentally sound or healthy or that the distribution of incomes and wealth in a country is fair.

Finally, let us look back at the discussion that started this chapter and see if we can make sense of it. Justine made an observation about the price of big-screen TVs falling, and Eric responded rather flippantly, "But that is just supply and demand." We now know that price can fall because either supply increased or demand decreased. Justine asked if Eric thought that the price fall was due to an increase in supply and Eric said, "Sure." Then came the really hard question: why would supply go up if price was falling? Eric once again responded that this was just supply and demand. Of course, we now know that Eric should have said that the supply had gone up—perhaps because of increased technology—and that increased supply caused the price to fall. That is, changes in supply cause changes in price, not the other way around.

All of this is summarized in **Figure 2.14**. In graph A, we see a movement from point *a* to *b*, which is an increase in the quantity demanded resulting from the fall in price caused by an increase in supply (S_1 to S_2). Graph B shows an increase in demand, which causes an increase in

FIGURE 2.14	Changes in the Quantity Demanded and Demand

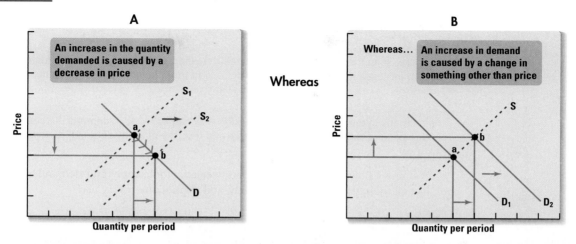

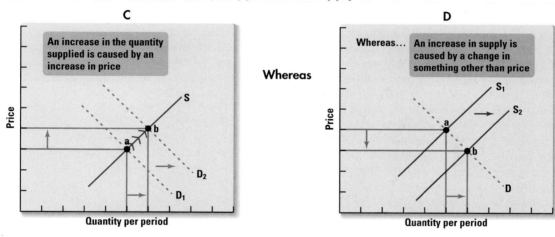

ADDED DIMENSION   The Famous Scissors Analogy

Since the time of Adam Smith, economists have emphasized the importance of understanding the role of price determination. Toward the end of the nineteenth century, there were two schools of thought about what determined price. The first was made up of those who believed that the cost of production was the main determinant—the supply-side view. The second was made up of those, including the famous economist Alfred Marshall, who believed that consumer demand was the main determinant—the demand-side view.

Marshall, writing at the end of that century, was the first to present a lucid synthesis of the two views and suggest that neither demand nor supply alone can provide the answer to the determination of price. His famous analogy of the scissors states, "We might as reasonably dispute whether it is the upper or the under blade of scissors that cuts a piece of paper as whether value [price] is governed by utility or cost of production. It is true that when one blade is held still, and the cutting is effected by moving the other, we may say with careless brevity that the cutting is done by the second; but the statement is not strictly accurate and is to be excused only so long as it claims to be merely a popular and not a strictly scientific account of what happens."[2]

[2] Alfred Marshall, *Principles of Economics,* 8th edition, Macmillan (1920). Reproduced with permission of Palgrave Macmillan.

price and in the quantity supplied (*a* to *b*). Graph C shows an increase in the quantity supplied (*a* to *b*), which follows an increase in price caused by an increase in demand (D_1 to D_2). Finally, in graph D, we see an increase in supply (S_1 to S_2) resulting in a fall in price and an increase in the quantity demanded (*a* to *b*). This allows us to conclude that:

> An increase in the quantity demanded results when an increase in supply pushes price down (A). An increase in demand increases price, and thus the quantity supplied increases (B).

> An increase in the quantity supplied results when an increase in demand pushes price up (C). An increase in supply decreases the price and thus the quantity demanded increases (D).

You now know what an important and versatile tool supply-and-demand analysis can be—but, like all tools, you must use it properly, and clean it after every use!

 ADDED DIMENSION Sales Always Equal Purchases

It is important not to confuse the terms "demand" and "supply" with "purchases" and "sales." As we have seen in this chapter, the quantity demanded and the quantity supplied are not always equal. However, purchases and sales, since they are two sides of the same transaction, must always be equal. The accompanying graph explains the differences in the terms.

The equilibrium price is $12, and at this price, the quantity demanded and supplied are equal at 40 units—this is the amount traded and is the same thing as the amount sold and purchased. However, if the price happened to be above equilibrium—$16—then the quantity demanded is denoted by *a* (30 units) and the quantity supplied by *b* (60 units). Clearly, the two quantities are not equal. But how much is bought and sold at this price? The answer is quantity *a*. It really does not matter how much is being produced, since at this price quantity *a* is the maximum amount that consumers are willing to buy. The difference *ab* represents the amount unsold, or a surplus of 30.

But what is the effect of a price that is below equilibrium? Suppose the price is $8, where the quantity supplied of 20 units

(*c*) is less than the quantity demanded of 50 units (*d*)? This time, how much is being bought and sold? The answer must be quantity *c*. It does not matter how much of this product consumers want to buy if producers are only making quantity *c* available. In general, the amount bought and sold is always equal to the smaller of the quantity demanded or the quantity supplied.

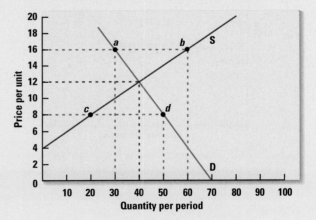

✓ **SELF-TEST**

8. The following are changes that occur in different markets. Explain what will happen to either demand or supply and to the equilibrium price and quantity traded.

   a) An increase in income on the market for an *inferior product*

   b) A decrease in the price of steel on the *automobile industry*

   c) A government subsidy given to operators of *day-care centres*

   d) A government subsidy given to parents who want their children to attend *day-care centres*

   e) A medical report suggesting that *wine* is very fattening

   f) A big decrease in the amount of Middle East oil exports on the *refined-oil market*

   g) An increase in the popularity of *antique furniture*

   h) An increase in the price of coffee on the *tea market*

Review

CHAPTER SUMMARY

In this chapter, you learned that in competitive markets, the price and quantity traded of any product depend on both the demand for and the supply of that product. Once equilibrium is achieved, price and quantity will not change unless either supply or demand changes. In order to fully understand this, you must also understand the following:

2.1a *Demand* is the price–quantity relationship of a product that consumers are willing and able to buy per period of time.

2.1b The demand curve is *downward sloping* because of the:
- substitution effect
- income effect

2.1c Products can be *related* in two ways:
- complements
- substitutes

2.1d *Market demand* is the conceptual summation of each individual's demand within a given market.

2.2a *Supply* is the price–quantity relationship of a product that producers are willing and able to sell per period of time.

2.2b *Market supply* is the conceptual summation of each firm's supply within a given market.

2.3 A market is a mechanism that brings buyers and sellers together.

2.4 Market equilibrium occurs when the quantity demanded and the quantity supplied are equal at a particular price.

2.5a All products are *either*:
- normal products, or
- inferior products

2.5b Market demand *changes* if there is a change in:
- consumers' preferences
- consumers' incomes
- the price of related products
- expectations of future prices, incomes, or availability
- the size of the market, or income and age distribution

2.5c An *increase in demand* will cause a shortage and result in both price and the quantity traded rising.

2.5d A *decrease in demand* will cause a surplus and result in both price and the quantity traded falling.

2.6a Market supply *changes* if there is a change in:
- the price of resources
- business taxes
- technology
- prices of substitutes in production
- future expectations of suppliers
- the number of suppliers

2.6b An *increase in supply* causes a surplus and results in price falling and the quantity traded rising.

2.6c A *decrease in supply* causes a shortage and results in the price rising and the quantity traded falling.

2.7 It is the demand for and the supply of a product that determine price and not price that determines demand and supply.

Practise and learn online with Connect, where you can find the Answered Questions and the Unanswered Problems for all chapters of this textbook's Study Guide section.

NEW GLOSSARY TERMS

ceteris paribus   45
change in demand   57
change in supply   63
change in the quantity demanded   46
change in the quantity supplied   51
complementary products   59
demand   45
demand schedule   46

equilibrium price   55
equilibrium quantity   57
income effect   48
inferior products   58
market   54
market demand   48
market supply   52
normal products   58

real income   48
shortage   61
substitute products   59
substitution effect   48
supply   50
supply schedule   50
surplus   62

STUDY TIPS

1. It is with this chapter that you will learn to appreciate the need for precision in the use of economic terms. For instance, the terms *demand* and *supply* have very clear definitions. "Demand" does *not* mean the amount a person wishes to buy or the amount bought. Demand is not a single quantity but a combination of different prices and quantities. Similarly, you cannot use the term "supply" synonymously with output, production, or quantity supplied. It is *not* a single quantity but a range of different quantities and prices.

2. If you have understood the first point, then this next one should make sense. A change in price cannot affect the demand, since price is part of what we mean by demand. That does not mean that a change in price does not affect consumers; generally, people change the amounts they purchase as a result of a price change. But this is a change in the quantity demanded, *not* a change in demand. Similarly, a change in price leaves supply unaffected. But it definitely affects the *quantity supplied*. These points are illustrated in the way that the demand and supply curves are affected. A change in price causes no change in the demand and supply curves but results in a movement *along* the curves. Only changes in other determinants, besides price, will cause a shift in the curves.

3. It is important for you to keep the concepts of demand and supply separate in your mind. A change in demand does *not* have any effect on supply. This means that the supply curve will not shift when the demand curve changes. Similarly, you must disconnect demand from supply. A change in supply has no impact on demand.

4. There is no alternative to learning the factors that do affect demand and supply. Memorize the five determinants of market demand and the six determinants of market supply. Note that, with the exception of expectations of future price changes, the factors that affect demand have no impact on supply, and vice versa. Try not to be too "cute" when trying to figure out the way in which various changes in determinants affect markets. It is possible to give a convoluted explanation of why, for example, a change in the number of suppliers can affect preferences and therefore the demand of customers of that product. While remotely possible, the effect would be of minor significance. Instead, use common sense and focus on the main effects. Remember that a change in one determinant will usually affect only demand or only supply but seldom both.

5. Do not skip the basics in this chapter, even if at times they seem a little obvious. For example, you need to know that if the price of good A increases, then the demand for the complement good B decreases. Similarly, if income increases, the demand for a normal good increases and the demand for an inferior good decreases.

6. Finally, the most important lesson to learn from this chapter is that the price of a product is determined by both demand and supply. Price is the effect and not the cause. This means that equilibrium price cannot change in a free market unless there has been a change in either demand or supply.

Answered Questions

These questions can also be found online on Connect.

Indicate whether the following statements are true or false:

1. **(LO 1) T or F**   The term "demand" means the quantities that people would like to purchase at various prices.

2. **(LO 4) T or F**   A change in the price of a product has no effect on the demand for the same product.

3. **(LO 1) T or F**   An increase in the price of a product causes a decrease in the real income of consumers.

4. **(LO 4) T or F**   An increase in the price of a product leads to an increase in supply.

5. **(LO 4) T or F**   Equilibrium price implies that everyone who would like to purchase a product is able to.

6. **(LO 4) T or F**   Surpluses drive prices up; shortages drive prices down.

7. **(LO 5) T or F**   An increase in incomes will lead to a decrease in the demand for an inferior product.

8. **(LO 7) T or F**   A decrease in the demand for a product will lead to a decrease in both price and the quantity traded.

9. **(LO 6) T or F**   An increase in business taxes causes the supply curve to shift left.

10. **(LO 6) T or F**   A decrease in supply causes price to fall and the quantity traded to increase.

Basic (Questions 11–22)

11. **(LO 1)** What does the term "demand" refer to?
    a) The amounts that consumers are either willing or able to purchase at various prices
    b) The amounts that consumers are both willing and able to purchase at various prices
    c) The quantity purchased at the equilibrium price
    d) The price consumers are willing to pay for a certain quantity of a product

12. **(LO 6)** What will a surplus of a product lead to?
    a) A reduction in supply
    b) A reduction in price
    c) An increase in price
    d) An increase in supply

13. **(LO 1)** What is the effect of a decrease in the price of a product?
    a) It will increase consumers' real income while leaving their actual income unchanged.
    b) It will increase consumers' actual income while leaving their real income unchanged.
    c) It will decrease demand.
    d) It will have no effect on income.

14. **(LO 5)** What is the effect of an increase in the price of coffee?
    a) It will lead to an increase in the demand for tea.
    b) It will lead to a decrease in the demand for tea.
    c) It will have no effect on the tea market.
    d) It will decrease the demand for coffee.

15. **(LO 1)** What is the slope of the demand curve?
    a) It is downward sloping because when the price of a product falls, consumers are willing and able to buy more.
    b) It is upward sloping because when the price of a product falls, consumers are willing and able to buy more.
    c) It is upward sloping because when the price of a product increases, consumers are willing and able to buy more.
    d) It is downward sloping because higher prices are associated with larger quantities.

16. **(LO 6)** What is the effect of an increase in the price of a productive resource?
    a) It will cause a decrease in the supply of the product.
    b) It will cause an increase in the supply of the product.
    c) It will cause a decrease in the demand for the product.
    d) It will cause an increase in the demand for the product.

17. **(LO 5)** In what way are Pepsi-Cola and Coca-Cola related?
    a) They are substitute products.
    b) They are complementary products.
    c) They are inferior products.
    d) They are unrelated products.

18. **(LO 6)** Which of the following could cause an increase in the supply of wheat?
    a) A decrease in the price of oats
    b) An imposition of a sales tax on wheat
    c) An increase in the price of fertilizer
    d) A decrease in the price of wheat

19. **(LO 5)** All of the following, *except one*, would cause an increase in the demand for a normal product. Which is the exception?
    a) An increase in consumers' incomes
    b) An increase in the price of a substitute product
    c) An increase in the size of the market
    d) Consumer expectations of a lower future price for the product

20. **(LO 5)** Which of the following pairs of goods are complementary?
    a) Coffee and tea
    b) Skis and ski boots
    c) Bread and crackers
    d) Popcorn and pretzels

21. **(LO 6)** All of the following, *except one*, would cause a decrease in the supply of product A. Which is the exception?
    a) An increase in the price of resources used to make product A
    b) An increase in business taxes
    c) An improvement in technology
    d) The expectation by suppliers that future prices of product A will be higher

22. **(LO 5)** Which of the following best describes a normal product?
    a) A product that people both need and like
    b) A product whose demand increases if incomes increase
    c) A product whose demand increases if incomes decrease
    d) A staple product that everyone needs

Intermediate (Questions 23–32)

23. **(LO 5)** How will a change in income affect the demand for an inferior product?
    a) The demand will increase if the incomes of consumers increase.
    b) The demand will increase if the incomes of consumers decrease.
    c) The demand for an inferior product is not affected by consumer incomes.
    d) The demand will remain the same, but the quantity demanded will increase if incomes decrease.

24. **(LO 5)** Which of the following factors will shift the demand curve left?
    a) An increase in the price of a substitute product
    b) A decrease in the price of a complementary product
    c) An increase in incomes if the product is an inferior product
    d) The expectation that future prices of the product will be higher

25. **(LO 6)** A rightward shift in the supply curve for a product could be caused by all of the following *except one*. Which is the exception?
    a) The expectation by suppliers that the future price of the product will be higher

b) A decrease in the price of a productive resource used in its manufacture
    c) A decrease in the price of a product that is a substitute in production
    d) A technological improvement in manufacturing methods

26. **(LO 6)** What is the effect of a decrease in the supply of a product?
    a) It will cause an increase in both price and the quantity traded.
    b) It will cause an increase in price but a decrease in the quantity traded.
    c) It will cause a decrease in both price and the quantity traded.
    d) It will cause a decrease in price but an increase in the quantity traded.

Table 2.11 depicts the market for mushrooms (in thousands of kilograms per month). Use this table to answer questions 27 and 28.

TABLE 2.11								
Price ($)	2.50	3.00	3.50	4.00	4.50	5.00	5.50	6.00
Quantity Demanded	64	62	60	58	56	54	52	50
Quantity Supplied	40	44	48	52	56	60	64	68

27. **(LO 4)** Refer to **Table 2.11** to answer this question. What are the values of equilibrium price and quantity traded?
    a) $3 and 52
    b) $3 and 62
    c) $4 and 58
    d) $4.50 and 56
    e) They cannot be determined from the data.

28. **(LO 4)** Refer to **Table 2.11** to answer this question. What will happen if the price of the product is $3?
    a) There would be a surplus of 18, which would lead to a decrease in price.
    b) There would be a shortage of 18, which would lead to an increase in price.
    c) There would be a shortage of 18, which would lead to a decrease in price.
    d) There would be a surplus of 18, which would lead to an increase in price.
    e) There would be neither a surplus nor a shortage.

29. **(LO 5)** In what way are products A and B related if an increase in the price of product A leads to a decrease in the demand for product B?
    a) Product A must be a resource used in the manufacture of product B.
    b) Product B must be a resource used in the manufacture of product A.
    c) The two products must be complements.
    d) The two products must be substitutes.
    e) The two products must be inferior products.

30. **(LO 3)** What is the effect of a shortage?
    a) It will cause a decrease in price, leading to an increase in the quantity supplied and a decrease in the quantity demanded.
    b) It will cause a decrease in price, leading to a decrease in the quantity supplied and an increase in the quantity demanded.
    c) It will cause an increase in price, leading to an increase in the quantity supplied and a decrease in the quantity demanded.
    d) It will cause an increase in price, leading to a decrease in the quantity supplied and an increase in the quantity demanded.

31. **(LO 7)** What is the effect of an increase in demand for a product?
    a) Its price will rise, and the quantity traded will decrease.
    b) Its price will rise, and the quantity traded will increase.
    c) Its price will fall, and the quantity traded will decrease.
    d) Its price will fall, and the quantity traded will increase.

32. **(LO 7)** Refer to **Figure 2.15** to answer this question. What will be the effect if the price is now $1200?
    a) There would be a surplus of 30.
    b) There would be a shortage of 30.
    c) 160 would be purchased.
    d) There would be a surplus of 60.
    e) The price will increase.

Advanced (Questions 33–35)

33. **(LO 7)** Refer to **Figure 2.15** to answer this question. Assume that there is a shortage of 60 units. What does this mean?

FIGURE 2.15

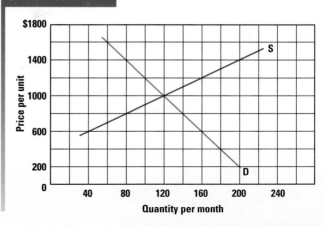

a) Purchasers would be willing to pay an additional $600 for the quantity they are now purchasing.
b) The price must be above equilibrium.
c) The price must be $1200.
d) The price must be $600.
e) None of the above is correct.

34. **(LO 7)** Refer to **Figure 2.15** to answer this question. Suppose that initially the market was in equilibrium and that demand increased by 60. What will be the new equilibrium as a result?
    a) A price of $1000 and quantity traded of 120
    b) A price of $1000 and quantity traded of 160
    c) A price of $1200 and quantity traded of 160
    d) A price of $1400 and quantity traded of 160
    e) A price of $1400 and quantity traded of 240

35. **(LO 7)** How will the demand and supply of a product be affected if both producers and consumers expect the price of a product to increase?
    a) It will cause an increase in demand but a decrease in supply.
    b) It will cause an increase in both demand and supply.
    c) It will cause a decrease in both demand and supply.
    d) It will cause an increase in supply but will have no effect on demand.
    e) It will cause an increase in supply but a decrease in demand.

Parallel Problems

ANSWERED PROBLEMS

36A. **(LO 1, 2, 4, 5, 6)** **Key Problem Table 2.12** shows the market for wool in the economy of Odessa (the quantities are in tonnes per year).
   a) Plot the demand and supply curves on **Figure 2.16**, and label them D_1 and S_1. Mark the equilibrium as e_1 on the graph.
   b) What are the values of equilibrium price and quantity?
      equilibrium price: _____
      equilibrium quantity: _____
   c) If the price of wool were $600, would there be a surplus or shortage?
      Surplus/shortage _____ of _____.
      Indicate the amount of the surplus or shortage on the graph.
   d) Suppose that the demand were to increase by 60. Draw and label the new demand curve as D_2. What are the new values of equilibrium price and quantity?
      equilibrium price: _____
      equilibrium quantity: _____
      Mark the new equilibrium as e_2 on the graph.
   e) Following the change in d), suppose that the supply were to increase by 50 percent. Draw and label the new supply curve as S_2. What are the new values of equilibrium price and quantity?
      equilibrium price: _____
      equilibrium quantity: _____
      Mark the new equilibrium as e_3 on the graph.

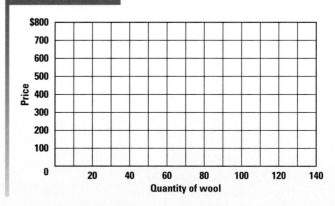

FIGURE 2.16

   d) An increase in the price of apple juice
   e) An increase in consumers' average income
   f) An improvement in the juicing process that lowers the cost of producing cranberry juice

38A. **(LO 3, 4, 6)** **Table 2.13** shows the market demand and supply for Fuji apples in Peterborough.
   a) What is the equilibrium price and quantity traded?
      price: _____ quantity: _____
   b) Suppose that supply increases by 30. What would be the price and quantity traded at the new equilibrium?
      price: _____ quantity: _____
   c) After the increase in supply, what would be the surplus/shortage at a price of $8?
      Surplus/shortage _____ of _____

TABLE 2.12

Price ($)	100	200	300	400	500	600	700
Quantity demanded	130	110	90	70	50	30	10
Quantity supplied	10	20	30	40	50	60	70

Basic (Problems 37A–44A)

37A. **(LO 5)** Circle which of the following factors will lead to an increase in the demand for cranberry juice (which is a normal good).
   a) A decrease in the price of cranberry juice
   b) A decrease in the price of cranberries
   c) The expectation by consumers that the price of cranberry juice is likely to increase

TABLE 2.13

Price	Quality Demanded	Quantity Supplied
0	180	90
2	170	110
4	160	130
6	150	150
8	140	170
10	130	190

39A. **(LO 1, 2, 5, 6)** In each of the two graphs in **Figure 2.17**, explain the change in equilibrium from a to b in terms of
   a) an increase or decrease in demand or supply
   b) an increase or decrease in the quantity demanded or supplied

FIGURE 2.17

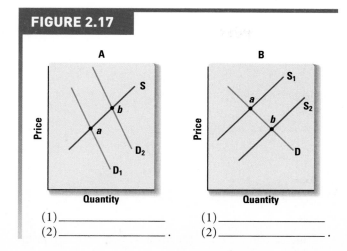

A

B

(1)_____   (1)_____

(2)_____.   (2)_____.

40A. (LO 4)

a) Given the data in **Table 2.14**, draw the demand curve on **Figure 2.18**.

b) What is the equilibrium price and quantity?

price: _____ quantity: _____

TABLE 2.14

Price	Quantity Demanded
1	80
2	70
3	60
4	50
5	40
6	30

FIGURE 2.18

Quantity of copy paper

41A. (LO 4, 5, 6)
Suppose that new medical research strongly indicates that the consumption of coffee can cause cancer of the colon. What effect will this news have on the equilibrium price and quantity traded of the following products?

a) Coffee beans

price: _____ quantity traded: _____

b) Tea, a substitute for coffee

price: _____ quantity traded: _____

c) Danish pastries, a complement to coffee

price: _____ quantity traded: _____

d) Teapots, a complement to tea

price: _____ quantity traded: _____

42A. (LO 5, 6)
What must have happened to demand or supply to cause the following changes?

a) The price of guitars falls, but the quantity traded increases.

Demand/supply _____ must have _____.

b) The price and quantity traded of saxophones decrease.

Demand/supply_____ must have _____.

c) The price of trombones increases, while the quantity traded falls.

Demand/supply _____ must have _____.

d) The price and quantity traded of clarinets increases.

Demand/supply _____ must have _____.

43A. (LO 1, 5)
What is the distinction between demand and the quantity demanded?

44A. (LO 1, 4)
Explain the effect of a shortage on prices.

Intermediate (Problems 45A–49A)

45A. (LO 4, 5, 6)
Consider the effects of each of the events outlined in **Table 2.15** on the market indicated. Place a (↑), (↓) or (−) under the appropriate heading to indicate whether there will be an increase, decrease, or no change in demand (D), supply (S), equilibrium price (P), and the quantity traded (Q).

46A. (LO 4)
Figure 2.19 shows the market for the new Guns and Butter album, "Live at Saskatoon."

a) Suppose that the album producers put it on sale for $8 each. How much will be the surplus or shortage? How many will be sold?

Surplus/shortage _____ of _____.

quantity sold: _____

b) What is the maximum price at which the quantity actually sold in a) could have been sold?

Maximum price: _____

c) If the album producers had actually put the album on the market at the price mentioned in b), what would have been the resulting surplus/shortage?

Surplus/shortage _____ of _____.

TABLE 2.15

Market	Event	D	S	P	Q
a) DVDs	A technological improvement reduces the cost of producing DVD players.				
b) Butter	New medical evidence suggests that margarine causes migraines.				
c) Newspapers	Because of worldwide shortages, the prices of pulp and paper increase dramatically.				
d) Low-quality toilet paper	Consumer incomes rise significantly.				
e) Movie rentals	Movie theatres halve their admission prices.				
f) Beef	World price of lamb increases.				

FIGURE 2.19

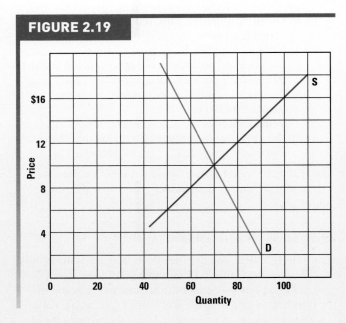

Quantity

47A. **(LO 1, 5)** "The prices of houses rise when demand increases. The demand for houses decreases when prices increase." Change one of these statements so that the two are consistent with each other.

48A. **(LO 5)** Briefly explain the five determinants of market demand.

49A. **(LO 4, 5)** Explain, step by step, how an increase in demand eventually affects both price and the quantity traded.

Advanced (Problems 50A–52A)

50A. **(LO 1, 4)** In Kirin, at a market price of $1 per kilo, there is a shortage of 60 kilos of avocados. For each 50-cent increase in the price, the quantity demanded drops by 5 kilos, while the quantity supplied increases by 10 kilos.
a) What will be the equilibrium price? _____.
b) What will be the surplus/shortage at a price of $4.50? Surplus/shortage _____ of _____ kilos.

51A. **(LO 4, 5, 6)** Identify any two possible causes and five specific effects involved in the movement from point a to b to c in **Figure 2.20**.

FIGURE 2.20

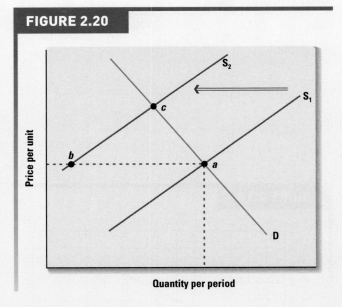

Quantity per period

52A. **(LO 6)** Suppose that in response to the high rent and low supply of affordable rental accommodation in the Toronto market, the city constructed 5000 additional rental units and put them on the market at below-equilibrium rents. Draw a supply-and-demand graph showing the effects on the rental market.

THE ALGEBRA OF DEMAND AND SUPPLY

THE ALGEBRA OF THE MARKET

We have described the marketplace in both tables and graphs. This appendix explains how we can also analyze demand and supply algebraically. Suppose that **Figure A1** shows the demand for soy milk in Canada.

FIGURE A1

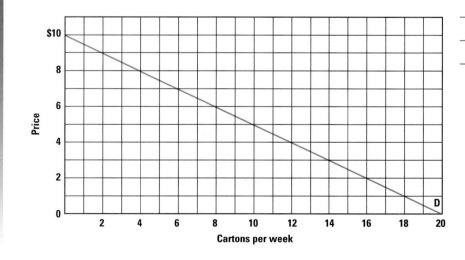

Number of Cartons per Week	
Price ($)	Quantity
0	20
1	18
2	16
3	14
4	12
5	10
6	8
7	6
8	4
9	2
10	0

You will remember from the Toolkit that, in general, the algebraic expression for a straight line is:

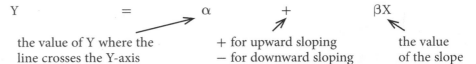

Y	=	α	+	βX
	the value of Y where the line crosses the Y-axis		+ for upward sloping − for downward sloping	the value of the slope

On our graph, price is shown on the vertical (Y) axis and the quantity demanded on the horizontal (X) axis. Therefore, the general expression for the demand curve is given as:

$$p = \alpha + \beta Q^d$$

Here, the value of a is equal to ($)10. This is where the demand curve crosses the price axis; that is, it is the highest price payable. The value of the slope is the ratio of change or rise over run. In terms of the demand curve, the slope shows by how much the quantity changes as the price changes.

$$\text{the slope} = \frac{\Delta \text{ (change in) P}}{\Delta \text{ (change in) Q}}$$

For our demand curve, that value equals:

$$\frac{1}{-2}$$

This means that each time the price changes by $1, quantity changes (in the opposite direction) by 2 units. The equation for this demand curve, then, is:

$$P = 10 - \frac{1}{-2} Q^d \text{ or } P = 10 - \frac{1}{2} Q^d$$

Though this is graphically the correct way to express it, in terms of economic logic, the quantity demanded is dependent on price rather than the other way around, so let us rearrange the terms, as follows:

$$Q^d = 20 - 2P$$

Now, let us look at the supply side of things. The table and graph in **Figure A2** show the supply of soy milk in the market.

FIGURE A2

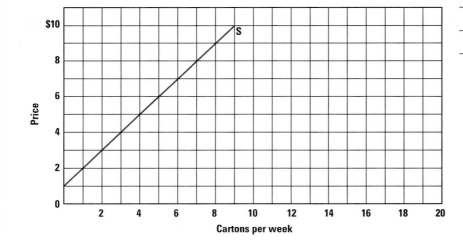

Number of Cartons per Week	
Price ($)	Quantity
0	—
1	0
2	1
3	2
4	3
5	4
6	5
7	6
8	7
9	8
10	9

The general equation for the supply curve is:

$$p = \alpha + \beta Q^s$$

As with the demand curve, α shows the value where the curve crosses the vertical (price) axis. This happens at a price of $1. The value of the slope is, again, the same as for the demand curve.

$$\frac{\Delta \text{ (change in) P}}{\Delta \text{ (change in) Q}}$$

For this supply curve, it equals:

$$\frac{1}{+1}$$

A $1 change in price causes a change of 1 unit in the quantity supplied. The equation for this supply curve, then, is:

$$P = 1 + Q^s$$

As we did with the demand curve, let us rearrange this equation in terms of Qs; thus:

$$Q^s = -1 + P$$

Bringing demand and supply together, in **Figure A3**, allows us to find the equilibrium values. From either the table or the graph, it is easy to see that the equilibrium price is equal to $7. At this price, the quantity demanded and the quantity supplied are both 6 units. Finding equilibrium algebraically is also straightforward. We want to find the price at which the quantity demanded equals the quantity supplied. We know the equations for each, and so we simply set them equal.

$$Q^d = Q^s$$

$$20 - 2P = -1 + P$$

That gives us:

$$3P = 21$$

Therefore,

$$P = 7$$

FIGURE A3

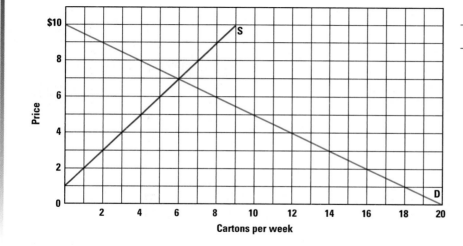

Number of Cartons per Week		
Price ($)	Q^d	Q^s
0	20	—
1	18	0
2	16	1
3	14	2
4	12	3
5	10	4
6	8	5
7	6	6
8	4	7
9	2	8
10	0	9

Substituting in either equation (and it is best to do both to make sure you are correct) gives us:

$$Q^d = 20 - 2(7) = 6$$

$$Q^s = -1 + (7) = 6$$

Doing things algebraically sometimes makes things easier. For instance, suppose market demand increased by 3 units; that is, the quantities demanded increased by 3 units at every price. What effect would this have on the equilibrium price and quantity? Algebraically, this is quite straightforward to calculate. The increase in demand means that the value of the (quantity) intercept increases by 3 and gives us a new demand equation:

$$Q^d_2 = 23 - 2P$$

The supply has not changed, and so we can calculate the new equilibrium as:

$$(Q^d_2 = Q^s) : 23 - 2P = -1 + P$$

This gives us:

$$3P = 24$$

Therefore,

$$P = 8$$

The new equilibrium quantity becomes 7. We can obtain this quantity by inserting the price of $8 into both equations, thus:

$$Q^d_2 = 23 - 2(8) = 7 \text{ and } Q^s - 1 + (8) = 7$$

Questions for Appendix to Chapter 2

ANSWERED PROBLEMS

1. If $Q^d = 40 - 2P$ and $Q^s = 10 + 3P$, what are the equilibrium values of price and quantity?

2. a) If $Q^d = 100 - 5P$ and $Q^s = 10 + P$, what are the equilibrium values of price and quantity?
   b) If demand increases by 12 and price remains the same as in a), will there be a surplus or a shortage? How much?
   c) If demand increases by 12, what will be the new equilibrium price and quantity?

3. a) If $P = 11 - 0.25Q^d$, what is the algebraic expression for Q^d?
   b) If $P = 16 + 2Q^s$, what is the algebraic expression for Q^s?
   c) What are the equilibrium values of price and quantity?

4. The following table shows the demand and supply of kiwi fruit in Montreal:
   a) What is the algebraic expression for the demand curve?
   b) What is the algebraic expression for the supply curve?
   c) Find algebraically the values of equilibrium price and quantity.

5. Suppose that the demand equation is $Q^d = 230 - 3P$ and the supply equation is $Q^s = -10 + 9P$.
   a) If the price is 15, will there be a surplus or a shortage? How much?
   b) If the price is 22, will there be a surplus or a shortage? How much?

6. Suppose that the demand equation is: $Q^d = 520 - 3P$ and the supply equation is $Q^s = 100 + 4P$.
   a) If the quantity presently supplied is 380, what is the price?
   b) At the price in a), what is the quantity demanded?
   c) At the price in a), is there a surplus or a shortage?

Price per Kilo	Quantity Demanded
0	675
$1	575
2	475
3	375
4	275
5	175

Price per Kilo	Quantity Supplied
0	0
$1	50
2	100
3	150
4	200
5	250

CHAPTER 3

MEASURING THE ECONOMY 1: GDP AND ECONOMIC GROWTH

WHAT'S AHEAD...

At the end of this chapter, you should be able to...

LO1 understand the circular flow of national income.

LO2 explain the concept of equilibrium and why national income can rise and fall.

LO3 understand the components of GDP accounting and be aware of some of the problems in determining official statistics.

LO4 know how to measure economic growth and appreciate the benefits of economic growth.

LO5 understand the importance of productivity in encouraging growth and some of the problems of unchecked growth.

What determines the level of an economy's national income and how that income relates to real output are at the heart of macroeconomics. In this chapter, we begin the explanation of this determination by introducing the circular flow of income approach. We then look at the methods for measuring national income. Next, we look at the immense importance of economic growth and explain how it is measured, which takes us to an examination of the sources of growth. Lastly, we look at some of the problems often associated with economic growth.

A Question of Relevance...

Suppose that you heard on the news that tax rates were being cut by government. It is easy for you to see immediately how this would affect you and other members of your family. Although people quickly recognize how some news items affect them directly, they fail to even note that other news items, are sometimes just as important. For example, suppose you read in the news that Canadians were saving much less this year than last, that Canadian exports were higher this year than last, or that interest rates would likely remain unchanged for the foreseeable future. How would you react to these news items? Do you consider them as significant as the item on tax cuts? The fact is that they might be just as significant. This chapter will help explain why.

In 2010, Canada's national income was $1622 billion. What are the major determinants of a country's income? How is national income measured? And what causes it to grow? More importantly, how can we ensure that we can sustain growth? Further, if economic growth is good for a nation, is more growth better than less? Finally, can an economy grow too fast? All these questions need reasonably well-thought-out answers. The first step in the process of finding these answers is to understand how income flows within an economy. To do this, we will construct a simplified model of the economy.

3.1 CIRCULAR FLOW OF INCOME

Flow of Factor Services

Imagine a simple economy with only two sectors: the household sector and the business sector. Clusters of individuals make up the household sector, whereas businesses of various types and sizes, from small family-run proprietorships to large corporations, make up the business sector. Next, recall the definition of the factors of production. As mentioned in Chapter 1, the factors (think of them as production inputs, if that is helpful) are divided into four categories: land, labour, capital, and enterprise.

LO1 Understand the circular flow of national income.

You may recall, also from Chapter 1, that economists consider *land* to be anything that is natural, such as minerals, all natural vegetation, natural harbours, supplies of water, and so on. The term *labour* is used in the broadest sense to describe a wide range of human endeavour, including that of a skilled surgeon, a construction worker, or a symphony musician. *Capital* is defined as the physical plant, tools, and equipment used to produce other goods or services. (In conventional language, capital is often equated with money. In economics, however, capital refers to the tools, equipment, and machines that are used to produce other goods. Money can be used to purchase capital goods, but it is not, in itself, a factor of production.) Finally, *enterprise* is the specialized human effort that organizes the other factors of production, innovates, and bears risks.

These four factors of production combine to produce the goods and services that individuals consume on a daily basis. In our private enterprise or market economy, the factors of production are, ultimately, owned by individuals. Individuals control the sale of their own labour; individuals own land and mineral rights; and individuals own the shares of a corporation's assets or (for our purposes) their capital.

We can now begin to build our model with a series of diagrams. The bottom blue loop in **Figure 3.1** represents the provision of factor services from the household sector to the business sector. Businesses use these factor services, which are provided by the household sector, in order to produce goods and services. This is illustrated by the upper blue loop flowing from the business sector to the household sector, which represents the provision of consumer goods and services from firms to households.

The Flow of Incomes

Next, let us turn to the financial flows that move in the opposite direction. The business sector must pay for the factor services they receive. This payment goes to the household sector, becomes income, and is divided into the specific categories of wages, interest, rent, and profits. Remember that many of these terms differ from their conventional usage. *Rent*, for instance, is the income received from the use of the factor land—that is, the payment for the use of a natural resource, such as royalty payments for a stand of timber—and is not the payment for the use of an apartment or other building. Wages means the income received for the use of labour services and includes

FIGURE 3.1   The Financial Flows

The inner blue circle represents the flow of factor services from households to business and the flow of consumer goods from business to households. The outer red circle shows the corresponding financial flows with a flow of factor spending (income) going from business to households and consumption spending flowing from households to business.

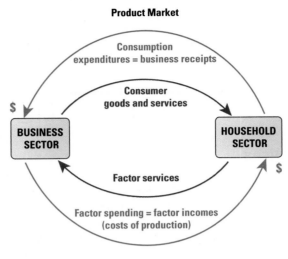

commissions, tips, and all employee benefits. *Interest* means the income received for the use of the factor capital, which again differs from conventional usage. Finally, by *profits* economists mean income that is left over after the three factors of production have been paid, and it can be thought of as a reward for the fourth factor: enterprise. Thus, the red lower loop in **Figure 3.1** represents the financial flow of factor incomes (costs of production to the firm), wages (w), interest (i), rent (r), and profits (π) from the business sector to the household sector.

Individuals in the household sector earn income by receiving payment for the factors they sell or rent. And what do these same individuals do with their incomes? Primarily, they engage in **consumption**—paying for the consumer goods and services received from the business sector. This flow represents an expenditure for households but is an income (in the way of business receipts) for the firms. This financial flow is the red upper loop. So, now we have two financial flows, as shown by the red circle in **Figure 3.1**.

consumption: the expenditure by households on goods and services.

> Households sell factor services to the business sector and earn incomes. With this income, they pay for the goods and services received from the business sector.

A number of complications are on the way, but each can be handled easily if you keep this basic circular flow clear in your mind.

We have now identified what economists call the **product market**, which is the buying and selling of goods and services (the upper loops); and the **factor market**, which is the buying and selling of the factors of production (the lower loops).

Also, note that every buy/sell transaction in either market is income to one sector and spending to the other. Thus:

product market: the market for consumer goods and services.

factor market: the market for the factors of production.

> National income is the *sum of all incomes* earned from economic transactions or the *sum of all spending.*

ADDED DIMENSION   François Quesnay and the Circular Flow

The circular flow concept owes a big debt to François Quesnay (1694–1774), court physician to Louis XV and Madame de Pompadour of France, and the founder of a group of scholars called the *Physiocrats*. This group was highly critical of the French government's interference in the economy, which had taken the form of a myriad of regulations and taxes. Quesnay published his Tableau Economique in 1758 to explain how income in an economy flows from one group in society to another. He believed that only nature was truly a creator of wealth, by generating what he called a surplus each year. Humans, he believed, merely "transformed" this surplus into various products. Further, this surplus eventually "flowed" to the landowners (the king, the aristocracy, and the church), and therefore only this group should be subject to taxation. He advocated that all other taxes should be abolished, leaving only a single tax on "wealth." Not surprisingly, his views were not well received in the circles of power.

The Flow of Income versus the Stock of Money

Before we move to some complications, there is a straightforward but very fundamental point that must be understood. We are building a circular flow of **income** model, and it is important that we distinguish between the flow of income and the stock of **money**. An example will help. Imagine a simple economy made up of only three businesses: Bill owns and operates a bakery, Wick is the proprietor of a candle-making business, and Tammy has a tailor's shop. Within this economy, there is only a single $10 bill, which is currently in the possession of Bill, the baker. So, we begin our story with three businesses (and three households), a stock of money equal to $10, and no income (yet). Let us assume that Wick has just produced some candles and that Bill, the baker, notices that his inventory of candles is getting low. He goes to Wick and buys $10 worth of candles and pays cash. Wick, in receipt of $10, decides he needs to purchase a new pair of jeans produced by Tammy, the tailor, which just happen to cost $10. Tammy has spent all day producing these jeans and for her efforts receives $10 from Wick. After all this effort, Tammy requires sustenance and makes her way to Bill, the baker, to buy some freshly baked bread, which has a price of $10. Bill, the baker, receives the $10 bill for his efforts. Let us summarize today's activities in this mini-economy:

income: the earnings of factors of production expressed as an amount per period of time.

money: any medium of exchange that is widely accepted.

- Total production came to a value of $30.
- Total spending came to $30; and total income is $30.
- All of this activity was financed by a single $10 bill.

Clearly, the stock of money and the flow of income are not the same thing! To cement this simple point, think of a retired couple with a lot of money—$200 000 in a bank account—but relatively little income—$16 000 a year in interest. Compare this with the young double-income professional couple just starting out, with an annual household income of $90 000 but almost no money in the bank, since all of the income is going to mortgage and car payments and the expenses of a fast-lane lifestyle. Again, the fundamental point—distinguishing between the flow of income and the stock of money—is important. In 2010, Canada's stock of money was approximately $258 billion. The flow of income during the same year was approximately $1622 billion. These figures tell us that the velocity of money in Canada for that year was 6.3 (that is, 1622 ÷ 258). This means that each unit of currency in Canada was used (changed hands) approximately six times during that year.

Closed Private Model

The simple economy described above seems to demonstrate that the value of (1) total production ($10 worth of candles, of bread, and of jeans); (2) total expenditure (the purchase of each of these three items); and (3) total income (what Wick, Bill, and Tammy each receive) are equal. Does this equality always hold true, or is it merely a coincidence? We will answer this question soon, but for now you should realize that a good part of macroeconomics is concerned with the link between these three aggregates: production, expenditure, and income.

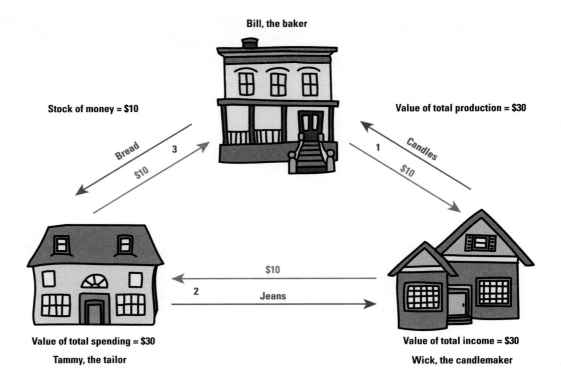

Bill, the baker

Stock of money = $10

Bread   3

$10

Value of total production = $30

1   Candles

$10

$10

2   Jeans

Value of total spending = $30

Tammy, the tailor

Value of total income = $30

Wick, the candlemaker

Keeping all this in mind, let us now return to the circular flow and introduce the first complication by asking: what else do individuals in the household sector do with their income besides spend on consumption? They save. **Saving** (S) can be defined as income (Y) received but not spent on consumption (C).

saving: the portion of income that is not spent on consumption.

$$S = Y - C \qquad\qquad [3.1]$$

leakage: income received within the circular flow that does not flow directly back.

Saving thus becomes a **leakage** from the circular flow of income. A leakage, then, is a flow of income that is diverted out of the circular flow and doesn't flow directly back. This is shown in **Figure 3.2**.

The reasons that people want to save can be quite varied: for retirement; for a major purchase in the future, such as a house, car, or a holiday trip; for a child's future education; or, quite simply, for a rainy day. In this model, the primary determinant of how much people are able to save is their level of income.

It should be noted as well that a business can also save by not paying out all of its after-tax profits in dividends. Nonetheless, our focus will be on saving by households. Savings make up the portion of wealth that is held in the form of financial instruments, such as bonds, term deposits, savings accounts, and chequing accounts. Normally, these savings are deposited with various **financial intermediaries**, such as banks, credit unions, and trust companies, and are available for loan as shown in **Figure 3.2**.

financial intermediaries: financial institutions, such as banks, that act as agents between borrowers and lenders.

Next, we want to add the concept of injection. An **injection** is any expenditure received by firms in the business sector that does not come from the household sector in the form of consumption and thus does not depend on the level of income.

injection: any spending flow that is not dependent on the current level of income.

One form of injection is **investment** spending. Investment is defined as spending that results in a physical increase in plant or equipment. Another way of thinking of investment is spending that increases the economy's stock of capital goods.

investment: spending on new capital goods.

FIGURE 3.2   The Saving Leakage and Investment Injection

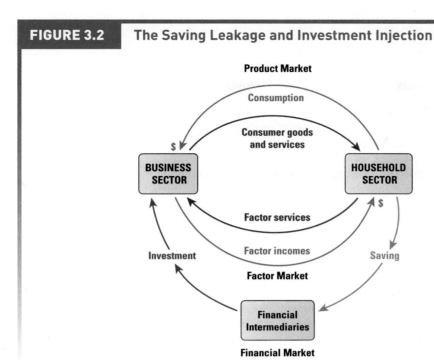

The financial intermediaries match the savings of the households with the desire of the business sector to borrow for investment.

Why would a firm invest in new machinery or equipment, thereby expanding its production capacity? Quite simply, to increase potential profit in the future.

You will note that that this definition of investment differs from the conventional use of the term. If you overheard a fellow student say: "I invested in some General Corporation shares today," you would correctly understand him to mean that he had bought some General Corporation shares. Yet, he has technically misused the term "investment," at least from the economist's point of view!

Let us get this sorted out. The person in our example was able to buy the shares through his broker only because someone else wanted to sell General Corporation shares. Someone sold the shares, someone bought them, brokers arranged the transaction and took a commission. From the point of view of the overall economy, what has changed? Very little. The portfolios of the two people in our example have changed, but the economy has not experienced any new investment.

Investment, then, is an increase in the economy's capacity to produce goods and services and is done by business for profit.

To re-emphasize:

> The reasons individuals save (for retirement, future purchases, and so on) differ from the reasons businesses invest. Saving (a leakage) and investment (an injection) are quite distinct actions.

Does this imply that there is no connection between saving and investment? Not at all. Most of the time, investment by business is financed with borrowed funds, and it is the savings in the economy that provide the pool of funds. In short, the savings available in the economy enable business investment to occur.

In other words, without savings there would be no investment. However, this does not mean that all savings will necessarily be invested:

> Saving is a *necessary but not sufficient* condition for investment.

imports: goods and services that are bought from other countries and constitute a leakage from the circular flow of income.

exports: goods and services that are sold to other countries and create an injection into the circular flow of income.

government spending: purchases of goods and services by government.

transfer payments: one-way transactions in which payment is made by the government but no good or service flows back in return.

Open Private Model

Putting saving and investment aside for now, let us turn to the second pair of leakages/injections: imports and exports. First, the leakage. Some of the goods and services that households buy, as well as some of the investment goods purchased by business, are goods and services imported from outside the domestic economy. Such expenditure does not flow back to the domestic economy but, instead, leaks out. We refer to this import spending in the model as plain **imports** (IM). Although it is usually business that does the actual importing of goods, we will illustrate this leakage as coming from the household sector, reflecting the fact that the ultimate consumers of most imports are individuals.

Conversely, the business sector receives payment for goods and services exported, and this payment is in addition to the consumption expenditure from (domestic) households. **Exports** (X) are therefore an injection into the circular flow of income. Note, then, that the value of exports does not depend on the level of income in this country but on the level of income in the rest of the world. The foreign sector, which is made up of the import leakages and the export injections, is illustrated in **Figure 3.3**.

Open Private Model with the Public Sector

The third pair of leakages/injections that we will consider is not so simply handled. First, we must add another sector to our analysis: government. The government sector taxes both the household sector and the business sector, and so taxes (T) are the third leakage. At the same time, the government sector purchases goods and services from the business sector, and so **government spending** (G) on goods and services is the third injection. In addition, government also disburses what are called **transfer payments** (TP). These are defined as payments made for which no goods

---

FIGURE 3.3   The Import Leakage and Export Injection

Households spend on imports, and the business sector exports to foreigners.

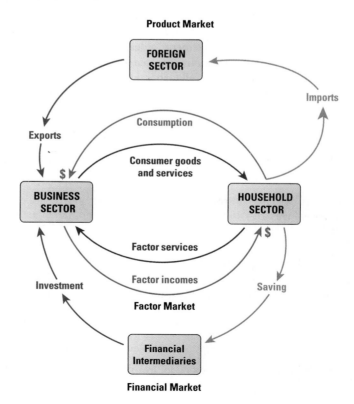

ADDED DIMENSION   The Rate of Savings and the Level of Income

There are many factors that influence the amount that a country saves, including the size of its population, the amount of government spending and taxation, the sophistication of its financial markets, and its cultural and historical mores. However, perhaps the most significant determinant is the level of income in the economy. Richer countries, on average, save more than poorer countries do, and it is significant that they also save proportionately more, as the following data clearly indicate. (The table shows the amount of savings as a percentage of GDP in 2008.)

Country	%	Country	%
Norway	40	Ireland	16
Japan	25	Portugal	11
Canada	24	Greece	4
U.K.	15		
U.S.	12		

Source: Based on data from OECD (2010), *OECD Economic Outlook*, Vol. 2010/1, OECD Publishing. http://dx.doi.org/10.1787/eco_outlook-v2010-1-en.

or services are given in exchange (at the time of the payment). Examples of transfer payments would be Employment Insurance payments, Canada Pension Plan payments, and subsidies to businesses. For simplicity's sake, we will treat all transfer payments as a flow from the government sector directly to individuals in the household sector. Since transfer payments are not strictly an injection, it is better to use the term **net tax revenue** (taxes minus transfer payments) to denote the true leakage. However, for simplicity's sake, we will continue to use the term "taxes." The addition of the government sector is illustrated in **Figure 3.4**.

net tax revenue: total tax revenues minus government transfer payments.

FIGURE 3.4   The Addition of Government

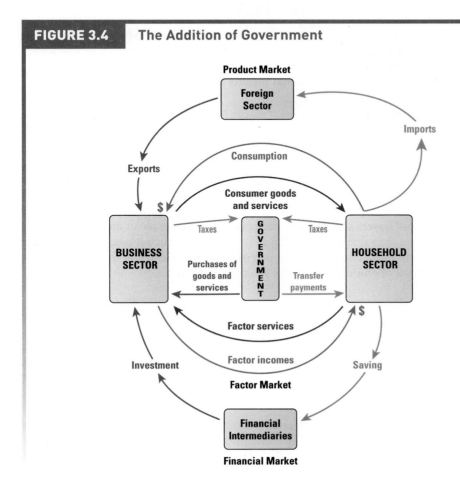

The circular flow of income in the whole economy includes three leakages:
- saving   (S)
- import   (IM)
- taxes   (T)

and the three injections:
- investment   (I)
- exports   (X)
- government spending   (G)

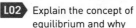 Explain the concept of
equilibrium and why
national income can
rise and fall.

equilibrium: a state of
balance between equal forces.

3.2 EQUILIBRIUM AND THE LEVEL OF NATIONAL INCOME

We are now ready to take on the first of two very basic views of **equilibrium** that we will encounter in our development of macroeconomic principles. The dictionary definition of this term is "a state of balance or equality between opposing forces." The opposing forces here are leakages on the one hand and injections on the other. If these two opposing forces are in balance if:

$$S + IM + T = I + X + G \qquad \text{[3.2]}$$

In this case, the level of national income will remain *unchanged* and can be said to be in equilibrium. On the other hand, if investment spending were to rise, then injections would exceed leakages, creating disequilibrium. The higher injections would cause the level of income to continue to *rise* until the resulting increases in saving, imports, and taxes were enough to create a new equilibrium. Conversely, if tax rates were to increase, then leakages would exceed injections and this would cause consumption spending to fall and income to continue to *fall* until the resulting decreases in saving, imports, and (total) taxes were sufficient to bring injections and leakages back into equilibrium. In summary, if:

$$I + G + X > S + T + IM \quad \text{then GDP rises} \quad \text{(economic growth)}$$

$$I + G + X < S + T + IM \quad \text{then GDP falls} \quad \text{(recession)}$$

A decrease in taxes would, of course, have the same effect as the increase in investment spending mentioned above. This gives an insight into a theme that we will be developing in subsequent chapters: changes in spending have a big impact on the level of income.

Thus, our first formal definition of **national income equilibrium** is:

national income equilibrium: that level of income where total leakages from the circular flow equal total injections.

> The level of income where the total of all three leakages equals the total of all three injections.

value of production: the total receipts of all producers.

There is a second view of equilibrium, which introduces the concept of the **value of production** (or the value of total output). We measure the value of production by adding up what producers get when they sell their output, that is, by summing the total receipts of producers. The amount that producers receive for their products is equal to the amount paid by those who buy the output, and, in turn, this total spending by buyers is called **aggregate expenditures**. Thus, the aggregate expenditures of buyers and the total receipts of the business sector are the same thing. But we can also measure the value of production in terms of how much it costs to produce that output. Since the costs of production (including profits) represent income to those who provide factor services, total costs of production must be equal to total income.

aggregate expenditures: total spending in the economy, divided into the four components: C, I, G, and (X − IM).

$$\text{Value of production} = \text{business receipts} = \text{aggregate expenditures} \qquad \text{[3.3]}$$

and

$$\text{Value of production} = \text{cost of production (including profits)} = \text{total income} \qquad \text{[3.4]}$$

To emphasize, when an economy is in equilibrium, aggregate expenditures are equal to total incomes, and both are equal to the value of production.

Let us use a simple example here. If, in a given period, aggregate expenditures (consumption spending, investment spending, government spending, and net exports) equal $100, then business receipts will, of course, also be $100. If we assume that inventories remain the same in this period, then it is also true that the value of production must have been $100, since this is the amount of goods that were bought. And how much income was generated in producing these goods? Exactly $100 worth—in the form of wages, interest, rents, and profits.

Once again, the fundamental point:

> **Equilibrium implies not only that total leakages equal total injections but also that aggregate expenditures equal total income.**

Now that this second definition of equilibrium is well in hand, we are ready to move on to the measurement of national income.

 SELF-TEST

1. If the economy is in disequilibrium because total income exceeds aggregate expenditure, what must be happening to inventories?

2. Does the term "consumption" refer to spending by households on domestically produced goods and services only? Does the term "investment" include the purchase of stocks and bonds?

3.3 MEASURING NATIONAL INCOME

L03 Understand the components of GDP accounting and be aware of some of the problems in determining official statistics.

The development of the circular flow of income model is complete. We now turn to the measurement of national income. Just as the circular flow diagram was helpful in conceptualizing equilibrium, it can also be helpful in recognizing that there are two different ways to measure income. The first is the *expenditures approach*. As the name implies, this approach adds up the four forms of expenditures, which, once again, are:

- C = consumption
- I = investment spending
- G = government spending on goods and services
- X = exports

and then subtracts spending on imports (IM) because what we are after is total spending on Canadian-produced goods and services.

In short, the basic expenditure—consumption of domestically produced goods—plus the three injections give us aggregate expenditures (AE). This gives us an equation you will become quite familiar with:

$$AE = C + I + G + (X - IM)$$ **[3.5]**

Defining **net exports** (X_N) as $X - IM$, we could rewrite this as:

$$AE = C + I + G + X_N$$

net exports: total exports minus total imports of goods and services, which can be written as $(X - IM)$ or as X_N.

The second conceptual approach to measuring national income—called the *incomes approach*—simply adds the four types of incomes that flow from the business sector to the household sector: wages, interest, rents, and profits.

Adding the total expenditures in the economy or adding the total incomes in the economy are both valid measurements of the value of production. When the economy is in equilibrium, these two sums will equal each other (after three technical adjustments, which we will soon explain). So, we have:

$$AE = C + I + G + X_N = \text{National Income} = w + i + r + \pi$$ **[3.6]**

Measuring National Income: The Mechanics

This section contains many terms that may seem a little tedious. Yet, every student of economics needs to have some understanding of how production is accounted for.

gross domestic product (GDP): the value of all final goods and services produced in an economy in a certain period.

national income (Y): total earnings of all the factors of production in a certain period.

The most-used economic statistic is **gross domestic product (GDP)**, which is defined as the money value of all final goods and services produced in the whole economy within a given year.

For our purposes, the other significant statistic is **national income (Y)**. (Government agencies use the symbol NI for national income, but we will use Y to be consistent with later chapters.) National income is defined as the total earnings of all factors of production within the economy in a given period.

There are two different ways to look at the value of any particular thing produced. The first and most straightforward is in terms of the price it finally sells for, for example, $3 for a tube of toothpaste off the retailer's shelf. Thus, one view is that the $3 is its price and thus will equal the amount spent on acquiring it. The other view, equally valid, is that there is $3 worth of income to distribute to all those factors that went into the activity of getting that tube of toothpaste to the retailer's shelf. So, the value of the toothpaste is the $3 of total income generated, which is paid to the various factors of production. In short:

> The value of output is determined by the income generated in getting it into the hands of the consumer and is equal to the amount that consumers have paid for it.

Conceptually, then, at *equilibrium* GDP, the value of output must equal AE, which must equal Y:

$$\text{GDP} = \text{AE} = \text{Y} \qquad\qquad \textbf{[3.7]}$$

Measuring GDP by the Expenditure Method

Let us next explain exactly what Statistics Canada includes in each item of expenditure. First, consumption includes spending on consumer goods and services and is subdivided into various components, such as consumer durables (for example, cars and household appliances); semi-durables (clothes); nondurables (food and beverages); and consumer services (educational, financial, health care, and legal).

The next item, investment, is composed of spending on machinery and equipment, changes in the value of inventories, and spending on all construction (including residential construction). (The change in business inventory from one period to the next is regarded by Statistics Canada as a form of investment and is what economists term *unplanned investment*.) The term *Ig* used below refers to **gross investment**—that is, before any depreciation is taken into account. Gross investment minus depreciation is known as **net investment**. The distinction between the two terms can be illustrated in terms of stocks and flows as follows:

gross investment: the total value of all new capital goods, both replacement and additional capital.

net investment: the addition to the capital stock during a year (equals gross investment less depreciation).

The capital stock of a country will grow as long as gross investment is greater than depreciation. The growth of the capital stock is what we mean by net investment, that is:

$$I_N = I_g - \text{depreciation} \qquad \text{[3.8]}$$

In many countries, during the Great Depression of the 1930s, depreciation exceeded gross investment so that these countries were not even able to replace worn-out capital; therefore, net investment was negative, and the size of the capital stock was decreasing. What this means is that there are two types of investment: depreciation (replacement capital) and net investment (additions to the capital stock), that is:

$$I_g = I_N + \text{depreciation} \qquad \text{[3.9]}$$

The next category of spending, government spending, is made up of the total spending on goods and services at all levels of government (including investment spending by government). Of course, governments spend on a huge variety of things: health services; education; military spending; security services, including the police, emergency services, courts, and prisons; pensions, including both Canadian Pensions and Old Age pensions; subsidies to firms; highway construction; salaries to bureaucrats and government administrators; as well as welfare payments and unemployment benefits. As we mentioned earlier, we must make a distinction between the two types of government spending: transfer payments, such as pensions, welfare, and unemployment benefits, which do not represent the payment for a good or service provided to government; and government spending on health, education and so forth, which does represent payment for a good or service rendered. In short, transfer payments are not included as part of government expenditures.

Finally, net exports is the total value of all exports (whether of consumer goods, capital goods, or government services) less the total value of all imports. The actual figures (in $ billions) for Canada in 2010 were as follows:

C	I_g	G	X_N (X − IM)
941	291	420	−30 (477 − 507)

Summing these four figures gives us a GDP of $1622 billion.

Note that the GDP measures the value (at market prices) of all goods and services produced *in Canada* in a year. Many of the other statistics we will be developing are concerned with production and incomes *by Canadians*. The term given to this latter statistic is **gross national product (GNP)**.

To calculate this number we need to add all the factor incomes earned by Canadians abroad (for example, a Canadian engineer working in Saudi Arabia or a Canadian firm earning interest from one of its foreign branch operations) and then subtract all the factor incomes of non-Canadian persons and firms that were earned in Canada (for example, an American academic at a Canadian university). Netting these two figures gives us "net foreign factor income," which can be either + or − in any given year. Thus, the calculations of GNP would be:

GDP at market prices	1622
Plus/minus net foreign factor income	− 28
= **GNP** at market prices	1594

gross national product (GNP): the total market value of all final goods and services produced by the citizens of a country, regardless of the location of production.

SELF-TEST

3. Identify the items in the statements below (from the point of view of the Canadian economy) according to the following codes:

C = consumption
I = investment
G = government spending
    on goods and services
N = not applicable

S = savings
IM = imports
T = taxes
X = exports

a) A student gets her haircut from a self-employed hairdresser.   C

b) The hairdresser buys a pair of scissors from the Ace Beauty Supply Company.   N

c) Out of each day's revenue, the hairdresser puts $5 in her piggy bank.   S

d) Each time she has enough set aside, the hairdresser buys a GM share.   I

e) GM expands its computer facilities in its head office.   I

f) American tourists go skiing in the Canadian Rockies.   C

g) Two Canadians go to Tokyo and stay at the Hilton Hotel.   N

h) Russia buys beef from Alberta cattle ranchers.   Ex

i) The Province of Saskatchewan pays for the building of a new highway.   G

Measuring GDP by the Income Method

Now, we turn to the income approach to measuring GDP. Statistics Canada uses five major groupings of income. The first is *wages and salaries*. This includes all benefits received and is expressed as gross earnings before taxes or deductions. Next is *interest and investment income*, which includes business interest only and not interest on consumer loans or on loans to government (the latter is regarded as a form of transfer payment). The third category is *gross profits*, the earnings of corporations before any distribution of dividends or payment of taxes.

Farmers' incomes is a self-explanatory category, though you might wonder why Statistics Canada has decided to single out farmers for special treatment. The reason is simply that it is difficult to know what portion of their total income comes from wages, what portion is profits, and what portion is from crop retention. (Yes, eating your own crops does not go unnoticed by government.) The fifth category, the clumsily titled *net income of nonfarm unincorporated business* (hereafter called *self-employed income*), includes the incomes of all businesses other than corporations (for example, sole proprietors and partners) and also includes some rent, as well as the profits of Crown corporations. The amounts for these categories in 2010 (again in $ billions) were as follows:

Wages	Interest	Gross Profits	Farmers' Income	Self-Employed Income
852	69	190	1	106

net domestic income: incomes earned in Canada (equals the sum of wages, profits, interest, farm, and self-employed income).

Therefore, total income or (to use Statistics Canada's official term) **net domestic income** equals $1218 billion.

This represents the total gross incomes in all forms received in Canada. As we did before, we need to make the same adjustment to find the total incomes received *by Canadians*.

Net domestic income	1218
Plus/minus net foreign factor income	− 28
= National income (of Canadians)	1190

Given what we learned about the circular flow of income earlier in this chapter, you may well be wondering why there is no separate category for rent. The absence of rent in the national income accounts is a practical problem rather than a conceptual one. Some profits are undoubtedly rent return, as are portions of farm income and even self-employed income. Statistics Canada, however, simply does not try to determine how much.

Reconciling GNP and National Income

Perceptive readers might have noted that the GNP (the expenditures approach) and national income (the incomes approach) totals do not agree! Didn't we say earlier that they are conceptually the same thing? Yes, they are, but in national income accounting, not all the receipts (the same as aggregate expenditures) of firms are paid out in the form of incomes. First, firms set up a fund for the replacement of worn-out capital. This is termed *depreciation* (or capital consumption allowance) and is not available for distribution, either to employees or to shareholders. If we subtract the amount of depreciation from the GNP, we have another statistic called **net national product (NNP)**. Thus, for 2010:

net national product (NNP): gross national product less capital consumption (or depreciation).

GNP at market prices	1594
Less depreciation	−230
= **NNP** at market prices	1364

In addition to depreciation, there is another item of income that firms receive but do not pay out as income to anyone, and that is the amount of sales taxes (indirect taxes, such as the harmonized sales tax [HST]) that firms are required to collect on behalf of government. If this amount (net of subsidies) is taken into account, we get:

NNP at market prices	1364
Less indirect taxes (net of subsidies)	−174
= **NNP** at factor costs	1190

After the two technical adjustments (depreciation and indirect taxes), the expenditures approach and the incomes approach do, indeed, balance at $1190 billion.

Table 3.1 illustrates that the flow of income and total expenditures are conceptually the same thing. As you can see on the left side of the table, when we add up aggregate expenditures and then adjust for net foreign factor income, depreciation, and indirect taxes, we get NNP at factor

TABLE 3.1

Expenditures			Incomes		
Consumption	$	941	Wages	$	852
Gross Investment	$	291	Interest	$	69
Government Spending	$	420	Gross Profits	$	190
Net Exports	$	−30	Farmers' Income	$	1
			Self-Employed Income	$	106
Gross Domestic Product	$	1622	**Net Domestic Income**	$	1218
+/− Net Foreign F. Income	$	−28	+/− Net Foreign F. Income	$	−28
Gross National Product	$	1594			
Less Depreciation	$	−230			
Net National Product	$	1364			
Less Indirect Taxes	$	−174			
NNP at Factor Costs	$	1190	**equals National Income**	$	1190

FIGURE 3.5

National income (after technical adjustments), aggregate expenditures, and the value of production are equal in equilibrium.

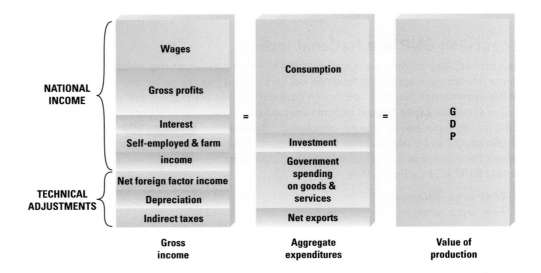

costs, which is $1190. On the right side of the table, if we add the five categories of income and then make the same adjustment for net foreign factor income, we get the same $1190 figure for national income, which is the same thing as NNP at factor cost. In short, the conceptual point that the expenditures approach and the incomes approach are the same thing is verified.

Figure 3.5 will help you understand the fundamental point that one person's spending is another person's income and that, at equilibrium, total spending (aggregate expenditures) is equal to total income, and both are equal to GDP (the value of production).

So, now you know that there is a technical difference between GDP and Y, and that it is important. Even more important, you also know that conceptually the two terms—GDP and Y—can be used interchangeably. We will do so throughout the text.

We might mention that the World Bank and the European Union prefer to report Gross National Income [(GNI) as opposed to GDP. GNI is the same thing as GNP (total income, including net foreign income) and is equal to national income plus depreciation and net indirect taxes.

personal income: income paid to individuals before the deduction of personal income taxes.

Our next focus is on the term **personal income**, which can be thought of as people's gross income, that is, income before payroll deductions. National income can be thought of as "earned" income whereas personal income is received income (before income tax). This means that we have to deduct from national income any items that people have earned but do not receive, and add in items that have been received but not earned. To do this, we need to make four adjustments (again we show the figures for 2010):

National income (or NNP at factor costs)	1190
Less undistributed corporate profits	69
Less corporate profit taxes	50
Plus government transfer payments	266
Less other income not paid out	61
= **Personal income**	1276

Let us explain the top two subtractions first. A corporation does one of three things with the profits it earns:

- pays taxes
- retains (saves) them (undistributed corporate profits)
- pays dividends to its shareholders (profit distributed to shareholders)

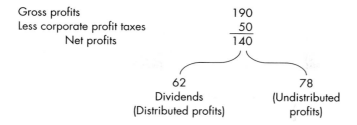

Gross profits   190
Less corporate profit taxes   50
Net profits   140

62   78
Dividends   (Undistributed
(Distributed profits)   profits)

Obviously, only the portion paid in dividends actually goes to individuals and thus becomes part of personal income. Therefore, the portion that goes to taxes and the portion that is saved are not part of personal income and thus must be subtracted from national income to get personal income.

Transfer payments (the very same ones talked about in the circular flow discussion earlier in this chapter) have to be added because they do become part of people's personal income but are not part of national income, since they have nothing to do with the payment to the factors of production. The last adjustment, other income not paid out, includes quite technical items, such as transfers from nonresidents and government investment income not paid out.

To complete our national income accounting framework, we need one final adjustment:

Personal income	1276
Less personal income taxes	− 266
= Disposable income	1010

Disposable income can be thought of as people's take-home, or net, income and is the amount received after deduction of income tax (and other payroll deductions). This is what is at the disposal of the household. From the point of view of national income accounting, however, households really have only two choices about what to do with their disposable income—they can spend it, or they can save it. Since we know how much they spent ($941 in 2010) personal saving must have been 69 (1010 disposable income less 941 spent on consumption). That is:

disposable income: the personal after-tax income of households.

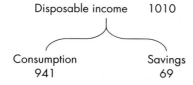

Disposable income   1010

Consumption   Savings
941   69

✓ SELF-TEST

4. If gross profits are $62, corporation taxes are $15, and dividends are $26, then what is the value of undistributed corporation profits?

5. Given the following data for the country of Hemlock:

net foreign factor income	−10
national income	600
government spending on goods and services	175
indirect taxes	50
gross investment	60
consumption	420
depreciation	20

determine the value of X_N.

6. Given the following data for the country of Seymour:

personal income	589
undistributed corporate profits	42
corporate profit taxes	41
other income not paid out	52
government transfer payments	172

determine the value of national income.

Problems in Measuring GDP

Since many policy decisions are based on the level and growth of GDP, it is important for you to understand that there are some limitations in collecting and measuring the various statistics.

The real problem is in deciding what should and should not be measured. Let us spell out exactly what it is that we are trying to measure: the value of all final goods and services produced in an economy in a year. By and large, this will mean the market value of all items produced, plus government-provided services (which are included at cost). However, we do not want to include the market value of everything that has been produced. For instance, we do not want to include both the value of tires produced and the finished value of the car they are a part of; the inclusion of these intermediate goods would represent double-counting. As the definition suggests, we want to include the value of final goods only.

Perhaps an example will make this clear. Suppose that in **Table 3.2** we are looking at the sale of bread at each stage of its production.

TABLE 3.2	Stages in the Production of Bread		
Producer	**Purchases**	**Value-Added**	**Value of Final Sale**
Mrs. Farmer	$ 0	$ 1200	$ 1200
Mr. Miller	1200	800	2000
Mrs. Baker	2000	1000	3000
Mr. Safeway	3000	2000	5000
Totals	**$6200**	**$5000**	**$11 200**

Let us initially suppose that Mrs. Farmer uses her own seeds to produce the wheat. The value added by each producer is the total of their expenses and includes a profit. The wheat is sold to Mr. Miller for $1200 and after his value is added, the flour is sold to Mrs. Baker for $2000. The bread is then sold to Mr. Safeway for $3000 who, after adding his services and profit, sells the bread to the final customer for $5000.

If we add the final sales of each producer, the total comes to $11 200, but this would be double-counting (more like quadruple-counting), since each producer's sales are included in the next producer's sales. To get the true value of productive activity, we can either take the value of the final product—Mr. Safeway's sales to consumers—of $5000 or we could add up the total of the value-added column. Statistics Canada uses both approaches: it takes the value of the final product ($5000), calculates the value of final sales of each producer, $11 200, and then subtracts inter-company sales (the purchases column) of $6200. In other words, we could either suggest that Statistics Canada exclude the sale of intermediate goods or that it exclude inter-company sales; it comes to the same thing.

Another obvious exclusion would be the sale and purchase of financial instruments, such as shares. Although they are market activities, they do not represent real production but merely the transfer of asset ownership between people. (The value of the services of the stockbroker who made this transfer would be included.) For a similar reason, public transfer payments (CPP, EI, and so on) and private transfers (such as gifts and donations) are also excluded. Also, because GDP is trying to measure current production only, second-hand sales would also be excluded, since their value was included when they were first produced. In summary, economic transactions that are not included in the measurement of GDP are:

- the sale of intermediate goods
- sales that merely transfer ownership of assets
- both public and private transfer payments
- the sale of second-hand goods

Finally, we should mention a number of items that are excluded in the measurement of GDP, even though they often do represent real productive effort. Some things are excluded because Statistics Canada does not hear of them. This includes all illegal activities and other activities that, though not illegal, are not reported to the tax collector (perhaps in-home hairdressing and child care). The existence of this "underground economy" means that the GDP may be seriously understated. Also excluded are productive services, such as the value of the activities of a home-maker, do-it-yourself work, and volunteer work. They are excluded because, again, they are nonmarket activities. A nonmarket activity is, quite simply, any economic activity that does not involve a payment (or the payment received is not reported to Revenue Canada). If this work were "paid for," then it would be included. This means, of course, that if one-half of the population were to do the housework of the other half and vice versa and each paid the other, then the GDP would increase dramatically!

It means also that one must be very careful when making comparisons of GDP over a period and between countries. It is certainly true that the GDP of Canada has grown substantially over the years. But a part of the reason is that many of the services now provided commercially were once provided on a nonmarket voluntary basis. We now have commercial home-makers, day-care centres, interior decorators, gardeners, and so on, whereas in the past these services were mostly nonmarket activities. In summary, productive activities that are excluded from the measurement of GDP are:

Maclean's/The Canadian Press (Phill Snell)

- underground activities
  - illegal activities
  - unreported (but legal) activities
- nonmarket activities
  - services of homemakers
  - do-it-yourself production
  - volunteer services

Squeegee labour would be considered part of the "underground economy." Although not illegal, the income is not reported to tax collectors and is therefore not part of GDP measurement.

▶ ADDED DIMENSION   How Well is Canada Doing?

In terms of real GDP per capita, Canada ranks well below many countries in the world. (Its ranking is something like 11th or 19th, depending on what exchange rate is used in the calculations.) Yet, when the United Nations "Human Development Index" (HDI) is used as a measure of the well-being of a country's citizens, Canada's ranking is very high—until recently it has been consistently in the top five. The UN's HDI is an attempt to measure peoples' choices as indicated by the view that "the most critical of these wide-ranging choices are to live a long and healthy life, to be educated, and to have access to resources needed for a decent standard of living." The HDI therefore includes not only real GDP per capita but also life expectancy rates and levels of literacy. The UN recognizes that additional choices could include political freedom, guaranteed human rights, and personal self-respect, but that "a quantitative measure of these aspects has yet to be designed." One could also argue that any attempt at constructing this type of composite-index of

well-being should include a measure of religious freedom, crime rates, levels of taxation, and an environmental index. (As of 2010, the UN uses years of schooling rather than literacy rates as its educational component. As a result, Canada slipped from 4th to 8th as the following table shows.)

UN list of the Top Ten Countries in 2010 (based on HDI)

1. Norway	6. Lichtenstein
2. Australia	7. Netherlands
3. New Zealand	8. Canada
4. United States	9. Sweden
5. Ireland	10. Germany

Source: United Nations Development Programme, *Human Development Report 2010*, published 2010. Reproduced with permission of Palgrave Macmillan.

✓ SELF-TEST

7. Forty years ago, few households employed a housekeeper, and almost no one had a nanny. Today, more and more households employ part-time housekeepers, and nannies are not uncommon. What has this change in employment pattern done to GDP? Is more produced as a result of this change?

8. How could reported GDP remain constant while real production rose?

  L04 Know how to measure economic growth and appreciate the benefits of economic growth.

economic growth: an increase in an economy's real GDP per capita, or an increase in the economy's capacity to produce.

3.4 ECONOMIC GROWTH

The discussion in Chapter 1 about growth as an economic goal established that growth has both positive and negative aspects. Before we discuss this in more depth, we need to define **economic growth**. Although the media often refer to any increase in GDP as economic growth, economists prefer to define it as an increase in an economy's *real* GDP (we explain the term "real" below). Often, this is extended to include an increase in real GDP per capita, which is real GDP divided by total population. This recognizes the fact that the population as a whole will not experience the benefits of growth unless real GDP grows faster than the population.

Let us first look at how modern economies measure economic growth, and later, we will see exactly why growth presents difficult challenges that all economies have to face. Economic growth undoubtedly improves the welfare of people today and also gives society opportunities to address social needs to an extent that was undreamed of by previous generations. But we need to recognize that growth is a double-edged sword that can also inflict costs on society.

Measuring Growth

nominal GDP: the value of GDP in terms of prices prevailing at the time of measurement.

We have seen that Statistics Canada measures the GDP of Canada by taking the market value of all final goods and services produced in the country in a year. It is possible, then, for GDP to increase from one year to the next simply because market prices rise. In fact, the economy may not have produced more. Thus, we need to make the important distinction between **nominal GDP** and real GDP. To see if an economy is growing, we need to know if it did actually produce more goods and services. In other words, we need to eliminate the effect of rising prices. Statistics Canada does this by measuring each year's output in terms of constant prices. This distinction between nominal and real GDP is so important that we need to go through a detailed example to really nail it down.

In **Table 3.3A**, let us assume a simple economy that produces four different goods—machines (a capital good), kilometres of road construction (a government good), bread, and cars (consumer goods). The value of production (nominal GDP) is simply the market value of those goods measured at current (year) prices. The total GDP, $42 000, is the sum of the four products.

TABLE 3.3A	GDP Year 1		
	Quantity of Output	Prices Year 1	Nominal GDP
Machines	100	$100	**$10 000**
Km of Road	50	300	**15 000**
Bread	500	2	**1 000**
Cars	20	800	**16 000**
Totals			**$42 000**

Now let us look at **Table 3.3B** and see how production changed in year 2. You will note that the quantities of output of machines, bread, and cars all increased compared with year 1, but the output of roads declined. You can also see that the prices of all four products increased in year 2 compared with year 1.

TABLE 3.3B	GDP Year 2				
	Quantity of Output	Prices Year 2	Nominal GDP	Prices Year 1	Real GDP
Machines	120	$120	$14 400	$100	$12 000
Km of Road	40	320	12 800	300	12 000
Bread	600	250	1 500	2	1 200
Cars	25	820	20 500	800	20 000
Totals			$49 200		$45 200

So, Nominal GDP increased from $42 000 to $49 200. However, this increase is partly due to the increase in production and partly to the increase in prices. In order to eliminate the effect of higher prices, the last two columns in **Table 3.3B** show the value of production if prices had remained constant at year 1's values. Using year 1's prices, we see that the value of **real GDP** is, in fact, only $45 200. In other words, what we mean by real GDP is the value of GDP assuming that prices do not change.

real GDP: the value of GDP measured in terms of prices prevailing in a given base year.

So, how much did this economy grow between year 1 and year 2? Well, in terms of nominal GDP, it increased by $7200, from $42 000 to $49 200, or by 17.14 percent. This is calculated using the following formula:

$$\text{Growth of Nominal GDP} = \frac{(\text{GDP in current year} - \text{GDP in previous year})}{\text{GDP in previous year}} \times 100 \quad \textbf{[3.10]}$$

However, if we measure the growth rate of *real* GDP, we find that it is only 7.6 percent ($3200 ÷ $42 000) × 100).

In summary, the annual economic growth rate is best measured in terms of the percentage change in real GDP from one year to the next, whereas real GDP is calculated by working out the value of production assuming that prices remain the same.

To further cement these ideas, let us see what happened to this economy in year 3 as shown in **Table 3.3C**.

TABLE 3.3C	GDP Year 3				
	Quantity of Output	Prices Year 3	Nominal GDP	Prices Year 1	Real GDP
Machines	130	$125	$16 250	$100	$13 000
Km of Road	50	350	17 500	300	15 000
Bread	650	3	1 950	2	1 300
Cars	26	840	21 840	800	20 800
Totals			$57 540		$50 100

Here, we see the outputs of each item has increased over year 2, as did all the prices. As a result, the value of nominal GDP increased to $57 540, which is an increase of $8340 or 16.95 percent ($8340 ÷ $49 200 × 100). But what about real GDP? Remember that to calculate real GDP, we need to assume that prices remain the same. But which prices do we use? We use the prices that were in effect in the base year. The choice of the *base year* is, in many ways, arbitrary.

Statistics Canada usually uses a census year (1971, 1981, and so forth) as the base year, but this is not always the case. In our example, we will make year 1 our base year. The last two columns of **Table 3.3C** show the value of year 3's production using base year (year 1) prices. Real GDP in year 3, then, comes to $50 100, an increase of $4900 or 10.8 percent ($4900 ÷ $45 200 × 100) over year 2.

So, calculating real GDP means that we have made allowance for the fact that inflation increases the GDP figures. However, as mentioned above, we may also want to consider the fact that while real GDP may have risen, population may have increased as well. If that were the case, then the average person may not be any better off. To calculate real GDP per capita (per head), we simply divide real GDP by the population.

$$\text{Real GDP per capita} = \frac{\text{real GDP}}{\text{population}} \qquad [3.11]$$

Suppose, for example, that the population of our hypothetical economy in year 1 was 1.1 million and it increased to 1.2 million in year 2 and 1.3 million in year 3. Assuming that our GDP data were all in millions of dollars, we can easily calculate real GDP per capita for all three years as shown in **Table 3.4**.

TABLE 3.4	Nominal GDP, Real GDP, and GDP per capita		
	Year 1	**Year 2**	**Year 3**
Nominal GDP (millions)	$42 000	$49 200	$57 540
Real GDP ($millions)	42 000	45 200	50 100
Population (millions)	1.1	1.2	1.3
Real GDP per capita	38 182	37 667	38 538

We can now see that the average person was actually worse off in year 2 compared with year 1 and was only slightly better off in year 3.

Our final piece of calculation is to show the change in real GDP per capita in percentage terms. The growth of real GDP per capita is, by far, the best and most important measure of how the average person's standard of living has changed.

$$\text{(Economic) growth rate} = \frac{(\text{Real GDP per capita in current year} - \text{Real GDP in previous year})}{\text{Real GDP in previous year}} \times 100 \qquad [3.12]$$

In year 2, the economy suffered negative growth.

$$\frac{(\$37\,667 - \$38\,182)}{\$38\,182} \times 100 = \frac{-\$515}{\$38\,182} \times 100 = -1.3\%$$

And year 3's growth rate (over year 2) was:

$$\frac{(\$37\,538 - \$37\,667)}{\$37\,667} \times 100 = \frac{+\$872}{\$37\,667} \times 100 = +2.3\%$$

It is interesting to see how Canada has performed in recent years. **Table 3.5** presents the data.

Note that over the whole ten-year period, Canada's real GDP per capita rose by $2758—an increase of 7.6 percent, or approximately 0.8 percent per year—but slowed down in recent years as Canada and other countries experienced a recession.

TABLE 3.5	Canada's Real GDP per Capita, 2001–2010				
Year	Nominal GDP	Real GDP (billions) (2002=100)	Population (millions)	Real GDP per Capita	Annual Growth Rate (%)
2001	1108	1119	31.0	36 097	0.9
2002	1152	1152	31.4	36 688	1.6
2003	1213	1176	31.7	37 098	1.1
2004	1291	1211	32.0	37 844	2.0
2005	1374	1248	32.3	38 638	2.1
2006	1450	1281	32.6	39 294	1.7
2007	1530	1307	32.9	39 726	1.1
2008	1600	1304	33.3	39 159	−1.4
2009	1527	1279	33.7	37 953	−3.2
2010	1622	1317	34.1	38 622	2.3

Source: Adapted from Statistics Canada CANSIM Database, http://cansim2.statcan.ca, Tables 380-0017 and 051-0001, 17 March 2011.

 ## SELF-TEST

9. The economy of Rustica produces only two products, carrots and tractors. In 2009, it produced 5 million kilos of carrots and 2000 tractors. In 2010, production of carrots increased to 6 million and tractors to 2200. If the price of carrots increased from $2 to $2.50 per kilo and of tractors from $50 000 to $52 000, calculate the value of nominal and real GDP in the two years.

 ## ADDED DIMENSION   Asian Tigers

The effects of a high growth rate, especially in an economy that starts off with a relatively low per-capita GDP, can be very dramatic, even over a short period. Let us take the hypothetical example of a developing Asian nation, over the last decade, whose per capita income starts at only one-half of that of a typical developed nation. Let us assume a growth rate in this Asian "tiger" of 8 percent (below the actual rates experienced by some of the fast-growing Asian economies in the early 1990s, by the way). We will assume a growth rate of 1 percent in the developed economy. The table shows what the results would be in only 12 years. With the higher growth rate, in just over a decade the tiger has not only caught up with the developed nation but surpassed it! And all of this is a result of growth rates that are not that wildly different—8 percent compared with 1 percent. Thus, you can see the power of high growth rates.

The Effect of Different Growth Rates on Real GDP per Capita		
Year	Asian Tiger: Real GDP per Capita	Developed Economy: Real GDP per Capita
1999	$ 10 000	20 000
2000	10 800	20 200
2001	11 664	20 402
2002	12 597	20 606
2003	13 605	20 812
2004	14 693	21 020
2005	15 868	21 230
2006	17 138	21 442
2007	18 509	21 657
2008	19 990	21 873
2009	21 589	22 092
2010	23 316	22 313

Despite all of this, students are often unimpressed by the concern that economists show over growth rates. What difference does it make, many wonder, if the annual growth rate of an economy is only 3 percent rather than 4 percent? Considering that in 2010 Canada's nominal GDP was $1622 billion (in current prices), a 1-percent difference in growth translates into $16.2 billion. If we divide the $16.2 billion by the approximately 10 million families in Canada, we get $1620. Could your family use an extra $1620 per year *every year* from now on? As you can see, even small differences in the growth rate can be significant over time.

Table 3.6 illustrates a fact that seems to come as a surprise to many Canadians. Canada's growth in real GDP has been good over the last few years. For example, it was the highest of all the G7 nations (the G8 minus Russia) for both the first part of the decade and for the recession-filled second part.

TABLE 3.6	Growth Rates of Real GDP for G7 countries	
Country	Average Growth of Real GDP 2001–2005 (%)	Average Growth of Real GDP 2006–2010 (%)
Canada	2.5	1.2
United Kingdom	2.5	0.4
United States	2.4	0.9
France	1.6	0.8
Japan	1.3	0.3
Italy	0.8	−0.4
Germany	0.6	1.2

Source: Based on data from OECD (2010), *OECD Factbook 2010: Economic, Environmental and Social Statistics*, OECD Publishing, http://dx.doi.org/10.1787/factbook-2010-en.

The Benefits of Economic Growth

For many of us, the benefits of high economic growth are easily observed and enjoyed. High growth equates to a higher standard of living, which, in turn, translates into more exotic vacations, big screen HD televisions, fancy smartphones, and bigger and better-equipped homes. But high economic growth can do so much more than merely providing us with more trinkets; it can transform our lives immeasurably. To see this, we need only look back a few pages in history to the time before the biggest transformation that has occurred on our planet: the Industrial Revolution. Prior to that revolution, economic growth was so small as to be immeasurable. The life of the average peasant living, say, in Southern Italy in the 1600s was little different from that of his father or his grandfather. In fact, in many ways, his life was probably little changed from that of peasants living 200, 400, or even 800 years earlier. In contrast, the life of the average person in Canada today is vastly different from a Canadian growing up 50 years ago, let alone back in the nineteenth century. And it is economic growth that has brought this about.

Economic growth does not just mean that we have more of everything; that is an obvious truism. It also brings about much more fundamental change in our social landscape. A rich country is not only able to ensure that its people are free from poverty and hunger, it also enables them to be far healthier and live longer. In the last 150 years, for instance. we have seen the almost total eradication of communicable diseases, such as diphtheria, typhoid fever, polio, and tuberculosis, which previously killed millions of people. The result is that life expectancy, especially in the richer countries, has increased dramatically in the last century or so. In Canada, life expectancy at birth in 1900 was less than 50 years; today it is over 81 years.

Not only is a rich country able to provide better and more accessible health services to its citizens, it can also offer them more education; grade 12 graduation has replaced grade 8 as a standard measure. Many poor countries cannot provide such a standard, and we know well that they have insufficient funds to provide the facilities. Nor can the parents afford to leave their children in school when they need them to get jobs to help support their families. In most rich countries, including Canada, education is regarded as a right and not a privilege, and the numbers enrolled in post-secondary education increases each year. In Canada, in 2008, almost 60 percent of 20- to 24-year-olds were enrolled in higher education—one of the highest rates in the world.

Besides the immensely important areas of health and education, economic growth provides other important benefits. It can enable a government to provide a good, well-maintained highway system, clean and plentiful parks and open spaces, funds to promote the arts and culture, and protection for the environment. A rich country offers its citizens the opportunity to work less and retire early without making a huge income sacrifice.

Finally, economic growth can enable a country to embrace social diversity. Through universal public education, it can also help countries eliminate discrimination against women and minorities, promote democracy, and uphold basic human rights. It comes as no surprise to most of us that those countries with the poorest records on human rights tend to be those that are economically the poorest and least developed. Economic growth, then, provides nations and people with the chance to achieve their greatest potential and can enable individuals to fulfill their aspirations. That does not necessarily mean they *will*, but the opportunity to do so is enhanced. To paraphrase Oscar Wilde, it is difficult to see the stars when your head is in the gutter. Economic growth can help lift us out of that gutter and make life a little less harsh and a little less cruel.

The benefits of economic growth include:

- better health services
- improved quality and length of education
- better transport, more support for the arts and culture, and better protection of the environment
- protection of human rights with increased democratic involvement

3.5 SOURCES OF ECONOMIC GROWTH

Let us start this discussion by pointing out that the most obvious sources of economic growth are people themselves. Since labour is the most important economic resource, an increase in the size of the labour force, caused by either population growth or a higher participation rate (a greater percentage of people in the labour force), will enable a country to produce more. But we must not get carried away with the idea that an increase in the working population will, by itself, guarantee economic growth. If that were so, then the world's most populous countries, China and India, would also be the most economically developed.

In reality, there is a growing consensus among economists that the *quality of an economy's labour resources* is the prime source of economic growth. A highly educated population results in a labour force that is both mobile and adaptable. As the world moves further into the twenty-first century, these traits of mobility and adaptability are likely to become more and more important. We are witnessing a shift in the paradigm (that is, the fundamental pattern) of what makes an economy successful.

Between 100 and 200 years ago, what would become today's successful economies shifted from an emphasis on agriculture to one on manufacturing. Tomorrow's successful economies are already in the process of a shift from a manufacturing base to an information/communications base, in which the whole world is the market. The areas in which new jobs are being created are changing—in fact, the definition and nature of work is also experiencing a paradigm shift. Gone are the days when a high-school graduate could step into a job at the local mill and earn, for a lifetime, an above-average income. Young people today will probably change careers three or four times in their working lives; training and education, both formal and self-taught, will be essential.

L05 Understand the importance of productivity in encouraging growth and some of the problems of unchecked growth.

Thus, the need to educate, and not just train, young people becomes increasingly important. And what of older workers who have been laid off from factories, which are now moving to other parts of the world? Here, we see the need for some form of retraining and encouragement to relocate. The old words used to describe a high-quality labour force might have been "hard working and dedicated." The new words are likely to be "smart, mobile, and adaptable."

What we are driving at in this discussion is a very important concept that economists call productivity. **Labour productivity** is the output per unit of labour input during a specific period.

labour productivity: a measure of the output produced per unit of labour input in a specific period.

$$\text{Labour productivity} = \frac{\text{output per period}}{\text{units of labour}} \qquad \textbf{[3.13]}$$

As an example, assume that 100 workers produce 6000 tonnes of paper in a week. Here, labour productivity would be 60 tonnes per unit of labour or per worker. If, in three years, that figure rises from 60 to 70 tonnes per worker, there has been an increase in labour productivity. To a large extent, economic growth is about just such increases in productivity. But as the nature of work changes, ideas about what is productive and what is not also change. In the industrialized countries of the world, the output per unit of a factory worker is becoming less important than the creativity of computer programmers, product designers, and organizational managers. All this brings a whole new meaning to the term "labour quality." This last point emphasizes the importance of what economists call **human capital**, which is defined as the accumulated skills and knowledge of human beings. An economy with a government that encourages human capital investment with well-funded and innovative education and training efforts, combined with a population that embraces the desire to improve its accumulated skills and knowledge, will be an economy with bright growth prospects.

human capital: the accumulated skills and knowledge of human beings.

A second fundamental source of economic growth is the amount of physical capital available within the economy. A worker with a mechanical backhoe will move more earth in a day than a worker with a hand shovel could in a week. Thus, an economy with a *higher capital/labour ratio* will be an economy with higher labour productivity.

Increasing the amount of capital stock in an economy is a direct result of more investment spending, which can be defined as a physical increase in the economy's plant and equipment. Canada has one of the highest capital/labour ratios in the world, and this, along with our rich supply of natural resources, has resulted in relatively high labour productivity in past years. However, things are now changing so fast that we cannot continue to rely on huge machines or natural resources to provide us with continued economic growth.

John A. Rizzo/Getty Images

The assembly line method of production is a traditional source of high productivity and growth. But is it still a major source?

The third source of economic growth is *technological change.* Here, we are referring not just to more machines (capital) but better machines, not just to finding more natural resources but finding and extracting them more efficiently. Technological change often involves better machines and equipment and always involves better methods of production, better ways of organizing work, and better ways of solving problems—in short, becoming more productive. A society that fosters and embraces technological change will soon be far ahead of one that does not. To some extent, this involves the attitudes of people as much as it does the brainpower that a society has at its disposal. Technological change can also be stimulated by spending, in both the public and the private sectors, on research and development—something that the Japanese have done more than any other society.

Finally, it is important to mention that the amount and quality of an economy's natural resources can be a source of growth. Canada is generously endowed in this area, and that does make growth easier. This was particularly true in the early development of this country, in which beaver, fish, lumber, grain, and minerals played a significant role in growth. But we should not assume that plentiful natural resources alone can ensure economic growth. Think of Brazil with its rich endowment and poor growth record. Nor should we assume that a scarcity of natural resources means no growth. Witness Japan, which has practically no natural resources but an above-average growth record.

In summary, the sources of economic growth for an economy are as follows:

- the quantity and quality of labour resources (the level of human capital)
- the amount of physical capital available
- the rate of technological change
- the amount and quality of natural resources

✓ SELF-TEST

10. Use the following information to calculate labour productivity (to one decimal place) per unit in both years. Approximately what percentage increase in labour productivity has occurred?

Year	Output	Labour Input
2010	12 400 tonnes	80 units
2011	14 400 tonnes	90 units

Growth and Economic Welfare

Despite the many benefits that flow from economic growth, we do need to add a word of caution to this discussion: *more* does not always mean *better*. It is true that economic growth is seen by many people as an indicator of the comparative "wellness" of an economy. After all, most people would feel that we are all better off if our economy grows, since most people view growth in a positive way. Although there is truth in this proposition, we should realize that GDP figures are not designed to measure welfare; they simply measure the market activity related to produced goods and services. In this context, we cannot always assume that a higher GDP necessarily means a better life. As we saw earlier, there are many services—such as child care and housework—that are now paid for, whereas previously they were provided by family and friends and thus not measured in GDP. This means that it is possible for measured GDP to grow, even though we are not actually producing more.

There are other problems with equating the level of GDP with the well-being of a population. GDP figures give no indication of the quality of goods produced, nor do they tell us what types of goods are being produced: a gun and an economics textbook are rated equally if they are priced the same. Nor can we assume that anyone is better off if population grows faster than GDP. For this reason, as we saw, it is better to express GDP in terms of GDP per capita. We could also mention that if people begin to value leisure time more and choose to work less, then GDP would grow more slowly but people would consider themselves better off despite the slower growth. Finally, the social and environmental costs of growth may well exceed the benefits.

Let us examine this further. Some critics say that a blind adherence to the growth gospel puts this planet at great risk. They point to the environmental degradation that often accompanies economic growth. We are all aware of the depletion of the ozone layer and the global warming that results from increased emissions of greenhouse gases into the atmosphere. These may well endanger all natural species, including humans. Economic growth has other undesirable side effects, such as the depletion of the world's rainforests and the destruction of fisheries around the world, including the Atlantic fisheries of Canada, as a result of serious overharvesting. Add to this the possibility that we will eventually run out of many resources such as oil and clean water. If that were not enough, economic growth produces not only a lot of "goods" but possibly even more "bads" in the form of waste, which also creates disposal problems.

Along with these environmental problems come a number of social costs that often accompany high economic growth rates. These include high stress levels, traffic jams, and the pressures that come with trying to accommodate to rapid change. Finally, a number of anti-growth critics suggest that rather than curing poverty, economic growth exacerbates it. They suggest that poverty is not the result of scarcity but of an unequal distribution of resources. They believe that Canada, for instance, has more than enough resources to ensure that no family lives in poverty. The problem is caused by a lack of political will and could be easily cured by a more equitable distribution of income rather than through even more growth.

In summary, economic growth does not necessarily mean that citizens are better off because

- a higher GDP may be the result of including the value of some services that were previously excluded.
- the quality or desirability of the goods produced is ignored.
- per-capita GDP will fall if population growth exceeds the growth of GDP.
- the social and environmental costs of higher GDP are ignored.

Using the single statistic of real GDP per capita as a measure of a country's overall well-being is often criticized as simplistic. This view has validity, and several attempts have been made to develop a better index of welfare. As we saw in an earlier Added Dimension box, the most significant of these attempts is the United Nations' Human Development Index [HDI]), which produced its 20th annual report in 2010. In it, life expectancy rates, number of years of schooling, and an education index are blended with the standard measurement of real GDP per capita to achieve a measure of human well-being. It is important to note that Canada has consistently ranked high on this index. A quote from U.S. economist Paul Krugman, in reference to the economic crisis of 2008–2010, is indicative of the respect that others hold for Canada: "We need to learn from those countries that evidently did it right. And leading that list is our neighbor to the north. Right now, Canada is a very important role model."

Review

CHAPTER SUMMARY

In this chapter, we used the circular flow of income model to give us a powerful overview of how a modern market economy works. The model showed how the level of income in an economy depends on the level of spending, and that equilibrium occurs when total spending = income = the value of production. Next, we looked at how Statistics Canada measures economic activity to derive such statistics as GDP, national income, and disposable income. Finally, we looked at economic growth, considering how it is measured as well as its benefits and costs.

3.1a The circular flow model illustrates both the financial and the real flows among the three sectors of the economy: business, household, and government.

3.1b Within this model, we find:
- three *leakages*: savings, imports, and taxes.
- three *injections*: investment, exports, and government spending on goods and services.
- the idea that if injections are greater than leakages then national income will rise, and if leakages exceed injections then national income will fall.

3.2 National income equilibrium occurs when:
- total leakages equal total injections.
- aggregate expenditures equal total income.

3.3a The expenditures approach to measuring national income involves adding up the four components of spending:
- *consumption* spending by households
- *investment* spending by businesses
- spending by foreigners on *net exports*
- *government spending* on goods and services

3.3b The incomes approach to measuring national income involves adding up the five types of income: *wages, interest, profits, self-employed income*, and *farming income*.

3.3c To reconcile these two approaches, it is necessary to make adjustments for:
- net foreign factor income.
- depreciation.
- indirect taxes.

3.3d For various reasons, national income statistics exclude:
- intermediate goods.
- transfers (both private and public).
- second-hand sales.
- sales taxes.
- the value of productive nonmarket activities and illegal activity.

3.4a Nominal GDP is calculated by finding the value of production using current year market prices; real GDP is calculated by finding the value of production at *base year prices*.

3.4b Real GDP per capita is computed by dividing real GDP by the size of the population.

3.4c The benefits of economic growth include:
- better health care services.
- improved quality and length of education.
- better transport, more support for the arts and culture, and better protection of the environment.
- protection of human rights with increased democratic involvement.

Practise and learn online with Connect, where you can find the Answered Questions and the Unanswered Problems for all chapters of this textbook's Study Guide section.

3.5a Long-term economic growth is dependant on improvements in labour productivity, which is defined as *output per period/units of labour.*

3.5b The major sources of long-term growth include:
- the quantity and quality of labour resources (the level of human capital).
- the amount of physical capital available.
- the rate of technological change.
- the amount and quality of natural resources.

3.5c Economic growth does not always mean that people are better off because:
- a higher GDP may include the value of some services that were previously excluded.
- the quality or desirability of the goods produced is ignored.
- per-capita GDP will fall if population growth exceeds the growth of GDP.
- the social and environmental costs of higher GDP are ignored.

NEW GLOSSARY TERMS AND KEY EQUATIONS

aggregate expenditures   92
consumption   86
disposable income   99
economic growth   102
equilibrium   92
exports   90
factor market   86
financial intermediaries   88
government spending   90
gross domestic product (GDP)   94
gross investment   94
gross national product (GNP)   95

human capital   108
imports   90
income   87
injection   88
investment   88
labour productivity   108
leakage   88
money   87
national income equilibrium   92
national income (Y)   94
net domestic income   96
net exports   93

net investment   94
net national product (NNP)   97
net tax revenue   91
nominal GDP   102
personal income   98
product market   86
real GDP   103
saving   88
transfer payments   90
value of production   92

Equations:

[3.1]	$S = Y - C$	page 88
[3.2]	$S + IM + T = I + X + G$	page 92
[3.3]	Value of production = business receipts = aggregate expenditures	page 92
[3.4]	Value of production = cost of production (including profits) = total income	page 92
[3.5]	$AE = C + I + G + (X - IM)$	page 93
[3.6]	$AE = C + I + G + X_N = \text{National Income} = w + i + r + \pi$	page 93
[3.7]	At equilibrium: GDP = AE = Y	page 94
[3.8]	$I_N = I_g - \text{depreciation}$	page 95
[3.9]	$I_g = I_N + \text{depreciation}$	page 95

[3.10] $$\text{Growth of Nominal GDP} = \frac{(\text{GDP in current year} - \text{GDP in previous year})}{\text{GDP in previous year}} \times 100$$ page 103

[3.11] $$\text{Real GDP per capita} = \frac{\text{real GDP}}{\text{population}}$$ page 104

[3.12] $$(\text{Economic}) \text{ growth rate} = \frac{(\text{Real GDP per capita in current year} - \text{Real GDP in previous year})}{\text{Real GDP in previous year}} \times 100$$ page 104

[3.13] $$\text{Labour productivity} = \frac{\text{output per period}}{\text{units of labour}}$$ page 108

17. **(LO 1)** What is flow 3?
    a) Consumer goods and services
    b) Factor services
    c) Factor incomes
    d) Investment

18. **(LO 1)** What are flows 4 and 5, respectively?
    a) Exports and imports
    b) Exports and taxes
    c) Savings and investment
    d) Investment and savings

19. **(LO 1)** All of the following, except one, are examples of the factor *land*. Which one is the exception?
    a) Minerals
    b) Natural harbours
    c) Mortgages held on land
    d) Supplies of fresh water
    e) Fertile soil

20. **(LO 4)** Which of the following is a valid description of economic growth?
    a) It is an increase in an economy's real GDP per capita.
    b) It is an increase in an economy's total output of goods and services.
    c) It usually implies an increase in labour productivity.
    d) All of the above.

21. **(LO 3)** What does the sum of national income, indirect taxes, and depreciation equal?
    a) Personal income
    b) Disposable income
    c) Gross domestic product
    d) Gross national product
    e) Net national product

Intermediate (Questions 22–32)

22. **(LO 3)** Which of the following is included by Statistics Canada in investment?
    a) An increase in business inventories from one year to the next
    b) The purchase of any durable good, such as a car or television
    c) An increase in total saving in the economy
    d) The change in the value of mutual funds from one year to the next

23. **(LO 1)** Which of the following is regarded as real capital?
    a) A savings account
    b) A Bank of Montreal share
    c) A dump truck
    d) A share certificate

24. **(LO 3)** Which of the following leads to an understatement of total production?
    a) The exclusion of work done by homemakers
    b) A decrease in the HST rate
    c) Government spending on an oil-spill cleanup
    d) The exclusion of intermediate goods

25. **(LO 3)** Which of the following will result in an increase in the stock of capital goods?
    a) Net investment is negative.
    b) Net investment is positive.
    c) Gross investment is less than consumption.
    d) Gross investment is negative.

26. **(LO 1)** What is the level of savings in an economy with no government and no international trade, if total factor income is $600 and consumption spending is $480?
    a) −$120
    b) $120
    c) $1080
    d) Cannot be determined from the information given

27. **(LO 1)** What does the simple circular flow show?
    a) Households are both buyers and sellers of products and resources.
    b) Businesses are sellers of resources and buyers of products.
    c) Households are buyers of products and sellers of resources.
    d) Businesses are sellers and households are buyers of both products and resources.
    e) Businesses both buy and sell products and resources, whereas households only buy.

28. **(LO 4)** What could cause an increase in nominal GDP?
    a) An increase in the output of goods and services but no change in prices
    b) An increase in the prices of goods and services but no change in their output
    c) An increase in both the output and the prices of goods and services
    d) All of the above

29. **(LO 2)** What is true about aggregate expenditure?
    a) It always equals national income
    b) At equilibrium it is equal to national income
    c) It equals C + I + X
    d) It depends on the rate of savings
    e) It is determined by inventory changes

30. **(LO 5)** A high economic growth rate may not mean a better life for the population. Which of the following statements supports that contention?
   a) Work such as housecleaning, which used to be entirely a nonmarket activity, is becoming more and more a market activity.
   b) Higher production has negative side effects, such as more pollution.
   c) In the measurement of GDP, no distinction is made as to the type of goods produced.
   d) All of the above.

31. **(LO 3)** What would be the effect if one half of the population did the housework for the other half of the population, and vice versa, and each group paid the other for these services?
   a) GDP would not be affected because the one set of transactions would cancel out the other.
   b) GDP would rise.
   c) GDP would fall.
   d) GDP would not be affected, but the personal incomes of people would be.

32. **(LO 3)** What is included in consumption and investment spending, respectively?
   a) Spending on domestically produced goods and services, and on real capital
   b) Spending on domestically produced and foreign-produced goods and services, and on real capital
   c) Spending on domestically produced goods and services and on net foreign investment income
   d) Spending on domestically produced goods and services, and on the purchase of stocks and bonds

Advanced (Questions 33–35)

33. **(LO 3)** How does government spending on goods and services differ from transfer payments?
   a) The former is done by the federal government and the latter by provincial governments.
   b) The former does not include investment spending, but the latter does.
   c) The former represents payments for services performed, but the latter does not.
   d) They are the same thing, and therefore there is no difference.

34. **(LO 2)** All of the following, except one, are true in equilibrium. Which is the exception?
   a) Total leakages equal total injections
   b) The value of production equals aggregate expenditures
   c) $Y = AE$
   d) The value of production equals consumer spending

35. **(LO 2)** In equilibrium, the value of production is equal to all of the following, except one. Which is the exception?
   a) The total receipts of all businesses
   b) Total income
   c) Output plus inventory accumulation
   d) Aggregate expenditures

Parallel Problems

ANSWERED PROBLEMS

36A. **(LO 1, 2, 3)** Key Problem **Figure 3.7** is the circular flow diagram for the economy of Argos.
   a) Place the numbers below in the appropriate blanks on the diagram in **Figure 3.7**.

Rent	$100	Savings	$100
Wages	400	Government spending	280
Profits	60	Exports	100
Interest	80	Imports	80
Taxes (HH only)	360	Investment	40
Transfer payments	120		

What are the values of the following?
   b) The costs of production _____

   c) Total factor payments _____
   d) Disposable income _____
   e) Aggregate expenditures _____
   f) The total revenue of all businesses _____
   g) Total injections and leakages (*Hint:* Use net tax revenue, that is, taxes less transfer payments.)
      Injections: _____
      Leakages _____
   h) The balance of trade (net exports)

      _____
   i) Government's budget surplus/deficit (*Hint:* Use net tax revenue.) _____

FIGURE 3.7

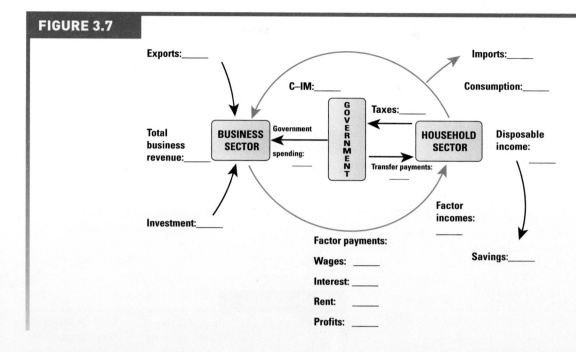

Basic (Problems 37A–47A)

37A. (LO 3) Identify the items in the statements below (from the point of view of the Canadian economy) according to the following code:

C = consumption	S = savings
G = government spending	T = taxes
X = exports	IM = imports
I = investment	N = not applicable

a) A Canadian tourist visits Athens. _____IM_____

b) A shipment of Canadian hot-house cucumbers is sent to the United States. _____X_____

c) A medical doctor in Alberta buys a new car that was built in Ontario. _____C_____

d) An accountant makes a regular monthly contribution to her RRSP fund. _____S_____

e) The federal government buys new equipment for the military. _____G_____

38A. (LO 3) In **Table 3.8**, you are given data for the country of Sequoia.

TABLE 3.8

Exports	130	Government spending	198
Consumption	430	Imports	118
Gross investment	126	Net foreign factor income	−22
Depreciation	64	Indirect taxes	80

a) What is the value of GDP? _____

b) What is the value of NNP at market prices? _____

c) What is the value of national income (net national product at factor costs)? _____

39A. (LO 3) In **Table 3.9**, you are given data for the country of Hemlock.

TABLE 3.9

National income	600
Personal income taxes	140
Other income not paid out	40
Corporate profit taxes	45
Undistributed profits	28
Transfer payments	90

a) What is the value of personal income? _____

b) What is the value of disposable income? _____

40A. (LO 3) Indicate which of the following are productive activities (P) and which are non-productive (N). Then indicate which of them are included (I) in national income statistics and which are excluded (Ex).

a) The sale of 100 shares of EA Sports _____ and _____

b) Child care at home _____ and _____
c) A person employed by the Tumbleweed Day Care Centre _____ and _____
d) The time spent by a person volunteering time at a local hospital _____ and _____
e) The money spent to renovate a storefront for a new retail business _____ and _____
f) The time spent by a householder to renovate a garden shed _____ and _____

41A. **(LO 4)** The data in **Table 3.10** show the total output (a mixture of consumer, capital, and government services) and the prices of each product for the distant country of Vindaloo. All figures are in billions of dollars, and the base year is 2009.
a) Complete the table, and answer the questions which follow (to one decimal place).
b) What is the value of nominal GDP in
   2010: $ _____ 2011: $ _____
c) What is the value of real GDP in
   2010: $ _____ 2011: $ _____
d) What is the annual growth rate of nominal GDP in 2010: _____ 2011: _____
e) What is the annual growth rate of real GDP in 2010: _____ 2011: _____

Suppose that the population in Vindaloo is as follows in **Table 3.11**.
f) What is the real GDP per capita in
   2009: $ _____ 2010: $ _____
   2011: $ _____
g) What is the growth rate in real GDP per capita in
   2010: _____% 2011: _____%

TABLE 3.11

2009	2010	2011
23 million	24 million	25 million

42A. **(LO 5)** **Table 3.12** shows labour data for Eturia.
a) Calculate the productivity rates for each year.
   _____, _____, and _____
b) In which year was labour productivity highest?
   _____

TABLE 3.12

Year	Output per Week (millions of cases)	Labour Input (millions of workers)
2009	120	8.00
2010	126	8.07
2011	130	8.55

TABLE 3.10

1	2	3	4	5	6	7	8	9	10	11	12	13	14
		2009			2010						2011		
Item	Qty	Prices Year 2009	Nom- inal GDP	Qty	Prices Year 2010	Nom- inal GDP	Prices Year 2009	Real GDP	Qty	Prices Year 2011	Nom- inal GDP	Prices Year 2009	Real GDP
Hot dogs	50	2	100	55	2.40				58	2.50			
DVDs	10	12	120	12	13				14	13.50			
Farm tractors	3	100	300	4	95				4	110			
Parking meters	4	50	200	4	60				5	70			
Totals			720										

43A. (LO 1) In **Figure 3.8**, replace each (*) with the appropriate term(s).

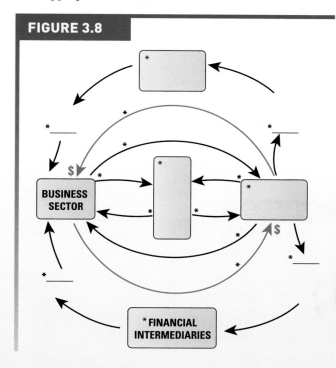

FIGURE 3.8

44A. (LO 3) In **Table 3.13**, fill in the missing data for the country of Birchwood.

TABLE 3.13

C	400
I$_g$	140
G	210
X$_n$	_____
GDP	850
Net foreign factor income	−50
GNP	_____
Depreciation	40
NNP	_____
Indirect taxes	60
National income	_____
Transfer payments	120
Undistributed corporate profits	35
Corporate profit taxes	50
Other income not paid out	25
Personal income	_____
Personal income tax	_____
Disposable income	500
Personal saving	_____

45A. (LO 3) **Table 3.14** shows actual 2006 data for Canada. Using these data, fill in the blanks. (You will find **Table 3.7**, page 113, to be a helpful framework).

TABLE 3.14

GDP at market prices:	_____ .
GNP at market prices:	_____ .
Net domestic income:	_____ .
National income:	_____ .
NNP at market prices:	_____ .
NNP at factor costs:	_____ .
Personal income:	_____ .
Disposal income:	_____ .
Self-employed income	100
Other income not paid out	42
Undistributed corporate profits	128
Consumption	804
Net foreign factor income	−11
Government spending on goods and services	319
Interest	65
Depreciation	185
Transfer payments	226
Personal income taxes	252
Gross investment	286
Gross profits	197
Wages	737
Indirect taxes	161
Corporate profit taxes	51
Farmers' income	1
Exports	525
Imports	488

46A. (LO 1) Distinguish between savings and investment.

47A. (LO 4) Define *economic growth*.

Intermediate (Problems 48A–53A)

48A. **(LO 3)** In **Table 3.15**, fill in the blanks in the data for the country of Baobob.

TABLE 3.15

C	_____
I_g	_____
G	340
X_N	20
GDP	800
Net foreign factor income	_____
GNP	780
Depreciation	70
NNP	_____
Indirect tax	_____
National income	550
Transfer payments	210
Undistributed corporate profits	30
Corporate profit taxes	80
Other income not paid out	20
Personal income	_____
Personal income tax	230
Disposable income	_____
Personal savings	50

49A. **(LO 3)** Table 3.16 shows the data for the country of Magnolia. Complete the national income accounting framework in **Table 3.7** (page 113).

TABLE 3.16

Disposable income	920
Dividends paid out by corporations	80
Imports	240
Investment (net)	80
Corporate profit taxes	60
Other income not paid out	20
Personal savings	120
Wages	530
Net exports	−40
Depreciation	120
Personal income taxes	160
Net foreign factor income	−20
Gross profits	180
Indirect taxes	220
Transfer payments	200
Government spending on goods and services	400
Interest	160
Farmers' income	90
Self-employed income	60

50A. **(LO 3)** Compare the expenditures approach to GDP measurement to the incomes approach.

51A. **(LO 1)** Explain the difference between the stock of money and the flow of income.

52A. **(LO 2)** What two things are true when an economy is in equilibrium?

53A. **(LO 3)** Are all productive activities that are not included in the measurement of GDP illegal?

Advanced (Problems 54A–57A)

54A. **(LO 3)** **Table 3.17** shows some of the national income accounts for the economy of Elmwood (all figures are in billions of dollars).

TABLE 3.17

Personal income taxes	160
Indirect taxes	130
Corporate profit taxes	40
Net exports	−40
Government spending on goods and services	240
Disposable income	820
Personal savings	100
Imports	85
Wages	620
Investment (net)	90
Net foreign factor incomes	+20
Gross corporate profits	130
Transfer payments	170
Depreciation	80
Dividends paid out by corporations	60
Other income not paid out	20

From this information, calculate the value of:
a) Consumption _____
b) GDP _____
c) GNP _____
d) National income _____
e) Personal income _____

55A. **(LO 3)** Suppose that new automobile purchases were treated like new housing purchases in national income accounts. How would that affect savings, consumption, investment, GDP, and DI? (*Hint:* This question is about reclassification, not about cause and effect.)

56A. **(LO 3)** Explain why transfer payments are excluded from the measurement of GDP.

57A. **(LO 5)** Explain why a high economic growth rate does not necessarily mean an improvement in economic welfare.

CHAPTER 4

MEASURING THE ECONOMY 2: UNEMPLOYMENT AND INFLATION

At the end of this chapter, you should be able to...

LO1 understand what unemployment is and how it is measured.

LO2 explain the different types of unemployment and understand the costs of unemployment.

LO3 understand what inflation is and how it is measured.

LO4 explain the two types of inflation and understand the costs of inflation.

WHAT'S AHEAD...

In this chapter, we continue our general introduction to macroeconomics with a focus on the measurements of unemployment and inflation—two eternal issues that tend to dominate the economic news. First, we describe how unemployment is measured and look at the different types of unemployment and how the cost of unemployment can be measured. Next, we look at how inflation is defined and two ways it is measured. Finally, we investigate the causes and costs of inflation.

A Question of Relevance...

The financial meltdown of 2008–09 and the consequent world-wide recession caused a great deal of anxiety for many. While most people were not directly affected by the economic slowdown, the accompanying unemployment was obvious to all and painful for the millions who lost their jobs. Will you be able to avoid being an unemployment statistic during your working life? Is inflation, the other "twin evil," really a big problem, and how does it affect you personally? These are questions that begin to take on more urgency as you approach the transition from student to active participant in the labour force with career aspirations. This chapter will help you think more deeply about these issues.

In this chapter, we continue the general topic of measuring the economy's performance by focusing our attention on two particular areas. We look first at unemployment: exactly what is it, what causes it and what are its real costs to individuals and society? The second issue is inflation—what are the costs of containing it, and are these costs too high? It is necessary to add that in this chapter, we are not attempting to provide complete answers to the causes of unemployment or inflation. (We will do this in the next chapter by constructing a model of the macroeconomy.) For now, we will focus on how we go about measuring unemployment and inflation and see some of the problems that are involved in doing so. This will give us a much better sense of what these terms mean.

4.1   UNEMPLOYMENT

L01 Understand what unemployment is and how it is measured.

In the purest sense, unemployment as a concept can apply to any of the three factor markets— labour, land, or capital. If the economy is not producing at full capacity, then some of the factors of production must be idle—or unemployed (assuming efficient methods of production). For our purposes, however, we will focus only on the labour market. **Unemployment** can be defined as the number of persons 15 years of age and older who are not in gainful employment but who are actively seeking employment.

unemployment: the number of persons 15 years old and over who are actively seeking work but are not employed.

Measuring Unemployment

To get us started on the actual measurement of Canada's unemployment rate, we turn to **Table 4.1** for some 2010 data.

TABLE 4.1	Population and Employment, Canada 2010 (millions)
Total population	34.2
Working-age population	27.7
Labour force	18.5
Employed	17.0
Unemployed	1.5

Source: Adapted from Statistics Canada CANSIM Database, http://cansim2.statcan.ca, Tables 282-0002 and 051-0001, 17 March 2011.

working-age population: in Canada, the total population, excluding those under 15 years of age, those in the armed forces, and residents of aboriginal reserves or the territories.

Economists use the term **working-age population**. In Canada, this is defined as the country's total population, *excluding*:

- those under 15 years of age.
- those living in the three territories or on aboriginal reserves.
- full-time members of mental and penal institutions or hospitals, and those in the armed forces.

As can be seen in the table, 6.5 million (34.2 minus 27.7) people fell into one of these three excluded categories. Next, Statistics Canada takes all those in the working-age population and subtracts those considered to be "not in the labour force." The result gives us the **labour force**. Those not in the labour force include retired people, those who are financially independent, and those who choose not to participate in the labour market for reasons such as devoting full attention to child rearing. As can be seen in **Table 4.1**, those in the labour force category totalled 18.5 million, while those not in the labour force totalled 9.2 million (27.7 − 18.5).

labour force: members of the working-age population, both employed and unemployed.

The information from **Table 4.1** can be represented visually.

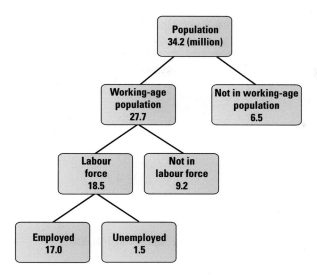

The actual mechanics of computing these data involve a random survey of 58 000 Canadian households done each month. Questions are asked of each household member 15 years of age and older. The questions used to determine if an individual is in the labour force are:

1. Is he or she currently gainfully employed for at least one hour per week or self-employed?
2. Is he or she employed but not on the job due to illness, vacation, or industrial dispute?
3. Is he or she laid off (within the last 26 weeks) but expecting to be recalled?
4. Is he or she not employed but starting a new job within 30 days?
5. Is he or she not employed, or laid off, but actively seeking employment?

If none of the above five categories applies, then that person is categorized as "not in the labour force." Having identified those who are in the labour force (employed and unemployed), the next distinction is between those who have gainful employment of at least one hour per week—those who are **employed** (categories 1 and 2 above)—and those who are **unemployed** (categories 3, 4, and 5), since they do not currently hold paid employment. It is important to note that the fact that a person does not have a job does not mean that he or she is unemployed. To be considered unemployed, the person must be available for work *and* actively seeking employment.

Out of these various categories come two important rates. First, the **participation rate**, which is the percentage of the working-age population who are in the labour force.

$$\text{Labour force participation rate} = \frac{\text{labour force}}{\text{working-age population}} \times 100 \qquad \text{[4.1]}$$

In Canada, for 2010, this rate was:

$$\text{Labour force participation rate} = \frac{18.5}{27.7} \times 100 = 66.8$$

Table 4.2 shows this rate as a total and for both genders over a 20-year period.

Over these 20 years, the female participation rate in Canada rose by 3.9 percentage points, while the male participation rate fell by 3.4 percentage points. This is confirmation of a 50-year trend of rising female labour force participation and represents a major change in the social reality of our nation. In addition, the size of Canada's overall labour force also grew.

employed: those who are in the labour force and hold paid employment.

unemployed: those who are in the labour force and are actively seeking employment, but do not hold paid employment.

participation rate: the percentage of those in the working-age population who are actually in the labour force.

TABLE 4.2	Labour-Force Participation Rates, Canada, Selected Years 1991–2010		
Year	Total (%)	Male (%)	Female (%)
1991	66.7	75.1	58.5
1996	64.9	72.4	57.6
2001	66.0	72.5	59.7
2006	67.2	72.5	62.1
2007	67.3	72.7	62.7
2008	67.8	72.9	62.8
2009	67.3	72.0	62.6
2010	67.0	71.7	62.4

Source: Adapted from Statistics Canada CANSIM Database <http://cansim2.statcan.ca>, Table 282-0002, 17 March 2011.

unemployment rate: the percentage of those in the labour force who do not hold paid employment.

The second important employment statistic is the **unemployment rate**, which is the percentage of the labour force actually unemployed. The equation for the unemployment rate is:

$$\text{Unemployment rate} = \frac{\text{number of unemployed}}{\text{labour force}} \times 100 \qquad \text{[4.2]}$$

We can use the 2010 data to illustrate:

$$\text{Unemployment rate} = \frac{1.5}{18.5} \times 100 = 8.1\%$$

Table 4.3 shows Canada's unemployment rates for selected years over the last 17 years and illustrates an important feature of the economy. Unemployment rates have generally declined, from a high of 11.4 percent as the country emerged from the recession of 1990–93 to a low of 6.0 in 2007 and then rose again as a result of the recession that began in 2009. It is interesting to note also that the unemployment rate for women is consistently lower than that for men. Since Canada is such a diverse nation, there are significant differences in unemployment rates across the country as **Table 4.4** illustrates.

TABLE 4.3	Unemployment Rates, Canada, Selected Years 1993–2010		
Year	Total (%)	Male (%)	Female (%)
1993	11.4	11.9	11.3
1996	9.6	9.9	9.3
2001	7.2	7.5	6.9
2006	6.3	6.5	6.1
2007	6.0	6.4	5.6
2008	6.1	6.6	5.7
2009	8.3	9.4	7.0
2010	8.0	8.7	7.2

Source: Adapted from Statistics Canada, CANSIM Database <http://cansim2.statcan.ca>, Table 282-0002, 2 February 2011.

TABLE 4.4 Unemployment by Province, 2010	
	Unemployment %
Newfoundland and Labrador	14.4
Prince Edward Island	11.2
Nova Scotia	9.3
New Brunswick	9.3
Quebec	8.0
Ontario	8.7
Canada	**8.0**
British Columbia	7.6
Alberta	6.5
Manitoba	5.4
Saskatchewan	5.2

Source: Adapted from Statistics Canada, CANSIM Database <http://cansim2.statcan.ca>, Table 282-0002, 2 February 2011.

As a final note on the measurement of unemployment, we should point out that the figures in **Tables 4.3** and **4.4**, as well as those often reported in the media, are actually what Statistics Canada calls "seasonally adjusted" unemployment rates. What this means is that increases and decreases in the unemployment rate that are *purely* the result of seasonal influences are removed. The rationale behind all this is that the seasonally adjusted rate is a better indicator of the economy's current performance than an unadjusted rate, which would always rise in the winter and fall in the summer.

✓ SELF-TEST

1. Suppose the population of Etrusca is 20 million, the working age population is 15 million, the number of employed is 9 million, and the number of unemployed is 1 million.

   a) What is the size of the labour force?

   b) What is the participation rate?

   c) What is the unemployment rate?

2. The working age population of Cortina is 32 million, its participation rate is 75 percent, and there are 20 million employed workers.

   a) What is the size of the labour force?

   b) How many workers are unemployed?

   c) What is the unemployment rate?

3. **a)** If a person is categorized as retired, would that person be included in the working-age population?

   b) What types of people are categorized as "not in the labour force"?

   c) Is it possible for the total number of people employed and the total number of people unemployed to rise at the same time?

4.2 THE DIFFERENT TYPES OF UNEMPLOYMENT

 L02 Explain the different types of unemployment and understand the costs of unemployment.

Now that we have seen how unemployment is measured, we must address a more fundamental question: what actually causes unemployment? In the next section, we will look at three distinct types of unemployment: frictional, structural, and cyclical.

Royalty Free/CORBIS

Unemployment can affect all ages.

frictional unemployment:
that part of total unemployment caused by the fact that it takes time for people to find their first job or to move between jobs.

Frictional Unemployment

In a free society, where employees have the right to quit a job and employers have the right to dismiss their employees, **frictional unemployment** is inevitable. This is simply a reflection of the fact that seldom does anyone who leaves, or is dismissed from a job on, say, Friday, start a new job on the following Monday. In more general terms, unemployment and unfilled job vacancies can exist simultaneously because it takes time for a match to be found between vacant jobs and people seeking employment.

In addition to this matching process, there are other aspects to frictional unemployment. The first involves the growing phenomenon of people searching for the right job rather than for just any job. These days, a growing percentage of households has more than one wage earner. Thus, if one partner earns a good income, the unemployed partner can take longer in the job-search process to increase the chances of finding a satisfying job. There is a benefit to society when more people have jobs closely matching their interests and skills. However, prolonging the job search would, of course, increase frictional unemployment.

Furthermore, many feel that Canada has, by world standards, generous employment insurance benefits that allow for people, in some circumstances, to accept periodic layoffs without actually searching energetically for other work. Examples of frictionally unemployed includes students who complete school and begin looking for a job, as well as homemakers who enter (or re-enter) the labour market. These people often do not find work immediately and are therefore frictionally unemployed until they do. Other examples would be a racetrack employee who is unemployed in the winter, and a contract college instructor who has no work in the summer.

Frictional unemployment is a part of a modern market economy. It will never be eliminated, and, in fact, we do not want to try to eliminate it. We need to recognize that it takes time to match people and jobs, and that some people take extra time to search for the right job. In addition, there are some on layoff who are not actively searching for alternative employment. We can therefore conclude that frictional unemployment in Canada is a significant portion of the official unemployment rate reported monthly in the popular press.

Structural Unemployment

structural unemployment:
the part of total unemployment that results from a mismatch in the skills or location between jobs available and people looking for work.

Next, we want to examine **structural unemployment**. Some have called this "long-term frictional," but such a description does not capture the sense of the major shifts continuously taking place in the economy that result in structural unemployment. A natural spinoff of a dynamic, growing economy is the fact that new industries continually emerge and enter the expansionary stage—think of computer software, communications technology, and cardboard packaging for the fast-food industry.

Other spinoffs include "sunset" industries, which have experienced declining employment for years—the East Coast fishery and paper manufacturing, for example. The root cause of structural unemployment, then, is changing tastes and technology. Over the years, peoples' preferences change, and their demands for certain products and services increase (winter vacations, soccer uniforms), while the demand for other things (newspapers, cigarettes) decrease. Similarly, new products are invented (iPods, laptops, smartphones) causing others (CD players, typewriters, fax machines) to become obsolete. These changes cause the rise and fall of firms and industries, and along with them, jobs and occupations.

People working in sunset industries may require both a geographical and an occupational move in order to transfer into one of the newly created jobs in the growth industries. Whether retraining is required or not, it undoubtedly takes some time for such adjustments to occur. In short, continuous structural changes within the economy always lead to a certain amount of structural unemployment. In addition, some economic observers argue that the forces of global-ization in the world today have increased the rate at which businesses, and even whole industries, leave Canada in order to set up in some other, lower-wage country. To the extent that this is true, structural unemployment becomes a bigger problem.

Cyclical Unemployment

In the next chapter, we will look at fluctuations in the economy called *business cycles*. These fluc-tuations are reflected in changes in the level of employment and unemployment. A complete cycle consists of an expansion phase followed by a contractionary phase. This sequence of expansion and contraction change is recurrent but not regular in length or duration.

When the business cycle is at its expansionary peak, the economy will likely be at, or near, what is called **full employment**. Another way of looking at this is to realize that "full employ-ment" refers to the situation in which any unemployment in the economy is a result of purely frictional and structural causes. **Cyclical unemployment** occurs in recessionary phases of the business cycle, so full employment only exists when there is no cyclical unemployment.

It is from the concept of zero cyclical unemployment that economists get the **natural rate of unemployment**. This exists when there is frictional and structural unemployment but no cyclical unemployment. When an economy is in a recession, cyclical unemployment exists because the total amount of unemployment is greater than the sum of frictional and structural unemployment, and is therefore above the natural rate.

Thus, we can say that full employment exists when the economy is experiencing only the natural rate of unemployment. This natural rate is considered to be the lowest unemployment rate an economy can achieve without accelerating inflation. In other words, it is possible to achieve a lower rate of unemployment, but only at the cost of higher prices. In addition, the natural rate of unemployment can vary from country to country and from time to time within the same country, as social and economic conditions change. For example, Japan, where the practice of changing jobs frequently is thought to show a lack of loyalty (and loyalty is a highly regarded virtue), is likely to have a much lower natural rate of unemployment than North America, where people frequently change jobs. As another example, some economists argue that Canada's natural rate of unemploy-ment increased in the 1970s following an overhaul of the employment insurance plan that increased coverage and benefits, as well as an increase in two-income families. Today, it appears that Canada's natural rate of unemployment is in the range of 5 to 7 percent, although it should be noted that there is no official rate generally recognized or accepted by everyone.

We should re-emphasize that regardless of the phase of the business cycle, there is always unem-ployment in the economy, and there are always job vacancies. The labour market is dynamic: the type and place of the vacancies are constantly in flux, and the people who are unemployed may or may not have the particular skills or experience to fill those vacancies. Many economists would argue that this points out the need for government-sponsored job placement and retraining services.

Thus, whatever the level of performance in the economy, there will always be thousands of existing job vacancies. In fact, the number of vacancies might well equal the number of unemployed people. This phenomenon serves to emphasize the notion that the natural rate of unemployment is the result of unavoidable mismatching in the labour market. When an economy is suffering from cyclical unemployment it has this mismatching problem combined with the fact that there are simply not enough jobs to go around; the number of unemployed people often greatly exceeds the number of available jobs.

full employment: frictional and structural unemployment exist, but cyclical unemployment is zero.

cyclical unemployment: occurs as a result of the recessionary phase of the business cycle.

natural rate of unemployment: the unemployment rate at full employment.

ADDED DIMENSION   Economic Growth and Recessions

A recession is defined by Statistics Canada as a decline in real GDP in two consecutive quarters. We know that a drop in real GDP will lead to layoffs in the economy and thus a rise in unemployment. Therefore, the average person is more likely to define a recession as an increase in the unemployment rate rather than a decrease in the growth rate. Are these two perspectives one and the same?

Although it is true that a negative or low positive growth rate is usually associated with high unemployment and that a high growth rate implies a low unemployment rate, this relationship is not exact. For example, in the early years of the Great Depression of the 1930s, the Canadian economy experienced negative growth rates and high unemployment. Then, from 1934 onward, the economy actually experienced positive growth in real GDP at an average annual rate of 7.1 percent, yet the unemployment rate remained at an annual average rate of 12.3 percent. More recently, growth rates began to increase in 2010 as we saw signs of the recession ending, but unemployment rates remained persistently high. That is, an economy in the recovery stage of a recession can expect to record positive growth rates but may not experience lower unemployment for some time. So, while there may be some truth that negative growth rates herald a recession, it would be a mistake to assume that positive growth rates always mean a quick fall in unemployment rates.

SELF-TEST

4. Categorize each of the following sets of circumstances as frictional, structural, or cyclical unemployment.

  a) Sanjit, a pulp-mill worker, is laid off because the mill's inventories are at an all-time high.

  b) Five weeks ago, Alison left a job she did not like and is still looking for another job.

  c) Ian was a fisher on the East Coast but sold his boat after years of hard work with little return. He has been unemployed for almost a year.

If the natural unemployment rate in Canada today is 5 to 7 percent, it is surely higher than it was just 25 or 30 years ago. There are three possible explanations for this increase in the natural rate of unemployment. First, as we mentioned above, changes in employment insurance (EI) legislation in the early 1970s significantly increased benefits. Second, a longer job-search time is being taken by job seekers, who are more affluent than they used to be and therefore can afford to extend the time spent looking for a satisfying job. Third, an increase in the female participation rate has contributed to an increase in the number of people looking for employment. If these explanations are valid, then the reductions in EI coverage and benefits in the mid-1990s and the expected levelling of the female participation rate may well result in a decrease in the natural rate of unemployment in Canada in the coming decades. In summary, the natural rate of unemployment could change if:

- employment insurance benefits change.
- the average job search time change.
- labour-force participation rates change.

Criticism of the Official Rate

The diagram on the next page helps us get a good overview of the labour market.

There are four grounds on which one could criticize the official unemployment rate, despite the fact that the interview and statistical techniques used by Statistics Canada to measure it are statistically valid and recognized around the world as among the best. The first two criticisms discussed below cause the official rate to be *understated*.

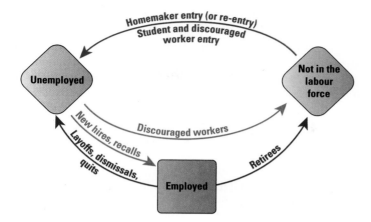

First, we must realize that people who respond that they worked only part time (and it may be as little as one hour a week) in the previous week will be classified as employed. However, if this under-employment is not what individuals were hoping for, then some real unemployment is being covered over in the reported statistics.

Second, we must consider what critics refer to as the **discouraged worker** phenomenon. According to the official definitions used by Statistics Canada, a person who is *not* actively seeking work is not in the labour force and thus would not be counted as unemployed. Yet, some argue that many individuals have become so discouraged in their attempts to secure employment that they have stopped looking. To exclude these discouraged workers is to understate the magnitude of the unemployment.

The third common criticism of unemployment statistics is one that may cause the official rate to be *overstated*. When people who are collecting EI or welfare payments are asked if they are actively seeking work, the response is very likely to be "yes." Yet, at least some of these individuals are not involuntarily unemployed but are, instead, simply waiting for benefits to expire (or their claim to be challenged) before returning to active participation in the job market.

The fourth cause of unreliability is the fact that there is a whole group in the underground economy who are working in illegal occupations and, for obvious reasons, are going to declare themselves unemployed. The same may well be true for people with legal jobs who are not declaring their incomes (to avoid paying income tax). They, too, would probably declare themselves unemployed.

We will make no attempt to judge whether reasons one and two, which tip the scale one way, outweigh reasons three and four, which tip it the other way. What is probably more important to note is that measuring the unemployment rate *consistently* is crucial if we are to make sense out of time comparisons. Measured consistently, the official rate allows valid conclusions to be drawn about the economy's performance in one year compared with another, and that is useful. In summary, the reported unemployment rates can be:

- understated because part-timers are included as full-timers.
- understated because they exclude discouraged workers.
- overstated because of false information from some EI recipients.
- overstated because of false information from those working in the underground economy.

discouraged worker:
an individual who wants work but is no longer actively seeking it because of the belief that no opportunities exist.

Costs of Unemployment

How serious a problem is unemployment? Should we really be concerned with it? Certainly, there are some obvious personal economic costs associated with unemployment. In addition, there are serious social costs that can affect all of us. Therefore, the true costs of unemployment cannot be measured simply in terms of EI or welfare payments going to those not working. In a sense, you might regard them as costs for the taxpayer, but obviously, from the recipient's point of view, they definitely represent a benefit. Overall, to an economist, they are not true economic costs at all but merely transfer payments. The true economic costs come from the fact that unemployment in an economy means that the quantity of goods and services being produced is less than it could be. (Like time, this lost production is gone forever.) This means that a country is producing below its potential, or in terms of Chapter 1's model, the economy is operating inside its production possibilities boundary. The amount of "lost" goods and services that were not produced because the economy was operating at less than full employment is what economists refer to as the **GDP gap**. In the form of an equation, it is shown as:

GDP gap: the difference between potential GDP and actual GDP (real or nominal).

$$\text{GDP gap} = \text{potential GDP} - \text{actual GDP (real or nominal)} \qquad \textbf{[4.3]}$$

An American economist, Arthur Okun, established a relationship between the amount of cyclical unemployment in the economy and the size of the GDP gap. **Okun's law** observes that for every 1 percent of cyclical unemployment, the economy's level of GDP falls 2.5 percent short of its potential. This gap can be calculated by using the following equation:

Okun's law: the observation that for every 1 percent of cyclical unemployment an economy's GDP is 2.5 percent below its potential.

$$\text{GDP gap} = 2.5 \times \text{cyclical unemployment (\%)} \times \text{actual GDP (real or nominal)} \qquad \textbf{[4.4]}$$

For example, in 2010, the unemployment rate was 8 percent (see **Table 4.3**). If one assumes 6 percent as the natural rate of unemployment, then Canada was experiencing cyclical unemployment of 2 percent. In that year, its nominal GDP was $1622 billion. Given this information, we are able to calculate the size of its GDP gap.

$$\text{GDP gap} = 2.5 \times 2\% \times \$1622 = \$81.1 \text{ billion}$$

This is a measurement of the economic cost of unemployment and is a significant figure. If Canada had been able to eliminate this cyclical unemployment, its potential GDP would have been $81 billion higher at $1703 billion, and each person in Canada would have earned on average an additional $2375 in that year ($81 billion/34.1 million).

As important as these dollar amounts are, the social costs to the individual and to society can represent an even greater waste. Cyclical unemployment of 2 percent, given Canada's labour force of 18.5 million, translates into approximately 371 000 people being involuntarily unemployed. In those 371 000 stories, one would find a lot of bitterness, disappointment, anger, loss of self-esteem, and a sense of failure. In addition, people who are unemployed for a significant period often lose some of the job skills that they had learned. Such feelings are not a recipe for social harmony. Alcoholism, accidents, claims on the health care system, violence, and crime all rise as a result. Furthermore, these social costs do not fall evenly across society. Young people and those with less education are hit the hardest, as are those who live in the Maritime provinces and Quebec.

Whether we try to categorize these costs as social, psychological, economic, or political, the fact remains that unemployment is expensive by any measure.

 SELF-TEST

5. What would happen to the size of the labour force if 100 000 unemployed people became discouraged workers? What effect, if any, would this have on the unemployment rate?

6. Given a natural rate of unemployment of 8 percent, an actual rate of 10 percent, and real GDP of $800 billion, calculate potential GDP.

4.3 INFLATION

Let us now turn to inflation. Public-opinion polls consistently show that people consider inflation, or the threat of inflation, to be a major problem facing society. In fact, people's concern about inflation usually ranks above their concern about unemployment. The reason for this is probably the simple fact that while unemployment in the economy directly touches only the unemployed and others close to them, inflation touches everyone daily. For our purposes, **inflation** can be defined as an increase in the general level of prices that is sustained over a period in an economy.

L03 Understand what inflation is and how it is measured.

inflation: a persistent rise in the general level of prices.

Price Indexes

Although inflation measures the amount that prices increase from one year to the next, this does not mean that the prices of all products increase. In fact, the price of some products may well decrease. As the definition suggests, inflation measures the change in the general, or average level of prices. However, Statistics Canada does not actually measure average prices—it uses an index of prices. Like any index, this is nothing more than converting the value of something in a particular year (called *the base year*) into the number 100 and then tracking the change in this value in subsequent years. The value of an index then is always equal to 100 in the base year. For example, if the value of the index increased by 8 percent in the following year, then the new index would have a value of 108.

When measuring price changes, Statistics Canada constructs many different price indexes which are of use to different groups: producers' price index, house construction price index, a farmers' price index and so on. The two most well-known and widely used indexes are the consumer price index (CPI) and the GDP deflator. Let us look first at the consumer price index.

Measuring Inflation Using the Consumer Price Index

Statistics Canada derives the **consumer price index** by first defining a representative bundle of goods and services and then collecting prices on each item every month. The basket reflects the spending habits of a family of four, and the prices are weighted to reflect a typical consumption pattern.

Suppose that we construct our own price index for a representative Canadian student using some simple, and very hypothetical, data. In the first year, we discover that an average student pays $600 per month for accommodation, lives on 30 pizzas a month (costing $8 each), and goes to the movies 8 times each month at a cost of $10 per ticket. Her spending is summarized in **Table 4.5A**.

consumer price index: a measurement of the average level of prices of the goods and services that a typical Canadian family consumes.

TABLE 4.5A	Monthly Spending by an Average Student, January 2011		
Item	**Quantity**	**Price**	**Cost**
Accommodation rental	1	$600	$600
Pizzas	30	8	240
Movie tickets	8	10	80
Total cost			**$920**

In January of the following year, we revisit this student to see how much she is now paying for these items. Perhaps not surprisingly, we find the prices of all three items have increased, as shown in **Table 4.5B**.

TABLE 4.5B	Monthly Spending by an Average Student, January 2012		
Item	**Quantity**	**Price**	**Cost**
Accommodation rental	1	$620	$620
Pizzas	30	8.60	258
Movie tickets	8	11	88
Total cost			**$966**

We can now convert this data into our own Student Price Index by simply assigning our basket of goods a value of 100 in the base year (2011), which enables us to find the value of the index in the next year, 2012.

$$CPI = \frac{\text{cost of basket in a given year}}{\text{cost of basket in base year}} \times 100 \qquad [4.5]$$

Using the above data gives us the value of the basket in 2012.

$$CPI = \frac{\$966}{920} \times 100 = 105$$

That is all there is to it. To find out the inflation rate, we simply calculate the percentage change in the value of the price index.

$$\text{Inflation rate} = \frac{(\text{price index this year} - \text{price index last year})}{\text{price index last year}} \times 100 \qquad [4.6]$$

Thus, for 2012:

$$\text{Inflation rate} = \frac{(105 - 100)}{100} \times 100 = 5\%$$

To reinforce these ideas, let us calculate the inflation rate in 2013, supposing that the value of our student's bundle of goods rose to $995. If that is the case, then using formula 4.5, the price index for 2013 would be:

$$CPI = \frac{\$995}{920} \times 100 = 108.15$$

And, using formula 4.6, the inflation rate for 2013 would be:

$$\text{Inflation rate} = \frac{(108.15 - 105)}{105} \times 100 = \frac{3.15}{105} \times 100 = 3\%$$

So, now that we know how to calculate inflation rates, let us look at **Table 4.6** for the actual CPI and inflation rates for Canada in recent years.

These inflation rates are low compared with those experienced in the 1970s and 1980s, when Canada's inflation went as high as 12.4 percent. (See **Figure 1.9B** for data since 1930.) In fact, inflation has never risen above 3.0 percent since 1991.

In addition to the CPI, Statistics Canada also publishes a *core CPI* which excludes items whose prices can fluctuate wildly from period to period. These items include fruits and vegetables, gas, fuel oil, mortgage interest, and tobacco. The core CPI then gives a better indication of long-term underlying inflation rates.

TABLE 4.6	**Consumer Price Index and Inflation Rates in Canada, Selected Years 1998–2010 (2002 = 100)**	
	CPI	**Inflation Rate (%)**
1998	91.3	1.0
2000	95.4	2.7
2001	97.8	2.5
2006	109.1	2.0
2007	111.5	2.2
2008	114.1	2.2
2009	114.4	0.3
2010	116.5	1.8

Source: Adapted from Statistics Canada, CANSIM Database <http://cansim2.statcan.ca>, Table 326-0021, 17 March 2011.

Measuring Inflation Using the GDP Deflator

Although the CPI is the most publicized of the price indexes and is generally the one used to measure inflation, it is not the only price index and is therefore not the only way of measuring inflation. In fact, many suggest that it is better to use the **GDP deflator** to measure the inflation rate of an economy because the bundle of goods that it uses does not simply consist of consumer goods. As the name suggests, the GDP deflator is a price index that measures the value of a bundle goods that includes the other goods that are included in GDP in addition to consumer goods—capital goods, exported goods, and government services. Also, because the GDP measures goods and services produced domestically, it excludes imports—the CPI is a reflection of consumer spending, and many of those products are made abroad. In other words, the CPI includes the prices of imported goods. You can see right away that since the two indexes measure different things, their values may well differ. For instance, if the prices of capital goods are rising much faster than the prices of consumer goods, then the GDP deflator will be higher than the CPI. Conversely, if the prices of imported goods are rising sharply, then the CPI will have a higher value than the GDP deflator.

GDP deflator: a measure of the price level of goods and services included in the GDP; calculated by dividing the nominal GDP by the real GDP and multiplying by 100.

The two indexes also differ significantly in the way that they are constructed. As we have seen, the CPI is derived from the expenditures of a representative consumer and tracks the value of a bundle of goods over time, assuming that the bundle of goods remains the same. It is referred to as an *explicit index*. By comparison, the GDP deflator is known as an *implicit index*, and as we shall see, the bundle of goods does, in fact, change from period to period. So, what bundle of goods does Statistics Canada use? It uses the actual goods and services currently produced, that is, the current GDP of the country. Let us work out the value of this deflator using the data that we used for a hypothetical economy in **Table 3.4** of the last chapter (partly reproduced in **Table 4.7**).

The value of nominal GDP in year 1 for this particular country was $42 000 (in millions of dollars). The following year, its GDP rose to $49 200. However, when we calculated its real GDP (its GDP using constant, year 1, prices), we found that it had only risen to $45 200. In other words, with no price change, its GDP was $45 200; including inflation it rose to $49 200. The relative

TABLE 4.7	**Nominal and Real GDP**		
	Year 1	**Year 2**	**Year 3**
Nominal GDP ($ millions)	42 000	49 200	57 540
Real GDP ($ millions)	42 000	45 200	50 100

difference between these figures must therefore represent the inflation rate. In other words, while nominal GDP rose by approximately 17 percent, real GDP rose only 8 percent. Inflation, therefore, must have been the difference, approximately 9 percent. To calculate the value of the GDP deflator, we measure the ratio of the two.

$$\text{GDP deflator} = \frac{\text{nominal GDP}}{\text{real GDP}} \times 100 \qquad\qquad \textbf{[4.7]}$$

We can therefore calculate the value of the GDP deflator for year 2.

$$\text{GDP deflator} = \frac{\$49\ 200}{45\ 200} \times 100 = 109$$

Again, looking at **Table 4.7**, we can calculate the value of the GDP deflator for year 3.

$$\text{GDP deflator} = \frac{\$57\ 540}{50\ 100} \times 100 = 114.9$$

To summarize, the value of the GDP deflator in year 1 was 100, rising in year 2 to 109, and in year 3 to 114.9. To calculate the inflation rates, using formula 4.6 is straightforward. In year 2, it came to 9 percent. (You could probably do that in your head!) The inflation rate in year 3 came to $(114.9 - 109) \div 109 = 5.4$ percent.

Having seen how we calculate inflation using each of the indexes, let us summarize their differences.

- The CPI is an explicit index using a constructed bundle of goods; the GDP deflator is an implicit index measuring the ratio of nominal to real GDP.
- The bundle of goods remains constant with the CPI; the bundle of goods in the GDP deflator changes each year.
- The CPI does not include capital or government goods and services; the GDP deflator includes them.
- The CPI includes imported goods; the GDP deflator excludes imported goods.

Finally, it is important to clearly understand the relationship among nominal GDP, real GDP, and the GDP deflator. For instance, if we know that nominal GDP in Canada in 2005 was \$1371 billion, and the value of its GDP deflator was 118.4 (1997 was the base year), it is a fairly simple matter to figure out the value of real GDP for that year by just rearranging formula 4.7.

$$\text{Real GDP} = \frac{\text{Nominal GDP}}{\text{GDP deflator}} \times 100 \qquad\qquad \textbf{[4.8]}$$

$$\text{Real GDP} = \frac{1371}{118.4} \times 100 = \$1157.9$$

Similarly, if we know the value of real GDP and the GDP deflator, it is straightforward to figure out the value of nominal GDP by rearranging this basic formula.

$$\text{Nominal GDP} = \text{real GDP} \times \frac{\text{GDP deflator}}{100} \qquad\qquad \textbf{[4.9]}$$

For instance, knowing that the real GDP in Canada in 2001 was \$1039 and its GDP deflator was 106.6, we can calculate the nominal GDP as:

$$\text{Nominal GDP} = \$1039 \times \frac{106.6}{100} = \$1107.6$$

✓ SELF-TEST

7. Fill in the blanks (to one decimal place) in the table of Etruria's GDP statistics.

	2010	2011	2012
Nominal GDP ($billion)	443	___	507
Real GDP ($billion)	374	389	___
GDP deflator (2002 = 100)	___	121.9	126.1
Population (millions)	26.1	26.4	27
Real GDP per capita	___	___	___

Measuring the Past

As we saw with the GDP deflator, one of the main purposes of a price index is to enable us to look at values from the past and compare them with the present. For instance, it would be difficult these days to get by on an annual salary of $10 000. However, a $10 000 salary thirty years ago could enable a person to live a fairly comfortable lifestyle. That is because one dollar 30 years ago went a lot further than it does today. Using a price index will allow us to compare past incomes (or other money values) with present incomes. We can do this by expressing all values, past and present, in terms of the same year's prices. Generally, the common year will be the base year. The following equation will help us to make this calculation:

$$\text{Real value (in Year B\$)} = \frac{\text{Nominal Value in Year A}}{\text{Price Index in Year A}} \times \text{Price Index in Year B (or base year)} \quad [4.10]$$

For instance, in **Table 4.8**, let us compare a $10 000 income earned in 1977, 1987, 1997, and 2007. (The base year is 2002.)

TABLE 4.8   Nominal and Real Income

Year	Nominal Income	Price Index	Real Income
1977	$10 000	33.6	$29 762
1987	10 000	68.5	14 599
1997	10 000	90.4	11 062
2007	10 000	111.5	8 969

To find real income then, we simply divide **nominal income** (or current income) by the price index and multiply the result by 100 (the price index in the base year of 2002). For example, the **real income** in 1977 was equal to:

$$\frac{\$10\ 000}{33.6} \times 100 = \$29\ 762$$

This table shows us how the real value of income has been eroded by inflation over the years. An income of $10 000 in 2007 was worth less than a third of what it was worth back in 1977.

To cement this idea a little more, let us look at some actual data for Canada over the past few years. **Table 4.9** presents information on average (after-tax) family incomes in Canada from 2001 to 2008 (2002 = 100).

nominal income: the present dollar value of a person's income.

real income: the purchasing power of income; that is, nominal income divided by the price level.

TABLE 4.9	Average After-Tax Family Income					
Year	Nominal Average Income	Nominal Income (%)	Price Index	Price Index (Inflation rate %)	Real Average Income	Real Income (%)
2001	$57 492	—	97.8	—	$58 785	—
2002	58 785	+2.2	100.0	2.2	58 785	0
2003	59 950	+2.0	102.8	2.8	58 317	−0.7
2004	62 526	+4.3	104.7	1.8	59 719	+2.4
2005	64 800	+3.6	107.0	2.2	60 560	+1.4
2006	67 601	+4.3	109.1	2.0	61 962	+2.3
2007	71 825	+6.2	111.5	2.2	64 417	+4.0
2008	74 600	+3.9	114.1	2.3	65 381	1.5

Source: Adapted from Statistics Canada, CANSIM Database <http://cansim2.statcan.ca>, Tables 326-0002 and 202-0603, 17 March 2011.

We can extend our understanding a little further by calculating how real income changed year by year. We can do this by working out the change in real income and expressing it as a percentage. For instance, real income in 2007 increased $2455 (from $61 962 to $64 417). As a percentage, this works out to:

$$\frac{\$2455}{\$61\,962} \times 100 = +4\%$$

The rest of the last column is worked out in a similar fashion. However, an alternative method would be to use the following formula which enables us to work out the change directly.

% change in real income = % change in nominal income − inflation rate   [4.11]

For example, **Table 4.9** shows us that nominal income changed by +6.2 percent in 2007, while the inflation rate for that year was 2.2 percent. Subtracting the inflation rate from the change in nominal income gives us a change in real income of 4 percent, which confirms our previous calculation.

One interesting use of the CPI is that it allows us to compare the actual price of a product in the past in terms of today's prices. For example, the actual price of a movie in 1958 was (about) $1, while today it is, say, $11 (it varies from city to city). On the other hand, we know that people's wages and incomes are also much higher in 2010 than they were in 1958. So, did the real price of a movie increase or not? We can answer this question using equation 4.9.

$$\text{Real value (in Year B\$)} = \frac{\text{Nominal Value in Year A}}{\text{Price Index in Year A}} \times \text{Price Index in Year B (or base year)}$$

Using this equation, and knowing the price indexes in 1958 and 2010, gives us:

$$\text{Real value in 2010} = \frac{\$1}{15.2} \times 116.5 = \$7.66$$

So, actually $11 is pretty expensive! If, alternatively, we want to know 1958 ticket prices in terms of 2002 (base year) prices, we would have:

$$\text{Real value in 2002} = \frac{\$1}{15.2} \times 100 = \$6.58$$

Along the same lines, which movie do you think is Hollywood's biggest box office hit? Well, the top-grossing movies world-wide (as of January 2011) will probably not come as a big surprise to most of you. They are (in millions of dollars) as follows:

	Domestic Sales	World Sales
1. Avatar (2009)	$760	$2782
2. Titanic (1997)	600	1843
3. Lord of the Rings: Return of the King (2003)	377	1119
4. Pirates of the Caribbean: Dead Man's Chest (2006)	423	1066
5. Alice in Wonderland (2010)	334	1024

One thing that they all share is the fact that they are recent movies—released within the last decade or so. However, we know that ticket prices are much higher today than they were in the past. If we allow for inflation, by adjusting the revenues of all movies to present day prices, the results (for domestic sales) are more than a little surprising.

6. Titanic	$1028
14. Avatar	779
45. Pirates of the Caribbean: Dead Man's Chest	517
51. The Lord of The Rings: Return of the King	493

So, in terms of revenue adjusted for inflation, what are the top box office hits of all time? Well, number one is *Gone With the Wind* ($1618), made in 1939, and number two is *Star Wars: A New Hope* ($1427) made in 1977, and number three is *The Sound of Music* ($1141) made in 1965. *Snow White and the Seven Dwarfs* ($873), made in 1937, is ranked 10th but does not even make it into the top 300 in actual dollars!

Finally, you must have heard stories from your parents or grandparents about "the good old days" and how it was possible then for a guy to take his girlfriend to the movies, have a meal afterwards, and still have enough change left over from a $5 bill to take the bus home. Right! We know of course that comparing prices of yesteryear with today means nothing unless we can compare them with today's prices in *real* terms. So, was everything really cheaper in bygone days? Well, it turns out that some things *really* were cheaper, but many other things were far more expensive. Here, for instance, are some items that have not changed very much in real terms in the past 50 years:

	Canadian Price in 1958	Real Value in 2008	Actual Price in 2008
Coffee (pound)	0.85	6.26	5.58
Bacon (pound)	0.63	4.64	4.22
Café breakfast	0.65	4.79	3.00–5.00
Chevrolet sedan	3295	24 284	26 000

But the following items are definitely more expensive now than they were 50 years ago:

	Canadian Price in 1958	Real Value in 2008	Actual Price in 2008
T-bone steak (pound)	0.89	6.56	15.96
Movie ticket	1.00	7.37	10.00
Newspaper	0.07	0.52	1.06
Bolshoi Ballet	2.00	14.74	30–80
Gasoline (litre)	0.08	0.59	1.12
Cigarettes (pack)	0.25	1.84	7.50

But then again, many other things are actually cheaper now than in the past:

	Canadian Price in 1958	Real Value in 2008	Actual Price in 2008
Record album	4.80	35.38	20.00
Flight Vancouver–London	623	4591	1200
RCA TV 21-inch	309	2271	>100

So, although the CPI tells us how average prices change over the years, we need to understand that not all prices change by the same rate. As our example shows, some prices rise far more than others.

The Rule of 70—A Helpful Tool

We have all heard how a few years of rapid inflation can ravage an economy or how compound interest can dramatically increase a given sum of money over time. The "rule of 70" (actually the number is closer to 72, but most people approximate it) is useful in estimating the time it will take for a figure to double in value given a certain percentage growth rate. The formula is:

$$\text{Number of years to double} = \frac{70}{\%\ \text{growth rate}} \qquad \textbf{[4.12]}$$

For example, if inflation is 5 percent per year, the CPI will double in:

$$\frac{70}{5} = 1.4\ \text{years}$$

Or $1000 in a savings account earning 10 percent will double in:

$$\frac{70}{10} = 7\ \text{years}$$

Another example would be an economy that is growing by 3.5 percent per year. It would experience a doubling of GDP in:

$$\frac{70}{3.5} = 20\ \text{years}$$

A final example has great import for us all. By 1960, the growth rate of the world's population reached 1.75 percent (it attained its maximum of over 2 percent by the mid-sixties). Although 1.75 percent does not sound a very big figure, it meant that the population was due to double in only 40 years (70 ÷ 1.75). And that is exactly what happened. In 1960, the world population had reached three billion. By 2000, it stood at six billion. Fortunately, this growth rate has slowed down in recent years: as of 2010, it was 1.3 percent. Even so, at this rate, the population will again double from its present 6.5 billion to 13 billion by the year 2064.

 SELF-TEST

8. If Kerri's nominal income increased during the year from $40 000 to $42 800, and the inflation rate for the year was 4 percent, by what percentage has her real income increased?

9. a) If the inflation rate is 7 percent, how long will it take for prices to double?

b) If a sum of money invested in the bank doubles in 7 years, what rate of interest is it earning?

4.4   THE COSTS OF INFLATION

Like unemployment, inflation involves some very heavy costs. However, the inflationary effects on the real income of different groups is quite uneven. The classic contrast is between an elderly couple living primarily on a private pension and a yuppie couple who both work in sales and receive, as income, a percentage of total sales volume. The real income of the elderly couple is eroded annually by inflation—in fact, during the high inflation years between 1972 and 1981, it was cut in half! Meanwhile, it is quite possible that the yuppie couple gained from inflation because their sales volume grew faster than the overall rate of inflation. When a society's real income is redistributed in undesirable ways by inflation itself, we refer to this as **redistributive costs**. Inflation can be unfair in that at times it hurts the economically weak and often leaves the strong unaffected or, perhaps, even benefits them. In general, those whose nominal income increases less than the rate of inflation will suffer because their real income decreases.

A second example of the effect of inflation is the experience of employees who have weak bargaining power in the market place—they might be non-unionized or working in a declining industry. In contrast, employees who are members of a powerful trade union or are working in a growing industry may well be able to keep up with inflation.

Inflation can also redistribute wealth, particularly if the inflation rate takes an unexpected jump. The easiest way to see this is to imagine yourself borrowing $1000 today, assuming a current inflation rate of 5 percent. This means that what costs you $1000 today will cost you $1050 a year from now. Anyone lending you $1000 now will definitely want to ensure they get the equivalent amount back. But in addition, they will want to earn a return on the money they lend, if for no other reason than the risk that the loan may never be repaid. Let us say that they want to earn a real return of 7 percent. In other words, the lender wants to earn 7 percent irrespective of the inflation rate. This is what is meant by the **real interest rate**: the rate of interest when inflation is zero, or put another way, the rate of interest assuming the value of the dollar remains constant. The lender would therefore charge you 5 percent to cover anticipated inflation + 7 percent = 12 percent, so:

Nominal interest rate = Real interest rate + inflation rate   **[4.13]**

So, let us say that you agree to the nominal rate of 12 percent and therefore to the repayment of $1120 in a year's time. If the actual inflation rate turns out to be 5 percent, then your friend will receive in real terms exactly what he expected to receive. But what would happen if the actual inflation rate turned out to be 10 percent? You will still pay back $1120 to your friend. But how

L04 Explain the two types of inflation and understand the costs of inflation.

redistributive costs: (of inflation) costs that are shifted from one group in society to another group by inflation.

real interest rate: the rate of interest measured in constant dollars.

much is this worth to him in purchasing power compared with the $1000 he lent to you a year ago? The answer is only approximately $1020 because of the increase in prices. Therefore, he earned, in real terms, only $20 on $1000, or 2 percent. In other words, rearranging 4.13 we have:

$$\text{Real interest rate} = \text{nominal rate} - \text{the inflation rate} \qquad \textbf{[4.14]}$$

Inserting the appropriate figures gives us:

$$\text{Real interest rate} = 12\% - 10\% = 2\%$$

This clearly hurts the lender of the $1000, while you are not hurt. If your real income rises because of the higher inflation, then you, the borrower, will actually gain. In general, an unexpected rise in inflation hurts lenders and can benefit borrowers, with the result being an unpredictable redistribution of wealth. On the other hand, an unexpected drop in the inflation rate will hurt borrowers and help lenders.

While these redistribution costs hurt some people, they help others. But inflation can have another cost that really does hurt everyone. These are what are termed the **output costs**.

output costs: (of inflation) costs of loss of output resulting from inflation.

Let us start this discussion by pointing out that long-term investment is an uncertain business at the best of times. Consider the example of a company that will have to spend $10 million to produce and market a new product. The financial viability of such a decision depends on many variables, from expected sales to production costs. If estimating these unknowns also requires that uncertain inflation rates—which will affect both revenue and production costs—must be factored in, then the risks may become too large to accept, and as a result, the company may shelve the launching of the new product. All the investment spending and new hiring that would have resulted is forgone.

The key phrase in the above paragraph is "uncertain inflation rate." Any inflation rate—0, 10, or 20 percent—is not a problem in the sense that we are discussing, as long as it remains unchanged and therefore predictable. It is the *uncertainty* associated with inflation that generates concern, making investment decision-makers nervous. If such hesitancy reduces the amount of investment in the economy, then the rate of economic growth slows and total output will be lower than it would have been.

Before leaving this discussion of the costs of inflation, it is worth taking a minute to look at the problems of the opposite situation—falling prices—which is called *deflation*. Japan, for example, has recently been facing just this situation. One of the effects of deflation is a reduction in both consumer and investment spending because when prices are falling, people put off purchases until the future in order to take advantage of the lower prices. In addition, investment spending is likely to be further affected because of the effects of deflation on the real interest rate. A number of studies have concluded that over the last 300 years or so the real rate of interest has gravitated around the 4 percent level. **Table 4.10** shows what the nominal rate needs to be in order to achieve a real rate of 4 percent.

For instance, if the inflation rate is 2 percent, then a nominal rate of 6 percent is needed to ensure a real rate of 4 percent, which will satisfy both lenders and borrowers. However, if the inflation rate rises to 12 percent, then a nominal interest rate of 16 percent is needed to yield a real rate of 4 percent. Now, consider the effects of deflation. If the *deflation* rate is 4 percent, then those who have money to lend can gain a real rate of interest of 4 percent by doing nothing except holding on to their money. Therefore, they will not be willing to lend, and since nominal interest

TABLE 4.10	Hypothetical Real Rates of Inflation	
Real Rate of Interest	Inflation Rate	(Needed) Nominal Interest Rate
4%	2%	6%
4%	12%	16%
4%	−4%	0%

rates cannot become negative, there is nothing that will change to correct this situation. In short, deflation freezes credit markets, and this also reduces output.

There are other examples of the output costs of inflation. The first is termed the *menu costs of inflation*. This refers to the business costs involved in changing prices, which is something that must be done more often in times of higher inflation. Let us take the case of Colonial Music, a small wholesaler of musical instruments, which are imported from Asia and sold to school boards across North America. Colonial Music produces three separate printed catalogues that it mails out—one for English Canada, one for French Canada, and one for the United States—as well as a Web site that has the same three categories. Since the company offers hundreds of instruments, the production of the catalogues and the updating of the Web site costs tens of thousands of dollars every year. Any increase in the inflation rate may necessitate the production of new catalogues sooner than the regularly scheduled time, and this clearly adds to the costs of doing business.

In addition, we know that inflation in Canada has a negative effect on the levels of Canadian exports. Higher inflation pushes up the prices of Canadian goods and reduces Canadian exports, unless the countries that we compete with also experience similarly high inflation. Furthermore, Canadian consumers will begin to substitute imports for the now higher-priced Canadian products. The result is less production in Canada, and this means less national income and fewer jobs. In summary, the output costs of inflation include:

- lower level of investment.
- menu costs.
- lower level of net exports.

Two Types of Inflation

In a very real sense, the entire catalogue of macroeconomic principles is necessary to understand what causes inflation. Nevertheless, it is useful to briefly identify two categories of causes at this point.

The first is referred to by economists as **demand–pull inflation**, which occurs when the total demand for goods and services in the whole economy exceeds its capacity to produce those same goods. That is to say, people are trying to buy more goods and services than the economy is capable of producing, even at full employment. This excessive demand will pull up prices and cause demand–pull inflation.

demand–pull inflation: inflation that occurs when total demand for goods and services exceeds the economy's capacity to produce those goods.

You may well ask, "But don't we also experience inflation at times when unemployment is high and, thus, when there is no demand–pull inflation?" Yes, we do, and this is the second classification of inflation, called **cost–push inflation**. This occurs on the supply side of the economy, whereas demand–pull inflation is a demand-side phenomenon. Cost–push inflation has three variations.

The first of these is *wage–push inflation*. For example, if a union succeeds in pushing the nominal wage rate up more than any recent increase in labour productivity would justify, then the employer's real cost will rise. If we assume that this increase was not simply a catch-up in response to inflation from some other cause, then we have the makings of inflation. If the employer who agreed to the increased nominal wage did so thinking that by increasing the price of the products she sells she can recoup the increased costs, and if the employer has sufficient market power, then we have a completed picture of wage–push inflation: increased wages pushing up costs, which push up prices. While the impact of one union and one employer probably is not noticeable, if the above scenario is typical of a general pattern, then the impact will become very apparent.

cost–push inflation: inflation caused by an increase in the costs of production or in profit levels, affecting the supply side.

The second variation of cost–push inflation, called *profit–push inflation*, can occur if firms have enough market power to enhance profits by simply increasing the prices of what they sell. This is more likely to occur in industries in which competition is weak and aggregate demand is strong.

The name of the third variation, *import–push inflation*, is almost self-explanatory. The classic example here is the OPEC oil price increases of the 1970s, which affected every economy in the world, particularly those that imported a significant percentage of the oil they consumed. Here, the cost of imported oil triggered price increases in all industries that were heavily dependent on oil. This had a snowballing effect throughout the economy.

ADDED DIMENSION   Galloping Inflation

In the twentieth century, some unfortunate countries have experienced the ravages of extreme rates of inflation that economists term *galloping* inflation or *hyperinflation*. The experience of Germany following World War I is both instructive and well documented. As a result of the Versailles Peace Treaty at the end of that war, Germany was presented, by the victorious nations, with a staggering reparations bill of 132 billion gold marks, which was an estimate of the war damage "caused" by Germany. Although the German government was allowed to pay this reparation in annual installments, the amount was far in excess of what it could reasonably raise through taxation or by borrowing. Germany, therefore, resorted to a method used by despotic kings, emperors, and corrupt governments throughout history—it simply printed more money in order to pay its bills. The result of "too much money chasing too few goods" was that prices rose by 5470 percent in 1922 alone. In 1923, things got even worse, and prices rose an astonishing 1 300 000 000 000 times! One egg cost 600 000 marks, a pound of butter cost 1.5 million marks, and a pound of meat cost 2 million marks. (If you put a dollar sign in front of these figures, you will sense the seriousness of the situation.)

Prices rose so rapidly at one point that waiters changed the amount charged for menu items throughout the meal. Workers demanded to be paid daily, and then, later, twice a day. And immediately upon being paid, people would rush to buy almost anything that was available for sale—especially nonperishable goods. Eventually, money was literally not worth the paper it was printed on. It was used by people to light the fire in stoves or by children to make building blocks. At this point, the economy collapsed, and unemployment and violence rose quickly. All of this contributed to one of the darkest chapters in human history—the rise of Hitler and the Nazi Party.

A more recent example of hyperinflation occurred in Zimbabwe where inflation, which had been growing over the past decade, peaked in November 2008 at a monthly rate of 7.96×10^{10}. This translates into a 98 percent daily rate, which means that prices were doubling every 25 hours! By June 2009, the country's government abandoned its own currency, which was replaced by the South African Rand, the British Pound. and the U.S. dollar.

If these figures are not scary enough, the world record inflation rate is held by Hungary, where prices in July 1946 rose by a staggering 41.9 quadrillion (that is 14 zeros) percent. This means that prices were increasing by 207 percent daily, or doubling every 15 hours!

This brief glimpse emphasizes that the cause of inflation can be either a demand-side or a supply-side phenomenon. We will explore this more thoroughly in a later chapter.

In summary, cost–push inflation can take three forms:

- wage-push
- profit-push
- import-push

A final note, as we complete our investigation of the "twin evils." As we shall see in Chapter 12, there is a great deal of evidence suggesting that many economies suffering from a recession with high unemployment generally have low inflation rates. Conversely, the good news for those economies suffering high inflation rates is that they seldom suffer high unemployment. The bad news is that efforts to reduce unemployment tend to push up inflation rates, and attempts to bring down inflation tend to increase unemployment. In other words, there seems to be a trade-off between the two (the famous Phillips Curve). In a way, it is a bit like a teeter-totter: as you push down on one side (unemployment), the other side (inflation) will rise.

SELF-TEST

10. a) If you borrowed a sum of money for one year at a nominal rate of interest of 11 percent, and during that same year the inflation rate was 4 percent, what real rate of interest did you pay?

b) Assume that you retire with a pension fixed at $12 000 per year, and that in each of the two years following retirement, the inflation rate is 5 percent. At the end of those two years, what will be the amount of your real income?

STUDY GUIDE

Review

CHAPTER SUMMARY

In this chapter, we first defined unemployment and discussed how economists measure unemployment and looked at both its personal and social costs. Next, we discussed the inflation and two ways of measuring it, along with its costs and causes. We will return to these topics later in the book.

4.1 Important definitions include:
- working-age population (excludes young people, those in the three territories, and people on aboriginal reserves or in institutions).
- employed (people who hold paid employment for more than one hour per week).
- unemployed (people who do not hold paid employment but are actively seeking work).
- participation rate (the percentage of the working-age population who are in the labour force).
- unemployment rate (the percentage of the labour force that is unemployed).

4.2a The three types of unemployment are:
- frictional (the movement of people between jobs).
- structural (resulting from structural changes in the economy's major industries).
- cyclical (caused by fluctuations in the economy's growth rate).

4.2b Criticisms of the official unemployment rates are that:
- part-time employees are regarded as fully employed.
- discouraged workers are excluded.
- some employment insurance recipients give false information.
- those working in the underground economy are not counted.

4.2c One way to measure the costs of unemployment is Okun's law, which relates cyclical unemployment to the GDP gap.

4.3a Inflation is measured by the percentage change in a price index from one period to the next.

4.3b There are two ways of measuring inflation:
- using the consumer price index (CPI), which tracks the value of a bundle of goods from period to period
- using the GDP deflator, which is calculated by dividing nominal GDP by real GDP and multiplying by 100

4.3c The differences between the CPI and GDP deflator are:
- the CPI is an explicit index using a constructed bundle of goods; the GDP deflator is an implicit index measuring the ratio of nominal to real GDP.
- the bundle of goods remains constant with the CPI; the bundle of goods in the GDP deflator changes each year.
- the CPI does not include capital or government goods and services; the GDP deflator includes them.
- the CPI includes imported goods; the GDP deflator excludes imported goods.

4.3d Real income is derived by dividing nominal income by the price index. The percentage change in real income can be calculated by dividing the change in real income by the original real income and multiplying by 100, or by subtracting the inflation rate from the percentage change in nominal income.

4.4a The costs of inflation are subdivided into redistributive costs and output costs. Redistributive costs include
- shifting income from the economically weak to the economically strong.
- from lenders to borrowers.

Because of increased uncertainty, output costs:
- reduce the level of investment and economic growth.
- increased menu costs (such as the cost of revising catalogues, Web sites, and so forth).
- reduce exports and increase imports.

Practise and learn online with Connect, where you can find the Answered Questions and the Unanswered Problems for all chapters of this textbook's Study Guide section.

4.4b The two causes of inflation are demand–pull and cost–push. Cost-push is subdivided into:

- wage–push
- profit–push
- import–push

NEW GLOSSARY TERMS AND KEY EQUATIONS

consumer price index (CPI)   131
cost–push inflation   141
cyclical unemployment   127
demand–pull inflation   141
discouraged worker   129
employed   123
frictional unemployment   126
full employment   127
GDP deflator   133

GDP gap   130
inflation   131
labour force   122
natural rate of unemployment   127
nominal income   135
Okun's law   130
output costs   140
participation rate   123
real income   135

real interest rate   139
redistributive costs   139
structural unemployment   126
unemployed   123
unemployment   122
unemployment rate   124
working-age population   122

Equations:

[4.1]   Labour force participation rate $= \dfrac{\text{labour force}}{\text{working-age population}} \times 100$ page 123

[4.2]   Unemployment rate $= \dfrac{\text{number of unemployed}}{\text{labour force}} \times 100$ page 124

[4.3]   GDP gap = potential GDP − actual GDP (real or nominal)   page 130

[4.4]   GDP gap = 2.5 × cyclical unemployment (%) × actual GDP (real or nominal)   page 130

[4.5]   CPI $= \dfrac{\text{cost of basket in a given year}}{\text{cost of basket in base year}} \times 100$ page 132

[4.6]   Inflation rate $= \dfrac{(\text{price index this year} - \text{price index last year})}{\text{price index last year}} \times 100$ page 132

[4.7]   GDP deflator $= \dfrac{\text{nominal GDP}}{\text{real GDP}} \times 100$ page 134

[4.8]   Real GDP $= \dfrac{\text{Nominal GDP}}{\text{GDP deflator}} \times 100$ page 134

[4.9]   Nominal GDP $= \text{real GDP} \times \dfrac{\text{GDP deflator}}{100}$ page 134

[4.10]   Real value (in Year B$) $= \dfrac{\text{Nominal Value in Year A}}{\text{Price Index in Year A}} \times \text{Price Index in Year B (or base year)}$ page 135

[4.11]   % change in real income = % change in nominal income − inflation rate   page 136

[4.12]   Number of years to double $= \dfrac{70}{\text{\% growth rate}}$ page 138

[4.13]   Nominal interest rate = Real interest rate + inflation rate   page 139

[4.14]   Real interest rate = nominal rate − the inflation rate   page 140

STUDY TIPS

1. The material covered in this chapter contains very little theory; the chapter is mostly descriptive or institutional. This does not mean that it is unimportant, but it probably does mean that you do not need to study it quite as much as some of the other chapters. If you have gained a sense of the limitations of the measurements, this is very good.

2. In a very real sense unemployment and inflation (along with economic growth) are the subjects of the entire course that we call *macroeconomics*. This chapter is meant to be an introduction to these topics and is not the final word. Therefore, you should not be concerned at this point if you are still unclear about the causes of unemployment the solutions to inflation. We still have a long way to go.

3. The concept of full employment and the definition of the natural rate of unemployment both play an important role in later chapters. Make sure that you understand that full employment does not mean zero unemployment.

4. Statistics Canada releases unemployment and inflation rates around the middle of each month. Often, the media coverage is extensive. If you start listening and looking for this coverage, you will become more attuned to the significance of what you are studying.

5. Many students tend to assume that a person who is not working is unemployed. You should recognize that many people who are not working are doing so either because they do not have to work (for example, they have accumulated enough money to live happily without a regular source of employment income) or because they choose not to work (such as a parent who chooses to stay home with young children). In short, people are unemployed only if they are actively seeking, but do not have, paid employment.

Answered Questions
These questions can also be found online on Connect.

Indicate whether the following statements are true or false:

1. **(LO 2) T or F** Frictional unemployment is likely to be greatest in sunset industries.

2. **(LO 2) T or F** The natural rate of unemployment is the unemployment rate at full employment.

3. **(LO 2) T or F** If the number of job vacancies in an economy is equal to the number of people unemployed, then cyclical unemployment is zero.

4. **(LO 1) T or F** Both male and female participation rates in Canada have been steadily rising for the past 20 years.

5. **(LO 4) T or F** The higher the rate of inflation, the lower is the redistribution effect of inflation.

6. **(LO 4) T or F** Cost–push inflation is caused by the total demand for goods and services exceeding the economy's capacity to produce those goods.

7. **(LO 3) T or F** The real interest rate is equal to the nominal interest rate plus the expected inflation rate.

8. **(LO 2) T or F** Real GDP is equal to nominal GDP divided by the GDP deflator times 100.

9. **(LO 3) T or F** If the annual inflation rate is 7 percent, then the price level will double in 10 years.

10. **(LO 1) T or F** The labour force participation rate is the percentage of the working age population that is included in the labour force.

Basic (Questions 11–21)

11. **(LO 3)** What is the real rate of interest if the nominal rate of interest is 10 percent and the rate of inflation is 4 percent?
    a) 6 percent
    b) 14 percent
    c) 10 percent
    d) 40 percent

12. **(LO 4)** Which of the following is a variation of cost–push inflation?
    a) Import–push inflation
    b) Demand–deficient inflation
    c) Galloping inflation
    d) National inflation

13. **(LO 3)** What can be said about Canada's inflation rate since 2001?
    a) It has never been below 3 percent.
    b) It has always been above 2.5 percent.
    c) It has always been below 3 percent.
    d) It was occasionally negative.

14. **(LO 2)** What type of unemployment is associated with recessions?
    a) Structural
    b) Cyclical
    c) Frictional
    d) Real

15. **(LO 4)** Which of the following does inflation affect?
    a) Both the level and the distribution of income
    b) The distribution but not the level of income
    c) The level but not the distribution of income
    d) Neither the level nor the distribution of income

16. **(LO 1, 2)** Suppose that there are 1.2 million unemployed workers, 0.6 million discouraged workers, and 12 million employed workers. What is the unemployment rate?
    a) 9.1 percent
    b) 10 percent
    c) 13 percent
    d) 15 percent

    Books wrong

17. **(LO 1)** According to the official Statistics Canada definition, what is the minimum amount of time a person must have worked in the previous week in order to be counted as employed?
    a) 5 hours
    b) 36 hours
    c) 40 hours
    d) 60 minutes

18. **(LO 3)** Which of the following statements is correct if we apply the "rule of 70" to a known rate of inflation?
    a) We would be able to calculate the corresponding rate of unemployment.
    b) We could determine when the value of a real asset will approach zero.
    c) We could calculate the number of years it will take for the price level to double.
    d) We could calculate the size of the GDP gap.

19. **(LO 3)** Which of the following statements is correct regarding the GDP deflator?
    a) It used to measure economic growth.
    b) It is calculated by dividing real GDP by nominal GDP and multiplying by 100.
    c) It is calculated by dividing real GDP by nominal GDP and dividing by 100.
    d) It is a price index that can be used to calculate the inflation rate.

20. **(LO 3)** How is real income calculated?
    a) By dividing the price level by nominal income
    b) By dividing nominal income by a price index and multiplying the result by 100
    c) By multiplying nominal income by the rate of inflation
    d) By adding the rate of inflation to the rate of increase in nominal income

21. **(LO 2)** What is the cause of cyclical unemployment?
    a) A downward fluctuation in the business cycle
    b) The declining importance of goods production and the growing importance of service production in our economy
    c) The normal dynamics of a free-market economy
    d) Technological change
    e) The changing nature of demand from one product to another

Intermediate (Questions 22–31)

22. **(LO 1)** What would be the effect on the unemployment rate if all the part-time workers were to become full-time workers?
    a) It would decrease.
    b) It would increase.
    c) It would remain unchanged.
    d) It depends on the size of the labour force.

23. **(LO 3)** All of the following, *except* one, are reasons why the CPI and GDP deflator differ. Which is the exception?
    a) The CPI is an explicit index using a constructed bundle of goods; the GDP deflator is an implicit index measuring the ratio of nominal to real GDP.
    b) The bundle of goods remains constant with the CPI; the bundle of goods in the GDP deflator changes each year.
    c) The CPI does not include capital or government goods and services; the GDP deflator includes both.
    d) The CPI excludes imported goods; the GDP deflator includes imported goods.

24. **(LO 2)** When is the Canadian economy considered to be at full employment?
    a) When 12 percent of the labour force is unemployed
    b) When 90 percent of the working-age population is employed
    c) When 90 percent of the labour force is employed
    d) When approximately 5 to 7 percent of the labour force is unemployed
    e) When everyone who wants a job has one

25. **(LO 2)** Which of the following statements concerning the natural rate of unemployment is correct?
    a) It is made up of both frictional and structural unemployment.
    b) It is the rate of unemployment at full employment.
    c) It is when the total number of job vacancies equals the number of people unemployed.
    d) It is probably about 5 to 7 percent in Canada today.
    e) All of the above.

26. **(LO 2)** What does Okun's law refer to?
    a) The relationship between job vacancies and unemployment
    b) The seemingly constant ratio between those in the labour force and the total population
    c) The relationship between the level of cyclical unemployment and the difference between potential and actual GDP
    d) The difference between an economy's real and nominal GDP
    e) The time it takes a number to double given a certain percentage growth rate

27. **(LO 4)** All of the following statements, *except* one, are correct concerning unanticipated increases in inflation. Which is the exception?
    a) It redistributes wealth and income in unpredictable ways.
    b) It increases the real value of savings.
    c) It decreases the purchasing power of money.
    d) It benefits debtors at the expense of creditors.
    e) It affects some individuals much more than others.

28. **(LO 3)** If the nominal GDP of a country is equal to $560 billion and its real GDP is $470 billion, what is the value of its GDP deflator?
    a) 1.19
    b) 83.93
    c) $2632
    d) 119.15

29. **(LO 3)** Which two pieces of information would allow us to calculate a GDP deflator?
    a) Prices and interest rates
    b) Nominal GDP and real GDP figures
    c) Unemployment rates and Okun's law
    d) Prices and the rule of 70
    e) GDP rates and the rule of 70

30. **(LO 1)** Which of the following categories would a 35-year-old, healthy male who does not work because he has inherited a large fortune most likely fall into?
    a) The labour force
    b) The working-age population
    c) Employed
    d) Unemployed

31. **(LO 1, 2)** Under what condition could the number of people employed and the number of people unemployed both increase?
    a) If the economy entered a severe recession
    b) If the number of people in the labour force increased more than the number of people employed
    c) If the total number of discouraged workers increased
    d) If the total population decreased
    e) If the number of people in the labour force grew more slowly than the increase in the number of people employed

Advanced (Questions 32–35)

32. **(LO 3)** How is real GDP calculated?
    a) By dividing nominal GDP by the GDP deflator and multiplying by 100
    b) By multiplying nominal GDP by the GDP deflator and dividing by 100
    c) By multiplying nominal GDP by the CPI and dividing by 100
    d) By dividing the GDP deflator by nominal GDP and multiplying by 100

33. **(LO 2)** What would be the effect of 100 000 unemployed people becoming discouraged workers?
    a) The unemployment rate would remain unchanged, and the size of the labour force would decline.
    b) Both the unemployment rate and the size of the labour force would decline.
    c) The unemployment rate would decline, and the size of the labour force would remain unchanged.
    d) Both the unemployment rate and the size of the labour force would rise.

34. **(LO 3)** How does Statistics Canada define a recession?
    a) A decline in real GDP during one quarter
    b) A decline in real GDP over two consecutive quarters
    c) An unemployment rate in excess of 8 percent along with a decline in GDP
    d) A decline in nominal GDP over one quarter
    e) An unemployment rate in excess of 8 percent

35. **(LO 4)** Why are economists concerned about deflation?
    a) Because it is associated with high rates of unemployment
    b) Because it could lead to very rapid and uncontrollable rates of growth
    c) Because it could drive the nominal interest rate to very high levels
    d) Because it could cause credit markets to freeze up, and, in turn, cause economic growth to stop

Parallel Problems

ANSWERED PROBLEMS

36A. **(LO 3)** **Key Problem** The data in **Table 4.11** shows the total output (a mixture of consumer, capital, and government services) and the prices of each product for the distant country of Vindaloo. (All figures are in billions of dollars, and the base year is 2010.)
    a) Complete the table, and answer the following questions (to one decimal place).
    b) What is the value of nominal GDP in
       2010: $ _____ 2011: $ _____
       2012: $ _____
    c) What is the value of real GDP in
       2010: $ _____ 2011: $ _____
       2012: $ _____

d) What is the value of the GDP deflator in
   2010: _____ 2011: _____
   2012: _____
e) What is the inflation rate (using the GDP deflator) in
   2011: _____% 2012: _____%
f) Suppose that the representative consumer in Vindaloo buys 5 units of each consumer good. What is the cost of each bundle in
   2010: $ _____ 2011: $ _____
   2012: $ _____
g) Converting the cost of each bundle into a consumer price index, what is the value of the index in each year using 2010 as the base year?
   2010: _____ 2011: _____
   2012: _____
h) What is the inflation rate using this price index?
   2011: _____% 2012: _____%

TABLE 4.11													
1	2	3	4	5	6	7	8	9	10	11	12	13	14
		2010			2011						2012		
Item	Qty	Prices Year 2010	Nomi-nal GDP	Qty	Prices Year 2011	Nomi-nal GDP	Prices Year 2010	Real GDP	Qty	Prices Year 2012	Nomi-nal GDP	Prices Year 2010	Real GDP
Pizzas	30	12		35	13				40	14			
Movie tickets	20	10		22	11				24	12			
Farm tractors	3	100		4	95				4	110			
Parking meters	4	50		4	60				5	70			
Totals													

Basic (Problems 37A–45A)

37A. **(LO 3)** The data in **Table 4.12** are for the country of Eturia. Answer the questions to one decimal place.

TABLE 4.12

	2010	2011	2012
Nominal GDP ($billions)	420	456	500
Real GDP ($billions)	400	422	447
Population (millions)	16	16.56	17.14

a) Calculate the GDP deflator for years:
2010: _____, 2011: _____, and 2012: _____
b) Calculate real GDP per capita for the three years:
2010: _____, 2011: _____, and 2012: _____.
c) Calculate the growth rate of real GDP per capita for years: 2011: _____ and 2012: _____

38A. **(LO 1)** The labour force data for Eturia (all in millions) are shown in **Table 4.13**.

TABLE 4.13

	2010	2011	2012
Population (millions)	20	21	22.05
Working-age population	12	12.5	12.8
Labour force	8.4	9	9.2
Unemployed	0.7	0.8	0.85
CPI (2002 = 100)	108.2	109	110.3

a) What are the (labour force) participation rates in each year? 2010: _____,
2011: _____, and 2012: _____
b) What are the unemployment rates in each year?
2010: _____, 2011: _____, and 2012: _____
c) What are the annual inflation rates in the years:
2011: _____ 2012: _____
d) What was the percentage increase in population in the years: 2011: _____ 2012: _____
e) If the population continues to increase at this rate, how long will it take for the population to double the number of years?

39A. **(LO 3)** The CPI in Eturia is as shown in **Table 4.14**. What are the annual inflation rates in years:
2010: _____ and 2011: _____

TABLE 4.14

	2009	2010	2011
CPI (2002 = 100)	116	121	128

40A. **(LO 3)** The population growth of Eturia is shown in **Table 4.15**.

TABLE 4.15

	2009	2010	2011
Population (millions)	16	16.56	17.14

a) What is the percentage growth in population in both 2010: _____ and 2011: _____
b) If the population continues to increase at this rate, how long will it take for the population of Eturia to double? _____

41A. **(LO 3)** The average nominal incomes earned in Eturia and the CPI are shown in **Table 4.16**.

TABLE 4.16

	2009	2010	2011
Nominal income	$28 000	$29 600	$32 000
CPI (2002 = 100)	116	121	128

a) Calculate real incomes for each year:
2009: _____, 2010: _____, and 2011: _____
b) By what percentage did real incomes rise in years:
2010: _____ and 2011: _____

42A. **(LO 3)** Interest rates in Eturia are shown in **Table 4.17**.

TABLE 4.17

	2009	2010	2011
Nominal interest rate	8%	6%	5.2%
Inflation rate	6.8%	4.3%	5.9%

Calculate the real interest rate in each year.
2009: _____, 2010: _____, and 2011: _____

43A. **(LO 3)** The data for three countries (all with the same base year, with figures converted to Canadian dollars) are shown in **Table 4.18**.

Calculate the real GDPs per capita for each country and rank them in size.

Country	Real GDP per capita
1. _____	$ _____
2. _____	$ _____
3. _____	$ _____

TABLE 4.18

	Population (in Millions)	Nominal GDP ($ Billions)	Price Index 2002 = 100
Altria	35	$ 715	140
Bergan	75	2200	120
Casper	150	2875	180

44A. **(LO 3)** What is the GDP deflator? How is it measured, and what is it used for?

45A. **(LO 2)** Distinguish between frictional and cyclical unemployment.

Intermediate (Problems 46A –51A)

46A. **(LO 1)** The information in **Table 4.19** is for the economy of Mensk.

TABLE 4.19

Working-age population	20.0
Number of people in full-time employment	11.5
Number of people in part-time employment	2.0
Number of people unemployed	1.5
Number of discouraged workers	1.5
CPI	117

a) What is the unemployment rate? _____
b) What is the participation rate? _____
c) How much inflation has occurred since the base year? _____

47A. **(LO 1, 2)** **Table 4.20** shows national data (in billions of dollars) for the economy of Westfall. Answer the questions to one decimal point.

TABLE 4.20

	2009	2010	2011
Nominal GDP	$ 850	$ 958	____
GDP deflator (1992 = 100)	109	____	118
Real GDP	____	833	____
Population (in millions)	30	____	31
Real GDP per capita	____	27 311	$28 390

a) Fill in the blanks in the table.
b) What is the inflation rate in 2010? _____
c) What is the growth rate of real GDP per capita in the year 2011? _____

48A. **(LO 3)** If the inflation rate unexpectedly rises from 2 to 5 percent, would each of the following individuals gain or lose as a result?
a) Nigel, who borrowed $20 000 last year, repayable over three years, to buy a new boat _____
b) Lars, an elderly man living on a fixed company pension _____
c) Yoko, who keeps her savings in a credit union that pays a fixed 4 percent on customers' deposits _____
d) Joan, an assembly-line worker whose employment is covered by a two-year union contract that calls for an annual wage increase of 5 percent _____
e) Robert, who owns shares in the company where Joan works _____

49A. **(LO 2)** The data in **Table 4.21** are for the economy of Merton, which has a natural rate of unemployment of 5 percent.

What is the size of the GDP gap for each of the three years? 2009: _____ 2010: _____ 2011: _____

TABLE 4.21

	2009	2010	2011
Real GDP	$600	$600	$630
Unemployment Rate	8%	6%	6%

50A. **(LO 1)** How are the participation rate and the unemployment rate measured?

51A. **(LO 4)** Give two examples of the output costs of inflation.

Advanced (Problems 52A–56A)

52A. **(LO 2)** Explain how an increase in the rate of unemployment might suggest an improvement in economic conditions.

53A. **(LO 2)** Suppose that the labour force is currently 5 million and the unemployment rate is 11 percent. On August 1, government announces that it will create 40 000 new jobs to be filled over the next three months. Only people who were unemployed on August 1 will be hired. As a result, 120 000 people immediately apply for the jobs; half of these people had previously not been actively seeking work.
   a) Has the labour force changed as a result of this announcement? Explain.
   b) What will be the unemployment rate before the jobs are filled?
   c) Once all the jobs are filled, what will the unemployment rate be?

54A. **(LO 3)** Suppose that James's income in year 1 is $36 000. Over the next four years, his income increases by 3 percent per year. At the same time, the economy experiences an inflation rate of 1.5 percent per year. At the end of four years, what will be James's real income?

55A. **(LO 2)** Suppose the actual real GDP in Merryland is $400 billion and its potential GDP is $450 billion. If the natural rate of unemployment is 6 percent, what is its present unemployment rate?

56A. **(LO 3)** The economy of Sumer produces only three products: rice, pajamas, and beer. The base year is 2009. The quantities and prices of these products in 2009 and 2010 are shown in **Table 4.22**.
   a) Calculate the nominal and real GDPs for the two years and the GDP deflator for 2010.

	2009	2010
Nominal GDP	$ _____	$ _____
Real GDP	$ _____	$ _____
GDP deflator		$ _____

   b) Supposing the average inhabitant of Sumer consumes 10 units each of beer and rice and 2 units of pajamas each year, calculate the CPI for 2010.

TABLE 4.22

	2009		2010	
	Quantities (in millions)	Price	Quantities (in millions)	Price
Rice	400 bushels	$ 5	430 bushels	$ 5.20
Pajamas	220	15	250	16
Beer	125 cases	20	130 cases	24

CHAPTER 5

AGGREGATE DEMAND AND SUPPLY

LEARNING OBJECTIVES

At the end of this chapter, you should be able to...

LO1 understand the concept of potential GDP, the business cycle, and the source of economic growth.

LO2 understand the concepts of aggregate supply, aggregate demand, and macroeconomic equilibrium.

LO3 understand what factors can affect aggregate demand and aggregate supply.

LO4 understand the causes of recessions and inflationary booms.

LO5 explain the main points of disagreement between neoclassical and Keynesian economics.

LO6 explain the modern view of aggregate demand and aggregate supply.

WHAT'S AHEAD...

This is the first of two chapters on what economists call the *product market*, the market in which consumer goods and services are bought and sold. In this chapter, we use an economic model that examines the interaction of aggregate demand and aggregate supply to determine the level of GDP, or national income, and the price level. We will use this same model in later chapters when we discuss various economic polices. The chapter concludes by looking at a fundamental question—whether a macroeconomy is capable of self-adjustment.

A Question of Relevance...

Which of the following acts do you think will improve economic conditions more, buying a new iPod nano for $300 or increasing your work productivity effort by 20 percent? Besides your obvious objection that neither action will have much impact on the whole economy, you would probably opt for the second one, since it seems to involve real production. After all, if we all became 20 percent more productive at our work, then the economy would surely be wealthier than if people simply bought more things. Surprisingly, in the short run, the two actions will have about the same effect on the economy. In the longer run, however, a sustained productivity increase will make for a healthier economy.

In the last two chapters, we looked at how economic growth, unemployment, and inflation are measured and briefly discussed some of the problems related to these issues. In this chapter, we want to be more analytical and develop a model that will help us understand the causes of these problems. As we shall see, economic growth, inflation, and unemployment are all interrelated, and in order to understand one, we need to understand all three. Our model of aggregate demand and aggregate supply will do that for us.

As we are all aware, the level of production and real GDP in Canada has risen over time. The reasons for this are not complicated. The size of the labour force grows, the amount of capital stock in the economy grows, and, most importantly, there are continuous advances in the level of technological knowledge. All of this leads to increases in productivity. However, it would be a mistake to assume that production and real GDP rise at a steady rate or even that they rise each and every year. In fact, in some years, firms find that their sales fall off and they need to cut their level of production. This leads to layoffs, rising rates of unemployment, and falling levels of income. When this happens, we say that the economy is in a recession. In other years, firms might well experience exactly the opposite set of circumstances with rising levels of sales, increased production, and additional hiring. These lead to falling rates of unemployment and rising levels of income. We can recognize, then, that there is an underlying trend that is pushing up production and income, but at the same time there are short-term fluctuations that sometimes push the economy beyond this trend (an economic boom) and sometimes below this trend (an economic recession). We shall begin developing our model by looking at this long-term upward trend.

5.1 POTENTIAL GDP

In Chapter 3, we defined economic growth as an increase in an economy's real GDP per capita. Although this is the standard definition used by most economists, Statistics Canada prefers to measure economic growth in terms of the growth in real GDP, ignoring the effects of a growing population. There is, however, an increasing number of economists who prefer to define economic growth as an increase in the economy's capacity to produce, rather than as a simple increase in actual production. The economy's capacity refers to the maximum level at which the country is able to produce, assuming that it is at full employment. In other words, it is the amount of GDP that would be produced if all of its labour and all other resources were fully employed (at normal levels of utilization). This is what is meant by **potential GDP**. It could also be called *full-employment GDP* or *economic capacity*. (Some economists refer to it as the *long-run aggregate supply*, or LAS. However, we prefer to use the term "potential GDP" because we believe that economies do not always reach their potential, though there may be forces at work which move them in that direction. The use of the term "long-run supply" implies, on the other hand, that this is what will happen to economies in the long run, and this is definitely not always the case.) In this sense, potential GDP can be looked at as the amount of GDP when the economy is at its natural rate of unemployment, that is, when there is no cyclical unemployment.

In emphasizing potential rather than actual GDP, economists are making the point that without increases in potential GDP, the prospects for sustained growth in the future are limited. There is an important difference, then, between actual growth in the present and sustainable growth in the future. This distinction can be illustrated using the production possibilities diagram in **Figure 5.1A**, where the production possibilities curve, PP1, shows the maximum quantities of capital and consumer goods that this economy is presently capable of producing.

You will recall that the curve itself does not show what the economy is actually producing or what it would like to produce (there is no indication of demand), it merely shows what it is capable of producing, that is, its potential levels of production. Let us assume that initially this economy is producing at point A in **Figure 5.1A**, and since this is inside the curve, it is producing less than it is capable of. In the following year, let us suppose that the economy increases its output of both capital and consumer goods, as depicted in the movement to point B. The economy has experienced economic growth and is now close to its potential output. Since an

L01 Understand the concept of potential GDP, the business cycle, and the sources of economic growth.

potential GDP: the total amount that an economy is capable of producing when all of its resources are being fully utilized.

| **FIGURE 5.1** | **Economic Growth and Production Possiblilities** |

Figure A shows the economy growing from point A to point B. But this growth may not be sustained, since its potential level (the PP curve) has not changed. Figure B shows similar economic growth from point A to point B. But in this case, the growth is more likely to be sustained, since its potential has similarly increased (from PP1 to PP2).

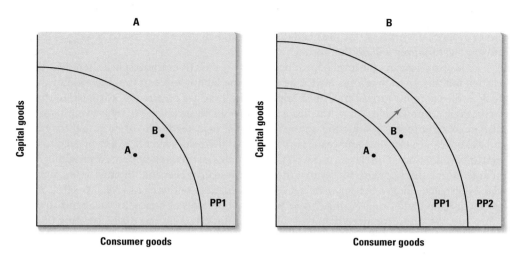

economy cannot (permanently) go beyond its production possibilities boundary, the amount by which it can increase production past point B is limited.

Now, contrast this to the situation in **Figure 5.1B**. Here, point A is the same starting point shown in **Figure 5.1A**, and the movement to point B is also the same. However, we also see that the production possibilities curve has shifted from PP1 to PP2, which indicates an increase in the economy's potential GDP. Obviously, the prospects for future growth in this case are much brighter. Economists would be more impressed by the growth depicted in **Figure 5.1B**, since not only is the economy producing more, it is also capable of sustaining this level of production in the future.

The ideas we have just presented can easily be shown in terms of a demand–supply diagram. On the vertical axis of **Figure 5.2**, we show the price level for the economy in terms of a GDP deflator. The horizontal axis shows the total output of all finished goods and services in the economy, in other words, its real GDP. The figures shown here are the approximate numbers for the Canadian economy in 2006.

| **FIGURE 5.2** | **Potential GDP** |

Potential GDP is a straight vertical line showing the amount of GDP at full employment. In 2006, it equalled $1360 billion.

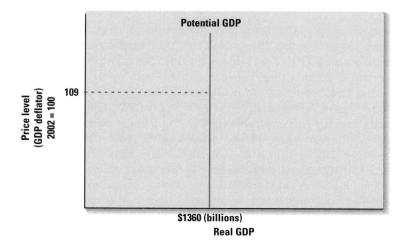

To calculate potential GDP is reasonably straightforward, making use of Okun's law, which we looked at in Chapter 4. The unemployment rate in Canada in 2006 was 6 percent, and the real GDP was $1327 billion. If we assume that the natural rate of unemployment is 5 percent, then its GDP gap is 1 percent (cyclical unemployment) × 2.5 × $1327, which comes to $33 billion. Potential GDP, therefore, was $1327 + $33, or $1360. This figure is not affected by the price level. The vertical nature of the potential GDP curve illustrates the fact that while a higher price level would raise *nominal* GDP, it would leave potential *real* GDP unaffected. Put another way, what an economy is physically capable of producing is not affected by the prices those goods and services happen to be sold at. Think of it like this: an economy has a certain size of labour force, a certain quantity of raw materials, and a certain amount of capital goods. If it were to perform at maximum efficiency using its best technology, then the potential GDP tells us the maximum output that could be produced *regardless of the price level*. In fact, as far as its potential GDP is concerned, the price level is irrelevant. Bear in mind also that potential GDP is merely a benchmark—albeit an important one—and does not tell us what the economy is actually producing or even what policy makers might want it to produce. We will look at actual production a little later.

SELF-TEST

1. Suppose the unemployment rate in Concordia is 8 percent and real GDP equals $600 billion. If the natural rate of unemployment is 5 percent, what is the amount of the GDP gap, and what is the value of potential GDP?

Next, we want to address the question of what makes an economy grow. What will cause an increase in an economy's potential real GDP? Graphically, this is a rightward shift in potential GDP and is, in many ways, analogous to asking, *"What factors will enhance (shift out) a country's production possibilities?"*

Sources of Economic Growth

We saw in Chapter 3 that the most important factor affecting a country's long-term economic growth is the level of its labour productivity. We also saw that this productivity itself depends upon a number of important determinants. Let us review them briefly. First and foremost, the quality of a country's human capital has a major impact on productivity and economic growth. By human capital we mean the accumulated knowledge, skills, and education of the labour force. But beyond this, it also depends on the imagination and ingenuity of its people as well as their motivation and the incentives that the country provides for them. Needless to say, the labour force participation rate also determines the amount of people who are actively engaged in production.

The second major factor that can improve labour productivity is the amount of physical capital that a country possesses. The quality of that capital is also of major importance. Is the country's physical plant and equipment modern and well-maintained, or is the country handicapped by having capital that is worn out and out of date?

The third productivity factor is the extent to which a country embraces and encourages technological change. One of the major indicators of the extent to which a country is willing to adopt new technology is the amount of its resources that it devotes to research and development. It comes as no surprise to learn that countries such as the United States, Germany, Japan, Canada, and, more recently, China, are at the forefront in terms of both research and development (R&D) and labour productivity.

Finally, the presence and accessibility of natural resources can help a long way in raising a country's growth rate. In fact, for many countries—Brazil immediately comes to mind—it may well be the most important factor.

ADDED DIMENSION   Economic Capacity

To economists, the idea of capacity can only be understood with reference to costs. Capacity does not literally mean the absolute maximum that can be produced in the short run. Firms can and do produce at full physical capacity from time to time, but it is a very expensive proposition in terms of overtime pay, high maintenance costs, and so on. Such high costs could not be sustained in the long run. Capacity, then, means the output level at which the firm can produce at the lowest per-unit cost, and this level may well be only 70, 80, or 90 percent of the physical capacity of the plant.

In summary, the sources of economic growth for an economy are:

- the quantity and quality of its labour resources (the level of human capital).
- the amount of physical capital available.
- the rate of technological change.
- the amount and quality of its natural resources.

The result of a change in any one of the factors just discussed would increase the economy's potential to produce. In **Figure 5.3**, potential GDP has increased by 3 percent each year from $1360 billion in year 1 to $1400 billion in year 2 to $1443 billion in year 3. This is illustrated by a rightward shift in the potential GDP line.

FIGURE 5.3   **Economic Growth and Potential GDP**

A positive change in any of the determinants of economic growth will result in a rightward shift of the potential GDP curve.

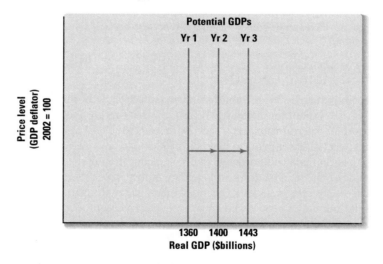

Economic Growth and the Business Cycle

Although Statistics Canada does not publish estimates of potential GDP on a regular basis, evidence suggests that it tends to increase by small, regular amounts each year. Research indicates that for Canada, potential GDP has grown, on average, by about 3 percent per year since the beginning of the 1990s.

TABLE 5.1	Canada's Rate of Growth in Real GDP
Year	**% Growth Rate of Real GDP**
1995	2.8
1996	1.7
1997	4.0
1998	3.1
1999	4.2
2000	4.5
2001	1.9
2002	2.0
2003	2.0
2004	3.0
2005	3.0
2006	2.7
2007	2.0
2008	−0.3
2009	−1.9
2010	2.9

Source: Adapted from Statistics Canada, CANSIM Database <http://cansim2.statcan.ca>, Table 380-0017, 3 February 2011.

However, actual economic growth is seldom so smooth and steady. **Table 5.1** shows the annual growth in actual real GDP for Canada for 1995 to 2010.

The average annual rate of growth for the period is 2.5 percent. As you can see from the data, however, the actual growth rate was nowhere near a steady 2.5 percent each year. This is true for most periods and most economies. In any period such as this, some years will have high growth rates, say, 4 or 5 percent, while other years will have rates below average or even negative rates. While the *average* long-run growth rate is positive for most economies, the year-to-year fluctuations can be quite unstable. In short, all economies experience **business cycles**—expansionary and contractionary phases in the rate at which real GDP changes. **Figure 5.4** illustrates this point using Canadian data. On the horizontal axis, we have time, starting with 1995, while on the vertical axis we have the growth rate (in real GDP).

business cycle: the expansionary and contractionary phases in the growth rate of real GDP.

You can see that the growth rate generally rose between 1996 and 2000, an expansionary phase, and then experienced a contractionary phase leading to a trough in 2001. After a minor peak and trough, the economy then entered another contractionary phase, leading to a major trough in 2009, before recovering in 2010. These expansionary and contractionary phases in the growth of real GDP form the business cycle—what goes up comes down, and vice versa.

In order to better understand the business cycle and explain why there are periodic fluctuations in the economy—in all economies, not just the Canadian economy—we need to look at the forces of supply and demand that lie behind them.

FIGURE 5.4   The Business Cycle

The rate of growth in real GDP reflects two major contractionary phases (in red) and two expansionary phases (in blue). The average annual growth rate for the period is 2.6 percent.

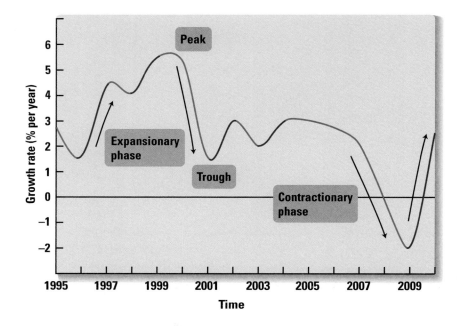

▶ ADDED DIMENSION   Robinson Crusoe and Economic Growth

Let us assume that Robinson Crusoe, the celebrated fictional castaway, is troubled by the prospects of making it on his own for an indefinite period on his new-found, uninhabited island. He obviously needs to catch a lot of fish to do more than just survive. He has a crude fishing pole and has been catching the odd fish recently, but he wonders if there is a better way to catch more and thus improve his standard of living. Perhaps there is another location on the island, where the fish are more plentiful, bigger, and easier to catch. But spending time looking for another place would leave less time for his current fishing efforts. Alternatively, he could stay where he is and hope that his fishing skills improve with experience and persistence (he curses the day he chose a course in Chinese cooking rather than a fishing class at night school). Finally, there is the possibility of fashioning a crude net or even building a boat, but again, either of these activities would take time away from actual

fishing. He has three choices in trying to improve his economic well-being.

- increase the resources available to him (find a better fishing spot)
- improve the level of his human capital (become a better fisher through experience)
- increase his physical capital (a net or a boat rather than just a pole)

Each of these choices requires that he sacrifice time plus the fish that would be caught during this time (consumption) but promises a richer harvest of fish in the future. In effect, every economy faces the same choices and sacrifices because economic growth involves more effort, less leisure, and less present consumption. The rewards, however, can be great and continue to pay off long into the future.

5.2 AGGREGATE SUPPLY AND DEMAND

In this section, we will construct our first simple model of the economy using the tools of aggregate supply and demand. Some of you will recognize that the basic principles behind their construction is not greatly different from supply, demand, and equilibrium in microeconomics. Let us begin with a look at the idea behind aggregate supply.

L02 Understand the concepts of aggregate supply, aggregate demand, and macroeconomic equilibrium.

Aggregate Supply

Aggregate supply refers to the total quantity of goods and services that firms in the economy would be willing and able to produce at various prices, assuming that the prices of factors of production remain constant. Essentially, this means that in the short term, wages and the prices of raw materials and of other resources are assumed to remain unchanged. This is not an unrealistic assumption. While most firms have little control over the market demand for their products, they can and do try to exercise as much control over their own supply as they can, and this certainly includes their own costs, both present and future costs. They can address future costs by entering into contracts with their suppliers and with their employees (or their unions) to achieve some certainty of future resource prices and wage rates. Because of these contracts, a firm is able to increase production (and therefore demand and employ more factor services) without experiencing an increase in the costs of those resources.

aggregate supply: the total quantity of goods and services that sellers would be willing and able to produce at various price levels.

This implies that if demand increases and firms can sell their products at a higher price, they will be only too willing to produce more (and employ more resources) because when resource costs remain constant (at least for a while), their total profits will rise. On the other hand, lower prices represent lower profits and will cause the firm to reduce production (and employment). In other words:

> The higher the price levels, the greater will be the aggregate quantity supplied; the lower the price level, the smaller will be the aggregate quantity supplied.

The aggregate supply curve therefore is upward-sloping. However, it is unlikely to be a straight line. The reason for this, as we shall discuss in detail later in the chapter, is that as production increases in the economy, productivity is likely to fall as firms are forced to use less suitable and less efficient resources. This will cause the unit cost of production to rise (even though the prices of resources remain the same) so that firms will only produce more at a higher price.

Figure 5.5 illustrates this idea: an increase in the price level from P_1 to P_2 will increase real GDP from Y_1 to Y_2.

Another, and more instructive, way of explaining the slope of the AS curve is in terms of the **real wage**. As we said at the outset, the AS curve is drawn on the (realistic) assumption that in the short run, factor prices—including wage rates—remain constant. Now, let us look at things from an employee's point of view. Given that her wages are constant, it is clear that if the price level in the economy were to rise, she will be worse off as she will not be able to afford to buy the same quantity of products as before. Put another way, her real wage will decline. The real wage then refers to the amount of goods and services that a worker can obtain for a given amount of **nominal wage**.

real wage: the amount of goods and services that an employee can buy for a given amount of nominal wage.

$$\text{Real wage} = \frac{\text{Nominal wage}}{\text{Price level}} \qquad [5.1]$$

nominal wage: the present day value of a current wage.

We can see from this equation that a person's real wage will decline if *either* her nominal wage were to fall *or* if the price level were to increase. The result of this—looking at things graphically—is that as we move up the AS curve, the real wage level prevailing in the economy declines.

FIGURE 5.5   **The Shape of the AS Curve**

An increase in the price level from P_1 to P_2 will increase the profits of firms and will lead to an increase in GDP from Y_1 to Y_2.

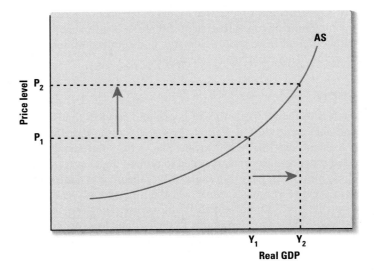

Now, let us look at things from the employer's point of view. Since it is the employer that is paying these wages, a higher price level—with wages remaining constant—means that real wage costs are declining. (From the employer's point of view it does not matter whether the lower real wage is the result of a higher price level or a lower nominal wage rate. In either case, the employer would benefit from a drop in the real wage because a lower real wage means higher profits per unit produced and will cause her to increase production.)

To recap: a higher price level, with wages remaining constant, will increase profit for the average firm and will cause a higher level of output. Conversely, a lower price level implies lower profit and a lower level of output.

✓ SELF-TEST

2. Using the accompanying graph, calculate the growth rate of real GDP for a price increase of 10 percent:

a) if the price level is currently 80

b) if the price level is currently 100

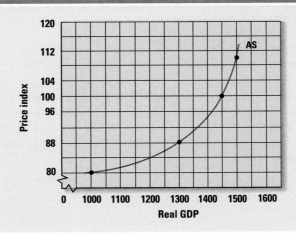

Aggregate Demand

Let us now turn our focus to **aggregate demand**, which is the total quantity of goods and services that people are willing to buy at different price levels. Its components are already familiar to you: consumption expenditures, investment spending, government purchases of goods and services, and net exports.

aggregate demand: the total quantity of goods and services that consumers, businesses, government, and those living outside the country would buy at various price levels.

Figure 5.6 shows an aggregate demand curve illustrating the output of goods and services that people will buy at various price levels. We have labelled the horizontal axis Real GDP and indicated the particular level at different prices as Y_1, Y_2, and so on. This reflects the fact that the value of production (real GDP) and the level of real income are always equal, as you learned in Chapter 3. The vertical axis is labelled Price Level, and you can think of this as the value of the GDP deflator—the weighted composite of prices for all goods and services. At price level P_1, real GDP is Y_1. At a lower price level, P_2, real GDP is higher, as seen in Y_2. Similarly, at price level P_3, real GDP is Y_3.

Now, we need to understand why aggregate spending is lower when the price level is higher, that is, why the AD curve is downward sloping. To most people, whether or not they have studied economics, one possible explanation seems fairly straightforward: if the price level goes up, people will simply buy less. But we need to be very careful here, since microeconomics suggests that one of the reasons for this is that people would substitute other products for the now more expensive ones. However, here we are looking at the average price level of all goods and services, and there are no substitutes for all goods—at least when we speak of domestically supplied goods.

The other possible reason for the downward slope (as we remember from microeconomics) is that with higher prices, people simply cannot afford as much. However, this explanation is equally invalid; while higher prices mean that buyers cannot afford as much, it also means that the incomes of sellers must also be rising, since they are receiving the benefit of the higher prices.

Our focus needs to be on the level of real GDP. If the price level were to go up, then the measured value of nominal expenditures and nominal GDP would increase proportionately, while the values of both real GDP and real consumption would remain unchanged. Therefore, what we need to work out is the effect on spending if both the price level and nominal incomes rise by the same proportion so that real income remains the same. You might suggest that under these circumstances expenditures may well remain unchanged. However, one portion of wealth that is affected by a price change is the real value of savings, which will decline as the price level rises.

| FIGURE 5.6 | The Aggregate Demand Curve |

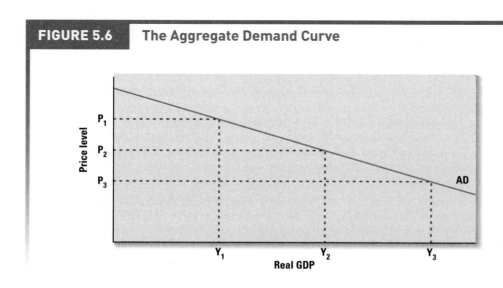

As the price level drops from P_1 to P_2 and to P_3, the quantity of goods and services that buyers are willing and able to purchase increases from Y_1 to Y_2 and to Y_3.

For instance, suppose that you have managed to save $10 000 (whether it is in a box under your bed or deposited in a savings account at a bank does not matter). The question is: what will happen to the value of those savings over the next year if the economy experiences an inflation of 10 percent? With the average price of products rising, your money will certainly not go so far if you decide to use it to make a purchase. Although the nominal value remains $10 000 (or a little higher if you earned interest at the bank), its real value has dropped by 10 percent. You are definitely worse off as a result of the inflation; in fact, your real wealth has declined as a result.

real-balances effect: the effect that a change in the value of real balances has on consumption spending.

This is what is referred to as the **real-balances effect**. Lower real wealth will cause people to cut down on spending. So, a higher price level leads to lower real wealth, lower consumption, and lower aggregate expenditures and will produce a lower level of real GDP. In **Figure 5.6**, therefore, a higher price level, such as P_1, will lead to a lower real GDP, Y_1. A lower price level will produce the opposite results: it will cause the value of real balances and consumption spending to increase, as we can see in the combination of P_3 and Y_3.

We have now established that the aggregate demand curve is downward sloping because consumption expenditures are inversely related to the price level. There are two additional explanations for the downward-sloping aggregate demand curve. First, a higher price level tends to push up interest rates, which, in turn, causes a reduction in investment spending and therefore aggregate expenditures. This is known as the **interest-rate effect**. In addition, higher Canadian prices make our exports less attractive while making imports more appealing to Canadians. This is called the **foreign-trade effect**. We will examine both these effects in detail in later chapters. So, in addition to lower levels of consumption, higher prices cause a drop in investment spending and in net exports. Lower prices will, of course, have the opposite effect.

interest-rate effect: the effect that a change in prices, and therefore interest rates, has upon investment; for example, higher prices cause higher interest rates, which leads to lower investment.

In summary, the aggregate demand curve is downward sloping due to the:

foreign-trade effect: the effect that a change in prices has upon exports and imports.

- real-balances effect.
- interest-rate effect.
- foreign-trade effect.

 SELF-TEST

3. Explain how a drop in the price level could affect consumption, investment, and net exports.

Macroeconomic Equilibrium

macroeconomic equilibrium: a situation in which aggregate demand equals aggregate supply.

Macroeconomic equilibrium exists when the quantity of aggregate demand equals the quantity of aggregate supply. Only at one price level will the total that people want to buy equal the total that is produced. This is illustrated in **Figure 5.7A**, where P_e and Y_e are the equilibrium values for the price level and real GDP.

Only at price level P_e are the quantity demanded and quantity supplied equal. It is possible that the price level, temporarily, may not be at equilibrium, but if this is the case, it is an unstable situation. This is illustrated in **Figure 5.7B**, where the price level is above equilibrium at P_2. At this higher price level, there is a surplus of goods and services because the quantity supplied exceeds the quantity demanded. To rid themselves of such surpluses, firms will be forced to cut prices and will continue to do so until the price level is back to equilibrium. In contrast, a lower price level of P_3, as seen in **Figure 5.7C**, would result in a shortage of goods and services, and prices would be pushed up until the economy is back at equilibrium, with neither surpluses nor shortages.

It is important to point out that there is no guarantee that equilibrium also means that the economy is operating at its potential (capacity) full-employment level of GDP. In fact, equilibrium could exist at any level of real GDP, as **Figures 5.8A**, **B**, and **C** illustrate.

FIGURE 5.7	Macroeconomic Equilibrium

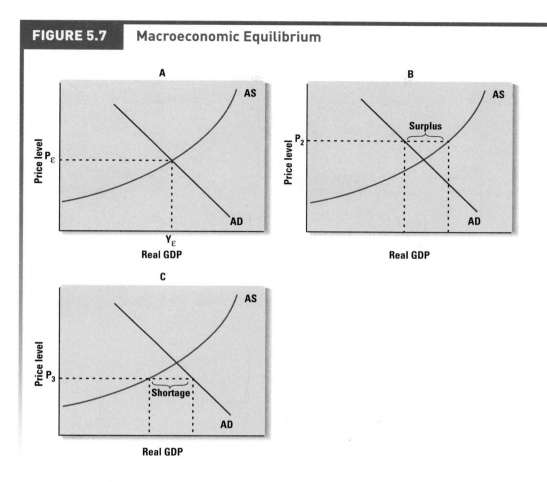

Equilibrium exists where the aggregate demand and the aggregate supply curves intersect. This determines the equilibrium price level P_ε and the equilibrium real GDP level Y_ε, as seen in Figure A. In Figure B, P_2 is a price level above equilibrium, and there is a surplus of goods and services. In this circumstance, firms will be forced to cut prices. At prices below equilibrium, as seen by P_3 in Figure C, there is a shortage, which will force the price level up.

These figures show three possible positions for an economy. In **Figure 5.8A**, the economy is in equilibrium because the quantity of aggregate demand is equal to the quantity of aggregate supply. In addition, this economy is also at potential GDP. In **Figure 5.8B**, the economy is suffering a **recession** because, while it is also in equilibrium (the AD curve intersects the AS curve at the level of real GDP, Y_ε), this equilibrium is below potential GDP, Y_{FE}. The difference between equilibrium GDP and potential full-employment GDP when the economy is in a recession is known as a **recessionary gap**. A recessionary gap implies that some of the factors of production are unemployed. In most people's minds, recession and unemployment therefore are synonymous. It was, of course, John Maynard Keynes who thought this was the situation in which many economies found themselves in the 1930s. During the whole decade, the economies of North America were in a sense caught in a low-level trap. Unemployment was high and production was low, but there was no incentive for firms to produce more because they were barely selling what they produced. Despite this recessionary gap, the economy was stable because there was neither a tendency nor an incentive to change.

Figure 5.8C shows the opposite situation. Here, again, the economy is in equilibrium at a real GDP level of Y_ε, but the equilibrium occurs above the full-employment potential GDP, Y_{FE}. In this situation, unemployment is below its natural rate, which means that labour is scarce relative to the demand for it. This is the situation of an **inflationary gap**. People are trying to buy more goods and services than the economy can produce on a sustainable basis. The level of aggregate demand, indicated by Y_ε, exceeds the level of sustainable potential output. The result is a situation that could be termed "too much spending chasing too few goods" but is often erroneously described as "too much

recession: a period when the economy is producing below its potential and has had two consecutive quarters of negative growth.

recessionary gap: the difference between actual real GDP and potential real GDP when the economy is producing below its potential.

inflationary gap: the difference between actual real GDP and potential real GDP when the economy is temporarily producing an output above full employment.

FIGURE 5.8   **Equilibrium and Full Employment**

Figure A shows an economy in equilibrium, and this equilibrium is also at full employment. In other words, the AD and AS curves intersect at potential GDP. Figure B shows equilibrium occurring below full employment, that is, there is a recessionary gap. In Figure C, equilibrium occurs above full employment, that is, there is an inflationary gap.

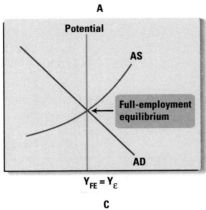

A

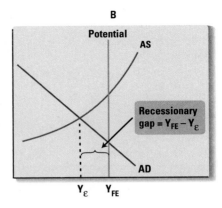

B

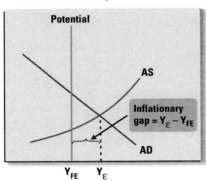

C

ADDED DIMENSION   Can an Economy Produce More Than It Is Capable of?

On the surface, this seems to be a ludicrous question! And yet our diagram suggests that an economy may be capable of producing in excess of its potential, thus creating an inflationary gap. How could this be so? Well, the answer lies in how we define the terms "capacity" and "full-employment." To an economist, capacity output (for a firm or an economy) does not mean the absolute maximum it is capable of producing. Rather, it implies the maximum production that can be sustained *in the long run* (alternatively, the output that produces the lowest average cost of production). Very few firms will want to produce at their maximum with the plant and all its available equipment working flat-out 24/7. It usually prefers to have some spare capacity to prevent "burn out." For most manufacturing firms in Canada, this is usually at around 75–80 percent of maximum capacity.

In a similar vein, full employment does not mean that employees are working every hour of every day. Instead, the idea of full employment is socially defined. In the nineteenth century, this could well have meant over 70 hours per week. Slowly over the past century, the number of weekly hours that constitute full employment has been reduced so that for most people, it is probably around 34 to 38 hours a week.

In all likelihood, a firm and its employees could, and often do, work in excess of full employment and capacity output, so suggesting that an economy could be above its potential GDP is not so far fetched. However, such a situation is not sustainable for the economy in the long run, since it tends to be very costly and therefore inflationary.

money chasing too few goods." We, however, know that money is a stock and spending is a flow, and we must be careful how we state things. Certainly, in such a situation, prices and wages will start to increase, but it may not have anything to do with the amount of money in the economy.

What is certainly true is that the amount of spending is in excess of the economy's present ability to produce goods. Such a situation is going to result in buyers bidding up prices in an effort to secure what they want and firms being forced to pay higher wages to attract labour, which is in high demand. Such price increases are, of course, inflationary, and the gap between Y_ϵ and Y_{FE} is the inflationary gap. This situation is not stable, since the economy simply cannot continue to produce a level of real GDP above its full-employment level on a sustained basis. In summary, equilibrium in the macroeconomy might:

- occur at full employment.
- result in a recessionary gap.
- result in an inflationary gap.

What we need to do now is look at how these various situations come about and what will happen as a result. In other words, we need to look at the dynamics of the model.

 SELF-TEST

4. Following are the aggregate demand and supply schedules for the economy of Tagara.

Price Index	Aggregate Quantity Demanded	Aggregate Quantity Supplied
90	$1200	$ 950
95	1150	1025
100	1100	1100
105	1050	1150
110	1000	1190
115	950	1220

a) What is the equilibrium level of prices and real GDP?

b) If the price level were 95, would there be a shortage or surplus? How much? What if the price level was 115?

5. Given the following graph and assuming that the economy is in equilibrium, calculate the inflationary or recessionary gap if:

a) potential GDP is $600.

b) potential GDP is $800.

c) potential GDP is $900.

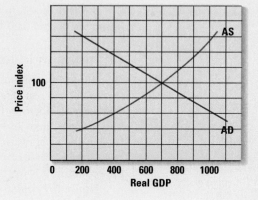

5.3 DETERMINANTS OF AGGREGATE DEMAND AND SUPPLY

The main thrust of our analysis in this chapter is to discover what brings about change in an economy's price level and its real GDP. These two important concepts are known as determinant variables; in other words, they are the result of other things changing. Their values depend on other things; they represent the effect, not the cause, of change. So, what can bring about change to the price level and real GDP? The answer is, anything that affects aggregate demand or aggregate supply. Let us look at aggregate demand first.

LO3 Understand what factors can affect aggregate demand and aggregate supply.

Determinants of Aggregate Demand

There are a number of factors that will cause aggregate demand to change and therefore cause the aggregate demand curve to shift. Remember that aggregate demand is simply the amount of total expenditure at various price levels. You will recall from Chapter 3 that the components of aggregate expenditures are consumption, investment, government spending on goods and services, and net exports. Anything that changes any one of these components will also change aggregate demand. We need to be very clear about the fact that we are talking about the aggregate demand curve *shifting*, and so we need to isolate the factors *other than a change in the levels of prices or real GDP* that change aggregate demand. In other words, if either the price level or real GDP changes, it will cause a movement along the aggregate demand curve, not a shift in it.

Changes in Consumption

Let us start with consumption spending. How might you react if the shares that you had bought a couple of months ago suddenly doubled in value? Would you go out and buy yourself something special? If so, your consumption level will go up despite the fact that your income and the price level have not changed. We have just isolated the first factor that can change consumption: *changes in wealth*. An increase in the nation's wealth therefore will cause an increase in aggregate demand, reflected in a rightward shift of the AD curve. It is interesting to note that the stock market can have a significant impact on the wealth of a big segment of the population. A sudden and serious drop in stock prices can have a significant effect on the real wealth of investors, and as a result, might cause them to curtail some of their planned consumer spending.

The second factor is the age of consumer durables. For most of us, when the car gets older and begins to wear out, we somehow find the means to either spend more on car repairs or maybe even buy a new car. This means that the greater the *age of consumer durables* in the economy, the more likely it is that they will be replaced, causing an increase in consumer spending.

A third factor involves consumer expectations. As confidence in the economy's future improves, people tend to loosen the purse strings and increase their consumption.

Changes in Investment

Turning to investment spending, a primary determinant of a change in investment spending is the rate of interest. The reason for this is straightforward—most major investment projects are funded with borrowed money, and if the cost of borrowing falls because of a decrease in the interest rate then investment spending will increase. Once again, note that this is true even though the level of national income or the price level has not changed. Since most economists regard the interest rate as a crucial factor in determining the amount of investment spending in the economy, it is worth our while to explicitly spell out the relationship.

Figure 5.9 depicts an investment demand curve. It is downward sloping because if interest rates are high, say, at r_1, then firms will not be inclined to spend very much on new capital goods because they will have to pay high interest costs to borrow funds to finance such spending. So, the level of investment spending will be a low I_1. On the other hand, if the interest rate was very low, say, r_2, then it would be very cheap to borrow and therefore firms will tend to invest more at I_2.

But what if firms do not need to borrow money in order to invest because they have sufficient funds themselves? Would the interest rate be irrelevant for such firms? No—it is still very relevant. For instance, suppose that a firm has an "idle" million dollars and is contemplating using these funds to purchase a new piece of equipment. However, these "idle" funds are unlikely to be that idle! In all likelihood, the firm has these funds deposited in a bank or other financial institution and is earning interest on them. The question for this firm then becomes: should we continue to *save* our money and earn X percent in the bank, or should we *invest* that money in our firm by buying the new equipment and thus earn for ourselves Y percent? You can see that

FIGURE 5.9 Investment Demand Curve

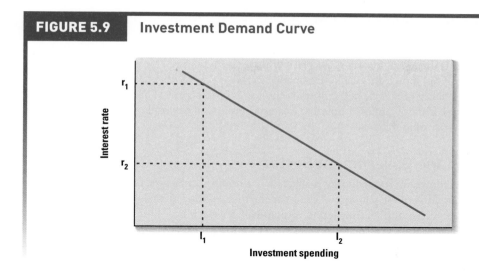

At a high rate of interest, r_1, investment spending will be small at I_1 because it will be costly to borrow. At a low interest rate of r_1, investment spending will be higher at I_1 because it will be cheap to borrow.

the lower the interest rate the firm is presently earning, the more it will be inclined to invest. Conversely, the higher the interest it is earning, the less likely will it be to invest.

To recap:

> A high interest rate will lead to low investment spending; a low interest rate will lead to high investment spending.

The second determinant of investment spending is the *purchase price and the installation, operating, and maintenance costs of the capital asset.* These might well be determining factors for a firm trying to decide whether or not to go ahead with a particular investment. If there is a sudden decrease in the purchase price of a new piece of equipment, many firms will be encouraged to go out and buy, thus increasing the amount of investment spending. This is especially true if their present equipment is fairly old or has been in constant use. Thus, the third determinant of investment is the age and *amount of spare capacity of the present capital stock.* A firm with new machinery that often sits idle is unlikely to embark on any new investment any time soon. Additionally, a firm may well be encouraged to invest if the future of the industry or the economy as whole looks bright, and will be disinclined if the future looks gloomy. Since investment spending can be postponed—unlike much of consumer spending—*business expectations* have an important role to play in determining the level of investment. Finally, *government policies and regulations*, which sometimes increase "red tape," can add considerably to the cost of doing business and might affect the potential profitability of investing.

An increase in investment as a result of a change in any of these factors will cause an increase in aggregate demand, reflecting a higher level of spending whatever the price level.

Changes in Net Exports

Three factors combine to determine the level of Canadian net exports. First is the *value of the exchange rate.* A lower Canadian dollar means that Canadian goods, in the eyes of foreigners, are cheaper and may result in more Canadian goods being sold abroad. In addition, a lower Canadian dollar will mean that Canadians will buy fewer imports because they are now more expensive. Higher exports and lower imports mean an increase in net exports and an increase in aggregate demand. Similarly, an *increase in the level of incomes abroad* will have the same positive effect on Canadian exports. If Americans are enjoying higher levels of income, they will spend more on consumption, including buying more Canadian goods. Third is the *price level of competitive (foreign) goods*. If the Brazilians raise the price of their short-range jet aircraft, then Bombardier Corporation will sell more of its Canadian-made aircraft.

The fourth determinant of net exports is the *tastes of foreigners*. For instance, if softwood lumber becomes a more popular building material around the world, then the demand for Canadian exports would increase.

Changes in the Government Sector

The role of government in the economy is affected by a number of factors, ranging from the social and cultural standards of the people and their expectations to the political philosophy of the governing party and the amount of time left in its mandate. Its specific role in directing the economy will be reflected in changes in government's revenue (through taxation), in its spending, or both. As we shall see when we look at fiscal policy in Chapter 7, these changes are designed to have an impact on the amount of spending in the economy. Aggregate demand will increase as a result of a decrease in taxes (whether it is a decrease in sales taxes, income taxes, or corporate profit taxes) or an increase in spending by government (whether on government-provided services, such as health or education, or on transfer payments, such as pensions or welfare). In addition, as Chapter 9 will explore in detail, a change in the money supply can also affect aggregate demand. This is because an increase in the supply of money, for instance, tends to push interest rates down, and, as we mentioned earlier, this will increase investment spending. This happens because lower interest rates imply a lower cost of borrowing, and this will encourage firms to borrow and invest those funds in their own operations. A decrease in the money supply, on the other hand, will reduce aggregate demand because it causes interest rates to increase and investment to fall.

If any of the determinants of aggregate demand were to change, it would mean that at any given price level buyers would be willing to buy more or less goods and services than before. This is illustrated in **Figure 5.10**.

In summary, the determinants of aggregate demand are as follows:

Consumption
- individual consumer wealth
- age of consumer durables
- consumer expectations

FIGURE 5.10   Shifts in the Aggregate Demand Curve

An increase in aggregate demand shifts the AD curve to the right, from AD_1 to AD_2. This means that at every price level, the quantity of goods and services demanded has increased. In contrast, a decrease in aggregate demand will shift the AD curve to the left, in this case from AD_1 to AD_3.

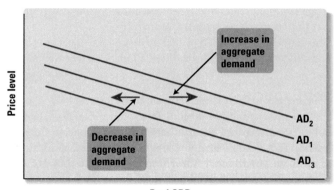

Investment

- interest rates
- purchase price, installation, and maintenance costs of capital goods
- age of capital goods and amount of spare capacity
- business expectations
- government regulations

Net Exports

- value of exchange rate
- income levels abroad
- price of competitive (foreign) goods
- tastes of foreigners

Government Spending and Tax Rates

Money Supply

 SELF-TEST

6. Which of the following factors will lead to an increase or decrease in aggregate demand (and a shift in the AD curve)?

a) A decrease in the stock market index

b) An increase in interest rates

c) A decrease in government spending

d) An increase in foreign incomes

e) A decrease in the exchange rate

Determinants of Aggregate Supply

We now need to work out the circumstances that would lead to an increase in aggregate supply. What factors, for instance, could lead firms to be willing and able to produce more than at present, *even though the price level remains the same*? Now, since firms are in business to make profits, it is clear that they will produce more at the same price only if their costs of production fall, and this will happen only if productivity increases or factor prices fall. Let us look at productivity increases first.

At the beginning of the chapter, we investigated those factors that would result in economic growth and enhance a country's potential GDP. Since each of these factors tends to increase an economy's productivity, each will, in turn, improve the profitability of its producers. Thus, an increase in aggregate supply will result from:

- an improvement in human capital.
- an increase in the amount of capital.
- technological improvement.
- an increase in natural resources.

Each of these factors will increase the productivity of producers. As a result, they will be able to produce at lower per-unit costs and thus make greater per-unit profits. Since profits are now higher, firms will be willing and able to produce more without the incentive of higher prices. In other words, if any of these four factors were to occur, it will increase aggregate supply, which means, graphically, a rightward shift in the AS curve.

In summary, then, if potential GDP increases, so, too, does aggregate supply. This is illustrated in **Figure 5.11**.

Figure 5.11 shows how, for instance, a technological improvement will increase an economy's potential GDP, shifting it from Y_1 to Y_2. In addition, technological improvements will also cut production costs and increase profits. This will cause an increase in the aggregate supply from AS_1 to AS_2.

FIGURE 5.11   An Increase in Aggregate Supply

An increase in the size or the quality of the labour force, an increase in the amount of capital stock and natural resources, or an improvement in technology shifts the aggregate supply curve to the right. (It also equally shifts potential GDP.)

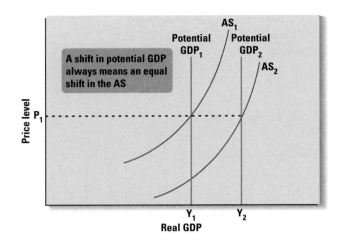

In addition to these productivity factors, there is one other thing that will affect the aggregate supply, and this is a drop in wage rates or in the prices of factor services. Lower wage rates will increase a firm's profits and lead to an increase in aggregate supply. So, too, will a fall in the prices of resources, such as oil, steel, wood—raw materials, in general. This, too, will lead to an increase in aggregate supply. On the other hand, an increase in resource prices (including wage rates) will cause profits to fall and lead to a reduction in aggregate supply. However, it is important to remember that a change in factor prices does not affect an economy's potential GDP.

A change in factor prices is shown in **Figure 5.12**. This figure shows the effect of, say, a significant reduction in the prices of imported inputs, such as oil. This will cause a drop in production costs in Canada and will encourage firms to produce more at the present price level. This implies a rightward shift in the aggregate supply curve from AS_1 to AS_2. Once again, since a change in factor costs has no effect on the productive capacity of the economy, there is no change in potential GDP.

FIGURE 5.12   Change in Factor Prices

A decrease in factor prices, such as lower prices of imported oil, will lower the costs of production and therefore shift the aggregate supply curve from AS_1 to AS_2 while leaving potential GDP unaffected.

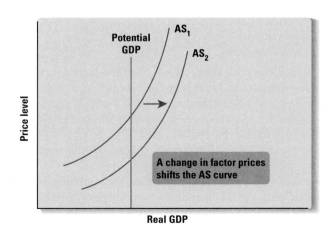

✓ **SELF-TEST**

7. What effect will the following changes have on aggregate supply and on potential GDP?

a) An increase in the price of imported crude oil

b) An increase in the number of immigrants entering Canada

c) The discovery of extensive oil deposits in northern Canada

d) A substantial increase in wage settlements

e) The introduction of a microchip that reduces computer processing time by 80 percent

8. Suppose the potential GDP for the country of Taymar is $1100 and the aggregate supply is as shown in the table.

a) Plot the aggregate supply curve, and show potential GDP.

b) Assume that the aggregate supply changed by $100 as a result of increased productivity. Plot the new AS curve, and show potential GDP.

Price Index	Aggregate Quantity Supplied
90	$ 950
95	1025
100	1100
105	1150
110	1190
115	1220
120	1240

5.4 DETERMINANTS OF REAL GDP AND THE PRICE LEVEL

It is now time to put this model to work and see how it explains various changes in the economy. It is clear that changes in the aggregate demand and aggregate supply can bring about changes in the price level and in real GDP, and so let us take each one in turn.

L04 Understand the causes of recessions and inflationary booms.

A Change in Aggregate Demand

Suppose that firms become more optimistic about future economic conditions in Canada and, as a result, start to loosen their purse strings and spend more on investment. The effect of this will be an increase in aggregate demand. But the important question here is: how much will aggregate demand increase? Will an increase in investment spending of, say, $10 billion increase aggregate demand by the same $10 billion? Surprisingly, the answer is no, and the reason is what economists call the **multiplier**, or expenditures multiplier, as some refer to it. Let us examine this important concept.

When firms spend this additional $10 billion, it means an increase in income for the contractors, suppliers, and their employees who provide the investment goods. And what will these people do with this increase in income? Well, some of it will be paid in taxes, some of it will be saved, and some of it will be spent on imports. However, a significant portion of it will be spent on domestically produced goods and services. Let us assume that 40 percent is paid in taxes, saved, or spent on imports, and that 60 percent, or $6 billion, is spent on the consumption of Canadian goods and services. When this $6 billion is spent, there is a further increase in income of the same $6 billion, which generates another round of tax payments, savings, import purchases, and the buying of more Canadian goods and services. This process continues, and we get a series of income increases.

Using **Figure 5.13**, we can track the total increase in income that results from the initial increase in investment spending of $10 billion.

multiplier: the effect on income of a change in autonomous spending, such as I, G, X, or autonomous C.

FIGURE 5.13   The Multiplier in Action

One person's spending becomes another person's income. However, in this example, at each round, only 60 percent of income gets spent (the rest is leaked to taxes, savings, and spending on imports). The spending in each round, therefore, is only 60 percent of the previous round's spending. But the process continues indefinitely.

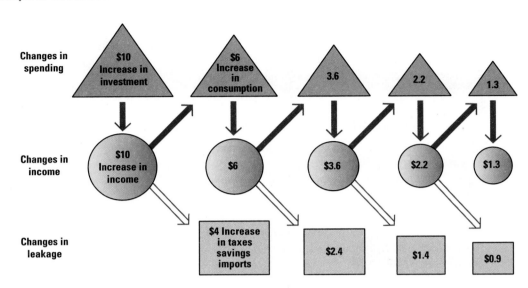

Initial round	$10.0 billion
Second round	6.0
Third round	3.6
Fourth round	2.2
Fifth round	1.3
All subsequent rounds	1.9
Total increase in income	25.0

In this example, an increase in investment spending of $10 billion will result in an increase in income of $25 billion, which means a multiplier of 2.5. If the portion spent on domestic production were higher, then the value of the multiplier would be larger. On the other hand, if taxes, savings, and imports were higher, then the value of the multiplier would be smaller. Also, we should point out that while our example illustrates the effect of an increase in investment spending, increases in other types of spending, such as exports, government spending, or consumption, would have the same effect.

This multiplier effect is illustrated graphically in **Figure 5.14**. We see here that the aggregate demand curve shifts to the right, from AD_1 to AD_2, as a result of the $10 billion increase in investment spending. If the price level (and for that matter, interest rates) were to remain unchanged, at P_1, then a multiplier of 2.5 would result in the level of real GDP increasing from $800 to $825, as seen by the movement from point *a* to *b*. However, since the AS curve is upward sloping, the increase in equilibrium real GDP will only be the movement of *a* to *c*, which is from $800 to, say, $815. What we are saying here is that the multiplier will have its full effect only if the AS curve is horizontal. Normally, some of the effect of the multiplier would be cancelled out by an increase in the price level associated with any increase in demand.

In summary, an increase in aggregate demand will lead to an increase in both the price level and in the level of real GDP. In contrast, a decrease in aggregate demand will decrease both the price level and real GDP.

FIGURE 5.14	The Effect of an Increase in Aggregate Demand on Real GDP

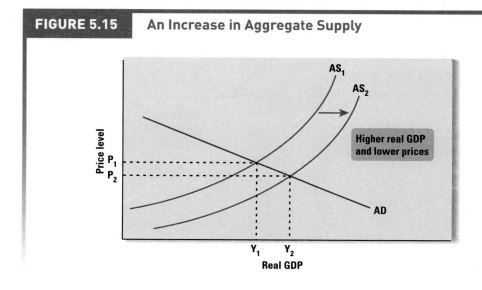

The increase in investment of $10 will increase aggregate demand by $25 from AD_1 to AD_2, which would result in an increase in real GDP from $800 to $825 (point *a* to *b*) if the price level did not change from its original level of P_1. However, since the equilibrium price level does rise to P_2, the increase in real GDP is smaller as seen by point *a* to *c*.

A Change in Aggregate Supply

As we have seen, a number of factors influence aggregate supply, but we want to focus on factor prices, since, as mentioned, they do not affect the potential GDP. Assume, for instance, that the price of imported oil were to fall. **Figure 5.15** illustrates the effect of such a change. When there is a decrease in factor costs, the aggregate supply curve will shift to the right, and the result is a decrease in the price level and an increase in real GDP. Other factors that might also cause an increase in aggregate supply include a decrease in the prices of raw materials, or a decrease in money wage levels. If any of these factors were to move in the opposite direction, this would produce a leftward shift and have the opposite result on the price level and the real GDP. We can generalize this to say that:

Any change in the price of any of the factors of production will shift the aggregate supply curve.

FIGURE 5.15	An Increase in Aggregate Supply

A decrease in the price of imported oil will improve profitability, causing the aggregate supply curve to shift to the right from AS_1 to AS_2. This change will cause the price level to drop from P_1 to P_2 and the level of real GDP to increase from Y_1 to Y_2.

What impact would a decrease in the price of imported oil have on the aggregate supply?

As we mentioned earlier, a change in productivity will also lead to a change in aggregate supply. In addition, it will cause a change in potential GDP. Assume, for instance, that the labour-force participation rate increases, which effectively means that the size of the labour force increases. Let us examine the effect of such a change on an economy. (We assume that the economy is initially at full-employment real GDP.) We know that in this case, both the aggregate supply and potential GDP will increase simultaneously, as illustrated in **Figure 5.16**.

As a result of the increase in the size of the labour force, the aggregate supply curve shifts to the right as does potential GDP. The new equilibrium is where the AD and the AS_2 curves intersect, which is at real GDP level, Y_2. The result of the change is a lower price level, P_2, and a higher level of real GDP, Y_2. Note that a recessionary gap now exists, since the new level of equilibrium real GDP is below the new level of potential real GDP, Y_3. As can be seen in **Figure 5.15**, the potential real GDP is now greater than the new output level. Actual real GDP has grown, but potential real GDP has grown more, resulting in a recessionary gap.

FIGURE 5.16   An Increase in Aggregate Supply and Potential GDP

An increase in the size of the labour force will shift the aggregate supply curve to the right (from AS_1 to AS_2) and also increase potential GDP. This change causes a reduction of the price level from P_1 to P_2 and an increase in real GDP from Y_1 to Y_2. The economy is now experiencing a recessionary gap; that is, the GDP is at Y_2, which is below the new potential GDP_2.

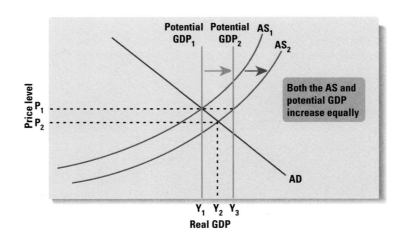

SELF-TEST

9. The following table shows the aggregate demand and aggregate supply schedules for the economy of Zee.

Aggregate Quantity Demanded	Price Index	Aggregate Quantity Supplied
$1950	90	$1620
1900	95	1700
1850	100	1760
1800	105	1800
1750	110	1830
1700	115	1850

a) What are the equilibrium values of price and real GDP?

b) Assume that aggregate demand decreases by $200 at every price level. What will be the new equilibrium values of price and real GDP?

10. Potential GDP for the economy of Ithica is $1500. The aggregate demand and aggregate supply schedules are shown in the following table.

Price Index	Aggregate Quantity Demanded	Aggregate Quantity Supplied
90	$1700	$ 950
95	1650	1150
100	1600	1300
105	1550	1420
110	1500	1500
115	1450	1540

a) What are the equilibrium values of price and real GDP? What type of equilibrium is this?

b) Assume that an increase in productivity increases aggregate supply by $300. What will be the new equilibrium values of price and real GDP? Is there now a recessionary gap or an inflationary gap? How much is the gap?

5.5 KEYNESIANS VERSUS THE NEOCLASSICAL SCHOOL

LO5 Explain the main points of disagreement between neoclassical and Keynesian economics.

The way in which changes in aggregate demand and supply affect the economy, and, indeed, what causes the changes, has been open to some dispute in economics over the last seventy years. There are two opposing camps: the long-established neoclassical school of thought and the Keynesian school, which represented a direct challenge to this orthodoxy. Although the heat has died down a little since the sometimes acrimonious debates that raged between the two in the decades following the publication of Keynes's *General Theory* in 1936, occasional flare-ups still break out.

The neoclassicists generally believed that the markets are competitive and efficient and will adjust rapidly whenever there is a general shortage or surplus. By adjustment, they meant that prices and wages would move up or down quickly and easily to ensure full employment. In addition, the economy would always remain at its potential full-employment level. This is illustrated in **Figure 5.17.**

The neoclassical school believed that the aggregate supply curve is a vertical straight line at the full-employment level of real GDP, Y_{FE}; that is, it is the same as potential GDP. The position of the curve is determined by the real variables that we discussed in reference to economic growth. The neoclassicists saw the aggregate demand curve as the normal downward-sloping demand curve. (To most neoclassical economists, the only factor that could really affect aggregate demand was the money supply.) This means that a change in aggregate demand will leave real GDP unaffected but will most definitely cause a change in the price level. Furthermore, wages

FIGURE 5.17   Neoclassical Aggregate Demand–Supply

The neoclassical AS is synonymous with potential GDP. This means that the price level has no effect on the quantity supplied. The aggregate supply curve will always be at the full-employment level of real GDP, labelled Y_{FE}. Changes in aggregate demand, therefore, have no effect upon real GDP and affect only the price level. An increase in aggregate demand from AD_1 to AD_2, for instance, will increase the price level from P_1 to P_2 but will leave real GDP unaffected at Y_{FE}.

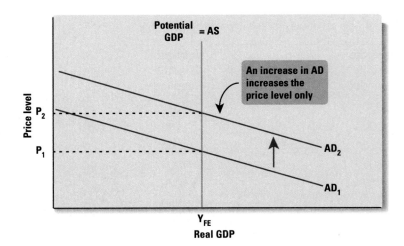

would change by the same percentage as the price level, leaving the real wage unaffected. At full employment, then, the real wage is constant. Since a change in the money supply is the only thing that can affect aggregate demand according to neoclassical economists, there could be only one type of inflation: demand–pull inflation. Moreover, they felt that the economy can only grow if there is a growth in the factors of production or in labour productivity. In their version of the model, a major depression or recession is impossible.

In contrast, Keynesian economists believed that the market is not very competitive because of the existence of big corporations and unions. They felt that this made prices and wages inflexible or "sticky." Changes in aggregate demand, therefore, have little impact on the price level. This is shown in **Figure 5.18**.

The aggregate supply curve is horizontal at the prevailing price level, P_1. Shifts in the aggregate demand can and will lead to changes in real GDP, but the price level will change little, if at all.

FIGURE 5.18   The Keynesian View of Aggregate Demand–Supply

The aggregate supply curve, according to Keynesians, is horizontal at the prevailing price level. Changes in aggregate demand, therefore, have no effect on the price level but do cause changes in real GDP. An increase in aggregate demand from AD_1 to AD_2 will cause an increase in real GDP from Y_1 to Y_2 but leave the price level unchanged at P_1.

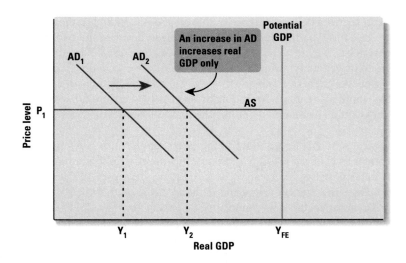

In addition, Keynesians believed that if there is a recessionary gap, wage levels would not drop and therefore the aggregate supply curve would remain unchanged. Only if the economy were at its potential full-employment GDP level would changes in aggregate demand affect the price level. However, without government intervention, there is nothing to guarantee that the economy will ever be at full employment.

We can use a metaphor to emphasize the contrast between the neoclassical and Keynesian viewpoints. Suppose there are two firms in town, Classical Cookies and Keynesian Kandies, both of which are facing a downturn in business. The manager of Classical Cookies calls a meeting of her staff and informs them that she has some good news and some bad news: "Despite the 20 percent reduction in orders this month, you'll be pleased to learn that we are not proposing any layoffs. You will all keep your jobs. Unfortunately, we have no choice under the circumstances but to reduce your pay by 20 percent. We will maintain production levels, but it does mean—please note, sales department—that in order to do so, we will be cutting prices by 20 percent starting tomorrow."

Meanwhile, over at Keynesian Kandies, another meeting is taking place between its manager and staff, and, similarly, there is both good news and bad news: "Despite the 20 percent reduction in orders this month, you'll be pleased to learn that we are not proposing any pay cuts for our staff. Unfortunately, we have no choice under the circumstances but to lay off 20 percent of you, starting tomorrow. We will maintain present prices, but it does mean—please note, production department—that we will be cutting production levels by 20 percent."

✔ SELF-TEST

11. Explain what will happen to nominal GDP and real GDP if there is an increase in aggregate demand according to:

a) Keynesians (if the economy is below full employment)

b) Neoclassicists

5.6 THE MODERN VIEW

Looking back on this historical debate, what can we say now? Who won the battle? Perhaps understandably, neither side. The modern view of the aggregate supply curve, as we mentioned earlier, is that it is neither horizontal nor vertical but an amalgam of both the neoclassical and Keynesian ideas. **Figure 5.19** shows the modern view of the aggregate supply curve.

 LO6 Explain the modern view of aggregate demand and aggregate supply.

At low levels of real GDP on the AS curve (the left portion), the curve is flat, illustrating the Keynesian belief that prices are inflexible. The right portion of the AS curve, where the GDP is higher, is very steep, reflecting the neoclassical view that real GDP is not affected by price changes. In between the two extremes is the intermediate range.

The shape of the AS curve has big implications for the economy should aggregate demand change. The effect of such a change will vary considerably, depending on what the present level of GDP is. **Figure 5.20**, for example, illustrates what will happen if aggregate demand increases.

We have seen that, as Keynes suggested, in a modern economy prices and wages tend to be inflexible. Given this, it is easy to increase production levels without causing either wages or prices to change appreciably. In addition, as production picks up in the economy, generally firms will be able to rehire productive workers, whom they may have been reluctant to lay off in the first place, and to make use of machines that have been sitting idle. An increase in aggregate demand from AD_1 to AD_2 in **Figure 5.20** will, therefore, have a big impact on real GDP (and employment), increasing it from Y_1 to Y_2 while not having much impact on either the per-unit costs or on prices, which hardly increase at all from P_1 to P_2.

| FIGURE 5.19 | The Modern View of the Aggregate Supply Curve |

The modern view of the AS curve is that at low GDP levels, the curve is quite flat (the Keynesian range) but gets progressively steeper as real GDP approaches full-employment (potential) GDP, where the curve becomes almost vertical (the neoclassical range). In between the two extremes is the intermediate range.

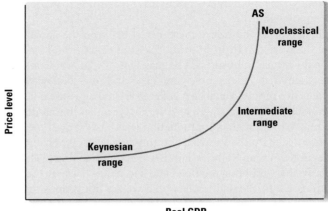

| FIGURE 5.20 | The Effect of an Increase in Aggregate Demand |

Because the AS curve is flat at low levels of income and gets steeper as the economy approaches its potential level, an increase in AD will have different effects, depending when it occurs. At low incomes, such as Y_1, most of the impact is on real GDP, increasing it to Y_2, while the price level only increase to P_2. At an income close to full-employment, such as Y_3, the same increase in AD impacts mostly on the price level, increasing it to P_4, while GDP increases only a little to Y_4.

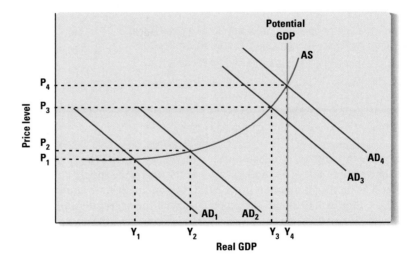

But now assume that the economy is close to full-employment potential GDP at Y_3, and a similar increase in aggregate demand, from AD_3 to AD_4, takes place. Here, productivity per worker will probably be less than when the economy was in a recession because now firms have to hire less-experienced and less-productive labour and are using older, less-efficient machines. In these circumstances, an increase in aggregate demand of the same magnitude as in the previous example will not increase GDP greatly—only from Y_3 to Y_4—but will have a big impact on both the per-unit costs and on the price level, pushing it up from P_3 to P_4.

To conclude, the impact that a change in aggregate demand has on the economy depends on the condition of the economy. The bigger the recession, the bigger will be the effect on GDP; in contrast, at or close to potential full-employment GDP, the effect of increased demand will be more inflationary.

Is the Economy Self-Adjusting?

Since modern macroeconomic theory is a synthesis of the two contrasting—Keynesian and neo-classical—schools of thought, we might ask the modern view on the possibility of a sustained recession. Remember that neoclassical economists felt that any recession would be short-lived, since the market economy is very efficient and adjusts quickly to bring an economy back to full employment. Keynes argued that this was highly unlikely because the modern world is not as perfectly competitive as the neoclassical economists suggest. As a result, the economy could be doomed to remain in a recession unless it was bailed out by government.

Again, the modern view is something of a compromise between the two positions. The view of most economists these days is that neither extreme view is valid. Although prices and wages are often inflexible in the short run, eventually they do adjust to the changing conditions of the economy. Let us explain exactly how this adjustment process works. Assume, as in **Figure 5.21**, that the economy finds itself in a recessionary-gap situation, with actual real GDP below potential real GDP.

The economy is currently in equilibrium at real GDP level, Y_1, where the aggregate quantity demanded is equal to the aggregate quantity supplied. However, the potential level of real GDP is at Y_{FE}. In this recessionary-gap situation, unemployment is above its natural rate. In other words, there is a certain amount of cyclical unemployment. That means firms find it easy to hire labour, and workers find it difficult to get jobs. Under these conditions, eventually nominal wage levels will be forced down. Remember that aggregate supply is based on a particular unchanging level of nominal wages; that is, the wage rate is constant along the AS curve. If the nominal wage level drops, this means that the aggregate supply curve will shift rightward. As this happens, firms hire more workers, production (real GDP) increases from Y_1 to Y_{FE}, and the price level falls from P_1 to P_2. As a result of this process, the economy finds equilibrium at Y_{FE}, where the new aggregate supply curve, AS_2, intersects the aggregate demand curve. This new equilibrium is at full employment.

Let us turn to the opposite situation and work out how the economy adjusts to an inflationary-gap situation. Assume that the economy finds itself in equilibrium at the real GDP level, Y_3, in **Figure 5.22**.

The economy is above full employment, which means that faced with a high demand, firms are producing more than they would consider their normal capacity output. Firms find it difficult to hire labour, and workers find it easy to get jobs. In this situation, nominal wage rates will be

FIGURE 5.21   Adjustment from a Recessionary Gap

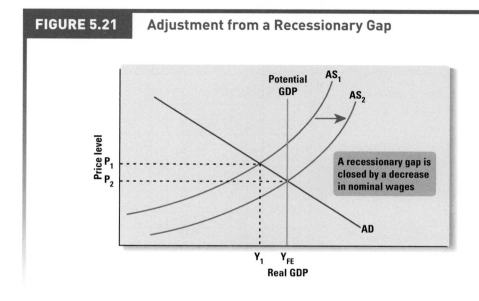

Initially, the economy is at price level P_1, and real GDP level, Y_1, below the full-employment level, Y_{FE}. This situation will put downward pressure on wages. As nominal wages fall, the aggregate supply curve shifts to the right until it is at AS_2. The net result will be a lower price level, P_2, and a full-employment real GDP, Y_{FE}.

| FIGURE 5.22 | Adjustment from an Inflationary Gap |

The economy is initially at equilibrium, with the AD curve intersecting AS_3 at the real GDP level, Y_3. With real GDP above its potential level, the unemployment rate is below the natural rate. The high demand for labour will push up nominal wage rates, causing aggregate supply to decrease and pushing the AS curve back to AS_2. The new equilibrium level of real GDP is now lower and the price level is higher than initially—price increases from P_3 to P_1.

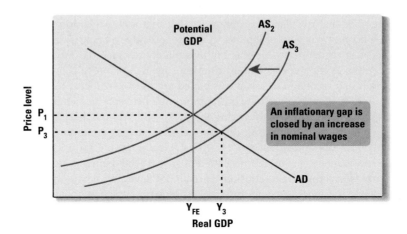

pushed up. This will cause the aggregate supply curve to shift left, pushing the price level up and real GDP down until the economy is back at potential full-employment equilibrium, with the aggregate demand curve, AD, intersecting the new aggregate supply curve, AS_2.

In all of this analysis, you might object that in the modern world, while price and wage levels do seem to increase year by year, they very seldom decrease. And yet, this model suggests that this is exactly what happens when there is a surplus of production or labour. The problem here is not so much a defect of the model but the limitation of picturing changes in terms of a two-dimensional graph. In reality, all economies are in a perpetual state of flux, with both the aggregate demand and supply constantly changing. If we could, it would be better to depict rates of change rather than actual changes, but then the analysis becomes unnecessarily complicated. In actuality, rather than the nominal wage level dropping, it rises, but at a slower pace than the price level.

This completes our discussion of the aggregate demand–supply model, which is the model that we will use to look at various issues in later chapters.

✓ SELF-TEST

12. Using the accompanying graph, explain the effect on the levels of GDP and the price level if aggregate demand increases by $400 when:

a) the present aggregate demand curve is AD_1.

b) the present aggregate demand curve is AD_2.

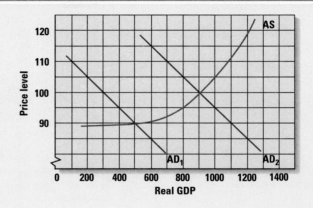

ADDED DIMENSION   Aggregate Demand and the Recession 2008–2010

The world-wide recession of 2008–2010 had less effect in Canada than it did in the United States and most of Europe. Even so, Canada's real GDP fell from a high of $1240 billion in November 2007 (on an annualized basis) to a low of $1186 billion in May 2009. This negative growth was reflected in the unemployment rate rising from 5.3% in October 2007 to a peak of 8.7% in May 2009. The major cause of this drop was the same as that in most countries: a fall in both consumer and investor confidence as share prices (world-wide) and house prices in the United States took a major tumble. In Canada, this was coupled with a decline

in exports to the United States, where the recession hit particularly hard. In terms of our AD–AS analysis, this caused a major drop in spending, causing aggregate demand to fall as shown in the following diagram.

The drop in aggregate demand in Canada caused a decline in real GDP from $1240 billion in late 2007 to $1180 billion in mid-2009. Since prices remained fairly constant in this period at 114 (2002 = 100), the full effect of the decreased demand was felt. If the price level had fallen a little, the real GDP would not have dropped as much (instead to, say, $1210 in the diagram.)

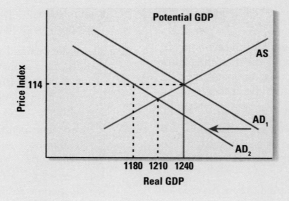

Review

CHAPTER SUMMARY

This chapter introduced you to the aggregate demand–aggregate supply model, which is a powerful tool that can be used to better understand the causes of unemployment and inflation as well as the effects of economic growth. You have learned to use the aggregate demand curve and the aggregate supply curve to illustrate and understand real-world events.

5.1a Potential GDP is the total amount that the economy is capable of producing at full employment (at the natural rate of unemployment). An increase in potential GDP is analogous to a rightward shift in the production possibilities curve.

5.1b Economic growth implies an increase in an economy's potential GDP and is illustrated by a rightward shift in its potential GDP line. The four sources of economic growth are:
- improved levels of human capital (an increase in the quantity or quality of labour employed).
- increases in physical capital stock.
- technological change.
- additional quantities of natural resources.

5.1c Economic growth rates are not steady, which means that economies are subject to business cycles—the periodic economic expansions and contractions that they all experience.

5.2a The aggregate quantity supplied varies directly with the price level because factor prices are constant and increases in the price level will raise profits, resulting in producers increasing output.

5.2b The aggregate quantity of goods and services demanded varies inversely with the price level because of the:
- real-balances effect.
- interest rate effect.
- foreign-trade effect.

5.2c Equilibrium real GDP occurs when the aggregate quantity of goods and services demanded equals the aggregate quantity supplied (the AD curve intersects the AS curve).

5.2d Equilibrium real GDP at a level other than full employment will mean one of the following:
- a recessionary gap, which means an output level below potential GDP
- an inflationary gap, which means an output level greater than potential GDP

5.3a Aggregate demand will change, causing the AD curve to shift, if the money supply changes or if there are changes in any of the four components of total spending.
- consumption spending as a result of changes in wealth, the age of consumer durables, or expectations
- investment spending as a result of changes in interest rate, purchase price, the age of capital goods, or expectations
- net exports as a result of changes in the exchange rate, income levels abroad, or the price of competitive (foreign) goods
- government spending on goods and services or taxes

5.3b A change in any of the four factors that cause economic growth will cause *both* potential GDP and aggregate supply to change, causing the potential GDP line *and* the AS curve to shift. If factor prices change, then only aggregate supply and the AS curve are affected; potential GDP remains the same.

5.4 AD will increase more than the initial change in spending because of the multiplier.
- An increase in AD will increase both real GDP and the price level.
- An increase in AS only will increase real GDP but decrease the price level.
- An increase in potential GDP will also increase AS and will increase real GDP and decrease the price level but will leave the economy below full-employment GDP.

5.5 At the heart of the historical debate between the Keynesians and neoclassicists is the question of whether the economy is capable of self-adjusting to an economic gap.

- Neoclassicists say that the economy can adjust and any gaps will immediately disappear.
- Keynesians say that that such gaps occur often and can last indefinitely.

5.6 Modern economists say that:
- recessionary gaps are eliminated by factor prices eventually falling and the AS curve shifting to the right.
- inflationary gaps are eliminated by factor prices eventually rising and the AS curve shifting to the left.

NEW GLOSSARY TERMS AND KEY EQUATIONS

aggregate demand 161	interest-rate effect 162	real-balances effect 162
aggregate supply 159	macroeconomic equilibrium 162	real wage 159
business cycle 157	multiplier 171	recession 163
foreign-trade effect 162	nominal wage 159	recessionary gap 163
inflationary gap 163	potential GDP 153	

Equations:

[5.1] $\text{Real wage} = \dfrac{\text{Nominal wage}}{\text{Price level}}$ **page 159**

STUDY TIPS

1. When you think about what a supply curve means, remember that it does not refer to the amounts that firms are actually producing *now* but what they would hypothetically produce under certain circumstances. In particular, aggregate supply is based on what firms are *willing and able* to produce at various prices if nominal wages and other resources prices do not change. On the other hand, potential GDP has nothing to do with this willingness but is tied totally to an economy's ability to produce. It is rather like a production possibilities curve that shows physical amounts a country is capable of producing. It tells you nothing about what a country is actually producing. Neither does it tell you how long it will take to reach maximum production or, for that matter, if it ever will.

2. Think of aggregate supply as having to do with profitability; anything that affects profitability will affect it. Think of potential GDP as having to do with productivity; anything that affects productivity will affect it.

In other words, imagine that there is a dollar sign above the supply curve. A change in nominal wages or in the price of imported resources will definitely affect profitability and, therefore, aggregate supply. These factors do not, however, affect a country's productive potential, that is, potential GDP.

3. A number of you will have difficulty at times disentangling those things that affect the demand side of things and those that affect the supply side. As in microeconomics, it is a good idea not to get too "cute" by thinking of ways in which a change in one thing can have an impact on other factors, however remote they may be. By some esoteric reasoning, it is possible to link pretty well all factors in life; in economics, it is better to stick to the more obvious. Learn the things that determine aggregate demand and aggregate supply, and remember that these factors affect only demand or supply, not both.

Practise and learn online with Connect, where you can find the Answered Questions and the Unanswered Problems for all chapters of this textbook's Study Guide section.

Answered Questions

These questions can also be found online on Connect.

Indicate whether the following statements are true or false:

1. **(LO 2) T or F** Aggregate demand is the total quantity of final goods and services that consumers, businesses, government, and those living outside the country would buy at different price levels.

2. **(LO 2) T or F** The foreign-trade effect is the effect that a change in exports and imports has on the price level.

3. **(LO 2) T or F** The aggregate supply curve is upward sloping.

4. **(LO 2) T or F** Macroeconomic equilibrium occurs where the aggregate demand is equal to potential GDP.

5. **(LO 3) T or F** A change in resource prices will shift both the aggregate supply and the potential GDP curves.

6. **(LO 4) T or F** An increase in potential GDP has no effect on macroeconomic equilibrium.

7. **(LO 4) T or F** An increase in aggregate demand will cause an increase in both real GDP and the price level.

8. **(LO 4) T or F** An increase in wage rates will cause an increase in both real GDP and the price level.

9. **(LO 5) T or F** According to Keynes, the aggregate supply curve is vertical.

10. **(LO 5) T or F** According to neoclassicists, an increase in aggregate demand will have no effect upon real GDP but will cause the price level to increase.

Basic (Questions 11–24)

11. **(LO 2)** Why is the AD curve downward sloping?
    a) Because production costs decline as real GDP increases
    b) Because higher prices cause an increase in wealth, which increases spending
    c) Because lower prices cause an increase in real balances, which increases spending
    d) Because lower prices cause interest rates to increase, which increases spending

12. **(LO 2)** Why is the AS curve upward sloping?
    a) Because firms will produce more if prices are higher, despite a lack of increase in profits
    b) Because firms will experience higher profits at higher prices and will therefore produce more
    c) Because aggregate demand rises with higher prices
    d) Because the potential GDP curve is also upward sloping

13. **(LO 3)** Which of the following will cause the aggregate demand curve to shift to the right?
    a) A decrease in the money supply
    b) A decrease in the interest rate
    c) An increase in the exchange rate
    d) A decrease in government spending

14. **(LO 2)** When does macroeconomic equilibrium occur?
    a) When aggregate supply equals potential GDP
    b) When the aggregate demand curve intersects the aggregate supply curve
    c) When the aggregate demand curve intersects the potential GDP curve
    d) When full employment occurs

15. **(LO 4)** What could cause the level of real GDP to rise but the price level to fall?
    a) A rightward shift in the aggregate demand curve
    b) A leftward shift in the aggregate demand curve
    c) A rightward shift in the aggregate supply curve
    d) A leftward shift in the aggregate supply curve

16. **(LO 3)** What can cause an increase in potential GDP?
    a) An increase in nominal wage rates
    b) A decrease in taxes
    c) Technological improvement
    d) A leftward shift in the AS curve

17. **(LO 2)** What does the *real-balances effect* mean?
    a) A higher price level will lead to an increase in the rate of interest thereby causing a decrease in consumption.
    b) A lower price level will lead to an increase in the rate of interest thereby causing a decrease in consumption.
    c) A higher price will increase the real value of financial assets thereby causing an increase in consumption.
    d) A higher price will decrease the real value of financial assets thereby causing an increase in consumption.
    e) A higher price will decrease the real value of financial assets thereby causing a decrease in consumption.

Refer to **Figure 5.23** to answer question 18.

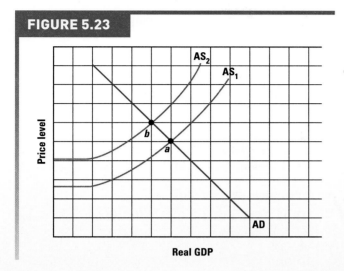

FIGURE 5.23

Price level (vertical axis)

AS₂

AS₁

b

a

AD

Real GDP

18. **(LO 3, 4)** What could cause a movement from point *a* to point *b*?
    a) An increase in government spending
    b) A decrease in labour productivity
    c) The discovery of new oil fields
    d) A decrease in taxes
    e) A decrease in the prevailing nominal wage

19. **(LO 4)** What effect will a decrease in aggregate demand have if the economy is in a recession?
    a) The price level will drop a great deal, but real GDP will fall only a little.
    b) The price level will drop a little, but real GDP will fall a great deal.
    c) The price level will drop a little, but real GDP will increase a great deal.
    d) The price level will drop a little, and real GDP will increase a little.
    e) Both the price level and real GDP will increase by the same amount.

20. **(LO 3)** What is the result of an increase in labour productivity?
    a) A decrease in aggregate supply
    b) An increase in potential GDP
    c) An increase in aggregate demand
    d) An increase in aggregate demand and aggregate supply

21. **(LO 1)** What is the business cycle?
    a) The periodic cycles of profits and losses that all firms experience

b) The natural evolution of new firms growing quickly at first, then slowing and fading into obsolescence
    c) The fact that real GDP falls as often as it rises
    d) The expansionary and contractionary phases in the growth rate of real GDP

22. **(LO 1)** What is meant by the term *human capital*?
    a) The sum of all financial assets owned by people
    b) The accumulated skills and knowledge of human beings
    c) The total amount of machines and physical overhead a country possesses
    d) The amount of physical capital that each worker has to work with

23. **(LO 1)** All of the following, *except* one, will contribute to economic growth. Which is the exception?
    a) Increased levels of human capital
    b) Higher prices
    c) Increases in the capital stock
    d) Technological improvement
    e) Increased quantities of natural resources

24. **(LO 3)** What are the four components of aggregate demand?
    a) Consumption, investment, government spending, and net exports
    b) Consumption, investment, productivity, and net exports
    c) Consumption, investment, productivity, and human capital
    d) Potential GDP, AD, AS, and the GDP deflator

Intermediate (Questions 25–30)

25. **(LO 3)** What will be the effect on trade of an increase in the Canadian price level?
    a) It will increase the volume of both Canadian exports and imports
    b) It will decrease the volume of both Canadian exports and imports
    c) It will increase the volume of Canadian exports but decrease the volume of imports
    d) It will decrease the volume of Canadian exports but increase the volume of imports

26. **(LO 3)** What is the domestic effect of an increase in the incomes of a country's major international trading partners?
    a) The aggregate demand curve will shift to the right.
    b) The aggregate demand curve will shift to the left.
    c) The aggregate supply curve will shift to the right.
    d) The aggregate supply curve will shift to the left.

Refer to **Figure 5.24** to answer questions 27 and 28.

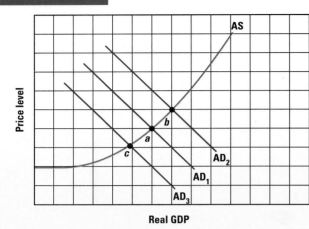

FIGURE 5.24

27. **(LO 4)** All of the following, *except* one, would cause a movement from *a* to *b*. Which is the exception?
   a) An increase in the price level
   b) An increase in wealth holdings
   c) An increase in government spending
   d) A decrease in the interest rate
   e) An increase in foreign incomes

28. **(LO 3, 4)** Which of the following would cause a movement from point *a* to point *c*?
   a) A decrease in the price level
   b) An increase in wealth holdings
   c) An increase in government spending
   d) An increase in the interest rate
   e) An increase in foreign incomes

Table 5.2 shows the aggregate demand and supply schedules for the economy of Adana. Refer to **Table 5.2** to answer questions 29–31.

TABLE 5.2

Aggregate Quantity Demanded	Price Index	Aggregate Quantity Supplied
$800	100	$550
750	105	650
700	110	700
650	115	740
600	120	770

29. **(LO 4)** What are the implications if the price level is 100?
   a) The price level is above equilibrium.
   b) There is a shortage of real output of $250.
   c) There is a surplus of real output of $250.
   d) There is a surplus of real output of $150.

30. **(LO 4)** If the aggregate quantity demanded falls by $100 at every price level, what will be the new equilibrium price level and real output, respectively?
   a) 100 and $550
   b) 105 and $650
   c) 110 and $650
   d) 115 and $500

Advanced (Questions 31–35)

31. **(LO 4)** At what level of real output will full employment occur in this economy?
   a) $600
   b) $650
   c) $700
   d) Cannot be determined from the information

32. **(LO 5)** What is the slope of the aggregate supply curve, according to neoclassical economists?
   a) Vertical, because prices tend to be inflexible
   b) Vertical, at the capacity level of output in the economy
   c) Horizontal, because wages are flexible
   d) Horizontal, because prices are flexible

Refer to **Figure 5.25** to answer questions 33 and 34.

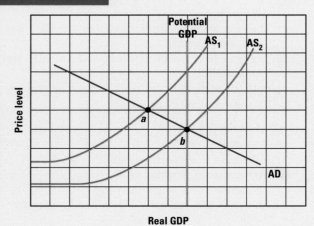

FIGURE 5.25

33. **(LO 6)** Which of the following statements is true if the economy is at point *a*?
   a) Firms will find it hard to hire labour, and people will find it easy to find jobs.
   b) Wages will eventually be forced down.
   c) An inflationary gap exists.
   d) Unemployment is at its natural rate.
   e) The achievement of full employment must await a decrease in aggregate demand.

34. **(LO 6)** If the economy was initially at point *a*, then what would a movement to point *b* suggest?
   a) The movement could be the result of an increase in aggregate demand.

b) The movement could be the result of a decrease in prices.
   c) The movement could be the result of a decrease in wages.
   d) It is a movement from one full-employment level of real GDP to another.
   e) The movement could be the result of expansionary monetary policy.

35. **(LO 5)** What is the slope of the AS curve according to Keynesians?
   a) Vertical, because prices tend to be inflexible
   b) Vertical, at the level of potential GDP
   c) Horizontal, because wages are inflexible
   d) Downward sloping, because wages are inflexible

Parallel Problems

ANSWERED PROBLEMS

36A. **(LO 1, 2, 3, 4, 5, 6)** **Key Problem** **Table 5.3** shows AD and AS for the economy of Everton. Potential GDP is currently 200.
   a) On **Figure 5.26** draw in and label curves AS_1 and AD_1.
   b) What are the equilibrium values for the price level and real GDP?
      Price: _____ Real GDP: _____
   c) Suppose that aggregate demand in Everton decreased by 60. Draw a new AD_2 curve on **Figure 5.26** to show this change. What are the new equilibrium values for the price level and real GDP?
      Price: _____ Real GDP: _____

FIGURE 5.26

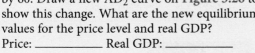

Price level (y-axis): 65, 70, 75, 80, 85, 90, 95, 100, 105, 110
Real GDP (x-axis): 40, 80, 120, 160, 200, 240, 280

TABLE 5.3

Price Index	Aggregate Quantity Supplied 1 (AS₁)	Aggregate Quantity Demanded 1 (AD₁)	Aggregate Quantity Supplied 2 (AS₂)
65*	$0	$260	$100
70*	100	240	180
75	160	220	220
80	200	200	245
85	230	180	260
90	250	160	270
95	260	140	274
100	270	120	275

(*The price level is inflexible downward at $70 for AS₁ and at $65 for AS₂)

d) Is there now a recessionary gap or an inflationary gap? What is the amount of this gap?
There is a(n) _____ gap of _____.

e) Put an "X" next to each of the following factors that could have caused the decrease in demand that you illustrated in c).
increased exports _____
higher taxes _____
higher interest rates _____
lower government spending _____

f) Assuming the original AD_1, suppose that aggregate supply changed as a result of a dramatic decrease in the price of oil as shown by AS_2 in **Table 5.3**. Draw in the new AS_2 in **Figure 5.26**. What are the equilibrium values for the price level and real GDP now?
Price: _____ Real GDP: _____

g) Is there now a recessionary or inflationary gap? What is the amount of this gap?
There is a(n) _____ gap of _____.

Basic (Problems 37A–45A)

37A. **(LO 1)** What are the four sources of economic growth?

38A. **(LO 1)** Suppose the real GDP of an economy is $480 billion dollars and its unemployment rate is 7 percent. If the natural rate of unemployment is estimated at 5 percent, what is the value of the country's potential GDP in billions of dollars? $ _____

39A. **(LO 3, 4)** Starting from full-employment equilibrium, indicate whether each of the following factors will affect aggregate demand (AD) or aggregate supply (AS) and whether the effect would be an increase or a decrease. Then, indicate what will happen to the price level and the level of real GDP and what type of equilibrium will result.
a) A decrease in interest rates: _____
Price level: _____ Real GDP: _____
Type of equilibrium

_____

b) An improvement in technology: _____
Price level: _____ Real GDP: _____
Type of equilibrium _____

c) An increase in the exchange rate: _____
Price level: _____ Real GDP: _____
Type of equilibrium _____.

d) A decrease in government spending: _____
Price level: _____ Real GDP: _____
Type of equilibrium _____

e) An increase in the money supply: _____
Price level: _____ Real GDP: _____
Type of equilibrium _____

f) An increase in the nominal wage rate: _____
Price level: _____ Real GDP: _____
Type of equilibrium _____

40A. **(LO 4)** Starting from equilibrium, explain in terms of changes in either AD or in AS (not both) how each of the following results could have occurred.
a) Real GDP increases, and the price level increases.
b) Real GDP decreases, and the price level increases.
c) Real GDP increases, and the price level decreases.
d) Real GDP decreases, and the price level decreases.

41A. **(LO 6)** Explain, in terms of a graph, how an increase in aggregate demand could have no effect on the price level.

42A. **(LO 4)** Assume that the potential GDP of the economy of Arion is $1000 and that the aggregate demand and the aggregate supply are as shown in **Table 5.4**.
a) What is the value of equilibrium real GDP and the price level? Is there a recessionary gap or an inflationary gap?
Real GDP: _____ Price level: _____
There is a(n) _____ gap of $ _____

b) If firms become more optimistic and aggregate demand increases by $65, what will be the new values of equilibrium real GDP and the price level?
Real GDP: _____ Price level: _____

c) Is there a recessionary gap or an inflationary gap? What is the size of the gap?
There is a(n) _____ gap of $ _____

TABLE 5.4

Aggregate Quantity Demanded	Price Index	Aggregate Quantity Supplied
$1080	96	$880
1060	97	940
1040	98	965
1020	99	985
1000	100	1000
980	101	1015
960	102	1025
940	103	1033
920	104	1040
900	105	1045

43A. **(LO 2)** Assume that the nominal wage rate increases from $18 to $20.80 per hour and, at the same time, the price index increases from 120 to 130. By how much has the real wage rate changed?

44A. **(LO 1)** What does the term *potential GDP* mean?

45A. **(LO 3)** What factors can cause an *increase* in aggregate demand?

Intermediate (Problems 46A–52A)

46A. **(LO 4)** Use the graph in **Figure 5.27** to illustrate the effect of the Great Depression on the Canadian economy, when prices, production, and employment all decreased dramatically in the 1930s. (Assume the economy was originally at full-employment equilibrium.)

FIGURE 5.27

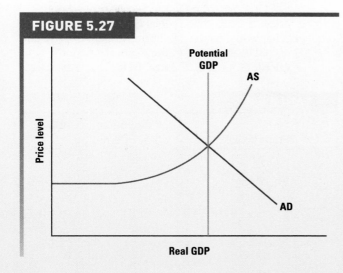

47A. **(LO 4)** In **Figure 5.28**, show a new equilibrium on the graph illustrating demand-pull inflation, and then name three things that could have caused the change.

a) _____
b) _____
c) _____

48A. **(LO 1)** Assume that the size of the labour force in the economy of Mersin remained unchanged in the year 2011, while labour productivity increased. If real GDP also remained unchanged, what change in the labour market must have occurred? _____

_____

FIGURE 5.28

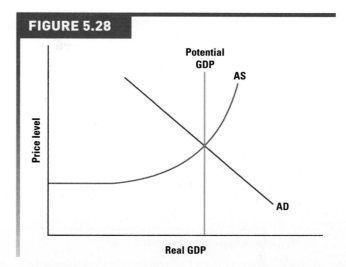

49A. **(LO 1)** **Figure 5.29** depicts the economy of Altrua, which is presently in equilibrium.
a) What is the size of its recessionary gap?
$ _____
b) What is the size of this gap as a percentage of its actual GDP$? $ _____
c) If the natural rate of unemployment is 6 percent, use Okun's law to calculate the amount of actual unemployment in Altrua. _____%

FIGURE 5.29

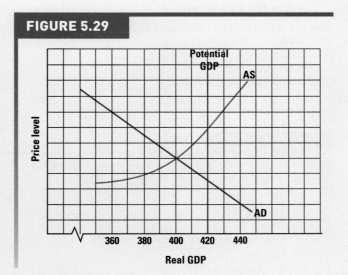

50A. **(LO 2)** You are given the following options:

1. ↑ aggregate demand   2. ↓ aggregate demand
3. ↑ aggregate supply   4. ↓ aggregate supply
5. ↑ aggregate supply and potential GDP
6. ↓ aggregate supply and potential GDP

Which of options 1–6 will occur as the result of the following changes?
a) An increase in investment spending
b) A decrease in imports
c) An increase in factor prices
d) A decrease in productivity
e) A decrease in factor prices
f) An increase in human capital

51A. **(LO 2)** What are the three reasons for the downward slope of the aggregate demand curve?

52A. **(LO 4)** Starting from full-employment equilibrium, explain what effect an increase in aggregate demand will have on price, real GDP, and equilibrium.

Advanced (Problems 53A–57A)

53A. **(LO 1, 4)** Villareal's nominal GDP increased from $168 billion to $220 billion last year. During the year, its economy experienced inflation, with its price index increasing from 105 to 110, while the number of persons employed increased from 20 million to 23.5 million. By what percentage did its labour productivity increase during the year? _____%

54A. **(LO 4)** Why does an increase in potential GDP leave the economy in a recessionary gap? _____
_____
_____
_____ .

55A. **(LO 5)** Table 5.5 shows the aggregate demand for the economy of Zandu. **Table 5.6** shows two aggregate supplies for the same economy.
a) Which of the two aggregate supply schedules, (1) or (2), is the neoclassical aggregate supply? Which is the Keynesian aggregate supply?
Neoclassical supply: _____
Keynesian supply: _____
b) According to the neoclassical school, what would be the equilibrium levels of price and real GDP?
Price: _____ Real GDP: _____
c) According to the Keynesian school, what would be the equilibrium levels of price and real GDP?
Price: _____ Real GDP: _____
Assume that the aggregate demand increased by $150.
d) What would be the equilibrium values of price and real GDP according to the neoclassical school?
Price: _____ Real GDP: _____
e) What would be the equilibrium values of price and real GDP according to the Keynesian school?
Price: _____ Real GDP: _____

TABLE 5.5

Price Index	Aggregate Quantity Demanded
75	$850
80	800
85	750
90	700
95	650
100	600
105	550
110	500

TABLE 5.6

Price Index	Aggregate Quantity Supplied (1)	Price Index	Aggregate Quantity Supplied (2)
75	$800	100	$600
80	800	100	650
85	800	100	700
90	800	100	750
95	800	100	800
100	800	100	850
105	800	100	900
110	800	100	950

56A. **(LO 4)** Suppose that the economy of Bunderland is initially at full-employment equilibrium. Explain, in terms of shifts in AD or AS, how the following results could occur:

  a) Real GDP increases; the price level increases; the economy is experiencing an inflationary gap.

  b) Real GDP increases; the price level decreases; the economy is experiencing an inflationary gap.

  c) Real GDP decreases; the price level increases; the economy is experiencing an inflationary gap.

57A. **(LO 6)** Suppose that the economy of Witland in Figure 5.30 is at full-employment equilibrium and the present nominal wage is $24 per hour.

  a) What is the real wage rate (in base year prices)? _____

  b) Suppose that the aggregate demand increases by $400. At the new equilibrium real GDP level, what will be the value of the real wage rate? _____

  c) As a result of the change in prices in b), suppose the nominal wage increases, causing aggregate supply to change by $400. At the new equilibrium, what will be the new real wage rate? _____
  At the new equilibrium in c), what is the value of the nominal wage rate? _____

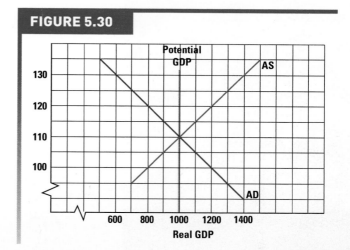

FIGURE 5.30

58A. **(LO 6)** How does the economy adjust if there is a recessionary gap? If there is an inflationary gap?

CHAPTER 6

AGGREGATE EXPENDITURES

At the end of this chapter, you should be able to...

LO1 understand the marginal propensity to consume and how consumption, saving, and investment relate to national income.

LO2 understand the concept of expenditures equilibrium.

LO3 explain how the multiplier produces big changes in national income as a result of small changes in spending.

LO4 see how government's budget balance and the balance of trade both relate to national income.

LO5 derive aggregate demand from aggregate expenditures.

WHAT'S AHEAD...

Like Chapter 5, this chapter focuses on the product market. Here, we use the expenditures model to analyze how the level of GDP or national income is determined. This model emphasizes how the various parts of the economy—from consumption spending and investment to government spending and exports—are interrelated. The term *equilibrium* takes on more than one meaning as the model unfolds around the discussion of the things that change equilibrium income.

A Question of Relevance...

You are probably aware that Canada is one of the best countries in the world in which to live. One reason is the country's relatively high level of national income, which, of course, means a high level of per capita income. But have you wondered what determines this level of national income? Why does it grow quickly at some times and not at all at other times? What role does consumer spending play in all this? And how is it influenced by business investment and exports? This chapter will help you answer these questions.

In the last chapter, we studied the aggregate demand/aggregate supply (AD/AS) model and saw how changes in both aggregate demand and aggregate supply can produce changes in production (and therefore income and employment) and in the price level (and therefore inflation). While changes in aggregate supply can cause long-term and radical changes to an economy, their short-term effect can go unnoticed. As well, such changes are difficult for governments and policy makers to instigate. However, changes in spending (demand) are likely to have a more obvious short-term effect and are more easily effected by governments.

For this reason, changes in spending lay at the heart of Keynes's *General Theory*, which was first published in 1936. Keynes realized that inadequate spending was the root cause of the Great Depression and that an increase in spending was necessary to cure it. In his General Theory, Keynes tended to downplay the role of prices and inflation (though he certainly did not ignore them), since for him and many others, the major problems facing the economy at that time were those of low (and negative) growth and massive unemployment. As a result, the price level plays a very minor role in the model that we will look at in this chapter.

In this chapter, we are concerned with the level of aggregate expenditures—what affects it and how it affects the economy. Aggregate expenditures and aggregate demand mean very much the same thing, except that we ignore the price level when we talk about aggregate expenditures, whereas aggregate demand is the total amount of aggregate expenditures at various prices. Since both are the total of consumption, investment spending, government spending, and net exports, anything that affects aggregate demand will also affect aggregate expenditures. At the end of the chapter, we will look more closely at how the two are linked.

We will begin by looking at a simplified model of the economy that includes only consumption and investment spending, and bring out some of the important interrelationships. Later in the chapter, we will include the government sector and finally derive a complete model by introducing the foreign sector. But let us begin gradually.

6.1 CONSUMPTION, SAVINGS, AND INVESTMENT FUNCTIONS

It is clear that the amount households spend on consumer goods and services (consumption) is closely related to household income. Quite simply, it seems obvious that high-income earners spend more than do low-income earners. The same is true for the whole economy: the higher the level of national income, the higher is the level of consumption. We will begin building our model for the hypothetical economy of Karinia by assuming its economy is both private and closed. By this we mean that in Karinia there is no government intervention (no government spending or taxation) and the economy is closed to international trade so that there are neither exports nor imports. **Table 6.1** shows how consumption spending is related to national income, which is equal to disposable income, since there is no taxation. (All the figures in this chapter are in billions of dollars.)

Since saving is that portion of income not spent on consumption, the savings column is derived by simply subtracting consumption from national income.

If you look closely at the consumption column, you can see that even at the zero level of income, there is still a certain level of consumption in Karinia (the people have to live, after all). This amount of spending—which is independent of the level of income—is referred to as **autonomous spending**. Autonomous spending (expenditures) is the absolute minimum level of spending that occurs. However, most of what people spend is the result of our earning an income; in other words, a good portion of consumption is induced by higher income levels. This is called **induced spending**. Thus:

$$\text{Total spending (aggregate expenditures)} = \text{autonomous spending} + \text{induced spending} \qquad \text{[6.1]}$$

LO1 Understand the marginal propensity to consume and how consumption, saving, and investment relate to national income.

autonomous spending (expenditures): the portion of total spending that is independent of the level of income.

induced spending: the portion of spending that depends on the level of income.

TABLE 6.1	Consumption and Savings Functions	
National Income (Y)	**Consumption (C)**	**Saving (S)**
0	50	−50
100	125	−25
200	200	0
300	275	25
400	350	50
500	425	75
600	500	100
700	575	125
800	650	150

So, we have both autonomous consumption and induced consumption. **Table 6.1** shows that the amount of autonomous consumption is $50 (the level of consumption at zero income). The amount of induced consumption varies with the level of income. The extra consumer spending that results from higher incomes is referred to as the **marginal propensity to consume** (MPC). In the form of an equation, this is:

marginal propensity to consume: the ratio of the change in consumption to the corresponding change in income.

$$\text{Marginal propensity to consume (MPC)} = \frac{\Delta \text{ consumption}}{\Delta \text{ income}} \qquad \text{[6.2]}$$

(Δ simply means "change in.")

You will note that **Table 6.1** shows income increasing by $100 at each level. Each time it does, consumption increases by $75 (from $25 to $100, from $100 to $175 and so on). The value of the MPC in Karinia is therefore equal to $75/$100 or 0.75. Given this information, we can spell out the precise relationship between the level of consumption and the level of income in a **consumption function**.

consumption function: the relationship between income and consumption.

$$C \quad = \quad 50 \quad + \quad 0.75Y$$
(Total consumption = autonomous consumption + induced consumption)

Presenting the consumption function algebraically allows us to calculate the values of consumption at levels of income not given in the table. For instance, when income is $360, we can easily calculate that consumption must equal 50 + 0.75 (360) = $320. And at an income level of $1000, consumption will equal 50 + 0.75 (1000) = $800.

Now, you might reasonably ask how householders in Karinia can possibly spend anything if they are not receiving any income? The answer is that they will be forced to make use of their own past savings or borrow (make use of someone else's past savings). This is referred to as **dis-saving**. At an income of zero, **Table 6.1** shows us that dis-saving equals $50. Note that as incomes increase not only do people spend more—consumption increases—they also save more. At incomes above $200, people are no longer dis-saving; there is now positive saving. The amount of extra saving that results from higher incomes is referred to as the **marginal propensity to save** (MPS). In the form of an equation, it is:

dis-saving: spending on consumption in excess of income.

marginal propensity to save: the ratio of the change in saving to the corresponding change in income.

$$\text{Marginal propensity to save (MPS)} = \frac{\Delta \text{ saving}}{\Delta \text{ income}} \qquad \text{[6.3]}$$

In this economy, the value of the MPS equals: 25/100 or 0.25. The equation for the **saving function** therefore is:

$$S \quad = \quad -50 \quad + \quad 0.25Y$$
(Total saving = autonomous dis-saving + induced saving)

saving function: the relationship between income and saving.

Now, since, by definition, the amount of income that is not spent must be saved (remember $Y = C + S$), it follows that:

$$MPC + MPS = 1 \qquad\qquad \text{(6.4)}$$

We can see this equality, if we add together the consumption and saving functions for Karinia.

$$
\begin{array}{rcl}
C & = & 50 + 0.75Y \\
S & = & -50 + 0.25Y \\
\hline
C + S & = & Y
\end{array}
$$

The consumption and saving functions are both graphed in **Figure 6.1**.

The value of the Y intercept (the point at which the consumption function crosses the vertical axis) is the amount of autonomous consumption. Similarly, where the saving function crosses the vertical axis is the amount of autonomous dis-saving. The slope of the consumption function is the value of the MPC, in this case 0.75, and the slope of the saving function is the MPS and is equal to 0.25. The higher the value of the MPC, the steeper will be the slope of the consumption function. (It will also imply a smaller MPS and flatter saving function.)

FIGURE 6.1   **Consumption and Saving Functions**

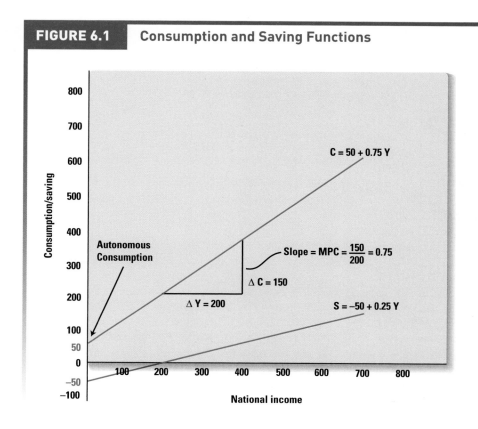

Both the consumption and saving functions are upward sloping, showing that both consumption *and* saving increase with incomes. The slope of the consumption function is equal to the MPC and the slope of the saving function is equal to the MPS. The points at which the curves cross the vertical axis show the amounts of autonomous consumption and autonomous dis-saving.

For simplicity's sake, in this chapter, we will assume that the MPC and MPS are constant. In reality, this may not be true, though a surprising amount of evidence suggests that in modern economies, it is not far from the truth. However, if we look at the long term, it does seem that the MPC tends to get smaller. In other words, as a country—and its people—grow richer, they tend to spend proportionately less and, consequently, save proportionately more of their income. Also, within most economies poorer members of society usually have a higher MPC than do richer ones. The implications of this are clear: a tax cut given to the poor will increase spending in the economy more than an identical tax cut given to the rich.

SELF-TEST

1. The following graph shows the consumption function for the economy of Astrid.

a) Complete the following table.

b) Draw in the saving line in the graph below.

National Income (Y)	Consumption (C)	Saving (S)
0		
200		
400		
600		
800		
1000		
1200		

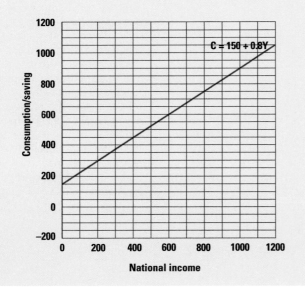

2. a) Complete the table, assuming that the MPC is constant.

b) What are the equations for the consumption and saving functions?

National Income	Consumption	Saving
0	60	—
200	220	—
400	—	20
600	—	60
800	700	—

Investment

In any modern economy such as Karinia's, investment spending is far more volatile than consumption; it can fluctuate unpredictably from year to year. There are a number of reasons for this, but an important one is the fact that investment can be postponed, which is not the case with consumption. (People are not likely to put off eating or wearing clothes until the economy improves.) More especially, and again in contrast to consumption, investment is not as closely related to national income. For instance, there have been a number of years in Canada's history when both GDP and investment increased, but there have been many other years in which the two went in opposite directions. For this reason, we will regard investment as autonomous from the level of income, as illustrated in **Table 6.2**.

The algebraic expression for the investment function therefore is straightforward.

$$I = 75$$

This graphs as a straight line, horizontal to the axis as illustrated in **Figure 6.2**.

This graph shows that regardless of the level of national income, investment remains a constant $75.

TABLE 6.2   Investment Function

National Income (Y)	Investment (I)
0	75
100	75
200	75
300	75
400	75
500	75
600	75
700	75
800	75

FIGURE 6.2   The Investment Function

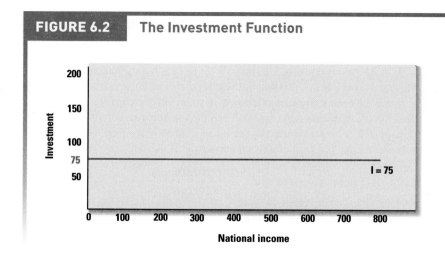

Investment is autonomous, which means it remains constant whatever the level of income. It therefore plots as a horizontal straight line.

6.2 EXPENDITURES EQUILIBRIUM

L02 Understand the concept of expenditures equilibrium.

Let us now combine the data we have on this economy's consumption and investment functions in **Table 6.3**.

TABLE 6.3	National Income and Aggregate Expenditures				
National Income (Y)	Consumption (C)	Saving (S)	Investment (I)	Aggregate Expenditures (AE) (C + I)	Surplus(+)/ Shortage (−) (Unplanned Investment)
0	50	−50	75	125	−125
100	125	−25	75	200	−100
200	200	0	75	275	−75
300	275	25	75	350	−50
400	350	50	75	425	−25
500	**425**	**75**	**75**	**500**	**0**
600	500	100	75	575	+25
700	575	125	75	650	+50
800	650	150	75	725	+75

Since there are two spending sectors in this simple economy, aggregate expenditures (AE) equal the total of consumption and investment spending combined. You can see that the aggregate expenditures column is similar to the consumption column in that there is an amount of autonomous spending ($125), and you can see that spending increases directly with the level of income. In other words, as we mentioned at the outset:

$$\text{Total AE} = \text{autonomous AE} + \text{induced AE}$$

The relationship between the change in aggregate expenditures and income is referred to as the **marginal propensity to expend** (MPE). In the form of an equation, it is:

marginal propensity to expend: the ratio of change in expenditures that results from a change in income.

$$\text{Marginal propensity to expend (MPE)} = \frac{\Delta \text{ aggregate expenditures}}{\Delta \text{ income}} \qquad \text{[6.5]}$$

The value of the MPE in Karinia is equal to 75/100 = 0.75. In fact, here it has the same value as the MPC, though as we expand our model, this will not remain the case. The marginal propensity to expend tells us how much of each extra dollar earned is spent on purchasing domestically produced goods. In other words, it tells us what fraction remains in the circular flow of income that we developed in Chapter 3. The remainder is the amount that leaks out. The **marginal leakage rate** (MLR) is therefore the fraction of extra income that leaks out:

marginal leakage rate: the ratio of change in leakages that results from a change in income.

$$\text{Marginal leakage rate (MLR)} = \frac{\Delta \text{ total leakages}}{\Delta \text{ income}} \qquad \text{[6.6]}$$

And since, together, the MPE and MLR add up to one, it follows that:

$$\text{Marginal leakage rate (MLR)} = (1 - \text{MPE}) \qquad \text{[6.7]}$$

In Karinia, the value of the marginal leakage rate is equal to $(1 - 0.75) = 0.25$ and has the same value as the marginal propensity to save (MPS), though this is true only in this simplified model.

The equation for the aggregate expenditure function, then, is:

$$AE = 125 + 0.75Y$$

As we mentioned at the outset, conceptually, we can regard gross domestic product (GDP, the value of production) as equal to national income. However, these two are not necessarily equal to aggregate expenditures. In fact, we can see in **Table 6.3** that at an income level of zero in Karinia, aggregate expenditures are equal to $125. At this level of income, spending is far in excess of production. The result would be a shortage of goods and services to the tune of $125. This amount is shown in the final column of **Table 6.3**, labelled *unplanned investment*, and can be calculated as the difference between national income and aggregate expenditures.

It is certainly pertinent to ask how, in an economy such as Karinia, people are able to physically buy $125 of goods and services if the country has, in fact, produced nothing—which must be the case since income is equal to zero. (We know that they are going to have to borrow in order to pay for them.) The answer is that buyers must be purchasing goods produced in previous years. In other words, they are buying up existing inventory. The last column of **Table 6.3** also shows us that the shortage of goods would be smaller at an income (and production) level of $100 and smaller still at an income level of $200. However, it is only at an income level of $500 that production is equal to aggregate expenditures. This is what is referred to as **expenditure equilibrium**. At income levels above $500, the opposite situation would prevail: production would exceed expenditures and the resulting surplus of goods would cause inventories to build up. Since a change in inventories is part of investment, we see why it is referred to as **unplanned investment**.

> **expenditure equilibrium:** the income at which the value of production and aggregate expenditures are equal.

> **unplanned investment:** the amount of unintended investment by firms in the form of a buildup or rundown of inventories, that is, the difference between production (Y) and aggregate expenditures (AE).

> Equilibrium income is that level of income (and production) at which there is neither a surplus nor a shortage of goods.

Before we can fully grasp all the details of the expenditure model, we need to return to our discussion of what *equilibrium* means. Try this. Imagine throwing a stone into a pond and watching the concentric ripples fade as they widen. In response to the shock of the stone striking the water's surface, that same surface immediately begins returning to normal or to a smooth state—returning to equilibrium. Thus, equilibrium can be thought of as a state of rest, or a state of normalcy, which can, from time to time, be disrupted by various shocks. In other words, the concept of equilibrium in economics contains not just the idea of equality between things but also a point of rest, or balance, toward which the economy will naturally move.

So, expenditure equilibrium not only means that income and production are equal to aggregate expenditures but also that if they are not equal, there will be forces in the economy that will help move them toward equality and equilibrium. And the motivating force is simply the desire by firms to make profits and avoid losses. All that this means is that if, in total, firms were producing in excess of sales (a surplus of goods), they would face a buildup of unsold inventories and have little alternative but to cut output (and possibly prices) in the next period. Alternatively, a shortage of goods would imply a depletion of inventories and cause firms to produce more in subsequent periods.

The concept of equilibrium can also be seen from a different viewpoint by recognizing (from our circular flow model) that it occurs when injections equal leakages. If you look at the bold-faced equilibrium row in **Table 6.3**, you can see that only at equilibrium do injections (investment) equal leakages (saving). These two ideas of equilibrium are illustrated in **Figure 6.3A**.

Here, we introduce a 45° line, which enables us to easily locate expenditure equilibrium. Any point on the 45° line indicates that what is being measured on the horizontal axis and what is being measured on the vertical axis are equal. (Of course, this assumes that the scales of the two

FIGURE 6.3   Expenditures Equilibrium

Autonomous aggregate expenditures are $125. The slope of the aggregate expenditures function is 0.75 so that expenditures increase by $75 for each increase of $100 in income. When income reaches $500, aggregate expenditures will have increased by $375 and will now equal income. This is expenditure equilibrium and is graphically indicated by the AE function crossing the 45° line.

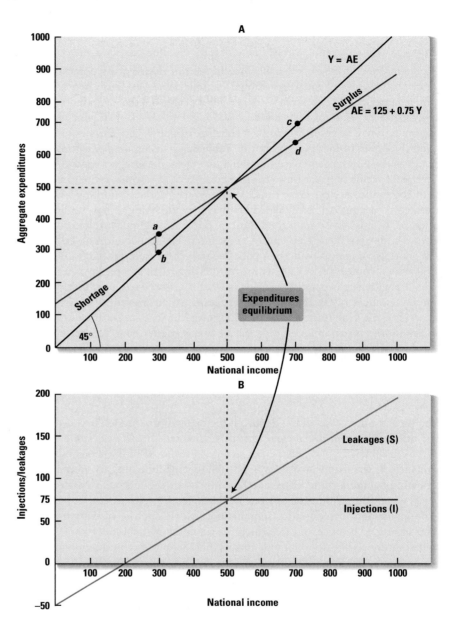

Total injections are an autonomous $75. Total leakages increase with income and are equal to injections at the equilibrium income of $500.

axes are the same.) We have labelled the 45° line Y = AE. Expenditure equilibrium occurs where aggregate expenditures equals income, and this is where the AE function crosses the 45° line. This occurs in our model at the $500 level of income. Note that at incomes below $500, the AE function is above the 45° line. This means that aggregate expenditures exceed national income.

Any gap between the two curves, say, the distance *ab*, represents the amount of shortage (unplanned dis-investment) that exists at that income level (the shortage equals $50 at the $300 income level in this case). At incomes greater than $500, the AE function is below the 45° line, which illustrates the fact that income (and production) exceeds aggregate expenditures, thus resulting in a surplus (unplanned increase in investment). For example, at an income level of $700, the distance *cd* (equal to $50) is the amount of the surplus. **Figure 6.3B** shows that at the equilibrium income of $500, total injections are equal to total leakages of $75.

Finally, let us see how we can derive expenditures equilibrium algebraically. Although we already know the algebraic expression for aggregate expenditures (AE = 125 + 0.75Y), it is revealing to derive it formally:

$$\begin{array}{rcl} C & = & 50 + 0.75Y \\ I & = & 75 + \\ \hline AE & = & 125 + 0.75Y \end{array}$$

By definition, expenditures equilibrium occurs where national income is equal to aggregate expenditures (Y = AE). So, if we substitute Y for AE in the above equation:

$$Y = 125 + 0.75Y$$

Therefore, $0.25Y = 125$

And $Y = 500$

✓ SELF-TEST

3. You are given the accompanying table for a private, closed economy.

a) What are the equations for the consumption, investment, and aggregate expenditures functions?

b) What is the value of expenditures equilibrium?

National Income	Consumption	Saving	Investment
0	100	−100	200
200	280	−80	200
400	460	−60	200

4. Given that for a private, closed economy C = 80 + 0.6Y and I = 120, what is the value of expenditures equilibrium?

6.3 THE MULTIPLIER

As we mentioned at the beginning of this chapter, spending—aggregate expenditures—lies at the heart of this Keynesian model of the economy, and therefore it is important that we get a handle on what determines the level of spending in a modern economy and what happens when it changes. Let us start by asking: what can cause a change in the level of spending? **Figure 6.4** illustrates two very different causes.

L03 Explain how the multiplier produces big changes in national income as a result of small changes in spending.

Figure 6.4A shows how spending rises (from $900 to $1200) as a result of an increase in the level of national income (from $800 to $1200). This is what we mean by an increase in induced spending. **Figure 6.4B** is very different. Again, spending has increased from $900 to $1200, but income has remained the same at $800. In other words, the change in spending was independent of the income level. This is what we mean by a change in autonomous aggregate expenditures. Let us look at some of the factors that affect autonomous spending.

| FIGURE 6.4 | Change in Induced Spending and Change in Autonomous Spending |

Figure A illustrates how an increase in income from $800 to $1200 increases aggregate expenditures from $900 to $1200 billion. This is an increase in induced expenditures, causing a movement along the AE curve. Figure B shows a similar increase in aggregate expenditures from $900 to $1200, though the income level remains at $800. This is caused by an increase in autonomous expenditures, causing a shift in the AE curve from AE_1 to AE_2.

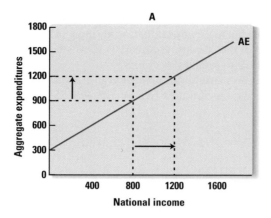

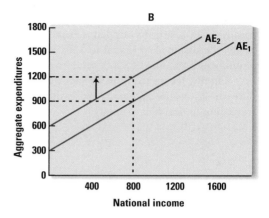

Determinants of Consumption

wealth effect: the direct effect of a change in wealth on consumption spending.

First, what will change autonomous consumption? Economists know that the wealth held by people can influence consumption spending. This is called the **wealth effect**. To use a micro-level example, imagine a middle-aged professional computer programmer driving home from work, reflecting on how well her life seems to be unfolding—good job, kids well on their way to growing up, spouse working at something he likes, and a mortgage that is now quite manageable. She then hears the day's closing stock quotations, which prompts her to do quick calculations after dinner on the current value of the $5000 she put into shares a couple of years back. She is pleasantly surprised to realize that the shares are now worth over $8000—at least on paper. Her thought is to surprise the family with a proposal for a spontaneous holiday or perhaps announce that the hot tub they had been discussing will, indeed, be purchased. The point is that the rise in wealth might well lead to increased consumption, even though income is unchanged.

Stockholders' wealth changes daily.

TSX	Dow	Germany	FTSE 100	C$
+41.95	**−47.38**	**−15.77**	**−2.18**	**−0.5**
1996.27	12548.37	7387.54	5923.69	US1.0263
S&P/TSX	**S&P 500**	**Nasdaq**	**Nikkei**	**Gold**
+14.19	**−8.30**	**−46.16**	**−90.47**	**−3**
13391.35	1329.47	2782.31	9558.30	US$1490.60
Hong Kong	**China (Shanghai)**	**India**	**Taiwan**	**Crude oil**
−315.64	**−21.96**	**−186.25**	**−94.90**	**−2.28**
22960.63	2849.07	18345.03	8911.71	US$97.37

Source: *The Financial Post*, May 17, 2011.

Next, let us recognize, as we did in Chapter 5, that the level of consumption also depends on the price level. A change in the price level will cause consumption spending to change. The reason for this may seem obvious. However, it is not simply a case of higher prices causing spending to drop because people can afford less, and of lower prices causing people to spend more because they can afford to. The proper explanation has to do with the real value of assets. Suppose, for instance, that both prices *and* your own money income were to increase by 10 percent so that your real income remained constant. Would this change have any real effect on your consumption? On the surface, the answer is no—in real terms, your financial status has not changed. However, even though your real income is unchanged, one portion of your wealth is adversely affected by the price increase: the value of your financial assets. Your wealth now has a lower purchasing power and has, in fact, declined in value. Under these conditions, you may well cut your consumption and save more to replenish your real wealth. Similarly, a drop in prices will increase the real value of your wealth and lead to an increase in consumption. The effect of a change in the price level on the level of real wealth and therefore on consumption, as you will remember from Chapter 5, is the real-balances effect.

Changes in the stock market can have a big impact on investors' wealth and on their spending.

A third factor that can affect the level of autonomous expenditures is due to the fact that most households today possess a number of durable goods, from kitchen appliances to iPhones, from cars to furniture. These things get replaced for two reasons. First, people get tired of them and can afford to replace them. Such action is obviously dependent on income. Second, durables get replaced simply because they wear out and must be replaced, regardless (within reason) of the current state of the householder's income flow. When the water heater quits, most of us just shrug, mumble that we will have to manage somehow, and arrange for a replacement. Thus, as the stock of consumer durables gets older, the likelihood of increased consumption spending grows as the need for replacement increases.

Finally, at any given time, there is a prevailing mood among an economy's consumers concerning the future state of the economy, particularly in the areas of job availability, trends in salary and wage rates, and expected changes in future prices. If this mood changes, say, from pessimistic to optimistic, then an autonomous increase in consumption spending is very likely to occur as well. In short, a change in consumer expectations can cause an autonomous change in consumption spending. In summary, the major determinants of autonomous consumption spending are:

- changes in wealth (wealth effect)
- changes in the price level (real-balances effect)
- changes in the age of consumer durables
- changes in consumer expectations

Determinants of Investment

In our simple model, there are two types of spending—consumer spending and investment spending—and a change in either will cause a change in aggregate expenditures. Let us now see what can cause a change in investment. You will recall that our model regards investment spending as totally autonomous of income. So, if the level of income does not affect investment, what does determines the level of investment spending in the economy? For most businesses, most of the time, investment spending is financed with borrowed money. That is, corporations do not just write a cheque for several million dollars to refit some of their production equipment. Instead, they borrow the money from a bank, or perhaps from some other financial intermediary via a bond issue. Given this, it is important to recognize the impact of a change in interest rates on the total interest cost of borrowing. As an example, look at the difference in interest costs when $10 million is borrowed at 10 percent simple interest for a 20-year period and when it is borrowed at 12 percent.

$$\$10 \text{ million @ } 10\% \text{ for } 20 \text{ years} = \$20 \text{ million}$$

$$\$10 \text{ million @ } 12\% \text{ for } 20 \text{ years} = \$24 \text{ million}$$

ADDED DIMENSION   Are Interest Rates Important?

Some might argue that there is a possible important omission from this list of the major determinants of consumption: interest rates. It is certainly true that increases in interest rates may cause some people to think twice before taking out consumer loans or buying a new car. (Remember from Chapter 3 that new house purchases are regarded—at least by Statistics Canada—as a form of investment and will definitely be affected by changes in interest rates.) If that is the case, then, why are most economists reluctant to include interest rates as a determinant of consumption? The reason is that research on the topic is inconclusive.

It could well be that higher interest rates mean some people will cut down on consumer loans and save more because of the higher return they can now expect. But other people may see the higher interest rates as a reason to cut back on their monthly saving, since they can put less aside yet still earn as much as they did before, given the higher interest rates.

Keynes himself felt that interest rates are not important determinants of consumption and saving. Most of us, he felt, are creatures of habit and it is a fairly painful exercise to re-adjust our spending patterns, which is what we would have to do if we adjusted our level of saving each time there was a change in interest rates. Income levels, as well as the other factors we have mentioned, are far more significant when it comes to figuring out our spending levels. Not everyone agrees with this. Some economists suggest that while low interest rates may, indeed, have little impact on consumer spending, very high interest rates may well choke off expenditures.

It is clear that a particular investment possibility may be judged to be "worth it" at, say, 10 percent interest but not at 12 percent because of the additional $4 million that must be paid in interest.

In short, whether an investment project appears profitable or not depends on the interest costs of the money that must be borrowed to finance it. Note also that even if the investment is self-financed by a company, the rate of interest is still a determining factor in deciding whether or not to invest, since the alternative to investing is simply to leave the money in some form of savings certificate, or in a savings account, and earn a guaranteed return.

In all of this, it is important to realize, as we mentioned in Chapter 4, that the real, not the nominal, rate of interest is the important determinant of investment spending. A firm that must pay a nominal rate of interest of 10 percent per annum over the next three years will be less inclined to borrow if it believes the rate of inflation is going to be 2 percent per annum over that period (making the real rate of interest it has to pay equal to 8 percent) than if it believes that inflation will be 7 percent (which would make the real rate equal to only 3 percent).

Besides the interest rate, the initial price that must be paid for equipment or building has a clear impact on whether that purchase will be profitable or not. Similarly, the maintenance and operating costs involved over the life of the new machine, equipment, or building must also be considered in calculating potential profitability.

Sometimes, new investment must be undertaken simply because equipment has worn out or a building is in a serious state of disrepair. As the age of an economy's capital stock increases, this sort of thing occurs with greater frequency, and investment spending is higher than it would otherwise have been. But it's not just the age of capital goods that determines how much investment will be done. The amount of investment will also depend on the amount of spare (unused) capacity that exists in that machines do not always run 24 hours a day and others sit entirely idle at times. If there is a lot of spare capacity in the economy, it is unlikely that firms will want to invest any time soon. In addition, investment spending may well increase when businesspeople are optimistic about the future, and decrease when pessimism sets in. These psychological factors have an important bearing on investment decisions.

Finally, bureaucracy or "red-tape requirements" add to costs and thus have an impact on the potential profitability of any proposed investment project. If red tape were cut, one would also expect investment spending to increase.

In summary, the major determinants of investment spending are:

- interest rates
- purchase price, installation, maintenance, and operating costs of capital goods
- the age of capital goods and the amount of spare capacity
- business expectations
- government regulations

One of the important ideas that Keynes popularized (though he did not invent it) was that of the multiplier. Simply put, the idea is that an increase in (autonomous) spending can have an impact on income well in excess of that spending. Perhaps the easiest way to see this is graphically.

The Multiplier Graphically

As we have seen, many factors influence the level of autonomous spending in a country, and we need to be able to work out the effect of these changes. Let us start with the assumption that businesses in Karinia become more optimistic about the future. As a result, they decide to increase spending on new investment projects. Instead of spending $75 billion on investment, as they did last year, let us suppose they increase investment spending to $125 billion. Karinian businesses place additional orders for new construction, equipment, computers, and other capital projects. This will, of course, increase production by $50 billion above that of the previous year and boost income by the same amount. But is that the end of the story? Is it simply the case that an extra $50 billion in spending translates into $50 billion of extra income? The answer is, in fact, no. As we shall soon see, income will increase by more than $50 billion. **Figure 6.5** helps explain this.

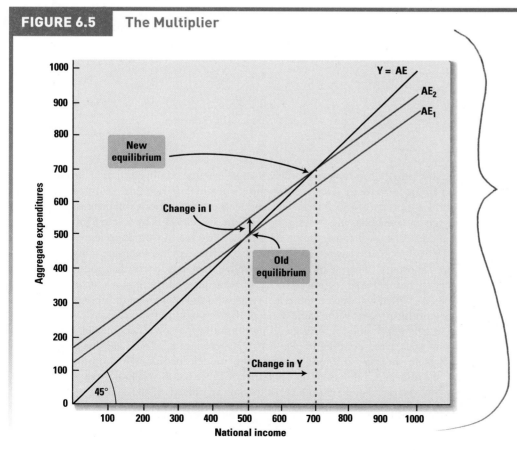

FIGURE 6.5   The Multiplier

The increase in autonomous spending of $50 has an immediate effect of increasing aggregate expenditures by $50. This results in a shortage. This will lead to an increase in production and, thus, income. The economy will eventually move to a new equilibrium, where the new AE function (AE_2) crosses the Y = AE curve. As a result, income here increases by a total of $200, four times as much as the initial increase in spending.

The increase in investment spending increases aggregate expenditures by $50 at every level of income so that there is a parallel shift up in the AE function from AE_1 to AE_2. After the shift, there would be a shortage of goods and services of $50 *at the original level of income of $500*. The result of the shortage is that production will increase. Even if income rises by $50 (the same amount as the increase in spending) to $550, there would still be a shortage of goods and services, since at this income level, AE_2 is still above the Y = AE line. The new equilibrium, in fact, occurs at the $700 level of income. In other words, income will increase by *four times* the amount of the increase in aggregate expenditures. The reason for this phenomenon is termed the *multiplier* (or expenditures multiplier as some refer to it), and it is one of the more intriguing aspects of macroeconomics.

The Multiplier Derived

Let us look at this decision to increase investment spending in more detail. **Table 6.4** illustrates the effect of an increase of $50 billion.

TABLE 6.4	The Multiplier Process				
Period	National Income (Y)	Consumption (C)	Investment (I)	Aggregate Expenditures (AE) (C + I)	Surplus(+)/ Shortage (−) (Unplanned Investment)
1	500	425	75	500	0
...	...	...	...	...	...
2	500	425	125	550	−50
3	550	462.5	125	587.5	−37.5
4	587.5	490.625	125	615.625	−28.125
5	615.625	511.72	125	636.72	−21.10
...	...	...	...	...	...
Final	700	575	125	700	0

Before the investment, Karinia's economy was in its original equilibrium of $500, and we will call this Period 1. The increase in investment spending of $50 in Period 2 will immediately create a disequilibrium—a shortage of $50. As a result, producers of capital goods will increase production by $50, raising the income of its employees, suppliers, and shareholders by $50 to $550 in Period 3. But if income increases, so will consumption. In Period 3, we see consumption increasing by 0.75 times $50, or by 37.5 to 462.5. However, this increase in the demand for more consumer goods will again create a shortage, this time of $37.5. In Period 4, then, producers of consumer goods will increase production and therefore income by $37.5. But this raises consumption a further 0.75 times $37.5, or by $28.125, which will cause another shortage. And thus it goes on in subsequent periods.

The essence of this process is the same concept that lies behind the circular flow model that we developed in Chapter 3: one person's spending is another person's income. The result is that each time income increases, spending increases by 75 percent of it. When will this process come to an end? When no shortage of goods exists. In our model, income will continue to increase until it finally gets to $700, as shown in the final row of **Table 6.4**. If you look back at **Figure 6.5**, you can verify that the new equilibrium level of income is, indeed, $700.

Note that, at this new equilibrium level of income, saving has increased from its original $75 to the new level of $125. It is now equal to the higher level of investment.

In summary, then, an initial increase in investment of $50 induced an increase of $200 in national income. On the surface, this seems to provide a dramatic solution to any recession and a simple formula for growth. We just need to encourage people to spend more! But as you probably suspect, there is a little more to it than that.

We have just seen the multiplier at work. This is the process by which changes in autonomous expenditures are translated into a multiplied change in national income:

$$\text{Multiplier} = \frac{\Delta \text{ income}}{\Delta \text{ autonomous expenditures}} \qquad \textbf{[6.8]}$$

In our model, the initial increase of $50 led to an increase in income of $200. In other words, the value of the multiplier was equal to 200/50 = 4.

To understand where this number came from, let us do a little algebra integrating the change in investment:

$$
\begin{aligned}
C &= 50 + 0.75Y \\
I &= 125 \qquad \text{(used to be 75)} \\
\hline
AE &= 175 + 0.75Y
\end{aligned}
$$

Equilibrium is where Y = AE, so:

$$Y = 175 + \underset{\text{(MPE)}}{0.75Y}$$

And
$$
\begin{aligned}
Y - 0.75Y &= 175 \\
\underset{\text{(MLR)}}{(1 - 0.75)Y} &= 175 \\
Y &= 175 \times \frac{1}{0.25} = \left(175 \times \frac{1}{\text{MLR}}\right) = 700
\end{aligned}
$$

The equation for the multiplier, therefore, is:

$$\text{Multiplier} = \frac{1}{(\text{MLR})} \text{ or } \frac{1}{(1 - \text{MPE})} \qquad \textbf{[6.9]}$$

In our example, the marginal propensity to expend (MPE) is 0.75, so the marginal leakage rate (MLR) is (1 − 0.75) = 0.25, and the multiplier is 1/0.25 = 4. This means that whenever autonomous spending (in this case, investment) changes by any amount, income will change four times as much.

It follows then that:

The higher the value of the MPE (the smaller the MLR), the bigger will be the multiplier.

Now, before we get carried away with this idea, the value of the multiplier will actually be much smaller than 4 (as we shall see later, when we fully expand our model). It should also be noted that the multiplier works in reverse: a drop in autonomous expenditures will produce a decline in income, which will also cause a decline in employment.

SELF-TEST

5. Given the following values for the MPE, calculate the values of the MLR and multipliers.

   a) 0.9

   b) 0.75

   c) 0.6

   d) 0.5

6. Note the accompanying graph.

   a) What is the algebraic expression for aggregate expenditures?

   b) What is the value of expenditures equilibrium?

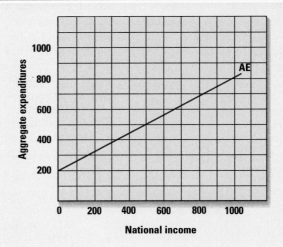

6.4   THE COMPLETE EXPENDITURE MODEL

L04 See how government's budget balance and the balance of trade both relate to national income.

We now need to make our model more realistic by including the other spending sectors of the economy. First, let us add in government spending and taxation.

The Government Sector

Suppose that taxation and spending are as shown in **Table 6.5**.

TABLE 6.5	Government Budget Function		
National Income (Y)	Tax Revenue (T)	Government Spending (G)	Budget Surplus (+)/ deficit (−) (T − G)
0	60	160	−100
100	80	160	−80
200	100	160	−60
300	120	160	−40
400	140	160	−20
500	160	160	0
600	180	160	+20
700	200	160	+40
800	220	160	+60

As with investment spending, government spending is treated as wholly autonomous, and its function in this example is:

$$G = 160$$

Now, you might object to this, and you may believe that the amount that government is able to spend is, in turn, determined by the amounts of tax and other revenues it receives. Since this tax revenue is dependent on income, wouldn't this mean that the amounts government spends are also dependent on the level of income? While there is some truth in this, it would be a gross simplification. In fact, governments can and do spend whatever they feel is necessary, irrespective of the tax revenues they receive. Therefore, we will regard government spending as autonomous. Making this assumption again offers the advantage of simplicity. We will return to this point later.

Note that in Karinia, taxes are $60, even when income is zero. This is the level of autonomous taxes. There are several examples of autonomous taxes, including highway tolls, user fees, property taxes, and so on. These taxes do not depend on the level of income. However, the majority of the Karinian government's tax revenue comes from induced taxes. These are taxes that depend directly on, or are related to, income levels. Examples would be personal income taxes, corporate taxes, and sales taxes.

Total taxes are made up of autonomous taxes and induced taxes:

$$\text{Total taxes} = \text{autonomous taxes} + \text{induced taxes} \qquad \text{[6.10]}$$

The rate at which tax revenues increase with national income is known as the **marginal tax rate** (MTR):

$$\text{Marginal tax rate (MTR)} = \frac{\Delta \text{ taxes}}{\Delta \text{ income}} \qquad \text{[6.11]}$$

marginal tax rate: the ratio of the change in taxation as a result of a change in income.

We can see in **Table 6.5** that as national income increases by 100, tax revenues increase by 20. Put another way, this means that for every additional $1 in income, $0.20 goes to taxes. The marginal tax rate for this economy is therefore equal to 20/100 = 0.2, and the tax function is:

$$T = 60 + 0.2Y$$

The government budget balance is simply the difference between its tax revenue and its spending (T − G). You can see in **Table 6.5** that as national income increases, government's budget deficit decreases and eventually becomes a surplus.

We illustrate these ideas in **Figure 6.6**.

In **Figure 6.6A**, since government spending is wholly autonomous, it plots (like investment spending) as a straight line horizontal to the axis. The tax function, however, varies directly with the level of income. It does not start at the origin, since there is $60 of autonomous taxation. The steepness of the tax function is determined by the value of the marginal tax rate. In Karinia, this has a value of 0.2, and this is the slope of its tax function. When government spending is above the tax function, the difference between them represents a budget deficit. When the tax function is above the government spending function, the difference is a budget surplus. There is a budget balance where the two lines intersect.

The condition of government's budget deficit is shown explicitly in the budget line in **Figure 6.6B**. It starts at a deficit of $100 and is upward-sloping; as the level of income increases (and along with it, the government's tax revenue) the size of the budget deficit gets smaller. It is balanced at an income of $500 and becomes a surplus at higher incomes.

Now, let us integrate both government spending and taxation into our model, going back to the original data with I = 75. This is done in **Table 6.6**.

FIGURE 6.6   **Government Spending, Taxation, and the Budget Line**

Figure A plots government spending as a horizontal line at $160. The tax function starts at an autonomous level of $60 and increases at a (marginal tax) rate of 0.2. The two curves intersect, and there is a balanced budget at an income level of $500. Below that level there are budget deficits, and above it there are budget surpluses.

Figure B shows government's budget position in the form of the budget line. It starts at a deficit of $100 at zero income and is upward sloping, since deficits get smaller (and surpluses bigger) as income rises. The budget line crosses the axis at $500, where the budget balance is zero.

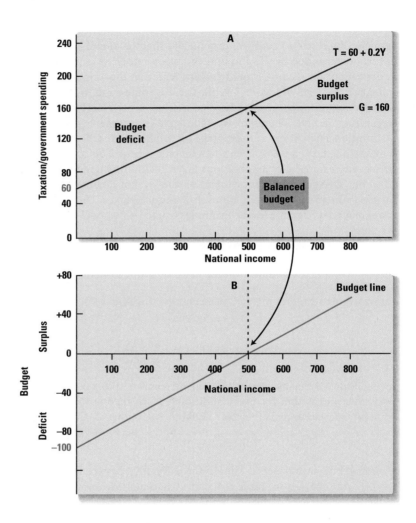

Our third column, Disposable Income, is simply (national) income after taxes:

$$\text{Disposable income} = \text{National income less tax} \qquad [6.12]$$
$$Y_D \qquad = \qquad (Y - T)$$

Our consumption function remains unchanged and is equal to $C = 50 + 0.75Y_D$. (Since we will be referring to both national and disposable incomes, we will abbreviate the former as simply Y and the latter as Y_D.) However, as a result of taxes, consumption and saving are both now lower for each level of national income.

The concept of expenditures equilibrium remains unchanged and occurs where national income is equal to aggregate expenditures. However, we now have an additional expenditure sector: government spending. Aggregate expenditures are therefore equal to the total of consumption (C), investment (I), and government spending (G). Expenditures equilibrium occurs at a national income level of $600.

TABLE 6.6		Expenditures Equilibrium					
National Income (Y)	Tax (T)	Disposable Income (Y_D)	Consumption (C)	Saving (S)	Investment (I)	Government Spending (G)	Aggregate Expenditures (AE) (C + I + G)
0	60	−60	5	−65	75	160	240
100	80	20	65	−45	75	160	300
200	100	100	125	−25	75	160	360
300	120	180	185	−5	75	160	420
400	140	260	245	+15	75	160	480
500	160	340	305	+35	75	160	540
600	**180**	**420**	**365**	**+55**	**75**	**160**	**600**
700	200	500	425	+75	75	160	660
800	220	580	485	+95	75	160	720

Besides adding another injection, we have also added another leakage: taxes (T). It remains true, however, that total injections are equal to total leakages at equilibrium. Thus:

$$I \quad + \quad G \quad = \quad S \quad + \quad T$$
$$(75 \quad + \quad 160 \quad = \quad 55 \quad + \quad 180 \quad = 235)$$

Equilibrium for our expanded model is illustrated in **Figure 6.7**.

The value of the Y intercept in **Figure 6.7A**, $240, is the amount of autonomous aggregate expenditures. This constitutes autonomous consumption of 5, investment of 75, and government spending of 160. The slope of the aggregate expenditures is equal to marginal propensity to expend. However, it is now smaller than it was in our simplified model. Its value is now equal to 60/100, or 0.6. Our spending is lower than before, simply because some of our income is going to taxation.

Earlier, we saw how to calculate the value of equilibrium income algebraically. The equation for aggregate expenditure is expressed as:

$$AE = 240 + 0.6Y$$

Setting this equal to Y:

$$Y = 240 + 0.6Y$$

Therefore:

$$0.4Y = 240$$

$$Y = 600$$

Note that since the value of the MPE is now smaller (0.6 compared with 0.75), the value of the marginal leakage rate is bigger (0.4), and the value of the multiplier is smaller (1/0.4 or 2.5).

As you can see, if the information about the economy is given to us as it is in **Table 6.6**, deriving an expression for aggregate expenditures and finding the value of equilibrium income is not difficult. However, we need to go one step further. To fully understand our model, we need to derive an expression for consumption related to national income as well as disposable income.

Let us begin by looking at how consumption relates to disposable income (Y_D), that is: $C = 50 + 0.75Y_D$. We also know that $Y_D = (Y - T)$ and that $T = 60 + 0.2Y$.

FIGURE 6.7   Expenditures Equilibrium

The autonomous aggregate expenditures are $240. The slope of the AE function is 0.6 so that expenditures increase by $60 for each $100 increase in national income. The expenditure equilibrium is where the AE function crosses the Y = AE (45°) line at an income of $600.

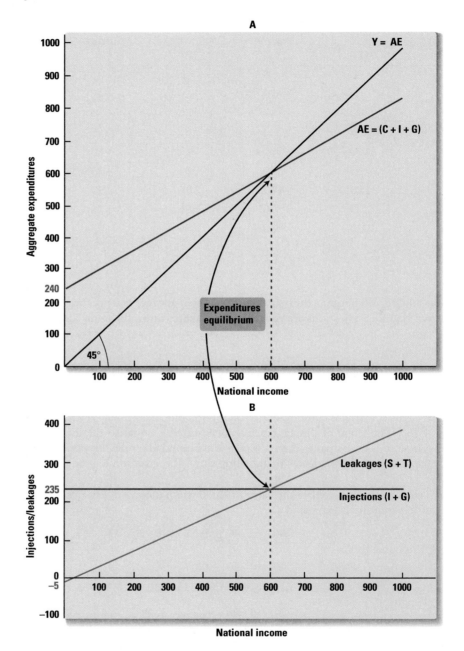

The total injections (I + G) are an autonomous $235. The total leakages increase with income and are equal to injections at the equilibrium income of $600.

Putting all this together gives us:

$$C = 50 + 0.75 \, (Y - [60 + 0.2Y]) \text{ or } C = 50 + 0.75(Y - 60 - 0.2Y)$$

Which we can reduce to: $C = 50 + 0.75Y - 45 - 0.15Y$

Therefore: $C = 5 + 0.6Y$

So, now we have two equivalent consumption functions, one related to disposable income ($C = 50 + 0.75Y_D$) and one related to national income ($C = 5 + 0.6Y$). Similarly, we have two marginal propensities to consume: one related to disposable income ($MPC_D = 0.75$) and one related to national income ($MPC = 0.6$). These two are related as follows:

$$\text{Marginal propensity to consume (MPC)} = MPC_D\,(1 - MTR) \qquad \textbf{[6.13]}$$

In our model, this gives us:

$$MPC = 0.75\,(1 - 0.2) \text{ or } 0.75 \times 0.8 = 0.6$$

Note also that the value of the MPE (0.6) is the same as the value of the MPC. However, this will *not* be the case when we introduce trade in the next section.

To find an expression for AE, we simply add together C, I, and G.

C	=	5 + 0.6Y
I	=	75
G	=	160
AE	=	240 + 0.6Y

This confirms the values that we obtained directly from the table. We should also note that, like investment, government spending is wholly autonomous. Should it increase, the effect will be a multiplied increase in national income; if it decreases, there will be a multiplied decrease in national income. An increase in autonomous taxes will, by contrast, decrease national income by a multiple, and a decrease in autonomous taxes will increase national income by a multiple.

To complete our model, we need to add one more injection, exports, and one more leakage, imports. In other words, we need to look at an open economy with international trade.

Adding the Foreign Sector

As we saw earlier, an increase in the level of income will lead to an increase in spending, whether this spending is on domestically produced or foreign-produced goods. This means that the amount that Canada imports is strongly related to our own national income, while our exports very much depend on the income levels in foreign economies. This means that our sale of goods abroad depends on foreign incomes and not on our own incomes, so exports are autonomous of national income. This is illustrated in **Table 6.7**.

However, the level of imports is directly related to the level of income. The relationship between imports and the level of income is known as the **marginal propensity to import** (MPM). Formally, this is:

marginal propensity to import: the ratio of the change in imports that results from a change in income.

$$\text{Marginal propensity to import (MPM)} = \frac{\Delta\text{ imports (IM)}}{\Delta\text{ income (Y)}} \qquad \textbf{[6.14]}$$

For Karinia, the value of the MPM is 0.1, since **Table 6.7** shows that for every \$100 increase in national income, imports increase by 10, that is, $10/100 = 0.1$.

Note that there is also an autonomous component to imports, since the level of imports is \$40 when income is zero. Presumably, since Karinia does not possess certain products and resources, it will need to import them from abroad, regardless of its income level. That is to say, import spending is both autonomous (the \$40) and induced (the MPM × the level of income), just as we saw when we looked at the consumption function.

The equation for the import function, therefore, is:

$$IM = 40 + 0.1Y$$

TABLE 6.7	Net Exports Function		
National Income (Y)	Exports (X)	Imports (IM)	Net Exports (XN) (X − IM)
0	100	40	+60
100	100	50	+50
200	100	60	+40
300	100	70	+30
400	100	80	+20
500	100	90	+10
600	100	100	0
700	100	110	−10
800	100	120	−20

✔ SELF-TEST

7. What does it mean to suggest that some amount of imports may be autonomous? Explain the phrase, and give examples to illustrate your answer.

net exports (balance of trade): the value of a country's export of goods and services less the value of imports.

Let us turn now to **net exports**, which is simply the difference between exports and imports. It is also referred to as the **balance of trade**, and this balance can be positive or negative. Note in **Table 6.7** that net exports are positive and highest when income is lowest. This is because autonomous exports are a constant $100, whereas imports are often induced and thus rise as income rises. In fact, at income levels above $600, imports rise to exceed exports. As a result, net exports become negative. This means that as Karinia enjoys a higher income it starts to see a reduction in its trade surplus and subsequently an increase in its trade deficit. This is illustrated in **Figure 6.8A**.

We see in **Figure 6.8A** that since exports are an autonomous $100, the export function is a horizontal line at that level. Since imports are partly autonomous, the import function starts at $40. However, it is also related to incomes so that the import function rises from that point. The slope of the import function is equal to the value of the MPM, which, you recall, has a value of 0.1 in Karinia.

Figure 6.8B shows that the net export function begins at a surplus of $60, since this is the amount of the difference between autonomous exports and autonomous imports. As income rises, imports also rise. However, exports do not change with income level so that *net* exports (or the trade surplus) decline. At an income level of $600, exports are equal to imports, which means that net exports are zero; that is, there is a zero balance of trade. This is indicated by the net export function crossing the horizontal line. In algebraic terms:

$$X_N = X - IM$$

Therefore, for our model, it is equal to:

$$X_N = 100 - (40 + 0.1Y), \text{ or}$$
$$X_N = 60 - 0.1Y$$

FIGURE 6.8   **The Net Export Function**

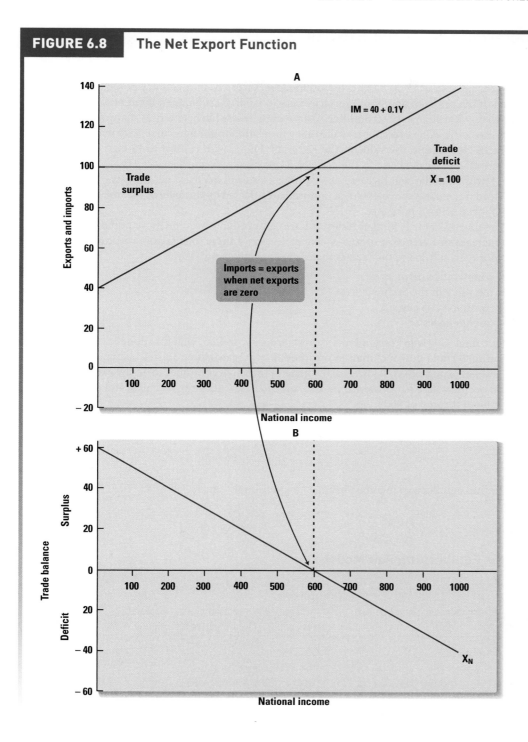

Figure A shows that imports increase as income levels increase so that the import function is upward sloping. Exports are autonomous of income levels, and therefore its function is a horizontal line. At low income levels, exports exceed imports, which results in a trade surplus. At higher income levels, however, imports exceed exports, which implies a trade deficit. At income level of $600, the trade balance is zero.

In Figure B, the net export function starts at a surplus of 60 but decreases in value as income increases. It has a value of zero (exports = imports) where the line crosses the axis at an income of $600.

Determinants of Net Exports

We have established that exports are wholly autonomous, whereas imports are partially autonomous and partly induced by income. There are four major factors affecting net exports.

First, net exports will be affected by the level of prices in a country compared with prices abroad. If the prices of goods and services were to fall in Karinia, then foreigners would be more likely to buy Karinian exports and Karinians would be less likely to buy as many foreign imports.

Second, the value of a country's currency in relation to foreign currencies will also affect net exports. A decrease in the value of the Karinian dollar (with respect to foreign currencies) has the same effect as a decrease in the price of Karinian goods and services. This means that a fall in the Karinian dollar will increase net exports; a rise will decrease net exports.

Third, Karinian exports (but not imports) are affected by the level of income in the countries that import Karinian products.

The fourth factor is foreign tastes. If Karinian products become more popular this will lead to an increase in Karinian exports. A change in any of these four factors will cause a change in net exports. In summary, the factors that determine net exports are:

- comparative price levels
- the value of the exchange rate
- income levels abroad
- foreign tastes

Our final task is to integrate net exports into our model, which is done in **Table 6.8**. With international trade now included in our model, aggregate expenditures become the total of C, I, G, and net exports (X_N). However, the general principle continues to apply: expenditure equilibrium occurs where national income and aggregate expenditures are equal, and this occurs only at a national income of $600.

The value of autonomous aggregate expenditure now equals $300, and the marginal propensity to expend is 50/100 or 0.5. The equation for the aggregate expenditure function is:

$$AE = 300 + 0.5Y$$

To find equilibrium income algebraically, we simply equate AE to Y:

$$Y = 300 + 0.5Y$$

TABLE 6.8										Expenditures Equilibrium: Full Model
National Income (Y)	Tax (T)	Disposable Income (Y_D)	Consumption (C)	Saving (S)	Investment (I)	Government Spending (G)	Exports (X)	Imports (IM)	Net Exports (X_N)	Aggregate Expenditures (AE) (C + I + G + X_N)
0	60	−60	5	−65	75	160	100	40	+60	300
100	80	20	65	−45	75	160	100	50	+50	350
200	100	100	125	−25	75	160	100	60	+40	400
300	120	180	185	−5	75	160	100	70	+30	450
400	140	260	245	+15	75	160	100	80	+20	500
500	160	340	305	+35	75	160	100	90	+10	550
600	**180**	**420**	**365**	**+55**	**75**	**160**	**100**	**100**	**0**	**600**
700	200	500	425	+75	75	160	100	110	−10	650
800	220	580	485	+95	75	160	100	120	−20	700

This gives us:

$$0.5Y = 300$$
$$Y = 600$$

We also know that equilibrium implies that injections equal leakages, and this can be confirmed by inspecting their values at equilibrium income:

$$I \ + \ G \ + \ X \ = \ S \ + \ T \ + \ IM$$
$$75 \ + \ 160 \ + \ 100 \ = \ 55 \ + \ 180 \ + \ 100 \ = 335$$

Equilibrium is also shown in **Figure 6.9A**. The value of the Y intercept is equal to $300, which is the value of autonomous aggregate expenditures. The slope is 0.5 and is equal to the value of the MPE. Expenditures equilibrium occurs where income and aggregate expenditures are equal or where the Y = AE (45°) line crosses the AE function. In **Figure 6.9** the two cross at a value of $600.

Figure 6.9B indicates that the injections (I + G + X) are all wholly autonomous and have a value of $335. The leakages (S + T + IM), however, are all directly related to national income. Another way to determine equilibrium income, then, is to find the level of income that will induce leakages of $335. This occurs at an income level of $600.

We could also have derived an equation for aggregate expenditures by summing each separate equation:

$$
\begin{aligned}
C \ &= \ 5 \ + 0.6Y \\
I \ &= \ 75 \\
G \ &= \ 160 \\
X_N \ &= \ 60 \ - 0.1Y \\
\hline
AE \ &= \ 300 + 0.5Y
\end{aligned}
$$

Note that with the addition of another leakage, imports, the values of the MPE and, thus, the multiplier have decreased. The equation for the MPE is now

Marginal propensity to expend (MPE) $= MPC_D(1 - MTR) - MPM$ or $MPE = MPC - MPM$ **(6.15)**

We can calculate its value for our full model, knowing that $MPC_D = 0.75$, MTR = 0.2, and MPM = 0.1:

$$MPE = [0.75 \times (1 - 0.2)] - 0.1) \text{ or } MPE = 0.6 - 0.1 = 0.5.$$

The value of the MLR is (1 − 0.5) = 0.5, and the value of the multiplier is 1/0.5 = 2. Alternatively, the MLR can be found by simply summing the 3 marginal leakages (all out of income), thus:

$$MLR = MPS + MTR + MPM$$ **(6.16)**

In our example, that would be: 0.2 + 0.2 + 0.1 = 0.5

You can see that the value of the multiplier in our full model is much smaller than it was in our original simplified model. Since the leakages in a modern economy do tend to be quite high, the multiplier is accordingly smaller. For instance, in Canada the estimated value of the MPC_D is 0.79 (MPS_D is 0.21), the MTR is 0.13, and the MPM is 0.3. This gives an MPE of 0.39, meaning that of every extra $100 of production (and income) in Canada, only $39 gets spent on Canadian-produced goods and services. The other $61 goes to saving, taxes, and imports. With an MLR of 0.61, the value of the multiplier for Canada, therefore, is estimated at 1.64 (1/0.61).

FIGURE 6.9   Expenditures Equilibrium: Full Model

The autonomous aggregate expenditures are $300. The slope of the AE function is 0.5 so that expenditures increase by $50 for each $100 increase in national income. The expenditure equilibrium is where the AE function crosses the 45° line at an income of $600.

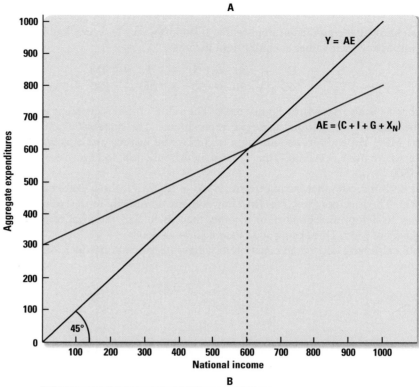

The total injections $(I + G + X)$ are an autonomous $335. The total leakages increase with income and are equal to the injections at the equilibrium income of $600.

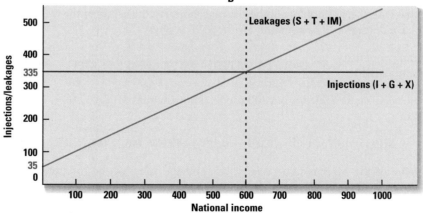

The following graphic summarizes more clearly the Canadian data from above:

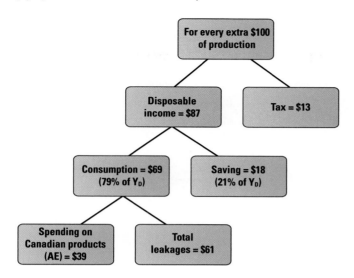

 ADDED DIMENSION   Real World Multipliers

In the modern world, the size of the expenditure multiplier is quite small. This is because savings, imports, and tax rates are quite high in most countries. The following table shows the estimated size of multipliers in the G8 countries using average rather than marginal rates. (Tax data are for 2008; all other data are for 2009.)

Value of the Multiplier for Selected Countries

Country	Savings/ GDP %	Imports/ GDP %	Taxes/ GDP %	Marginal Leakage Rate	Multiplier
Canada	17.7	30.4	12.9	0.61	1.64
France	16.4	25.0	21.4	0.63	1.59
Germany	21.5	35.9	11.8	0.69	1.45
Italy	16.0	24.4	22.6	0.63	1.59
Japan	23.6	12.2	11.9	0.48	2.08
Russia	22.7	20.4	15.8	0.59	1.69
U.K.	12.2	30.0	28.5	0.71	1.41
U.S.	9.8	13.9	10.1	0.34	2.94
World Average	18.5	23.3	16.0	0.58	1.72

Source: International Bank for Reconstruction and Development/The World Bank: World Development Indicators, 2010.

SELF-TEST

8. If T = 50 + 0.25Y; G = 200; IM = 30 + 0.1Y; and X = 120, what are the budget balance (T − G) and the trade balance (X − IM) at the following income levels?

    a) 400   **b)** 600   **c)** 900   **d)** 1200

9. You are given the following table for the economy of Narkia. Assuming that the MPC, MTR, and MPM are constant and I, G, and X are all autonomous.

    a) Fill in the table.

    b) Calculate the value of the expenditures equilibrium.

10. Find the value of MPE, MLR, and the multiplier, if $MPC_D = 0.9$; MTR = 0.25; MPM = 0.075.

Y	T	Y_D	C	S	I	G	X	IM	X_N	AE
0	20	—	30	—	50	—	—	10	—	_____
100	—	60	102	—	—	70	—	—	−2	_____
200	60	—	—	—	—	—	20	—	—	_____
300	—	220	246	−26	—	—	—	—	−26	_____

The Expenditures Model: A Summary

The level of national income is determined by the level of aggregate expenditures. An increase in any of the following will cause the level of income to increase:

- autonomous consumption
- investment
- exports
- government spending

The size of the increase is determined by the value of the multiplier.

Of course, a decrease in any of the above items will cause a multiple decrease in income. Furthermore, an increase in either of the following will cause a decrease in national income.

- autonomous taxes
- autonomous imports

Finally, the value of the multiplier will *increase* if any of the following *decrease*:

- marginal propensity to save (either MPS_D or MPS, since they move together)
- marginal tax rate
- marginal propensity to import

    The above summary brings out the essence of the expenditures model. Income depends on the level of autonomous spending; if this spending changes, income will change by some multiplied amount. That is to say, small changes can have a larger effect on the level of income.

    Also, we realize that the model demonstrates that the macroeconomy is always driving income to its equilibrium level. But we should add a cautionary note by asking: is it a desirable level of income? Not necessarily. Simply because an economy is at an expenditure equilibrium tells us nothing about how well it is performing. The economy could well be in a low-level trap. It is at equilibrium, but that equilibrium is well below the full-employment level. This is the message of Keynesian economics: though competitive markets naturally tend to move toward equilibrium, they do not necessarily move toward full employment. In fact, according to Keynes, the only way to move toward full employment is by achieving the *right level* of aggregate expenditures. This is a topic we will explore in detail in Chapters 7 and 9.

SELF-TEST

11. a) Which of the following circumstances would lead to an increase in national income?

   i) An increase in the marginal propensity to import

   ii) An increase in autonomous consumption

   iii) A decrease in the marginal tax rate

   iv) a decrease in government spending

   v) an increase in the marginal propensity to consume

   vi) a decrease in investment

b) Which of them would result in an increase in the size of the multiplier?

6.5 DERIVING AGGREGATE DEMAND

To wrap up this chapter, let us show how aggregate demand that we looked at in Chapter 5 is an extension of, and is derived from, aggregate expenditures.

L05 Derive aggregate demand from aggregate expenditures.

We have already discussed three ways that a change in the price level can have an impact on total expenditures. We saw that an increase in the price level reduces the level of real consumption by affecting the real value of money balances. In addition, we know that a change in domestic prices affects net exports: a higher domestic price reduces exports and increases imports. Finally, we noted that higher prices will push up interest rates and reduce investment spending.

We now want to show explicitly how a price change affects aggregate demand. Since aggregate demand equals the amount of aggregate expenditures at various price levels, we want to find the quantity of aggregate expenditures at price levels P_1, P_2, P_3, and so on. **Figure 6.10** shows how we can derive an aggregate demand curve directly from the expenditures equilibrium diagram.

In **Figure 6.10A**, the initial expenditure equilibrium is at Y_1, where AE_1 crosses the Y = AE (45°) line. This spending is done at a particular price level. Let us call this price level P_1 and show in the bottom **Figure 6.10B** that when the price level is P_1, equilibrium real GDP is at Y_1. You should note that we have made a change in the way we label the horizontal axes. When we use aggregate expenditures on the Keynesian 45° graph, the horizontal axis is labelled National Income. When we use the aggregate demand graph, we label the horizontal axis Real GDP. Of course, real GDP and real income are conceptually the same, but this change will help you keep the two graphs distinct.

Now, we want to figure out the effect on aggregate expenditures if the price level is higher. We just mentioned that a higher price reduces the real value of money balances (as well as other assets denominated in money). Earlier in the chapter, we called this the real-balances effect and suggested that the result of people holding assets with reduced values will be a reduction in their consumption spending. In addition, higher domestic prices also make our products less competitive in international markets so that the value of exports will fall and domestic consumers will be encouraged to buy comparatively cheaper foreign goods. It will also lower investment because interest rates will rise. As a result, net exports will decline.

Lower consumption, lower net exports, and lower investment will mean a lower level of aggregate expenditures at each level of income. This implies a downward shift in the aggregate expenditure curve, as shown in **Figure 6.10A**, from AE_1 to AE_2. This results in a lower level of real income, from Y_1 to Y_2. Therefore, we see in **Figure 6.10B** that a higher price level, P_2, is matched with a corresponding lower real GDP of Y_2. A lower price level will produce the opposite results: it will cause real balances, consumption spending, investment, and net exports to increase in value. A lower price level will therefore shift the AE curve up from the original AE_1 to AE_3. This leads to a higher equilibrium income level, Y_3. **Figure 6.10B** shows that a lower price level (P_3) means a higher level of real GDP (Y_3). As you can now see, every point on the aggregate demand curve is a point of equilibrium between aggregate expenditures and income. Simply put, the aggregate demand curve is downward sloping because consumption, net exports, and investment are inversely related to the price level.

FIGURE 6.10   The Aggregate Expenditures and Aggregate Demand Curve

Figure A shows that at price P_1, equilibrium GDP is Y_1. A higher price of P_2 lowers aggregate expenditures to AE_2 and leads to a lower income of Y_2. A lower price of P_3 increases aggregate expenditures to AE_3 and increases income to Y_3.

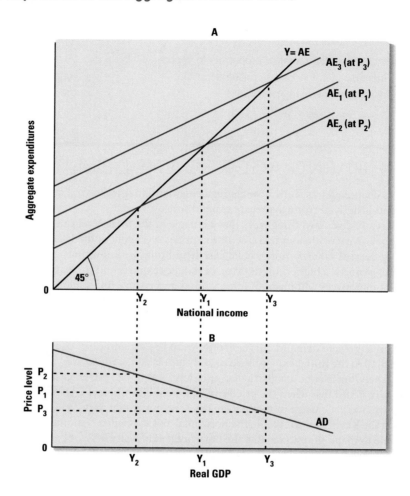

In Figure B, we see that joining these points produces a downward-sloping aggregate demand curve.

SELF-TEST

12. Which of the following will increase if prices fall, and why?

    a) exports

    b) investment

    c) government spending

    d) imports

    e) consumption

Review

CHAPTER SUMMARY

In this chapter, we constructed a model of the economy that highlights the interrelationships between the major spending sectors. We started by analyzing consumption, savings, and investment, and explained what can cause them to change and what happens when they do. We then introduced the government sector, and finally the international sector, again explaining what determines their levels of spending and how changes will affect the whole economy. The important concept of the multiplier was briefly introduced. We finished the chapter by demonstrating the link between aggregate expenditures and aggregate demand.

6.1a Production generates income that goes to households. Individuals use this income to:
- buy domestically produced goods and services and imports
- save
- pay taxes

6.1b Both consumption and saving have autonomous and induced portions. The marginal propensity to consume (MPC) relates the change in consumption to the change in income that induced it. Similarly, the marginal propensity to save (MPS) relates the change in saving to the change in income that induced it.

6.1c Investment is regarded as wholly autonomous with respect to national income.

6.2a Expenditures equilibrium occurs where:
- $Y = AE$
- injections = leakages
- there is no unplanned investment (neither a surplus or shortage)

It can be shown graphically where the AE function intersects the 45° ($Y = AE$) line.

6.3a The multiplier refers to the fact that an increase in autonomous spending leads to a multiplied increase in income. Its formula is:

$$\text{Multiplier} = \frac{1}{\text{MLR}} \text{ or } \frac{1}{(1 - \text{MPE})}$$

6.3b Changes in *autonomous consumption* are a result of:
- the wealth effect
- the real-balances effect
- changes in the age of consumer durables
- changes in consumer expectations

6.3c Changes in *autonomous investment* are a result of:
- changes in the interest rate
- changes in the purchase price or maintenance costs of capital goods
- changes in the age of capital goods
- changes in business expectations
- changes in government regulations

6.4a Government spending is regarded as wholly autonomous with respect to national income. Taxes, however, are partly autonomous and partly induced.

6.4b The marginal tax rate (MTR) is defined as ratio of change in taxes to a change in income.

6.4c Exports are regarded as wholly autonomous with respect to national income. Imports, however, are partly autonomous and partly induced.

6.4d The marginal propensity to import (MPM) is defined as ratio of change in imports to a change in income.

6.4e The MPE for the full model is equal to MPC − MPM or $\text{MPC}_D (1 - \text{MTR}) - \text{MPM}$.

Practise and learn online with Connect, where you can find the Answered Questions and the Unanswered Problems for all chapters of this textbook's Study Guide section.

6.4f Changes in exports are a result of:
- comparable price levels
- the value of the exchange rate
- income levels abroad

6.4g National income will increase as a result of:
- an increase in autonomous C, I, G, or X
- a decrease in autonomous T or IM

6.4h The size of the multiplier will increase as a result of a decrease in the MPS, MPM, or MTR.

6.5 We can derive the *aggregate demand curve* used in the previous chapter from the aggregate expenditures graph.

NEW GLOSSARY TERMS AND KEY EQUATIONS

autonomous spending
  (expenditures)   193
consumption function   194
dis-saving   194
expenditure equilibrium   199
induced spending   193

marginal leakage rate   198
marginal propensity to consume   194
marginal propensity to expend   198
marginal propensity to import   213
marginal propensity to save   194

marginal tax rate   209
net exports (balance of trade)   214
saving function   195
unplanned investment   199
wealth effect   202

Equations:

[6.1]	Total spending (aggregate expenditures) = autonomous spending + induced spending	page 193

[6.1]   Total spending (aggregate expenditures) = autonomous spending + induced spending   **page 193**

[6.2]   Marginal propensity to consume (MPC) $= \dfrac{\Delta \text{ consumption}}{\Delta \text{ income}}$ **page 194**

[6.3]   Marginal propensity to save (MPS) $= \dfrac{\Delta \text{ saving}}{\Delta \text{ income}}$ **page 194**

[6.4]   (In a closed, private economy) MPC + MPS = 1   **page 195**

[6.5]   Marginal propensity to expend (MPE) $= \dfrac{\Delta \text{ aggregate expenditures}}{\Delta \text{ income}}$ **page 198**

[6.6]   Marginal leakage rate (MLR) $= \dfrac{\Delta \text{ total leakages}}{\Delta \text{ income}}$ **page 198**

[6.7]   Marginal leakage rate (MLR) = (1 − MPE)   **page 198**

[6.8]   Multiplier $= \dfrac{\Delta \text{ income}}{\Delta \text{ autonomous expenditures}}$ **page 207**

[6.9]   Multiplier $= \dfrac{1}{\text{(MLR)}}$ or $\dfrac{1}{\text{(1 − MPE)}}$ **page 207**

[6.10]   Total taxes = autonomous taxes + induced taxes   **page 209**

[6.11]   Marginal tax rate (MTR) $= \dfrac{\Delta \text{ taxes}}{\Delta \text{ income}}$ **page 209**

[6.12] $Y_D = (Y - T)$ **page 210**

[6.13]   Marginal propensity to consume (MPC) = MPC_D (1 − MTR)   **page 213**

[6.14]   Marginal propensity to import (MPM) $= \dfrac{\Delta \text{ imports (IM)}}{\Delta \text{ income (Y)}}$ **page 213**

[6.15]   Marginal propensity to expend (MPE) = MPC_D(1 − MTR) − MPM or MPE = MPC − MPM   **page 217**

[6.16]   Marginal leakage rate (MLR) = MPS + MTR + MPM   **page 217**

STUDY TIPS

1. It is essential that you understand the distinction between autonomous spending, which does *not* depend on the level of income, and induced spending, which does.

2. Be careful when you draw your diagrams that the vertical and horizontal axes are drawn to the same scale. If they are not, your line will not be 45° and your graph will be misleading. When constructing graphs in this chapter, it is important that you construct reasonably large, accurate graphs. It is worth the extra effort.

3. Note that the vertical axis in math is often referred to as the *Y axis*, and the horizontal is called the *X axis*. This might occasionally be confusing, since economists use the letter Y to stand for income. In macroeconomics, income (Y) is placed on the X axis.

4. Probably the area of this chapter that causes most confusion for the student is the distinction between national income (GDP) and disposable income. If it helps, think back to Chapter 3, and recall all the additions and subtractions that had to be made to GDP to arrive at a figure for disposable income. In this model, all of those adjustments have been lumped together into a single heading: Tax. Again, remember from GDP accounting that how much people consume and how much they save are determined by *disposable* income and not by *national* income.

5. Some students have difficulty with the fact that Y stands for both the *concept* of income and the *value* of income. When the letter Y occurs in an equation such as Y = 100 + 0.6Y, for instance, the Y is short for 1Y.

6. Be careful when deriving disposable income that taxes are deducted from and not added to income. For example, if autonomous taxes are $100 and induced taxes are 20 percent of national income, then total taxes are (100 + 0.2Y). This *whole term* is subtracted from national income to give disposable income:

$$Y_D \quad = \quad Y \quad - \quad (100 + 0.2Y)$$

(disposable income)   (national income)   (taxes)

When you remove the brackets from the tax function, the plus sign becomes a minus:

$$Y_D = Y - 100 - 0.2Y$$

Answered Questions
These questions can also be found online on Connect.

Indicate whether the following statements are true or false:

1. **(LO 1) T or F**   Autonomous spending depends on the level of income, whereas induced spending does not.

2. **(LO 2) T or F**   Equilibrium income occurs where the value of production is equal to aggregate expenditures.

3. **(LO 4) T or F**   Induced taxes do not change with income, but autonomous taxes do.

4. **(LO 5) T or F**   A change in the price level shifts the aggregate expenditures curve but does not shift the aggregate demand curve.

5. **(LO 3) T or F**   The real-balances effect refers to the effect that a change in interest rates has on the real value of wealth.

6. **(LO 3) T or F**   A decrease in the interest rate will cause an increase in investment spending.

7. **(LO 3) T or F**   The value of the multiplier is equal to the inverse of the marginal leakage rate.

8. **(LO 4) T or F**   Growth in an economy's GDP (if not caused by a change in exports) results in a larger trade deficit or in a reduction of a previous trade surplus.

9. **(LO 4) T or F**   If taxes increase, disposable income will fall, but consumption will remain the same. *induced, autonomous*

10. **(LO 4) T or F**   If the marginal tax rate increases, then the marginal propensity to expend will be smaller, and the marginal leakage rate will be larger.

Basic (Questions 11–22)

11. **(LO 3)** What does the multiplier effect indicate?
    a) That a small increase in income will generate a large decrease in aggregate expenditures
    b) That a change in autonomous expenditures will cause income to change by a larger amount
    c) That a small increase in income will generate a large increase in aggregate expenditures
    d) That a change in induced expenditures will cause income to change by a larger amount

12. **(LO 4)** What is the marginal propensity to expend?
    a) It is the fraction of income that is not spent.
    b) It is the ratio of change in income that results from a change in expenditures.
    c) It is the ratio of change in expenditures that results from a change in income.
    d) It is the fraction of income that is taxed.

13. **(LO 4)** What is the effect of a decrease in government spending?
    a) It leads to an even larger increase in income.
    b) It leads to an even larger decrease in income.
    c) It leads to a smaller increase in income.
    d) It leads to a smaller decrease in income.

14. **(LO 4)** What effect does an increase in exports have?
    a) It leads to an even larger increase in income.
    b) It leads to an even larger decrease in income.
    c) It leads to a smaller increase in income.
    d) It leads to a smaller decrease in income.

15. **(LO 4)** What is the effect of a decrease in the MTR?
    a) The MLR will increase, and the multiplier will increase.
    b) The MLR will decrease, and the multiplier will increase.
    c) The MLR will increase, and the multiplier will decrease.
    d) The MLR will decrease, and the multiplier will decrease.

16. **(LO 3)** What is the most important determinant of the level of consumption?
    a) The level of prices
    b) Consumer expectations
    c) The stock of wealth
    d) The level of income

17. **(LO 4)** What circumstance will lead to a smaller multiplier?
    a) If the MPS becomes bigger
    b) If the MPC becomes bigger

c) If the MPM becomes smaller
d) If the MLR becomes smaller

18. **(LO 2, 4)** All of the following statements concerning the equilibrium level of income are correct, except one. Which is incorrect?
    a) There will be no tendency for firms to increase or decrease production.
    b) The government's budget will be balanced.
    c) Unplanned investment in inventories will not occur.
    d) Leakages equal injections.
    e) Aggregate expenditures equal income.

Refer to **Figure 6.11** to answer questions 19 and 20.

FIGURE 6.11

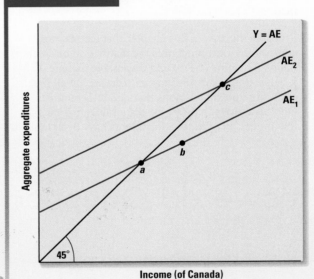

19. **(LO 3, 4)** What could cause a change from *a* to *b*?
    a) An increase in American income
    b) An increase in government spending
    c) A decrease in interest rates
    d) An increase in Canadian income
    e) A decrease in autonomous taxes

20. **(LO 3, 4)** All of the following, except one, could cause a change from *a* to *c*. Which is the exception?
    a) An increase in Canadian income
    b) A decrease in interest rates
    c) A decrease in the Canadian exchange rate
    d) A decrease in autonomous taxes
    e) An increase in American income

21. **(LO 1)** What are induced consumption and the marginal propensity to consume, respectively?
    a) The amount of income that results from higher levels of consumption and the change in income divided by the change in consumption
    b) The amount of consumption that results from higher levels of income and the change in consumption divided by the change in income
    c) The amount of consumption that occurs at zero income and the change in consumption divided by the change in income
    d) The amount of consumption that occurs at zero income and the change in income divided by the change in consumption

22. **(LO 2)** How is the AE function placed onto the 45° graph?
    a) It starts at zero income and rises with a slope equal to the MPE.
    b) It starts on the vertical axis at the level of autonomous expenditures and rises with a slope equal to the MPE.
    c) It starts at zero income and falls with a slope equal to the MPE.
    d) It starts on the vertical axis at the level of autonomous expenditures and falls with a slope equal to the MPE.

Intermediate (Questions 23–30)

23. **(LO 2)** If the MPE is equal to 0.4, what is the value of the MLR?
    a) 0.6
    b) 2.5
    c) 0.4
    d) 40

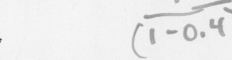

24. **(LO 2)** If the MPE is equal to 0.4, what is the value of the multiplier?
    a) 1.67
    b) 2.5
    c) 0.25
    d) 0.167

25. **(LO 4)** If X is an autonomous $90 (there are no autonomous imports) and the MPM is 0.2, what is the value of X_N at an income of $500?
    a) + $10
    b) − $10
    c) + $90
    d) + $590

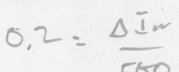

26. **(LO 3)** What does the real-balances effect refer to?
    a) The effect that a change in savings has on the real rate of interest
    b) The level of income where it is exactly equal to the level of consumption
    c) The effect that a change in interest rates has on the real value of savings
    d) The effect that a change in the price level has on the real value of wealth
    e) The effect of a change in consumption on the real value of wealth

27. **(LO 4)** Which of the following variables in the expenditure model are wholly autonomous, and which are partly induced?
    a) I, G, and S are autonomous; X, IM, and C are partly induced.
    b) I, G, and C are autonomous; S, IM, and X are partly induced.
    c) I, G, and X are autonomous; S, IM, and C are partly induced.
    d) G, X, and IM are autonomous; S, C, and I are partly induced.

28. **(LO 4)** Which two of the four components of aggregate expenditures are wholly autonomous?
    a) C and I
    b) C and G
    c) I and G
    d) I and X_N
    e) C and X_N

29. **(LO 4)** What happens to income earned in Canada?
    a) It is spent on exports, imports, and investment, and saved.
    b) It is spent on consumption, imports, and taxes, and saved.
    c) It is spent on consumption, exports, and taxes, and saved.
    d) It is spent on consumption, imports, taxes, and investment.
    e) It is spent on imports, taxes, and government spending.

30. **(LO 4)** Graphically, when is the balance of trade equal to zero?
    a) When the rising IM line intersects the horizontal X line
    b) When the rising X line intersects the horizontal IM line
    c) When the rising IM line intersects the horizontal axis
    d) When the rising X line intersects the horizontal axis

Advanced (Questions 31–35)

Refer to **Table 6.9** to answer questions 31 and 32. (You can assume that the MPC, MTR, MPM, X, I, and G are all constants.)

TABLE 6.9

Y	T	Y_D	C	S	I	G	X	IM	X_N	AE
0	25	−25	___	___	80	___	___	50	___	___
100	50	50	90	___	___	___	___	60	___	___
200	75	125	150	___	___	100	90	70	+20	___
300	100	200	210	−10	___	___	___	80	___	___
400	125	___	270	+5	80	100	90	90	0	450
500	150	___	330	___	80	100	90	100	−10	500
600	175	425	___	35	___	___	___	___	−20	___

31. **(LO 4)** What is the value of expenditures equilibrium?
    a) $300
    b) $400
    c) $500
    d) $600
    e) $1000

32. **(LO 4)** What is the value of the multiplier?
    a) 0.5
    b) 1
    c) 2
    d) 2.5
    e) 5

Answer questions 33–35 based on the parameters for an economy shown in **Table 6.10**. (All figures are in billions of dollars.)

TABLE 6.10

$$G = 1200$$
$$I = 400$$
$$C = 100 + 0.6Y$$
$$X_N = 700 - 0.2Y$$

33. **(LO 4)** What is the value of the multiplier in this economy?
    a) 1
    b) 1.54
    c) 1.67
    d) 2
    e) 5

34. **(LO 4)** What is the value of equilibrium income in this economy?
    a) $3840
    b) $3967
    c) $4000
    d) $4133
    e) $5000

35. **(LO 4)** At equilibrium, what is the balance of trade?
    a) A surplus of $100
    b) A deficit of $100
    c) A surplus of $300
    d) A deficit of $300
    e) A zero balance of trade

Parallel Problems

ANSWERED PROBLEMS

36A. **(LO 4)** **Key Problem** Table 6.11 shows some of the expenditure amounts in the economy of Arkinia. The MPC, the MTR, and the MPM are all constant, as are the values of the three injections.

TABLE 6.11

Y	T	Y_D	C	S	I	G	X	IM	X_N	AE (C + I + G + X_N)
$0	___	___	___	___	60	150	50	___	___	___
100	___	50	___	−10	___	___	___	___	30	___
200	75	___	120	5	___	___	___	___	___	___
300	100	___	180	___	___	___	___	40	___	___
400	125	___	___	35	___	___	___	50	___	___
500	___	___	300	___	___	___	___	60	___	___
600	___	425	___	___	___	___	___	___	___	___
700	___	___	420	___	___	___	___	___	___	___
800	___	575	___	95	___	___	___	___	−40	___

a) Complete **Table 6.11**, and in **Figure 6.12** graph a 45° line and the aggregate expenditure function, labelled AE₁. Identify expenditure equilibrium with the letter *e*.

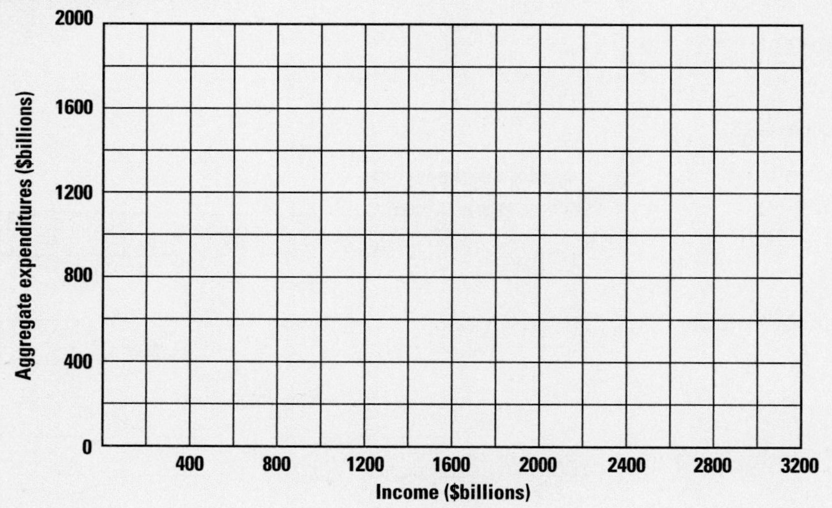

b) What is the value of equilibrium income?
   Income: $ _____

c) What are the values of total injections and total leakages at equilibrium?
   Total injections: _____
   Total leakages: _____

d) What is the value of the MPE in Arkinia? MPE: _____

e) What is the value of the multiplier in Arkinia?
   Multiplier: _____

f) Suppose that exports from Arkinia were to increase by $150. Draw the new aggregate expenditure function on **Figure 6.12**, and label it AE₂. Identify the new expenditure equilibrium.

g) What is the value of the new equilibrium income, and at equilibrium, what is the value of net exports?
   Income: _____
   Net exports: _____

FIGURE 6.12

Aggregate expenditures ($billions) vs Income ($billions)

Basic (Problems 37A–46A)

37A. **(LO 4)** The economy of Irinika has the following parameters:
Autonomous exports = $400 million
Autonomous imports = $100 million
MPM = 0.25
a) What is the balance of trade at an income of $800?
_____
b) What is the balance of trade at an income of $2000? _____
c) At what income level is there a zero balance of trade? _____

38A. **(LO 1)** Use the information in **Table 6.12** to answer questions about the economy of Watis.
a) Complete the table assuming that the MPC is constant.
b) What are the values of the MPC and MPS?
MPC: _____
MPS: _____
c) What are the equations for the consumption function and the saving function?
C = _____
S = _____

FIGURE 6.13

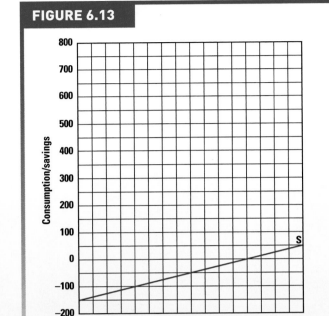

TABLE 6.12

Y	C	S
0	40	_____
50	70	_____
100	_____	_____
150	_____	20
200	_____	40

TABLE 6.13

National Income	Consumption	Saving
0		
100		
200		
300		
400		
500		
600		
700		
800		

39A. **(LO 1)** **Figure 6.13** shows the saving function for an economy.
a) Complete **Table 6.13**.
b) Add the consumption function to **Figure 6.13**.

40A. **(LO 3)** The simple economy of Altria shown in **Table 6.14** has no government or taxes and no international trade. Its investment is autonomous and its MPC is constant.
a) Complete **Table 6.14**.
b) What is the value of expenditures equilibrium?
Equilibrium: _____
c) What is the value of the multiplier?
Multiplier: _____

TABLE 6.14

Y	C	S	I	AE
0	100	_____	150	_____
200	250	_____	_____	_____
400	_____	0	_____	_____
600	_____	_____	_____	_____
800	_____	_____	_____	_____
1000	_____	100	_____	_____

41A. **(LO 3)** The following are the parameters for the simple economy of Minnerva which has no government involvement and no international trade:

$$C = 240 + 0.68Y \qquad I = 440$$

a) What is the value of expenditures equilibrium?
Equilibrium: _____

b) What is the value of the multiplier?
Multiplier: _____

c) If investment increases by 80, what will be the new value of expenditures equilibrium?
New equilibrium: _____

42A. **(LO 2)** Suppose that a simple economy has the following parameters:

$$C = 100 + 0.5Y \qquad I = 300$$

a) Complete **Table 6.15**.

TABLE 6.15

Y	C	S	I	AE
0	___	___	___	___
100	___	___	___	___
200	___	___	___	___
300	___	___	___	___
400	___	___	___	___
500	___	___	___	___
600	___	___	___	___
700	___	___	___	___
800	___	___	___	___
900	___	___	___	___
1000	___	___	___	___

b) What is the value of expenditures equilibrium? Verify your answer algebraically.
Equilibrium: _____

c) What are the values of injections and leakages at expenditures equilibrium?
Answer: _____

d) In **Figure 6.14**, plot C, S, I, and AE. Show equilibrium in terms of both Y = AE and injections = leakages.

FIGURE 6.14

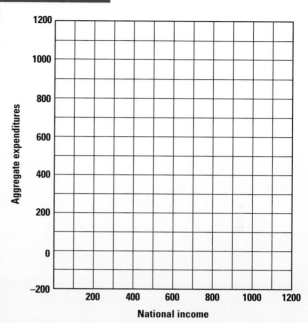

43A. **(LO 3)** Irkania's aggregate expenditures function is shown in **Figure 6.15**.

FIGURE 6.15

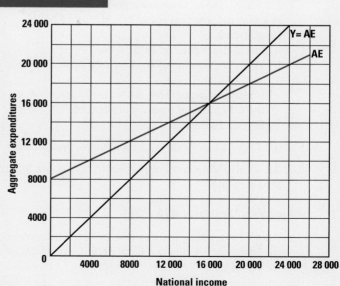

TABLE 6.16

Y	T	Y$_D$	C	S	I	G	X$_N$	AE	Unplanned Investment
$400	$40	___	$320	$40	$60	$50	+$10	___	___
450	___	___	___	45	___	___	−5	___	___
500	___	___	___	___	___	___	___	___	___
550	___	___	___	___	___	___	___	___	___

TABLE 6.17

Y	T	Y$_D$	C	S	I	G	X	IM	X$_N$	AE
___	___	___	___	110	80	180	___	80	10	800

a) What is the value of equilibrium income? _____

b) What is the value of the multiplier in Irkania? _____

c) If investment in Irkania were to decrease by $4000, what would be the new level of equilibrium income? _____

d) If investment were to increase by $2000, what would be the new level of equilibrium income? _____

44A. **(LO 4)** The partial data in **Table 6.16** are for the economy of Arinaka. Planned investment, government spending, and *all* taxes are autonomous. Furthermore, you may assume that the MPC, MPS, and MPM are constant.
a) Fill in the blanks in **Table 6.16**.
b) What is the value of equilibrium income? _____

c) If planned investment decreases by 20, what is the new value of equilibrium income? _____

45A. **(LO 1)** What is meant by *autonomous expenditures*?

46A. **(LO 4)** Explain marginal propensity to import. What is its formula?

Intermediate (Problems 47A–53A)

47A. **(LO 4)** In Arkania, income rose by $200 million over the past year. During the same period, tax revenue increased by $40 million, savings rose by $16 million, and imports rose by $24 million. What are the values of its MPE, MLR, and multiplier?
MPE: _____ MLR: _____
Multiplier: _____

48A. **(LO 4)** The following parameters are for Nirakia:
MPCD = 0.9   MTR = 0.25   MPM = 0.175
What are the values of its MPE, MLR, and multiplier?
MPE: _____ MLR: _____
Multiplier: _____

49A. **(LO 4)** Complete the balancing row in **Table 6.17** for the economy of Kaniria, which is in equilibrium.

50A. **(LO 4)** **Table 6.18** provides information for the economy of Zawi.

TABLE 6.18

C = 42 + 0.65Y	X$_N$ = 18 − 0.15Y
I = 120	G = 220

a) What is the value of equilibrium income? _____

b) Set up a balancing row to verify your calculations (the tax equation is: T = 60 + 0.2Y and X = 200).

Y	AE

c) If exports decrease by 50, what is the new equilibrium income? _____

51A. **(LO 4)** **Table 6.19** provides information for the economy of Patria.

TABLE 6.19

C = 32 + 0.9Y$_D$	T = 30 + 0.1Y
I = 110	IM = 42 + 0.06Y
G = 170	
X = 57	

a) What is the value of expenditures equilibrium? _____

b) What are the values of total leakages and injections at expenditures equilibrium? _____

c) What is the value of the multiplier? _____

52A. **(LO 2)** What is meant by the term *expenditures equilibrium*? What are the three equivalent ways of expressing it?

53A. **(LO 3)** What four factors will cause a change in autonomous consumption?

Advanced (Problems 54A–58A)

54A. **(LO 3)** **Figure 6.16** shows the economy of Itassuna.

FIGURE 6.16

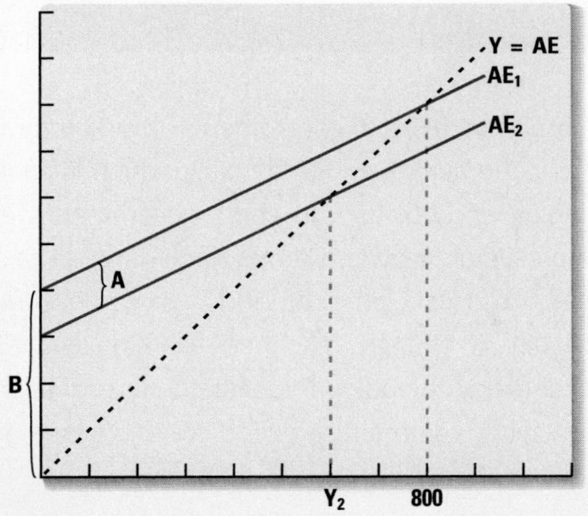

a) If the value of A is 50 and the multiplier is 4, what is the value of Y_2? _____.

b) If the value of Y_2 is 700 and the value of A is 60, what is the value of the multiplier? _____.

c) Given AE_1, if the value of the multiplier is 2, what is the value of B? _____.

55A. **(LO 4)** **Table 6.20** shows the parameters for the economy of Hutu.

TABLE 6.20

$C = 80 + 0.6Y$	$X_N = 140 - 0.1Y$
$I = 200$	$G = 300$

a) What is the value of equilibrium income? _____

b) If exports were to increase by 30, what would be the new value of equilibrium income? _____

c) Given your answer in b), what is the new value for X_N? _____

d) Given the equilibrium income in a), if full employment income is 1350, what change in government spending is necessary to move the economy to this level? _____

56A. **(LO 4)** The following data provide information on Akinira's economy in a particular year:

Y = \$500	investment spending = \$100
savings = \$120	government spending = \$200
taxes = \$180	balance of trade = + \$70

a) Explain which variables depend on others.

b) Is the economy in equilibrium, and what has happened to the country's level of inventories in this particular year? _____

c) Comment on what implications this might have for the following year's GDP. _____

57A. **(LO 4)** The data in **Table 6.21** are for the economy of Nubia.

a) Complete the AE column.

b) Write out expressions for the tax function, the consumption function (related to national income [Y]), the net export function, and the AE function.

T = _____ C = _____

X_N = _____ AE = _____

c) Use algebra to find out the value of equilibrium income. Y = _____

58A. **(LO 4)** What is the difference between expenditures equilibrium and full-employment equilibrium?

TABLE 6.21

Y	T	Y_D	C	S	I	G	X	IM	X_N	AE
0	50	−50	20	−70	60	70	100	50	+50	_____
100	60	40	92	−52	60	70	100	62	+38	_____
200	70	130	164	−34	60	70	100	74	+26	_____
300	80	220	236	−16	60	70	100	86	+14	_____
400	90	310	308	+2	60	70	100	98	+2	_____

CHAPTER 7

FISCAL POLICY

LEARNING OBJECTIVES

At the end of this chapter, you should be able to...

LO1 understand why the federal government's budget depends on the rate of taxation, the size of the GDP, and its own spending.

LO2 explain the pros and cons of a budget policy aimed at achieving full-employment equilibrium.

LO3 explain the pros and cons of a budget policy aimed at achieving a balanced budget in each fiscal year.

LO4 explain the pros and cons of a budget policy aimed at achieving both full employment and a balanced budget over the life of the business cycle.

LO5 discuss the cause, size, and problems of the national debt.

WHAT'S AHEAD...

We now turn to one of most important tasks of governments around the world—making economic policy. The focus here is on fiscal policy, which is each government's approach to spending and taxation: in short, government's annual budget. We begin by defining several important terms, including net tax revenue, budget deficits, surpluses, and national debt, and then go on to discuss what can cause each of these to change. We then examine two distinct approaches to the use of fiscal policy, including the shortcomings of each one. This leads to a discussion of a third, compromise policy. We end with a discussion of the national debt.

A Question of Relevance...

Do you remember what you were doing the evening the last federal budget was unveiled in Parliament? Probably not. Furthermore, you quite likely think that "it has nothing to do with me." Yet, the truth is that government's annual budget affects you more than almost any other regularly scheduled event in your life, other than such personal events as birthdays and anniversaries. It determines the taxes you pay, the chances of your getting a job next summer, the likelihood of getting a student loan, and even the size of your classes next year. This chapter will help you learn more about the budget.

It is a truism that governments have to spend, and therefore they have to tax. So, what should government's attitude toward its own spending and taxation be? How small or large should this spending and taxation be? Should the two be equal? Does the condition of the economy have anything to do with the answers to these questions? For example, when the economy is in the middle of a recession with high unemployment—as was the case just a few short years ago—what should the attitude of government be? Should government decrease its own spending, increase it, or change nothing? Alternatively, should we expect it to cut taxes, to increase taxes, or to change nothing? These are the types of questions we will be looking at in this chapter. But first, we need to define some terms.

ADDED DIMENSION   How Much Should a Government Spend: Canada versus the United States?

There is much discussion today about the growing size of government spending which often morphs into a political debate about whether this is a welcome result of growing affluence (we are richer now and can "buy" more government-provided services) or a threat to future prosperity (the associated higher taxes will stunt economic growth). Comparisons between Canada and the United States are also often mixed into this debate.

Let us make some comparisons. Before World War II, the size of government spending as a percentage of GDP was below 15 percent in both countries. Today, the percentages are around 35 percent in Canada and 32 percent in the United States Clearly, government spending has grown considerably. If we look at the major categories of spending we may get an insight into why.

In the years before World War II, income security (social assistance and public pensions) and public health expenditures were nearly nonexistent, while education expenses were much smaller than today. As short as this explanation is, it just about sums up the growth in government spending over the past hundred years. People have access to comprehensive health care, more kids are completing high school and going into higher education, and we now have a public pension program; thus government spending as a percentage of GDP has increased. And what are the major differences in public spending between the United States and Canada? In this country, we have more income security and less national defence.

Category of Spending	Percentage of GDP: Canada	Percentage of GDP: US
Income Security	11	7
Education, Health, and General Public Service	15	15
Housing, Culture, and Recreation	1.5	0.8
Public Safety	2	2
National Defence	1.2	4

Source: Data derived by authors from information found in Department of Finance Canada, Working Paper 2003–05. Reproduced with the permission of the Minister of Public Works and Government Services, 2011.

7.1   FISCAL POLICY AND THE BUDGET

Fiscal policy refers to a government's approach toward its own spending and taxation. When the minister of finance brings down the budget in Parliament each spring, this reveals government's fiscal policy for the coming year. The annual projected budget contains estimates of government revenues and expenditures. Budget day is headline news, and TV screens across the country are filled with political comments about how good or bad the new budget is.

Table 7.1 shows the federal government's budget for the fiscal year ending March 31, 2010. All figures are actual revenues and expenditures in billions of dollars.

L01 Understand why the federal government's budget depends on the rate of taxation, the size of the GDP, and its own spending.

fiscal policy: government's approach toward its own spending and taxation.

TABLE 7.1	Federal Government's Budget for Fiscal Year Ending March 2010 (in $ billions)
REVENUES	
Personal income taxes	103.9
Corporate and other income taxes	36.0
E.I. premiums	16.8
GST, excise, and energy taxes	40.6
Nontax revenues	21.6
Total Revenues	**218.6**
OUTLAYS	
Transfers to persons	68.6
Spending grants to other levels of government	57.0
Public debt charges	29.4
Direct program spending	119.2
Total Outlays	**274.2**
Budget Deficit	**55.6**

Source: Department of Finance Canada, Fiscal Reference Tables. Reproduced with the permission of the Minister of Public Works and Government Services, 2011.

Revenues are government's total receipts, which were $218.6 billion for the fiscal year 2009–2010, which began on April 1, 2009. This figure represents approximately 14.3 percent of Canada's GDP in 2009. These revenues do not include the CPP payments that are made by Canadians, since this program is administrated independently of the budget. By far the largest source of revenue is *personal income tax* which is estimated to be $103.9 billion, while *E.I. premiums* are $16.8 billion. *Corporate income and other taxes* are taxes on profits paid by companies and non-residents; they totalled $36.0 billion. GST and excise taxes of $40.6 billion include the federal sales tax as well as excise taxes on gasoline, alcohol, and cigarettes, plus tariff revenues on certain imports. *Nontax revenues*, at $21.6 billion, include income from government crown corporations and other government investments, plus Bank of Canada earnings.

Total outlays were $274.2 billion. *Transfers to persons* totalled $68.6 billion and include payments toward Old Age Security, Guaranteed Annual Income Supplements, Spouse's Allowances, and the EI program. Once again, CPP payments are not included here. *Spending grants to other levels of government*, at $57.0 billion, was the amount of spending on postsecondary education, health, and social assistance, as well as equalization payments, which are aimed at six provinces (all but Alberta, B.C., Newfoundland and Saskatchewan). Aid to the developing nations and dues to international organizations, such as the United Nations, are also included in this category. *Public debt charges*, at $29.4 billion, are the interest payments on government's national debt; these are also treated as a form of transfer payment in national income accounting. The last item, *direct program spending* of $119.2 billion, is part of the total spending on goods and services (G) that we first identified in the circular flow treatment in Chapter 3 and includes everything from computers for government offices to salaries of the civil servants working in those offices. The total budget

The Canadian Press (Tom Hanson)

Finance Minister Jim Flaherty responds to a question on his budget during Question Period in Ottawa in February 2008.

deficit for the year is $55.6 billion, with total government outlays exceeding total revenues. This compares with a deficit of $5.8 billion for the previous year. (The federal government stated that $21 billion of the total deficit was the result of its Action Plan designed to help fight the recession.)

The distribution of revenues and outlays is shown in the following pie graph:

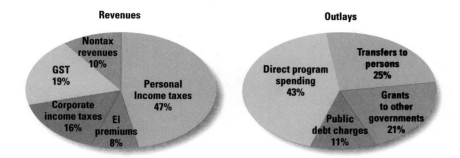

We now need to define **net tax revenue**:

$$\text{NTR} = \text{tax revenue} - \text{transfer payments} \qquad [7.1]$$

Government's budget balance is defined as the difference between net tax revenues and government spending:

$$\text{budget balance} = \text{NTR} - \text{G} \qquad [7.2]$$

A positive balance means a **budget surplus**, since net tax revenue would be greater than spending on goods and services. Conversely, a negative balance means a **budget deficit**, since net tax revenues would be lower than government spending. It is important to note that government tax revenues, spending, and the deficit (or surplus) are all flows because they occur over a period. If we were to add up all the deficit flows over the years and then subtract the sum of all the surpluses over the same period, we would get the **national debt**. The national debt, or as it is sometimes called, the *public debt*, is a stock concept because it is the total outstanding at any particular point in time and is the summation of the flows of all previous deficits and surpluses. We will return to this topic at the end of the chapter.

In **Table 7.2** we take a brief historical look at the federal government's budget balance. Deficits were a permanent feature in the 1970s and 1980s, and were close to $40 billion per year in the early 1990s. This led to increasing pressure on government to change policy and balance the budget. You can see in **Table 7.2** that the size of the deficit started to fall in 1995 and turned into a surplus in 1998. What was behind this rather dramatic turnaround? The answer is twofold. First, the federal government cut transfer payments to the provinces, which squeezed the delivery of health care and higher education services across the country. This resulted in growing waiting lists for surgery and a reduction in the number of hospital beds, while college and university classes grew in size and professors' salaries were frozen. Second, despite the cut in government spending, the rate of economic growth, fuelled by increased exports to the United States, accelerated and raised government revenues, since more people were working and paying income tax and total spending was up, which meant more consumption tax (GST/HST) revenue.

As the twenty-first century began, government faced a new issue: debate over what to do with the budget surpluses. In 2008, after eleven consecutive years of budget surpluses, the country, along with all other industrialized nations, entered a severe recession with the result that the government started to run up deficits as tax revenues fell and spending on income support programs rose. In addition to this, the government embarked on an Action Plan designed to stimulate the economy by pumping in over $60 billion (over two years) in extra government spending. The result was Canada's highest budget deficit ever, in 2009–2010.

net tax revenue: total tax revenue received by government less transfer payments.

budget surplus: net tax revenue in excess of government spending on goods and services.

budget deficit: government spending on goods and services in excess of net tax revenues.

national debt: the sum of the federal government's budget deficits less its surpluses.

TABLE 7.2	Budget Surpluses/Deficits and the Net National Debt (current $ billion)		
Year	Budget Surplus	Budget Deficit	Net National Debt
1940	—	0.1	3.3
1963	—	0.8	15.7
1973	—	1.9	24.0
1983	—	29.0	136.7
1993	—	39.0	449.0
1997	—	8.7	562.9
1998	3.0	—	559.9
1999	5.8	—	554.1
2000	14.3	—	539.9
2001	19.9	—	520.0
2002	8.0	—	511.9
2003	6.6	—	505.3
2004	9.1	—	496.2
2005	1.5	—	494.7
2006	13.2	—	481.5
2007	13.8	—	467.3
2008	9.6	—	457.6
2009	—	−05.8	463.7
2010	—	−55.6	519.1

Source: Department of Finance Canada, Fiscal Reference Tables, October 2010. Reproduced with the permission of the Minister of Public Works and Government Services, 2011.

Changes in the Economy and Government Revenues

It is important to emphasize that changes in the economy can have an impact on government revenues. A prime example of this occurred between the budget years of 1996 and 1997. In those two years, the size of the budget deficit dropped from $30 billion to $8.7 billion. As we mentioned, while transfer payments did decrease, the reduction in the deficit was greatly helped by the continued by growth in the economy, which raised government revenues. This illustrates an important generalization in the model we are building: NTR and GDP are directly related.

In addition, you may recall from our discussion in Chapter 3 on the circular flow of income that we treat government spending on goods and services as autonomous of (independent from) the level of real GDP. That is to say, both the government transfer payments to persons and the public debt charges are included in the calculation of NTR, leaving the categories of grants to provinces and Direct Program Expenses making up what we call G below. We put revenue and spending together in Figure 7.1.

In Figure 7.1A, the horizontal line, G, reflects the autonomous nature of government spending on goods and services. We also have assumed that when GDP is zero, so, too, are tax revenues and transfer payments so that the net tax revenues (NTR) line begins at the origin. Since government's tax revenue is greater and transfer payments are lower at higher levels of GDP, the NTR line rises as the level of GDP rises. At a GDP level of Y_1, NTR is less than the level of government spending, and there would be a budget deficit equal to ab. At a GDP level of Y_3, NTR exceeds G, and there would be a budget surplus equal to de. When GDP is at a level indicated by Y_2, there

FIGURE 7.1   Government Deficits and Surpluses

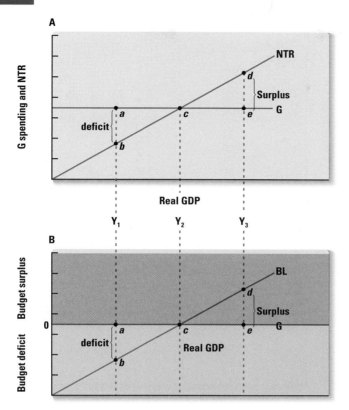

At real GDP level Y_2, government spending and net tax revenues are equal, and therefore there is a balanced budget, as illustrated by point c in figure A. In Figure B, a balanced budget is also indicated by point c, which is where the budget line, BL, crosses the zero axis. At real GDP level Y_3, net tax revenues exceed government spending, and therefore there is a budget surplus, indicated by de in both graphs. Conversely, at real GDP level Y_1 there is a budget deficit of ab.

would be neither a budget surplus nor a deficit, as illustrated by point c. The effect of different levels of GDP on the budget itself is shown explicitly in **Figure 7.1B**. Here, we introduce the budget line, BL—which is simply NTR minus G at all levels of GDP—and show the same deficit, ab, at GDP level Y_1 and the same surplus, de, at GDP level Y_3. Point c on both figures represents a **balanced budget**.

Figure 7.1 shows that there are two things besides the level of GDP that will affect a government's budget and therefore the position of the budget line: a change in either the amounts of government spending or net tax revenues. An increase in government spending, for instance, will increase the amount of the budget deficit (or reduce the surplus) at every level of GDP and result in the budget line shifting down. This is shown in **Figure 7.2**. Here, we see that an increase in government spending will shift the G curve up from G_1 to G_2. With the government increasing its level of spending, the budget deficit is higher (or the budget surplus lower) at each level of income. This means that the budget line shifts down from BL_1 to BL_2. The result is that the government is now able to achieve a balanced budget only at a higher level of income, at Y_2 instead of at Y_1.

You can perhaps work out for yourself that an increase in autonomous taxes would cause a smaller deficit (or increased surplus) at every level of income and is shown as a parallel shift upward in both the NTR line and the budget line. In contrast, an increase in the tax rate would also see a shift upward in both the NTR and budget lines; however, the shift would be greater at higher levels of GDP than at lower levels. We could call this an upward pivot in both lines. The essential point is that:

balanced budget: net tax revenues equal government spending on goods and services.

> The state of government's budget depends on the level of GDP in the economy as well as on tax rates and its own spending.

FIGURE 7.2	The Effect of an Increase in Government Spending

An increase in government spending shifts the G line up from G_1 to G_2 in figure A, and as a result shifts *down* the budget line from BL_1 to BL_2 in Figure B.

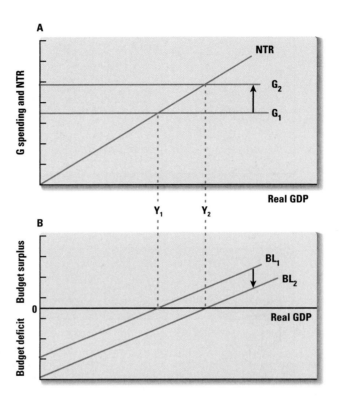

A question that often springs to people's minds at this point is: how is government's budget deficit financed? There is no mystery. It is financed by borrowing. For example, when people buy a government bond (such as a Canada Savings Bond or a treasury bill), they are, in effect, lending some of their savings to government so it can finance a deficit. Government can also borrow from the Bank of Canada. In this case, government would issue bonds and sell them to the Bank of Canada. However, there is a big difference between the Bank of Canada buying bonds and somebody else buying them. If a private individual or corporation buys government bonds, there is simply a transfer of money from that individual's bank account to the government account at a commercial bank. That is, the overall supply of money stays the same. But when the Bank of Canada buys government bonds, the money it uses to pay for them involves an injection of new money into the economy; in other words, the money supply is increased. The effect of this is much the same as government printing money to pay its bills. This method of borrowing, known as **monetizing the debt** or quantitative easing, is not used to a great extent in Canada today. But it has been frequently used by desperate governments in the past to finance extravagance, or wage war, or to help a country survive extreme economic conditions. We will return to this topic in the chapter on monetary policy.

monetizing the debt: when government borrows from its central bank to finance increased spending.

Two Schools of Thought on Fiscal Policy

We now want to address one of the more important questions posed at the beginning of this chapter. What, if anything, should government do when the economy faces unemployment, or for that matter, inflation? There are two distinct schools of thought on this question. On the one hand, we have economists and policymakers, interventionists, who believe that government needs to deliberately intervene in the economy and over-spend, or under-spend, from time to time in order to help the economy achieve the goals of full employment and stable prices. On the other hand, noninterventionists believe that these goals can be achieved best if there is no government intervention. We shall look at both of these different philosophies, as well as a third option that is something of a compromise between these opposing schools of thought. We will start with the interventionist philosophy called *countercyclical fiscal policy*.

 SELF-TEST

1. Draw a graph similar to **Figure 7.2**, showing the effect of a decrease in autonomous taxation.

2. Assume that current net tax revenues are $200 billion, government spending on goods and services is $180 billion, and the national debt at the beginning of the period was half the size of current net tax revenues. What is the size of the national debt at the end of the period?

3. Suppose that government spending is an autonomous $50 and net tax revenues are as shown in the table.

Real GDP	0	40	80	120	160
Net tax revenues	20	30	40	50	60
Budget balance	—	—	—	—	—

Complete the table, and plot the corresponding budget line.

7.2 COUNTERCYCLICAL FISCAL POLICY

Interventionist philosophy is rooted in a very particular period of our history—the lost decade of the 1930s that we call the Great Depression. Prior to this devastating experience, the prevailing view was that government should play a minimal and "neutral" role in the economy—spend little, and tax just enough to cover this minimal spending. But the Great Depression was very severe. Millions of people were forced to the very edge of existence with unemployment rates as high as 25 percent and no social welfare net in place to buffer the fall in incomes. Many families were dependent on a single wage earner. Prices were falling, yet producers' sales were dropping—manufactures could not sell their cars, new house construction all but disappeared (despite record low interest rates), even farmers could not sell their food—and net investment in the economy became negative. Furthermore, it lasted the whole of the decade.

The result was that many people began to question the viability of capitalism as an economic system—and this was in the wake of "the ten days that shook the world"—the communist revolution in Russia. The fear that gripped society was not helped by the fact that economists as a group were frozen into silence, apparently unable to suggest what might be done to turn things around.

But there was one economist who was able to see through the fog. Using the analysis of the circular flow of income that you learned in Chapter 3, the Englishman John Maynard Keynes built a model of the economy based on the level of aggregate expenditures: the $AE = C + I + G + X_n$ equation that you are familiar with. Keynes argued that the depression was caused by a series of events that dramatically reduced the level of AE in the economy and that only an increase in spending—an increase in aggregate demand—would pull the world's economies out of depression. He further reasoned that consumption (C) was not going to rise because unemployed people had no income to spend and that those who were still employed were so frightened by the future that they held their spending to a minimum. Investment spending was not going to increase because no one would build new factories or buy new machinery when so many of the existing factories were idle. Net exports (X_n) were not going to increase because world trade had virtually collapsed. Thus, he called for a dramatic increase in government spending on goods and services (G), financed by borrowing, as the only way to get incomes up and unemployment down, and thus save the economic system itself.

L02 Explain the pros and cons of a budget policy aimed at achieving full-employment equilibrium.

This was radical stuff, and the reaction of most people was predicable: they screamed that the idea of "spending ourselves to prosperity" was totally insane! But, as history has shown before, it is in times of great strife that radical thinking rises to the surface. Keynes's groundbreaking idea, and the mostly negative reaction to it, were given a few years to stew before something even more dramatic occurred—the outbreak of World War II. As first France, England, and Canada, and then later the United States entered the war, each nation dramatically increased government spending on armaments and "hired" hundreds of thousands of soldiers.

The economy returned to full employment almost overnight and the total output quickly exceeded even the most optimistic hopes of the war planners. This was exactly what Keynes had predicted. The Keynesian revolution in macroeconomics was complete when, following the end of the war, government after government passed various forms of "full-employment acts" in hopes of preventing the great depression from ever happening again. The idea that the government had a role in guiding the economy to a state of relatively full employment became cemented in peoples' consciousness and in law. This philosophy is what we today call **countercyclical fiscal policy**.

Very much in the spirit of the Keynesian revolution, the interventionists today advocate countercyclical fiscal policy to close recessionary and inflationary gaps. That is, figuratively speaking, government policy should lean against the prevailing winds. If, for example, aggregate demand is weak and a recessionary gap exists, expansionary policy should be used to deliberately stimulate demand with higher government spending or lower taxes (or both). However, if aggregate demand is so strong that an inflationary gap exists, then contractionary policy should be used to dampen down demand through cuts in government spending or increases in taxes. The recessionary gap situation is illustrated in **Figure 7.3**.

Given the current aggregate supply curve, AS_1, and the aggregate demand curve AD_1, equilibrium GDP is Y_1. Since this level of GDP is below potential GDP of Y_{FE}, we have a recessionary gap of $Y_{FE} - Y_1$. Countercyclical fiscal policy would call for either increased government spending or decreased taxes. This would have a multiplied impact on aggregate demand, as indicated by the shift from AD_1 to AD_2. If such a policy were well crafted, aggregate demand would increase just enough to eliminate the recessionary gap by moving the economy to Y_{FE}.

Next, let us assume the economy is experiencing an inflationary gap. Here, the appropriate countercyclical fiscal policy would be to decrease government spending or increase taxes in order to reduce the level of aggregate demand. This is illustrated in **Figure 7.4**.

countercyclical fiscal policy: deliberate adjustments in the level of government spending and taxation in order to close recessionary or inflationary gaps.

FIGURE 7.3   Countercyclical Fiscal Policy with a Recessionary Gap

A recessionary gap exists if the current level of GDP is below the full-employment level as illustrated by $Y_{FE} - Y_1$. Countercyclical fiscal policy is aimed at increasing the level of aggregate demand by either increasing government spending or decreasing taxes. It shifts the aggregate demand curve to the right from AD_1 to AD_2 and closes the recessionary gap.

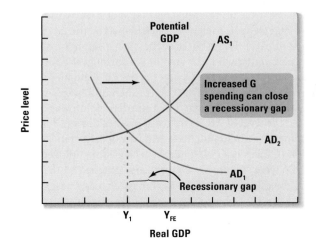

FIGURE 7.4	Countercyclical Fiscal Policy with an Inflationary Gap

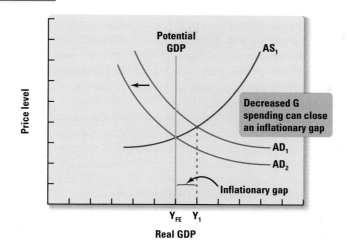

If the economy is experiencing an inflationary gap, such as $Y_1 - Y_{FE}$, then the appropriate counter-cyclical fiscal policy aimed at closing the gap is to lower the level of aggregate demand by either reducing government spending or increasing taxes. This is illustrated by a leftward shift in the aggregate demand from AD_1 to AD_2.

An inflationary gap is present because the equilibrium level of GDP, Y_1, is above the full-employment level, Y_{FE}. Closing the gap requires a lower level of aggregate demand, as illustrated by the shift from AD_1 to AD_2. This could be accomplished by government reducing its spending or increasing taxes.

It is important to note here that the goal of countercyclical fiscal policy is to achieve full employment with minimal inflation. That is, what is being balanced is the economy. This mean that the government's budget would sometimes be in deficit (stimulating demand) and sometimes in surplus (dampening down demand). The idea here is to "balance the economy not the budget."

In summary, countercyclical fiscal policy means that:

- when aggregate demand is low and the economy is experiencing a recessionary gap, governments should spend and tax in a way that *increases* aggregate demand.
- when aggregate demand is high and an inflationary gap is present, governments should spend and tax in a way that *reduces* the level of aggregate demand.

In this way, government policy helps to stabilize the economy and take some of the sting out of fluctuations in the business cycle.

 SELF-TEST

4. In the following cases, indicate the direction in which the aggregate demand curve will shift (right or left).

   a) Taxes increase.

   b) Government spending on goods and services decreases.

c) Countercyclical fiscal policy is used to close a recessionary gap.

d) Countercyclical fiscal policy is used to close an inflationary gap.

Shortcomings of Countercyclical Fiscal Policy

For some thirty years, beginning in the 1970s, countercyclical fiscal policy received a good deal of criticism. To better understand why, we look at three potential problems associated with the use of countercyclical fiscal policy.

The first involves the fact that interventionists see the essence of countercyclical fiscal policy as that of fine-tuning the economy. This is done by adjusting government spending or taxation by just the right amounts to achieve a level of aggregate demand sufficient to bring about full-employment GDP with stable prices. Critics, however, argue that in practice, the use of counter-cyclical fiscal policy is like fine-tuning with a sledgehammer. Even if just the right amount of adjustment can be determined, (which critics think is problematic) countercyclical fiscal policy takes time to implement and is slow to take effect. This means that the economy may suffer from an overdose of spending when the policy does take full effect. In other words, the application of countercyclical fiscal policy is *subject to serious delays*.

For example, consider a government that has just determined that the economy is in need of a $4 billion spending stimulant. This government cannot simply increase spending by $4 billion without first identifying how it is going to spend the money and then getting parliamentary approval for its fiscal plans. The next problem is that a number of procedures are necessary before the actual spending can begin, the most significant of which is putting out contracts for bids by various firms in the private sector. All of this takes time, and since major projects, such as a new port facility, may last a number of years, the full effect of the increased spending may manifest a long way down the road, by which time the need for such spending may no longer exist.

The experience of the Canadian government's $60 billion stimulus program in 2009 is interesting here. The Prime Minister said that this program would save the economy from a serious depression and the economic performance of Canada in 2010, compared with the United States, could be used as evidence that he was right. However, critics point out that the Canadian government strayed a long way from practical infrastructure projects—such as upgrading roads, bridges, water, and sewage works—and went, instead, on a quest for "shovel-ready" projects that provided great photo-ops for politicians and directed money in ways that benefited some businesses much more than the citizenship in general. Perhaps this was done precisely because of the time-delay problem.

All of this begs the question of economic planning by government in general. Some would argue that "good" government should have a catalogue of needed infrastructure projects conceptualized, with engineering studies complete and parliamentary approval achieved, on the shelf and ready to go when the next need for fiscal stimulus arises. In that way, stimulus spending could be on the "right" kind of projects much more quickly.

The second perceived problem with countercyclical fiscal policy is that many believe it is ineffective *because it has a built in inflationary bias*. Suppose, for instance, that government uses countercyclical fiscal policy to get an economy out of a recession. The result will be an increase in aggregate demand, as shown in **Figure 7.5**.

FIGURE 7.5   **The Effect of Countercyclical Fiscal Policy on the Price Level**

If the economy is experiencing a recessionary gap, countercyclical fiscal policy will increase the level of aggregate demand. This is illustrated by the shift from AD_1 to AD_2. The recessionary gap closes as real GDP increases from Y_1 to Y_{FE}. However, the price level will also increase from P_1 to P_2.

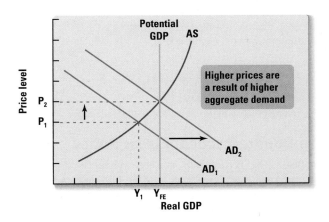

An increase in government spending (or a reduction in taxes) would shift the aggregate demand curve to the right, from AD_1 to AD_2. Clearly, the level of GDP increases from Y_1 to Y_{FE}. Unfortunately, the price level also rises, in this case from P_1 to P_2. Countercyclical fiscal policy is therefore subject to an inflationary bias. Just how serious this bias might be depends on the steepness of the aggregate supply curve. As you may recall from Chapter 6, as we approach the full-employment level of GDP, the rise in prices accelerates. While this inflationary bias is certainly possible, how serious this is may be does not depend on Canada's inflation rate alone but more on its rate of inflation compared with that in the countries that buy Canadian goods.

The third, and some believe the most serious, problem with countercyclical fiscal policy is that *it completely ignores the effect it has on government's budget.* Over the last half century, Canada's countercyclical fiscal policy has been aimed mainly at attempting to close recessionary gaps. Such policy involves either higher levels of government spending or lower levels of taxation. Either of these will have a deficit-inducing effect on the current budget. The result will be an increase in the size of an already-existing budget deficit or a decrease in the size of an already existing budget surplus. This is best illustrated with **Figure 7.6.**

Suppose that the current level of GDP in **Figure 7.6A** is Y_1. This means that the economy is experiencing a recessionary gap equal to the distance between full-employment level of GDP, Y_{FE}, and the current level, Y_1. We can also see, in **Figure 7.6B**, that at GDP level Y_1, government has a budget deficit of *ab*. The recessionary gap can be closed by the use of countercyclical fiscal policy. This would imply an increase in government spending or a decrease in taxation. The effect, graphically, would be to shift aggregate demand from AD_1 to AD_2. However, the greater government spending or lower taxation would also increase the size of government's budget deficit. This is illustrated in the downward shift in the budget line from BL_1 to BL_2, where the deficit immediately increases to *ac*. The overall result is that the economy moves to full-employment equilibrium at Y_{FE}. We can see that as GDP increases, the size of the deficit is reduced from *ac* to *de*

FIGURE 7.6   **Effect of Countercyclical Fiscal Policy on Budget Deficits**

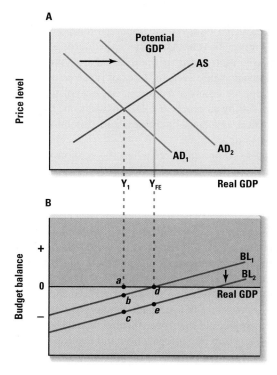

Suppose the economy is originally at GDP level Y_1 with a budget deficit of *ab*. Countercyclical fiscal policy aimed at increasing aggregate demand from AD_1 to AD_2 will also shift the budget line down from BL_1 to BL_2. The result is a larger budget deficit, *de*, at the new equilibrium income of Y_{FE}.

(a movement up the BL_2 curve) as a result of an increase in net tax revenues. However, this will still leave the economy with a larger overall deficit (*de*) than it began with (*ab*).

If the deficit-inducing effects occur often and are allowed to accumulate over a period, the size of government's national debt will grow substantially. Increased deficits mean increased borrowing, and this further requires government to use a larger percentage of its total spending to service its debt, leaving a smaller percentage for spending on such things as health care and education.

In summary, the three criticisms of countercyclical fiscal policy are that:

- it is subject to serious time lags
- it has an inflationary bias
- it can cause serious budget deficits

 SELF-TEST

5. What effect will countercyclical fiscal policy aimed at closing an inflationary gap have on the level of national income and prices?

L03 Explain the pros and cons of a budget policy aimed at achieving a balanced budget in each fiscal year.

balanced-budget fiscal policy: the belief that a government's budget should be balanced in each budget period.

automatic stabilizers: provisions of tax laws and government spending programs that automatically take spending out of the economy when it is booming and put spending in when it is slowing down.

7.3 BALANCED-BUDGET FISCAL POLICY

Some politicians and political commentators, and even a few economists, alarmed at the effect of countercyclical fiscal policy on the size of budget deficits, argue that government should balance its spending and tax revenues in *each budget period*. This is known as a **balanced-budget fiscal policy** and is the second of the budget philosophies we consider. Advocates of a balanced-budget fiscal policy use three observations to support their position. First, they consider the three short-comings of countercyclical fiscal policy that we just discussed as a serious indictment of that approach and see the balanced-budget approach as the only alternative.

Second, advocates of a balanced-budget fiscal policy approach believe that because of **automatic stabilizers**, the modern economy has enough built-in safeguards to ensure that it avoids extremes of high inflation or unemployment. Automatic stabilizers are government programs that ensure that spending remains relatively stable even in times of rapid economic change. For instance, as we have seen, when an economy enters a recession, because of the progressive nature of taxes, disposable incomes do not fall by as much as GDP. In addition, the amount paid out in unemployment benefits and welfare assistance increases, and this buoys up disposable income and therefore consumption spending.

Automatic stabilizers also come into force when the economy is booming and in danger of "overheating." In this case, the higher levels of GDP generate proportionately higher taxes, and at the same time, the amounts paid out for unemployment benefits and welfare are also reduced. These both have the effect of dampening down expenditures.

The third point used in support of a balanced-budget fiscal policy is by far the most significant. As mentioned earlier, noninterventionists believe that if either a recessionary or an inflationary gap exists, the economy is capable of returning to full-employment equilibrium by itself through a *self-adjustment process*, unaided by interventionist polices of any kind. Let us review the argument that was presented in Chapter 5.

The key to understanding this position which we termed the modern view in Chapter 5 is the belief that any temporary excesses of aggregate demand (inflationary gap) or a lack of aggregate demand (recessionary gap) would disappear through changes in prices and wage rates. If the economy were to experience a drop in aggregate demand leading to a recession, then eventually wage rates will be forced down, which implies an increase aggregate supply. This would lead to

FIGURE 7.7   **Adjustment from a Recessionary Gap**

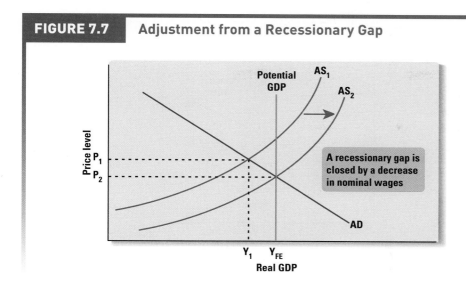

If the economy is in a recession at income Y_1, eventually wages will be forced down thus increasing aggregate supply. The AS curve will continue to shift right until the economy is returned to full-employment GDP, Y_{FE}. This will also decrease the price level from P_1 to P_2.

an increase in profits and production at the same time that prices were dropping further. Eventually, prices and wages will continue to fall until the economy has recovered and is back at full-employment equilibrium. This is illustrated in **Figure 7.7**.

Similarly, suppose that the economy is initially in equilibrium, and experiences an increase in demand. This will lead to higher prices and an inflationary gap. However, this above full-employment equilibrium will eventually lead to higher wages, thus decreasing aggregate supply until the economy is back at full employment equilibrium.

The essence of the argument by advocates of a balanced budget, then, is that government intervention is unnecessary, since the economy is quite capable of returning the economy to full-employment unaided. (Even Keynes admitted this; however, he felt that the adjustment process took too long and caused unnecessary suffering. As he said, "In the long run, we are all dead!")

In summary, the arguments in support of a balanced-budget fiscal policy are as follows:

- Countercyclical policy does more harm than good.
- The economy has effective automatic stabilizers.
- The economy is capable of returning to full-employment equilibrium through a self-adjustment process.

The Shortcomings of Balanced-Budget Fiscal Policy

We now need to examine the economic effects when a government actually follows a balanced-budget fiscal policy. In doing so, we will find that the effects are significant and they are not at all neutral.

Suppose in **Figure 7.8A** that the economy is at income level Y_1. Since income is below potential GDP, the economy finds itself in a recession. As is often the case in a recession, because of falling tax revenues, government is suffering a budget deficit, as shown by the distance *ab* in **Figure 7.8B**. If government is intent on balancing the budget regardless of the condition of the economy, then it will have no choice but to reduce government spending and/or increase taxation. The result, graphically, will be an upward shift in the budget line from BL_1 to BL_2 in **Figure 7.8B** so that at income level Y_1, the budget is initially balanced. However, the effect of cutting government spending or increasing taxes will have an impact on the economy as well as on the government budget. The result will be a reduction in aggregate demand. This is shown graphically in **Figure 7.8A** as a leftward shift in the aggregate demand curve, from AD_1 to AD_2.

FIGURE 7.8	Reduced Government Spending and the Deficit

An attempt to eliminate the budget deficit that exists at Y_1 would call for a reduction in government spending or an increase in taxes. Thus, the budget line shifts up from BL_1 to BL_2, and the budget deficit appears to be eliminated (point *a*). However, this action reduces aggregate demand from AD_1 to AD_2, which causes the level of equilibrium GDP to decrease to Y_2, and at this lower level of GDP there is still a budget deficit of *cd*.

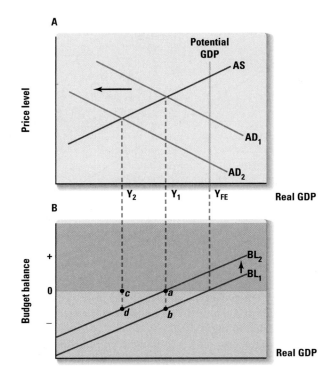

procyclical: action by government that tends to push the economy in the same direction it is leaning in.

The drop in aggregate demand will cause GDP to drop by a multiple of the decrease in aggregate expenditures. At the lower equilibrium level of Y_2, NTR will be smaller, with the result that the budget deficit (*cd*) will persist (although it is now smaller than it was at *ab*).

What we have just seen is that if the economy is experiencing a recessionary gap and a budget deficit, then the pursuit of a balanced-budget fiscal policy will be **procyclical**. To understand this, note that a recession implies that there is unemployment in the economy. If government takes action to try to eliminate the budget deficit rather than the unemployment, then the level of unemployment will rise, since the level of GDP falls. In short, the recessionary phase of the business cycle creates a given level of unemployment, and government's fiscal policy aimed at reducing the deficit results in even *higher* unemployment.

Would a balanced-budget fiscal policy result in the same procyclical tendencies if the economy was experiencing an inflationary gap? The answer to this depends on the state of the budget associated with the gap. Recall that an inflationary gap is a result of high aggregate demand, which generates a level of income that is temporarily higher than the full-employment level of GDP.

Let us assume that this high GDP level generates sufficient tax revenue to create a government budget surplus. Strict adherence to a balanced-budget fiscal policy would then necessitate that either taxes be lowered or spending be increased to eliminate the budget surplus. Such fiscal policy action would *raise* aggregate demand and thus the level of GDP. This would increase the size of the inflationary gap, and we again see the procyclical effect of a balanced-budget fiscal policy in this situation.

To review, a balanced-budget fiscal policy will likely be procyclical when the economy is experiencing a recessionary gap, since the low levels of income will generate low levels of tax revenue, which create budget deficits. Similarly, such a policy will also be procyclical when the economy is experiencing an inflationary gap if the inflationary gap comes with a budget surplus.

The Arithmetic of a Balanced Budget

Let us now examine another aspect of the procyclical nature of the balanced-budget philosophy in more detail. We will again assume that the budget is balanced and that the economy is at full-employment equilibrium. Now assume that a new government, which promised lower government spending, is elected. This new government is intent on carrying out its promise of cuts in spending. However, in consideration of the already balanced budget and given the fact that the economy is at full employment, it also announces that taxes will be reduced by a similar amount. Since government spending and taxes are to be cut by the same amount, won't both the government's budget balance and the level of GDP be unaffected? That is to say, isn't it true that what government takes out of the economy in the form of reduced spending is exactly offset by what it puts back into the economy in the form of reduced taxes? It comes as a surprise to most people that the answer to this question is no.

Suppose that the economy is at a full-employment equilibrium of $1000, government spending is $200, and taxes—which, for simplicity, we assume are entirely autonomous—are also $200. Furthermore, suppose that the value of the multiplier is 2 and that the portion of additional income that consumers spend (the MPC_D) is 0.8. As we know, a reduction in government spending will definitely reduce aggregate demand and therefore the level of GDP. Suppose government spending is cut by $40. With a multiplier of 2, this will reduce GDP by $80. Next, we know that the corresponding cut in taxes will increase aggregate demand and the level of the GDP. But how much will GDP increase? Will it increase by the same $80?

Well, a cut in taxes of $40 will immediately raise disposable income by the same $40. Does this mean that consumers will spend all of this additional disposable income? The answer is no, since we know that with an MPC_D of 0.80, the increase in spending will only be 0.8 × $40, or $32 (the other $8 will be saved). This additional $32 in spending, not the whole $40 cut in taxes, is the amount that gets multiplied.

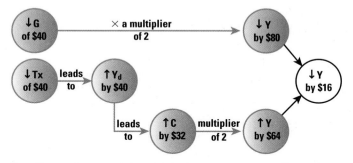

The effect on income of changing both government spending and taxes.

The cut in government spending reduces the level of GDP by $80, whereas the cut in taxes increases it by only $64. The net result is a drop in GDP of $16. In short:

> **A policy of decreasing both government spending and taxes by the same amount results in a lower real GDP and higher unemployment.**

This means that a balanced budget does not have a neutral effect on the economy, as some have suggested. Instead, any change in the size of the government's budget—even if the budget remained balanced—will result in the level of GDP either rising or falling; it will not remain unchanged.

We want to emphasize that the two contrasting approaches to fiscal policy have dramatically different results. The essence of a countercyclical fiscal policy, which is aimed at the level of GDP and unemployment, is to use fiscal policy to address recessionary and inflationary gaps that might exist in the *economy*. In simple terms, it attempts to balance the economy, not the government's budget. By contrast, the essence of the balanced budget fiscal policy, which is aimed at the government's budget, is to use fiscal policy to balance that *budget*, not the economy.

It is now clear that the issues regarding the use of fiscal policy to address recessionary and inflationary gaps, and the question of the budget deficit are more complex than one would first imagine. It is true that some people object to countercyclical fiscal policy because such an approach ignores the issue of budget deficits and the associated level of the national debt. However, the balanced-budget fiscal policy has the potential to exacerbate the economy's situation because of its procyclical tendencies. Is there another approach that could be used? In fact, the answer is yes. We now turn to a discussion of what could be described as a blend of the two philosophies just discussed.

✓ SELF-TEST

6. Assume that the economy is in a recession and that government is experiencing a budget deficit. If fiscal policy is used to try to eliminate the deficit, what will happen to:

a) unemployment

b) GDP

c) NTR

d) the deficit

Next, assume the same conditions, but this time, fiscal policy is used to try to reduce unemployment. How will your four answers to the above change?

7. Given the following data, and assuming all taxes are autonomous, calculate equilibrium income.

$$C = 20 + 0.75Y_D$$
$$X_N = 60 - 0.25Y$$
$$I = 50$$
$$G = 80$$
$$T_O = 80$$

Next, assume that government increases both its spending and autonomous taxes by 20. Calculate the new equilibrium income. Is this action by government neutral, or does it have some impact on income?

7.4 CYCLICALLY BALANCED BUDGET FISCAL POLICY

L04 Explain the pros and cons of a budget policy aimed at achieving both full employment and a balanced budget over the life of the business cycle.

Without overstating the obvious, one could ask what is so sacred about a year as far as budgets are concerned? Why not balance the budget each month, each week, or for that matter each day? Well, a week or a month would simply not be practical because government's flow of income and expenditures is not regular. Some weeks or months would have high deficits, whereas others would have high surpluses.

The same is true during any one year. Given this and the fact that a government's budget also depends on the level of GDP in the economy, some economists—including Keynes himself—suggest that governments should, instead, try to balance the budget, not on an annual basis but *over the life of the business cycle*. A typical business cycle can last for several years, so the use of fiscal policy to smooth out the business cycle would be viewed from a longer perspective than just each budget period. In these circumstances, deficits might be big in some years, as the economy enters a recession, which causes lower tax revenues and higher transfer payments. Conversely, when the business cycle moves into an expansionary phase, the result should be budget surpluses. This longer-view approach would continue to use countercyclical fiscal policy to lean against the prevailing winds while addressing the concerns of many people about budget deficits and the size of the national debt.

In a sense, this policy is a compromise of the two approaches discussed above and is known as a **cyclically balanced budget fiscal policy**. This is the use of countercyclical fiscal policy to balance the budget over the life of the business cycle. Such a policy would require governments to spend more (or tax less) at some times, and to spend less (or tax more) at other times.

Although it does seem like a sound idea, there are two potential problems with this cyclically balanced budget fiscal policy. The first is that there is no guarantee that the size and length of the recessionary gap, when government is running a budget deficit, will be exactly offset by the size and length of the inflationary gap, when government is running a budget surplus. As a result, the end of the business cycle may still show a net budget deficit.

The second, and perhaps the most difficult, problem is that most governments find it easier to increase spending in bad times than to decrease it in good times. Can you imagine a government cutting its spending on some needed social project because the economic times are so good? In short, pursuing a cyclically balanced budget fiscal policy would take a remarkable amount of discipline on the part of government, and understanding on the part of the electorate. In addition, most business cycles are longer than the term of office of any particular government. This invites the existing government to leave the problem of balancing the budget to the succeeding government.

Fiscal policy is a powerful tool, and getting it right is sometimes difficult. What we have established in this chapter is that when the economy takes a nosedive—as it did in the early 1930s or in 2008—there are three fundamentally different ways that a government can react. The first is to stimulate the economy with additional spending or tax reductions. The second is to address the resulting budget deficits caused by the economic downturn and cut spending or raise taxes. Finally, the third option is to do nothing.

We can briefly mention here that the Canadian government used countercyclical fiscal policy to counteract the effects of the 2008–2010 recession that followed the global financial crisis. We will examine this action more closely and contrast it with the actions of other governments in Chapter 13.

> **cyclically balanced budget fiscal policy:** the use of countercyclical fiscal policy to balance the budget over the life of the business cycle.

7.5   FISCAL POLICY AND THE NATIONAL DEBT

The size of the national debt is a topic that has received a great deal of attention lately. The use of countercyclical fiscal policy usually leads to growth in the debt, and thus its use has created a lot of debate. Let us examine all this more closely by asking: just what is so bad about budget deficits and therefore a growing national debt?

First, let us establish to whom this debt is owed. Any Canadian individual, corporation, or bank that buys a Canada Savings Bond, a treasury bill, or other type of government bond is lending money to government. The payment of interest and the redemption of the bond is the responsibility of government. In this sense, it can be regarded as a debt that we Canadians owe to ourselves. However, one of the major problems with the debt is that the "we" and the "ourselves" in the last sentence do not refer to the same groups of people. We, the taxpayers, are responsible for paying off the interest and principal to ourselves, the bondholders. But while all bondholders are taxpayers, not all taxpayers are bondholders. And therein lies one of the problems: as the size of the debt increases, and with it the interest payments, increasing amounts must be raised in taxes, and those amounts are then transferred to bondholders. Since it is normally the comparatively wealthy who hold the majority of bonds, while taxes are paid by rich and poor alike, the payment of interest on the national debt could represent a major *redistribution of income*.

For another angle on this redistributional aspect, let us assume that the debt is entirely internal and that in response to public pressure, it was decided to repay the entire debt of approximately $519 billion (as of 2010). How could this be done? The most straightforward answer is for the government to raise $519 billion additional dollars through increased taxes, of which all

> **LO5** Discuss the cause, size, and problems of the national debt.

Canadians would pay some small part. What then would Ottawa do with this incredible rush of additional revenue? Turn around and send it back to those Canadians who hold Canada Savings Bonds and those institutions holding the other bonds. The net effect: all Canadians pay $519 billion in additional taxes, and some Canadians receive $519 billion in bond repayments. As many might argue, why bother? Why not leave it where it was in the first place?

Before considering some of the problems associated with big government deficits and debt, let us look at the facts. It is unfortunate that public discussion of the national debt often runs to hyperbole, and we used to hear mention of a "staggering" debt of "enormous" proportions as a result of "crippling" deficits. Dollar amounts in billions are certainly enormous from an individual's perspective, but one seldom hears the size of Canada's GDP described as staggering. We therefore need to put things in perspective. Just how big is our national debt? It might help if we look at it over a period. **Table 7.3** shows some figures for selected years.

TABLE 7.3	Net National Debt (nominal $billions)				
1926	**1940**	**1946**	**1967**	**1991**	**2010**
2.4	3.3	13.4	17.7	377.7	519.1

Source: Adapted from the Statistics Canada CANSIM database http://cansim2.statcan.ca, Table 385-0010, 17 March 2011, and Department of Finance Canada, Fiscal Reference Tables, 1926–2010. Reproduced with the permission of the Minister of Public Works and Government Services, 2011.

It certainly seems like a "staggering" increase. But since the population of Canada has increased appreciably during the past hundred years, it might be better to show the figures in terms of per capita debt, as in **Table 7.4**.

TABLE 7.4	Per Capita Net National Debt (nominal $billions)				
1926	**1940**	**1946**	**1967**	**1991**	**2010**
254	287	1090	868	13 475	15 222

Source: Adapted from the Statistics Canada CANSIM database http://cansim2.statcan.ca, Table 385-0010, 17 March 2011, and Department of Finance Canada, Fiscal Reference Tables, 1926–2010. Reproduced with the permission of the Minister of Public Works and Government Services, 2011.

So, the average debt per person has increased from a mere $254 in 1926 to over $15 000 eighty years later. It certainly looks like a fairly staggering increase. But we need to make one further adjustment to allow for the effects of inflation over the years. So, let us show the total debt, but this time, in constant 2002 dollars, as in **Table 7.5**.

TABLE 7.5	Net National Debt ($2002, billions)				
1926	**1940**	**1946**	**1967**	**1991**	**2010**
25.8	40.9	140.0	94.2	445.4	424.1

Source: Adapted from the Statistics Canada CANSIM database http://cansim2.statcan.ca, Table 385-0010, 17 March 2011, and Department of Finance Canada, Fiscal Reference Tables, 1926–2010. Reproduced with the permission of the Minister of Public Works and Government Services, 2011.

Finally, let us combine both factors in **Table 7.6** to give us figures in terms of constant dollars per capita.

This puts things in perspective. In real terms, the per capita debt increased 32 percent in the 14 years leading up to World War II; it more than tripled during the war, declined to less than half by 1967, but has tripled again in the last 40 years.

TABLE 7.6	Per Capita Net National Debt ($2002)				
1926	1940	1946	1967	1991	2010
2730	3594	11 391	4152	16 618	12 477

Source: Adapted from the Statistics Canada CANSIM database http://cansim2.statcan.ca, Table 385-0010, 17 March 2011, and Department of Finance Canada, Fiscal Reference Tables, 1926–2010. Reproduced with the permission of the Minister of Public Works and Government Services, 2011.

Although **Table 7.6** is helpful, it still does not tell us whether Canada's national debt is too big. The best measure of the size of any debt is relative to the ability to repay, and this is relative to income. **Table 7.7** shows the size of Canada's debt relative to the country's income, that is, as a percentage of GDP (of GNP until 1967).

TABLE 7.7	Percentage of Net National Debt/GD(N)P				
1926	1940	1946	1967	1991	2010
47%	49%	113%	23%	56%	34%

Source: Adapted from the Statistics Canada CANSIM database http://cansim2.statcan.ca, Table 385-0010, 17 March 2011, and Department of Finance Canada, Fiscal Reference Tables, 1926–2010. Reproduced with the permission of the Minister of Public Works and Government Services, 2011.

In recent years, the percentage has steadily declined. In fact, since 1995, Canada's debt burden has fallen from being the second highest to the lowest of the G8 countries. (The United States sits at 61 percent, Italy at over 109 percent, Greece at 148 percent, and Japan topping the list at 184 percent).

These figures show clearly that one of the major causes of the growth of Canada's debt was the financing of World War II. During a major war, few nations are able to finance their military expenditures through taxation alone. They are often left with little choice but to borrow, and the majority of this borrowing is from the nation's own citizens. Most would feel this is a legitimate reason to increase the debt and might also agree that there are other legitimate reasons for the increased debt—for example, deficit financing to prevent or escape from a recession, or the financing of necessary infrastructure such as bridges and airports. The third explanation for the increased Canadian debt, especially since the early 1970s, has been the increase in the size of income-support programs. Here, controversy about whether this is a good reason for the debt to increase heats up; some have suggested that these programs are too generous in comparison with those of some other countries.

Finally, it should be noted that the very high interest rates between the mid-1970s and the 1990s compounded the size of the debt. (As we saw, some economists suggest that the reason that interest rates were so high in the first place was the result of borrowing by governments. Complicated world, isn't it?) Leaving the statistics behind, let us examine some of the problems associated with the debt.

Problems of the National Debt: Fact or Fantasy?

The first perceived problem involves the size of the foreign portion of the debt. Private financial agencies give ratings for government bonds sold around the world, to help their clients who wish to invest. The lower the rating for a particular government's bonds, the higher the perceived risk and therefore the higher the interest payments that must be paid. In early 1995, there was a *perception* that Canada's national debt was too large. The result was a lower bond rating, and the outflow of interest payments on the foreign-held debt increased. (It should be noted however that in Canada's case 84 percent of the debt is owed to Canadians, with only 16 percent owed to foreign individuals, corporations, and financial institutions.)

Second, we noted that payment of interest on the debt represents a redistribution of income from lower-income Canadians to higher-income Canadians. This is because only higher-income Canadians receive interest payments that come out of the taxes of all Canadians, including middle- and low-income Canadians.

As a third point, large interest payments also mean that each year government must earmark several tens of billions of dollars in interest payments before it can even start to consider other spending claims. This obviously curtails its ability to satisfy other demands in the economy. (The annual total interest payments in the 1990s were approximately $40 billion, which is higher than the annual deficits during the period.) This is a conundrum: if government did not have to pay these interest charges, then it could balance the budget. But because it did not balance the budget in the past, it has to pay these interest charges.

A final criticism comes from the fact that a federal government has almost unlimited power to spend. Theoretically (and legally), there is no upper limit to how big a deficit can be. That does not mean that big deficits are not harmful to an economy; it simply means that a national government has supreme power to tax, to borrow, and to print money. This means that without checks on its spending, a government can become power hungry and wasteful in its fiscal affairs. And for this we would all suffer.

In summary, the problems with high deficits and debt are:

- the interest payments that must be paid on foreign-held debt
- the income redistribution effects of large interest payments
- the reduced ability of government to meet the needs of its citizens
- the possible increased power grabbing and wastefulness of government

Let us now take a brief look at what are sometimes seen as problems of the debt, but really are not.

One of the bogus arguments about the national debt seeks to draw an analogy between a household or a business and the operations of the federal government. It suggests that just like an individual or a business, if revenue falls short of expenses for a long enough period, then bankruptcy will follow. This is just not a legitimate concern when applied to a federal government, which, as we just mentioned, has unlimited powers of taxation and borrowing, and has direct control over the nation's supply of money. Therefore, it is highly unlikely that the federal government of a large economy such as Canada will "go broke" as a result of *internal* borrowing. It is true that the German government went broke following World War I, but this was a result of external debt imposed on it by France and the United Kingdom. If urban decay and high taxes drive many higher-income taxpayers and businesses out of a city, that city might go broke in that it could default on interest payments on the bonds it sold to borrow money. The same might be said, although this would be stretching it, of a particular province or state, but not of a country as large and as desirable to live in as Canada.

Another argument suggests that a big national debt means that we are encumbering future generations, who will eventually have to pay it. It is true that our children and grandchildren will inherit a larger debt and the interest charges associated with it. However, it is also true that future generations will inherit the Canadian-held portion of the assets (bonds) represented by that debt. That is, if our descendants have to pay extra taxes to service a larger debt, they also, as a generation, will get those same taxes back as the interest payments are made to whoever holds those bonds.

While it is true that the federal government is in debt to the tune of hundreds of billions of dollars, it is also true that the government owns assets—airports, military hardware, land, buildings, and so on—that also total a great deal. Is the debt too large relative to the assets owned?

Most observers suggest that a debt/GDP ratio of less than 50 percent is not particularly worrisome. Canada's debt in the early 1990s was cause for some concern, but as we saw in **Table 7.7**, the national debt in 2007 has been reduced to a manageable 33 percent.

ADDED DIMENSION   Is a World Financial Crisis Possible?

In today's turbulent world, there is no shortage of disaster scenarios ranging from global warming to coordinated terrorist attacks on a massive scale. There is even one scenario within the field of economics.

Doomsday economists raise the spectre of a global debt crisis rooted in the fact that so many countries—wealthy as well as poor—have exceeded national debt thresholds. If just one sovereign country defaults on its debt, this might trigger a firestorm that could quickly spread into a global depression on a scale beyond that experienced in the 1930s.

In late 2011, Greece was at the centre of just such a concern. Its budget deficit in 2009 alone was more than 13 percent and its total national debt equalled 126 percent of its GDP. More seriously, Greece is not a special case. Some of the world's largest developed countries have budget deficits almost as large, relative to the size of their economies. Both the United Kingdom's and Spain's deficits were running at 11 percent of GDP, and that of the United States at 10 percent. The debt-to-GDP ratio in Japan (178 percent) and Italy (106 percent) certainly gives one pause. Enormous debt loads used to be a problem only in emerging economies, but today those burdens are also a problem for some higher-income countries.

The doomsday aspect comes into play when one realizes that debts this high are in context of very low interest rates. If some major bond defaults were to occur, then lenders would demand higher-risk premiums in interest rates and the strain of carrying a large debt would be magnified. As a final thought, all of the above is in context of an aging population that would very much feel the pinch if there were a crisis in government-funded pension programmes.

It is estimated that governments of mature, safe economies will issue upwards of $5 trillion worth of bonds each of the next several years. This raises the possibility that some major countries may face debt restructurings or debt defaults—or both.

Sovereign defaults can wreck economies. Banks can quickly become shaky as the prices of the government bonds they hold plunge to a fraction of their face value, reducing those governments' ability to make new loans. Devaluation of the currency would almost certainly follow, and this reduces consumers' buying power. For example, the Mexican peso crisis of 1994 walloped the rest of Latin America, and as late as 2002 some Brazilian government bonds were trading as low as 50 percent of their face value.

A Wrap-Up and a Plea for Common Sense

When discussing policy issues, it is important to focus on the economic issues that are important to the well-being of the citizenship of a country as a whole. This means that in a recession, unemployment is a serious concern for all of us, not just those without work. In this situation, the appropriate action should be expansionary fiscal policy implying a deficit in the government budget. However, it should also be recognized that government must keep the size of the national debt—as a percentage of GDP—under control. In the long run, these goals can be achieved if government policy is adjusted to fit the inevitable changes in the immediate economic circumstances. This means government budget surpluses in good times as well as budget deficits in times of recession. This long-run approach implies balancing the budget over the life of the business cycle, and will serve the economy far better than getting caught up in any kind of single-minded ideology about how to manage fiscal policy in any particular year. By and large, Canadian governments of the past have done rather well in achieving all of this.

 SELF-TEST

8. Under what circumstances is it inappropriate for government to run up a budget deficit?

Review

CHAPTER SUMMARY

This chapter focused on three distinct budget polices. The first is countercyclical policy, aimed at closing any GDP gaps that may exist in the economy. The second is an annually balanced budget policy, aimed at balancing the budget each budget period. The third is a cyclically balanced budget policy, which calls for the budget to be balanced over the life of the business cycle.

7.1 The state of the government's budget depends on:
- its net tax revenues, which, in turn, depend on both the rate of taxation and the size of the GDP
- its own spending

7.2a Countercyclical fiscal policy:
- increases the level of government spending or decreases the level of taxation when a recessionary gap exists
- decreases the level of government spending or increases the level of taxation when an inflationary gap exists

7.2b There are three potential shortcomings with counter-cyclical fiscal policy.
- There can be time delays involved in closing a GDP gap.
- It may be inflationary.
- It can cause serious budget deficits.

7.3a Balanced-budget fiscal policy balances the government's revenues and overall spending each budget year and:
- highlights the effect of automatic stabilizers
- argues that the economy is capable of achieving full-employment equilibrium through a self-adjustment process

7.3b The problem with a balanced-budget policy is that it is almost always procyclical and can make an existing economic condition, such as unemployment, more serious.

7.4 A cyclically balanced budget policy attempts to meld the countercyclical and balanced-budget fiscal policies into a single policy where the budget is balanced, but over the life of the business cycle and not in every budget year.

7.5a The size of the national debt should be viewed in terms of:
- per capita debt in constant dollars
- a percentage of real GDP

7.5b Canada's national debt has grown because of:
- deficit-financing to prevent or escape from a recession
- borrowing to finance World War II
- an increase in the size of income-support programs
- high interest rate costs in the last 25 years of the twentieth century

7.5c The potential problems with the national debt are:
- the interest that must be paid on foreign-held debt does not go to Canadians
- the income distribution effects of large interest payments
- the reduced ability of government to meet the needs of its citizens
- the possible increased greed and wastefulness of government

NEW GLOSSARY TERMS AND KEY EQUATIONS

automatic stabilizers 246
balanced budget 239
balanced-budget fiscal policy 246
budget deficit 237
budget surplus 237

countercyclical fiscal policy 242
cyclically balanced budget fiscal
  policy 251
fiscal policy 235
monetizing the debt 240

national debt 237
net tax revenue 237
procyclical 248

Equations:

[7.1] NTR = tax revenue − transfer payments

page 237

[7.2] budget balance = NTR − G

page 237

STUDY TIPS

1. Students sometimes have difficulty understanding the concept behind the term "procyclical." It simply means a tendency to push things further in the direction that they are already moving. Here is an example. Assume that 100 new forest fires are caused in a particular area by an evening thunderstorm. If the next day turns out to be sunny and very hot with some wind, the weather will certainly add to the size of the fires; that is, it will be procyclical. Conversely, if the day turns out to be cool, with some rain and no wind, then the weather will be countercyclical.

2. You should realize that all governments have some kind of fiscal policy. Just what kind of policy a government has depends on its attitude toward spending, taxation, and budgets. No government would ever set out to deliberately make an economy already in a recession even worse with a procyclical policy that pushed down GDP and raised unemployment even more. However, if a government decided to balance its budget regardless of cost, pursuing a policy of reducing government spending (or increasing taxation) when the economy is in recession, then it would do just that.

3. It is probably useful to state outright that the cause-and-effect relationship between a change in taxes and GDP operates both ways. A change in the level of taxation will certainly have an impact on GDP. But it is also true that if GDP changes, then the tax revenue received by government will change. To keep these effects clear, you need to focus on which is the cause and which is the effect. It is the same as saying that a change in income will affect consumption and that a change in consumption will affect income. It is important to distinguish between induced and autonomous consumption, and induced and autonomous taxes.

Answered Questions
These questions can also be found online on Connect.

Indicate whether the following statements are true or false:

1. **(LO 5) T or F**   The national debt is the sum of the federal government's past budget deficits less its surpluses.

2. **(LO 2) T or F**   The Great Depression ended when World War II began.

3. **(LO 2) T or F**   If aggregate demand increases as a result of countercyclical fiscal policy, prices will rise, and GDP will fall.

4. **(LO 2) T or F**   Countercyclical fiscal policy aimed at closing an inflationary gap is illustrated graphically by the aggregate demand curve shifting to the left.

5. **(LO 1) T or F**   Both net tax revenues and government spending on goods and services are a function of GDP.

6. **(LO 2) T or F**   A decrease in government spending on goods and services will shift the budget line up.

7. **(LO 2) T or F**   A decrease in autonomous taxes would pivot the NTR line up.

8. **(LO 2, 3) T or F**   Countercyclical fiscal policy is aimed at balancing the budget, whereas a balanced-budget fiscal policy is aimed at balancing the economy.

9. **(LO 3) T or F**   If government spending on goods and services is increased by exactly the same amount that taxes are increased, the level of GDP will not change.

10. **(LO 2) T or F**   In trying to cure a recession, countercyclical fiscal policy may increase a budget deficit.

Practise and learn online with Connect, where you can find the Answered Questions and the Unanswered Problems for all chapters of this textbook's Study Guide section.

Basic (Questions 11–24)

11. **(LO 1)** What is fiscal policy?
    a) It is government's policy on spending.
    b) It is government's policy on taxation.
    c) It is government's policy on both spending and taxation.
    d) It is the central bank's policy on interest rates.

12. **(LO 2)** Which of the following will close an inflationary gap?
    a) An increase in government spending
    b) A decrease in government spending
    c) A decrease in taxes
    d) An increase in exports

13. **(LO 5)** To what group is the largest portion of the national debt owed?
    a) The Canadian public, that is, individuals, businesses, and banks in Canada
    b) Foreign individuals, banks, and businesses
    c) The Bank of Canada
    d) The government of Canada

14. **(LO 2)** What is net tax revenue?
    a) It is the total of all taxes collected by government.
    b) It is the total of all taxes collected by government minus spending by government on goods and services.
    c) It is the total of all taxes collected by government plus transfer payments.
    d) It is the total of all taxes collected by government minus transfer payments.

15. **(LO 2)** When does a government budget surplus exist?
    a) When government spending of all types exceeds net tax revenue
    b) When net tax revenue is less than government spending of all types
    c) When government spending on goods and services exceeds net tax revenue
    d) When net tax revenue exceeds government spending on goods and services

16. **(LO 5)** What is true about the national debt since the 1960s?
    a) It has grown both absolutely and as a percentage of GDP.
    b) It has grown absolutely but has declined as a percentage of GDP.
    c) It has grown absolutely but remained constant as a percentage of GDP.
    d) It has declined absolutely but increased as a percentage of GDP.

17. **(LO 2)** What is the effect of a countercyclical fiscal policy?
    a) It intensifies changes in GDP caused by the business cycle.
    b) It dampens changes in GDP caused by the business cycle.
    c) It has no effect on changes in GDP caused by the business cycle.
    d) It allows a government to balance its budget.

18. **(LO 2)** What would cause the aggregate demand curve to shift to the right?
    a) An increase in taxes
    b) A decrease in government spending on goods and services
    c) An increase in net tax revenues
    d) Countercyclical fiscal policy used to eliminate a recessionary gap

19. **(LO 2)** What can cause an upward (left) shift in the budget line?
    a) An increase in GDP
    b) An increase in taxes
    c) An increase in government spending
    d) A decrease in taxes

20. **(LO 2)** Which of the following statements about countercyclical fiscal policy is correct?
    a) It is an appropriate policy response to a recessionary gap but not to an inflationary gap.
    b) It is an appropriate policy response to an inflationary gap but not to a recessionary gap.
    c) It involves only higher government spending.
    d) It involves only higher taxes.
    e) It is the use of spending or taxation policies by government to push the economy in a direction opposite to the way it was moving.

21. **(LO 2)** Which of the following did not occur in the great depression of the thirties?
    a) Unemployment rose to historical highs
    b) Interest rates rose to historical highs
    c) Investment spending dropped to dramatic lows
    d) International trade nearly disappeared

22. **(LO 3)** What are automatic stabilizers?
    a) Imports and exports that automatically change with the state of the economy so as to stabilize the economy
    b) Investment spending that automatically changes with the state of the economy to stabilize the economy
    c) Tax provisions and government spending program that automatically put spending into a recessionary economy and take it out in a boom economy
    d) Consumption spending that automatically changes with the state of the economy to stabilize the economy

23. **(LO 4)** What is a cyclically balanced budget fiscal policy?
   a) A policy of balancing the budget each fiscal year
   b) A policy of using the budget to balance the economy each fiscal year
   c) A policy of balancing the budget over the life of the business cycle
   d) A policy of using the budget to balance the economy over the life of the business cycle

Refer to **Figure 7.9** to answer questions 24, 25, and 26.

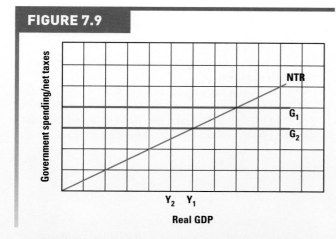

FIGURE 7.9

24. **(LO 4)** Which of the following statements is verified by the graph?
   a) A budget surplus exists if government spending is G_1 and real GDP is Y_1.
   b) A budget deficit exists if government spending is G_1 and real GDP is Y_1.
   c) If government spending was reduced from G_1 to G_2, the budget surplus at Y_2 would decrease.
   d) NTR is a function of the level of government spending.

Intermediate (Problems 25–32)

25. **(LO 2)** What is most likely to happen if the level of GDP is Y_1 and government reduces its spending from G_1 to G_2 in an attempt to balance its budget?
   a) The budget would be balanced at the new GDP level, Y_2.
   b) GDP would remain at Y_1, but the budget would be in deficit.
   c) GDP would be Y_2, and the budget would be in deficit.
   d) GDP would be Y_2, and the budget would be in surplus.

26. **(LO 2)** If government spending is G_1 and GDP is Y_1, why won't a reduction in government spending by the size of the budget deficit eliminate the deficit?

a) Because GDP and NTR will decrease as a result of the decrease in government spending
b) Because government spending is a function of income
c) Because GDP will rise as a result of the decrease in government spending
d) Because NTR will rise as a result of the decrease in government spending

27. **(LO 5)** Which of the following statements concerning a budget deficit is true?
   a) It is smaller if the economy is in the midst of a severe recession.
   b) It is smaller if the economy is experiencing strong aggregate demand.
   c) It reduces the size of the national debt.
   d) It can be measured in terms of the amount of unemployment that it causes.

28. **(LO 3)** Which of the following is true if government attempts to balance its budget when the economy is in a recession and government is running a budget deficit?
   a) Inflation would result.
   b) The unemployment rate would decrease.
   c) Government spending would have to increase.
   d) GDP would increase.
   e) The action would be procyclical.

29. **(LO 2)** What is the effect of countercyclical fiscal policy on price level?
   a) It will increase in the case of a recessionary gap.
   b) It will increase in the case of a inflationary gap.
   c) It will decrease in the case of a recessionary gap.
   d) It will have no effect in the case of a recessionary gap.
   e) It will have no effect in the case of an inflationary gap.

30. **(LO 3)** Which of the following is part of the argument that, in the face of a recession, the economy is self adjusting?
   a) The use of countercyclical fiscal policy
   b) The desirability of keeping the national debt privately held
   c) The value of "shovel-ready" public works plans
   d) Flexible prices

31. **(LO 2)** All of the following, except one, are arguments *against* the use of countercyclical fiscal policy to close a recessionary gap. Which is the exception?
   a) Countercyclical fiscal policy can be inflationary.
   b) Countercyclical fiscal policy is subject to serious time lags.
   c) Countercyclical fiscal policy can lead to serious increases in the budget deficit.
   d) Countercyclical fiscal policy can reduce budget deficits, but this would also lower the exchange rate.

32. **(LO 3)** What is the result of balanced-budget fiscal policy when both a recessionary gap and a budget deficit exist?
    a) The recessionary gap would be reduced, and the budget deficit would fall.
    b) The recessionary gap would increase, and the budget deficit would fall.
    c) The recessionary gap would be reduced, and the budget deficit would rise.
    d) The recessionary gap would increase, and the budget deficit would rise.

Advanced (Problems 33–35)

33. **(LO 4)** Which of the following is least likely to occur?
    a) A recessionary gap and a budget surplus
    b) An inflationary gap and a budget surplus
    c) A recessionary gap and a budget deficit
    d) High employment and economic growth

34. **(LO 2)** Keynes argued that the economy could escape the great depression by:
    a) Stimulating investment spending with low interest rates
    b) Dramatically increasing the level of government spending
    c) Encouraging consumers to spend more through an increase in taxes
    d) Stimulating exports by adopting a flexible exchange rate
    e) All of the above

35. **(LO 3)** Suppose that an economy is simultaneously experiencing a budget deficit and an inflationary gap. If government attempts to balance the budget, what will be the effect?
    a) Real GDP will increase, and the deficit will increase.
    b) Real GDP will increase, and the deficit will decrease.
    c) Real GDP will decrease, and the deficit will increase.
    d) Real GDP will decrease, and the deficit will decrease.

Parallel Problems

ANSWERED PROBLEMS

36A. **(LO 2, 3) Key Problem** Figure 7.10 shows the aggregate demand/supply and the government budget line for the economy of Mahdi. The economy is presently at equilibrium. For every $1 change in government spending, aggregate demand changes by $3.
   a) What is the present level of GDP and the price level in Mahdi? GDP: _____ ; price level: _____
   b) Is there a recessionary or an inflationary gap? How much? Gap: _____ ; amount: _____
   c) Does government have a budget deficit or a surplus? How much? Deficit or surplus: ____ ; amount: ____
   d) By how much must aggregate demand increase or decrease in order to move the economy to full-employment equilibrium? Draw in the new aggregate demand curve, labelled AD₂. Increase or decrease: _____ ; amount: _____
   e) What change in government spending is necessary in order to move the economy to full-employment equilibrium? Increase or decrease: _____ ; amount: _____ .
   f) What effect will this have on the level of GDP and price level? New GDP: ____ ; new price level: _____
   g) If government makes the change in e), draw in the new budget line, labelled BL₂. What will be the new value of government's budget at this new GDP?

   Returning to the original equilibrium, suppose that government is committed to a balanced budget. Deficit or surplus: _____ ; amount: _____
   h) What change in government spending is necessary in order to balance the budget at the present income level? Draw in the new budget line labelled BL₃. Increase or decrease: _____ ; amount: _____
   i) What effect will the change in h) have on aggregate demand? Draw in the new curve, labelled AD₃. Increase or decrease: _____ ; amount: _____
   j) As a result of this change in aggregate demand, what will happen to the value of GDP and price level? New GDP: _____ ; new price level: _____
   k) What will be the new value of government's budget at this new GDP? Deficit or surplus: _____ ; amount: _____ .

Basic (Problems 37A–43A)

37A. **(LO 1)** Table 7.8 shows the revenue and spending of the Canadian federal government from 2005–2006. For simplicity, assume that all of the *spending grants to other levels of government* were spent in Canada on goods and services.
   a) What are the projected NTRs in this budget plan?

   _____
   b) What is the value of NTR less government spending on goods and services (G)? _____

FIGURE 7.10

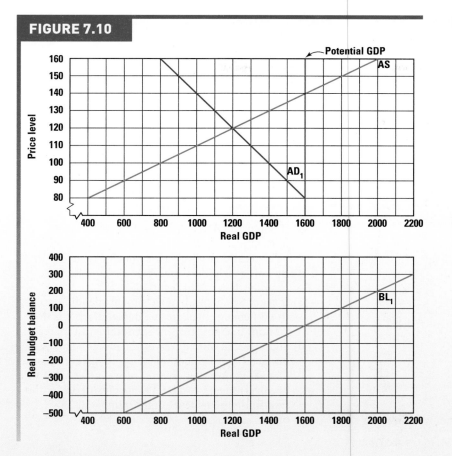

What percentage of total revenue is:
c) personal income taxes? _____
d) corporate income taxes? _____

What percentage of total outlays is:
e) transfer payments to persons? _____
f) public debt charges? _____

38A. **(LO 1)** Government spending in Robok is $140 billion, and its only tax is an income tax with a marginal tax rate of 0.35.
  a) What is the balance on the government's budget at a GDP level of $360 billion? _____
  b) What is the balance on the government's budget at a GDP level of $500 billion? _____
  c) At what level of GDP will the economy of Robok have a balanced budget? _____

39A. **(LO 2)** Figure 7.11 shows the economy of Tagara. Its aggregate demand is currently AD_1 and the budget line is BL_1.
  a) What effect would an increase in government spending have on each of the graphs?
    Graph A: the aggregate demand curve would shift from _____ to _____
    Graph B: the budget line would shift from _____ to _____

  b) What effect would an increase in taxes have on each of the graphs?
    Graph A: the aggregate demand curve would shift from _____ to _____
    Graph B: the budget line would shift from _____ to _____

TABLE 7.8	Federal Government's Budget Plan for Fiscal Year Beginning April 2005		
REVENUES		**OUTLAYS**	
Personal income taxes	$103.7	Transfers to persons	52.6
Corporate income taxes	31.7	Spending grants to other levels of government	42.8
Other income taxes	4.5	Public debt charges	33.8
GST and excise taxes	46.2	Direct program spending	81.8
EI premiums	16.5	**Total Outlays**	**209.0**
Other revenues	19.6	**Projected Budget Plan Surplus**	**13.2**
Total Revenues	**222.2**		

Source: Data derived by authors from information found in Department of Finance Canada, Budget Plan, 2005–2006. Reproduced with the permission of the Minister of Public Works and Government Services, 2011.

FIGURE 7.11

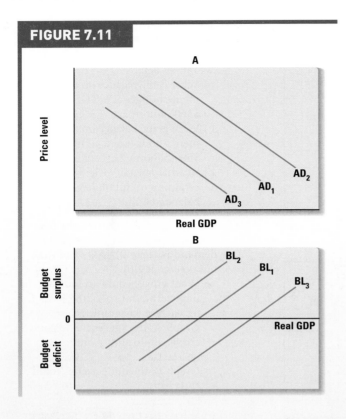

A

Price level

Real GDP

AD_2
AD_1
AD_3

B

Budget surplus

0

Budget deficit

BL_2
BL_1
BL_3

Real GDP

TABLE 7.9

Year	Budget Surplus	Budget Deficit	National Debt	GDP	Debt/ GDP %
2006	/	/	280	700	—
2007	/	14	—	725	—
2008	—	—	323	730	—
2009	8	/	—	—	45.0
2010	—	—	310	720	—
2011	/	6	—	750	—

a) If potential GDP is $540, and the economy is presently in equilibrium, is there an inflationary or a recessionary gap? How much of a gap?
b) By how much must aggregate demand increase in order to close this gap? _____
c) If every $1 change in government spending leads to a $4 change in aggregate demand, what is the amount that government spending must increase?
d) Suppose that initially government has a balanced budget. If government increases its spending as in c) and tax revenues are 0.25 of real GDP, what will be government's real budget surplus/deficit at the new full-employment equilibrium? _____ of _____

40A. **(LO 5)** Complete **Table 7.9** for the economy of Smetana.

41A. **(LO 1, 2)** The economy of Morin is shown in **Figure 7.12**.

FIGURE 7.12

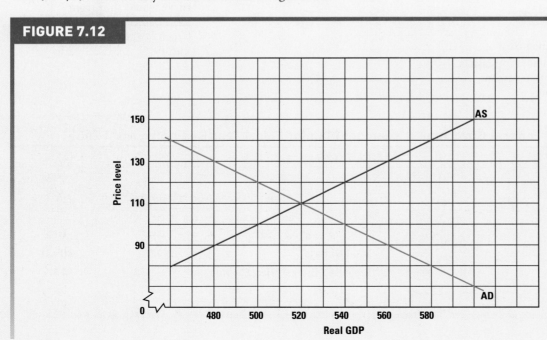

42A. **(LO 1)** Define *fiscal policy.*

43A. **(LO 5)** To whom does the federal government owe most of its debt?

Intermediate (Problems 44A–51A)

44A. **(LO 2)** Answer the questions below for the economy of Motak, using the graph in **Figure 7.13**.
   a) If GDP is $800 and government spending is G_1, what is the size of Motak's budget deficit? Answer: _____ .
   b) If government spending is decreased by the size of the deficit in a), and the multiplier is 2, what is the new level of equilibrium GDP? Answer: _____ .
   c) What is the size of Motak's deficit at this new level of equilibrium GDP? Answer: _____ .

45A. **(LO 1, 2, 3)** The aggregate demand and supply for Cancum are shown in **Table 7.10**. Potential GDP is $1500 billion.
   a) If the economy is in equilibrium, is the economy experiencing an inflationary or a recessionary gap? _____ How much? _____
   b) Suppose government uses countercyclical fiscal policy to close the gap. By how much and in what direction would AD have to change in order to achieve full employment? _____
   c) As a result of this change, what would be the inflation rate? _____

46A. **(LO 3)** The following are data for the economy of Moksha:

$$C = 25 + 0.6Y \qquad G = 160$$
$$I = 60 \qquad X_N = 55 - 0.1Y$$

   a) Calculate equilibrium GDP. Equilibrium GDP: _____
   b) Calculate the multiplier. Multiplier: _____
   c) If the tax function is $T = 20 + 0.2Y$, calculate the size of the budget deficit or surplus. (deficit/surplus) _____ of $ _____
   d) Now, change government spending by the amount of the surplus or deficit in an attempt to balance the budget. What will be the new equilibrium income? Equilibrium GDP: _____
   e) What is the budget surplus or deficit at the new equilibrium? (deficit/surplus) _____ of $ _____

47A. **(LO 2, 3)** Suppose that a federal election is called at a time when the economy is experiencing a recessionary gap and there is a budget deficit. The leader of Party A promises, if elected, to immediately balance the budget by slashing government spending. The leader of Party B promises, if elected, to stimulate the economy with a tax decrease. What would be the effect of each party's proposed policy on each of the following?
   a) The level of GDP. _____ .
   b) The level of NTR. _____ .
   c) The level of unemployment. _____ .
   d) The budget deficit. _____ .
   e) The price level. _____ .

48A. **(LO 2)** Given the graph of government spending and net tax revenues in **Figure 7.14A**:
   a) Draw the corresponding budget line in **Figure 7.14B**.
   b) If government spending were to decrease by 40, draw in the new government spending and budget lines.
   c) After the change in government spending, what is the budget balance at a GDP level of 500? (deficit/surplus) _____ of $ _____

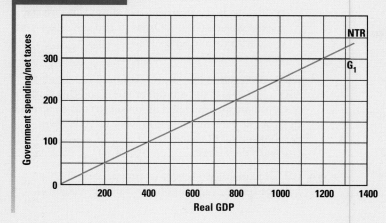

FIGURE 7.13

TABLE 7.10		
Price Index	**Aggregate Quantity Demanded**	**Aggregate Quantity Supplied**
105	1600	400
110	1500	800
115	1400	1100
120	1300	1300
125	1200	1400
130	1100	1500
135	1000	1600
140	900	1650

FIGURE 7.14

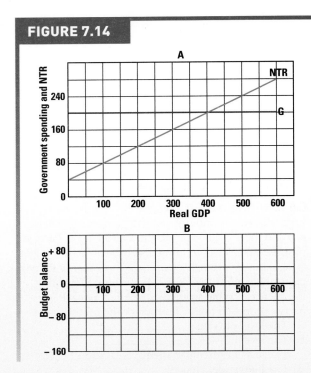

A

B

49A. **(LO 2)** Explain some of the problems associated with a countercyclical fiscal policy.

50A. **(LO 2)** What is the primary goal of countercyclical fiscal policy? What are three criticisms of it?

51A. **(LO 5)** Explain how paying off the national debt would redistribute income.

Advanced (Problems 52A–56A)

52A. **(LO 2, 3)** The following is information for the economy of Tandor, where taxes are wholly autonomous.

$$C = 40 + 0.8Y_D \qquad G = T_O = 340$$
$$I = 100 \qquad X_N = 107 - 0.1Y$$

a) What is the value of equilibrium income? _____
b) At equilibrium, what is the amount of the budget?
   Deficit/Surplus _____ of $ _____
c) If government increased both its spending and taxes by $60, what would be the new equilibrium income? _____

53A. **(LO 3)** The following is information for the economy of Tindor:

$$C = 60 + 0.8Y_D \qquad T = 200 + 0.25Y$$
$$I = 600 \qquad X_N = 700 - 0.2Y$$

Assume that government is constrained by law to maintain a balanced budget; that is, $G = T$ (where $T = 200 + 0.25Y$).

a) What is the value of equilibrium income?
   Equilibrium GDP: _____
b) What are the values of G and T at equilibrium income? G = _____ T = _____
c) What is the value of X_N at expenditures equilibrium?
   X_N = _____
d) What is the value of the multiplier?
   Multiplier: _____

54A. **(LO 2, 3, 4)** The government of Osiris believes in balancing its budget over a seven-year cycle. Over the first six years, it has maintained its spending at $150 billion and its MTR at 0.25. (There are no autonomous taxes in Osiris.) Column 2 of **Table 7.11** shows the level of GDP in each of the first six years in the cycle.

TABLE 7.11

(1) Year	(2) GDP ($ billion)	(3) Deficit/Surplus
1	600	_____
2	580	_____
3	560	_____
4	612	_____
5	620	_____
6	608	_____

a) Fill in column (3), showing the actual amounts of the budget deficit or surplus for each year. Suppose that the estimated level of GDP in Year 7 is projected to be $600.
b) What level of government spending (assuming no change in the tax rate) is necessary for the government of Osiris to end the seven-year cycle with its budgetary goal on target? Answer: _____ .
c) Alternatively, what change in the tax rate (assuming no change in government spending) is necessary for the government of Osiris to end the seven-year cycle with its budgetary goal on target? Answer: _____ .

55A. **(LO 2, 3)** Assume that in the economy of Malud, the MPC_D is 0.8 and the multiplier is 2.5 and that both government spending and autonomous taxes increase by $100. By how much and in what direction will equilibrium GDP change?
(increase/decrease) _____ of $ _____

56A. **(LO 3)** Explain two sets of circumstances where a balanced-budget fiscal policy would be procyclical.

CHAPTER 8

MONEY AND BANKING

WHAT'S AHEAD...

This is the first of two chapters on the money market and monetary policy. We look at the origins of money, its current definition, and the part that money plays in our modern economy. We examine the role of our modern banking system and emphasize the ability of that system to create new money and how this helps the economy grow.

A Question of Relevance...

You and four friends decide to go out for a fancy meal to celebrate another successful year at college. When the bill arrives, you split it into five shares. Frederick pays by cheque. Sian pays by credit card. Althea digs deep into her pocket and comes up with 20 loonies. Bosie gives an IOU to the manager (a friend of his). Finding that you have none of the above means, you have to pay by "volunteering" to wash up (for yourself and 200 other diners). You all paid in different ways. But who used money? Some of you? All of you? So, what does constitute money in our modern economy?

Money has been called humanity's greatest invention and its greatest curse. People fret about it, and they sweat for it. For some, it is the root of all evil and for others the source of all joy. Economists, being less fanciful and poetic, refer to it merely as a medium of exchange. The reason economists do not wax quite so lyrical when they discuss money is that they regard it as merely one form of wealth-holding. After all, it is possible to be extremely wealthy but literally have no money. In fact, there is a problem with holding wealth in the form of money because money generally does not accumulate. That is, you cannot earn a return from money alone. This is not the case with other forms of wealth, such as stocks and bonds, real estate, or a term deposit in a bank. The other reason economists remain subdued on the topic of money is because they are not so concerned with the effect of money on the individual (in that respect, most economists revere money as much as the next person) but rather on the role of money in the whole economy.

On this subject, economists over the centuries have held differing views. Adam Smith suggested that money is a veil that often conceals the phenomenon of real production that lies behind it. He compared money to a river in that it helps bring goods to the market but does not in any way affect the actual volume of goods. However, today, we realize that money can, in fact, have a determining influence over the "real" variables, such as production and employment. For example, we saw in Chapter 5 how an increase in the money supply can result in an increase in real GDP. It is these and other aspects of money that we will examine in the next two chapters—including one obvious role of money: it has an important role in determining prices.

As the market economy was emerging in the sixteenth and seventeenth centuries, many people had personal experience of how the amount of money (and, more specifically, changes in the amount of money) in a society could affect prices. The huge influx of gold from the new American colonies into Europe produced a persistent and pernicious increase in prices in most European countries. Gold meant money, and if the amount of money quickly increases while the volume of production changes slowly, then you get the makings of what we previously called demand–pull inflation. This is sometimes characterized as "too much money chasing too few goods."

A group of young students in Toronto take turns playing the "My Money" game. The former stockbroker who designed the game for the Bank of Montreal hopes it will help children learn to invest wisely once they get some money of their own.

CP/Toronto Star/Bernard Weil

In the same vein, consider an apocryphal story that came out of World War II, relating a devious scheme by the Germans to disrupt the Allied war effort. This plan involved the dispatch of bombers over Britain, equipped not with bombs but with millions of counterfeit pound notes. These were to be rained down on the major British towns and cities. The effects would have been obvious. The British people, as heirs to this sudden windfall, would do the predictable: they would spend it, the demand for the limited quantity of consumer goods would rise dramatically, and since production could not increase immediately, the effect would be the bidding up of prices. Britain would have been faced with the same devastating phenomenon that the Germans themselves had experienced in the early 1920s: galloping inflation or hyperinflation. This story is used to illustrate the very strong link between changes in the supply of money and the level of prices. More on this later.

✔ SELF-TEST

1. What do you think Adam Smith might have meant by the statement, "Money is a veil"?

8.1 THE FUNCTIONS AND CHARACTERISTICS OF MONEY

So far, we have discussed some aspects of money without actually defining it. Let us continue to skirt around the definition for now with a question: what is money good for? The answer? To spend, of course. In fact, it has been suggested that money imparts value only in parting. The first, and prime, function of money is that it acts as a **medium of exchange**. Without money, people would be forced to barter goods and services directly, but barter requires what is called the *double coincidence of wants*. This simply means that if I am to trade with you, you must have what I want, and I must have what you want. If this is not the case, then we must try to find a third, fourth, or fifth party to act as intermediary. This would mean that to obtain a bare minimum of goods and services through barter, a person would spend far more time and effort in exchanging than in producing. Thus, economists describe the barter system as having high transactions costs.

The use of money reduces the wasted effort associated with barter as long as people will readily accept money as a medium of exchange. Money can be almost anything, but its most important characteristic is that it should be widely acceptable. In addition, if we are going to carry it around with us, it should be reasonably portable.

But money is not just used for exchange. Some of us like to keep it. In other words, money can be used as a **store of wealth**. This is its second function. As we mentioned, wealth can be stored in other forms—from stocks and bonds to real estate, or from savings accounts to art collections—but these other forms are not as convenient as money and often involve more risk. Compared with all other forms of wealth, money is the most liquid; that is, it can be used directly as a means of payment. If it is to act as a store of wealth, money should obviously possess other desirable characteristics. Besides portability, it should also be reasonably durable and of such a nature that *people are willing to hold it*.

Finally, money is used as a **unit of account** (or measure of value). Think of the problems in trying to value a commodity in a moneyless community. Assume, for instance, that a suit of clothes is worth ten litres of beer, that a litre of beer is worth two loaves of bread, and that you need a hundred loaves of bread to buy a table—how many suits of clothes does it take to buy a table? The answer is five suits, but the answer does not come quickly. By providing a single uniform measure of values, money simplifies comparisons of prices, wages, and incomes.

In summary, the functions of money are as:

- a medium of exchange
- a store of value
- a unit of account

In a money-using society, each product and service can be valued in terms of a single commodity, money. If we measure everything in money terms, that is, in dollars and cents, we might ask what money itself is worth. The answer must be in relative terms—it is worth what we can

medium of exchange: something that is accepted as payment for goods and services.

store of wealth: the function of money that allows people to hold and accumulate wealth.

unit of account: the function of money that allows us to determine easily the relative value of goods.

ADDED DIMENSION   Money Increases Wealth

A society possessing no money would be very simple and materially very poor. This is because exchange would be difficult and time consuming. Imagine a person possessing a pound of honey but wanting a package of medium-sized, flat-head screws. How long might it take to find someone with the right screws who just happened to want some honey? In short, almost everybody would be forced to produce most of the necessities of survival for themselves. Few could earn a livelihood by specializing in producing just one product and then trading it for other products. This lack of specialization, along with the high cost of exchange, would ensure an existence in which a minimal quantity of goods and services was exchanged. This is how the use of money increases a nation's wealth.

get in exchange for it. And what we can get is determined by prices; the lower the price, the more we can obtain and the higher the value of money. The *value of money* is, therefore, inversely related to the price level. If prices were to increase, then the value of a unit of money would decrease.

Although anything can be (and most things have been) used as money, some things are definitely better than others. For instance, let us imagine a (particularly silly) society that hit upon the idea of using stones as a form of money. Well, certainly stones are durable, portable, divisible (big stones and little stones), and easily recognized by the general public, which are characteristics that all money needs. The problem is that without very much trouble at all, everybody would spend time collecting piles of stones and think they had become fabulously rich. The result would, of course, be rampant inflation. This would happen because although the amount of money has increased, the amount of goods and services available has not. As a result, the prices of all products would rise significantly as demand far exceeds supply. To avoid this outcome, the supply of money in an economy needs to be sufficient to facilitate trade and economic growth but it also needs to be controlled by a central authority so that the supply does not become too large relative to the real wealth of the country. We might add that it should also be of a standardized form (each unit of currency should be like all others) and of a form that cannot be easily copied. In short, money needs to be all of the following:

- acceptable
- durable
- portable
- divisible
- standardized, and easily recognized but not easily copied
- controlled by a central authority

Timeline for the History of Money

Source: © MacNeil-Lehrer Production. Reprinted with permission.

 SELF-TEST

2. Given the clothes/table example above, how many suits of clothes would it cost to buy a table if a litre of beer is worth only one loaf of bread?

 L02 Recognize the various kinds of money and understand what fractional reserve banking means.

commodity money: a type of money that can also usefully function as a commodity.

8.2 DIFFERENT KINDS OF MONEY AND FRACTIONAL RESERVE BANKING

When such things as beads, whales' teeth, salt, or shells are used as money, they have intrinsic value in themselves as well as having value as money. This type of money is called **commodity money**. Even today, in situations such as jails and prisoner-of-war camps, where people have no access to the outside community, such things as cigarettes or playing cards act as forms of commodity money.

One particularly important commodity that has been used as money throughout the ages is gold (and, less often, other precious metals). Gold certainly fills the bill in terms of portability, durability, and scarcity. However, it has one serious drawback: gold (or any other precious metal) does not come in standardized units. The gold needs to be weighed out each time a transaction is made. To overcome this problem, standardized metal *coins* of specific sizes and weights were introduced in the fifth century BCE. The trouble with using coins made of gold is that they are open to abuse. Gold is a particularly soft metal, so in earlier times, it was possible for some people to make money out of money. They did this by such practices as sweating the currency (shaking the coins up in a bag so as to produce a residue of gold dust in the bottom) or by clipping the currency (shaving a thin sliver from the outside of un-milled coins). Perhaps the worst offenders were the sovereigns whose portraits on the coins were supposedly a mark of trust and integrity. An important event, such as a coronation or royal wedding, was an occasion for the sovereign to call in the old coins and replace them with newly minted coins. However, in the process of melting down the old coins, a base metal, such as lead, was often added to the vat of gold. Over time, the currency became more and more debased. This resulted in inflation, so that the new coins became worth only their weight in lead.

In addition, gold has another serious defect as a form of money: it is very heavy. Because of this and because of the dangers of carrying about large sums of money, people in Europe in the Middle Ages started to deposit their money in the goldsmith's (jeweller's) vault. In return for making a deposit (for which they were required to pay a fee), they received a certificate from the goldsmith acknowledging the deposit. In time, these certificates were considered as reliable as gold and could be easily transferred from one person to another as a form of payment. In other words, *paper money* was introduced. (It is interesting to note that paper currency had appeared in China even earlier than in Europe.) With the formation of commercial banks in the early eighteenth century, many of the functions of the goldsmiths were taken over by these banks— including that of issuing paper money. Since 1935, in Canada, the only bank with the power to issue currency—sometimes called **fiat money** because is declared legal tender by law—is the Bank of Canada. As we will see later, Canada's central bank no longer acts as a commercial bank, as it once did, but now acts solely as an agent of government.

fiat money: anything that is declared as money by government order.

As commercial banks became more prominent, bank notes became more acceptable. But just as people, in earlier times, were wary of carrying large sums of gold and coins, they also preferred to deposit their bank notes in the banks. Thus, the nineteenth century saw the development of the last form of modern money: *chequebook money*. In return for depositing notes and coins with the bank, the customer could now receive a chequebook from the bank. A cheque is nothing more than a standardized form of instruction by a customer to the bank, telling it to transfer a sum of money from the customer's account to the person specified on the cheque. As such, a cheque is not money but merely a method of accessing it. It is the deposit in your bank account that constitutes money. Generally speaking, this order from one of its customers presents the bank with no great problem. The average bank certainly has enough cash. However, banks do not act simply as big safety deposit boxes, guarding your money until you require it. This means that if all of the customers of a particular bank were to descend *en masse* demanding a return of their deposits, that bank (and any bank in the modern banking world) would find itself acutely embarrassed. It simply would not have that amount of cash on hand. So, what happened to the cash that you and all the other customers deposited in the past? The answer is that the bank loaned it out. Banks only keep a small fraction of the amounts of cash that have been deposited, so they may be vulnerable to a run on the bank, that is, when more money is being withdrawn than is being deposited. So, how did such a state of affairs come to be? Before answering this question, let us summarize the different kinds of money.

- Commodity money (including gold and other precious metals)
- Coins
- Paper money
- Fiat money (anything designated as money by government)
- Chequebook money (bank deposits)

Many transfers that were once carried out using cheques are now completed using electronic banking machines.

ADDED DIMENSION   Electronic Money

Cash has a number of advantages, including the fact that the transaction costs of using it are low. If I want to buy something, I just hand over the cash. I do not need to register the transfer, and the seller need not record that she received the cash from me. Also, in the case of cash, possession implies ownership. But this is also one of its great disadvantages. Cash is easy to steal and difficult to recover once gone. For this reason, many people look forward to the day when we can dispense with cash.

In fact, the day has already arrived. In many cities around the world, experiments with using "electronic money" are taking place. Small plastic cards embedded with computer chips have been introduced that will record the value of each transaction and the remaining balance on the card. For instance, you could buy a $30 card (say, from a bank) that enables you to spend up to that amount using only your card. You could use the card to pay for such items as transit fares, parking meters, telephone calls, and so on.

Could this idea be extended to chequing accounts, too? Well, the debit card, which is an electronic form of cheque writing, is a step in that direction. Some observers predict that chequebook money may also disappear as people shift from paper currency and chequebooks to electronic cash (e-cash). This vision sees smart-cards becoming the customary circulating medium along with *privately* supplied digital cash, which is stored in computer hard drives and used over the Internet to facilitate e-commerce.

Obviously, for all this to happen, people will have to trust and feel comfortable with the new e-money as well as with e-commerce itself. However, there are potential drawbacks to this idea. What would happen, for instance, if the private company that issued the card went out of business? Who is going to honour the e-money then? Furthermore, there are many people in society who would be concerned about leaving an electronic trail of their purchases. This includes not only members of the underworld but also ordinary consumers who may not want merchants and card issuers to obtain detailed information about their spending habits.

Now, let us go back to the goldsmiths. Goldsmiths discovered, very early on in the game, that most of the time the gold and coins sitting in the vaults did just that: they sat there. Most unproductively! Certainly, customers came in from time to time to withdraw some of their cash, but that same cash usually got re-deposited with the same goldsmith rather soon. Certainly, money was turning over. But the goldsmiths realized that on any given day of the week, about as much gold was deposited as was withdrawn.

So, what would be the harm in the goldsmiths lending out the gold that was not needed? Unless all of the customers arrived on the doorstep at the same time—a very remote possibility—there would be no harm done. So, lend it they did. In fact, the goldsmiths also learned that when they started offering loans, most people did not particularly want to receive gold but preferred to receive one of the goldsmiths' certificates of deposit. The goldsmiths could simply make loans by giving customers a piece of paper. Thus was born the basis of modern banking: the **fractional reserve system**. In a similar manner, with the rise of commercial banking, bankers discovered that they, too, only needed to keep a small fraction of their customers' deposits in the form of cash reserves. As we mentioned earlier, today, banks in Canada keep only a very small percentage of their customers' deposits in the form of cash. The fact that modern banks operate on a fractional reserve basis has important implications for the monetary system and for monetary policy, as we shall see later.

fractional reserve system: a banking system in which banks keep only a small fraction of their total deposits on reserve in the form of cash.

 SELF-TEST

3. Explain the difference between commodity money and fiat money.

L03 Explain what is and is not money, and describe the main functions of banks as money lenders.

8.3   AND AT LAST A DEFINITION

The following definition of **money** encompasses the vital elements: money is any item that is widely accepted as a medium of exchange, gives direct and immediate access to goods and services, and can be used to settle debts.

In the next chapter, we will see that changes in the amount of money in an economy can have significant consequences. Also in the next chapter, we will see that the Bank of Canada needs to control the supply of money to the economy. It needs to be able to clearly define and measure the amount. What may come as a surprise to many is the fact that there really is not one single accepted measure of the money supply. Let us start with the simplest, most basic definition, called the **M1** definition, which includes currency in circulation (coins and paper bank notes) plus **demand deposits** in the chequing accounts of all commercial banks. The word *demand* in demand deposits refers to the fact that depositors can demand their deposits in cash at any time.

The money supply (in billions of dollars) in Canada in December 2010 was:

$$M1 = \text{currency plus demand deposits}$$
$$263 = \quad 57 \quad + \quad 206$$
$$(22\%) \qquad (78\%)$$

Some have suggested, however, that this definition is too narrow. They argue that if chequing accounts (demand deposits) are included as part of the money supply, then why not also include savings accounts and other types of **notice deposit**? Notice deposits, as the name suggests, require the depositor to give notice to the bank before making a withdrawal. Surely these accounts, in practice, are no different from chequing accounts, since banks seldom enforce the requirement of giving notice before withdrawal. So, we have a wider definition of money, called **M2**, which includes all of M1 plus all notice deposits (savings accounts on deposit for an undefined length of time) and what are called personal term deposits, which are on deposit for a specific term, such as six months. The amounts in December 2010 were:

$$M2 = \text{M1 plus notice deposits and personal term deposits}$$
$$1027 = \quad 263 \quad + \quad 764$$
$$(26\%) \qquad (74\%)$$

Finally, an even broader measurement, **M3**, includes M2 but adds to it term deposits of businesses (known as *certificates of deposit*), which are easily convertible into chequable deposits. The M3 measurement, then, includes all of M2 plus certificates of deposits. Again, for December 2010, the amounts were:

$$M3 = \text{M2 plus certificates of deposits}$$
$$1422 = \quad 1027 \quad + \quad 395$$
$$(72\%) \qquad (28\%)$$

You can see from this that the various measures are ranked in order of liquidity, i.e. the closeness to cash, with M1 being the most liquid and M3 the least. The visual on the right illustrates the relative sizes of these three measures of money.

At this point, you may well ask what is the point of multiple measures of the money supply—in short, who cares about the differences between M1 and M2 or M3? In Chapter 9, we will examine the role of monetary policy in stabilizing the economy and avoiding inflation. Since this kind of policy-making involves controlling the money supply, just how we define "the money supply" becomes very important.

For reasons of expediency, we will confine our discussion and analysis of money to the simplest definition, M1—currency in circulation plus demand deposits (chequing accounts). This helps keep things simple and recognizes the essential characteristic of money: the direct and immediate control over goods and services.

money: anything that is widely accepted as a medium of exchange and therefore can be used to buy goods or to settle debts.

M1: currency in circulation plus demand deposits.

demand deposit: money deposited in a chequing account which is available on demand.

notice deposit: money deposited in a savings account which is available only after notice is given.

M2: M1 plus all notice and personal term deposits.

M3: M2 plus non-personal term deposits known as *certificates of deposits*.

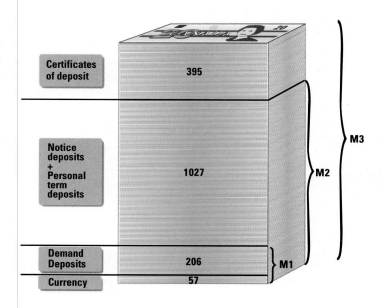

What is Not Money?

Not all currency issued by the Bank of Canada is included as money, only the portion that is in circulation. In other words, the currency in the vaults or tills of banks is not included in any definition of money.

This is because when you deposit currency in a bank, the balance of your bank account increases, and since the amount of deposits in your accounts is part of the money supply, it would be double-counting to count both the increase in your accounts and the increase in the bank's tills. In other words, when people deposit currency in a bank, the amount of currency *in circulation* goes down and the amount in deposit accounts goes up. This means that:

> **A new bank deposit of currency changes the composition of the money supply but does not change its total.**

Another exclusion from the money supply is gold. (Try paying for your designer jeans with a bar of gold.) Similarly, such financial securities as stocks and bonds are also excluded. So, too, is the available credit people have on their credit cards. Credit cards, as well as the more recent debit cards, are merely a means of accessing money but are not money in themselves. You might argue that in many instances, credit cards are more acceptable than personal cheques, and that is true. However credit cards merely represent a loan that you have negotiated with a finance company. More importantly, you cannot pay off a debt with a credit card. Certainly, you can obtain cash with a credit card, but that is the clue: you can use a credit card to get money; it is not itself money. Similarly, cheques are not money but simply give you access to the money in your chequing account.

near-banks: financial institutions, such as credit unions or trust companies, that share many of the functions of commercial banks but are not defined as banks under the *Bank Act* (they are also known as *nonbank financial intermediaries*).

The final exclusion from the modern definition of money is chequing accounts at **near-banks**. Near-banks include credit unions, trust companies, and mortgage and loan associations. In other words, all of our three alternative definitions of money—M1, M2, M3—refer to accounts only at commercial banks. Canada's central bank, the Bank of Canada, exercises a degree of control over the commercial banks but has a lesser degree of power over near-banks (also termed *nonbank financial intermediaries*). The central bank prefers to count as money only the currency it can control directly, hence the exclusion of accounts at near-banks. Nonetheless, the Bank of Canada also measures what it calls M2+, which includes demand and notice deposits at near-banks, and M2AA which further includes Canada Savings bonds and other non–money market funds.

Chartered banks include the six major commercial banks in Canada (all of which received a charter under the Bank Act) and a few dozen much smaller banks. They are referred to as *chartered* banks because each was set up by federal charter, that is. by parliamentary approval. Starting a bank is not the same as starting your own business; banking is a very special business.

As we have now seen, it is important that we are able to clearly distinguish money from other types of assets that people (and institutions) hold. **Table 8.1**, which shows other types of wealth-holdings listed in order of liquidity, may help.

TABLE 8.1	Forms of Wealth Holdings	
Money	**Description**	
Currency	Coins and notes	
Chequable deposits	Deposits in chequing accounts	
Notice deposits	Deposits in savings accounts	
Financial Assets		
Term deposits	Funds deposited for a fixed period (generally short-term) at a fixed interest rate	
Treasury bills	Short-term security (usually for 3 months) in speific denominations issued by the federal government	
Bonds	Securities (IOUs) issued by the governments and corporations, at a fixed rate of interest at a fixed term (often from 1 to 10 years)	
Stocks (shares)	A part-ownership of a corporation which entitles the owner to a claim on its assets and profits (in the form of dividends)	
Mutual funds	A part-ownership of a fund that has invested its clients' money in various assets, including shares in corporations	
GICs	Guaranteed Investment Certificates are securities issued by financial institutions like investment and insurance companies.	
Real Assets		
Personal assets	Ownership of things like cars, boats, jewellery	
Real estate	Ownership of houses and land	

 ADDED DIMENSION   Canada's Big Banks

The five largest banks in Canada in order of size are: Royal Bank, TD Canada Trust, Scotiabank, Bank of Montreal, and the Canadian Imperial Bank of Commerce (CIBC). Credit Unions, which are regulated provincially, are major players in British Columbia and in Quebec, where they are called *caisses populaires*. Recently, the world has seen a trend of big bank mergers. However, the attempted merger a few years ago between the Bank of Montreal and the Royal Bank of Canada, which was blocked by the federal government, indicates some resistance to this trend in Canada. And just how big are our Canadian banks? It might be instructive to compare them with the world's biggest banks (at July 2010):

	Assets ($ billions Can)			Assets ($ billions Can)
1. BNP Paribus (France)	3009		36. Royal Bank (Can)	617
2. Royal Bank of Scotland (U.K.)	2791		43. TD Canada Trust (Can)	525
3. Credit Agricole (France)	2477		48. Scotiabank (Can)	468
4. HSBC (U.K.)	2400		54. Bank of Montreal (Can)	366
5. Barclays (U.K.)	2268		62. CIBC (Can)	317
10. Citigroup (U.S.)	1884			

Source: *The Banker,* July 2010.

SELF-TEST

4. a) If David deposits $240 cash into his chequing account at a commercial bank, has the money supply changed?

b) If, later on, David transfers this $240 from his chequing account to a saving account in the same bank, has M1 changed? Has M2?

5. Given the following data (all in billions of dollars):

Coins	13
Certificates of deposit	137
Demand deposits	72
Notice and personal term deposits	215
Notes	27

What are the values of M1, M2, and M3?

The Canadian Banking System

spread: the difference between the rate of interest a bank charges borrowers and the rate it pays savers.

Banks, like other corporations, are in business to make profits. Their major source of profits comes from lending out any excess deposits they might have. Their profit comes from the **spread**, the difference between the interest rate a bank charges to borrowers and the interest rate it pays to depositors. There is not much difference in the spread among Canada's major banks. The total profits of a bank come more from the total volume of its transactions rather than from a difference in the spread. Like any other business, banks do not like to carry excess inventories. In the case of banks, their inventory is money. They do not earn a return on idle money balances; therefore, they will always try to ensure that the amount of reserves they retain is kept to a minimum, consistent with security.

target reserve ratio: the portion of deposits that a bank wants to hold in cash.

Until recently, the Bank Act specified exactly how much commercial banks had to keep in reserve. Although this is no longer required, banks still hold reserves and maintain what is referred to as a **target reserve ratio**, which is the proportion of demand deposits that a bank wants to hold in the form of cash in its vaults or with the Bank of Canada. These target reserves provide some degree of security for the bank's customers. However, the main security for depositors comes from insurance. All banks are required by law to take out insurance on customers' deposits. The deposits are insured with the Canada Deposit Insurance Corporation up to a maximum of $100 000 per depositor per bank.

The Canadian banking system is remarkably secure. (There were only three bank failures in all of the twentieth century, although two occurred within the last thirty years.) What economists call a branch banking system accounts for this stability. This is a system dominated by a few large banks, each of which has many branches operating across the entire country. For example, Canada's six big banks each have several hundred branches coast to coast. The sheer size and geographical diversity of this type of structure spreads the risk and therefore minimizes the possibility of bank failure.

Contrast this with a unit banking system, which, though currently in transition, is still the basic system in the United States. This system is made up of thousands of relatively small banks that have either only one branch or multiple branches that are confined to a single state. Such a system is less secure. For example, the First National Bank of Dalton (Nebraska) is small compared with the average branch of any one of Canada's big six banks. Furthermore, most of the loans by First National would be to local wheat farmers for equipment, seed, and so on. If a bad hailstorm wipes out the local wheat crop and most of the farmers go bankrupt, then the bank could face the same fate.

Chances are that your bank does not look like this. Canada's six major banks have several hundred branches across the country.

Does this mean that the Canadian banking system is superior? From a security sense, yes. But the source of this security is a system dominated by only six big banks, and this means that competition within the system is weak. There are several consequences of this lack of competition. First, the merely irritating: long lineups for routine transactions, short operating hours (closed on Saturdays and Sundays)—though this has certainly been changing in recent years—and the inability of customers to deal face-to-face with the decision makers.

More significantly, the size of the spread in the Canadian banking system is historically wider than that in the American system. Finally, there is the issue of the banks' loan policies. From time to time throughout history, one can find references to a recurring complaint by small businesses in Canada: large banks do not recognize the unique circumstances of a small business, and they do not make loans to unproven companies or ideas. Although one can understand the position of the large banks on this issue, it is also obvious that the whole economy does, from time to time, fail to benefit from the potential success of a new business or product because of the lack of loans needed to get started. In summary, the Canadian branch banking system is very secure and stable, but it is also very conservative.

Some of this may be changing. Foreign banks have recently been allowed to operate in Canada, although there are constraints on size. This should, at least to some extent, increase competition in this industry.

Balanced against all this is the fact that compared with most banking systems around the world, Canada's is one of the safest. The financial and economic meltdown experienced by most economies (especially the American and European economies) around the world in 2008 left Canada's banking system pretty much unaffected. This is largely because the Canadian banking regulations did not allow the extreme risk taking that was commonplace elsewhere—particularly in the United States. We will have more to say about this in Chapter 13.

 ADDED DIMENSION   Financial Institutions

The financial market consists of different types of financial institutions. All of these institutions have one thing in common: they are intermediaries and act as agents among households, businesses, and governments that have funds available for lending and others who want to borrow those funds. Canadian banks are the biggest borrowers as well as lenders.

Other institutions came into existence because banks were originally forbidden to provide certain types of loans. Mortgage companies specialized in long-term loans (mortgages) for people wishing to purchase real estate, such as houses or apartments. Trust companies looked after the pensions and trust accounts of both firms and individuals. Credit unions (*caisses populaires* in Quebec) sprang up because many small firms were unable to obtain loans from the banks.

As the following table makes clear, in Canada the banks are, by far, the biggest source of credit.

	Debt Outstanding 2008 ($millions)	% of Total Debt
Domestic banks	289 121	53
Finance (incl. mortgage) companies	55 368	10
Other banks (incl. trust companies)	94 371	17
Credit unions	57 232	10
Other lending institutions	58 298	10
Total	$554 390	100

Source: Adapted from the Statistics Canada's Summary Tables, http://www40.statcan.ca/l01/cst01/busi04-eng.htm, 17 March 2011.

8.4   THE CREATION OF MONEY BY THE BANKING SYSTEM

As we have mentioned, the Bank of Canada is solely responsible for determining the amount of currency in the economy. The public decides what fraction of this currency it wants to hold and what fraction it wants to deposit with banks and other financial institutions. The banks will then, decide how much of these deposits they wish to keep as reserves and how much they want to lend.

To understand how just a small amount of reserves can support many loans and deposits, we need first to understand a few very basic accounting terms.

Assets, Liabilities, and Balance Sheets

assets: the part of a company's balance sheet that represents what it owns or what is owed to it.

liabilities: the part of a company's balance sheet that represents what it owes.

net worth: the total assets less total liabilities of a company— also called *equity*.

Essentially, we need to understand a few basic features of a balance sheet. (The profit and loss statement is of no concern here.) A balance sheet presents the financial condition of an institution at a particular moment in time. On one side are listed all the assets and on the other side the liabilities. **Assets** represent what a company owns or what others owe it. **Liabilities** represent what a company owes to others. The difference between the two is the **net worth** of the company, otherwise known as equity. Equity is the book value of the company to its shareholders. (The company's market value may be more or less than its book value.) The following is a simplified balance sheet of the Saymor Bank Limited:

Balance Sheet of Saymor Bank Ltd. as of December 31, 2011			
Assets		**Liabilities and Equity**	
Reserves	$ 10 000	Demand deposits	$100 000
Loans to customers	60 000	Shareholders' equity	20 000
Securities	30 000		
Fixed assets	20 000		
	$120 000		$120 000

The assets are all listed in terms of liquidity (closeness to cash), with the most liquid at the top. Reserves are the currency held, in part, by the bank as cash on hand (vault cash) and, in part, on deposit with the Bank of Canada. Loans to customers represent one of the income-earning assets of the bank and are their most important and most lucrative assets. Securities are shares (gilt-edged, that is, very secure—"as good as gold") or bonds (usually government bonds and treasury bills). Fixed assets include the buildings, equipment, and furniture of the bank. The major liability, and the only one shown here, is demand deposits, which represents the total amount of depositors' accounts owed by the bank to its customers. (We will ignore notice or savings deposits.) The equity figure shows that the book value of this bank is $20 000 (in millions of dollars).

Let us practice a few simple transactions to familiarize ourselves with bookkeeping entries. Standard accounting procedures require that every transaction involve two entries. After making any entries, the balance sheet should remain in balance. (The totals may change, but the assets should still equal liabilities plus equity.)

Transaction 1: Fred, a customer of the bank, deposits $200 cash in the bank. The reserves of the bank would, therefore, increase by $200. The other entry? Fred's bank balance will increase by $200. (An asset for Fred, of course, but a liability for the bank, since it now owes Fred $200 more.) So, demand deposits increase by $200. In other words, both assets and liabilities have increased.

Transaction 2: Penny withdraws $500 cash from her account. This is straightforward, since it is just the reverse of Transaction 1. The bank's reserves are reduced by $500, and the demand deposits go down by $500; both assets and liabilities are reduced.

Transaction 3: The bank buys some securities for $200 cash. In this case, reserves decrease by $200, and securities increase by $200; one asset decreases, and another increases. The net effect on total assets is zero.

The next transaction is of more significance, since it is the foundation for the commercial banks' ability to create money.

Transaction 4: Suppose that the bank grants you a loan. What exactly does this imply? Generally speaking, it does not mean that the bank gives you cash. Instead, in exchange for your written acceptance of the terms and conditions for repayment of the loan, the bank will give you immediate credit in your chequing account for the amount of the loan. Now, whether you actually draw out cash or write a cheque for all or part of the amount is up to you. But what the bank has given you is "direct and immediate access to goods and services" and the ability to settle a debt. It has, in other words, by a single bookkeeping entry, created money for you. The two accounts affected are an increase in loans (an asset) and an increase in demand deposits (a liability). Cash reserves are unaffected.

Each time that a bank issues a loan, it creates money.

Now, having been granted the loan you might do one of three things.

Transaction 4a: You decide that you are going to withdraw some or all of the loan in cash. This means the bank's reserves decrease by the amount of the withdrawal, and the demand deposits are decreased by the same amount.

Transaction 4b: You write a cheque to buy an airline ticket. Suppose that the airline uses the same bank. In that case, your demand deposit balance is reduced by the amount of the cheque, and that of the airline company is increased by the same amount. Here, the total amount of demand deposits remains unchanged. In addition, note that the bank's reserves were unaffected.

Transaction 4c: You write a cheque to buy a new sofa from the Sogood Sofa company. Sogood Sofa deposits your cheque at its bank, which is a different bank from yours. At the end of the day, its bank will come to yours for payment of the cheque. The cheque is then cleared against your bank, whose reserves will drop as a result. Therefore, your bank's reserves and demand deposits will be reduced, while the other bank's reserves and demand deposits will increase.

 SELF-TEST

6. Give the necessary bank bookkeeping entries for each set of circumstances below.

   a) The bank makes a $2000 loan to Fadia.

   b) Fadia writes a $2000 cheque to Middle East Travel, which has its accounts at a different bank.

The Money Multiplier

That is enough bookkeeping for the present. Now, what we want to figure out are the implications for a bank and for the banking system when a bank holds more than its targeted reserves. Let us start off the analysis by assuming that the Saymor Bank and all other banks are just meeting their target reserves of ten percent. Remember that this means that each bank wants to hold a minimum of ten percent of its demand deposits in the form of cash reserves.

$$\text{Target reserves} = \text{target reserve ratio} \times \text{demand deposits} \qquad \text{[8.1]}$$

For instance, assume that Saymor starts from the position indicated in this balance sheet:

Balance Sheet of Saymor Bank Ltd. as of December 31, 2011			
Assets		**Liabilities and Equity**	
Reserves	$ 10 000	Demand deposits	$100 000
Loans to customers	60 000	Shareholders' equity	20 000
Securities	30 000		
Fixed assets	20 000		
	$120 000		$120 000

Now, assume that Tom, rummaging about under his bed one morning, comes across $1000 in currency. Not knowing what to do with it, he decides to deposit it in the bank. The bank credits the $1000 to his account. Its reserves now equal $11 000, and its demand deposits equal $101 000. The bank now finds that it has excess reserves, since it wants to hold only 10% × $101 000, or $10 100. It is over-reserved to the tune of $900, that is:

$$\text{Excess reserves} = \text{Actual reserves} - \text{target reserves} \qquad \text{[8.2]}$$
$$900 = 11\ 000 - 10\ 100\ (10\% \times 101\ 000)$$

Or look at it another way: of the $1000 that Tom deposited, the bank aims to keep only 10 percent in the form of cash reserves and, therefore, has $900 more than it considers necessary to hold. As we mentioned before, banks do not like to have such idle cash; they want to earn some return on it. They will be very happy to lend it out.

Now, let us assume Wing Kee happens to come into the bank the next day in need of a $900 loan. The loan is happily granted, and he walks out with $900 more in his chequing account. Within a few hours, Wing Kee purchases a used Volkswagen from the New Star Car Company. A New Star employee deposits his cheque in another bank called the J.M.K. Bank. Recall our assumption that the J.M.K. bank, prior to the deposit by New Star, had no reserves in excess of its targeted amount. After J.M.K. Bank clears Wing Kee's cheque against the Saymor Bank, the following accounts at J.M.K. Bank will be affected:

Reserves + $900   Demand deposits + $900

excess reserves: reserves in excess of what the bank wants to hold as its target reserves.

We assume that the J.M.K., like all other banks, also wants to keep 10 percent of the increased demand deposits, that is, 10% × $900, or $90. It therefore has $810 in **excess reserves**. It, too, is anxious to lend these reserves out. Now, let us assume that Sue is in need of $810 to pay off a debt to her friend Sarbjit and manages to negotiate an $810 loan from J.M.K., in the form of an increased credit balance to her chequing account. She immediately pays Sarbjit by cheque. Sarbjit deposits the cheque at his bank, which we will call the M.P.C. Bank. After he makes this deposit and Sue's cheque clears, the balance sheet of the M.P.C. Bank changes:

Reserves + $810   Demand deposits + $810

The M.P.C. Bank now finds itself with excess reserves (over its targeted amount). It wants to keep back only 10 percent of the $810, or $81, as cash reserves. Therefore, it has $810 minus $81, or $729, in excess reserves. Let us assume that this amount is loaned out. Regardless of whom it is loaned to, and regardless of how the loan is spent (assuming that recipients of the cheque deposit it back into a bank), sooner or later one of the banks in the banking system will find itself again with excess reserves and be ready and able to lend. Although the cash moves from bank to bank, the banking *system* seems unable to get rid of this additional cash. A bank lends it out, but each time it gets spent and returns to some other bank. However, each time it returns, the receiving bank retains ten percent of that new deposit in additional reserves. Let us follow the trail resulting from Tom's initial deposit of $1000.

Reserves	Loans	Deposits
+1000		+1000 (Tom)
	+900 (to Wing Kee)	+900 (New Star)
	+810 (to Sue)	+810 (Sarbjit)
	+729	+729
	. . .	. . .
	. . .	. . .
	. . .	. . .

You can see that both the loans and deposits columns above follow a geometric pattern. What we are interested in finding out is the total of the deposits column. Why would we be interested in this figure? Because *it is money*. Think back to the definition of money (M1): currency in circulation plus demand deposits. The banks' cash reserves are not part of the money supply, but the total amount in peoples' chequing accounts certainly is.

So, what will be the total of all demand deposits that result from Tom's initial deposit of $1000? They will be 1000 + 900 + 810 + 729 + . . . It is reasonably easy to solve if you remember the formula for summing a geometric progression. But let us tackle the problem from a different perspective by looking at part of the balance sheet of the *whole banking system*. Assume it was as follows prior to Tom's deposit:

Reserves	$100 000	Demand deposits	$1 000 000
Loans	$900 000		

Staying with our assumption that banks want to keep a ten percent reserve ratio, the banking system illustrated above is neither over- nor under-reserved. If the target reserves must equal 10 percent of deposits, it means that demand deposits will equal 10 times the amount of reserves. Now, Tom deposits $1000 in one of the banks so that reserves equal $101 000. Demand deposits can potentially rise to a maximum of 10 × $101 000, or $1 010 000. As a result of the lending process we described, the new combined balance sheet would look like this:

Reserves	$101 000	Demand deposits	$1 010 000
Loans	$909 000		

In other words, if the target reserve ratio is ten percent, a new deposit of $X will lead to an increase in total deposits throughout the *whole* banking system of ten times $X. As you probably recognize, what we have here is another multiplier; this time, the **money multiplier**.

$$\text{Money Multiplier} = \frac{\Delta \text{ deposits}}{\Delta \text{ reserves}} \qquad \textbf{[8.3]}$$

$$\text{Money Multiplier} = \frac{1}{\text{target reserve ratio}} \qquad \textbf{[8.4]}$$

money multiplier: the increase in total deposits that occur in the whole banking system as a result of a new deposit in a single bank.

In our example, the target reserve ratio is 10 percent, or 0.1, and so the money multiplier is 1/0.1, or 10. If the target reserve ratio was 5 percent, or 0.05, it would mean that banks want to keep a smaller amount of reserves and therefore would have more to lend out. In this case, the money multiplier would be 1/0.05, or 20.

The principle of the money multiplier is based on the fact that banks only keep a small fraction of deposits in the form of cash reserves. Excess reserves allow banks to increase loans and, therefore, increase deposits by a multiple of the excess reserves. The money multiplier shows what will happen in the whole banking system over a period.

Be careful not to confuse the effect of the money multiplier working through the whole banking system with the circumstances facing a single bank. Simply because a single bank happens to find itself with excess reserves does not mean that it could increase loans by a multiple of those excess reserves. For instance, look at the following circumstances for the Saymor Bank:

| Reserves | $100 | Demand deposits | $1000 |

The target reserve ratio is ten percent. Someone now deposits cash of $50. Excess reserves would then equal $45 (90 percent of $50), and this is all Saymor wants to lend. It could not lend out $450, since the bank would be in a very embarrassing situation if the borrower immediately asked for cash. In short:

> A single bank has to tread carefully and limit its loans to the amount of its excess reserves.

 SELF-TEST

7. Assume that the nation's banking system is over-reserved by $20 million. What is the value of the money multiplier, and what is the maximum possible expansion in the money supply if the target reserve ratio is:

a) 10%

b) 2%

c) 5%

Can Banks Ever Be Short of Reserves?

It can certainly happen that at the end of a day's business, a bank might find it has less reserves than it targeted. In that case, what can it do? It would need to borrow. The Bank of Canada will lend money to a commercial bank, but the bank must pay interest equal to the **bank rate** to the Bank of Canada. However, since the bank rate is regarded by the banks as a penalty rate (since they can borrow from the public or from other banks at a much lower rate), commercial banks will try to ensure that they pay off any loans from the Bank of Canada as quickly as possible. As a result, such loans tend to be very short-term ones.

bank rate: the rate of interest that the Bank of Canada charges a commercial bank for a loan.

The Money Multiplier Also Works in Reverse

Are there other consequences if a single bank—Saymor, for instance—finds itself under-reserved? Well, after receiving a loan from the Bank of Canada, Saymor will have to increase its reserves in some more permanent way. Although it is not difficult for a single bank to increase its reserves, doing so will be at the expense of some other bank's reserves.

To explain, let us assume that Saymor calls in an outstanding loan that was made earlier to the New Star Car Company. New Star will be forced to quickly sell off some of its inventory. The car buyers involved in this selloff will be reducing their deposits in other banks as they pay for their purchases. This will result in other banks finding themselves under-reserved and thus forced to call in some of their loans. Soon, we will find the total loans in the whole banking system decreasing and, as a result, deposits also reduced by an amount determined by the money multiplier. As an example, look at the following combined balance sheet of a banking system:

| Reserves | $ 95 | Demand deposits | $1000 |
| Loans | $905 | | |

If the target reserve ratio is 10 percent, the banking system is under-reserved in the amount of $5. How can the whole banking system produce another $5 worth of reserves? It cannot. What will happen, in fact, is that over a period, the banking system will be forced to call in outstanding

loans. In this case, the money multiplier is 10, and so the banks in total will have to call in 10 ×
$5, or $50, to get their reserves back in line with the deposits. After this contraction, the balance
sheet will look like this:

| Reserves | $ 95 | Demand deposits | $950 |
| Loans | $855 | | |

We emphasize that banks can neither create nor destroy *currency*. What they can do is create
or destroy loans and demand deposits, and this is what they do whenever they are over- or under-
reserved. It is in this sense that we say that banks can create and destroy *money* (demand deposits).
However, as we will see in the next chapter, it is the Bank of Canada that ultimately controls the
money supply by determining the amount of currency held by the commercial banks.

A Smaller Money Multiplier?

Occasionally, the size of the money multiplier will be diminished. As we have already seen, if a
bank increases its target reserves it lends less, and the money multiplier is reduced. But in a modern
banking system, banks keep their targets as low as is safely possible, since they earn no return on
idle cash. It is also possible that people may decide to keep a larger portion of their assets in the
form of cash. This increase in cash holdings will mean fewer deposits into the banking system
and would reduce the size of the multiplier. (This is referred to as *currency drain.*) Further, simply
because a bank has excess reserves does not mean that it will make more loans. It is possible that
the banks may determine that there are not enough creditworthy applicants for loans and that
their excess reserves would persist. Finally, it should be noted that in a recession banks often find
it difficult to make loans because many people simply do not want to accumulate more debt.
Here, again, the banks' excess reserves would persist and reduce the size of the multiplier. In summary, there are four factors that may reduce the size of the money multiplier:

- an increase in the banks' target reserves
- an increase in the amount of cash that people hold
- an insufficient number of creditworthy applicants for loans
- a reduced demand for loans by people in times of recession

✓ SELF-TEST

8. The following is the balance sheet for the Islanders' Bank:

Reserves	5 000	Demand Deposits	60 000
Loans	41 000	Shareholder's Equity	10 000
Securities	18 000		
Fixed Assets	6 000		
	70 000		70 000

a) If the target reserve ratio is eight percent, what is the
amount of its target reserves?

b) If the target reserve ratio is five percent, what is the
amount of its target reserves?

9. a) Given the Islanders' Bank balance sheet in question 8,
how much does it have in excess reserves if the target
reserve ratio is eight percent?

b) How much does it have in excess reserves if the target
reserve ratio is five percent?

10. What will be the increase in total deposits in the whole
banking system following a new deposit of $2000 into
the XYZ bank in each of the following circumstances?

a) a target reserve ratio of twenty percent

b) a target reserve ratio of five percent

11. The J.M.K. Bank has demand deposits of $60 000 and
reserves of $6000. By how much can it increase its loans if:

a) the target reserve ratio is eight percent

b) the target reserve ratio is five percent

c) Assume the same $60 000 and $6000 applied to the
entire banking system. What are your new answers to
a) and b)?

Review

CHAPTER SUMMARY

In this chapter, you examined the functions and characteristics of money and came to understand that there is more than one measurement of money. The central idea in this chapter is the process of money creation which occurs as a result of banks making loans and thereby increasing the amount of deposits, via the money multiplier, in the whole banking system.

8.1a The functions of money are as a:
- medium of exchange
- store of value
- unit of account

8.1b Money must be:
- acceptable
- durable
- portable
- divisible
- standardized, easily recognized but not easily copied
- controlled by a central authority

8.2a The various types of money are:
- commodity money (including gold and other precious metals)
- coins
- paper money
- fiat money (anything designated as money by government)
- chequebook money

8.2b In our modern banking system, individual banks keep in their vaults only a fraction of the money that they have received in deposits and lend out the balance of the money. This is known as *fractional reserve banking*.

8.3a The modern definition of money includes:
- M1, which is currency plus demand deposits
- M2, which is M1 plus notice deposits and personal term deposits
- M3, which is M2 plus certificates of deposit

8.3b Money is only one type of financial asset; others include bonds, stocks, mutual funds, and so forth. In addition, people also own real assets like personal assets and real estate.

8.4a Modern banks keep only a small fraction of their deposits on reserve and loan out the balance. This fact allows the whole banking system to create money, since the new demand deposits of any one bank are spent and redeposited into other banks, and then loaned out again. This is the important money multiplier process. The money multiplier varies inversely with the target reserve ratio; that is, if the reserve ratio falls, the multiplier gets larger.

8.4b The money multiplier will be smaller if:
- banks increase their target reserve ratios
- people hold more cash
- there are insufficient creditworthy applicants for loans
- people do not wish to take loans, for example, in a recession

NEW GLOSSARY TERMS AND KEY EQUATIONS

assets   276
bank rate   280
commodity money   268
demand deposit   271
excess reserves   278
fiat money   269
fractional reserve system   270

liabilities   276
M1   271
M2   271
M3   271
medium of exchange   267
money   271
money multiplier   279

near-banks   272
net worth   276
notice deposit   271
spread   274
store of wealth   267
target reserve ratio   274
unit of account   267

Equations:

[8.1]   Target reserves = target reserve ratio × demand deposits   **page 278**

[8.2]   Excess reserves = Actual reserves − target reserves   **page 278**

[8.3] $\text{Money Multiplier} = \dfrac{\Delta \text{ deposits}}{\Delta \text{ reserves}}$ **page 279**

[8.4] $\text{Money Multiplier} = \dfrac{1}{\text{target reserve ratio}}$ **page 279**

STUDY TIPS

1. Many students have trouble with the material in this chapter. For a long time, we had difficulty in understanding this, especially because the concepts involved are not complicated. We have now come to believe that the source of the student's difficulty is, yet again, the temptation to equate money with income. The chapter is about how the banking system can create money. Students who (consciously or unconsciously) confuse this with creating income seem to "freeze up" at this prospect and never really understand much that follows. On the one hand, only by combining resources in production can we create wealth and real income. On the other hand, a banking system is quite capable of creating more money, even though no more real income has been created. Obviously, if this is done in excess, prices will be driven up because more money will be chasing the same quantity of goods. There is nothing mysterious going on here—do not let yourself get spooked into thinking that there is.

2. When working with the many balance statements in this chapter, remember that the key entry is the amount of demand deposits. This is the bank's (or the system's) primary liability, and reserves must be large enough to cover expected net withdrawals (new withdrawals minus new deposits in the future). The target reserve ratio is always a percentage of demand deposits.

3. Students sometimes have difficulty understanding what might happen if a bank becomes under-reserved. The bank might be able to get a loan and thus increase its reserves by the amount that it borrows; that is easy to comprehend. Not quite so easy is the idea that the only other way out of being under-reserved is for the bank to decrease its demand deposits. A bank does this by calling in loans that it has previously made. Obviously, a bank cannot call in a fixed-term mortgage that it made to someone a year or two ago. However, many loans to businesses are what are called *demand loans* and are subject to being called in "on demand," if necessary.

Practise and learn online with Connect, where you can find the Answered Questions and the Unanswered Problems for all chapters of this textbook's Study Guide section.

Answered Questions

These questions can also be found online on Connect.

Indicate whether the following statements are true or false.

1. **(LO 1)** **T or F**   Money acts as a medium of exchange, a store of wealth, and a unit of account.

2. **(LO 1)** **T or F**   Individuals in a society that had no medium of exchange would be forced to use barter to exchange goods.

3. **(LO 1)** **T or F**   The most important characteristic of money is that it be portable.

4. **(LO 3)** **T or F**   Canada's largest commercial bank is the Bank of Canada.

5. **(LO 3)** **T or F**   M1 is defined as currency in circulation plus notice deposits in commercial banks.

6. **(LO 3)** **T or F**   The target reserve ratio is that portion of a bank's deposits that it wishes to loan out.

7. **(LO 3)** **T or F**   The spread is the difference between the interest rate that a bank pays to borrowers and the interest rate it charges depositors.

8. **(LO 3)** **T or F**   A bank will try to lend out all of its excess reserves.

9. **(LO 4)** **T or F**   The bank rate is the rate of interest that the Bank of Canada charges a commercial bank for a loan.

10. **(LO 4)** **T or F**   If some of the recipients of bank loans keep a portion of the loan in the form of cash, the money expansion process would expand.

Basic (Questions 11–25)

11. **(LO 3)** What is the basis of the modern banking system?
    a) Fractional reserves
    b) Commodity money
    c) A medium of exchange
    d) Gold

12. **(LO 4)** What is the value of the money multiplier?
    a) One, divided by the target reserve ratio
    b) The reciprocal of the MPC
    c) M1 divided by the multiplier
    d) It is always 2

13. **(LO 3)** What kind of banking system does Canada have?
    a) A unit banking system
    b) A branch banking system

c) A money banking system
d) A provincial banking system

14. **(LO 1)** If you were working out the cost of attending school next year, which function of money would you be using?
    a) A medium of exchange
    b) A unit of account
    c) A store of wealth
    d) The commercial function

15. **(LO 1)** If you wrote out a cheque to buy textbooks, which function of money would you be using?
    a) A medium of exchange
    b) A unit of account
    c) A store of wealth
    d) The commercial function

16. **(LO 3)** What is *the spread*?
    a) The difference between a bank's actual reserves and its target reserves
    b) The interest rate difference between what a bank charges borrowers and what it pays savers
    c) The difference between a bank's demand deposits and its total loans to customers
    d) The geographical distribution of banks across the country

17. **(LO 4)** Why is the banking system able to increase loans and demand deposits by a multiple of its excess reserves?
    a) Because reserves lost by one bank are gained by another
    b) Because the MPC of borrowers is positive
    c) Because one person's debt becomes another person's income
    d) Because the target reserve ratio is greater than one

18. **(LO 3)** What is the definition of M1?
    a) Currency in circulation only
    b) Currency in circulation plus demand deposits and savings accounts
    c) Currency in circulation plus demand deposits and Canada Savings Bonds
    d) Currency in circulation plus demand deposits

19. **(LO 1)** Which of the following statements about the value of money is correct?
    a) It varies inversely with the price level.
    b) It varies directly with the interest rate.
    c) It varies directly with the price level.
    d) It varies directly with the quantity of money.

20. **(LO 4)** Which of the following are assets to a bank?
    a) Demand deposits, equity, and reserves
    b) Reserves, loans to customers, and securities
    c) Reserves, property, and equity
    d) Equity, property, and demand deposits

21. **(LO 4)** Suppose that the Canucks Bank has excess reserves of $6000 and demand deposits of $100 000. If its targeted reserve ratio is 10 percent, what is the size of the bank's actual reserves?
    a) $4000
    b) $16 000
    c) $10 000
    d) $14 000

22. **(LO 1)** All of the following, except one, are characteristics that money should possess. Which is the exception?
    a) It should have general acceptability.
    b) It should be divisible.
    c) It should be convertible into gold or other precious metals.
    d) It should be portable.
    e) It should be durable.

23. **(LO 4)** Suppose that a banking system has $10 000 000 in demand deposits and actual reserves of $1 200 000. If the target reserve ratio for all banks is 10 percent, what is the maximum possible expansion of the money supply?
    a) $2 200 000
    b) $115 000
    c) $200 000
    d) $12 000 000
    e) $2 000 000

24. **(LO 3)** What is the difference between M1 and M2?
    a) M1 includes currency in circulation, and M2 does not.
    b) M2 includes certificates of deposit, and M1 does not.
    c) M2 includes notice deposits and personal term deposits, and M1 does not.
    d) M2 is always smaller than M1.

25. **(LO 4)** How is the money multiplier calculated?
    a) Divide the target reserve ratio by 1
    b) Divide 1 by the target reserve ratio
    c) Multiply the target reserve ratio by M1
    d) Multiply the target reserve ratio by 1

Intermediate (Questions 26–31)

26. **(LO 2)** Historically, why were goldsmiths able to create money?
    a) Because consumers and merchants preferred to use gold rather than currency for transactions
    b) Because they always kept 100 percent reserves
    c) Because only a few of their customers would redeem their notes for gold at any one time
    d) Because they held the right to print money

27. **(LO 4)** Suppose that Adam Ricardo deposits $1000 cash into the Penguins Bank. On the same day, David Smith negotiates a loan for $4000. By how much has the money supply changed?
    a) It has increased by $3000.
    b) It has decreased by $3000.
    c) It has increased by $4000.
    d) It has increased by $5000.

28. **(LO 3)** The currency held by banks is considered to be part of what definition of money?
    a) M1
    b) M2
    c) M3
    d) Part of all three—M1, M2, and M3
    e) Not part of any definition of money

29. **(LO 4)** If Guy and Laraine both have chequing accounts at the same bank and Guy writes a cheque for $1000, payable to Laraine, what will happen to the bank's accounts?
    a) They will not be affected.
    b) Assets and liabilities will both decrease by $1000.
    c) Liabilities will decline and the bank's equity will increase by $1000.
    d) Reserves and demand deposits will both decrease by $1000.
    e) Demand deposits will increase and loans to customers will decrease by $1000.

30. **(LO 4)** Which of the following statements is correct if a bank is holding excess reserves?
    a) It is in a position to make additional loans.
    b) Its reserves exceed its loans.
    c) It is making above-normal profits.
    d) Its actual reserves are less than its targeted reserves.
    e) Its loans to customers exceed its required loans.

31. **(LO 4)** Suppose that the Just Right Coffee Company negotiates a $100 000 loan from the Blackhawks Bank and takes $40 000 in the form of cash, leaving the remainder in its account. What has happened to the supply of money?
    a) It has increased by $100 000.
    b) It has decreased by $100 000.
    c) It has increased by $40 000.
    d) It has increased by $60 000.
    e) It has not changed.

Advanced (Questions 32–35)

32. **(LO 4)** All of the following statements, except one, are correct. Which is the exception?
    a) A bank's total reserves are equal to its excess reserves plus its target reserves.
    b) A bank's assets plus its net worth equals its liabilities.
    c) When a bank makes a loan, it creates demand deposits.
    d) A single bank can safely lend out only an amount up to the value of its excess reserves.
    e) If a bank transaction decreases the value of one of its assets, then either some other asset must increase in value or one of its liabilities must decrease in value.

33. **(LO 3)** What is true about deposits in near-banks, such as credit unions?
    a) They are part of M1 but not M2.
    b) They are part of M1 and M2 but not M3.
    c) They are part of M3 only.
    d) They are not part of the money supply at all.

34. **(LO 4)** What is true if a bank's balance sheet has $1.2 million in assets and $1 million in liabilities?
    a) The bank must have been profitable this year.
    b) The bank has shareholders' equity of $0.2 million.
    c) Demand deposits must be $0.2 million.
    d) Cash reserves must be $0.2 million.

35. **(LO 4)** Suppose that Bank Apollo has a target reserve ratio of 5 percent, $10 000 in demand deposits, and $1000 in reserves. Assume that the bank makes a loan equal to its excess reserves and the borrower spends this amount at a business that does not use Bank Apollo. What is the net effect on Bank Apollo?
    a) It will be neither under- nor over-reserved.
    b) It will be over-reserved by $500.
    c) It will be under-reserved by $500.
    d) It will be under-reserved by $25.
    e) Its reserve status will be unaffected.

Parallel Problems

ANSWERED PROBLEMS

36A. **(LO 4)** **Key Problem** Table 8.2 is the current balance sheet for the Maple Leafs Bank. Answer the following questions, assuming that the bank's target reserve ratio is five percent.

TABLE 8.2	Maple Leafs Bank Balance Sheet as of the Current Date		
Assets		**Liabilities/Equity**	
Reserves	$ 100 000	Demand deposits	$1 000 000
Loans	650 000	Shareholders' equity	250 000
Securities	300 000		
Fixed assets	200 000		
Totals	$1 250 000		$1 250 000

a) Is this bank over- or under-reserved, and by what amount? Answer: _____

b) Suppose that a loan, in the amount of the excess reserves found in a), is made to Sats Mundin. What effect does this transaction have on the bank's balance sheet? Answer: _____

c) Suppose that Sats immediately spends all of his loan by writing a cheque to his psychologist, Freda Freud. She deposits it in her bank account, which happens to also be at the Maple Leafs Bank. What effect do these transactions have on the bank's balance sheet? Answer: _____

d) Is the Maple Leafs Bank now over- or under-reserved? If so, by how much? Reserved? _____ ; amount? _____ .

e) Suppose, instead, that the bank makes a loan for the amount of your answer in a), which then clears against the Maple Leafs Bank. How much excess reserves does the bank have now? Answer: _____

Suppose that there are nine other banks in the economy and that the balance sheet for the whole banking system is presented in **Table 8.3**. You can assume that each of the other banks also has a target reserve ratio of five percent.

f) In **Table 8.3**, show the balance sheet of the banking system when it is fully loaned up.

g) What is the increase in the money supply as a result of all the banks becoming fully loaned up? Answer: _____

h) Finally, returning to the balance sheet in **Table 8.3**, what would be the consequence of the economy's central bank imposing a 12.5 percent required reserve ratio on all banks? What amount of loans would have to be called in? Answer: _____

TABLE 8.3	Whole Banking System Balance Sheet				
Assets			**Liabilities/Equity**		
Reserves	$1 000 000	_____	Demand deposits	$10 000 000	_____
Loans	6 500 000	_____	Shareholders' equity	2 500 000	_____
Securities	3 000 000	_____			
Fixed assets	2 000 000	_____			
Totals	$12 500 000	_____		$12 500 000	_____

Basic (Problems 37A–44A)

37A. **(LO 4)** Identify the necessary bookkeeping entries in the accounts of the Friedman Bank to record the following transactions:
   a) The Friedman Bank sells some of its old computers for $20 000 in cash. _____
   b) The bank buys $50 000 worth of government bonds from one of its customers and pays by cheque. _____
   c) The Friedman Bank calls in the $5000 loan of Kim's, who pays in cash. _____
   d) The bank grants a loan of $10 000 to Radim. _____
   e) Radim, a customer of the Friedman Bank, writes a cheque for $10 000 payable to his father, who deposits it in his own account at the same bank. _____

38A. **(LO 4)** Table 8.4 shows the balance sheet of the Bruins Bank.

TABLE 8.4	Bruins Bank Balance Sheet		
Assets		**Liabilities/Equity**	
Reserves	$ 24	Demand deposits	$400
Loans	280	Shareholders' equity	20
Securities	80		
Fixed assets	36		
Totals	$420		$420

By how much is the Bruins Bank over- or under-reserved, if the target reserve ratio is
   a) 2 percent _____
   b) 5 percent _____
   c) 8 percent _____
   d) 12 percent _____

39A. **(LO 4)** What is the value of the money multiplier if the target reserve ratios of all banks in the banking system are as follows:

   a) 2 percent _____
   b) 5 percent _____
   c) 8 percent _____
   d) 12 percent _____

40A. **(LO 4)** Table 8.5 is the balance sheet for the Oilers Bank, which has a target reserve ratio of five percent.

TABLE 8.5	Oilers Bank Balance Sheet as of the Current Date		
Assets		**Liabilities/Equity**	
Reserves	$ 6 000	Demand deposits	$ 80 000
Loans	68 000	Shareholders' equity	20 000
Securities	17 000		
Fixed assets	9 000		
Totals	$100 000		$100 000

   a) By how much is the Oilers Bank over- or under-reserved? Answer: _____
   b) If the bank makes a loan equal to the excess reserves and the borrower writes a cheque (for the full amount of the loan) to another customer of the bank, who then deposits it, what will be the new amount of excess reserves? Answer: _____
   c) If, instead, the cheque written by the borrower is cleared against the Oilers Bank (the cheque was written to a customer of another bank), what will be the amount of excess reserves held by Oilers Bank? Answer: _____

41A. **(LO 4)** Table 8.6 is the balance sheet for all banks combined in the banking system. All banks have a target reserve ratio of eight percent.
   a) What is the amount of excess reserves? Answer: _____
   b) What is the maximum amount that loans and deposits can be increased? Answer: _____

TABLE 8.6	Whole Banking System Balance Sheet		
Assets		**Liabilities/Equity**	
Reserves	$78 000	Demand deposits	$900 000
Loans	720 000	Shareholders' equity	100 000
Securities	100 000		
Fixed assets	100 000		
Totals	$1 000 000		$1 000 000

c) If the system becomes fully loaned up, by how much will the money supply have increased?
Answer: _____

42A. **(LO 4)** In which of the following circumstances has the money supply changed?
a) Mario deposits $1000 at his bank.
Yes _____ No _____
b) Mario withdraws $1000 from his bank.
Yes _____ No _____
c) Mario lends Luigi $1000.
Yes _____ No _____
d) The bank lends Mario $1000.
Yes _____ No _____
e) Mario lends the bank $1000.
Yes _____ No _____

43A. **(LO 1)** What are the three functions of money?

44A. **(LO 3)** What is meant by the term *the spread*?

Intermediate (Problems 45A–50A)

45A. **(LO 3)** Answer the questions below from the data in Table 8.7. (All figures are in billions of dollars.)
a) What is the total currency in circulation?
Answer: _____
b) How much larger is M1 than the total currency in circulation?
Answer: _____
c) How much larger is M2 than M1?
Answer: _____

TABLE 8.7	
Total currency issued by the Bank of Canada	$ 20
Total personal savings deposits	192
Total demand deposits	23
Deposits of the federal government at the Bank of Canada	2
Currency held by commercial banks	2
Government bonds owned by public	100
Nonpersonal fixed-term deposits (certificates of deposit)	46

d) How much larger is M3 than M2?
Answer: _____

46A. **(LO 4)** Fill in the blanks in the balance sheet of the Flames Bank in **Table 8.8**, assuming that the value of fixed assets is the same as shareholders' equity and that the bank is fully loaned up. The target reserve ratio is five percent.

TABLE 8.8	Flames Bank Balance Sheet		
Assets		**Liabilities/Equity**	
Reserves	$ _____	Demand deposits	$100 000
Loans	_____	Shareholders' equity	20
Securities	10 000		_____
Fixed assets	_____		
Totals			$120 000

47A. **(LO 4)** Table 8.9 is the balance sheet for the Senators Bank. The target reserve ratio is ten percent.
a) What is the size of the bank's excess reserves?
Answer: _____
b) Change the balance sheet to show the effect of the bank loaning out an amount equal to its excess reserves.
c) Now change the balance sheet to show the effect of a cheque for the amount of the loan in b) clearing against the bank.

TABLE 8.9	Whole Banking System Balance Sheet				
Assets			**Liabilities/Equity**		
Reserves	$60 000	_____	Deposits	$400 000	_____
Securities	80 000	_____	Shareholders' equity	60 000	_____
Loans	260 000	_____			
Fixed assets	60 000	_____			
Totals	$460 000	_____		$460 000	_____

d) Suppose, instead, that the target reserve ratio is twenty percent. What is the bank's reserve situation, and what action will it take?
Answer: _____

48A. **(LO 3)** Many students think that government (or the Bank of Canada) still has a pile of gold somewhere that "backs" our money. Since this is not true, what does back Canadian money?

49A. **(LO 4)** What is included in a list of a bank's assets?

50A. **(LO 4)** What does it mean for a bank to be over-reserved?

Advanced (Problem 51A–55A)

51A. **(LO 4)** The central bank of Muldovia has issued $100 000 in Muldovian dollars. What is the size of the Muldovian money supply if:
a) Muldovians have deposited none of the currency in Muldovia's banks? Answer: _____
b) Muldovians have deposited all of the currency in Muldovia's banks, and the banks have a 100 percent target reserve ratio? Answer: _____
c) Muldovians have deposited 50 percent of the currency in Muldovia's banks, and the banks have a 100 percent target reserve ratio?
Answer: _____
d) Muldovians have deposited 50 percent of the currency in Muldovia's banks, and the banks have a 10 percent target reserve ratio and are fully loaned up? Answer: _____

52A. **(LO 4)** Table 8.10 is the balance sheet for all the banks combined in the banking system.
a) Which one of the above figures is part of the money supply? Answer: _____
b) If all banks maintain 100 percent reserves, what happens to the money supply if eventually $500 cash is deposited into one of the banks in the system? Answer: _____
c) If none of the banks maintains reserves, what happens to the money supply if $500 cash is deposited into one of the banks in the system? Answer: _____

TABLE 8.10		Whole Banking System Balance Sheet	
Assets		**Liabilities/Equity**	
Reserves	$50 000	Demand deposits	$500 000
Loans	450 000	Shareholders' equity	50 000
Securities	30 000		
Fixed assets	20 000		
Totals	$550 000		$550 000

53A. **(LO 4)** Table 8.11 is the combined balance sheet for all the banks in a banking system. Each bank has a target reserve ratio of four percent.
a) Fill in the blanks in column 1 reflecting the complete effect of all excess reserves being loaned out.
b) What is the maximum possible increase in the money supply? Answer: _____
c) If the target reserve ratio changes to ten percent, what quantity of loans will the system be forced to call in? Write in the figures in column 2 that show this process completed.

54A. **(LO 4)** Rearrange the items in the balance sheet shown in Table 8.12 so each is in the correct position. Change one figure only to reflect the bank achieving a five percent target reserve ratio.

TABLE 8.12		Balance Sheet of Senators Bank Ltd	
Assets		**Liabilities/Equity**	
Reserves	$50	Demand deposits	$500
Loans	630	Securities	220
Shareholders' equity	80	Fixed assets	180

55A. **(LO 3)** Many people believe that the ability to buy goods with credit cards makes such cards "money." Explain why a credit card is not money. Do you think that debit cards are money?

TABLE 8.11	Whole Banking System Balance Sheet						
Assets		1	2	**Liabilities/Equity**		1	2
Reserves	$ 200	_____	_____	Deposits	$3000	_____	_____
Loans	1800	_____	_____	Shareholders' equity	600	_____	_____
Securities	1300	_____	_____			_____	_____
Fixed assets	300	_____	_____			_____	_____
Totals	$3600	_____	_____		$3600	_____	_____

CHAPTER 9

THE MONEY MARKET AND MONETARY POLICY

LEARNING OBJECTIVES

At the end of this chapter, you should be able to...

LO1 understand the determinants of money demand and supply and explain how equilibrium in the money market is achieved.

LO2 explain how the Keynesian transmission process works by targeting the money supply.

LO3 understand why Monetarists believe that controlling the money supply is vital.

LO4 explain why many economists are critical of attempts to target the money supply.

LO5 understand why most central banks around the world believe targeting the interest rate is the most effective monetary tool.

LO6 understand why anti-inflationary policy emphasizes targeting the interest rate.

LO7 understand some of the recent criticisms of anti-inflationary monetary policy.

WHAT'S AHEAD...

In Chapter 7, we saw how government is able to have a strong impact on the economy through the use of fiscal policy. In this chapter, we look at the other time-honoured method of bringing about economic change: the use of monetary policy. We begin by looking at the money market and see how inter-related it is to the product market. We emphasize the importance of the interest rate that connects these two markets. The rest of the chapter then examines three different approaches to policymaking. The first is the Keynesian approach, which proposes that the central bank should target the money supply as the major tool to achieve full employment and stable prices. The second approach is that of the Monetarist school, which believes that the central bank should not be given such power over the money supply and its role should, in effect, be replaced by a simple monetary rule. The third approach is that presently used by the Bank of Canada, which seeks to exercise control only over inflation by targeting the interest rate.

A Question of Relevance...

Have you ever watched one of the many money shows on TV? Did you notice the emphasis that analysts put on interest rates? "I expect the stock market to remain strong, as long as interest rates stay low," is a sentiment often expressed. Low interest rates are certainly good for the stock market, but are they also good for the economy and for you and me? Generally, the answer is yes. So, if low interest rates are so important, why aren't they always kept low? Is it because they have to be kept in line with those in the United States? Or are there sometimes good reasons for high interest rates? This chapter will help answer these questions.

9.1   THE MONEY MARKET

Few people would dispute the usefulness of money to both individuals and society. In fact, most economists consider it one of the fundamental elements of a wealthy society, even though they do not consider money itself to be a form of wealth for a nation. However, as we shall see, economists most definitely disagree on the role of money in producing real change in the economy. In order to see just how money can affect things like production and employment, we need to understand the workings of the money market. The idea of a market for money might sound a little strange, if by this we mean a place where people come to buy and sell money. (What do you use to buy money?) But as we shall see, money is a commodity, and like any commodity there is a demand for it, and a supply of it; as such, there is certainly a price for money. To begin with, let us look at the supply side of the money market.

L01 Understand the determinants of money demand and supply, and explain how equilibrium in the money market is achieved.

The Supply of Money

For simplicity's sake, we will use the narrow definition of the money supply, M1, in our discussion. Thus, the supply of money, if you remember, is composed of currency in circulation and the total of all demand deposits at chartered banks. The Bank of Canada determines exactly how much currency is issued, but it is the public that decides what portion of this it wishes to keep in circulation (in our pockets, in the tills of shops, in office safes, and so on) and what portion is deposited with banks. The portion that is deposited constitutes the banks' reserves, which, in turn, determine the amount of loans and demand deposits they are able to support. We will see later how the Bank of Canada is able to affect the amount of money in the economy. The important point we wish to make at this stage is that, to all intents and purposes:

> The supply of money is determined by the Bank of Canada, which can change the supply as it sees fit.

In economics, *supply* refers to "the quantities supplied at various prices." And what exactly is the price of money? In terms of opportunity costs, it is what is sacrificed as a result of holding money rather than holding some other financial instrument on which an income could have been earned. In other words, the cost of money is equal to the interest rate that is forgone. For now, we will assume that the Bank of Canada does not automatically increase or decrease the quantity of money as a result of a change in the price level (the interest rate). In the short run, we can say that the money supply is autonomous with respect to its price—and the price of money, as we shall see, is the same thing as the **interest rate**. Graphically, then, the money supply plots as a straight vertical line, as shown in **Figure 9.1**. If the money supply were to increase, the curve would shift right; a decrease would move it left.

interest rate: the annual rate at which payment is made for the use of money (or borrowed funds); a percentage of the borrowed amount.

FIGURE 9.1   **The Money Supply**

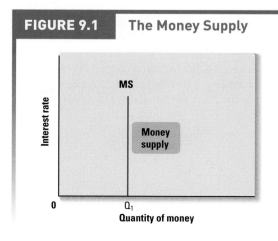

Since the Bank of Canada can set money supply (MS) independently of the rate of interest, it plots as a perfectly inelastic (vertical) supply curve at the present quantity, Q_1

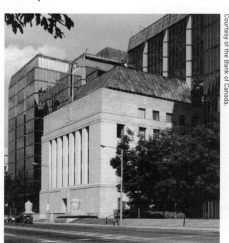

The Bank of Canada building in Ottawa

Courtesy of the Bank of Canada.

Since it is the Bank of Canada, and not government, that controls the supply of money and is responsible for enacting monetary policy, we need to understand exactly what its role is.

Functions of the Bank of Canada

In general, the Bank of Canada operates much like other central banks throughout the world. Some central banks are state owned—the Bank of Canada and the Bank of England—whereas others are privately owned, as is the case of the Federal Reserve Board in the United States. However, for all intents and purposes, ownership is unimportant. What is important is what central banks have in common. The following comments about the Bank of Canada apply equally, therefore, to most central banks.

The first traditional function of the Bank of Canada is that it is the *sole issuer of currency*. It acts as a reservoir in that it will issue more currency to the banks when needed (just before Christmas, for instance), and at other times, it will take back any surplus above the banks' and the public's requirements. You may recall that only the portion of the outstanding currency that is in the hands of the public is considered part of the money supply; the portion in bank vaults is excluded.

A second traditional function is that the Bank of Canada acts as *government's bank*. It is the institution that looks after government's banking needs. More recently, however, individual government ministries have been given authority to deal with whichever commercial bank they choose, making this function of the Bank of Canada less important. In addition, the Bank of Canada *manages reserves of foreign currencies* (and gold) on behalf of government. This includes the buying and selling of Canadian dollars and other currencies, in consultation with government and consistent with its policies.

The Canadian Press (Tom Hanson)

A visitor to the currency museum in the Bank of Canada building in Ottawa looks at the half-burnt Canadian dollar. The display illustrates how old currency is disposed of.

Another important function of the Bank of Canada is to act as the *bankers' bank*. This means that each of the commercial banks has an account with the Bank of Canada to facilitate the borrowing and lending of funds between the two. The central bank stands prepared to make extraordinary loans to a commercial bank that is experiencing a liquidity problem to avert a loss of depositor confidence. In this respect, it is often known as the "lender of last resort."

The Bank Act also stipulates that the Bank of Canada is to act as *auditor and inspector of the commercial banks*, and the latter are required to submit periodic reports to the Bank of Canada and to open their books and accounts for inspection and audit.

The final function of the Bank of Canada is the most important, and that is to *regulate the money supply*. It is interesting to note in this regard that although the federal government, through Parliament, has the power and the responsibility to effect fiscal policy, it does not itself directly control monetary policy: this is the prime function of the governor and the board of directors of the Bank of Canada. It is possible, therefore, at least in theory, for government and the Bank of Canada to be in conflict regarding the direction in which they want to move the economy. In fact, there was such a conflict between the two in the late 1950s. This does not happen often, however. This is not because the two always agree but because a conflict in policy would be regarded as something of a political failure and thus something that the policymakers wish to avoid. In summary, the functions of a central bank, such as the Bank of Canada, are to act as:

- the issuer of currency
- government's bank and manager of foreign currency reserves
- the bankers' bank and lender of last resort
- the auditor and inspector of commercial banks
- the regulator of the money supply

ADDED DIMENSION The Bank of Canada and Government

It is worth emphasizing that while the governor and directors of the Bank of Canada are appointed by the federal cabinet (through the Governor General), their roles are meant to be nonpolitical. Appointments are not politically motivated by patronage but rather based on merit and expertise. In addition, their seven-year terms exceed the life of a government, and the governor's appointment can be terminated only by an act of Parliament. In these ways, it is hoped that the bank will operate independently of government and pursue monetary policy without being affected by short-term political considerations. Government could, through the minister of finance, attempt to formally dictate to the governor what policy it wished him to follow. (So far, all governors have been men, including the incumbent, Mark Carney.) However, being forced to act openly in this manner signals a marked political failure on the part of government—which may well have negative economic repercussions—and is, therefore, rare.

Let us now look at the other side of the equation: the demand for money.

The Demand For Money

Before you start thinking that the average person's demand for money is unlimited, remember that we are not talking about income. The average person's demand for *income* might well be unlimited, but we are speaking about (the stock of) money. As we noted in Chapter 8, money is a stock and is only one of many possible forms of wealth that people might hold.

Like any other form of wealth-holding, money has certain advantages and disadvantages. Except in times of high inflation, money maintains a reasonably stable value, unlike such things as land or stocks and bonds, whose value can vary greatly, both up and down. From this point of view, money involves less risk. The other advantage is that money is highly liquid. In contrast, real estate is not liquid in that it may take weeks or even months to convert it to money. Balanced against that is the fact that holding money does not produce a return, whereas most other forms of wealth can offer at least the prospect of some small return in the form of interest or dividends. In general, the safer the investment, the lower is the return; the greater the risk, the higher is the return.

So, why bother holding money at all? Why not, on receipt of income, immediately transfer it into some sort of financial investment? The reason is obvious: we need to keep a portion of our wealth in a chequing account or as currency simply because other forms of wealth are unacceptable as a means of payment. It is certainly true that over the years, the introduction of credit cards, debit cards, and Internet banking has meant that we need to keep only a smaller proportion of our wealth in the form of money. Nevertheless, many of our transactions still require that we pay for them with money.

One reason to hold money, therefore, is what economists call the **transactions demand for money**. Simply put, we need money in order to transact many of our regular daily purchases. What determines this transactions demand? The value of transactions we make. And what determines the value of our transactions? The answer is: the level of our income. The higher the income level of individuals, the more they will spend and the higher will be the transactions demand for money. This is similarly true for the whole economy. The higher the level of the gross domestic product (GDP), the higher will be the transactions demand for money.

Note here that we are speaking of nominal GDP. This means that a higher demand for money can come about either because real GDP increases or because prices increase. The major determinants of the transactions demand for money, then, are the level of real income and the level of prices; a change in either can cause a change in the transactions demand for money. (It should also be added that institutional factors, such as the increased use of credit cards, the regularity with which people get paid, the efficiency of the banking system in clearing cheques, and so on, can also affect the transactions demand in the long run.)

Exactly what does this mean in terms of the average consumer? Well, twenty years ago, one of the authors could easily get through the week by taking out $50 in cash from the bank. This was more than enough to pay his immediate expenses for lunches, bus fares, and the occasional drink.

transactions demand for money: the desire of people to hold money as a medium of exchange, that is, to effect transactions.

FIGURE 9.2   Transactions Demand for Money

The transactions demand is independent of the interest rate and plots as a vertical line. An increase in the price level or in real GDP will shift the curve to the right; a decrease in either will shift it to the left.

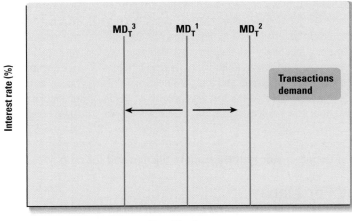

These days, there is no way that $50 will last out the week; he finds that he needs double this amount. Why is that so? Well, the first reason is simple: prices have gone up considerably over the last twenty years. He needs more money just to buy the same amount of purchases that he did twenty years ago. But on top of this, he has found that his real income is a lot higher these days and he tends to buy more than he ever could afford in his younger days. So, a higher price level and a higher real income will both increase the transactions demand for money.

Figure 9.2 shows the transactions demand for money graphically.

Since the transactions demand for money does not depend on the prevailing interest rate, it plots as a straight vertical line. An increase in either the price level or in real GDP means that the value of transactions will increase—simply put, people will need more money to buy the goods and services. This will be reflected in a rightward shift in the transactions demand curve. A decrease in either the price level or in real GDP will have the opposite effect, causing the curve to shift left.

Another way of looking at the transactions demand is that it is related to the way money functions as a medium of exchange. But, as we have already noted, money is also used as a store of wealth. Under what circumstances will it be a popular form of wealth-holding? Presumably, when other forms of wealth-holding are not attractive. If, for instance, the return on bonds was a mere 1 percent, and the value of stock markets and real estate was declining, then most people would start to regard money as a very secure "investment." So, when the return on other assets is low, people's demand for money tends to be high. This motive for holding money as a store of wealth is termed the **asset demand for money**. Conversely, when the average return on other types of financial investment is high, people tend to economize on their money balances and try to keep as little as possible beyond their transactions needs. In general, the rates of return on bonds tend to move in concert with the rate of interest. There is, therefore, an *inverse* relationship between rates of interest and the asset demand for money. When interest rates are high, asset demand is low; when rates are low, asset demand is high. This idea is illustrated in **Figure 9.3**.

We can now bring together the transactions and asset demands for money to derive the total demand for money curve.

Figure 9.4A illustrates the fact that the transactions demand for money is unrelated to the rate of interest. We need a certain amount of money—in this example, $30 billion—regardless of how high or low the rate of interest is. As we said earlier, this demand would increase with a rise in real incomes or prices and decrease with a fall in either.

asset demand for money: the desire of people to use money as a store of wealth, that is, to hold money as an asset.

FIGURE 9.3   The Asset Demand for Money

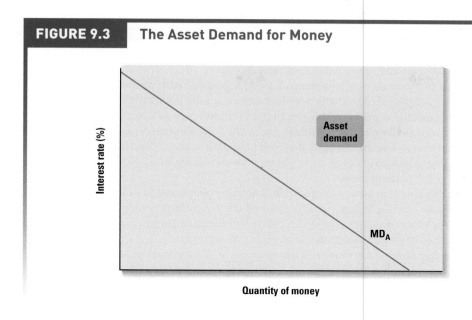

When the rate of interest is high, people will economize on the amount of asset money they hold. At a lower interest rate people will be willing to hold a bigger quantity of asset money. There is, therefore, an inverse relationship between the rate of interest and the quantity of asset money.

Figure 9.4B shows the inverse relationship between the asset money demand for money and the rate of interest. At an interest rate of eight percent, the quantity of asset money demanded will be relatively low at $20 billion. At this high rate of interest, people will economize as much as possible in their holdings of money simply because holding money as an asset yields a zero percent rate of return. Thus, they will try to put any excess cash into some form of income-earning asset. At an interest rate of 2 percent, however, the asset demand at $50 billion is high. At this low rate of interest, many people are fairly indifferent about holding other financial investments and would just as soon hold onto money, especially if they believe that the interest rate is likely to rise.

Figure 9.4C shows the total demand for money, which is simply the addition of the transactions and asset demands. (The two curves are just summed together horizontally.) It shows that when the rate of interest is at 8 percent, the total demand for money is $50 billion. This total is composed of $30 billion transactions demand plus $20 billion, the amount of idle money or asset

FIGURE 9.4   Transactions, Asset, and Total Demand for Money

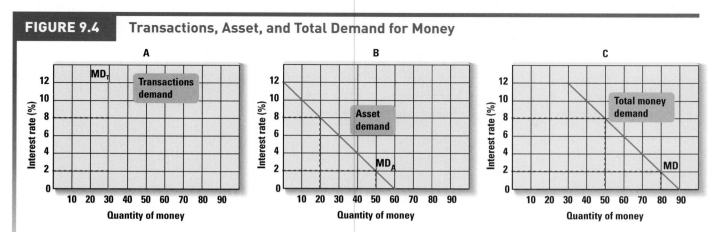

Graph A shows the transactions demand for money, which is equal to $30.
Graph B shows the asset demand for money. When the rate of interest is 8 percent, the quantity of money demanded for asset purposes is $20, and at an interest rate of 2 percent, it is $50. The final graph, C, shows the total demand for money, which is obtained by summing the first two graphs horizontally.

demand. When the rate of interest is 2 percent, the total demand for money is $80 billion, composed of transactions demand of $30 billion and asset demand of $50 billion.

What we have then is that people will hold enough money to finance their daily transactions but will often possess an additional amount of "idle balances," which is what we have called the *asset demand*. There is controversy among economists regarding such idle balances. Keynes, for example, gave other explanations of why people might rationally hold such additional balances of money. He suggested it is perfectly rational to hold idle balances in situations where holding bonds is risky. This might happen if the interest rate is low (and bond prices are high) and people expect the interest rate to rise. In this case, they will hold onto money. If the interest rate does go up, they will be able to purchase bonds more cheaply (as we will see later). Keynes called this the speculative motive for holding money.

Besides offering this explanation, Keynes felt that many people might hold cash as a form of security, or insurance, for the future (what he termed the *precautionary motive*). Even allowing for the fact that the value of money erodes through inflation, many people may still want to hold on to money because of its immediate accessibility in an emergency.

In summary, the demand for money in the economy is determined by:

- the level of transactions (real GDP)
- the average value of transactions (the price level)
- the rate of interest

✓ SELF-TEST

1. Assume you are given the following asset demand for an economy:

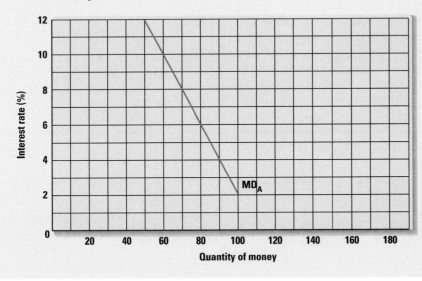

a) Assume that the nominal GDP in this economy is $800 and that the transaction demand for money is equal to 10 percent of nominal GDP. Draw the *total* demand for money curve.

b) If the money supply is $150 billion, draw in the money supply curve.

c) What is the equilibrium interest rate and the quantity of money?

d) If the interest rate, is 10 percent, is there a surplus or shortage of money? How much?

Equilibrium in the Money Market

We have now looked at both the supply of money and the demand for money in an economy. Hopefully, you know what is coming next? To find out under what circumstances the public will be happy to hold the amount of money that the Bank of Canada has supplied, we need to put the two together. **Figure 9.5** does this.

FIGURE 9.5	Surplus and Shortage of Money

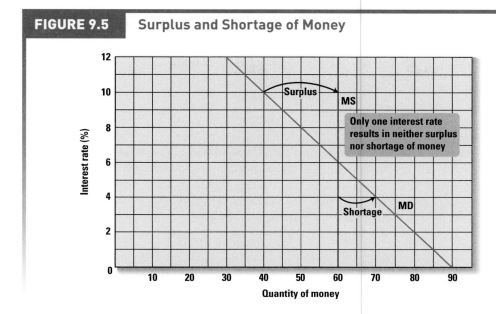

At an interest rate above equilibrium (such as at 10 percent), there is a surplus of $20 of money. People will buy bonds, which will increase the price of bonds, thus reducing the interest rate. Conversely, at interest rates below equilibrium (such as at 4 percent), there will be a shortage of $10 of money causing people to sell off bonds. The effect of this will be to push down bond prices, causing the rate of interest to rise. Only at equilibrium interest rate of 6 percent will people be happy to hold the amount of money that is supplied by the Bank of Canada.

The supply of money, as mentioned before, is determined by the Bank of Canada, and we will regard it as independent of the rate of interest. It is simply a fixed autonomous amount equal to $60 (billion). The demand for money curve is merely a repeat of **Figure 9.4C**. The graph shows that only at an interest rate of 6 percent will the quantities of money supplied and demanded be equal, and we have equilibrium in the money market.

But what will happen if the money market is not in equilibrium? For instance, what will happen if the interest rate happens to be above the equilibrium at, say, 10 percent? At this rate of interest, there is obviously a surplus of money; that is, the quantity supplied exceeds the quantity demanded of $20. The quantity demanded is less because at higher rates of interest, people are going to reduce their money holdings; they will want to keep their money balances to a minimum and will want to buy some other financial instrument, such as a bond.

Bonds are nothing more than loans that are issued for a set period—one year, five years, and so on—and have a nominal face value, such as $100 or $1000, and pay a fixed rate of interest (the coupon rate) to the holder of the bond. They are issued by corporations, by banks, and by various levels of government: municipal, provincial, and federal. An essential feature of a bond is that it can easily be bought and sold in the market. This means that the return you earn on a bond depends not just on the coupon rate but also from the profit (or loss) on its sale. Suppose, for instance, that a new one-year $100 bond was issued that pays a coupon rate of 5 percent. Suppose also that you can earn 10 percent return on most other financial investments with similar degrees of risk. You can imagine that not many people are going to buy the bond for this price. As a result, soon after its issue, the price will quickly drop. How low will the price drop? Until it earns the same return, 10 percent, that is being offered on other financial investments. In other words, the price will drop to approximately $95. Buyers will now earn $5 from when the bond is redeemed a year later, and will earn $5 from the interest paid to it, for a total of $10. (It is actually a little over 10 percent, but that is a feature we can skip over.)

A pressman stacks some of the new Canada Premium Bonds as they come off the presses at the Canada Bank Note Company in Ottawa.

The Canadian Press (Tom Hanson)

We could state this in terms of an equation.

$$\text{Rate of return (rate of interest)} = \frac{\text{coupon interest} +/- \text{ change in the bond price}}{\text{Price paid for bond}} \times 100 \quad \textbf{[9.1]}$$

In our example, the rate of return is:

$$\frac{\$5 + \$5}{95} \times 100 = 10.53\%$$

To cement this idea a little, let us suppose that a $5000 bond with a coupon rate of 4 percent (= $200) with one year left until redemption is sold at the following prices. In each case, let us work out the rate of return (interest).

$$\text{Purchase price: } \$4700\text{: Rate of return} = \frac{(\$200 + \$300)}{4700} \times 100 = 10.64\%$$

$$\$4900\text{: Rate of return} = \frac{(\$200 + \$100)}{4900} \times 100 = 6.12\%$$

$$\$5100\text{: Rate of return} = \frac{(\$200 - \$100)}{5100} \times 100 = 1.96\%$$

In other words, the lower the price of bonds, the higher will be the return that you earn (the rate of interest). It also means that the higher the price of bonds, the lower the yields (rates of return). In effect, this will mean a lower rate of interest. In short:

> **The lower the price of bonds, the higher is the rate of return; the higher the price of bonds, the lower is the rate of return.**

 ADDED DIMENSION   Gold and Wealth

One of the reasons that Adam Smith's *The Wealth of Nations* became the seminal work in economics is because it attempted to look beyond the economic fears and aspirations of the individual and shift the focus to a study of the whole economy. The title of Smith's opus is, after all, *The Wealth of Nations*, not *The Wealth of People*. It would have been a very simple task for Smith to have defined what constitutes wealth as far as the individual is concerned. It is far less obvious and far more interesting to figure out what comprises the wealth of nations.

At first glance, it would seem that it is made up of the total wealth of all individuals plus any assets that are held in common. However, there was major disagreement as to whether or not money should be included as a form of wealth. Although gold could certainly be used as an international medium of exchange, did it mean that the more gold a country had, the richer it was? What if a country's stock of gold were to increase appreciably—would the country be any richer? Well, by and large, people in possession of gold are able to buy more foreign goods. However, they probably want to buy more domestic goods, too. Since there is no reason for the amount of goods produced to change, the only thing that is likely to happen is an increase in prices. Eventually prices will increase in line with the increased amount of gold. The net result is that people are no better off than they were before.

What Smith tried to do in his book was to redirect people's views regarding wealth. Being wealthy for Smith meant that a nation was able to produce and had produced an abundance of goods and services—not that it merely owned a stock of glittering pieces of metal, such as gold. Gold is not wealth in the same way that labour and capital goods are forms of wealth. The latter are regenerative in that they can recreate themselves; gold, in contrast, is totally sterile.

Let us return to **Figure 9.5**. Suppose that the interest rate is above equilibrium at 10 percent. At this comparatively high rate of interest, people will only wish to hold a small quantity of money, $40, which is less than the quantity supplied of $60. The result is a surplus of $20 of money—people will wish to reduce their money holdings by buying bonds. This increase in the demand for bonds will cause bond prices to increase and, as we saw, cause the rate of interest to fall until it is at the equilibrium rate of 6 percent.

Let us now look at the effect of an interest rate lower than equilibrium, say, 4 percent.

At this lower interest rate, people will be more than willing to hold the quantity of money of $70, since the return on bonds and other financial securities is low. However, since the quantity of money supplied, $60, is less than the amount people wish to hold, there is a money shortage of $10. To obtain more money, people will be forced to sell off bonds or other financial instruments. The effect of this action will be to increase the supply of these types of instruments as people cash them in. This causes their price to fall and the rate of interest to rise, until the money market is back in equilibrium at an interest rate of 6 percent.

What we see, then, is that the interest rate is determined by *both* the demand for and supply of money, and a change in either will cause the interest rate to be affected. This means that the interest rate will increase if there is either an increase in the demand for money or a drop in the supply of money. Similarly, a decrease in the interest rate is caused by either a drop in the demand for money or an increase in the supply of money. We will look at changes in the money supply in the next section; here, we will concentrate on changes in the demand for money.

When we say that there is an increase in the demand for money, we mean that people are willing and able to hold more money whatever the current rate of interest. In effect, an increase in the demand for money can only be caused by an increase in the transactions demand for money, and this, in return, must be the result of an increase in either the price level or in real GDP. (Additionally it might be caused by a change in institutional factors—how often people get paid and so on.) A higher demand for money will cause the interest rate to increase; a fall in the demand will cause the interest rate to also fall. In summary:

> An increase in the interest rate is caused by either a rise in the demand for money or a fall in the supply of money.

> A decrease in the interest rate is caused by either a fall in the demand for money or a rise in the supply of money.

So far, this whole discussion (in fact, this whole book) has spoken of *the* interest rate as if there were one single rate. In fact, what we have in any economy is an interest-rate *structure* made up of many rates: the rate paid by banks on savings accounts, the rate charged by banks for loans of different types (mortgages, personal loans, or credit card charges), and the bank rate, which we will look at shortly. For convenience, however, we will continue to speak of "the interest rate," and the reader can use the context of the discussion to determine whether it would be for saving or for borrowing.

Now that we have examined the mechanics of the money market, it is time to look at how the Bank of Canada (and other central banks) brings about changes in the money market and how this impacts on the product market. We will be looking at three different philosophies. The first two, those of Keynes and the Monetarists, emphasize controlling the money supply; the third and more recent philosophy is that of those who advocate anti-inflationary **monetary policy**, which seeks instead to control interest rates.

monetary policy: policy designed to change the money supply, credit availability, and interest rates.

SELF-TEST

2. Assume that the money demand for a particular economy is as follows. (All figures are in billions of dollars.)

Rate of Interest (%)	Asset Demand ($)	Transactions Demand ($)	Total Demand ($)
12	50	80	_____
11	55	80	_____
10	60	80	_____
9	65	80	_____
8	70	80	_____
7	75	80	_____
6	80	80	_____

Complete the table, and answer these questions:

a) If the money supply equals $150, what must be the equilibrium interest rate?

b) If the money supply equals $140, what must be the equilibrium interest rate?

c) If the rate of interest is 11 percent and the money supply is $150, what are the implications?

9.2   TARGETING THE MONEY SUPPLY: KEYNESIAN MONETARY POLICY

L02 ▸ Explain how the Keynesian transmission process works by targeting the money supply.

The essence of Keynesian monetary policy is that the various macroeconomic markets, the money market, the product market (that we looked at in Chapters 5 and 6) and the international market (that we will investigate in Chapter 11) are all intrinsically linked. Changes in one market will bring about changes in the other(s). In his General Theory, Keynes was especially interested in the product market (since production, economic growth, and employment are directly related to it) and sought to understand and explain what caused change in this market. We saw in Chapter 7 how fiscal policy can directly influence this market. We will now look at Keynes' belief that changes in the money market could also indirectly impact the product market. The agent of change here is the central bank, which has a degree of control over the supply of money and can thus affect interest rates. Before we take a look at that process, let us first examine the two tools that are at the disposal of the Bank of Canada when it wishes to change the supply of money.

Monetary Tools

expansionary monetary policy: a policy that aims to increase the amount of money in the economy and make credit cheaper and more easily available.

contractionary monetary policy: a policy in which the amount of money in the economy is decreased and credit becomes harder to obtain and more expensive.

open-market operations: the buying and selling of securities by the Bank of Canada on the open (to the public) market.

Let us assume that the Bank of Canada wishes to effect an **expansionary monetary policy** (also called an *easy money policy*). This involves increasing the money supply. How could this be done? Well, we know from Chapter 8 that if the Bank could increase the amount of cash reserves held by the commercial banks, then any reserves that banks consider in excess of their target reserves would be loaned out and, through the money multiplier process, would lead to an increase in demand deposits (the main portion of money supply). **Contractionary monetary policy** (or a *tight money policy*) implies the opposite.

One simple way the Bank of Canada can increase the commercial banks' cash reserves would be to give them additional amounts of reserves. However, some of us might complain about a free gift of cash to the banks! The Bank of Canada therefore has to use a more subtle and businesslike process known as **open-market operations**, so called because it involves the Bank of Canada (or at least its agent) buying or selling treasury bills (short-term bonds) in a market that is open to anyone.

In other words, the Bank of Canada buys and sells government bonds in the same way that any individual or corporation might. It should be noted that these are "second-hand" bonds—bonds that government has previously issued and sold to the public.

To better understand just how this market works, we need to understand the role of treasury bills. A treasury bill is a type of short-term bond, or fixed-term debt, issued by the Bank of Canada, acting as the agent of government. Fortunately, it is often the case that from time to time, corporations, commercial banks, life insurance and pension fund companies, and other organizations find themselves with excess cash. Usually, this cash will be needed by these organizations in the near future, and so the question of what to do with, say, $2 million for 60 days can arise. One of the most popular revenue-earning assets are these treasury bills (or T-bills), which can be bought in various denominations for either a three- or six-month term. They differ from longer-term government and corporate bonds in that they are short-term and do not pay interest. Instead, return is earned on them because they are purchased at a discount (at a price below the face value) and are then redeemed at the end of the fixed term at face value.

If it wished to increase the amount of cash reserves of the commercial banks, the Bank of Canada would buy outstanding T-bills in the open market. The seller of the T-bills would receive a cheque from the Bank of Canada, which would then be deposited in the seller's bank account. At the end of the day, the commercial bank involved would look to the Bank of Canada for collection. This could be achieved by the Bank of Canada transferring the required amount of reserves to the commercial bank in question. Rather than doing this, however, the Bank of Canada just credits the account that the commercial bank has with the Bank of Canada. It, in effect, tells the commercial bank that the amount of credit it has "on reserve" at the Bank of Canada has been increased. The commercial banks' reserves have therefore increased, and this recently acquired surplus will be loaned out, thus leading to a multiple expansion of money in the economy, as we discussed in Chapter 8.

To reduce the money supply, the Bank of Canada would, of course, do the opposite and sell T-bills to whoever wished to purchase them. These people would have to make payments to the Bank of Canada. Their bank account balances would be thus reduced, and so would the reserves of the commercial banks. As a result, banks would be forced to call in loans, and this would reduce the amount of money in the economy.

Open-market operations are not the only tool of monetary policy, but they are a frequently used and important method. This is because they can be initiated on short notice, take effect quickly, and can be done in any amount.

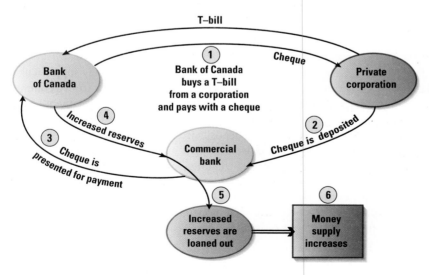

The sequence of events when the central bank uses open-market operations to expand money supply.

✓ SELF-TEST

3. In terms of the banking system's ability to create money, what difference, if any, does it make if the Bank of Canada buys bonds from a commercial bank rather than from a member of the public?

▶ ADDED DIMENSION   The Bank of Canada's Balance Sheet

The operations of the Bank of Canada affect the economy, but they also affect the balance sheet of the bank itself. The following table shows the Bank of Canada's balance sheet in simplified form as of December 31, 2010. All figures are in millions.

The biggest asset of the bank is its holdings of government bonds and treasury bills, and it is the sale and purchase of these that we term *open-market operations*. The major liability

of the bank, as you can see, is the amount of notes in circulation. Although these notes are assets to members of the public who own them, they represent a liability to the issuing bank, the Bank of Canada. The other major liability is the reserves that the commercial banks deposit with the Bank of Canada. Such reserves are, of course, an asset to the commercial banks but a liability to the Bank of Canada.

Assets		Liabilities	
Cash and foreign deposits	5	Notes in circulation	57 874
Short-term loans to banks	2087	Government of Canada deposits	1869
Treasury bills of Canada	24 906	Deposits of banks	48
Government bonds	33 589	Other deposits	640
Other assets	298	Other liabilities	324
Total	60 885	Share capital	130
		Total	60 885

Source: Adapted from the *Bank of Canada Annual Report, 2010.*

A second way that the Bank of Canada can affect the money supply is by *switching government deposits*. For instance, if the Bank of Canada wants to contract the money supply it can, with the approval of the finance ministry, transfer some of government's deposits from a commercial bank to the Bank of Canada. It does this, in effect, by writing a cheque on government's account at the commercial bank made payable to the Bank of Canada. Conversely, if it wished to increase the money supply, it would switch government deposits from the Bank of Canada to the commercial banks. The effect of switching deposits is similar to open-market operations. In both cases, demand deposits and reserves are affected. Switching deposits has become an increasingly popular monetary tool for the Bank of Canada.

As we shall see when we look at the policy of targeting interest rates rather than the money supply, the Bank of Canada has two additional monetary tools available to it: targetting the overnight rate and moral suasion. More about these later.

SELF-TEST

4. Given here are balance sheets for the commercial banking system and for the Bank of Canada (all figures are in billions). Show the effects on the balance sheets of both the Bank of Canada and the commercial banks as a result of the Bank of Canada buying $2 billion worth of securities directly from the commercial banks.

5. Suppose that the banking system's target reserve ratio is 10 percent and the Bank of Canada switches $100 million of government funds from government's account with the Bank of Canada to an account at a commercial bank. Since neither government's accounts with commercial banks nor the commercial banks' reserves are considered to be part of the money supply, how could such a switching of funds have any effect on money supply?

All Commercial Banks

Assets		Liabilities	
Reserves:		Deposits	$800
In vaults	$ 70		
On deposit with the Bank of Canada	10		
Securities	120		
Loans	600		
Totals	$800		$800

Bank of Canada

Assets		Liabilities	
T-bills and bonds	$80	Notes in circulation	$65
		Deposits of Banks	10
		Other liabilities	5
Totals	$80		$80

Now that we have looked at the mechanics of how the Bank of Canada is able to affect the money supply, let us see how Keynes believed such changes affect the whole economy.

Expansionary Monetary Policy and the Transmission Process

Keynesian monetary policy envisions an active process of setting macroeconomic goals and then adjusting policy to achieve those goals. As an example, the Bank of Canada used Keynesian monetary policy for some time after the bank was established in 1935. The Bank's mandate then was:

> To regulate credit and currency in the best interests of the nation... and to mitigate by its influence fluctuations in the general level of production, trade, prices, and employment.

As you can see, implied here is the use of monetary policy to assist in achieving four separate goals:
- steady growth in real GDP
- an exchange rate that ensures a viable balance of trade
- stable prices
- full employment

ADDED DIMENSION   Bills and Bonds

Bonds and bills are nothing more than types of IOUs, but whereas bonds are issued by all types of institutions, including corporations and governments (at all levels), treasury bills (T-bills) are issued only by the federal government. Both bills and bonds are freely negotiable financial instruments, which means that they can be easily bought and sold at any time at their current market value (which may well be different from their nominal, or face, value). Although bonds and T-bills are offered in any number of denominations, $500, $1000 and so forth, the major difference between the two is that bonds are long-term IOUs, whereas bills are usually of short duration, with the typical T-bill issued for a 91-day period. Another difference between them is that a bond pays a fixed interest rate (the coupon rate) annually, whereas a T-bill does not pay any interest at all. Consider, for instance, the issuance of a T-bill at a face value of $1000 that will be redeemable in 91 days. Since no one would pay $1000 for a bill that will give them $1000 in three months' time, T-bills are sold at a discount.

Now, suppose this bill is sold at a discounted price of $975. This means that anyone buying it will expect to earn a return of $25 in just three months. As a percentage of the investment outlay, this represents a return of 25/975 × 100 or 2.564 percent. To find the annual return, we multiply this rate by 365/91, which gives us a rate of return (interest rate) of 10.28 percent. The formula is:

$$r = \frac{F - P}{P} \times \frac{365}{\# \text{ days to maturity}} \qquad [9.2]$$

where r = annual interest rate, F is the face value and P is the price paid for the T-bill. So, to confirm our calculation:

$$r = \frac{25}{975} \times \frac{365}{91} = 0.1028 \text{ or } 10.28\%$$

But suppose the annual interest rate being earned on similar investments is only 6 percent. In that case, this T-bill would be in great demand. The result will be that the market value of the bill will immediately rise. And it will continue to rise until this bill is neither more nor less attractive than those other investments. Its price will rise until it offers a return equal to 6 percent. Rearranging equation 9.2 will help us work out its value.

$$P = \frac{\dfrac{365}{\# \text{ days to maturity}} \times F}{\dfrac{365}{\# \text{ days to maturity}} + r} \qquad [9.3]$$

Therefore,

$$P = \frac{\dfrac{365}{91} \times 1000}{\dfrac{365}{91} + 0.6} = \frac{4011}{4.07} = \$985.50$$

So, the price will rise to $985.50; anyone buying it will earn $14.50 in 91 days, or 14.50/985.50 × 100 or approximately 1.5 percent in 91 days. That comes to 365/91 × 1.5 percent or 6 percent per annum.

This confirms what we already know. The higher the price of a bond (or bill), the lower is the rate of interest earned.

transmission process: the Keynesian view of how changes in money affect (transmit to) the real variables in the economy.

Keynesian theory also suggests, as we mentioned earlier, that the money market and the product market are intrinsically linked: changes in one will bring about changes in the other. Not only that, but for the economy to achieve a stable equilibrium, *both* the product and the money markets need to be in equilibrium. How exactly does this work out? Well, suppose that the Bank of Canada wishes to effect expansionary monetary policy in order to stimulate an economy that is suffering a recession. Let us work through how a change in the money supply affects the product market. In doing this, we will see that what is called the **transmission process** puts the emphasis on the interest rate, which provides the link between the two markets.

We start our analysis with **Figure 9.6A**, which shows the money market initially in equilibrium. Now let us see what happens when the Bank of Canada increases the money supply from MS_1 to MS_2. This will immediately cause a surplus of money, which will lead individuals and institutions to rid themselves of this surplus by buying bonds. This increased demand for bonds will push up their prices, thus lowering the interest rate. You may recall from Chapter 5 that a lower interest rate will increase the quantity of investment spending, as firms will be induced to borrow more and invest the proceeds in new capital goods, as depicted in **Figure 9.6B**. This higher level of investment spending will increase aggregate expenditures and shift up the aggregate expenditures curve from AE_1 to AE_2, as shown in **Figure 9.6C**. We know from Chapter 5

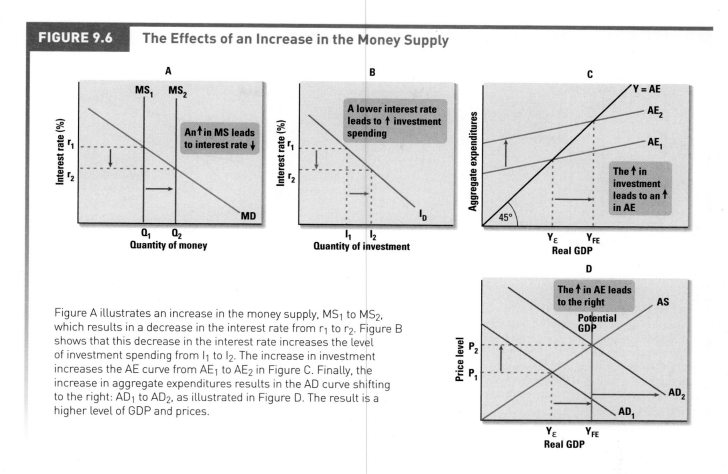

FIGURE 9.6   The Effects of an Increase in the Money Supply

Figure A illustrates an increase in the money supply, MS₁ to MS₂, which results in a decrease in the interest rate from r₁ to r₂. Figure B shows that this decrease in the interest rate increases the level of investment spending from I₁ to I₂. The increase in investment increases the AE curve from AE₁ to AE₂ in Figure C. Finally, the increase in aggregate expenditures results in the AD curve shifting to the right: AD₁ to AD₂, as illustrated in Figure D. The result is a higher level of GDP and prices.

that anything (apart from a change in the price level) that increases aggregate expenditures will also increase aggregate demand. Thus, the aggregate demand curve in **Figure 9.6D** will shift to the right from AD_1 to AD_2. This will then increase both the price level (increasing it from P_1 to P_2) and the level of real GDP (raising it from $Y\varepsilon$ to Y_{FE}).

In short, increases in money supply will shift the AD curve to the right, thus increasing both the level of real GDP and the price level. It is important for you to realize that the shift from AD_1 to AD_2 is larger than the increase in investment spending from I_1 to I_2. The existence of the multiplier is the reason for this. As we saw in earlier chapters, the increase in investment spending will trigger a series of increases in income and spending. The multiplier ensures that the increase in aggregate demand from AD_1 to AD_2 will be greater than the investment increase from I_1 to I_2.

The following graphic shows the chain of events which results from an increase in money supply:

	Money Market Changes			Transmit into	Product Market Changes
$M_s\uparrow \Rightarrow$	Surplus of Money $\Rightarrow$	Purchase of Bonds $\Rightarrow$	Bond Prices $\uparrow$	$\Rightarrow r\downarrow \Rightarrow$	$I\uparrow \rightarrow Y\uparrow$ (Shift in AD curve)

FIGURE 9.7   The Effect of Contractionary Monetary Policy

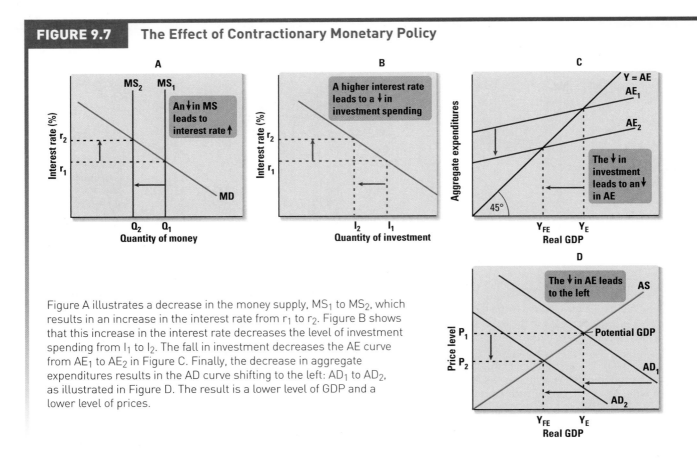

Figure A illustrates a decrease in the money supply, MS$_1$ to MS$_2$, which results in an increase in the interest rate from r$_1$ to r$_2$. Figure B shows that this increase in the interest rate decreases the level of investment spending from I$_1$ to I$_2$. The fall in investment decreases the AE curve from AE$_1$ to AE$_2$ in Figure C. Finally, the decrease in aggregate expenditures results in the AD curve shifting to the left: AD$_1$ to AD$_2$, as illustrated in Figure D. The result is a lower level of GDP and a lower level of prices.

Contractionary Monetary Policy to Fight Inflation

Now let us see how monetary policy can be used to fight an inflationary boom. Suppose that initially the economy is producing a GDP of Yε which is above the potential GDP, Y$_{FE}$ as in **Figure 9.7D**. In this situation, Keynesian monetary policy would call for contractionary monetary policy. The Bank of Canada would, therefore, reduce the money supply from MS$_1$ to MS$_2$, as shown in **Figure 9.7A**. This will cause a shortage of money that, in turn, will cause people to sell bonds to increase their money holdings. The result will be a drop in bond prices, causing the interest rate to rise from r$_1$ to r$_2$. **Figure 9.7B** shows that the increase in the interest rate reduces investment spending from I$_1$ to I$_2$, which will then decrease the level of aggregate expenditures in **Figure 9.7C** from AE$_1$ to AE$_2$. Finally, the lower level of aggregate expenditures will reduce aggregate demand from AD$_1$ to AD$_2$ in **Figure 9.7D**. The important part of this last figure is the fact that while GDP falls to Y$_{FE}$, the price level also drops from P$_1$ to P$_2$. In summary, inflation is reduced by contracting the money supply, thereby increasing interest rates and reducing overall spending in the economy.

 SELF-TEST

6. Which of the four former goals of the Bank of Canada are in conflict with each other, and which are compatible?

7. If the Bank of Canada wanted to decrease the money supply, should it buy or sell government bonds?

In summary, Keynesian monetary policy aims to stabilize the level of spending in the economy. If the economy is under-spending and a recessionary gap exists, then expansionary monetary policy would be used to raise spending. Similarly, if an expansionary gap exists as a result of over-spending in the economy, then contractionary monetary policy would be used to reduce that spending.

You can appreciate from the analysis that this transmission process involves several steps of cause and effect. We will see in the next section that Keynesians believe that the effect of a change in the money supply on the economy may not be very powerful. In contrast, Monetarists believe that the effects of changes in the money market are much simpler, far more direct, and certainly more potent than Keynesians believe. Let us take a look at this view.

9.3   TARGETING THE MONEY SUPPLY: MONETARIST POLICY

L03 Understand why Monetarists believe that controlling the money supply is vital.

Monetarism refers to a school of thought popularized by Nobel Prize–winning economist Milton Friedman. From the Monetarist perspective, GDP determination can be summarized in a single equation referred to as the **equation of exchange**:

$$MV = PQ \qquad \text{[9.4]}$$

M is the supply of money that we have been discussing in this chapter. V refers to the **velocity of money** (also called the "velocity of circulation") and needs some explanation. If, for example, the GDP in a given year was $800 billion and the supply of money was $80 billion, the velocity would be ten. What this means is that every loonie, every $5 bill, every $10 bill, and so on, changes hands, from person to person, an average of ten times during the year. The velocity of money is, therefore, the rate at which the money supply turns over in generating income.

Q refers to the quantity of goods and services sold (real GDP), whereas P is a composite (or index) of their prices.

Remember the very simple economy that we briefly looked at in Chapter 3. In this economy, Bill, the baker, suddenly discovers that he is short of candles and so rushes over to the shop of Wick, the candle-maker, who has just produced ten candles and is selling them for $1 each. Bill pays with a $10 bill. With this $10 income, Wick decides to buy a new pair of jeans produced by Tammy, the tailor, and pays for them with the $10 bill. Feeling a little hungry after working on the jeans, Tammy decides to indulge herself by spending the $10 bill on five loaves of fresh bread, at $2 a loaf, from Bill, the baker. (All right, so she is more than a little hungry!) Now, in summarizing this economic activity, we could use the method that Statistics Canada uses, as described in Chapter 4, by adding the market value of each product—that is, by multiplying the quantity of each product (Q) by its price (P) and then aggregating the totals.

monetarism: an economic school of thought that believes that cyclical fluctuations of GDP and inflation are usually caused by changes in the money supply.

equation of exchange: a formula that states that the quantity of money times the velocity of money is equal to nominal GDP (price times real GDP).

velocity of money (or circulation): the number of times per year that the average unit of currency is spent (or turns over) buying final goods or services.

$$
\begin{aligned}
10 \text{ candles @ \$1} &= \$10 \\
1 \text{ pair of jeans @ \$10} &= \$10 \\
5 \text{ loaves @ \$2} &= \$10 \\
(Q \times P) & \qquad \$30
\end{aligned}
$$

However, we could have worked out the value of market sales by simply noting that these sales were financed by a single $10, which was used (spent) three times.

$$
\begin{aligned}
\$10 \times 3 &= \$30 \\
(M \times V)
\end{aligned}
$$

In other words, we can see that:

$$\text{Nominal GDP} = Q \times P \qquad \text{[9.5]}$$

ADDED DIMENSION   The Velocity of Money

The velocity of money can also be used to describe the number of times that money is actually used each year. In this case, we are looking at money used to finance all sorts of expenditures, including stock market transactions, second-hand sales, and all those other transactions that we do not include in GDP. Defining V this way results in the following equation of exchange:

$$MV = PT$$

where V relates to the number of times money is used to finance *all transactions* and T is the number of transactions (not just those involving GDP items).

We are usually more interested in looking at the effect of money changes on GDP rather than its effects on all transactions

in an economy during a year. However, it is only a short step from one formulation to the other, since the level of GDP is usually closely related to the total of all transactions that take place.

Determining the actual size of V in Canada very much depends on which definition of money is used. This is because the actual velocity cannot be directly measured but is obtained by dividing nominal GDP (P × Q) by the size of the money supply (M). If we use the narrow (M1) definition, empirical data show that the value of V increased steadily from approximately 7.5 in the early 1960s to over 17 in the early 1990s. Using the broader (M2) definition of money yields a value of V that has remained a fairly constant 3 over the last 30 years.

But could also be measured as:

$$\text{Nominal GDP} = M \times V \qquad \textbf{[9.6]}$$

It, therefore, follows that MV equals PQ, in that they both equal nominal GDP. In short, the two terms equal each other *by definition*.

Now that this basic equation has been established, we can explore some of its implications. A fundamental assumption of the Monetarists is that one can treat V (the velocity of money) as a constant, thus:

$$M\bar{V} \equiv PQ$$

(The line above V indicates that the term is a constant; the triple equality symbol means that this is an identity—it is true by definition—rather than just an equality.)

If velocity is, indeed, constant, then we immediately know that any change in M will have an impact on the right side of the equation: on prices or on the quantity of goods that, combined as we just saw, is the same thing as nominal GDP. That is, if M were to rise by 10 percent, then either the price level or quantity of goods and services produced or a combination of the two would also rise by 10 percent.

If we were to assume further that the economy is currently at full-employment output, then Q would not be able to rise (at least not permanently), and any increase in M would have a direct and proportional impact on P—the price level. That is, if both V and Q are constant, then increases in M translate into inflation—pure and simple. Thus the phrase "inflation is a monetary phenomenon."

We should also point out that Monetarists believe that V is constant because they feel that individuals only demand money for transaction purposes; that is, there is no asset demand for money. For Monetarists, it is irrational for anybody to hold "idle balances" of money for any purpose. They suggest that there are a whole host of financial instruments (bonds, term deposits, and so on) that are as safe and convenient as money but also provide the individual with an income. Therefore, if people find themselves with excess cash balances—because, for example, of a recent increase in the supply of money—they will divest themselves of these excess balances by purchasing either financial instruments or goods and services rather than hold those balances.

According to the Monetarist position, an increase in the money supply would cause a big drop in interest rates and a significant increase in investment spending. It will *also* cause an increase in consumption of major consumer goods, such as cars, as people try to rid themselves of what they see as excess cash balances. If the economy is experiencing a recessionary gap, then this additional demand will raise the *real* GDP. If, however, the economy is already at full-employment equilibrium, then the increase will directly raise only *nominal* GDP by pushing up prices.

> ### ⏵ ADDED DIMENSION   Milton Friedman: Mr. Monetarist
>
> Milton Friedman, the 1976 Nobel Prize winner for economics, had an enormous influence on modern economic thinking. As a lifetime professor at the University of Chicago, he was most famous for his work in the field of monetary policy. However, he was also influential in many other areas, as illustrated by his seminal works on the consumption function, the role of expectations, the idea of a negative income tax, and the concept of
>
> the natural rate of unemployment. Also, he gained fame outside of economics as a journalist for *Newsweek*, in a television documentary series, and as adviser to then-presidential candidates Barry Goldwater and Richard Nixon. His book *Capitalism and Freedom* is an elegant presentation of his laissez-faire views. He died in November 2006.

Contrasting Keynesian and Monetarist Policies

We can graphically illustrate the big difference between the two schools of thought in the diagrams that follow. The two graphs in **Figure 9.8** represent the view of Keynes who believed that the asset demand for money was fairly sensitive to changes in the interest rate. Consequently, the money demand curve is quite flat; that is, the demand is elastic. But Keynes also believed that the investment demand by firms was inelastic (not very sensitive to interest rate changes), since there are many other factors that influence their decisions. Therefore, a small change in interest rates is unlikely to have much of an impact on firms. This implies a fairly steep investment demand curve. The combination of a flat (elastic) money demand curve and a steep (inelastic) investment demand curve means that a change in money supply has only a small impact on investment and, thus, on real GDP.

Keynes believed that sometimes it is quite sensible for people to hold cash as an asset. If the money supply were to increase, it would not affect interest rates much. It is true that some people might get rid of the extra money and buy bonds, which will push up bond prices and thus reduce interest rates. However, only a small drop in interest rates would be required to make people feel comfortable holding increased amounts of money. In **Figure 9.8A**, then, an increase in the money supply of $20 billion has very little impact on the interest rate and it falls only from 6 to 5 percent. **Figure 9.8B** shows that this reduction in the interest rate does not seem to impress businesses greatly, since it encourages them to increase their investment spending only from $25 billion to $30 billion.

FIGURE 9.8	Keynesian View of an Increase in Money Supply

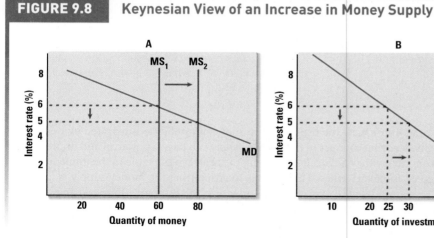
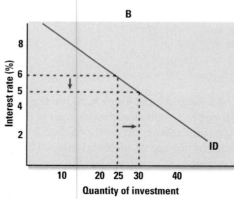

In Figure A, an increase of 20 in the money supply reduces the rate of interest from 6 to 5 percent. In Figure B, this decrease of 1 percentage point only increases investment spending by $5 (from $25 to $30).

FIGURE 9.9   Monetarist View of an Increase in Money Supply

In Figure A, an increase in the money supply from $60 to $80 causes the interest rate to drop from 6 percent to 2 percent. In Figure B, this drop causes a big change in investment spending, increasing it from $25 to $65.

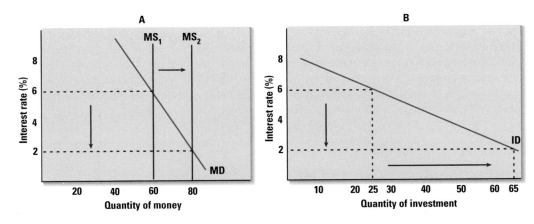

The Monetarist school, in contrast, believes that people would be foolish to hold idle cash balances because there are many types of financial investments that are as secure as cash but offer a return. Therefore, Monetarists believe an increase in the money supply would lead people to quickly get rid of the extra money by buying bonds, causing a big increase in bond price and a big drop in interest rates. In **Figure 9.9A**, an increase in the money supply from $60 to $80 causes interest rates to fall from 6 to 2 percent.

In contrast to Keynes, Monetarists believe that firms are particularly sensitive to interest rate changes, thus implying a flat investment demand curve as shown in **Figure 9.9B**. A drop of 4 percentage points has a very big impact on investment spending causing it to increase from $25 billion to $65 billion as firms take advantage of this low rate of interest.

In summary, then, the same $20 billion increase in the money supply would increase investment spending by a meagre $5 billion according to the Keynesians, but by a whopping $40 billion according to the Monetarists.

 SELF-TEST

8. If the price level increases, what effect will this have on interest rates, investment, and the aggregate quantity demanded?

9. What would be the effect on the level of investment and real income if the money supply were reduced?

10. a) If M is $100, P is $2, and Q is 500, what is the value of the velocity of money?

b) Given the same parameters as in a), if the velocity of money stays constant and assuming the economy is at full employment, what will be the level of P if M increases to $120?

Monetarist economists view the use of activist monetary policy as advocated by Keynesians with alarm. They believe that changes in the money supply can have a powerful and unpredictable impact on the economy, so they advocate restricting the central bank's role to the implementation of certain pre-agreed monetary rules. Their goal is to ensure that the money supply is increased only enough to accommodate the expected real growth in the economy. Emphasizing long-run stability, they suggest that the central bank's function is merely to ensure that the money supply is increased smoothly and predictably in line with estimates of the long-run economic growth rate. The result, they suggest, is the creation of a stable and predictable economic climate, which will be beneficial for all. In effect, this policy would replace the central bank by a simple monetary rule or at least with a computer capable of implementing such a rule.

In addition, Monetarists are highly critical of the stated goals of Keynesian monetary policy as interpreted by central banks around the world. They feel that using such policy to stimulate economic growth, while also promoting full employment, ensuring an acceptable exchange rate, and fighting inflation, is hugely over-ambitious and thus doomed to fail. It would be better, they argue, to achieve a few goals rather than fail to achieve many. Monetary policy should be geared solely to achieving the monetary goals of "preserving the internal and external value of the currency." In other words, the Bank of Canada should do what it does best: keep prices and the exchange rate stable. As we shall see, this is the present-day focus of many central banks around the world.

But it was not just Keynesian monetary policy that was attacked in the early 1990s. The Keynesian and Monetarist views both came under severe criticism and led to a whole new approach to monetary policy. Let us look at these new ideas.

9.4 CRITICISMS OF MONEY SUPPLY TARGETING

A number of economists became critical of both the Keynesian and Monetarist views because both emphasized the importance of the central bank's ability to control the money supply, which they believed was impossible. But why, exactly, do they think the Bank of Canada is unable to control the money supply?

L04 Explain why many economists are critical of attempts to target the money supply.

Firstly, although the Bank of Canada may well be able to control the amount of cash reserves in the banking system through open market operations, it cannot subsequently control the total money supply (cash plus deposits) because it cannot control the process of deposit expansion by the commercial banks. For instance, although a commercial bank may find itself with excess reserves as a result of open market operations by the Bank of Canada, it may be unwilling or unable to increase customer loans, and may not, therefore, increase the amount of deposits. As we saw in Chapter 8, a commercial bank may decide not to increase loans even though it has excess reserves if it feels that there are not enough credit-worthy customers looking for loans. As well, in times of a recession (which is when the Bank of Canada might well want to enact expansionary monetary policy) people that the banks consider credit worthy may be fearful of getting into further debt.

A second reason the Bank of Canada does not target the money supply is that even if it had total control over the money supply, it cannot know for certain what is the level of demand for money is. This means that it cannot predict in advance the extent of people's reaction to holding any given size of surplus or shortage of money. We learned earlier that if people are holding more or less money than they wish to hold, they will buy or sell bonds, thus affecting bond prices and therefore interest rates. However, since the Bank of Canada does not know how sensitive the public may be to changes in money holdings resulting from an interest change (in technical terms it cannot be certain of the slope of the money demand curve), then it cannot be sure of the extent that interest rates will be affected by a change in the money supply. And it is the interest rate that is the key variable in bringing about a change in aggregate demand. Besides all this, there are many institutional factors that also affect the demand for money. For instance, the demand for money has changed a great deal in recent decades with the increased use of credit and debit cards, the rise of Internet banking and the creation of new types of bank accounts. All this means that there are many factors affecting the demand for money and their impact is unpredictable, thus making the effect of changes in the money supply very difficult to predict.

In summary, the Bank of Canada no longer tries to target the money supply because:

- the Bank of Canada cannot control the creation of loans by the commercial banks
- the Bank of Canada cannot know for certain what the demand for money is and cannot therefore predict with certainty what effect a change in the money supply will have.

9.5 TARGETING THE INTEREST RATE

L05 Understand why most central banks around the world believe targeting the interest rate is the most effective monetary tool.

By the late 1980s, the Bank of Canada (along with many other central banks) abandoned the Keynesian monetary policy, believing that it attempted to achieve too much with too little. In addition, it rejected both the Keynesian and Monetarist policies for emphasizing the money supply as the key variable. Instead, the Bank of Canada began targeting interest rates as the main policy variable and, in addition, restricted its own role to that of controlling inflation rates. Let us see graphically what this entails by looking at **Figure 9.10**.

Suppose that the Bank of Canada wishes to dampen spending in the economy by raising interest rates. The market rate is presently 3 percent and the quantity of money demanded is Q1. If the Bank of Canada successfully targets a higher interest rate of 4 percent, then the quantity of money demanded will fall to Q2. What the bank must then do is to *accommodate* this change in the money demanded by reducing the money supply. In other words, the Bank of Canada adjusts the money supply to whatever quantity the public wishes to hold at a particular interest rate.

But why does the Bank of Canada target the money supply in this way? The answer is that, as we shall see, it has much more control over interest rates than it does over the money supply. In addition, it is easier for the Bank of Canada to communicate its policy if it targets interest rates rather than the money supply. After all, most of us are aware of the impact on us personally of a rise in interest rates; on the contrary, we are generally ignorant of, and oblivious to changes in the money supply. In other words, the Bank of Canada can more easily communicate its monetary policy when it targets interest rates rather than the money supply.

Now we need to look a little more closely at how the Bank of Canada goes about targeting interest rates. As we shall see in a moment, there is no such thing as *the* interest rate—there are, in fact, many different interest rates. However, they are all related to the "official" interest rate, which sets the trend for all other rates. The key rate for the Bank of Canada is the **overnight interest rate**, which refers to the rate of interest that commercial banks charge each other on short-term loans. As we saw in Chapter 8, it is often the case that one commercial bank may find itself with insufficient reserves after cheques have been cleared for the day, while another bank may have surplus reserves. The rate at which these loans are transacted is called the *overnight interest (or lending) rate* and can fluctuate daily as the cash requirements of the banks change. Now, the Bank of Canada can exercise a huge influence on this overnight rate. It does this by setting a target for that rate (it does

overnight interest rate: the interest rate that commercial banks charge one another on overnight loans.

FIGURE 9.10

The present equilibrium rate is 3 percent and the quantity of money demanded Q$_1$. When the bank targets a higher interest rate of 4 percent, it must reduce the money supply to Q$_2$ to accommodate the lower quantity demanded.

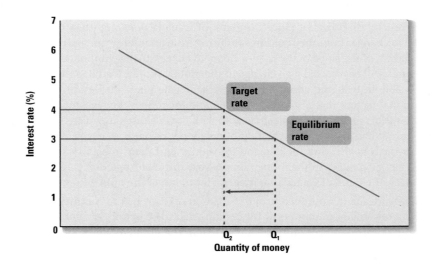

this eight times a year on pre-announced dates) and this **target for the overnight rate**, as it is called, is the midpoint of the Bank's 50-basis-point (0.5 percent) operating band—the range of acceptable interest rates. For example, when the operating band extends from 2.25 percent to 2.75 percent, the target for the overnight rate is set at 2.5 percent. The **bank rate** is the upper limit (2.75 percent) of this band and is the rate at which the Bank will lend to commercial banks. The lower limit (known as the *Bankers' deposit rate*) is the rate that the Bank will pay on any deposits made by those same institutions.

The overnight interest rate will always be within the Bank of Canada's operating band. Why should that be? Well, suppose that the bank rate (the top of the operating band) happens to be 2.75 percent and the actual overnight rate is 3 percent. Why would a commercial bank that is short of cash reserves borrow from the other banks at 3 percent when it could easily borrow funds from the Bank of Canada at 2.75 percent? It wouldn't. Alternatively, suppose that the overnight rate is 2 percent, which is below the bankers' deposit rate (the bottom of the range) of 2.25 percent. In this instance, why would a commercial bank that finds itself with excess reserves lend money to another bank at 2 percent when it could earn 2.25 percent by depositing the money with the Bank of Canada? Again, it wouldn't. In short, the overnight interest rate must fall somewhere within the Bank of Canada's operating band.

However, that is not good enough for the Bank of Canada; it tries to ensure that the overnight rate is as close as possible to its target rate. It accomplishes this using open-market operations (the ones we discussed earlier). For instance, if the overnight rate is above the Bank's target, it will *buy* bonds so that the amount of money is increased, thereby pushing the interest rate down. Conversely, if the overnight rate is below the Bank's target, it will *sell* bonds, decreasing the money supply and increasing the interest rate.

The target for the overnight rate is often referred to as the Bank's *key interest rate* or *key policy rate* in that it is a trend-setting rate for the whole economy. This rate may be changed on any of the eight "fixed" dates during the year. When the interest rate is changed, it sends a clear signal about the way the Bank wants interest rates to go. To the average consumer considering the purchase of a new house or car, the interest rate is one of the most important of all economic statistics. It has the power to shape the future of most of us, whether we are interest earners or interest payers. To a company considering capital investment, a change in interest rates—compared with its expected rate of return—will often tip the decision of whether or not to go ahead.

It is important to realize that the bank rate is just one of the many rates that make up the whole interest-rate structure. For example, the rate that commercial banks charge their best customers, the prime rate, is just slightly higher than the bank rate. Moving up the scale, the mortgage rate would be next and then, above that, the personal loan rate. All the various rates on savings would be below the bank rate, with the highest interest rate paid on large sums of money that are committed for a long time, and the lowest interest rate paid on small sums invested for short periods. When we speak of a change in the interest rate, we are referring to the whole interest-rate structure.

target for the overnight rate: the Bank of Canada's key policy interest rate; it is the midpoint of the Bank's 50-basis-point operating band.

bank rate: the rate of interest payable by the commercial banks on loans from the Bank of Canada.

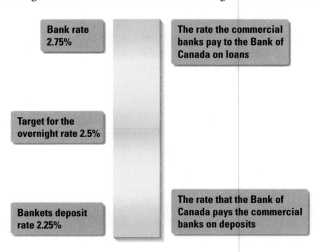

The following visual gives you some idea on interest rate structure with approximate rates at March 2011.

Credit card rate	**20**%
Personal loan rate (3-year)	**8.5**%
Mortgage rate (5-year)	**4.75**%
Prime rate	**3.0**%
Bank rate	**1.25**%
Savings rate (long term, large amount)	**1.25**%
Savings rate (short term, small amount)	**0.05**%

Therefore, a drop in the bank rate signals expansionary policy, which we now know means that credit is more freely available and cheaper. Conversely, a contractionary policy, which means credit is harder to obtain, is reflected in a higher bank rate.

9.6   TARGETING INTEREST RATES: ANTI-INFLATIONARY MONETARY POLICY

L06 Understand why anti-inflationary policy emphasizes targeting the interest rate.

As we have mentioned, the Bank of Canada now targets the interest rate rather than the money supply as its main tool of policy. However, perhaps more significant than that is the change in its targeted goal. Its present approach is to:

> Contribute to solid economic performance and rising living standards for Canadians by keeping inflation low, stable, and predictable.

In other words, the Bank tries to preserve both the internal value and the external value of currency. The Bank's current mission is to maintain low inflation rates and a stable exchange rate. Its recent target has been an inflation rate between 1 and 3 percent per year. In this, it has been markedly successful. Recent inflation rates are in stark contrast to the experience of most of the 1970s and 1980s. Following the OPEC-imposed oil price increases of the early 1970s, inflation rates around the world, Canada included, were in the range of 8 to 12 percent per year. In addition to holding the rate of inflation down, the bank is also concerned with the external value of the currency (the exchange rate), with an eye to maintaining its stability.

Those who support this new monetary policy argue that the underlying purpose of preserving the internal as well as external value of a country's currency is to create the right atmosphere for investment. Price stability is the key condition for stimulating investment and thus in maintaining the highest possible levels of productivity, real incomes, employment, and global competitiveness. As we saw in Chapter 4, the worst enemy of new investment is uncertainty. High rates of inflation, or even unpredictable changes in the inflation rate, create an atmosphere of uncertainty. Foreign investors, in particular, need the assurance that both the external value (the

ADDED DIMENSION   The Correct Measure of Inflation?

When the Bank of Canada sets an inflationary-control target range, such as the 1 to 3 percent range mentioned in this chapter, it has always been an unstated assumption that this range referred to changes in Canada's CPI (consumer price index) as measured monthly by Statistics Canada. Other central banks around the world (but, interestingly, not the U.S. Federal Reserve Board) that also have explicit inflation targets also target domestic consumer-price indexes, such as the CPI.

However, some central bankers are now suggesting that the prices of such assets as houses and shares should also be taken into account. That is because surging house prices (for example) can occur, even though inflation, measured in the conventional sense, is tame. The result is distorted price signals that encourage too much investment in housing and, as a result, too little saving in the economy as a whole. This would, in turn, result in too little investment in other industries in the economy.

It is easy to see how this idea has recently surfaced. Thanks to low inflation in most countries around the world in the last few years, interest rates have remained at near record lows. To achieve these low interest rates, more liquidity has been pumped into the economy, and this additional liquidity has, in the last few years, spilled over into rapidly rising house prices rather than an increase in the CPI. So, where might this leave us? Perhaps the conventional idea that inflation can be described as "too much money chasing too few goods" now should be revised to say "too much money chasing too few assets."

exchange rate) and the internal value (the price level) of a currency will not change dramatically in the near future. In short, uncertainty and the lower levels of investment spending that go with it reduce the rate of economic growth and the prosperity of the nation.

Given this, the federal government and the Bank of Canada made a joint statement in December 1993 attempting to generate confidence in the economy. They announced their objective of keeping inflation between 1 and 3 percent. Furthermore, government and the bank made it clear that more target-range announcements would be forthcoming.

We have already seen that controlling inflation means preventing aggregate demand from becoming too strong, and this is done by keeping the pace of monetary expansion in line with economic growth and, occasionally, by using contractionary monetary policy.

Let us now turn to the other part of the Bank of Canada's new mandate—preserving the value of Canada's flexible exchange rate. Is this possible if the bank is focused primarily on an anti-inflationary monetary policy? In fact, not only is it possible, but these two goals are quite compatible. The most noticeable effect of a tight monetary policy is a higher interest rate. These same higher interest rates, which dampen spending and keep inflation low, will also encourage foreigners to hold Canadian securities, which as we shall see in more detail in Chapter 11, increases the demand for the Canadian dollar and strengthens its value on international money markets. The higher Canadian dollar will decrease Canadian exports and cause an increase in imports. Net exports, then, will decrease. Because of flexible exchange rates, monetary policy becomes a far more effective anti-inflation tool. We can show this schematically.

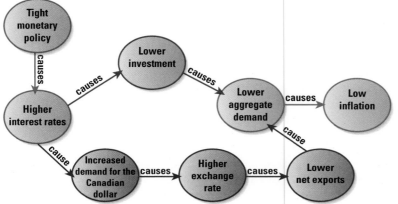

Contracting the money supply results in lower inflation.

9.7 CRITICISMS OF INTEREST RATE TARGETING

L07 Understand some of the recent criticisms of anti-inflationary monetary policy.

The most serious criticism of anti-inflationary monetary policy is that because the Bank of Canada is overly concerned about controlling inflation, it will lose sight of other equally valid goals, such as economic growth and low unemployment.

An example of this concern can be found in a study done by Professor Pierre Fortin of the University of Quebec. Fortin points out that between 1981 and 1989, real short-term interest rates were about 1 percent higher in Canada than in the United States, but between 1990 and 1996, the gap rose to 3.6 percent. He attributes these higher interest rates to the zeal with which the Bank of Canada pursued an anti-inflationary monetary policy. Further, Fortin and others argue that these high interest rates cost the Canadian economy dearly in the form of lost GDP and higher unemployment. Along the same lines, a recent American study argues that a modest amount of inflation, say, 2 to 3 percent, is a necessary lubricant for economic growth.

The second criticism of anti-inflationary policy is that by using high interest rates to control inflation, the central bank has helped increase the cost of servicing the national debt. Just a 1 percentage point difference in interest rates translates into a $5 billion difference in the annual interest payments that government has to make. Many observers have suggested that especially in the early 1990s, the Bank of Canada could have reduced interest rates significantly without triggering inflation. The benefit of doing so would not only have meant higher growth and employment as previously mentioned, but also lower budget deficits and debt.

Review

CHAPTER SUMMARY

In this chapter, you learned that the interest rate is the price of money and, like other prices, it is determined by the forces of supply and demand. The rest of the chapter looked at three contrasting monetary policies. The first two, the Keynesian and the Monetarist approaches, both target the money supply though supporters disagree on how this works and how effective it is. The third approach is the one currently used by the Bank of Canada and targets the interest rate.

9.1a The Bank of Canada is able to control the amount of money in the economy because it controls the amount of currency (reserves). It also acts as:

- government's bank
- the bankers' bank
- auditor and inspector of the commercial banks
- regulator of the money supply

9.1b *Money demand* can be subdivided into:

- the transactions demand, which depends on the level of nominal GDP
- the asset demand, which varies inversely with the rate of interest

9.1c The *interest rate* is the price of money and, like other prices, it is determined by the interaction of supply and demand.

- A higher interest rate is caused either by an increase in the demand for, or a decrease in the supply of, money.
- A lower interest rate is caused either by a decrease in the demand for, or an increase in the supply of, money.

9.2a Keynesian monetary policy puts emphasis on the power of the central bank to control the money supply. It does this using one of two tools: open market operations and the switching of government deposits.

9.2b The aim of the policy is to produce steady economic growth, an exchange rate that ensures a viable balance of trade, stable prices and full employment.

9.2c Expansionary monetary policy, according to Keynes, operates through the transmission process: an increase in the money supply reduces the interest rate, which increases investment spending and, therefore, aggregate expenditures and demand. The result is higher real GDP and a higher price level. Contractionary policy implies a reduction in the money supply, an increase in the interest rate, and lower investment, aggregate expenditure, and demand. The result is lower prices (and, therefore, inflation) and a lower real GDP.

9.3a Monetarism is based on the equation of exchange:

$$MV = PQ$$

9.3b Monetarists believe that changes in money supply have a big impact on the economy because the money demand curve is steep and the investment demand curve is flat. Keynesians believe that the money demand curve is flat and the investment demand curve is steep, so changes in money supply have only a small impact on the economy.

9.4 Attempts to target the money supply have been criticized because:

- the Bank of Canada cannot control the creation of loans by commercial banks
- the slope of the money demand curve is uncertain
- the position of the money demand curve is uncertain

9.5 The Bank of Canada sets a target for the overnight interest rate at the mid-point of a 0.5 percent operating band. It then *accommodates* the supply of money to whatever the quantity demanded might be at that interest rate.

Practise and learn online with Connect, where you can find the Answered Questions and the Unanswered Problems for all chapters of this textbook's Study Guide section.

9.6 The present policy of the Bank of Canada is to keep inflation within the range of 1 to 3 percent. In doing so, it aims to preserve the internal and the external value of the currency. This can be done by keeping interest rates high, which reduces domestic spending and encourages foreign investment.

9.7 The Bank of Canada's current anti-inflationary policy has come under criticism for keeping interest rates higher than they need be. The result has meant lower growth, higher unemployment, and big government budget deficits because of the high interest costs.

NEW GLOSSARY TERMS AND KEY EQUATIONS

asset demand for money   294
bank rate   313
contractionary monetary policy   300
equation of exchange   307
expansionary monetary policy   300

interest rate   291
monetarism   307
monetary policy   299
open-market operations   300
overnight interest rate   312

target for the overnight rate   313
transactions demand for money   293
transmission process   304
velocity of money (or circulation)   307

Equations:

[9.1] $\text{Rate of return (rate of interest)} = \dfrac{\text{coupon interest} +/- \text{change in the bond price}}{\text{Price paid for bond}} \times 100$ **page 298**

[9.2] $r = \dfrac{F - P}{P} \times \dfrac{365}{\text{\# days to maturity}}$ **page 304**

[9.3] $P = \dfrac{\dfrac{365}{\text{\# days to maturity}} \times F}{\dfrac{365}{\text{\# days to maturity}} + r}$ **page 304**

[9.4] $MV = PQ$ **page 307**

[9.5] $\text{Nominal GDP} = Q \times P$ **page 307**

[9.6] $\text{Nominal GDP} = M \times V$ **page 308**

STUDY TIPS

1. Once again, it is very important not to confuse the concepts of money and income. Money is a commodity, and like all commodities there are substitutes for it and a price attached to its ownership. The price of money, as we point out in this chapter, is the rate of interest. When we talk about the demand for (the stock of) money, we are not thinking of (the flow of) income. So, try to think of money as something that can be bought and sold like any other commodity.

2. Perhaps you can get a good handle on the idea of what drives the transactions demand for money by realizing how it changes over the years. Thirty-five years ago, when one of the authors was still at school, he needed only $50 in cash to make normal day-to-day purchases for a week. These days, he finds himself having to take out twice that amount. Although he is somewhat richer,

the main reason for his increased demand for money is the increase in prices of goods and services that has occurred over the years. Inflation, by itself, will cause the demand for money to increase. In addition, the transactions demand for money will also increase as both individuals and countries get richer in real terms.

3. The relationship between interest rates and bond prices is quite straight-forward. Allowing for differences in risks and term lengths, the rates of return (the interest rate) on various bonds tend to be very similar. Let us say you earn $5 a year on a bond that sells for $50. This is the same return (10 percent) as earning $2 on a bond selling for $20. What if it were possible to earn $5 on some other bond worth $20—a return of 25 percent a year. Everyone would be clamouring to purchase these higher-yielding bonds. And what would happen to their price?

It would increase and continue to increase until its return was the same as all other similar securities. When it gets to a price of $50, it is no more or less attractive than other bonds. As the price of a bond rises, the interest earned by the bond holder declines.

4. Though the idea of open-market operations at first seems unnecessarily subtle and complicated, it involves nothing more than the transfer of cash for bonds between the Bank of Canada and anyone who wants to buy or sell bonds. But since the central bank is doing the buying and selling, the effect is a little different from normal trading. For instance, if I buy a bond from you, I will have less money, but you will have more. The net effect on the economy's money supply is zero. However, when money goes into the Bank of Canada, the nation's money supply is reduced, and when money comes out, its money supply is increased.

5. Try not to confuse the primary sale of bonds (or any other security) and the secondary sale of bonds. When an institution (including government) "floats" a new issue, that institution receives the proceeds of the sale. Any subsequent sale of the same bond is a private transfer and, apart from registering the name of the new owner, does not involve the issuing institution at all. The sale of government bonds by the Bank of Canada is a primary sale, and the proceeds go to government. Open-market operations involve mostly the buying and selling of "pre-owned" bonds; that is, they are secondary sales.

6. Do not interpret the fact that there are three approaches to monetary policy as evidence that economics is unnecessarily complicated or that economists never agree with each other. This is a natural evolution in policy-making as economic circumstances change over time.

Answered Questions

These questions can also be found online on Connect.

Indicate whether the following statements are true or false:

1. **(LO 1) T or F**   The transactions demand for money is determined by how much money people need.

2. **(LO 1) T or F**   The quantity of asset demand for money that people wish to hold increases as the rate of interest falls.

3. **(LO 1) T or F**   The interest rate is determined by savings and investment.

4. **(LO 1) T or F**   An interest rate above equilibrium will lead to a surplus of money.

5. **(LO 2) T or F**   One way that the Bank of Canada can increase the money supply is to purchase bonds in the open market.

6. **(LO 2) T or F**   The biggest asset on the balance sheet of the Bank of Canada is notes in circulation.

7. **(LO 2) T or F**   Contractionary monetary policy will result in a rightward shift in the AD curve.

8. **(LO 2) T or F**   An increase in money supply, according to Keynes, will cause investment and real GDP to increase.

9. **(LO 3) T or F**   The velocity of money refers to the number of times a particular product is bought and sold in the period of a year.

10. **(LO 3) T or F**   The equation of exchange is: MV = PQ.

Basic (Questions 11–23)

11. **(LO 5)** What is the name of the interest rate that the Bank of Canada charges to the commercial banks?
    a) The prime rate
    b) The commercial rate
    c) The bank rate
    d) The loan rate

12. **(LO 1)** What is the demand for money?
    a) The same as the demand for income
    b) The transactions demand plus asset demand
    c) The transactions demand minus asset demand
    d) Whatever the Bank of Canada determines it to be

13. **(LO 2)** What is the effect of an increase in the money supply?
    a) It will lower the interest rate.
    b) It will increase the interest rate.
    c) It will decrease the demand for money.
    d) It will decrease the quantity of investment spending.

14. **(LO 2)** What is the effect of expansionary monetary policy?
    a) The money supply increases, and interest rates rise.
    b) The money supply increases, and interest rates fall.
    c) The money supply decreases, and interest rates rise.
    d) The money supply decreases, and interest rates fall.

15. **(LO 2)** What is true about the quantity of asset money demanded?
    a) It varies directly with nominal GDP.
    b) It varies inversely with nominal GDP.
    c) It varies inversely with the interest rate.
    d) It varies directly with real GDP.

16. **(LO 2)** What is the effect of expansionary monetary policy?
    a) It causes the aggregate demand curve to shift right.
    b) It causes the aggregate demand curve to shift left.
    c) It causes a movement down the aggregate demand curve.
    d) It causes a movement up the aggregate demand curve.

17. **(LO 2)** When does the demand for money curve shift to the left?
    a) If nominal GDP increases
    b) If the interest rate increases
    c) If the price level decreases
    d) If real GDP increases

Table 9.1 contains data relating to the money market. Refer to this table to answers questions 18 and 19.

TABLE 9.1

Rate of Interest (%)	Asset Demand for Money ($)	Transactions Demand for Money ($)	Total Demand for Money ($)
4	100	70	_____
5	90	70	_____
6	80	70	_____
7	70	70	_____
8	60	70	_____

18. **(LO 2)** If the supply of money is $150, what is the value of the equilibrium interest rate?
    a) 4 percent
    b) 5 percent
    c) 6 percent
    d) 7 percent

19. **(LO 2)** What are the implications if the current supply of money is $160 and the interest rate is 7 percent?
    a) The interest rate will fall.
    b) The interest rate will rise.
    c) The asset demand will fall.
    d) The transactions demand will fall.

20. **(LO 1)** Which of the following is the most important function of the Bank of Canada?
    a) The collection and clearing of cheques among commercial banks
    b) Regulating the supply of money
    c) Holding the reserves of commercial banks
    d) Issuing new currency

21. **(LO 3)** Suppose that in a particular economy M = 200, P = 2, Q = 500, and V = 5. What is the value of nominal GDP?
    a) 200
    b) 400
    c) 500
    d) 1000

22. **(LO 2)** According to the Keynesian transmission process, what effect will an increase in the money supply have?
    a) An increase in the interest rate, an increase in investment spending, and an increase in GDP
    b) An increase in the interest rate, an increase in investment spending, and a decrease in GDP
    c) An increase in the interest rate, a decrease in investment spending, and a decrease in GDP
    d) A decrease in the interest rate, an increase in investment spending, and an increase in GDP
    e) A decrease in the interest rate, a decrease in investment spending, and a decrease in GDP

Refer to **Figure 9.11** to answer questions 23, 24, and 25.

23. **(LO 2)** What does curve MD2 represent?
    a) The asset demand for money
    b) The transactions demand for money
    c) The investment demand
    d) The stock of money
    e) The total demand for money

Intermediate (Questions 24–31)

24. **(LO 2)** How would people react if the interest rate were 3 percent?
    a) They would sell bonds, which would cause bond prices to fall and the interest rate to rise.
    b) They would buy bonds, which would cause bond prices to fall and the interest rate to rise.

FIGURE 9.11

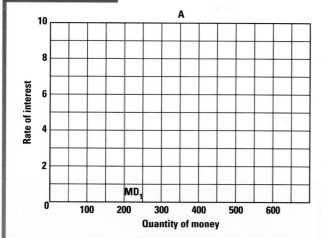

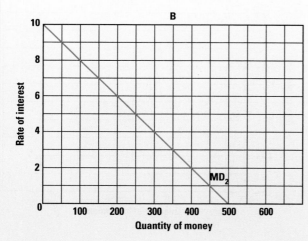

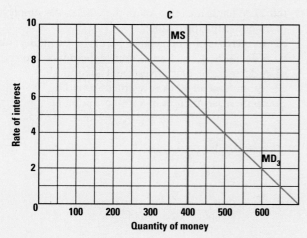

c) They would sell bonds, which would cause bond prices to rise and the interest rate to rise.
d) They would buy bonds, which would cause bond prices to rise but have an uncertain effect on the interest rate.

25. **(LO 2)** Suppose that the economy is in equilibrium and each dollar held for transaction purposes is spent, on average, five times per year. What can we infer from this?
a) That nominal GDP is $1000.
b) That real GDP is $1200.
c) That money supply is $1000.
d) That nominal GDP is $400.
e) None of the above can be inferred.

26. **(LO 1)** In which of the following cases would the quantity of money demanded be the greatest?
a) When nominal GDP is $200 billion and the interest rate is 6 percent
b) When nominal GDP is $100 billion and the interest rate is 6 percent
c) When nominal GDP is $100 billion and the interest rate is 8 percent
d) When nominal GDP is $200 billion and the interest rate is 8 percent

27. **(LO 1)** What effect will a lower price of bonds have on interest rates?
a) It will raise interest rates.
b) It will lower interest rates.
c) It could either raise or lower interest rates.
d) There is no connection between the price of bonds and interest rates.

28. **(LO 2)** Advocates of Keynesian monetary policy see all of the following, except one, as goals that monetary policy can help achieve. Which is the exception?
a) Steady interest rates
b) Steady growth in real GDP
c) Stable prices
d) Full employment

29. **(LO 2, 5)** Which of the following would be appropriate in an economy experiencing an inflationary gap?
a) A tighter monetary policy that decreased money supply
b) An easy monetary policy that increased money supply
c) Lower interest rates
d) A lower exchange rate

30. **(LO 2, 5)** Which of the following would be appropriate in an economy experiencing a recessionary gap?
    a) A tighter monetary policy that decreased money supply
    b) An easy monetary policy that increased money supply
    c) Higher interest rates
    d) A higher exchange rate

31. **(LO 7)** What is the most serious criticism of anti-inflationary monetary policy?
    a) Monetary policy is probably ineffective in fighting inflation.
    b) Overemphasis on controlling inflation ignores the equally valid goals of low unemployment and economic growth.
    c) Maintaining internal price stability means losing control of the exchange rate.
    d) The monetary rules implied by this version of monetary policy are too rigid.

Advanced (Questions 32–35)

32. **(LO 6)** Why does the Bank of Canada presently focus its monetary policy on maintaining the value of the Canadian dollar internally and externally?
    a) Because it believes that a monetary rule approach to monetary policy is the best way to go
    b) Because it believes that this approach will also achieve full employment
    c) Because it believes that this approach will help achieve a balanced budget
    d) Because it believes that interest rates must remain stable
    e) Because it believes that the twin goals of stable prices and low unemployment are not compatible

Refer to **Figure 9.12** to answer questions 33, 34, and 35.

33. **(LO 2)** If the money supply is equal to 180, what are the values of the interest rate and investment spending?
    a) 4 percent and 150
    b) 8 percent and 130
    c) 10 percent and 120
    d) 12 percent and 110
    e) 12 percent and 120

34. **(LO 2)** What is the effect of an increase in the money supply of 20?
    a) Money demand increases by 20.
    b) The quantity of money increases by 40.
    c) The rate of interest increases by 2 percentage points.
    d) Investment spending increases by 10.
    e) Investment spending decreases by 20.

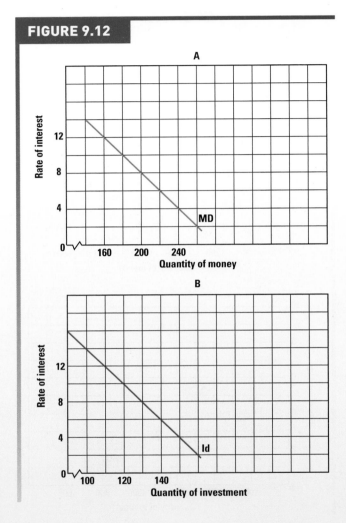

FIGURE 9.12

35. **(LO 2)** What is the effect of an increase in the supply of money from 160 to 200?
    a) An increase of 4 percentage points in the interest rate
    b) A decrease in the transactions demand for money
    c) A decrease of 40 in investment spending
    d) An increase of 40 in investment spending
    e) An increase of 20 in investment spending

Parallel Problems

ANSWERED PROBLEMS

36A. **(LO 1, 2, 6)** The money market in the country of Everton is depicted in **Figure 9.13** (all figures are in billions of dollars). The investment demand curve is shown in **Figure 9.14** and the product market in **Figure 9.15**. Both the money market and the product market are in equilibrium.

Suppose that the central bank of Everton wishes to use expansionary monetary policy and increases the money supply by $10 billion.

FIGURE 9.13

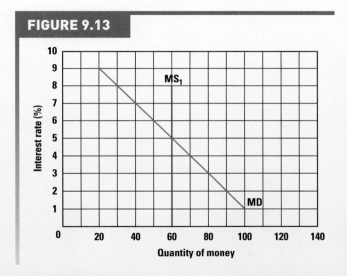

FIGURE 9.14

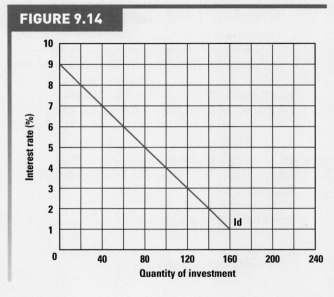

FIGURE 9.15

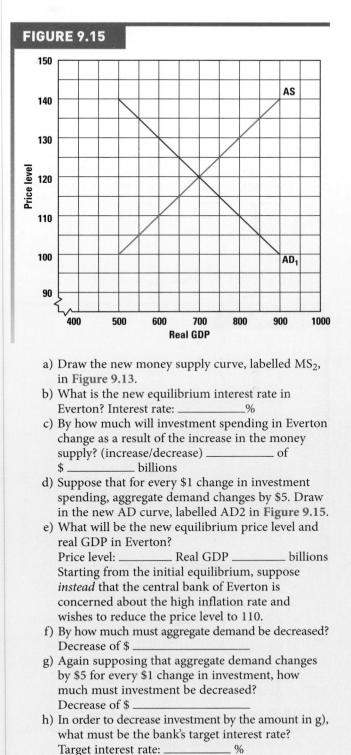

a) Draw the new money supply curve, labelled MS_2, in **Figure 9.13**.
b) What is the new equilibrium interest rate in Everton? Interest rate: _____%
c) By how much will investment spending in Everton change as a result of the increase in the money supply? (increase/decrease) _____ of $ _____ billions
d) Suppose that for every $1 change in investment spending, aggregate demand changes by $5. Draw in the new AD curve, labelled AD2 in **Figure 9.15**.
e) What will be the new equilibrium price level and real GDP in Everton?
   Price level: _____ Real GDP _____ billions
   Starting from the initial equilibrium, suppose *instead* that the central bank of Everton is concerned about the high inflation rate and wishes to reduce the price level to 110.
f) By how much must aggregate demand be decreased? Decrease of $ _____
g) Again supposing that aggregate demand changes by $5 for every $1 change in investment, how much must investment be decreased? Decrease of $ _____
h) In order to decrease investment by the amount in g), what must be the bank's target interest rate? Target interest rate: _____ %

i) At this new interest rate, by how much must the money supply be decreased in order to accommodate the new quantity of money demanded?
Decrease of $ _____

Basic (Problems 37A–45A)

37A. (LO 3) In the country of Sparta, money supply equals 11 million drams, real GDP is 70 million drams, the price level is 1.1, and the velocity of money is 7.
a) What is the value of its nominal GDP?
_____

b) If, in the next year, V remains constant and real GDP increases to 77 million drams, what must happen to money supply in order to keep prices stable?
_____

38A. (LO 2) The economy of Carlsberg is presently in equilibrium but is suffering a recession as depicted in **Figure 9.16**. The central bank of Carlsberg is introducing an expansionary monetary policy to get the economy back to the full-employment level of real GDP.

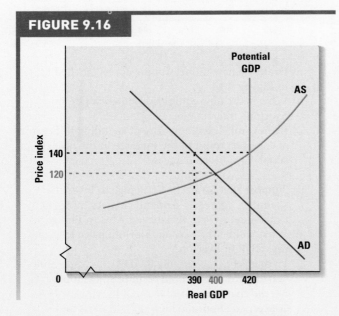

FIGURE 9.16

a) What increase in aggregate demand is necessary to achieve this? Answer: _____
b) If successful, what will be the growth rate?
Answer: _____
c) If successful, what will be the inflation rate?
Answer: _____

39A. (LO 3) In the country of Juventus, money supply is equal to $40 (billion), the velocity of circulation is 5, and real GDP is $100 (billion).

a) What is the price level in Juventus, and what is the value of its nominal GDP?
Price level: _____ Nominal GDP: _____
b) If money supply increases by 20 percent, what will be the new values of the price level and nominal GDP, assuming that V and real GDP remain constant?
Price level: _____ Nominal GDP: _____
c) What does this suggest about the connection between money supply and price level?

40A. (LO 1) Andra has just been given a $5000 one-year bond with a coupon rate of 7 percent per year. However, she needs the money now and is surprised to find that the market value of the bond has increased to $5200. What rate of return (interest) would a prospective buyer earn on this bond?
_____

41A. (LO 2) **Figure 9.17** illustrates the money demand and investment demand for the economies of Pabst and Kokanee.
a) If money supply is increased by 10, what will be the new interest rate?
Pabst: _____ Kokanee: _____
b) What will be the increase in investment spending as a result of this new interest rate?
Pabst: _____ Kokanee: _____
c) If the multiplier is 2 in each economy, what will be the increase in GDP?
Pabst: _____ Kokanee: _____
d) In which economy would monetary policy be more effective in closing a recessionary gap?

42A. (LO 2) **Figure 9.18** shows information for the economy of Tantalus.
a) If money supply is equal to 60, what are the values of equilibrium interest rate and investment spending?
Interest rate: _____% Investment: _____
b) If money supply is equal to 100, what are the values of equilibrium interest rate and investment spending?
Interest rate: _____% Investment: _____
c) If money supply is equal to 80, and money demand increases by 40, what are the values of equilibrium interest rate and investment spending?
Interest rate: _____% Investment: _____

43A. (LO 1) Explain why (or why not) each of the following will cause an increase in the transactions demand for money.
a) An increase in price level _____ .
b) An increase in real income _____ .
c) An increase in nominal income _____ .
d) An increase in both price level and nominal income by same percentage _____ .

FIGURE 9.17

Pabst

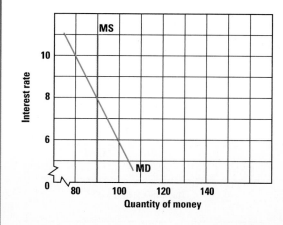

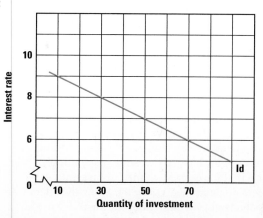

Kokanee

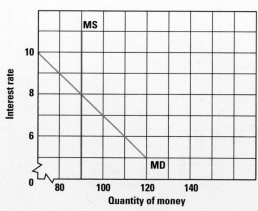

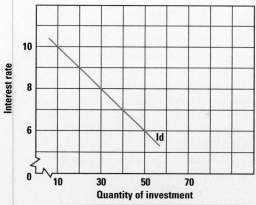

FIGURE 9.18

A

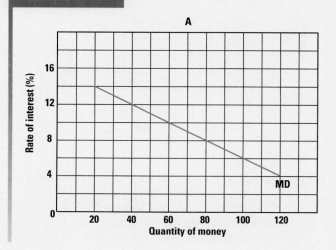

B

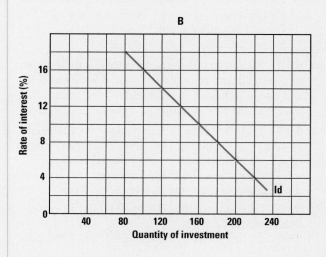

44A. **(LO 1)** What are the two determinants of the transactions demand for money?

45A. **(LO 1)** What do we mean when we say a treasury bill is sold at a discount?

Intermediate (Problems 46A–53A)

46A. **(LO 2)** **Figure 9.19** shows information for the economy of Heart.
   a) In **Figure A**, illustrate the effect of an increase in money supply, which reduces the interest rate to four percent, and in **Figure B**, the effect of the lower interest rate on the level of investment spending.
   b) What is the new level of investment spending?
   c) Suppose that for each $1 change in investment, aggregate demand changes by $4. Show the effect of this change in investment spending in **Figure C**.
   d) What is the new level of real GDP? GDP: $ _____

47A. **(LO 1)** **Table 9.2A** shows abbreviated balance sheets for the central bank in the country of Beckland. **Table 9.2B** shows tables for its whole commercial banking system. The target reserve ratio for the banks is 10 percent. (All figures are in billions of dollars.)
   a) Suppose that the Bank of Beckland buys $1 billion of government securities (T-bills) from the commercial banks. Show the immediate effects of this transaction on the balance sheets in column (1) of **Tables 9.2A** and **B**.
   b) What effect does this transaction have on the money supply of Beckland?
   Change in money supply: _____ .
   c) What effect does the transaction have on the banking system's excess reserves? _____
   d) If the banks were to fully loan-up, show the result in column (2) of the banking system's balance sheet.
   e) By how much has money supply now changed?
   Change in money supply: +/– _____ of $ _____

48A. **(LO 1)** Assume that the original price of a three-month treasury bill with redeemable value of $100 was $96, and one month later, it was sold for $96. What is the change in the rate of return on this bill? _____

49A. **(LO 3)** **Table 9.3** shows actual data for the Canadian economy for the period 1993–1997 (all money figures in billions of dollars). For each year, calculate the velocity of money. (*Hint:* You may need to rearrange the equation of exchange and divide by 100.)

What is the value of the velocity of money in each of the five years?
1993 _____ 1994 _____ 1995 _____ 1996 _____ 1997 _____

FIGURE 9.19

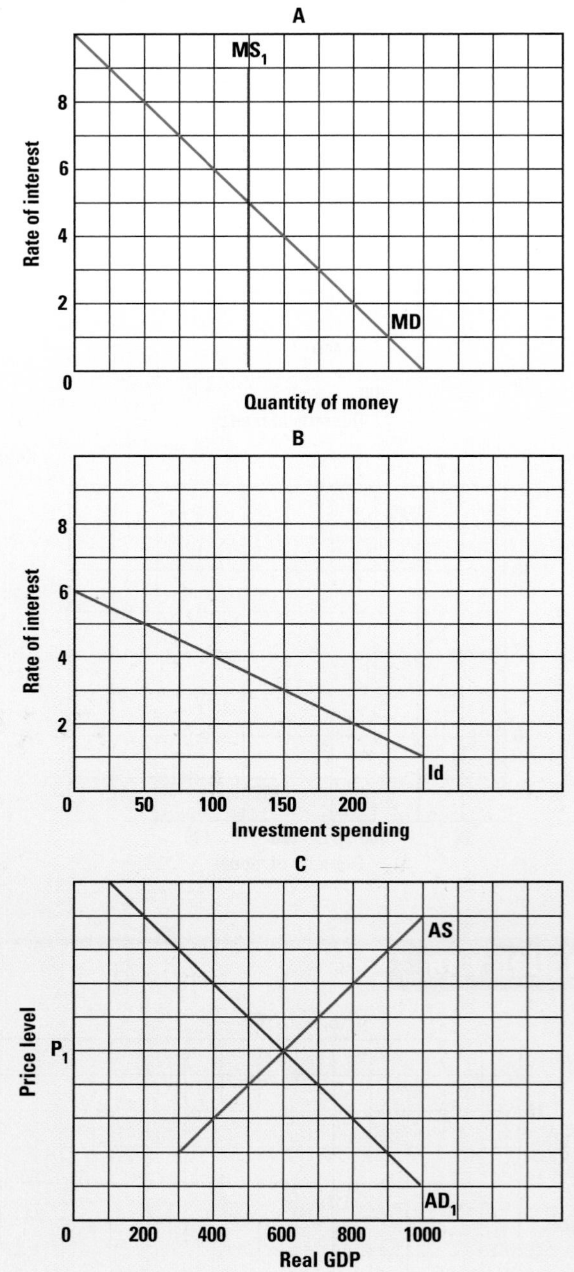

50A. **(LO 1)** Justin's grandfather left him a $10 000 bond with exactly one year left until redemption. Its coupon rate is 8 percent per annum. The current rate of interest on similar bonds is 5 percent. Unfortunately, Justin has to sell this bond to raise

TABLE 9.2

A) Central Bank of Beckland

Assets		(1)	Liabilities		(1)
Treasury bills	190	_____	Notes in circulation	185	_____
Short-term loans to banks	5	_____	Government deposits	6	_____
			Deposits of banks	4	_____

B) Beckland's Banking System

Assets		(1)	(2)	Liabilities		(1)	(2)
Reserves: in vaults	8	_____	_____	Deposits	120	_____	_____
in Bank of Beckland	4	_____	_____	Short-term loans from Bank of Beckland	5	_____	_____
Securities	30	_____	_____				
Loans to customers	90	_____	_____	Equity	7	_____	_____

TABLE 9.3

Year	M1	Price Level (1992 = 100)	Real GDP (GDP at 1992 price level)
1993	48.3	101.2	716
1994	54.2	102.4	744
1995	57.1	105.1	760
1996	63.1	106.6	770
1997	73.5	107.1	798

FIGURE 9.20

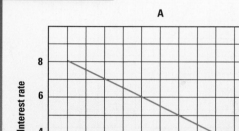

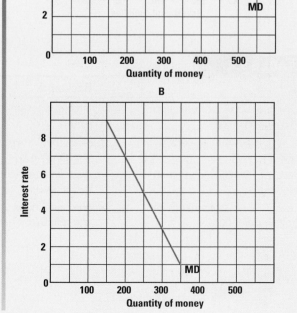

money for tuition next semester. Ignoring brokerage fees and other transaction costs, approximately how much will Justin get for his bond?

51A. **(LO 1)** How does a surplus of money disappear?

52A. **(LO 2)** Why does contractionary monetary policy imply a leftward shift in the aggregate demand curve?

53A. **(LO 2, 3)** Explain how an increase in money supply affects the interest rate, investment, and income. How do the Keynesians and the Monetarists differ in their views of this?

Advanced (Problems 54A–58A)

54A. **(LO 1)** Adriana's cousin has sent her a $20 000 bond, which pays annual interest of $1600. The bond has two years left until redemption. Adriana wants to cash in the bond to buy a truck. The current interest rate is 5 percent. Ignoring brokerage and other costs, approximately how much will Adriana get for the bond?

55A. **(LO 3)** Use **Figure 9.20** and **Figure 9.21** to answer the following questions.

FIGURE 9.21

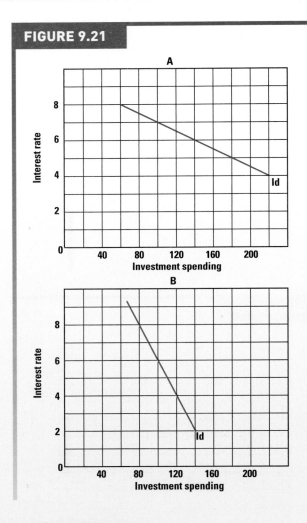

a) Which graph in **Figure 9.20** depicts the Keynsian view of the money market? Which is the Monetarist view? Keynesian view: graph _____ . Monetarist view: graph _____

b) Which graph in **Figure 9.21** depicts the Keynsian view of investment demand? Which is the Monetarist view? Keynesian view: graph _____ . Monetarist view: graph _____

c) According to the Keynesians, how much would investment spending change if money supply were to increase by $100? Increase/Decrease _____ by $ _____

d) According to the Monetarists, how much would investment spending change if money supply were to increase by $100. Increase/Decrease _____ by $ _____

56A. **(LO 2)** **Table 9.4** shows the effect of changes in various economic variables in the countries of Beckland and Heineken.

a) What is the effect of an increase of $10 million in money supply on the price level and the level of real GDP in both countries? Beckland Price change: _____ GDP change: _____ Heineken Price change: _____ GDP change: _____

57A. **(LO 2)** Would Keynesian monetary policy be more effective in dealing with a recessionary gap or an inflationary gap? Why?

58A. **(LO 3)** What do Monetarists say about the asset demand for money? Why do they believe this?

TABLE 9.4

	Beckland	Heineken
For every $10 million change in money supply:	Interest rates change by 1 percentage point.	Interest rates change by 2 percentage points.
For every 1 percentage point change in interest rates:	Investment spending and net exports change by a total of $20 million.	Investment spending and net exports change by a total of $10 million.
For every $10 million change in expenditures:	Aggregate demand changes by $20 million.	Aggregate demand changes by $30 million.
For every $10 million change in aggregate demand:	The price index changes by 1 point; and real GDP changes by $5 million.	The price index changes by 2 points; and real GDP changes by $3 million.

CHAPTER 10

INTERNATIONAL TRADE

LEARNING OBJECTIVES

At the end of this chapter, you should be able to...

L01 explain why nations trade with each other.

L02 explain why nations import certain goods, even though they can be made more cheaply at home.

L03 explain how the gains from trade are divided between trading partners.

L04 describe why some groups win and others lose as a result of freer trade, and explore trade restrictions.

L05 identify some arguments against free trade.

WHAT'S AHEAD...

We start this look at the international market of trade and finance by asking why people trade with each other and, in answering that question, we discover that all nations trade for exactly the same reason. We explain Ricardo's theory of comparative advantage which, approximately 170 years ago, helped to sort all this out. We then look at the terms of trade and show how this determines who gets what share of the increased production that results from trade. Finally, we examine some of the reasons nations have restricted trade in the past.

A Question of Relevance...

Have you looked at the little tag on your jeans lately? Were they made in Canada? What about your camera? Your fishing rod? Your tennis racket? Your MP3 player? Does it concern you that they all might well have been made abroad? It will probably not come as a surprise to you that Canada imports approximately 40 percent of all its products. Is this good for the country? Surely, it would be in Canada's interests to produce its own goods. Or would it? This chapter looks at the question of whether Canada is better or worse off as a result of international trade.

People have traded in one form or another since the dawn of time, and most of the great powers in history have also been famous traders: the Phoenicians and the Greeks; medieval Venice and Elizabethan England; and the early American colonies and modern Japan. It seems obvious that great benefits are obtained from trading, but there has always been the underlying suspicion that someone also loses as a result. For many, a great trading nation is one that consistently and, through shrewd practice, always manages to come out on top during trade negotiations. This "beggar thy neighbour" attitude was no great concern for writers immediately preceding Adam Smith, who thought it was part of the natural state of affairs that there are always winners and losers in trade. It was the job of policy makers, they felt, to ensure that their own country was always on the winning side.

It took the mind of Adam Smith to see that whenever two people enter into a voluntary agreement to trade, both parties must gain as a result. If you trade a textbook in exchange for your friend's new Guns 'n' Butter CD, you obviously want that CD more than the textbook, and your friend must want the textbook more than the CD. Trade is to the advantage of both of you, otherwise it would not take place. When we look at international trade between nations, we are simply looking at this single transaction multiplied a billion-fold. It is not really nations that trade, but individual people and firms buying from foreign individuals and firms. In many ways, the reason you trade with a friend is the same reason you buy products from a Toronto brewery, Winnipeg car dealer, or Tokyo fishing rod manufacturer: you hope to gain something as a result, and what you give up in return (usually money) is of less value to you than the thing you obtain in return.

All of which raises the question of why you personally (or a whole nation for that matter) would want to buy something rather than make it at home. In other words, why are people not self-sufficient? Why do they not produce everything that they personally consume? Well, Adam Smith had an answer for this (as for many things):

> It is the maxim of every prudent master of a family, never to make at home what will cost him more to make than to buy.[1]

There, in essence, is the main argument for trade: why make something yourself if you can buy it cheaper elsewhere? If it takes Akio three hours to make a certain product, but he can buy it elsewhere from the income he gets from one hour's work in his regular job, then why would he bother? It would pay him to do his own job for three hours; he could afford to buy three units of the product. An additional consideration is the fact that Akio cannot make most of the things he wants—or could make them only after extensive training and with the help of very expensive equipment.

---

[1] Adam Smith, Wealth of Nations (Edwin Cannan edition, 1877), p. 354.

10.1 SPECIALIZATION AND TRADE

Specialization is the cornerstone of trade. As we have seen in earlier chapters, big advantages can be gained from specialization. From an individual point of view, each of us is better suited to one thing than to another. Rather than trying to grow all our own food, make our own clothes, brew our own beer, and so on, it makes more sense to specialize in our chosen occupation and, with the proceeds, obtain things that other people can make better and more cheaply. Similarly, firms will be far more productive if they specialize in the production process, that is, make use of the division of labour. As we shall see in this chapter, there are also great benefits to be enjoyed by countries by specializing rather than by trying to be self-sufficient.

L01 Explain why nations trade with each other.

Specialization and trade go hand in hand, so it follows that more specialization means more trading. Modern nations, firms, and individuals have become increasingly specialized, and with this has come a huge increase in the volume of trade, domestically and internationally. But is there a limit to specialization? From a technical point of view, Smith thought not. But he did believe that specialization would be limited by the size of the market: the smaller the market, the smaller is the output and, therefore, the less opportunity or need for extensive specialization. The larger the market, the greater is the opportunity for specialization which would then lower the cost of producing goods. The prime driving force behind the expansion of markets is that it enables firms to produce in higher volumes at a lower cost. All things being equal (including demand), it is the cost of production, and therefore the price of the product, that induces trade. If you can produce a product more cheaply than I can, then it makes no sense for me to try to produce it myself. And why are you able to produce certain products more cheaply than I can? The answer presumably is that you possess certain advantages over me. Let us look at these advantages.

▶ ADDED DIMENSION Canada, the Great Trader

Canada is certainly one of the world's great trading nations, at least in relative terms. In 2010, for example, Canada exported $475 billion worth of goods and services and imported $507 billion. Each of these figures represents approximately 30 percent of Canada's GDP. Only a few developed countries, such as Austria and the Netherlands, trade a larger fraction. The United States and Japan, in comparison, trade only about 12 percent of their GDPs (though, of course, in actual dollars, this represents a lot more). The United States is Canada's predominant trading partner, purchasing more than all other countries combined (buying approximately 70 percent of our exports). In fact, Canada sells over twice as much to the United States as it does to all other countries combined and buys approximately 62 percent of all of its imports from the United States.

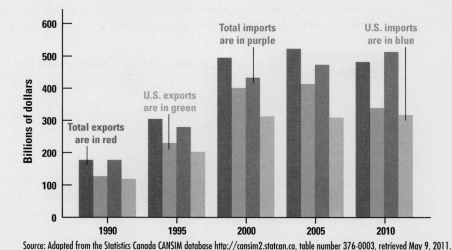

Source: Adapted from the Statistics Canada CANSIM database http://cansim2.statcan.ca, table number 376-0003, retrieved May 9, 2011.

Factor Endowment

One person has an advantage in production over others if he or she is endowed with certain natural or acquired skills or has more or better equipment or other resources. Just as there are many reasons why some people are better gardeners or truck drivers or hockey players than others, so it is with countries. A country will have a great advantage in producing and trading pineapples, for instance, if it possesses the right type of soil and climate. But the same country may well be at a disadvantage in growing coniferous trees. Another country has an advantage in producing electronic equipment if it has the right capital, the technical expertise, and a well-educated labour force. It may not, however, be able to compete with other countries in raising sheep. Just as with people, countries are well endowed in certain areas and impoverished in others. Japan has a well-educated and motivated workforce, possesses great technical expertise, and is highly capitalized, yet it is very poorly provided with arable land and possesses very few mineral resources.

It is often suggested that countries trade primarily to buy resources that they do not naturally possess. Although there is some truth in this, it often obscures the main motivation. Canada, for instance, is not endowed with a warm and sunny climate throughout the year and is unable to produce bananas commercially. However, using geodesic domes with artificial light and heating, it could grow its own bananas, but the cost would be enormous. The reason it does not grow bananas is not because it cannot but because it is cheaper to buy them from countries that grow them more easily. Most countries can overcome a resource deficiency by using different methods or other resources, but it does not make sense if this production method results in more expensive products than those obtainable from abroad.

Theory of Absolute Advantage

A country will gravitate to producing in those areas where, because of its own factor endowments, it possesses a cost advantage over other producing countries: Canada produces wheat, lumber, and minerals; Chile produces copper and other metal ores; Australia exports mineral fuels; Japan produces cars and electronic equipment; and so on. **Figure 10.1** shows the distribution of exports for these particular countries. This is what Adam Smith proposed when he put forward his *theory of absolute advantage*. Nations, like firms and individuals, should specialize in producing goods and services for which they have an advantage, and they should trade with other countries for goods and services for which they do not enjoy an advantage.

Let us work through a simple example of this theory. We will concentrate on just two countries and suppose that they produce just two products. We will assume that the average cost of producing each product remains constant. In addition, to begin with, we will further assume that each country is self-sufficient and that no trade is taking place. **Table 10.1** shows the productivity per worker (average product) of producing wheat and beans in Canada and Mexico.

TABLE 10.1	Output per Worker by Country and Industry		
	NUMBER OF BUSHELS PER DAY		
	Wheat		**Beans**
Canada	3	or	2
Mexico	1	or	4

We can see at a glance that Canada is more productive than Mexico at producing wheat, whereas Mexico is more productive than Canada at producing beans. Let us examine the possibility of gains if both countries were to specialize—Canada in wheat and Mexico in beans.

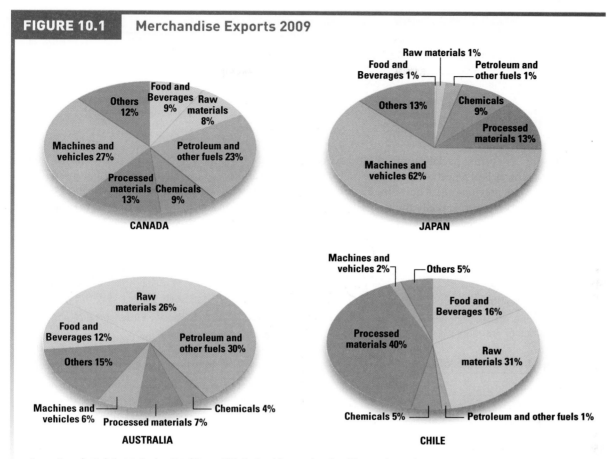

FIGURE 10.1   Merchandise Exports 2009

Source: *Commodity Trade Statistics Database,* United Nations, 2010. The United Nations is the author of the original material.

Let us suppose that initially the two countries do not trade with each other and that the working population in each country is 16 million, divided equally between the two industries. **Table 10.2** shows what the two countries produce.

TABLE 10.2	**Total Outputs before Trade**	
	TOTAL NUMBER OF BUSHELS PER DAY (in millions)	
	Wheat	**Beans**
Canada	24	16
Mexico	8	32
Total	32	48

In this case, half the working population of Canada—8 million workers—is producing wheat. Since each person is capable of producing 3 bushels of wheat, the total production of wheat is 8 million times 3, or 24 million bushels. The other figures are similarly derived.

Now, suppose that the two countries decide to enter into a free trade agreement, with each country totally specializing in what it does best: Canada producing wheat and Mexico producing beans. With the whole of the working population of 16 million in Canada producing wheat and all 16 million people producing beans in Mexico, the totals can be seen in **Table 10.3**.

TABLE 10.3	Total Outputs after Trade	
	TOTAL NUMBER OF BUSHELS PER DAY (in millions)	
	Wheat	Beans
Canada	48	0
Mexico	0	64
Total	48	64

With specialization, the two countries combined could produce an additional 16 million bushels of wheat (48 minus the previous 32) and an additional 16 million bushels of beans (64 minus the previous 48). These are referred to as the *gains from trade*. Strictly speaking, the increased total production is really the result of increased specialization. But if a country is going to specialize, it will need to trade in order to obtain those products that it is not producing. Specialization, then, implies trade, and it would be impossible to have one without the other.

✓ SELF-TEST

1. The following table shows the productivity per worker in the beer and wine industries of Freedonia and Libraland:

Output in Hundreds of Litres

	Beer		Wine
Freedonia	4	or	1
Libraland	3	or	4

a) Which country should specialize in which product?

b) Suppose that initially the working population of each country is 20 million, with 10 million working in each industry. What is the total output of the two countries?

c) Now, suppose that each country decides to specialize in the product in which it has an advantage. What will be the total output of each product, and what are the gains from trade?

10.2 THEORY OF COMPARATIVE ADVANTAGE

LO2 Explain why nations import certain goods, even though they can be made more cheaply at home.

The eminent economist David Ricardo, following in the footsteps of Adam Smith, agreed in principle with Smith, adding a subtle but important refinement to Smith's theory of trade. To see the effect of his modification, let us change our example to that of theoretical trade between the United States and the Philippines, keeping the same two products, wheat and beans. The output per worker in each country is shown in **Table 10.4.**

TABLE 10.4	Output per Worker by Country and Industry	
	NUMBER OF BUSHELS PER DAY	
	Wheat	Beans
United States	4	4
Philippines	1	3

You can see from the table that U.S. wheat production is four times that of the Philippines; similarly, the United States is one and one-third times as productive as the Philippines in producing beans. If we were to follow Smith's dictum, then presumably the United States should produce both products itself. After all, how can it possibly be of any advantage to trade with the

Philippines, since it could produce both products more cheaply? The heart of Ricardo's idea is that it is not *absolute advantage* but **comparative advantage** that provides the mutual gains from trade. Let us see exactly what this means, through an example.

Suppose you happened to be absolutely the best lawyer in town. Not only that, but you are also its greatest secretary. Given this, why would you bother to hire a secretary to do your clerical work, since you are faster and, by all measurements, more efficient than anyone you could possibly hire? The answer is that you would still hire a secretary because you could not afford not to. That is because you are very productive. Your high productivity is both a blessing and a curse. It is a blessing because you earn a great deal as a lawyer; it is a curse because you sacrifice a great deal in not being a secretary. In other words, your opportunity cost of being a lawyer is the lost salary of not being a secretary. Your opportunity cost of being a secretary is your lost earnings as a lawyer. But because you can earn *comparatively* more as a lawyer than as a secretary, you would be advised to concentrate on that career and hire someone (admittedly less productive than yourself) to act as your secretary.

Ricardo's idea of comparative advantage directs attention away from making comparisons between countries and, instead, focuses on the comparison between products. In **Table 10.4**, for instance, we might ask: how much does it cost the United States to produce wheat? One way to answer this would be to express it in dollars and cents. However, knowing that the value of money varies over time and that it is often misleading to translate one currency into another, Ricardo was at pains to express costs in more fundamental terms. One way of doing this is to express costs in terms of the number of hours it takes to produce something. For instance, if in our example the average worker in the United States can produce four bushels of beans in an average 8-hour day, then the cost of one bushel of beans would be 8/4, or 2 hours. In contrast, the cost of one bushel of beans in the Philippines would be 8/3, or about 2.66 hours. So, beans are more expensive to produce in the Philippines. However, it is more illuminating to measure costs is in terms of *opportunity costs*. This is the method chosen by Ricardo.

You will remember that the opportunity cost of producing one thing can be measured in terms of another thing that has to be sacrificed in order to get it. As far as the United States and the Philippines are concerned, the cost of producing more wheat is the sacrifice of beans, and the cost of increased bean production is the loss of wheat. Let us work out these costs for each country. The cost of employing a worker in the wheat industry is what that worker could have produced in the bean industry, assuming that the country is fully employed. In other words, for every 4 bushels of wheat that an American worker produces, the country sacrifices 4 bushels of beans. In per-unit terms, in the United States 4 bushels of wheat costs 4 bushels of beans, so 1 bushel of wheat costs 1 bushel of beans, and 1 bushel of beans costs 1 bushel of wheat.

In the Philippines the cost of 1 bushel of wheat is 3 bushels of beans, and the cost of 1 bushel of beans equals 1/3 bushel of wheat. Let us summarize these figures in **Table 10.5**.

comparative advantage: the advantage that comes from producing something at a lower opportunity cost than others are able to do.

TABLE 10.5	Opportunity Costs of Production	
	COST OF PRODUCING ONE UNIT	
	Wheat	**Beans**
United States	1 beans	1 wheat
Philippines	3 beans	1/3 wheat

Now you can understand the significance of comparative costs. If you measure the costs in absolute terms, using hours as we did in our example above, then beans are cheaper to produce in the United States. But in comparative terms, they are very *expensive*. Why is that? Because to produce beans, the United States has to make a big sacrifice in the product in which it is even more productive: wheat. Similarly, although beans, in absolute terms, are very expensive in the Philippines, they are cheap in comparative terms; to produce them the Philippines sacrifices little in wheat production because productivity in the wheat industry is low.

In this example then, the United States should specialize in producing wheat, since the opportunity cost is only one unit of beans compared with three units of beans in the Philippines. Conversely, the Philippines can produce beans comparatively cheaply, at the cost of 1/3 unit wheat, while in the United States the cost is one unit of wheat. Although the United States has an absolute advantage in both products, it has a comparative advantage only in wheat production and the Philippines has a comparative advantage in bean production.

Let us extract some further insights by showing the production possibilities of the two countries on the assumption that the size of the labour force in both the United States and the Philippines is 100 million, and that unit costs are constant.

We are assuming constant unit costs to keep the analysis simple. If you remember from Chapter 1, in reality the law of increasing costs applies, which means that the slope of the production possibilities curve is concave. Assuming constant costs means that the production possibilities curves in this chapter plot as straight lines.

The respective production possibilities for the United States and the Philippines are shown in **Table 10.6**. The 400 bushels of wheat, under option A in the United States, is the maximum output of wheat if all of the 100 (million) workers were producing 4 bushels of wheat each. Similarly, if the 100 million American workers produced only beans and no wheat, then they would also produce 400 bushels of beans as seen under option F. The figures for B, C, D, and E are derived by calculating the output if 80, 60, 40, and 20 million workers are employed in wheat production, while 20, 40, 60, and 80 million workers are employed in bean production. The figures for the Philippines are similarly obtained.

TABLE 10.6	**Production Possibilities**					
UNITED STATES: OUTPUT (millions of bushels per day)						
	A	**B**	**C**	**D**	**E**	**F**
Wheat	400	320	240	160	80	0
Beans	0	80	160	240	320	400
PHILIPPINES: OUTPUT (millions of bushels per day)						
	A	**B**	**C**	**D**	**E**	**F**
Wheat	100	80	60	40	20	0
Beans	0	60	120	180	240	300

Suppose that initially the countries do not trade with each other, with the United States producing combination C and the Philippines producing combination B. Before specialization and trade, therefore, their joint totals are as shown in **Table 10.7**.

TABLE 10.7	**Output of Both Countries before Specialization and Trade**	
	TOTAL OUTPUT (millions of bushels per day)	
	Wheat	**Beans**
United States	240	160
Philippines	80	60
Total	320	220

If the two countries now specialize, the United States producing wheat and the Philippines producing beans, their output levels would be as shown in **Table 10.8**.

TABLE 10.8	Output of Both Countries after Specialization and Trade	
	TOTAL OUTPUT (millions of bushels per day)	
	Wheat	**Beans**
United States	400	0
Philippines	0	300
Total	400	300

You can see by comparing the before and after specialization positions of the two countries that production of both products is now higher. **Table 10.9** outlines the gains from trade.

TABLE 10.9	Gains from Specialization and Trade
TOTAL OUTPUT (millions of bushels per day)	
Wheat	**Beans**
+80	+80

Thus, we can conclude that:

> As long as there are differences in comparative costs between countries, regardless of the differences in absolute costs, there is a basis for mutually beneficial trade.

What this example shows is that it is possible for both countries to gain from trade, but several questions remain. Will they? How will the increased production be shared? Will it be shared equally, or will one country receive more than the other? Discussion of the terms of trade will help answer these questions.

 SELF-TEST

2. Suppose that the labour force in Freedonia is 10 million. Six million people are producing apples, and the rest are are producing pears. Libraland's labour force is 16 million, divided equally between the production of apples and the production of pears. The labour productivity in the two countries is given in the following table:

	Output per Worker (bushels per day)		
	Apples		**Pears**
Freedonia	5	or	2
Libraland	1	or	3

Make a production possibilities table for Fredonia (A to F) and for Libraland (A to E).

a) Which is Fredonia's present combination (A–F)?

b) Which is Libraland's present combination (A–E)?

3. a) Given the data in Self-Test 2, what is the total output of the two countries for both products?

b) If each country were to specialize in the product in which it has a comparative advantage, what will be the total output of the two countries for both products?

c) What will be the gains from trade?

ADDED DIMENSION   WTO: Forum for International Cooperation or Engine of Destruction?

The World Trade Organization (WTO), created in 1995 and with 153 member nations, is the only international organization that deals with the rules of trade among nations. It catapulted into people's consciousness during the violent street protests in Seattle in November 1999. Thousands of protestors voiced their displeasure with the trend toward globalization—which they saw as being fostered by the WTO—by disrupting the organization's meetings. Although the intensity of the debate about the "good" or "evil" of globalization and the WTO has subsided recently, the issue is still an important one. Let us list some of the pros and cons of the issue.

Pros:
1. Most of those who work within the organization are seasoned bureaucrats or academics from well-known universities around the globe. The importance of growing world trade can be seen in the fact that every post–World War II example of a nation breaking out of the vicious cycle of poverty and underdevelopment has been a nation that dramatically increased its exports.
2. It is easier for concerned nations with strong labour, safety, and environmental standards to put pressure for change on nations whose standards are weak, if they are already participants in the WTO.
3. Increased trade, fostered by the WTO, has shown some dramatic benefits. An example comes from a World Bank study (using 2000–2001 data) concluding that the number of people in the world living on less than $1 a day decreased in the last twenty years by over 600 million. At no time in human history have such a large number of people been lifted out of abject poverty in so short a period.

Cons:
1. The WTO is an undemocratic organization whose members are not elected. It poses one of the biggest threats to the sovereignty of independent nations and ignores the social and cultural differences among nations.
2. Globalization reduces the effectiveness of labour, safety, and environmental standards across the globe as each nation becomes trapped in a race to the bottom as it competes to attract more foreign investment from the large transnational corporations.
3. Globalization increases the income gap between the rich and poor nations of the world. It also increases the disparity of incomes within a country, since a few big business people gain at the expense of ordinary citizens.
4. The WTO's dispute resolution panels are loaded with members who represent a corporate bias, which works against the interests of ordinary people.

We hasten to add that some very famous economists—Alan Blinder and Paul Krugman, for example—are raising serious concerns about the process of freer trade and globalization as they might affect Canada. They argue that communications technology, which allows services to be delivered electronically from afar, will put many North American middle-class jobs in jeopardy in the next two decades. The late Paul Samuelson, a giant among economists, said that "most economists oversimplify complexities about globalization" and that we need to slow this trend to help poor nations build domestic industries and give rich nations more time to retain displaced workers.

10.3   TERMS OF TRADE

L03 Explain how the gains from trade are divided between trading partners.

terms of trade: the average price of a country's exports compared with the price of its imports.

The expression **terms of trade** refers to the price at which a country sells its exports compared with the price at which it buys its imports. Statistics Canada regularly measures Canada's terms of trade using the following formula:

$$\text{Terms of trade} = \frac{\text{Average price of exports}}{\text{Average price of imports}} \times 100 \qquad \textbf{[10.1]}$$

If the worldwide demand for Canadian softwood lumber were to increase, for example, it would increase the average price of Canadian exports, with the result that the terms of trade would be said to have moved in Canada's favour. The result would be the same if Canadian prices remain the same but the price of imports drops. In either case, the sale of our exports would enable us to purchase more imports. Conversely, the terms of trade would shift against Canada if Canadian export prices dropped and/or the price of imported goods rose (see **Figure 10.2**).

FIGURE 10.2   Terms of Trade

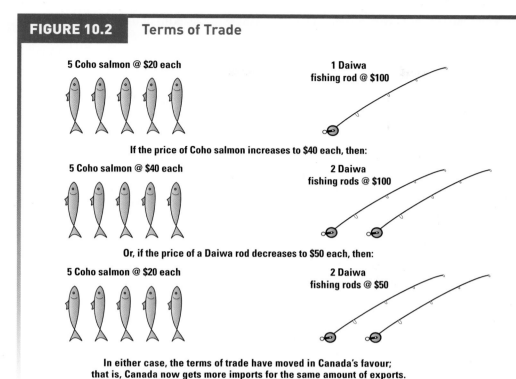

5 Coho salmon @ $20 each   1 Daiwa
                                              fishing rod @ $100

If the price of Coho salmon increases to $40 each, then:

5 Coho salmon @ $40 each   2 Daiwa
                                              fishing rods @ $100

Or, if the price of a Daiwa rod decreases to $50 each, then:

5 Coho salmon @ $20 each   2 Daiwa
                                              fishing rods @ $50

**In either case, the terms of trade have moved in Canada's favour;
that is, Canada now gets more imports for the same amount of exports.**

Changes in the terms of trade can have a significant effect on Canada's economic performance. This ratio of our exports to import prices directly affects our nominal trade balance, and indirectly affects the level of real GDP in Canada. A higher ratio reflects a situation in which most Canadians are better off since our exports would be high—which means more jobs—and the price of imports that Canadians buy would be lower. Canada's terms of trade peaked at a ratio of approximately 112 in 1973 when world commodity prices were very high, then declined to 70 in 1998. By 2003, the ratio had risen to 106 and has continued to rise as Canada's oil exports from the Alberta oil sands continue to grow and the price of oil remains high.

In our previous United States/Philippines example, we found that the country which gains the most from trade depends on the terms of trade. But let us look at what would be acceptable prices from the two countries' points of view. Remember that the United States is the wheat producer and exporter. A glance back at **Table 10.4** shows that *in the United States, one bushel of wheat costs one bushel of beans.* Given this, what price would it be willing to sell its wheat for? Presumably for as high a price as it can get, but certainly not for less than one bushel of beans. What about the Philippines? How much would it be willing to pay for wheat? Remember, **Table 10.4** tells us that *in the Philippines, one bushel of wheat costs three bushels of beans.* Therefore, we can conclude that the Philippines would certainly not pay any higher than this price and would be happy to pay less. As long as the price is above the American minimum and below the Philippines' maximum, both countries would be willing to trade. In other words, trade is possible if the price of one unit of wheat is anywhere between one and three units of beans.

We could have just as easily expressed things in terms of beans, and a glance back at **Table 10.5** shows that feasible terms of trade would be anywhere between one-third and one bushel of wheat for one bushel of beans. In other words, the feasible terms of trade will be between the costs of each product in the two countries. The final terms of trade will depend on the strength of demand in the two countries for these products.

Let us choose one particular rate among the many possible terms of trade and work out the consequences. Suppose, for instance, that the terms end up at *1 bushel of wheat = 2 bushels of beans (or 1 bushel of beans = 1/2 bushel of wheat)*. Let us now assume, since we need some point to start from, that the Philippines is quite happy consuming the 60 million bushels of beans that it was producing before it decided to specialize, as was shown in **Table 10.6**. However, because of specialization, it is now producing only beans and will therefore have 300 − 60 = 240 million bushels of beans available for export, which it sells to the United States at a rate of one bushel of beans for half a bushel of wheat. It will receive back 120 million bushels of wheat and will finish up with 60 million bushels of beans and 120 million bushels of wheat. Because of trade, it will have gained an additional 40 million bushels of wheat compared with its self-sufficient totals shown in the "Before Trade" column in **Table 10.10**.

The United States will also gain. It was the sole producer of wheat, and of the total of 400 million bushels produced, it has sold 120 million bushels to the Philippines in exchange for 240 million bushels of beans. It will end up with 280 million bushels of wheat and 240 million bushels of beans, which is 40 million bushels of wheat and 80 million bushels of beans more than when it was producing both products as shown by comparing the "Before Trade" and "After Trade" columns for the United States. In reviewing **Table 10.10** recall that we are assuming that the Philippines consumes the same 60 million bushels of beans before and after trade.

Terms of Trade and Gains from Trade, Graphically

Let us now look at each country's trading picture separately. Using a graphical approach, **Figure 10.3** shows the production possibilities curve for the United States. Before it decided to trade, this was also its consumption possibilities curve, since it could obviously not consume more than it produced. The slope of the curve is 1, which is the cost of 1 bushel of beans (that is, it equals 1 bushel of wheat).

TABLE 10.10

		PHILIPPINES	
		Before Trade	After Trade
	Beans produced	60	300
	Beans exported	0	−240
Beans consumed		**60**	**60**
	Wheat produced	80	0
	Wheat imported	0	+120
Wheat consumed		**80**	**120**
		Gain = 40 Wheat	
		UNITED STATES	
		Before Trade	After Trade
	Beans produced	160	0
	Beans imported	0	+240
Beans consumed		**160**	**240**
	Wheat produced	240	400
	Wheat exported	0	−120
	Wheat consumed	**240**	**280**
		Gain = 80 Beans and 40 Wheat	

ADDED DIMENSION   Public Opinion about NAFTA

In 1993, Canada, the United States, and Mexico formalized the North American Free Trade Agreement (NAFTA) despite considerable political opposition in both Canada and the United States. This agreement was an expansion of the earlier Canada–U.S. Free Trade Agreement of 1988. Unlike the European Union, NAFTA does not create a set of supranational governmental bodies: nor does it create a body of law that supersedes national law.

Since NAFTA, trade has increased dramatically among the three nations. For instance, from 1993 to 2004, total trade between Canada and the United States increased by 129.3 percent. Public opinion in Mexico, Canada, and the United States tends to be positive toward NAFTA. A July 2004 survey conducted in

Mexico showed that 64 percent of the Mexican public favoured NAFTA. A Canadian poll conducted in June 2003 found that 70 percent of Canadians supported NAFTA. Another survey reported in January 2004 that 47 percent of Americans thought NAFTA has been good for the United States, and 39 percent thought it had been bad for the country.

Despite their support for NAFTA, polls in Canada and Mexico have tended to show that citizens see their own country as the loser in NAFTA, and see the United States as the winner. The U.S. public has viewed Mexico as the winner and has been narrowly divided about whether the United States is a winner or loser in NAFTA.

The curve to the right is its trading possibilities curve, which shows how much the United States could obtain through a combination of specializing its production and trading. Note that the slope of the trading possibilities curve is equal to 0.5. This is the terms of trade established between the two countries: 1 bushel of wheat for 2 bushels of beans.

You can see from this graph that the United States, at one extreme, could produce the maximum quantity of 400 million bushels of wheat and keep all of it. However, before trade, the maximum amount of beans available was 400 million bushels. Now, if it wished, the United States could produce 400 million bushels of wheat, trade *all* of it, and receive in exchange 800 million bushels of beans. (We presume it is able to buy these beans from other countries as well as from the Philippines, given that the latter can only produce 300 million bushels of beans.) More likely, of course, it will opt to have a combination of both products, such as 280 million bushels of wheat and 240 million bushels of beans, as in our numerical example above.

FIGURE 10.3   U.S. Production and Trading Possibilities Curves

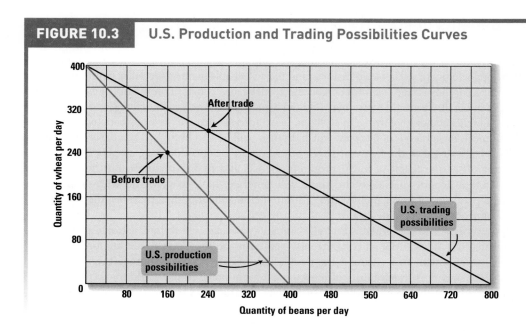

The slope of the production possibilities curve shows the cost of producing beans in the United States is equal to 1 bushel of wheat = 1 bushel of beans. The slope of the trading possibilities curve shows the terms of trade and equals 1 bushel of wheat = 2 bushels of beans. The previous maximum obtainable quantity of beans was 400 million bushels, when the United States was self-sufficient. Its new maximum, as a result of trading, is now 800 million bushels.

FIGURE 10.4   Philippines Production and Trading Possibilities Curves

The Philippines specializes in the production of beans, and its trading possibilities curve lies to the right of the production possibilities curve. In other words, whether it trades or not, the cost of beans remains the same; the cost of wheat, however, is now lower as a result of trade, since it can now obtain wheat at a cost of 2 bushels of beans per 1 bushel of wheat, whereas producing its own wheat costs 3 bushels of beans per 1 bushel of wheat.

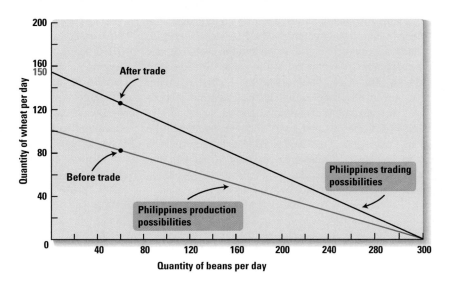

Figure 10.4 shows the situation from the point of view of the Philippines. The inside curve is its production (and therefore its consumption) possibilities curve, representing the maximum of both products that can be produced when the country is self-sufficient. The slope of the curve represents the cost of 1 bushel of beans and is equal to 1/3 bushel of wheat. The outer curve is the trading possibilities curve if the terms of trade are 1 bushel of beans = 1/2 bushel of wheat. You can see that trading allows the Philippines to enjoy increased consumption as well. After specialization, the maximum amount of beans remains unchanged at 300 million bushels. However, the maximum amount of wheat has increased from 100 (if produced in the Philippines) to 150 (by trading all of its 100 million bushels of beans for this quantity of wheat).

The Benefits of Free Trade

Ricardo's theory of comparative advantage, which we have been looking at, is very important because it clearly highlights the major benefits of trade. Free and unrestricted trade gives nations and individuals the opportunity to sell in world markets, and this will enable them to specialize in products where they enjoy a cost advantage over others. The effect will be lower costs of production generally, which translates into *lower prices* for consumers. This, in turn, will reduce the cost of living and enable them to enjoy a higher standard of living. In addition, free trade will increase the levels of output worldwide and will mean *higher levels of incomes*, which, in turn, will lead to improved standards of living.

This boils down to the fact that specialization increases productivity, so people as a group are better off as the result of lower production costs and higher incomes. But not only that, countries that do not specialize and trade will generally have to make do with domestically produced products of lower quality and of limited choice; with global markets, the variety and quality of products are much greater.

A final benefit of free trade is that all companies are exposed to international competition. This means that they cannot sit complacently behind protective barriers but are forced to compete for business with firms around the world. This also tends to discourage the formation of monopolies, since it is much more difficult to be a monopolist in the world market than it is to be a monopolist in the home market. In summary, free trade has the following advantages:

- Lower prices as the result of lower costs of production
- Higher incomes

| FIGURE 10.5 | Canadian Exports to the United States and the Rest of the World |

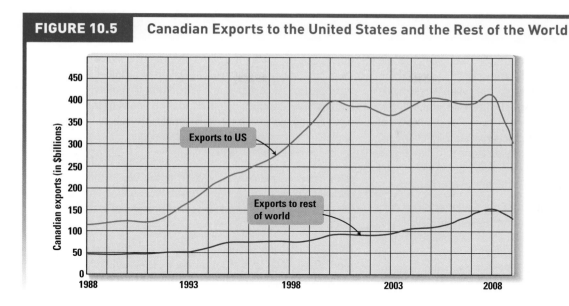

- A greater variety and quality of products
- Increased competition

The 1988 Free Trade Agreement with the United States caused a dramatic increase in the volume of trade that Canada has done with that country, as **Figure 10.5** demonstrates.

Some Important Qualifications

We need to point out that when comparing the wage rates of two countries engaged in international trade, the country with lower nominal wages will not necessarily have an advantage over a country that has higher nominal wages. The productivity of the workers in the two countries must also be considered. If the higher wage country also has a labour force that has higher labour productivity then they may not be at a disadvantage.

These are, indeed, powerful arguments in favour of free trade, but before we leave the topic, let us look at some of the qualifications that must be introduced. First, free trade is never free because there will always be transport, insurance, and other freight charges, which must be added to the cost of production and which will usually reduce the trading advantage of foreign sellers. (However, in a country as large as Canada, it is often cheaper to transport products to the American states bordering the country than it is to transport them from one end of the country to the other.)

In addition, selling in a foreign country is always going to be more difficult (and often more expensive) than selling in the domestic market because of the differences in language, culture, taxation, regulations, and so on. Besides cost differences, the analysis we have presented so far has assumed constant costs. This leads to the result in our examples that countries should specialize in, perhaps, a single product and produce that product to a maximum. However, as we learned in Chapter 1, if any country tries to concentrate on a single product, its production is subject to the law of increasing costs. This means that one country only enjoys a cost advantage over others *up to a point*. As it tries to push production levels higher, its cost will start to increase so that it no longer enjoys a competitive advantage. This is the reason why few countries specialize entirely and why many countries both produce *and* import the same product. The presence of increasing costs will also lessen the advantages that one country enjoys over another in trade.

Even allowing for these cautions, it is still true that there are a number of benefits to be obtained from trade. This leads us to ask: why does free trade tend to be the exception rather than

ADDED DIMENSION   Other Organizations of Major Importance for Trade

IMF: The International Monetary Fund (IMF) was created at the Bretton Woods Conference in 1944 in response to the experience of the interwar period (1918–1939) when world trade collapsed. Headquartered in Geneva, Switzerland, the IMF has 184 member countries and is dedicated to the promotion of international monetary cooperation, exchange stability, economic growth, and international trade. It makes loans to national governments—at the request of governments themselves—and provides a very sophisticated level of technical assistance.

OECD: The Organization for Economic Cooperation and Development (OECD) is a Paris-based organization with 30 developed-nation members and working relationships with some 70 less developed countries. The mission of the OECD is to promote policies that achieve sustainable economic growth and development of the world economy, help countries realize sound economic expansion and development, and help world trade grow on a multilateral, nondiscriminatory basis.

EU: The European Union (EU) currently has 27 members and grew out of the six-member former European Economic Community, which was established in 1957. The EU has its capital in Brussels and is the largest economic/social experiment ever attempted among nations. It continues to be a work in progress. Over time, the EU has established a common market for goods, services, capital, and labour. Given the size of its population (495 million people) and huge contribution to the world's GDP, its decisions on competition, labour and safety standards, and environmental policies have profound effects on the behaviour of other nations.

G8: This group of eight nations consists of Canada, the United Kingdom, France, Germany, Italy, Japan, the United States, and, recently, Russia. It represents (along with China and Spain) the ten largest economies in the world. The heads of state of these eight countries hold summits (in various locations around the globe) in which the world's pressing economic, political, and social issues are discussed.

G20: This is an expanded version of the **G8**. In this case, the ministers of finance and heads of the central banks of the 20 member nations meet to promote financial stability in the world's markets.

UNCTAD: The United Nations Conference on Trade and Development (UNCTAD) was established in 1964 and is located in Geneva. UNCTAD aims to help developing countries integrate into the world economy. UNCTAD provides a forum for intergovernmental discussions while also supporting research, data collection, and policy analysis helpful to the developing countries, along with the provision of some technical assistance.

NAFTA Secretariat: The North American Free Trade Agreement (NAFTA) Secretariat was established with the signing of the 1994 agreement that formed the world's largest free trade area made up of Canada, the United States, and Mexico. The mandate of the Secretariat is to provide administrative support to panels and committees established by the agreement to provide dispute resolutions. The Secretariat has three locations: Ottawa, Mexico City, and Washington, D.C.

the rule throughout history? Why does the question of free trade still divide countries and lead to such acrimonious debate? To understand part of the reason, let us look at an example illustrating that not everyone within a country will benefit from free trade.

 SELF-TEST

4. The following table shows the average productivity in Freedonia and Libraland:

Output per Worker (bushels per day)		
	Apples	Pears
Freedonia	6 or	3
Libraland	3 or	2

Assuming the two countries wish to trade, would terms of trade of 1 bushel of pears = 2.5 bushels of apples be feasible? What about 1 bushel of pears = 1 bushel of apples? 1 bushel of pears = 1.75 bushels of apples?

5. From the data contained in **Figure 10.3** or **Table 10.6**, how many beans can the United States obtain if it is self-sufficient and producing 240 million bushels of wheat? If, instead, it specializes in wheat production and can trade at terms of 1 bushel of wheat = 2 bushels of beans, how many bushels of beans could it have to accompany its 240 million bushels of wheat? What if the terms were 1 bushel of wheat = 3 bushels of beans?

10.4 THE EFFECT OF FREE TRADE

L04 Describe why some groups win and others lose as a result of freer trade, and explore trade restrictions.

Let us set up a scenario in which initially we have two self-sufficient countries, France and Germany, each producing wine. The demand and supply conditions in the two countries are different, of course, with both the demand and supply being greater in France than in Germany, as is shown in **Table 10.11**.

TABLE 10.11	The Market for Wine in France and Germany (millions of litres per month)					
FRANCE			**GERMANY**			
Price ($ per litre)	**Quantity Demanded**	**Quantity Supplied**	**Price ($ per litre)**	**Quantity Demanded**	**Quantity Supplied**	
3	19	7	3	17	2	
4	17	11	4	15	3	
5	**15**	**15**	5	13	4	
6	13	19	6	11	5	
7	11	23	7	9	6	
8	9	27	**8**	**7**	**7**	

The equilibrium price in France is $5 per litre and the equilibrium quantity is 15. In Germany, the equilibrium price and quantity are $8 and 7, respectively. These are shown graphically in **Figure 10.6**.

Now, suppose that the two countries decide to engage in free trade. To keep things simple, let us assume there are no transport costs. If free trade is now introduced, what will be the price of wine in the two countries? Since we have assumed there are no transport costs, the price in the two countries should be the same. To find this price, all we need to do is look at the combined market of France and Germany. In other words, we simply need to add the demands and supplies of the two countries, as shown in **Table 10.12**.

The total market demand is obtained by adding together the French demand and the German demand at each price. For instance, at $3 per litre, the quantity demanded in France is 19 and in Germany 17, giving a total for the two countries of 36. Similarly, the quantity supplied at $3 is 7 in France and 2 in Germany, giving a total market supply of 9. This is done for all prices. The new market price (let us call it the world price), then, will be $6 per litre, and at that price, a total of 24 million litres will be produced and sold.

FIGURE 10.6	Demand and Supply of Wine in France and Germany

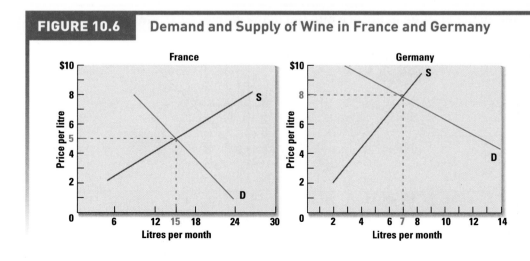

In France, the demand and supply of wine are both higher than in Germany. The consequence is a greater quantity of wine traded in France: 15 million litres, compared with 7 million in Germany. The price of wine, however, is lower in France than in Germany.

TABLE 10.12	Deriving the Total Market Demand and Supply of Wine for France and Germany (in millions of litres per month)					
	FRANCE		GERMANY		TOTAL MARKET	
Price ($ per litre)	Demand	Supply	Demand	Supply	Demand	Supply
3	19	7	17	2	36	9
4	17	11	15	3	32	14
5	15	15	13	4	28	19
6	13	19	11	5	24	24
7	11	23	9	6	20	29
8	9	27	7	7	16	34

Now, let us look at the effect in each market. French winemakers are delighted at the situation because the world price for wine is higher and their volume of business is higher. French winemakers are now producing 19 million litres, up from the 15 million litres produced before trade, and the price they receive is $6, up from $5. Note also that in France, the quantity produced (19) exceeds the demand from French consumers (13). What happens to the surplus of 6 million litres? It is being exported to Germany. And what is the situation in that country? Well, certainly German consumers are delighted because the new world price of $6 is lower than the previous domestic price of $8. But we can imagine that the German winemakers are far from happy. The new lower world price has caused a number of producers to cut back production, and presumably some producers are forced out of business and some employees have lost their jobs. Therefore, although the populations of both France and Germany as a whole benefit, not everyone within those populations gains. At the world price of $6, German producers are only producing 5 million litres, below the German demand of 11 million litres. How is this shortage going to be made up? The answer is: from the import of French wine. This simply means that the French export of 6 million litres equals the German import of 6 million litres. These points are illustrated graphically in **Figure 10.7**.

Bottled wine aging in storage.

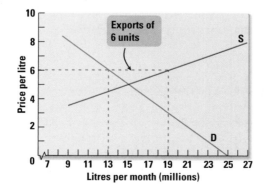
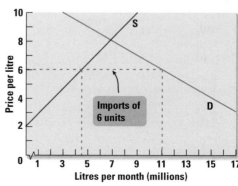

FIGURE 10.7   Demand and Supply of Wine in France and Germany with Free Trade

The new world price of wine is above the previous French price but below the previous German price. The result is a surplus of wine in France of 6 million litres but a shortage in Germany of 6 million litres.

So, who loses and who gains as a result of markets being opened up? The answer in our example is that both German wine consumers and French wine producers gain and French wine consumers and German wine producers lose. Free trade has cost French consumers $1 a litre, and it has cost German winemakers $2 per litre. Previously, German winemakers were selling 7 million litres at $8 per litre, for a total revenue of $56 million. Now, they are selling only 5 million litres for $6 per litre, for a total revenue of $30 million. In total, then, these producers, of whom there may be fewer than 100, have collectively lost $26 million in revenue. It is easy to see why these producers may not be in favour of free trade! In fact, it would pay them to lobby their own parliament and to launch publicity campaigns in an attempt to keep out "cheap" French wines. If they are successful and efforts do not cost more than $26 million, they will be ahead of the game.

It is easy to see why powerful lobby and special interest groups have been very vocal throughout history in trying to persuade government and the public that it is in the country's interests to ban or curtail foreign imports. This is an activity that economists call *rent seeking*. Such **protectionism** can take many forms, which we will now examine.

The Imposition of Import Quotas

The most obvious way to restrict imports is to ban them entirely or partially, and this is exactly what is meant by a **quota**. An import quota can take a variety of forms, ranging from a total restriction to a maximum limit being placed on each individual foreign exporter, or perhaps the requirement that each foreign exporter reduce its exports by a percentage of the previous year's sales. The essence of an import quota is to reduce or restrict the importation of certain products. And what will the effect of such restriction be? Suppose, in our wine example, that German winemakers were successful in their efforts to keep out French wines, and the German government imposed a total ban on French wines. At the current price of $6 per litre, there will be an immediate shortage in Germany. The result of the shortage is to push up the price of wine. It will continue to rise, encouraging increased German production until the price returns to the pre–free-trade price of $8. In France, the immediate effect of the German quota will be to cause a surplus of French wine, which will depress the price of French wine until it, too, is back at the pre-trade price of $5 per litre.

Let us move on from our European example and look at trade from the Canadian perspective. Unlike our example where the market price was determined by the total demand and supply in just two countries, in reality the prices of wine and of most products traded internationally are determined by the world's demand and supply. That is to say, for any one small country, such as Canada, the world price is a given; the country's action will have little impact on the world price. This situation is illustrated in **Figure 10.8**.

Figure 10.8 shows the domestic demand (D_d) and supply (S_d) of wine in Canada. P_d would be the domestic price and Q_d the domestic production if Canada was totally closed to foreign trade. Suppose that the world price is P_w and that Canada now freely allows imports into the country. This means that if the world price of Pw prevails within Canada, the amount produced by domestic Canadian producers is a, and the amount demanded is c. Since Canadian consumers want to purchase more than Canadian producers are willing to produce, the difference of ac represents the amount of imports.

Now, suppose that the Canadian government yields to pressure from Canadian wine producers and imposes a quota of ab on imported wine. In effect, the total supply is equal to the domestic supply plus the amount of the quota. This is represented by the new supply curve, $S_d + quota$. Since the total available has now been reduced, the price will increase to Pq, and the quantity will fall to Q_q.

From this, it can be seen that the losers will be Canadian consumers (who are paying a higher price and are having less quantity and variety of wines) and foreign winemakers whose exports are being restricted. The winners will be Canadian winemakers, who are producing more wine and receiving a higher price.

protectionism: the economic policy of protecting domestic producers by restricting the importation of foreign products.

quota: a limit imposed on the production or sale of a product.

FIGURE 10.8   The Effects of a Quota

Initially, the Canadian domestic demand and supply are D_d and S_d, and the world price is P_w. The quantity demanded in Canada at the world price P_w equals c, of which Canadian producers would produce a and foreign producers would export ac to Canada. A quota of ab would raise the price to P_q. As a result, domestic production will increase, and imports would drop to the amount of the quota.

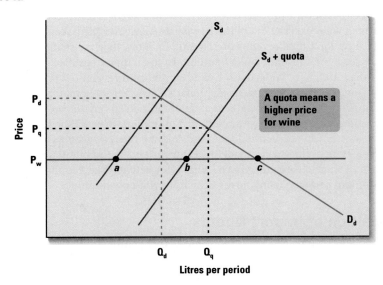

The Imposition of Tariffs

tariff: a tax (or duty) levied on imports.

A second way of restricting imports is by the use of a **tariff**, which is a tax on imports. It is implemented more often than import quotas because governments can derive considerable revenue from tariffs. The effects of a tariff are much the same as those of a quota because in both cases the price of the product will increase. With a quota, however, the domestic producers get the whole benefit of the higher price, whereas with a tariff the benefit is shared between the domestic producers and government. An additional benefit of a tariff over a quota is that a quota tends to treat foreign producers indiscriminately because each and every producer is treated in the same way; with a tariff, only the more efficient producers will continue to export, since only they will be able to continue to make a profit. A tariff discriminates against the less efficient producers, and therefore, from an efficiency point of view, it is superior to a quota.

In **Figure 10.9**, suppose, again, that we are describing the Canadian wine market. At the world price of P_w, Canadian producers are supplying a, and Canadian consumers are buying b. The difference, ab, is the amount of imported wine. Suppose that the Canadian government imposes a tariff of t per unit. The price in Canada will rise to P_t. Note that at the higher price, Canadian producers (who do not pay the tariff) will receive the whole price P_t, and will increase production to Q_f. Canadian consumers will reduce consumption to Q_g. In addition, imports will fall to a level represented by the distance $Q_f - Q_g$. The result is very similar to what we saw in the analysis of quotas. Again, it is Canadian consumers and foreign producers who lose out and Canadian producers who gain.

The other winner in this scenario is the Canadian government, which will receive tax revenue equal to the shaded rectangle in **Figure 10.9**.

Other Trade Restrictions

currency-exchange controls: government restrictions limiting the amount of foreign currencies that can be obtained.

Besides the two most popular protectionist measures of tariffs and quotas, a number of other available methods deserve mention. **Currency-exchange controls** are similar to quotas, but instead of a restricting the importation of goods, currency-exchange controls limit the availability of foreign currencies (that is, foreign exchange). The effect is the same because foreigners wish to be paid in their own currencies, and importers who are unable to get their hands on the appropriate currency will not be able to buy the foreign goods.

FIGURE 10.9	The Effects of the Imposition of a Tariff

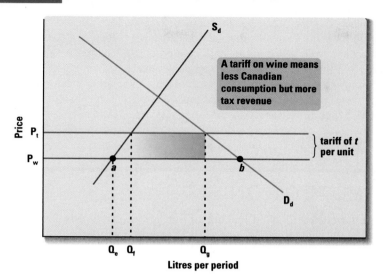

A tariff on wine means less Canadian consumption but more tax revenue

tariff of t per unit

Litres per period

The imposition of a tariff, t, will increase the price of wine in Canada to P_t from P_w. As a result, Canadian production will increase from Q_e to Q_f and imports will drop to $Q_g - Q_f$. The tax revenue to government is equal to t times the quantity of imports, $Q_g - Q_f$, the shaded area.

The controls might be across-the-board restrictions, or restrictions on particular currencies or on particular products or industries. The effect in all cases will be to increase the domestic price of the products affected, which will be to the benefit of the domestic producer at the expense of the domestic consumer. Another more subtle but often equally effective way to cut imports is by way of *bureaucratic regulations*, though not all regulations have that intent. A government might make trade so difficult or time-consuming for the importer that the amount of trade is significantly reduced. For instance, the customs department of a particular country might tie the importer up with red tape by requiring that all imports must be accompanied by ten different forms (all in triplicate) obtainable from ten different government departments. Or perhaps the product must meet certain very unrealistic standards of safety or packaging, or hygiene standards that are not required for domestically produced items.

A more recent type of trade restriction is known as **voluntary export restrictions (VERs)**. Rather than imposing tariffs and import quotas, the importing country requests that the exporting country itself voluntarily restrict the amount being exported. In this way, the exporting country is given the power to administer the quotas, which will also prevent the importing country from receiving tariff revenue on the imports. Since the restrictions are voluntary, the exporting country does not have to comply. However, since the importing country has other weapons at its disposal, these restrictions are usually adhered to.

In summary, there are five types of trade protection:

- Import quotas
- Tariffs
- Currency-exchange controls
- Bureaucratic regulations
- Voluntary export restrictions

voluntary export restriction (VER): an agreement by an exporting country to restrict the amount of its exports to another country.

 SELF-TEST

6. In **Table 10.12**, if the demand for wine in Germany increased by nine (million litres) at every price, how much wine would now be produced in Germany, and how much would be imported from France?

ADDED DIMENSION   The Softwood Lumber Dispute

In 2006, Canada and the United States finally reached an agreement to end the dispute over Canadian exports of softwood lumber to the United States. The seven-year agreement removed a U.S. tariff on softwood lumber that Canada claimed was illegal under the terms of NAFTA. However, it also included an export tax imposed on Canadian shipments of wood to the United States if the market price dropped below a certain level. This tax ranges from 5 percent to 15 percent, depending on how low the market price dropped below a certain base level. This long simmering dispute centred on the stumpage fees that Canadian provincial governments impose on lumber companies for the right to harvest trees on crown land. The Americans felt that these fees were too low, which resulted in a de facto subsidy to Canadian lumber companies.

10.5   PROTECTIONISM

L05 Identify some arguments
against free trade.

In this chapter, we have tried to avoid making an outright declaration in favour of free trade, though the flavour of the chapter would suggest that there are many benefits to be derived from trade, and probably the majority of economists feel that the freer the trade, the better. But even a notable free-trader, such as the astute Adam Smith, recognized that there may be occasions when a degree of protectionism in the way of tariffs and quotas might be called for. He suggested, for instance, that a country's strategic industries should be offered protection so that, for instance, the country does not become dependent on foreign manufacturers for the production of military hardware and related technology. The problem with this *strategic industry argument*, however, is that most industries would claim that they are of "strategic importance" to a nation and, therefore, deserve similar protection from foreign competition.

In addition, Smith suggests that in order to have a level playing field for both domestic and foreign producers, if the produce of domestic industry is being taxed, then foreign imports should be taxed by a similar amount. He also felt that if a foreign country is placing tariffs and import quotas on your country's exports, then you should do likewise to its exports—not, it should be noted, for retaliation but to help the foreign country to recognize the folly of its actions and to persuade it to restore free trade.

Finally, Smith was prescient enough to realize that if a country has had a long history of protectionism, the sudden arrival of free trade is likely to cause dramatic shifts of labour and capital away from industries that can no longer compete to those industries that are growing. This dislocation may cause a great deal of suffering in the short term, so Smith felt that a wise government would introduce free trade gradually, to mitigate any suffering. This caveat is of particular importance in terms of the North American Free Trade Agreement discussions. Although many felt that there would be great long-term benefits for all the participating countries, it is equally certain that in the short term, a great deal of suffering would be experienced by those industries, firms, and individuals who, through no fault of their own, found themselves unable to compete. This is why tariffs were reduced in stages over a 10-year period.

It should also be mentioned that some economists believe certain "infant" industries should be given a helping hand by government until they are sufficiently mature to take on foreign competition. This *infant industry argument* is strongest when government feels that undue reliance on the exportation of a few staple products would leave the country in a vulnerable position if a future change in demand or technology were to occur. In order to diversify the economy and develop other industries, many feel that these "infants" should be sheltered from competition. The trouble is, these infant industries often never grow up! In addition, even if there are persuasive arguments in favour of protecting or assisting certain industries, it may be better for government to give this aid in the form of direct subsidies rather than by interfering with normal trading patterns through the imposition of tariffs and quotas.

A third argument against free trade is the *cultural identity argument*. This one is difficult to dismiss solely on economic grounds. Many commentators feel that free trade brings with it mass production and standardization, which may harm the importing country's sense of individuality and cultural identity. As a result, some are totally against free trade, whereas others feel that it should not extend into such areas as communications, health, and education. They firmly believe that a country's radio and television stations, its newspapers and magazines, and its educational institutions and hospitals should not be owned or controlled from abroad.

A fourth argument is the belief that the environmental and labour standards of developed nations may be eroded as they try to compete with countries whose standards may be considerably lower and who may have a cost advantage as a result. This could trigger a "race to the bottom" as standards are lowered in all countries.

In summary, there are four arguments against free trade:

- The strategic industry argument
- The infant industry argument
- The cultural identity argument
- The lower environmental and labour standards argument

 SELF-TEST

7. Which industry in Canada do you feel deserves protection in each of the following categories?

   a) Strategically important

   b) Infant

   c) Culturally important

   d) Environmentally important

 ADDED DIMENSION   Does Free Trade Cost Jobs?

During the recession that began in 2008, a number of countries introduced rescue packages designed to boost their own industries. Many thought that such aid should only be given to those firms and industries able to guarantee that money would flow directly into boosting domestic production and jobs. There was a concern that a great deal of the extra spending might instead benefit foreign producers.

In the United States, for example, President Barack Obama was enjoined to ensure that any stimulus spending by the government would be to "Buy American." There is nothing new in this. Whenever a country is suffering economically, there are always those who advocate restrictions on foreign imports on the basis that importing costs jobs, that is, by buying from abroad, we are effectively exporting jobs to other countries.

There is some truth in this. Certainly in the case of Canada, employment in the textile industry has declined as jobs have shifted to India and other countries. But before we jump to the conclusion that Canada needs protection from low-wage countries that are able to "unfairly" compete with us, let us stop to consider which have been the top trading nations in the world over the last half century. The list would surely include the United States, Japan, Germany, the United Kingdom, and—Canada. And which countries have the highest wage rates in the world? Again, the United States, Japan,

Germany, the United Kingdom, and—Canada. The reason for this is straightforward. It may be true that labour costs determine which country can produce certain products more cheaply, but labour costs are not determined solely by wage rates. For example, suppose that a Canadian steelworker earns $30 an hour, whereas the going wage in Mexico is just $5 an hour. A big advantage to Mexico, it would seem. However, let us further suppose that the Canadian worker is able to produce 15 units of steel an hour compared with only 2 units by the Mexican. The cost of a unit of steel in Canada is, therefore, equal to $30/15 or $2 per unit, whereas in Mexico a unit of steel costs $5/2 or $2.50. In summary, Canada will be more competitive than Mexico in steel production because although it has higher wage rates, it has even higher productivity rates.

But let us return to the original idea: does buying abroad cost us jobs in Canada? In a sense, the answer is yes, since we are importing products made by foreign labour and, therefore, exporting jobs. But whenever we export products, we are importing jobs into Canada. So, what jobs should we export, and what should we import? Presumably, we should specialize in products and jobs in which we have some expertise: automobile production, high-tech electronics, financial services, and telecommunications. And we should buy products and jobs that other countries can produce more cheaply: T-shirts, textiles, and soy beans.

Review

CHAPTER SUMMARY

In this chapter, you learned that the benefits of free trade are rooted in specialization and that a nation's comparative advantage determines what products it should export. The way that the gains from trade are divided between trading partners is determined by the terms of trade between them. You also learned that when a nation embraces free trade there are both winners, usually consumers, and losers, usually inefficient producers of certain products.

10.1a If trade is voluntary, then both parties to the trade must benefit.

10.1b Differences in factor endowments between nations and the theory of absolute advantage explain why, for example, Canada exports lumber and imports bananas.

10.2a The theory of comparative advantage explains why one nation is willing to trade with another nation, even though it may be more efficient in producing both (all) the products involved.

10.2b The trade in any two products between any two nations will result in gains from trade unless the opportunity costs of production happen to be exactly the same in each country.

10.3a The way in which the gains from trade are divided between the trading partners is determined by the terms of trade, calculated as the average price of exports divided by the average price of imports times 100.

10.3b The major benefits of free trade are:
- lower prices
- higher incomes
- a greater variety and quality of products
- increased competition

10.4a Although the population of a country as a whole gains from free trade, not everyone within that population wins.

10.4b The two most common forms of *trade restrictions* are tariffs and quotas, both of which:
- increase the domestic price of a product that is imported
- reduce the quantities traded of that product

The other two types of restrictions are:
- exchange controls
- voluntary exports restrictions

10.5 Four arguments against free trade are:
- the strategic industry argument
- the infant industry argument
- the cultural identity argument
- the lower environmental and labour standards argument

NEW GLOSSARY TERMS AND KEY EQUATION

comparative advantage   335
currency-exchange controls   348
protectionism   347

quota   347
tariff   348
terms of trade   338

voluntary export restriction
(VER)   349

Equations:

[10.1] $\text{Terms of trade} = \dfrac{\text{Average price of exports}}{\text{Average price of imports}} \times 100$

STUDY TIPS

1. The argument for free trade is based on Ricardo's theory of comparative advantage. It is important that you fully understand the basic idea of opportunity costs that lies behind this theory. A good way to test yourself is to make up your own figures for a two-country, two-product world; draw the corresponding production possibilities curves; and work out which country has an advantage in which product and why.

2. Some students have difficulty understanding that if we are dealing with only two products, and if a country has a comparative advantage at producing one product, it must by definition have a comparative *disadvantage* in the other product.

3. To get an understanding of the terms of trade, again make up some numbers for yourself and plot them on a production possibilities diagram. For instance, start off with a country that could produce 30 units of wool or 20 computers and has an advantage in wool production. If it could trade at 1 wool = 1/2 computer, what combinations could it have? Try 1 unit of wool = 1 computer, 1 unit of wool = 2, 3, 5 computers and so on.

Draw each resulting trading possibilities curve. Note that both the trading and production possibilities curves reflect opportunity costs. The former case shows what must be given up in trading; the latter case shows what must be given up in production.

4. To understand the idea behind world markets, note, as in **Figure 10.7**, that what one country is exporting, another country must be importing. This means that if one country produces a trade surplus, then the other country must be experiencing a trade deficit. In the exporting country, the world price must be higher than the domestic price. In the importing country, the world price must be lower than the domestic price.

5. You will get a good grip on the effects of tariffs and quotas by drawing a simple demand-and-supply curve and noting, first, the effect of a price set above market equilibrium (which is what a tariff produces) and, second, a quantity below market equilibrium (which is what an import quota produces). This approach suggests that the effect of both tariffs and import quotas is to produce higher prices and lower quantities.

Answered Questions

These questions can also be found online on Connect.

Indicate whether the following statements are true or false:

1. **(LO 2) T or F**   A country has a comparative advantage over another only if it is able to produce all products more cheaply.

2. **(LO 2) T or F**   David Ricardo first introduced the theory of comparative advantage.

3. **(LO 1) T or F**   If a country wishes to specialize its production, it will also want to engage in trade.

4. **(LO 2) T or F**   If a country is able to produce all products more cheaply than any other country, then there is no advantage in trade.

5. **(LO 3) T or F**   The terms of trade relate to the laws and conditions that govern trade.

6. **(LO 3) T or F**   If the prices of a country's exports decrease and the prices of imports increase, then the terms of trade will move in its favour.

7. **(LO 3) T or F**   If a country's trading possibilities curve lies to the right of its production possibilities curve, there are no gains from trade.

8. **(LO 5) T or F**   Protectionism is the economic policy of protecting domestic producers by putting restrictions on exports.

Practise and learn online with Connect, where you can find the Answered Questions and the Unanswered Problems for all chapters of this textbook's Study Guide section.

9. **(LO 4) T or F** A tariff is a tax on exports; a quota is a tax on imports.

10. **(LO 5) T or F** Domestic producers gain and domestic consumers lose as a result of the imposition of tariffs or quotas.

Basic (Questions 11–26)

11. **(LO 1)** What is the meaning of the term *gains from trade*?
    a) The surplus of exports over imports
    b) The increase in output resulting from international trade
    c) The fact that everyone gains from international trade
    d) The increase in revenue that government receives from tariffs

12. **(LO 4)** What is a tariff?
    a) It is a tax imposed on an import.
    b) It is a tax imposed on an export.
    c) It is a tax imposed on production.
    d) It is a tax imposed on consumption.

13. **(LO 1)** What are the two largest categories of goods that Canada exports?
    a) Energy and forestry products
    b) Agricultural and forestry products
    c) Forestry products and industrial materials
    d) Automotive products and machinery/equipment products

14. **(LO 3)** What is the definition of the *terms of trade*?
    a) It is the average price of a country's imports divided by the average price of its exports.
    b) It is the average price of a country's exports divided by the average price of its imports.
    c) They are the rules and regulations governing international trade.
    d) The value of a country's currency compared with that of its biggest trading partner.

15. **(LO 2)** What does it mean if the opportunity costs differ between two countries?
    a) Then comparative costs must be the same.
    b) There can be no gains from trade.
    c) It is possible for both countries to gain from specialization and trade.
    d) Then absolute costs must be the same.

16. **(LO 3)** On what basis are the gains from trade divided between countries?
    a) According to the terms of trade
    b) According to international trade agreements

c) According to the quantity of resources possessed by each
d) According to each country's comparative advantage

17. **(LO 2)** Under what circumstances will there be no opportunity for mutually advantageous trade between two countries?
    a) When the terms of trade are the same
    b) When comparative costs are the same
    c) When comparative costs are different
    d) When tariffs exist

18. **(LO 3)** Suppose that originally the average price of Happy Island's exports was 180 and the average price of its imports was 120. Now, the price of its exports drops to 160, and the price of its imports drops to 100. What effect will this have on Happy Island's terms of trade?
    a) There will be no change in the terms of trade.
    b) The terms of trade have moved in Happy Island's favour.
    c) The terms of trade have moved against Happy Island.
    d) The terms of trade have both increased and decreased.

19. **(LO 5)** All the following, except one, are forms of protectionism. Which is the exception?
    a) Import subsidies
    b) Tariffs
    c) Exchange controls
    d) Quotas

20. **(LO 2)** Suppose that the cost of producing one unit of wine in Happy Island is two units of rice; in Joy Island, one unit of wine costs four units of rice. What does this mean for the two countries?
    a) Happy Island should specialize in, and export rice to, Joy Island.
    b) Happy Island should specialize in, and export wine to, Joy Island.
    c) Happy Island should specialize in rice but export wine to Joy Island.
    d) Happy Island should specialize in wine but export rice to Joy Island.

21. **(LO 3)** Suppose that the cost of producing one unit of wine in Happy Island is two units of rice; in Joy Island one unit of wine costs four units of rice. What might be possible terms of trade between the two countries?
    a) 1 rice = 3/8 wine
    b) 1 rice = 3 wine
    c) 1 rice = 6 wine
    d) 1 wine = 1 rice

22. **(LO 5)** What is the difference between a tariff and
a quota?
a) A tariff causes an increase in the price, whereas
a quota does not affect the price.
b) Both a tariff and a quota will affect the price, but
a tariff has no effect on the quantity, whereas a
quota will lead to a reduction.
c) Both a tariff and a quota will affect the price, but
a tariff has no effect on the quantity, whereas a
quota will lead to an increase.
d) A quota affects all foreign producers equally,
whereas a tariff does not.
e) A tariff affects all foreign producers equally,
whereas a quota does not.

Refer to **Figure 10.10** to answer questions 23–26.

FIGURE 10.10

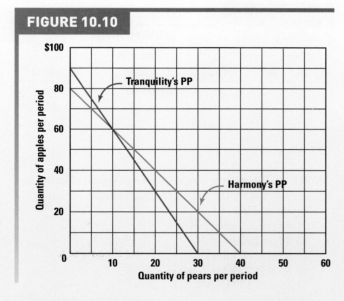

23. **(LO 2)** What is the opportunity cost of producing
1 apple in Harmony and in Tranquility?
a) 2 pears in Harmony and 3 pears in Tranquility
b) 1/2 pear in Harmony and 1/3 pear in Tranquility
c) 2 pears in Harmony and 1/3 pear in Tranquility
d) 1/2 pear in Harmony and 3 pears in Tranquility
e) 3 pears in Harmony and 2 pears in Tranquility

24. **(LO 2)** What do the comparative opportunity costs in
the two countries suggest?
a) That there are no advantages to be gained from trade.
b) That Harmony should specialize in apples but
export pears.
c) That Tranquility should specialize in apples but
export pears.

d) That Harmony should specialize in pears but
export apples.
e) That Harmony should specialize in pears and
Tranquility should specialize in apples.

25. **(LO 3)** Suppose that both Harmony and Tranquility are
producing 20 pears. What will be the total gains from
trade for the two countries?
a) 20 apples and 0 pears
b) 30 apples and 10 pears
c) 20 apples and 10 pears
d) 20 apples and 30 pears
e) 0 apple and 20 pears

26. **(LO 3)** What could be possible terms of trade between
the two countries?
a) 1 apple = 0.25 pear
b) 1 apple = 2.5 pears
c) 1 apple = 3 pears
d) 1 pear = 0.5 apple
e) 1 pear = 2.5 apples

Intermediate (Questions 27–31)

Refer to **Table 10.13** to answer problems 27–31.

TABLE 10.13

| | AVERAGE PRODUCT PER WORKER | | | |
Country	Broomsticks			Swords
Rings	1	or		4
Potter	6	or		3

27. **(LO 2)** What is the cost of producing one sword in Rings?
a) 4 broomsticks
b) 0.25 broomstick
c) 0.67 broomstick
d) 1.5 broomsticks

28. **(LO 2)** What is the cost of producing one broomstick
in Potter?
a) 2 swords
b) 0.5 sword
c) 0.33 sword
d) 3 swords

29. **(LO 2)** Supposing that there are 200 workers in Rings,
how many broomsticks could be produced if 200 swords
were produced?
a) 40 broomsticks
b) 50 broomsticks
c) 150 broomsticks
d) 160 broomsticks

30. **(LO 2)** Supposing that there are 200 workers in Potter, how many swords could be produced if 540 broomsticks were produced?
    a) 0 swords
    b) 110 swords
    c) 120 swords
    d) 330 swords

31. **(LO 2)** Supposing that there are 200 workers each in Rings and Potter. If, originally, half the workers were employed in each industry, what would be the gains from trade if the countries completely specialized in the products in which they have a comparative advantage?
    a) + 200 broomsticks, − 100 swords
    b) + 200 broomsticks, + 100 swords
    c) + 500 broomsticks, + 100 swords
    d) + 700 broomsticks, + 700 swords

Advanced (Questions 32–35)

Refer to **Figure 10.11**, which shows the market for cloth in Smith Island, to answer questions 32, 33, and 34.

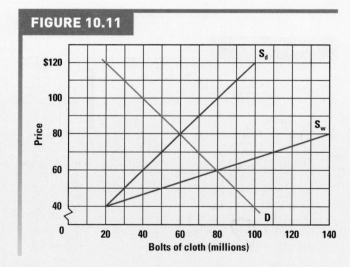

FIGURE 10.11

32. **(LO 1)** At the world price, how much is Smith Island trading?
    a) It is importing 30 units.
    b) It is importing 40 units.
    c) It is exporting 30 units.
    d) It is exporting 40 units.

33. **(LO 5)** If Smith Island introduced an import quota of 20, what would be the new price of cloth in Smith Island?
    a) $55
    b) $60
    c) $70
    d) $90

34. **(LO 5)** If Smith Island introduced an import quote of $20, how much would be imported?
    a) 0 units
    b) 10 units
    c) 20 units
    d) 40 units

Table 10.14 shows the output of kumquats per month. Refer to this table to answer question 35.

TABLE 10.14

Price ($ per kilo)		SMITHLAND	
	Demand	Domestic Supply	Imports
3	100	40	30
4	90	50	40
5	80	60	50
6	70	70	60

35. **(LO 1)** What is the world (free trade) price of kumquats, and what quantity of this product is being consumed domestically?
    a) $4 and 50 kilos
    b) $4 and 90 kilos
    c) $5 and 80 kilos
    d) $6 and 70 kilos
    e) $6 and 130 kilos

Parallel Problems

ANSWERED PROBLEMS

36A. **(LO 2, 3)** **Key Problem** Suppose that Richland and Prosperity have the output figures shown in **Table 10.15**.

TABLE 10.15

	AVERAGE PRODUCT PER WORKER		
Country	Wheat		Wine
Richland	4 bushels	or	2 barrels
Prosperity	2 bushels	or	6 barrels

Assume that cost and productivity remain constant.
a) What is the opportunity cost of producing one bushel of wheat in Richland? _____ .
b) What is the opportunity cost of producing one barrel of wine in Richland? _____ .
c) What is the opportunity cost of producing one bushel of wheat in Prosperity? _____ .
d) What is the opportunity cost of producing one barrel of wine in Prosperity? _____ .
e) In what product does Richland have a comparative advantage? _____ .
f) In what product does Prosperity have a comparative advantage? Suppose that the labour force in each country is 10 million. _____ .
g) Fill in the missing production possibilities data for both countries in **Table 10.16**.

TABLE 10.16

	RICHLAND'S PRODUCTION POSSIBILITIES (millions of units)				
	A	B	C	D	E
Wheat	40	30	20	10	0
Wine	___	___	___	___	___

	PROSPERITY'S PRODUCTION POSSIBILITIES (millions of units)				
	A	B	C	D	E
Wheat	___	___	___	___	___
Wine	0	15	30	45	60

Suppose that both countries are presently producing combination C.
h) Fill in the blanks in the following table:

Total output in millions of units:		
	Wheat	Wine
Richland	_____	_____
Prosperity	_____	_____
Total: both countries	_____	_____

Now, suppose that each country specializes in the product in which it has a comparative advantage.
i) Show the results below:

Total output in millions of units:		
	Wheat	Wine
Richland	_____	_____
Prosperity	_____	_____
Total: both countries	_____	_____

j) What is the joint gain from trade?
Wheat: _____ Wine: _____

Suppose that the two countries establish the terms of trade at 1 wine = 1.5 wheat, and Prosperity decides to export 12 wine to Richland.
k) Show how the two countries will share the gains from trade in the table below:

Gains for each country in millions of units		
	Wheat	Wine
Richland	_____	_____
Prosperity	_____	_____
Total: both countries	_____	_____

Basic (Problems 37A–43A)

37A. **(LO 3)** If the terms of trade for the country of Onara equals 0.9 and the average price of its imports is 1.4, what is the average price of its exports?

_____ .

38A. (LO 2) In Onara, the average worker can produce either five bags of pummies or three kilos of clings, whereas in Traf the average worker can produce either four bags of pummies or six kilos of clings. Which country can produce pummies more cheaply and which can produce clings more cheaply? Show the cost in each country.

Pummies: _____ Cost: _____

Clings: _____ Cost: _____

39A. (LO 2, 3) The following shows the maximum output levels for Here and There:

	Cloth		Computers
Here	100	or	50
There	60	or	120

a) What is the cost of 1 unit of cloth and a computer in Here?
 1 unit of cloth: _____
 1 computer: _____
b) What is the cost of 1 unit of cloth and a computer in There?
 1 unit of cloth: _____
 1 computer: _____
c) In what product does each country have a comparative advantage?
 Here: _____
 There: _____
d) What is the range of feasible terms of trade between the two countries?
 1 unit of cloth: _____
 1 computer: _____

40A. (LO 2) The following table shows the productivity for the countries of Yin and Yang:

	Machines		Bread
Yin	2	or	10
Yang	3	or	2

a) If the working populations of Yin and Yang are both 40 million, divided equally between the two industries in each country, how many machines and bread are currently being produced in Yin and Yang?

	Machines	Bread
Yin	_____	_____
Yang	_____	_____
Total	_____	_____

b) If the two countries decide to specialize, in which product does each country have a comparative advantage?
 Yin: _____ Yang: _____
c) If the two countries were to totally specialize, show the totals in the table below.

	Machines	Bread
Yin	_____	_____
Yang	_____	_____
Total	_____	_____

d) What are the gains from trade?

	Machines	Bread
	_____	_____

41A. (LO 2, 3) Table 10.17 shows the production possibilities for Concordia and Harmonia.

TABLE 10.17

		CONCORDIA'S PRODUCTION			
Product	**A**	**B**	**C**	**D**	**E**
Pork	4	3	2	1	0
Beans	0	5	10	15	20

		HARMONIA'S PRODUCTION			
Product	**A**	**B**	**C**	**D**	**E**
Pork	8	6	4	2	0
Beans	0	6	12	18	24

a) What are the costs of the two products in each country?
 Concordia: 1 unit of pork costs _____
            1 unit of beans costs _____
 Harmonia: 1 unit of pork costs _____
            1 unit of beans costs _____
b) What products should each country specialize in and export?
 Concordia: _____
 Harmonia: _____
c) If, prior to specialization and trade, Concordia produced combination C and Harmonia produced combination B, what would be the total gains from trade?
 Pork: _____
 Beans: _____

d) What would be the range of feasible terms of trade between the two countries? _____ .

42A. **(LO 3)** What is meant by *terms of trade*?

43A. **(LO 1)** What is meant by *factor endowment*?

Intermediate (Problems 44A–50A)

44A. **(LO 2)** The graph in **Figure 10.12** shows the domestic supply of and demand for mangos in India.

FIGURE 10.12

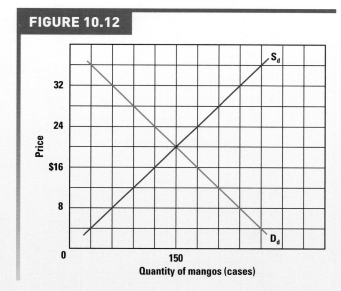

Quantity of mangos (cases)

The world price is $16 a case, and India is open to free trade.

a) Will India export or import mangos?

_____ .

b) What quantity will domestic producers supply?

_____ .

c) What quantity will India export or import?

_____ .

d) If the world price is $28, will India export or import mangos? How much?
   (Exports/import): _____
   Quantity: _____

45A. **(LO 1, 5)** **Table 10.18** shows the market for wool in Canada, which is closed to trade.

a) What is the present equilibrium price and domestic production?
   Price: _____
   Domestic production: _____

TABLE 10.18

Price per Tonne ($)	Quantity Demanded Domestically	Quantity Supplied Domestically
1700	145	45
1800	140	60
1900	135	75
2000	130	90
2100	125	105
2200	120	120
2300	115	135
2400	110	150

b) Suppose that Canada now opens to free trade and the world price of wool is $2000 per tonne. How much wool will Canada produce domestically, and how much will it import?
   Domestic production: _____
   Imports: _____

c) Assume that the Canadian government, under pressure from the Canadian wool industry, decides to impose an import quota of 20 tonnes. What will be the new price, and how much will the Canadian industry produce?
   Price: _____
   Domestic production: _____

d) Now suppose that the Canadian government decides to replace the import quota with a tariff. If it wishes to maintain domestic production at the same level as with a quota, what should be the amount of the tariff, and how much revenue will government receive?
   Tariff: $ _____
   Tariff revenue: $ _____

46A. **(LO 4)** **Table 10.19** shows the production possibilities for Canada and Japan. Prior to specialization and trade, Canada is producing combination D and Japan is producing combination B.

a) On the graph (**Figure 10.13**), draw the production possibilities curve for each country, and indicate their present output positions.

b) Suppose that the two countries specialize and trade on the basis of 1 DVD player = 1 wheat. Draw the corresponding trading possibilities curves.

TABLE 10.19

CANADA'S PRODUCTION POSSIBILITIES					
Product	A	B	C	D	E
DVD players	30	22.5	15	7.5	0
Wheat	0	10	20	30	40

JAPAN'S PRODUCTION					
Product	A	B	C	D	E
DVD players	40	30	20	10	0
Wheat	0	5	10	15	20

47A. (LO 2) The following incomplete table (**Table 10.20**) shows the productivity levels of producing beer and sardines in Canada and Mexico.

TABLE 10.20

PRODUCTION PER WORKER (average product)		
	Beer	Sardines
Canada	6	4
Mexico	3	_____

What should be the Mexican productivity per worker in the sardine industry for no advantage to be gained from trade? _____ .

48A. (LO 5) Suppose the Canadian demand for and the Japanese supply of cars to Canada is shown in **Table 10.21** (quantities in thousands).
  a) The present equilibrium price is $ _____ and quantity is _____ (thousand).
  b) Suppose that the Canadian government imposes a $2000 per car tariff on imported Japanese cars. Show the new supply in the last column above.
  c) The new equilibrium price is $ _____ and quantity is _____ (thousand).
  d) The total revenue received by government will be $ _____.
  e) Assume, instead, that government imposes an import quota of 100 000 cars. The new equilibrium price is $ _____ and quantity is _____ (thousand).
  f) Does government now receive any revenue?

49A. (LO 1) How are trade and specialization related?

50A. (LO 3) List three arguments against free trade.

FIGURE 10.13

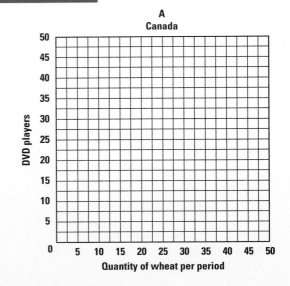

A
Canada

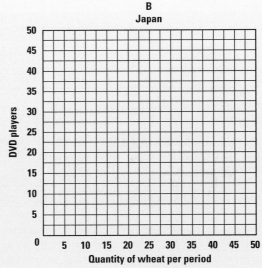

B
Japan

Advanced (Problems 51A–55A)

51A. (LO 2, 3, 4) Latalia has a labour force of 12 million, half in the wool industry and half in rice farming. The labour productivity in the wool industry is 40 kilos per worker per year, and in rice farming it is 100 kilos per worker per year. Latalia has discovered that the international terms of trade are two kilos of rice per one kilo of wool. It is happy with its current consumption of rice but would like to obtain more wool.

TABLE 10.21

Price($)	Quantity Demanded	Quantity Supplied (before tariff)	Quantity Supplied (after tariff)
$12 000	180	60	_____
13 000	160	80	_____
14 000	140	100	_____
15 000	120	120	_____
16 000	100	140	_____
17 000	80	160	_____
18 000	60	180	_____
19 000	40	200	_____

a) Assuming constant per-unit costs, on the graph in **Figure 10.14**, draw the production and trading possibilities curves for Latalia.

b) If Latalia were to specialize and trade, what product should it produce?

_____ .

c) What would be Latalia's gain from trade?

_____ .

d) On the graph, indicate the consumption levels before and after trade.

52A. **(LO 2, 3)** Suppose three countries have productivity data as shown in **Table 10.22**.

FIGURE 10.14

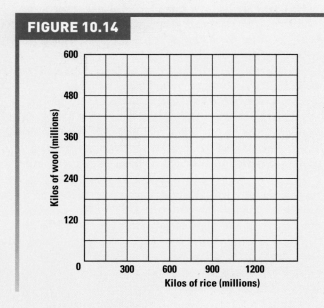

Kilos of wool (millions) vs Kilos of rice (millions)

TABLE 10.22

	PRODUCTIVITY PER WORKER	
	Wheat	Beans
Alpha	1	2
Beta	4	2
Gamma	2	2

a) What is the cost of wheat in each country?
   In Alpha, 1 unit of wheat costs _____.
   In Beta, 1 unit of wheat costs _____.
   In Gamma, 1 unit of wheat costs _____.

b) Which country can produce wheat the most cheaply (comparatively)?

_____ .

c) Which country can produce beans the most cheaply (comparatively)?

_____ .

d) Suppose that the international terms of trade were 1 wheat = 3/4 beans. Which countries would export wheat? Which countries would import wheat?

_____ .

e) Suppose, instead, that the international terms of trade were 1 wheat = 1½ beans. Which countries would export wheat? Which countries would import wheat?

_____ .

53A. **(LO 2, 3)** Table 10.23 shows the annual demand and supply of cell phones in Canada (in tens of thousands), where D_C is the domestic demand, D_W is the rest of the world demand, S_C is the Canadian supply, and S_W is the quantity supplied by manufacturers in the rest of the world.

TABLE 10.23

Price	D_C	D_W	D_T	S_C	S_W	S_T
$ 25	200	1200	_____	20	1200	_____
50	180	1100	_____	30	1250	_____
75	160	1000	_____	40	1300	_____
100	140	900	_____	50	1350	_____
125	120	800	_____	60	1400	_____
150	100	700	_____	70	1450	_____
175	80	600	_____	80	1500	_____
200	60	500	_____	90	1550	_____
225	40	400	_____	100	1600	_____

a) Complete the total demand (D_T) and total supply (S_T) columns.

b) What are the world price and quantity?
   Price: _____ Quantity: _____

c) If Canada was closed to international trade, what would be the price and quantity in Canada?
   Price: _____ Quantity: _____

d) If Canada were open to international trade, how much would Canada import from the rest of the world? Quantity imported: _____

e) If the Canadian government were to impose a quota and limit the amount of imported cell phones to 90 (tens of thousands), what would be the new price and quantity in Canada?
   Price: _____ Quantity: _____

54A. **(LO 2, 5)** If comparative cost is the basis for trade, why are the developing countries (which have very low wage rates) not the world's greatest trading nations?

55A. **(LO 1, 2)** Explain the theory of comparative advantage. How does it differ from the theory of absolute advantage?

EXCHANGE RATES AND THE BALANCE OF PAYMENTS

LEARNING OBJECTIVES

At the end of this chapter, you should be able to...

LO1 calculate the value of the Canadian dollar in terms of other currencies and understand the purchasing power parity theory.

LO2 identify who wants to buy and sell Canadian dollars in foreign exchange markets.

LO3 explain why the value of the Canadian dollar fluctuates.

LO4 compare flexible and fixed exchange rate systems.

LO5 understand the meaning of a balance of payments surplus and deficit.

WHAT'S AHEAD...

We now turn our focus to exchange rates and international finance. This is the last step on our way to revisiting economic policy making in Chapter 12. In this chapter, we begin by discussing a nation's exchange rate and then examine why this rate might appreciate or depreciate. We then look at the consequences of such changes in the exchange rate under a flexible-exchange-rate system. This sets up our discussion about fixed-exchange-rate systems. Finally, we explain how international transactions of trade and finance are recorded in a nation's Balance of Payments statement.

A Question of Relevance...

One of the more dramatic changes in the Canadian economy in the last several years has been the increase in the value of the Canadian dollar when measured in terms of the American dollar. In November of 2001, $1 Canadian could be bought for $0.63 U.S. Four years later, it took $0.85 U.S. to buy $1 Canadian. Then, in the fall of 2007, the Canadian dollar went over par and hovered there for the next few years reaching several cents above par in the summer of 2011. These dramatic moves are, to some extent, a reflection of Canada's rich endowment of commodities, such as oil, gold, copper, and grain, which often experience wide swings in prices. Are there other reasons for this change? And is a rising Canadian dollar necessarily a good thing for Canada? This chapter will help answer these questions.

Suppose that a resident of Alberta buys a product that was made in Quebec. This involves an economic exchange that we all understand. The product is moved west and the money payment flows east, and that is that. But now, suppose that the same Alberta resident buys a product that was made in Japan. How is this exchange any different? In one sense, there is no difference, in that the product goes one way and the payment the other. But in another sense, it is different—here, two currencies are involved. The Alberta resident will want to pay in Canadian dollars, and the Japanese seller will want to be paid in yen. This means that an exchange between the two currencies will have to occur as the one currency is converted to the other. This exchange will involve at least one bank. Import and export regulations and procedures are also involved. Thus, international trade is more complicated than domestic trade, and the most obvious complication is the exchange rate itself. Let us now go to a discussion of exchange rates.

11.1 EXCHANGE RATES

L01 Calculate the value of the Canadian dollar in terms of other currencies and understand the purchasing power parity theory.

For most people, an exchange rate is an enigma, and yet it is nothing more than the comparative value of one currency in terms of another. It is, if you like, the relative price of a currency. Until fairly recently, it was possible to state the value of a currency in terms of an international medium of exchange: gold. When countries were on the gold standard, each currency could be valued in terms of a comparative amount of gold. Today, however, if you want to know how much a Canadian dollar is worth, the answer can be expressed only in terms of how many American dollars, British pounds, Swiss francs, or some other currency it can buy.

Before we look at the determinants of exchange rates, let us make sure that you are able to easily convert one currency into another. For instance, if the Canadian dollar is worth $0.80 American, then how much is an American dollar worth in Canada? The answer is $1.25 (not $1.20). If you are not sure why, then ask yourself, what is the value of an American dollar if a Canadian dollar is worth $0.50 American—$1.50? $2? The answer is $2 Canadian.

Both the $0.50 and $2 are **exchange rates**: Canadian for American, and American for Canadian. In general, to convert one currency into another, we simply take the reciprocal.

exchange rate: the rate at which one currency is exchanged for another.

$$\frac{\text{1 Canadian dollar}}{\text{(in units of foreign currency)}} = \frac{1}{\text{foreign currency (in Canadian dollars)}} \qquad \text{[11.1]}$$

$$\frac{\text{1 unit of foreign currency}}{\text{(in Canadian dollars)}} = \frac{1}{\text{Canadian dollars (in foreign currency)}} \qquad \text{[11.2]}$$

If a Canadian dollar is worth 5 Mexican pesos, then one Mexican peso is worth 1/5, or $0.20 Canadian. If a Canadian dollar is worth 0.50 British pounds, then a British pound would be worth 1/0.50, or $2 Canadian. And if the Canadian dollar is worth 0.80 American dollars, then an American dollar is worth 1/0.80, or 1.25 Canadian dollars.

Exchange rates fluctuate, sometimes rising and sometimes falling. Such an increase or decrease is always in terms of another currency. For example, assume that instead of one British pound equalling $2 Canadian, it now equals $4 Canadian. How much is the Canadian dollar worth now? The answer is 0.25 pounds. In other words, when one **currency appreciates** in terms of another, the other **currency depreciates** in value automatically. This is not a case of cause and effect; it is simply true by definition.

currency appreciation: the rise in the exchange rate of one currency for another.

currency depreciation: the fall in the exchange rate of one currency for another.

Another point worth making is the fact that just because the Canadian dollar might be depreciating against the American dollar, it does not mean that it is also depreciating against other currencies. In fact, it may well be *appreciating* against the Japanese yen or against the euro.

We need to answer two questions in this chapter. What determines the value of any given currency? And what are the causes of changes in this value? The exchange rate is simply the relative price of a currency, and that price may be determined by either the interaction of demand and supply in the marketplace, or it may be determined by government decree. In the first case, we are looking at **flexible** (or floating) **exchange rates** and in the second, at **fixed** (or pegged) **exchange rates**. We will look at each in turn.

Before we get into a detailed analysis of currency value determination, we should mention a well-established economic theory known as the **purchasing power parity theory** of exchange rates. This theory suggests that in the long run, exchange rates will adjust so as to equate the purchasing power of each country's currency. This means, for instance, that a pint of beer should have the same real price in every country. (You will have to use a different currency in each, of course.) It also means that a thousand Canadian dollars should have the same spending power in Canada as the equivalent number of euros in France or Japanese yen.

On the surface, this seems difficult to accept. Most international jetsetters (and anybody who shops south of the border) realize that commodities in some countries are relatively cheap for Canadians and one can have a reasonably good time for very little (in parts of Africa and Asia and in most Latin American countries, for example), whereas commodities in other countries are prohibitively expensive for the average Canadian (such as Japan, the Scandinavian countries, and Switzerland). So, why would anyone suggest that the cost of living in various countries should become comparable over time?

In answering this question, we will work through a model in which we assume that transport costs are negligible and that each country produces products that are identical to those from other countries. For instance, suppose that Sweden produces and sells coal at 1000 Swedish krona a tonne; Canada also produces and sells coal, for $200 a tonne. Further, suppose that the exchange rate is $1 Canadian = 5 kronas. The price of coal, therefore, is the same in both countries. Now, what would happen if the price of coal in Canada were to rise to $250 a tonne? If the exchange rate remained the same, everybody would buy their coal in Sweden. But, of course, the exchange rate would not remain the same. People would be demanding kronas in order to buy Swedish coal. The krona would appreciate (as would, in all likelihood, the price of Swedish coal). But how much would it appreciate? Well, as long as there was a difference in prices, it would pay some enterprising company to buy coal in Sweden, where it is cheap, and sell it in Canada, where it is expensive.

Assuming that the price of coal in Sweden remains at 1000 kronas a tonne, then the krona will appreciate until the prices in Canada and Sweden are the same—that is, until $250 is equal to 1000 krona. In other words, the krona will appreciate until one Canadian dollar is worth only four kronas instead of five kronas.

Once again, purchasing power parity theory says that if the same product is sold at different prices in different countries, it would be worthwhile buying it where it is cheap and selling it where it is expensive. This is referred to as **arbitrage**. But this action, by itself, will cause the exchange rates to adjust until there is no longer any difference in the relative prices.

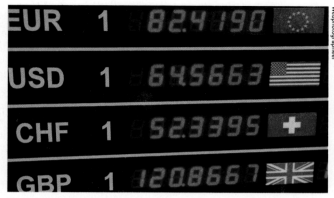

Most banks and exchange bureaus post the exchange rates on display boards so that they are readily accessible to travellers.

flexible exchange rate: a currency exchange rate determined by the market forces of supply and demand and not interfered with by government action.

fixed exchange rate: a currency exchange rate pegged by government and, therefore, prevented from rising or falling.

purchasing power parity theory: a theory suggesting that exchange rates will change so as to equate the purchasing power of each currency.

arbitrage: the process of buying a commodity in one market, where the price is low, and immediately selling it in a second market where the price is higher.

ADDED DIMENSION Strong Currencies

The international value of a currency is, unfortunately, regarded by some people (even at times by some economists) as an indicator of a country's economic strength and prestige on the international stage. Thus, when the Canadian dollar appreciates in value, it is sometimes described as a "stronger" dollar. Exchange rates are nothing more than the price (in terms of some other currency) of a currency, and how can one possibly talk of strong or weak prices? If this made any sense, we could certainly say that the price of beer is getting much stronger in Canada. Exchange rates appreciate and depreciate. They do not get stronger or weaker.

Yet, prices are not the same worldwide. Why? First, if the price of a haircut in Edmonton is only half the price of a haircut in New Orleans, we would not really expect a mass exodus of Edmontonians heading down to Louisiana to get their locks shorn. In other words, certain goods and services are not transportable, and therefore, differences in the prices of these things may well persist over time between countries. Second, if transport and other shipping costs are taken into account, price differences might continue. Third, tariffs and import quotas limit the quantity and increase the costs of trade and lead to price differences between countries. Fourth, products are not identical. Some people do prefer, say, Japanese cars over North American cars. Fifth, and finally, exchange rates do not equate the purchasing power among countries because they are also greatly affected by the international sale and purchase of financial assets. Sometimes, there is a strong demand by foreigners for Canadian shares and bonds. At other times, Canadians may have a strong demand for foreign shares and bonds.

So, there are five factors that explain differences in purchasing power between countries:

- The fact that many services, such as haircuts, are not traded internationally
- The existence of transportation and insurance costs
- The existence of tariffs and other trade restrictions
- The expression of particular preferences by consumers
- The effect on the value of currencies of trade in financial assets

Despite all of these reservations, many economists still hold that, with globalization and the freer movement of products and factors, in the long run there is a tendency for exchange rates to move toward equalizing the purchasing power of currencies. Whether or not this is true, we still need to explain day-to-day and year-to-year fluctuations in exchange rates.

 ADDED DIMENSION   The Big Mac Purchasing Power Parity Theory

Since 1986, the *Economist* magazine has published a "Big Mac" Index comparing the relative prices of a Big Mac around the world and, with it, the relative value of currencies. Since countries no longer use gold as an international currency of exchange (and, therefore, of comparison), the *Economist* decided to use the Big Mac instead. So if a Big Mac costs $3.80 in the United States and 13.73 yuan in China (as of January 2011), then 13.73 yuan should be worth $3.80 or one U.S. dollar should be equal to 13.73/3.80, or 3.61 yuan. The actual exchange rate was, in fact, 6.62 yuan per dollar. Most commentators would, therefore, suggest that the yuan is mightily undervalued against the U.S. dollar. Here are some comparisons with other countries (as at January 2011).

However, this comparison could be interpreted differently. For instance, if purchasing power were equal on all products between the United States and Norway, then the price of a Big Mac in Norway should be the same as it is in the United States (converted at the actual exchange rate of 5.82 krone per $U.S.). It should cost, therefore, 3.80 × 5.82 = 22.12 krone. The actual price is, in fact, 46.36 krone. This would suggest that the krone is overvalued. However, it is possible that the high price of a Big Mac in Norway is simply a reflection of the higher wages rates for workers in the fast food industry in Norway, compared with the wage rates in the United States.

Country	Price in Local Currency	Big Mac ER (local currency price/US price)	Actual ER	Over-/Under-valued
Norway	46.36 krone	12.20 krone	5.82 krone	+118%
Switzerland	6.70 franc	1.76 franc	0.94 franc	+92%
Canada	4.26 $ Canadian	1.12 $ Canadian	1.00 $ Canadian	+12%
Japan	312 yen	86 yen	82 yen	+5%
UK	2.32 £ British	0.61 £ British	0.65 £ British	−2%
Mexico	12.26 peso	8.60 peso	12.26 peso	−28%
Russia	73.1 ruble	19.2 ruble	30.6 ruble	−32%

Source: www.Maxi-Pedia.com.

✓ SELF-TEST

1. a) Assume that a Swedish krona is worth $0.20 Canadian. How much is a Canadian dollar worth in krona?

b) Assume that one Canadian dollar equals 70 Japanese yen. How much is a yen worth in Canadian dollars?

11.2 FLEXIBLE EXCHANGE RATES

In the absence of government involvement, exchange rates are determined by the interplay of demand and supply in a free market. Canada has officially had a flexible exchange rate since the early 1970s, during which time the value of the Canadian dollar has fluctuated from a high of approximately $1.04 U.S. in 1973 to a low of $0.63 U.S. in 2001, then back up again to trade above par in the spring of 2011. However, even when governments do not actually fix exchange rates, they still often feel it necessary to intervene in international exchange markets so as to influence the value of currencies. They become, therefore, active players in the game of buying and selling currencies. For the time being, however, we will ignore such involvement and concentrate on the determination of exchange rates entirely by market forces.

L02 Identify who wants to buy and sell Canadian dollars in foreign exchange markets.

Demand for the Canadian Dollar

Apart from Canadians, who else wants to obtain Canadian dollars? The first and most obvious group are foreigners who want to obtain Canadian goods and services. The demand for Canadian exports, such as forest products and automobiles, therefore, creates a demand for the Canadian dollar. Note, however, that some services can only be enjoyed in Canada. We are thinking here of restaurant, hotel, and other tourist services required by foreigners travelling in Canada. Tourism in Canada, therefore, represents a (significant) Canadian export. Conversely, spending by Canadians on imported goods or by travel abroad represents a Canadian import.

A second demand for the Canadian dollar involves foreigners who want to purchase Canadian investments. These investments might include the purchase of Canadian real estate or real assets, which are called **direct investment**, or it might include the purchase by foreigners of Canadian shares or bonds, known as **portfolio investment**. In either case, a demand is created for the Canadian dollar with which to purchase these investments. The level of portfolio investment in Canada by foreigners is partly driven by the interest rate paid on savings in Canada relative to that paid elsewhere. If Canadian bonds are paying an average of 6 percent while similar bonds in the United States are paying only 4.5 percent, then portfolio investment into Canada and the demand for Canadian dollars will be strong.

direct investment: the purchase of real assets.

portfolio investment: the purchase of shares or bonds representing less than 50 percent ownership.

This brings us to the third group of people who demand Canadian dollars: Canadians who receive income, gifts, or transfers from abroad. This includes, for instance, people who have previously bought foreign investments. These people will be earning returns on these investments, which will be paid to them in foreign currencies. As Canadians, of course, they do not have much use for foreign currencies, and they will want to convert these currencies into Canadian dollars.

A fourth group that wants to buy Canadian dollars is speculators. Speculators who deal in foreign exchange are no different from other types of speculators. They hope to buy when the price is low and sell later when the price is high. Speculators buying Canadian dollars are, therefore, hoping for an appreciation of the Canadian dollar relative to foreign currencies some time in the future, when they will then sell. The level of currency speculation depends a great deal on the expectations that people hold toward the currency. If people expect the Canadian exchange rate to fall, then speculators will sell Canadian dollars in exchange for other currencies. This action will have the effect of pushing the actual value of the dollar down and thus fulfilling people's expectations.

The Canadian Press (Chuck Stoody)

Railway trains carrying grain for export are constantly on the move at the United Grain Growers elevator in Vancouver.

There is another group of currency dealers who also buy and sell Canadian dollars, but for a different reason. They buy Canadian dollars (or any other currency) whenever they see a difference in quoted exchange rates on different international exchanges. For instance, let us say that the Canadian dollar is quoted at $0.985 American on the Zurich exchange but is being quoted at $0.988 on the Tokyo exchange. Then, someone will find it profitable to buy Canadian dollars in Switzerland (where they are cheap) and sell them in Japan (where they are relatively more expensive). As we mentioned earlier, this is known as *arbitrage*. Note that, unlike speculators, those engaged in arbitrage are not concerned with the future value of the Canadian dollar and are not holding them to sell at some later date; they are selling immediately.

To sum up, five groups have a demand for the Canadian dollar:

- Foreigners who want to buy Canadian exports or who travel in Canada
- Foreigners who want to purchase Canadian investments
- Canadians who receive income or gifts or transfers from abroad
- Currency speculators
- Arbitragers

Finally, as noted above, governments also sometimes buy and sell currencies, but more on this later.

Now, remember what we mean by the demand for a currency. It is no different from the demand for any other product or service; that is, it is defined as the quantities that people are willing and able to buy at various prices in the foreign exchange market. As you would expect, the demand curve for the Canadian dollar is downward-sloping, as shown in **Figure 11.1**.

Note that on the vertical axis, we need to express the price of the Canadian dollar in terms of another currency. It would be a bit silly to express the price of the Canadian dollar in Canadian dollars because then it would always equal one. The currency you choose to express it in, other than the Canadian dollar, is of no importance. On our graph, we have used the pengo, the currency of the mythical and fascinating country of Pengoland. We do this to emphasize that any given currency can be expressed in any other currency.

FIGURE 11.1   The Demand for the Canadian Dollar

The demand curve for the Canadian dollar is downward sloping, reflecting the inverse relationship between the price of the currency and the quantity demanded. At P_1 the quantity demanded is Q_1.

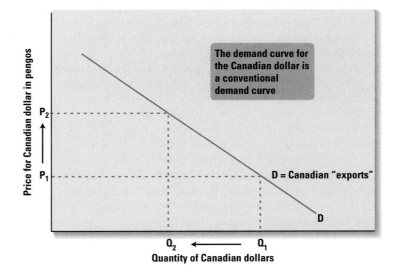

The demand curve for the Canadian dollar is a conventional demand curve

Price for Canadian dollar in pengos

P_2

P_1

D = Canadian "exports"

D

Q_2 ← Q_1

Quantity of Canadian dollars

The demand curve is, of course, downward sloping, which implies that at a higher exchange rate the quantity of Canadian dollars demanded will be low; at a low exchange rate, the quantity demanded will be high. Now, let us figure out why that should be so. Remember that the demand for the Canadian dollar comes, by and large, from foreigners buying our goods, services, and investments, that is, from Canadian exports in the broad sense. To help you remember this, we have added the label Canadian "Exports" to the demand curve. However, remember that the demand for the Canadian dollar comes not just from people who want to buy our products, but from those who want to buy our assets as well as those speculators and arbitragers who just want the dollars themselves.

Let us start off by assuming that the Canadian dollar is worth one pengo and that one of our major exports to Pengoland is smoked salmon, which is priced at $100 a box in Canada and therefore sells for 100 pengos in Pengoland. Now, what would happen if the value of the Canadian dollar were to appreciate so that $1 Canadian is now equal to two pengos? (Note that as the Canadian dollar appreciates, the pengo depreciates; it is now worth only 50 cents). The effect of such an appreciation is summarized in **Table 11.1**.

TABLE 11.1

Price of One Canadian Dollar	Price in Canada of a Box of Salmon	Price in Pengoland of a Box of Salmon
1 pengo	$100	100 pengos
2 pengos	$100	200 pengos

Despite the fact that the price of smoked salmon in Canada remains unchanged, its effective price has increased as far as the Pengolians are concerned. Whereas earlier they paid 100 pengos, now they will have to pay 200 pengos for the same box. One would expect therefore that they would buy less smoked salmon. In other words, when the Canadian dollar appreciates, the effective prices of Canadian exports increase, and total exports are likely to decline.

You can see why a high Canadian dollar is likely to be unpopular among Canadian exporters and in the high-export provinces of Canada. For example, even a small increase in the Canadian dollar can have big implications in terms of sales, profits, and employment in the B.C. lumber industry and is looked on with alarm. Not only that, a higher Canadian dollar also means that the effective price of Canadian financial investments will be higher for foreigners so that foreign investment is likely to decrease.

The depreciation of the Canadian dollar, however, has the opposite effect. Assume, for instance, that starting from $1 Canadian = 1 pengo, the Canadian dollar were to fall to $1 Canadian = 0.5 pengo. (The pengo now equals $2 Canadian; that is, it has appreciated). The same box of Canadian smoked salmon that used to cost the Pengolians 100 pengos can now be obtained for a mere 50 pengos. This will then cause exports of smoked salmon to increase. In general, therefore, when the Canadian dollar depreciates, the effective prices of Canadian exports decrease, and total exports are likely to increase. Exporters will prefer a low Canadian dollar to a high Canadian dollar, since this makes Canadian products more competitive abroad.

We can summarize these results as follows:

> When the Canadian dollar depreciates, the effective prices of Canadian exports decrease, and total exports are likely to rise.

> When the Canadian dollar appreciates, the effective prices of Canadian exports increase, and total exports are likely to fall.

ADDED DIMENSION   The Effective Exchange Rate

There is no single commodity whose value remains constant and against which all currencies can be measured. This means the Canadian dollar might well be *depreciating* against one currency, such as the American dollar, but at the same time appreciating against all other currencies. It is possible, however, to work out an average of what is happening to the Canadian dollar. This is what is referred to as the *effective exchange rate*.

The effective exchange rate compares the value of the Canadian dollar in terms of the average value of the currencies of all the countries with which Canada trades. It is a weighted average, which means that the value of the American dollar, for instance, would carry more weight than, say, the Swiss franc in calculating its value, since Canada does much more trade with the United States than it does with Switzerland. The effective exchange rate is also based on an index value of 100, assigned in the base year, which was 1992. The accompanying graph shows how Canada has performed against the effective exchange rate and against major currencies this past decade.

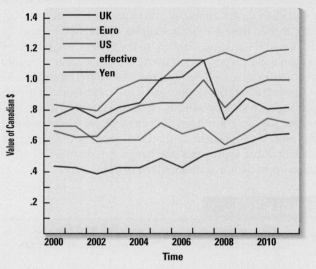

SOURCE: Bank of Canada, *Banking and Financial Statistics*, May 2011, Table I1.

It should be pointed out, as this example makes clear, that a drop in the value of the Canadian dollar is not—as many people think—by itself a bad thing. Although there are some undesirable aspects that we will look at later, for such a big exporting country as ours, a lower dollar may be very good news, since it stimulates export spending, which, in turn, will boost employment and incomes.

 SELF-TEST

2. Given the events described below, indicate whether the demand for the Canadian dollar would appreciate, depreciate, or not change.

a) Canadian exports rise.

b) Vancouver hosts the Winter Olympics in 2010.

c) IBM, ITT, and the provincial government announce the construction of a $2 billion data processing and informational transfer complex in Halifax.

d) Migration from the Maritime provinces to Ontario increases appreciably.

Supply of Canadian Dollars

Let us now look at the other side of the coin, the supply of Canadian dollars on the foreign exchange market, and examine who exactly provides this supply. Most people probably think it is government or the Bank of Canada. That may be true under certain circumstances, as we shall see later. However, in a free market system, it is not really necessary for these institutions to supply Canadian dollars to foreigners, since through normal international trade, transactions dollars will be made available automatically on the world's money market. How does this come about? The simple fact is that if Canadians wish to purchase foreign currencies, then we will use Canadian dollars to make these purchases. Thus, in obtaining foreign currencies, we must automatically supply Canadian dollars. In other words, if we send Canadian dollars to France to buy euros so that we can buy, say, French wine, France will now have Canadian dollars that it can use

| FIGURE 11.2 | The Supply of the Canadian Dollar |

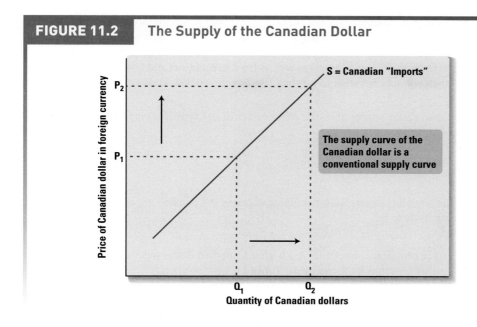

The supply of the Canadian dollar is upward sloping, reflecting the direct relationship between the price of the currency and the quantity supplied. At price P_1, the quantity supplied is Q_1.

to buy Canadian products. In general, therefore, the supply of Canadian dollars comes from our demand for foreign currencies. This relationship between the supply of and demand for currencies is important enough to emphasize:

Demand for foreign currencies = Supply of Canadian dollars
Demand for Canadian dollars = Supply of foreign currencies

The supply of Canadian dollars is graphed in **Figure 11.2**.

Why is the supply curve upward sloping? It is for the usual reason—an increase in the price (of a currency) will lead to an increase in the quantity supplied. Or, put another way, an appreciation of the Canadian dollar will lead to an increase in imports because we will be able to afford to buy more foreign goods with our dollars. Let us make sure that we understand this. Suppose that Pengoland is famous for its production and export of wonderful smoked hams, which presently sell for 100 pengos each. At an exchange rate of $1 Canadian for 1 pengo, the hams costs Canadians $100 each. Now, let us see the effect of the Canadian dollar appreciating so that, for instance, the Canadian dollar is now worth 2 pengos. (The pengo has depreciated to $0.50 Canadian.) This is good news for Canadians since they will now have to pay only $50 for a ham because the $50 will now give them the 100 pengos necessary to purchase the ham. Since a lower pengo is the same thing to Canadians as lower priced ham, the sale of ham to Canada will increase, and so, too, will the quantity of Canadian dollars exchanged. The effect of the appreciation of the Canadian dollar is summarized in **Table 11.2**.

TABLE 11.2		
Price of One Canadian Dollar	Price in Pengoland of Smoked Ham	Price in Canada of Ham
1 pengo	100 pengos	$100
2 pengos	100 pengos	$50

Just as we added an extra label to the demand curve, we have added the label Canadian "Imports" to the supply curve to remind you that the supply comes from Canadians wishing to buy foreign currencies so that they can import foreign products. Again, we should add the caution that the supply also comes from purchases of assets as well as from speculators and arbitragers, who do not want to import any products but wish to just buy foreign currencies. Thus we have the following:

> **When the Canadian dollar appreciates, the effective prices of Canadian imports decrease, and total imports are likely to rise.**

Conversely...

> **When the Canadian dollar depreciates, the effective prices of Canadian imports increase, and total imports are likely to fall.**

This brings us to one simple question. Is a higher Canadian dollar a good or a bad thing? Let us start to answer this question by focusing on **Table 11.3**.

TABLE 11.3

	Exports	**Imports**
Canadian dollar appreciates	FALL Canadian commodity producers are hurt; tourism is down; foreigners invest less in Canada	RISE Canadians shop more in the United States; more foreign cars sold in Canada; Canadians invest more abroad
Canadian dollar depreciates	RISE Canadian commodity producers are helped; tourism booms; foreign investment in Canada is up	FALL U.S. shoppers start showing up in Canada; more domestic cars are sold; Canadians invest less abroad

In terms of Canadian jobs and income levels, we can see from the table that a lower Canadian dollar is preferable. But we must be careful to recognize that the *reason* the dollar is high or low is crucial to answering our question. If the Canadian dollar appreciates because the world wants more Canadian goods, and therefore exports are booming, it is "a good thing." But if the Canadian dollar appreciates because the rest of the world is rushing into the Toronto Stock Exchange to speculate on new oil and gold discoveries, it is "a bad thing."

So, now, we need to think about what causes the dollar to appreciate and depreciate.

Equilibrium in Foreign-Exchange Markets

To obtain an equilibrium exchange rate, we put together the supply and demand curves, as is done in **Figure 11.3**.

Note that at the equilibrium exchange rate, the quantity demanded for the Canadian dollar is equal to the quantity supplied. The demand comes from foreigners (Canadian exports) and the supply comes from Canadians (Canadian imports). Can foreigners always get their hands on sufficient Canadian dollars to purchase Canadian goods? Certainly. It does not require any assistance from the Canadian government or from the Bank of Canada. With truly flexible exchange rates, sufficient Canadian dollars are made available by Canadians themselves, who automatically supply dollars when purchasing foreign currencies. Note also that at equilibrium, not only are the

FIGURE 11.3	The Demand for and Supply of the Canadian Dollar

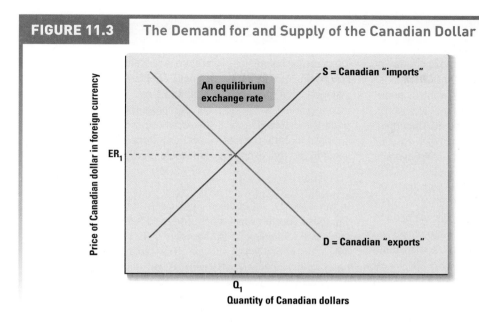

The intersection of the demand and supply curves yields the equilibrium exchange rate: ER_1. At ER_1 the quantity of dollars demanded and the quantity supplied are equal.

quantity supplied and the quantity demanded of Canadian dollars equal, but the quantities demanded and quantity supplied of foreign currencies in Canada will also be equal. Remember that foreign currencies are made available to Canadians whenever a foreigner purchases Canadian products or investments; at equilibrium, such foreign currencies will just be sufficient to satisfy the demand from Canadians for these currencies.

A further point worth mentioning about foreign exchange markets is that they provide "textbook" approximations of the perfectly competitive market. All the ingredients are present—large numbers of buyers and sellers, homogeneous product, easy entry and exit, and so on—plus arbitrage and speculation, both of which are unique to competitive markets.

 SELF-TEST

3. Imagine that the Canadian dollar appreciates.

  a) What would happen to Canadian imports?

  b) What would happen to Canadian exports?

11.3 CHANGES IN DEMAND AND SUPPLY

Since the value of a currency is determined by the interplay of supply and demand, it follows that any change in supply or demand will change its value. We now focus on what could cause a change in demand or supply and how such a change will affect a currency's value. Let us start on the demand side. What could cause people to demand more Canadian dollars, even though there has been no change in the currency's value? Well, the first and most straightforward reason would be a rise in incomes in the countries that buy Canadian goods. It seems reasonable to suggest that if *foreign incomes* increase, then the demand for all available products, including Canadian ones, will increase. Let us trace through the effects using **Figure 11.4**.

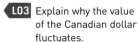 **LO3** Explain why the value of the Canadian dollar fluctuates.

ADDED DIMENSION   Real Exchange Rates

How would you feel about emigrating to the fictitious country of Albioni, where the average monthly salary is 20 000 albions? Before you could decide, you would probably want to know, among many other things, what 20 000 albions are worth. Suppose that you learned that 1 albion equalled $1 Canadian, would that help you decide? If you still cannot make up your mind, perhaps some more data would be helpful. An average meal in Albioni will cost you 200 albions per person, a pair of socks cost 20 albions, and a new car will cost you 200 000 albions. Now, a rational decision is easier to make. In other words, in order to compare the values of currencies, we need to know not only the exchange rate but *also* the average price level in each country. This is what the real exchange rate measures. Its formula is:

$$\text{real exchange rate} = \frac{\text{price level in Canada}}{\text{price level in other country}} \times \text{nominal exchange rate}$$

The nominal exchange rate is simply the value of the Canadian dollar, measured in terms of the foreign currency ($0.98 American, 90 yen, and so on). As an example, suppose that a brand new Toyota costs 1 800 000 yen in Japan and that an equivalent Ford car in Canada costs $20 000. If the exchange rate was equal to 90 yen per Canadian dollar, then you can see that the two cars have equivalent value.

$$\text{real exchange rate} = \frac{20\ 000}{1\ 800\ 000} \times 90 = 1$$

The real exchange rate, therefore, measures the comparative purchasing power of a currency. The formula tells you, for instance, that the value of Canada's real exchange rate will increase if either the nominal exchange rate or the Canadian price level increases, or if the Japanese price level falls. Now, suppose that the price of a new Ford dropped to $15 000. The value of the real exchange rate would change.

$$\text{real exchange rate} = \frac{15\ 000}{1\ 800\ 000} \times 90 = 0.75$$

In other words, a Canadian Ford owner is now poorer than a Japanese Toyota owner, since if he sold his car and converted it into yen (obtaining 15 000 × 90 or 1 350 000 yen), he could only afford to buy 3/4 of a Toyota. The Toyota owner, on the other hand, could now buy 4/3 Fords. Given this, you can imagine that Japanese buyers will be flocking to buy Canadian Fords, which have become a real bargain. The result of this increased demand (for both Fords and for the Canadian dollar) is that both of them will increase. Can you figure out how far they will increase? Until the real exchange rate is again equal to 1. This is the reason economists suggest that there is a long-run tendency for the purchasing power of all currencies to move toward par.

FIGURE 11.4   **An Increase in the Demand for a Currency**

A rightward shift in the demand for the Canadian dollar will cause the equilibrium exchange rate to rise from ER_1 to ER_2 and the equilibrium quantity to increase from Q_1 to Q_2.

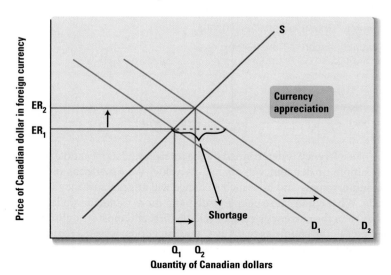

The initial demand curve is D_1. The increase in foreign income and the resulting increase in the demand for Canadian exports will increase the demand for Canadian dollars. This is illustrated by the shift in the demand curve to D_2. The increase in demand creates a shortage of Canadian dollars, which results in the exchange rate rising from ER_1 to ER_2. At this higher exchange rate, we obtain a new equilibrium. This higher exchange rate means that the attractiveness of Canadian exports is reduced because they are effectively more expensive. However, the volume of trade has still increased *despite* the higher Canadian dollar.

Note that imports and exports have increased. Why have imports increased? Remember that the higher exchange rate, ER_2, makes imports cheaper, and therefore, more are bought. In other words, an increase in the demand for Canadian goods and services will increase Canadian exports, even though it has caused the Canadian dollar to appreciate. The amount of Canadian imports has also increased, but this is because of the appreciation.

Perhaps a small reminder is in order. The level of Canadian exports is independent of Canadian income; it is determined by the level of foreign income. Conversely, the level of Canadian imports definitely does depend on the level of our income: the greater our income, the more we import.

Other things will also cause a change in the demand for Canadian dollars. For example, the *price of Canadian products that are traded abroad* will have an impact on demand. A decrease in the price of these goods will cause the worldwide demand for such products to increase. It must be added, however, that it is not the absolute level of prices of traded goods that is important but rather the relative level compared with that of other countries. An increase in the prices of foreign goods that compete with Canadian exports will have the same effect on the demand for Canadian exports, as would the decrease in Canadian prices.

Another factor affecting the demand for a currency is the view foreigners have of Canadian goods—in short, *foreigners' tastes*. For example, if tastes shifted away from wood-frame houses toward metal-frame houses, this could well decrease Canada's lumber exports.

A final factor affecting the demand for Canadian dollars is *interest rates*. When foreigners are deciding whether or not to put money into Canada, they will look at a number of factors, but the rate of interest that they can obtain is certainly one of the most important. Traditionally, rates of interest in Canada have been kept above those in the United States expressly to encourage the inflow of American money and to discourage the outflow of Canadian dollars to the United States. Obviously, the higher the rate of interest, the higher the level of foreign currency flow into Canada. This will mean a higher demand for Canadian dollars. As with prices, it is not the absolute level of interest rates that is important but the difference between Canadian rates and those in other countries. The demand for the Canadian dollar would therefore increase with a drop in interest rates abroad. In summary, the demand for the Canadian dollar is determined by four important factors:

- The level of foreign incomes
- The price of Canadian products relative to the price of foreign products
- Foreigners' tastes
- Comparative interest rates

We now need to recognize that any change in the demand for the Canadian dollar will have effects on the domestic economy. If the demand for the Canadian dollar has increased because Canadian exports have increased, aggregate demand will also have increased. Whether this increase in exports is because of higher foreign incomes, lower Canadian prices, or a change in tastes in favour of Canadian goods does not matter. The higher exports mean greater aggregate demand. This is illustrated in **Figure 11.5**.

An increase in Canadian exports does, indeed, raise the value of the dollar (and also imports), but it also raises Canadian GDP (assuming that the increase in exports is greater than the increase in imports, which is almost always the case). This process is often called an export-led boom. Foreigners buy more Canadian goods, and this raises aggregate demand within Canada, creating new jobs, raising GDP, and finally raising the price level.

FIGURE 11.5	The Effect of an Increase of Exports on Aggregate Demand

An increase in Canadian exports increases aggregate demand, as illustrated by the shift from AD_1 to AD_2. This results in a rise in both the price level and in GDP.

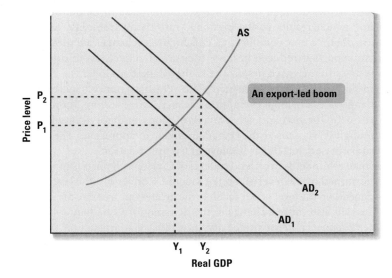

ADDED DIMENSION   Foreign Investment and Interest-Rate Parity

The amount of international funds looking for a good (profitable) home is enormous. International investors are constantly seeking opportunities where they can earn the highest returns on their funds. Hundreds of billions of dollars are traded every day in foreign-exchange markets. (In contrast, the demand for Canadian dollars to buy Canadian products is less than $1 billion per day.)

An investor buying foreign financial assets can earn a return from both the interest and from an appreciation in the value of the currency in which it is denominated. For instance, suppose I buy a South African bond that has a value of 5000 rands and pays annual interest of 8 percent. If the exchange rate is 5 rands to the dollar, it will cost me $1000 to buy the bond. At the end of the year, I receive 5400 rands. Now, suppose that during the year, the rand has appreciated to 4.5 rands to the dollar. Converting my rands back into dollars gives me $1200. I have, therefore, earned $200, or 20 percent, on my original $1000. I earned 8 percent in interest and 12 percent from the appreciation of the rand.

This also means that if the currency I hold drops in value, the interest earned is wiped out by the loss on the exchange rate. Foreign investors, therefore, are concerned not only with interest

to be earned but also with what might happen to the value of the foreign currency. This is the reason there are often big differences in interest rates around the world.

Ask yourself this: if Canadians can earn only 5 percent interest in Canada but can earn 20 percent in Mexico, why wouldn't all the funds flow out of Canada and into Mexico? The answer is that in order to earn that 20 percent per year, you have to convert your dollars into pesos and leave them in pesos for a whole year. But many are fearful that during the year, the value of the peso might fall against the dollar. How much does the average investor think it will fall? Presumably by 15 percent. Why this amount? Because they will earn a certain 20 percent in interest on their funds but expect to lose 15 percent on the depreciation of the peso, netting them 5 percent—the same amount they can earn in Canada. In other words, if you take into consideration both the interest earned and the gain or loss on the foreign currency, the rate of return you can earn is more or less equal around the world. This is often referred to as *interest-rate parity*, though perhaps it would be better to refer to it as *rate-of-return parity*.

FIGURE 11.6	An Increase in the Supply of Canadian Dollars

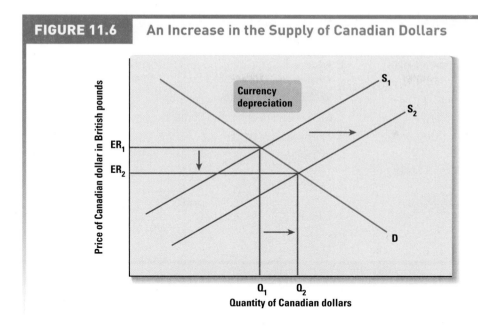

An increase in the supply of Canadian dollars is represented by the shift from S_1 to S_2. As a result of this increase, the value of the Canadian dollar decreases and the quantity of Canadian dollars bought and sold increases.

You should also note that we can see here that this export-led boom may have the effect of reducing the size of the Canadian multiplier. This is because the boom will, as we just mentioned, likely increase the prices of Canadian products and, further, will raise the value of the Canadian exchange rate. Both of these effects will tend to dampen the effect of the initial rise in exports.

A very important point in all this discussion is that the exchange rate does not move in isolation from the domestic economy. What happens on the international market very much affects what happens internally. This has always been true, but it is becoming increasingly pertinent as the world's economies become more integrated, as we saw in Chapter 10.

Let us now work through a situation that affects Canadians' demand for imported goods. Assume that Canada were to remove the tariffs on British products coming into Canada. To the Canadian consumer, this lowers the price of British products; and we would expect the quantity demanded of such goods by Canadians to increase. This means that the Canadian demand for the British pound increases, and this, in turn, implies that Canadians will be supplying more Canadian dollars on the world market. This last point is illustrated in Figure 11.6.

As Canadians demand more imports from the United Kingdom and thus more pounds, the supply curve of Canadian dollars shifts outward from S_1 to S_2. This will cause the exchange rate to drop to a lower level at ER_2. The removal of tariffs on British imports will tend to lead to a depreciation of the Canadian dollar and an appreciation of the pound.

In other words, British exports to Canada will increase *despite* the higher pound. In addition, British imports of Canadian products will increase *because* of the higher pound. The total value of trade will, therefore, increase.

The intellectual appeal of market-determined flexible exchange rates is strong among most economists today. If the supply of or the demand for a currency changes for any one of a variety of reasons, the exchange rate itself changes, and the economy adjusts automatically without any need for government policy and with a minimum of disruption to the domestic economy. Although, as we shall see, the benefits of a fixed exchange regime may seem very appealing, advocates of flexible exchange rates feel that the costs are far greater. Perhaps the best way to really understand all this is to now move to a discussion of fixed exchange rates and then to compare the two systems.

SELF-TEST

4. Which of the following factors would cause the Canadian dollar to appreciate?

a) A big increase in the popularity of wood-built homes in China.

b) A drop in Canadian interest rates.

c) A big increase in Canadian incomes.

d) Significantly higher inflation rates in the United States than in Canada.

e) A big economic growth in Japan.

5. Assume that the demand for Canadian exports decreases. What would be the effect on:

a) The value of the Canadian dollar

b) The level of aggregate demand

c) The level of GDP

d) The price level

11.4 FIXED EXCHANGE RATES

L04 Compare flexible and fixed exchange rate systems.

Fixed exchange rates have been the rule rather than the exception over the centuries. Until the 1970s, most governments throughout the world were persuaded that they needed to exercise control of the value of their currencies by fixing their exchange rate at a predetermined value expressed historically in gold and then in American dollars after World War II. However, Canada's experience was different, since we had a flexible rate system for most of the 1950s, while other countries remained on fixed rates. During this time the value of the Canadian dollar rose above par with the American dollar and peaked, with 1 Canadian dollar being equal to 1.08 American dollars. In 1962, Canada adopted a fixed rate of $0.925 U.S. at the urging of the IMF, but returned to a flexible exchange rate in 1970.

It is suggested that by its very nature, international trading is fraught with problems and uncertainties. If, as a Canadian company, you want to trade with a firm in Japan, Germany, or any other country, you need to understand the different commercial laws and government regulations, the language and culture, the customs and history, and a host of other factors. What you do not need is the addition of another problem: fluctuating exchange rates. After all, if you have spent a good deal of time and money negotiating a contract with some foreign firm, you do not want to run the risk of seeing all your profit wiped out by an unforeseen shift in exchange rates.

Certainly, fixed exchange rates can add a degree of certainty to international trade. Without this security, many feel that the volume of international trade would be considerably less. But besides this, if flexible exchange rates change, both exports and imports are immediately affected. This means that employment and profits in the firms within these sectors can take rather abrupt swings up or down. An appreciation of the exchange rate, for instance, will lead to a decline in exports and an expansion of imports. This will be good news for those firms that do the importing, but it will involve layoffs, cancellation of contracts, and postponement of investment plans for export industries.

The import industries, conversely, will be gearing up for the higher volumes by hiring additional staff, buying new equipment, and expanding capacity. What happens if the exchange rate now starts to depreciate? Everything will be thrown into reverse, with the export industries now booming, but the import industries suffering. Thus, it is argued, flexible exchange rates can lead to a great deal of domestic disruption and make long-term planning very difficult.

A corollary of this is the fact that flexible exchange rates can be affected by the actions of a small group of speculators. Why, it is asked, should the fortunes of many firms and the livelihoods of many people be in the hands of a few speculators who are out for private gain and cannot be held accountable for their actions? It is true that fixed exchange rates are also open to currency speculation. However, this generally happens only occasionally when pressure to devalue or revalue starts to mount. With flexible exchange rates, speculation occurs continuously.

Finally, it should be mentioned that in some people's minds, there is a great deal of national prestige tied up in exchange rates. These people feel that their nation should have a "strong" currency. When the Canadian dollar was trading well below the value of the U.S. dollar, many Canadians felt that our dollar was "weaker" than theirs—but we are dealing with two different countries and two separate currencies. There is no reason that, except through coincidence, they should be at par. Hardly anyone would suggest that the Canadian dollar should be at par with the pound sterling, the euro, or the Japanese yen, and yet the comparison of the Canadian dollar with the American dollar persists.

In summary, there are four basic arguments in favour of fixed exchange rates:

- They add a degree of certainty to international trade.
- They prevent instability in the export and import industries.
- They discourage currency speculation.
- They appeal to people who tend to equate the exchange rate with national prestige.

These are the arguments for a fixed exchange rate. Let us now delve into how such a system would function.

Fixed Exchange Rates and an Increase in Demand

Assume that the government of Canada fixed the exchange rate. This means that anyone buying or selling Canadian dollars could only do so at the official rate decreed by government. Let us begin with the rate fixed at the equilibrium market rate. Suppose that later, however, an increase in the demand for Canadian exports and thus the Canadian dollar occurs. The situation is illustrated in **Figure 11.7**.

Given a fixed exchange rate, an increase in demand for the Canadian dollar results in the dollar being undervalued compared with what its free-market value would be (the market rate ER_2 is above the fixed rate, ER_f, in this case). Foreigners see Canadian goods as very attractive buys. At the fixed rate of ER_f, the quantity demanded (Q_d) of Canadian dollars exceeds the quantity supplied (Q_s). Since government has fixed the exchange rate, it must ensure, for normal trading to continue, that enough Canadian dollars are made available to meet world demand. In other words, the Bank of Canada will have to supply this shortage by expanding the money supply. This strong demand for Canadian exports and the continual increase in money supply by the Bank of Canada will eventually be inflationary. If this inflation goes on long enough, the price

---

FIGURE 11.7   **An Increase in Currency Demand under Fixed Exchange Rates**

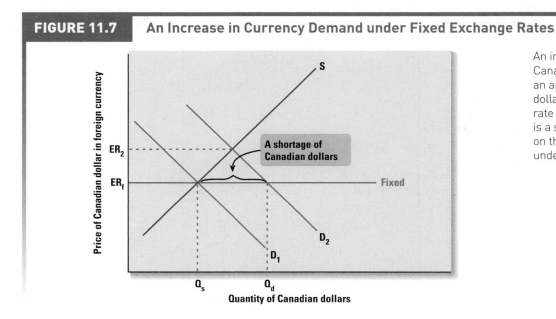

An increase in the demand for the Canadian dollar does not lead to an appreciation of the Canadian dollar under a fixed exchange rate system. The result, therefore, is a shortage of Canadian dollars on the world market and an undervalued dollar.

of Canadian goods will rise, causing the export of these goods to fall. Eventually this will reduce the demand for Canadian dollars to equilibrium on curve D_1. However, during this period of adjustment, the economy will experience inflation.

Another implication for an undervalued currency is its effect on other countries. For instance, many observers considered that the Chinese yuan, which from 1995 to 2005 was fixed to the American dollar at a rate of 8.28 yuan per American dollar, that is, 1 yuan is worth US 12 cents, was seriously undervalued and its market rate was likely much higher. Of course, this undervalued rate meant that Chinese exports were considerably cheaper than they would otherwise have been. More significantly, it also meant that exports to China were very much more expensive. The result was big trade deficits with China for the United States and other countries. This was the cause of a great deal of friction between them. In 2005, under pressure, the Chinese authorities allowed the value of the yuan a degree of flexibility and consequently it rose to 12.3 US cents. By May 2011, it had appreciated further, to 15.4 US cents, an appreciation of 28 percent from its previous fixed value.

Let us now look now at the second scenario. Many people view this scenario as more serious for an economy, so we will examine it in some detail.

Fixed Exchange Rates and a Decrease in Demand

Again, suppose that the Canadian government fixes the value of the Canadian dollar at ER_f. This time, however, the demand for the dollar drops, as shown in **Figure 11.8**.

The fixed exchange rate ER_f is now above what would be the free-market equilibrium rate ER_2, and thus, there is a surplus of Canadian dollars on the world market. Let us examine what is happening. Before the change in demand, the quantity of dollars foreigners wanted to buy was equal to the quantity supplied of dollars on the foreign exchange market. Then, the demand for the dollar dropped. Since foreigners are now buying fewer Canadian goods and services and, therefore, buying fewer Canadian dollars, the amount of foreign currencies available for Canadians to buy is reduced. Thus, this situation can be seen as either one of a surplus of Canadian dollars on the foreign exchange market or as a shortage of foreign currencies in Canada. Whichever way you look at it, the fixed exchange rate ER_f is overvalued. So, what happens next?

In instituting fixed exchange rates, the central bank must take responsibility for any surplus or shortage of currencies. Faced with an insufficient supply of foreign currencies from normal

| FIGURE 11.8 | A Decrease in Currency Demand under Fixed Exchange Rates |

A decrease in the demand for the Canadian dollar does not lead to a lower Canadian dollar under a fixed exchange rate system. The result is a surplus of Canadian dollars on the foreign exchange market and an overvalued dollar.

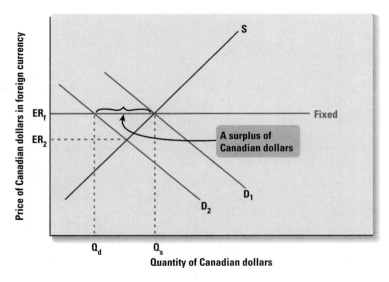

trading, government (through the Bank of Canada) must make good the deficiency. One of the major assets of the Bank of Canada, apart from government bonds, is reserves of gold and foreign currencies. (In November 2007, for instance, these stood at approximately $39 billion U.S., of which $19 billion was in American dollars.) These official international reserves, or at least as much as necessary, have to be made available to Canadians. So, along with an overvalued fixed exchange rate, as in **Figure 11.8**, comes the depletion of the central bank's foreign reserves. Canada, like all other countries, possesses only a limited amount of gold and foreign currencies. Because of this, the draining of foreign-currency reserves cannot continue indefinitely, and government will, as a result, be forced to take some kind of action. There are few options open, and none of them is attractive.

One possible tactic to stem the demand for foreign currencies would be to introduce quotas or tariffs to reduce Canadian imports. However, introducing such trade policies to try to reduce the amount of imports would violate international trade agreements and probably result in retaliation against Canadian exports. Direct **subsidies** to increase Canadian exports could, again, be in violation of trade agreements and would be expensive for government.

A policy of introducing foreign-exchange controls has been used by some governments in the past. Here, instead of directly restricting imports, government restricts the amount of foreign currencies available to Canadians. In other words, it rations the relatively scarce foreign currencies, in effect saying: this is the amount of currency being made available by foreigners buying our goods and services, and this amount only can be obtained by Canadians. This restricts the amount of imports.

These foreign-exchange controls can take many forms, including quotas on foreign currencies available for foreign travel, placing currency quotas on importing companies or industries, or giving preference to certain imports over others. The problem with foreign-exchange controls is that they distort trade and production, favour some importers over others, and restrict consumer choice.

Another alternative would be for the Canadian government to convince countries that are big exporters to Canada to agree to voluntary export restrictions. This would restrict imports to Canada. This is not often an easy option to exercise but has been achieved by a few countries recently.

There is only one other policy option for a government facing an overvalued fixed exchange rate. Since imports are a function of income, a reduction in imports could be achieved by reducing income. This involves reducing aggregate demand through specific policies that we will discuss in the next two chapters. In short, the adjustment mechanism for an overvalued exchange rate may be the deliberate creation of a recession.

In summary, a government can defend an overvalued exchange rate in four ways:

- Introducing quotas or tariffs
- Introducing foreign-exchange controls
- Negotiating voluntary export restrictions
- Creating a recession at home

A government that finds it politically impossible to impose any of the above policies or that finds that those policies fail after being tried will be forced to **devalue** its currency, that is, refix the exchange rate at a lower level.

Devaluation of a currency has serious political ramifications. It is often interpeted as a failure of a government to control its own destiny and, from that point of view, may lead to a loss of confidence generally in a government's economic policies. Furthermore, once even the possibility of a devaluation is recognized by the market, international currency dealers will ask only "when" and not "if." This lack of confidence by itself may make devaluation an inevitability because dealers will not want to hold the currency when there is the possibility that it may be devalued. Their actions, in selling off the currency that is under siege, then become a self-fulfilling prophecy.

In sum, the adjustment mechanism for an under- or overvalued fixed exchange rate is very painful and throws the economy into either an inflationary situation or a recession.

One final criticism of fixed exchange rates should be mentioned. If a country decides to peg the value of its currency to that of another, it is the "fixing" country's responsibility to ensure that that value is maintained by buying or selling its own currency. But, just as importantly, it must

subsidy: a payment by government for the purpose of increasing some particular activity or increasing the output of a particular good.

devaluation: the refixing by government of an exchange rate at a lower level.

also ensure that its interest rate is maintained at the level of the other country's. Even the smallest difference in interest rates would cause a huge amount of money to flow between the countries. This is because financial investors need not be concerned about fluctuations in the value of currency; the only deciding factor for them will be interest rate differentials. In effect, then, the fixing country has to peg both the value of its currency *and its interest rate* to that of the other country. As a result, it effectively abandons the idea of having an independent monetary policy.

For many countries, this may be too big a sacrifice. For this reason, most economists favour the flexible exchange rate system. This is the main reason that Canada led the world to a return to flexible exchange rates in 1970, with the result that fixed exchange rates have been rare in the past 30 years (one exception to this is China). However, truly flexible rates are almost as rare. Instead, most countries operate a system of managed exchange rates, or a **dirty float**. This means that the degree to which a currency is allowed to float (or fluctuate) is managed by the central bank in order to stabilize the exchange rate.

In Canada's case, the Bank of Canada buys and sells foreign currencies to keep the value of the dollar within what it perceives to be permissible limits. In order to prevent too rapid a depreciation of the dollar, government sells foreign reserves and buys dollars so as to hold up the demand for the dollar. Similarly, to keep the dollar from appreciating too quickly, government will do the opposite and sell dollars in exchange for foreign currency. This hybrid of the fixed and flexible exchange rate systems will probably be the choice of governments for the foreseeable future.

dirty float: an exchange rate that is not officially fixed by government but is managed by the central bank's ongoing intervention in the market.

SELF-TEST

6. Assume that the demand for the Canadian dollar increases. Describe the adjustment mechanism to this change, given:
a) flexible exchange rates, and b) fixed exchange rates.

 L05 Understand the meaning of a balance of payments surplus and deficit.

balance of payments: an accounting of a country's international transactions that involves the payment and receipt of foreign currencies.

current account: a subcategory of the balance of payments that shows the income or expenditure related to exports and imports.

capital account: a subcategory of the balance of payments that reflects changes in ownership of assets associated with foreign investment.

official settlements account: a subcategory of the balance of payments that shows the change in a country's official foreign exchange reserves.

11.5   THE BALANCE OF PAYMENTS

The Canadian **balance of payments** (or, more correctly, the balance of international payments) is an accounting of the international buying and selling of the Canadian dollar. In a sense, the term is a misnomer, since it is more like an income statement than a balance sheet. The balance of payments has three main sections: the **current account**, the **capital account**, and the **official settlements account**. What it shows are the various categories of international buying and selling that involve the Canadian dollar during a year. **Table 11.4** is a simplified balance of payments for Canada for 2010.

In a sense, the current account shows income and expenditures from international trading. The first line, exports and imports of goods and services, is self-explanatory. The difference between the two represents the **balance of trade** (what we called "net exports" in earlier chapters). Recall that imports create a supply of Canadian dollars; exports create a demand. However, when looking at the balance of payments, it is often more illuminating to look at the corresponding flows of foreign currencies. In other words, imports create a demand from Canadians for foreign currencies and exports produce a supply of foreign currencies. Traditionally, Canada has had, until recent years, a *positive* balance of trade. With the onset of a world recession, Canadian exports fell off considerably in 2009 and 2010, and in the latter year, Canada achieved a record trade deficit of $32 billion (compared with a record surplus of $61 billion a decade earlier). This means that trade in goods and services, again until the last few years, has usually produced a net inflow of foreign currencies to Canada. The higher Canadian dollar has also caused the trade balance to fall a little compared with earlier years.

TABLE 11.4	Canada's Balance of International Payments 2010 ($ billions)			
Demand for Canadian Dollars		**Supply of Canadian Dollars**		**Balance**
Current Account				
Exports of goods & services	475	Import of goods & services	507	
		Balance of Trade		−32
Foreign factor income from abroad	61	Factor income paid abroad	77	
		Net foreign factor income		−16
Transfers received from abroad	9	Transfers paid abroad	11	
		Transfers (net)		−2
		Balance on Current Account		**−50**
Capital Account				
Foreign Investment in Canada	154	Canadian Investment abroad	94	
		Net foreign Investment		60
		Balance on Capital Account		**60**
		Statistical Discrepancy		−6
		Overall Balance (current + capital + statistical discrepancy)		**+4**
Official Settlements Account				
(Foreign reserves bought)		Canadian dollars sold		−4
Total Balance (Current + Capital + Official Settlements)				0

Source: Adapted from the Statistics Canada CANSIM database <http://cansim2.statcan.ca>, Tables 376-0001, 376-0002, 376-0003, and 376-0004, March 10, 2011.

balance of trade: the value of a country's exports of goods and services less the value of its imports.

The next line, **foreign factor income** from abroad, includes the total amount of interest, dividends, and wages that Canadians received in this particular year from their previous foreign investments. This income produces an inflow of foreign currency into Canada. Foreign factor income paid abroad represents an outflow of foreign currencies. Since, over the entire history of Canada, foreigners have invested more in Canada than Canadians have invested abroad, the income going abroad as a result of this investment almost always exceeds the income flowing into Canada. In 2010, there was a net outflow of $16 billion.

Transfers—the last line in the current account—includes gifts and other remittances (pensions, for example) as well as foreign aid. In 2010, the outflows exceeded the inflow by $2 billion.

The balance on the current account equals −50, which means that $50 billion more in foreign reserves left Canada than entered Canada. Again, until recently, the current account has had a positive balance every year since 1998. The years 2009 and 2010 were certainly challenging ones for Canada as far as international trade was concerned.

The capital account shows the changes in international investment holdings during the year. Foreigners purchased $60 billion more in the way of shares, bonds (portfolio investment), and companies (direct investment) than Canadians purchased abroad during the year. This, therefore, represented an inflow of $60 billion

foreign factor income: income (such as wages, interest, or dividends) that nationals receive from providing their services to another country.

Gold has been a means of international payment for centuries.

into Canada. The total of the current and capital accounts (allowing for a statistical discrepancy of $6 billion) gives us a $4 billion surplus in the balance of payments. (The statistical discrepancy comes about because we do not have a complete record of funds crossing borders, especially in the case of the underground economy.)

This surplus means that, overall, foreigners were buying Canadian currency more than Canadians were buying foreign currencies. The Bank of Canada made up the shortage of Canadian dollars for trading from its own reserves. In the balance of payments statement this shows up in the final section, the Official Settlements Account. This section shows the involvement of the Bank of Canada in international transactions. In 2010, there was an outflow (a negative balance) of $4 billion. However, this is an outflow of Canadian dollars, which means that the Bank of Canada received the equivalent of $4 billion Canadian in return in international reserves. A balance of payments surplus, then, means that foreign reserves are coming into the country. (A balance of payments deficit means an outflow of foreign reserves leaving the country.)

The total balance of current, capital, and official settlements accounts sums to zero. This will always be the case, since it includes both private and government (Bank of Canada) currency dealings. If there is a deficit, government will make up the shortage of foreign currencies; if there is a surplus, government will make up the shortage of Canadian dollars. Only with complete, instantaneous flexible exchange rates will there be no central bank intervention and never a balance of payments deficit or surplus.

Let us now raise a new question. Since, with flexible exchange rates, the balance of payments is automatically achieved, can balance of payments problems ever arise? Yes, because it really does make a difference what a country is importing and what it is exporting. Canada can earn foreign currencies by exporting goods or services or by selling assets. Exporting goods and services does not lead to any future obligations on the part of anyone in Canada. However, selling off Canadian assets obliges some Canadians to pay out future income to foreigners and represents a drain on our foreign reserves in the future.

It is important that we clear up one particular myth relating to these flows. It is often suggested that Canada needs to encourage the inflow of foreign investment because we need this inflow to pay off the deficit that Canada, until recently, has had on its current account. Perhaps you have figured out why this is a myth. The reason Canada generally has a deficit on the current account is because of the amount of investment income that has to be paid abroad. This is high because of high levels of foreign investment in the past.

If we express this in terms of the individual, it might make more sense. Picture a student who defends her excessive borrowing every year by pointing out that she needs to borrow because her expenditures always seem to exceed her income, so she is left with no choice. But the reason her expenses are so high is because she is must make huge interest payments on her previous loans. In a similar fashion, many people suggest that if Canada were to cut down its dependence on foreign investment, it would not have current account problems in the future.

However, as **Table 11.5** shows, because of Canada's good trading performance, at least until the last two years, the current account has shown some impressive surpluses.

TABLE 11.5	Canada's External Performance (balances in $ billions)				
Year	Balance of Trade—USA	Balance of Trade—All Countries	Current Account Balance	Balance of Payments Overall Balance	Value of $ Canadian (in $US)
1995	+ 25	+ 25	−6	+ 4	0.74
2000	+ 87	+ 61	+ 29	+ 5	0.65
2001	+ 92	+ 63	+ 25	+ 3	0.65
2002	+ 87	+ 50	+ 20	0	0.64
2003	+ 81	+ 45	+ 15	−5	0.71
2004	+ 92	+ 55	+ 29	−3	0.77
2005	+ 99	+ 50	+ 26	+ 2	0.83
2006	+ 86	+ 35	+ 20	+ 1	0.88
2007	+ 73	+ 29	+ 13	+ 5	0.93
2008	+ 74	+ 24	+ 7	+ 2	0.94
2009	+ 20	−27	−44	+12	0.88
2010	+ 22	−32	−50	+ 4	0.97

Source: Adapted from the Statistics Canada CANSIM database <http://cansim2.statcan.ca>, Tables 376-0001 and 376-0002, March 29, 2011.

 SELF-TEST

7. Fill in the blanks in this hypothetical balance of payments statement:

Demand for Canadian Dollars		Supply of Canadian Dollars		Balance
Current Account				
Exports of goods & services	164	Import of goods & services	_____	
		Balance of Trade		+2
Foreign factor income from abroad	8	Factor income paid abroad	_____	
		Net foreign factor income		−15
Transfers received from abroad	26	Transfers paid abroad	_____	
		Transfers (net)		_____
		Balance on Current Account		−17
Capital Account				
Foreign Investment in Canada	_____	Canadian Investment abroad	186	
		Net Foreign Investment		+18
		Balance on Capital Account		_____
		Statistical Discrepancy		0
		Overall Balance (current + capital)		_____
Official Settlements Account				
(Foreign reserves bought)		Canadian dollars sold		_____
Total Balance (Current + Capital + Official Settlements)				_____

Review

CHAPTER SUMMARY

This chapter began with a discussion of the exchange rate and what is meant by the appreciation or depreciation of a currency. The main focus of the chapter was an examination of how exchange rates are determined under a flexible exchange rate system and how this contrasts with a fixed exchange rate system. The chapter concluded with a discussion of the balance of payments.

11.1a The exchange rate of any currency is calculated by dividing one by the unit value of the other currency.

11.1b The purchasing power parity theory suggests that the purchasing powers of different currencies will tend to become equal over time.

11.1c Several factors prevent this:
- the lack of international trade in many services
- transportation and insurance costs
- tariffs and other trade restrictions
- consumer preference for the products of one particular country over another
- the effect on currency value of trade in financial assets

11.2a The demand for the Canadian dollar on the international market comes from:
- foreigners who want to buy Canadian exports or who travel in Canada
- foreigners who want to buy Canadian assets
- Canadians who receive factor income from abroad
- currency speculators
- arbitragers

11.2b The supply of Canadian dollars on the international market comes from:
- Canadians want to buy foreign goods or who travel abroad
- Canadians who want to buy more foreign assets
- foreigners receive more Canadian factor income
- currency speculators and arbitragers

11.2c Appreciation of the Canadian dollar will increase the effective price of exports and cause exports to fall and imports to rise. Depreciation of the Canadian dollar will decrease the effective price of exports and cause exports to rise and imports to fall.

11.3 Changes in the demand for the Canadian dollar come from:
- changes in the level of foreign incomes
- changes in the price of Canadian goods
- changes in foreigners' preferences
- changes in comparative interest rates

11.4a The arguments for a fixed exchange rate are:
- it adds a degree of certainty to international trade
- it prevents instability in the export and import industries
- it discourages currency speculation
- it appeals to people who tend to equate the value of the exchange rate with national prestige

11.4b Many economists favour a flexible exchange rate system because:
- it avoids the necessary adjustment of inflation, which results when a fixed exchange rate is undervalued
- it avoids the necessary adjustment of recession, which results when a fixed exchange rate is overvalued

11.5 The balance of payments is an accounting of a country's international transactions and is made up of:
- the current account, which adds the balance of trade (export of goods and services minus imports), net investment income, and transfers
- the capital account (the net flow of all changes in the ownership of international assets)
- the official settlements account, which shows the movement of foreign reserves in and out of the Bank of Canada

NEW GLOSSARY TERMS AND KEY EQUATIONS

arbitrage   365
balance of payments   382
balance of trade   383
capital account   382
currency appreciation   364
currency depreciation   364

current account   382
devaluation   381
direct investment   367
dirty float   382
exchange rate   364
fixed exchange rate   365

flexible exchange rate   365
foreign factor income   383
official settlements account   382
portfolio investment   367
purchasing power parity theory   365
subsidy   381

Equations:

[11.1] $\dfrac{\text{1 Canadian dollar}}{\text{(in units of foreign currency)}} = \dfrac{1}{\text{foreign currency (in Canadian dollars)}}$ page 364

[11.2] $\dfrac{\text{1 unit of foreign currency}}{\text{(in Canadian dollars)}} = \dfrac{1}{\text{Canadian dollars (in foreign currency)}}$ page 364

STUDY TIPS

1. A lot of this chapter is about the idea of price being determined by supply and demand, something that students have little difficulty in accepting. We focused on the price of currencies, and the fact that (given a flexible exchange rate system) a currency's price (exchange rate) is determined by the supply and demand for that currency. Just keep thinking of currencies as commodities, and do not get hung up on the fact that they are also moneys. You will find there is nothing unduly mysterious or difficult about the topic.

2. The value of any currency always has to be expressed in terms of another currency. The question, "What is the price of the Canadian dollar?" makes no sense. "What is the price of the Canadian dollar in yen?" is a sensible question.

3. It is important for you to keep in mind that (flexible exchange) rates are determined by the supply and demand for a currency, and *not* the other way around. Thus, any question that starts with "if the exchang rate changes" has to be handled carefully because one needs to know what caused the exchange rate to change in the first place.

Answered Questions

These questions can also be found online on Connect.

Indicate whether the following statements are true or false:

1. **(LO 1) T or F**   If the Panamanian balboa is worth $0.20 Canadian, then $1 Canadian is worth 4 balboas.

2. **(LO 1) T or F**   The purchasing power parity theory suggests that exchange rates adjust so as to equate the purchasing power of each currency.

3. **(LO 2) T or F**   A major source of demand for the Canadian dollar in the international money markets is the desire of foreigners to buy Canadian exports.

4. **(LO 2) T or F**   A resident in Canada receiving a British pension will have a demand for the British pound.

Mc Graw Hill **connect**™

Practise and learn online with Connect, where you can find the Answered Questions and the Unanswered Problems for all chapters of this textbook's Study Guide section.

5. **(LO 3) T or F**   An increase in Canadian interest rates will lead to an appreciation of the Canadian dollar.

6. **(LO 2) T or F**   When the Canadian dollar depreciates, the effective price of Canadian exports increases and, as a result, total exports are likely to fall.

7. **(LO 2) T or F**   If the Canadian dollar appreciates, cross-border shopping by Canadians will increase.

8. **(LO 4) T or F**   If Canada were on a fixed exchange-rate system, an increase in the demand for the Canadian dollar would result in the dollar being undervalued.

9. **(LO 4) T or F**   A fixed exchange rate above the market value will lead to an outflow of foreign currencies.

10. **(LO 5) T or F**   An increase in imports will have a negative effect on the current account balance.

Basic (Questions 11–24)

11. **(LO 1)** What is the value of the euro in dollars if a French importer can buy 8 dollars for 10 euros?
    a) $1.25
    b) $0.8
    c) $80
    d) $2

12. **(LO 1)** If the Canadian dollar appreciates in value against the Mexican peso, what happens to the value of the Mexican peso against the dollar?
    a) It appreciates.
    b) It depreciates.
    c) It might appreciate or depreciate.
    d) It remains unchanged.

13. **(LO 2)** What currency will an American resident who receives interest on the Canadian savings bond she holds be demanding?
    a) Canadian dollars
    b) U.S. dollars
    c) Euros
    d) British pounds

14. **(LO 2)** What is arbitrage?
    a) The cost of shipping and insuring exported goods
    b) The buying of a currency at one price and its immediate sale at another price
    c) The cost of holding goods whose price is expected to increase in the future
    d) Speculation on the future price of a currency

15. **(LO 3)** If Canada and the United Kingdom are both on flexible exchange rate systems, what would happen if the United Kingdom experiences rapid inflation, while prices remain steady in Canada?
    a) The Canadian dollar will depreciate.
    b) The British pound will depreciate.
    c) The British pound will appreciate.
    d) The exchange rate will not change.

16. **(LO 3)** Which of the following would result from an increase in Canada's GDP?
    a) Canadian exports would rise.
    b) Both Canadian exports and imports would rise.
    c) Canadian exports would rise, but imports would decrease.
    d) Canadian imports would rise.

Table 11.6 contains hypothetical data for Canada's balance of payments accounts for a particular year. (Figures are in billions of dollars.) Refer to **Table 11.6** to answer questions 17, 18, and 19.

TABLE 11.6

Exports of goods and services	$150
Imports of goods and services	145
Foreign factor income received from abroad	10
Foreign factor income paid abroad	30
Net transfers	–5
Foreign investment in Canada	200
Canadian investment abroad	190

17. **(LO 5)** What is Canada's balance of trade?
    a) A surplus of $150 billion
    b) A surplus of $5 billion
    c) A deficit of $15 billion
    d) A deficit of $10 billion

18. **(LO 5)** What is Canada's current account balance?
    a) A surplus of $10 billion
    b) A surplus of $15 billion
    c) A deficit of $10 billion
    d) A deficit of $20 billion

19. **(LO 5)** What is Canada's capital account balance?
    a) A deficit of $10 billion
    b) A surplus of $10 billion
    c) A surplus of $5 billion
    d) A surplus of $30 billion

20. **(LO 2)** All of the following groups, except one, demand Canadian dollars. Which is the exception?
    a) An American tourist visiting Canada
    b) Canadians who received dividends from American corporations
    c) Texans who purchase Alberta beef
    d) Americans who receive interest on their holdings of Canadian savings bonds
    e) International speculators who think that the Canadian dollar will soon appreciate

21. **(LO 2)** Which of the following would increase the supply of Canadian dollars on the international money market?
    a) Canadians travelling abroad
    b) An American corporation investing in Canada
    c) A Canadian resident receiving interest payments on a foreign bond
    d) A Canadian exporter selling products abroad
    e) A retired American, living on Vancouver Island, receiving a U.S. Social Security pension cheque

22. **(LO 4)** If a country is suffering perennial balance of payments deficits, all of the following, except one, will help solve the problem. Which is the exception?
    a) The introduction of quotas on imported goods
    b) An increase in interest rates
    c) The introduction of exchange controls
    d) The reduction in tariffs on imported goods
    e) An increase in subsidies to exporting industries

23. **(LO 4)** What does *managed* (or *dirty*) *float* mean?
    a) That a country's currency is fixed to the price of gold
    b) That a country's currency is fixed to the value of the U.S. dollar
    c) That a country's balance of payments is persistently in deficit
    d) That the country's central bank fixes the value of its currency
    e) That a country's central bank buys and sells currencies in order to smooth out short-run fluctuations in its own currency

24. **(LO 1)** What is purchasing power parity theory?
    a) A theory suggesting that exchange rates will change to equate the purchasing power of each currency
    b) A theory suggesting that exchange rates tend to diverge over time
    c) A theory suggesting that all currencies will be, in time, at par
    d) A formula used to calculate the exchange rate of one currency for another

Intermediate (Questions 25–31)

25. **(LO 2)** What will be the result of a change in exchange rates if fewer Mexican pesos are needed to buy a Canadian dollar?
    a) Canadians will buy more Mexican goods and services.
    b) Mexicans will buy fewer Canadian goods and services.
    c) Canadians will buy fewer Mexican goods and services.
    d) Mexicans will buy more Mexican goods.

26. **(LO 3)** Assuming a flexible exchange rate system, what would happen to the value of the Canadian dollar and the Mexican peso if Canadian interest rates increased while Mexican rates remained the same?
    a) The price of dollars in terms of the peso would increase.
    b) The price of pesos in terms of dollars would increase.
    c) The peso in terms of dollars would appreciate.
    d) The Canadian dollar in terms of the peso would depreciate.

27. **(LO 2)** Which of the following statements is true about the supply curve for the Canadian dollar?
    a) It is downward sloping because a lower price for the dollar means Canadian goods are cheaper to foreigners.
    b) It is downward sloping because a higher price for the dollar means Canadian goods are cheaper to foreigners.
    c) It is upward sloping because a lower price for the dollar means foreign goods are cheaper to Canadians.
    d) It is upward sloping because a higher price for the dollar means foreign goods are cheaper to Canadians.

28. **(LO 4)** Assuming a fixed exchange rate system, which of the following would contribute to a Canadian balance of payments deficit?
    a) Leonard Cohen and Shania Twain team up for a giant outdoor concert in Shanghai.
    b) The number of Indian tourists visiting Canada increases significantly.
    c) The United States increases its tariff on Canadian softwood lumber.
    d) A wealthy Taiwanese family builds a mansion in Calgary.
    e) Honda builds a new assembly plant outside Montreal.

29. **(LO 1)** All of the following, except one, would help explain differences in purchasing power among countries. Which is the exception?
    a) Many services not traded internationally
    b) Financial assets seldom traded internationally
    c) The existence of transportation and insurance costs
    d) The expression of particular preferences by consumers
    e) The existence of tariffs and other trade restrictions

30. **(LO 1)** Refer to Table 11.7 to answer this question. What is the price of one Canadian dollar in Year 2?

TABLE 11.7

	Price of one Canadian Dollar	Price of a Gallon of Maple Syrup in Canada	Price of a Gallon of Maple Syrup in Japan
Year 1	80 yen	$20	1600 yen
Year 2	_____	$20	1760 yen

    a) 72 yen
    b) 80 yen
    c) 88 yen
    d) Cannot be determined

31. **(LO 1)** Refer to Table 11.8 to answer this question. Which of the following statements is correct?
    a) The Canadian dollar has appreciated, and the Japanese yen has depreciated.
    b) The Canadian dollar has depreciated, and the Japanese yen has appreciated.
    c) The Japanese yen is now worth less in terms of the Canadian dollar.
    d) The Canadian dollar is now worth more in terms of the Japanese yen.

TABLE 11.8

	Price of one Canadian Dollar	Price of a Gallon of Maple Syrup in Canada	Price of a Gallon of Maple Syrup in Japan
Year 1	80 yen	$20	1600 yen
Year 2	72 yen	$20	1440 yen

Advanced (Questions 32–35)

32. **(LO 5)** What does it mean for a country that is on a fixed exchange rate system to have a balance of payments surplus?
    a) The quantity supplied of its currency on the international money market will exceed the quantity demanded.
    b) The exchange rate is overvalued.
    c) There is an inflow of foreign currencies into the country.
    d) The balance of payments surplus is matched by a balance of trade deficit.
    e) There is an outflow of foreign currencies from the country.

Figure 11.9 shows the market for the U.S. dollar.

FIGURE 11.9

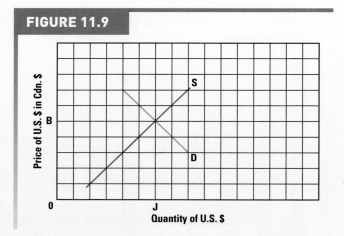

33. **(LO 2)** Refer to the graph in Figure 11.9 to answer this question. What is the value of the U.S. dollar if a flexible exchange rate system is in effect?
    a) 0J Canadian dollars for one U.S. dollar
    b) 0B Canadian dollars for one U.S. dollar
    c) 1/0B U.S. dollars for one Canadian dollar
    d) 0J U.S. dollars for one Canadian dollar
    e) 0B U.S. dollars for one Canadian dollar

34. **(LO 3)** Assuming flexible exchange rates, which of the following would result in an increase in a country's exchange rate?
    a) The purchase by the central bank of its own currency
    b) The purchase by the central bank of foreign currencies
    c) The sale by the central bank of its own currency
    d) The central bank decreasing the country's interest rates
    e) Government imposing an export tax

35. **(LO 4)** The country of Lancores, which was on a fixed exchange rate system and had an undervalued currency, has just adopted a flexible exchange rate system. Which of the following statements is correct?
    a) Lancores's currency will depreciate, and its exports will increase.
    b) Lancores's currency will appreciate, and its exports will increase.
    c) Lancores's currency will depreciate, and its exports will decrease.
    d) Lancores's currency will appreciate, and its exports will decrease.

Parallel Problems

ANSWERED PROBLEMS

36A. **(LO 2, 3, 4, 5)** **Key Problem** Suppose that the international demand and supply of Canadian dollars (in billions) is as shown in **Table 11.9**. This represents the total market for Canadian dollars (that is, no transfers, speculation, or arbitrage).
    a) Calculate and fill in the total demand and total supply columns of the table.
    Suppose that Canada is operating with a flexible exchange rate system.
    b) What is the equilibrium value of the Canadian dollar? _____ .
    c) What is the value of its balance of trade? _____ .
    d) What is its current account balance? _____ .
    e) What is its capital account balance? _____ .
    f) What is the overall balance of payments (current and capital accounts)? _____ .
    Now, suppose that Canada fixes its exchange rate against the U.S. dollar at a value of $1 Canadian equals $0.96 American.
    g) What is the value of its balance of trade? _____ .
    h) What is its current account balance? _____ .
    i) What is its capital account balance? _____ .
    j) What is the overall balance of payments (current and capital accounts)? _____ .
    k) What is the balance on its official settlements account? _____ .

TABLE 11.9

| Value of Canadian Dollars (in U.S. dollars) | DEMAND FOR CANADIAN DOLLARS | | | | SUPPLY OF CANADIAN DOLLARS | | | |
| | Foreign Factor | | | | | | | |
	Export of Goods & Services	Income Earned Abroad	Foreign Investment in Canada	Total	Import of Goods & Services	Foreign factor Income Paid Abroad	Canadian Investment Abroad	Total
$0.84	120	70	180	_____	80	67	146	_____
0.86	119	70	175	_____	83	67	148	_____
0.88	118	70	170	_____	86	67	150	_____
0.90	117	70	165	_____	89	67	152	_____
0.92	116	70	160	_____	92	67	154	_____
0.94	115	70	155	_____	95	67	156	_____
0.96	114	70	150	_____	98	67	158	_____
0.98	113	70	145	_____	101	67	160	_____
1.00	112	70	140	_____	104	67	162	_____
1.02	111	70	135	_____	107	67	164	_____
1.04	110	70	130	_____	110	67	166	_____

Basic (Problems 37A–44A)

37A. **(LO 1)** If a Canadian hockey stick has a price of $42, how much does it cost in:
   a) Europe, assuming an exchange rate of 1 euro = $1.40 Canadian _____ .
   b) The United Kingdom, assuming an exchange rate of 1 pound = $2.10 Canadian _____ .

38A. **(LO 1)** Fill in the blanks.
   a) If one Canadian dollar equals $0.75 American, then one U.S. dollar equals _____ Canadian dollars.
   b) If one Canadian dollar equals 80 yen, then one yen equals _____ Canadian dollars.
   c) If one euro equals 1.6 Canadian dollars, then one Canadian dollar equals _____ euros.

39A. **(LO 2)** Refer to the following list, and explain who will be buying Canadian dollars and who will be selling.
   a) A Canadian businesswoman visiting Japan.
   _____ .
   b) A Russian tourist visiting Cape Breton.
   _____ .
   c) An American corporation building a new plant in Saskatoon. _____ .
   d) A Canadian bank expanding its operations in the United States. _____ .

40A. **(LO 2)** Refer to the following list, and identify who would be hurt and who would benefit from an appreciation of the Canadian dollar.
   a) An Italian father spending the summer with his daughter in Calgary _____ .
   b) A Canadian research scientist living in Washington, D.C., who is paid a monthly salary in Canadian dollars by his Ottawa employer
   _____ .
   c) A retired couple living in Ontario whose major source of income is from a British pension
   _____ .
   d) A nurse living in Windsor who works at a hospital in Detroit _____ .

41A. **(LO 3)** What effect will the following events have on the value of the Canadian dollar versus the Mexican peso?
   a) Canadian interest rates rise significantly above Mexican rates. _____ .
   b) An especially bad winter causes tens of thousands of Canadians to escape to the Mexican Riviera for vacations. _____ .
   c) A Canadian telecommunications firm sells equipment to the Mexican government. _____ .
   d) The winter vegetable crop in Mexico is destroyed by unusually cold temperatures. _____ .

TABLE 11.10

Foreign investment in Etruria	90
Transfers (net)	+4
Foreign factor income from abroad	11
Imports of goods and services	153
Exports of goods and services	157
Etruria investment abroad	68
Foreign factor income paid abroad	29

42A. **(LO 5)** Arrange the data in **Table 11.10** into the form of a balance of payments for Etruria. (All figures are in billions of dollars.)
   a) What is the value of the balance of trade?
   _____ .
   b) What is the balance on the current account?
   _____ .
   c) What is the balance on the capital account?
   _____ .
   d) Is there a balance of payments surplus or deficit? How much? _____ .

43A. **(LO 2)** Where does the supply of Canadian dollars on foreign exchange markets come from?

44A. **(LO 2)** What is arbitrage?

Intermediate (Problems 45A–50A)

45A. **(LO 1)** Karen operates a small foreign-currency exchange business. She begins each day with three boxes of cash. Each box contains 10 000 units of Canadian currency and 10 000 units of another currency. **Table 11.11** shows Karen's holdings of each currency at the end of a day's business.

TABLE 11.11

Box 1	euros	8000	and	$12 800 Cdn.
Box 2	Japanese yen	7000	and	10 050 Cdn.
Box 3	U.S. dollars	6400	and	15 000 Cdn.

What is the value of the Canadian dollar in terms of the three currencies?

Dollar in terms of the euro: _____

Dollar in terms of the yen: _____

Dollar in terms of the U.S. dollar: _____

46A. **(LO 5)** A country that experiences a capital account surplus for many years will, eventually, experience many years of current account deficits. Explain.

47A. **(LO 3)** Assume that the demand for the Canadian dollar increases because of a rising GDP level in the United States. What will happen to the value of the Canadian exchange rate, Canada's GDP, and the unemployment rate in Canada?

Exchange rate: _____

GDP: _____

Unemployment rate: _____

48A. **(LO 3)** The graph in **Figure 11.10** illustrates hypothetical supply and demand curves for the Canadian dollar. Use the graph to answer the questions below.

FIGURE 11.10

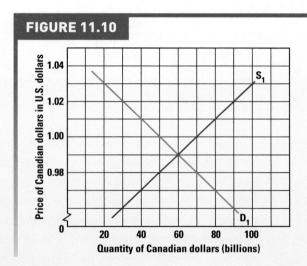

Quantity of Canadian dollars (billions)

a) What is the quantity of dollars exchanged, given D_1 and S_1? _____ .

b) What is this quantity worth in U.S. dollars? _____ .

c) If you increase the demand for the dollar by 20 (draw in), what would be the dollar volume of exchange if the exchange rate is fixed? _____ .

d) What is the quantity of Canadian dollars exchanged if the exchange rate is flexible? _____ .

e) What is this quantity worth in U.S. dollars? _____ .

49A. **(LO 2)** What happens to the effective price of Canadian products if the Canadian dollar appreciates? What happens to the volume of Canadian exports?

50A. **(LO 4)** Contrast flexible exchange rate and fixed exchange rate.

Advanced (Problems 51A–55A)

51A. **(LO 3)** An increase in the demand for Canadian products will cause the Canadian dollar to appreciate. Yet, an appreciation of the dollar causes the demand for Canadian products to fall. How can you reconcile these two statements?

52A. **(LO 4)** Explain why a country with a fixed exchange rate loses control over its money supply as an effective policy tool.

53A. **(LO 3)** Suppose that a certain type of SUV costs $32 000 in Canada, whereas it sells for 18 000 British pounds in the United Kingdom. Suppose that the nominal exchange rate is one Canadian dollar = 0.45 British pounds.

a) What is the value of the real exchange rate?

_____ .

b) In which country is the SUV cheaper? _____ .

54A. **(LO 1)** Table 11.12 shows some hypothetical data concerning exchange rates and the prices of Big Macs in the summer of 2005.

a) Using the relative prices of Big Macs, determine the Big Mac exchange rate in the three countries.

1 yuan = $ _____

1 Singapore dollar = $ _____

1 Hong Kong dollar = $ _____

b) Compared with the Big Mac exchange rates, are the actual exchange rates overvalued or undervalued?

Chinese yuan _____

Singapore dollar: _____

Hong Kong dollar: _____

c) Given your answers in b), would you expect Canadian imports from each of these countries to increase or decrease in the future?

Chinese: _____

Singapore: _____

Hong Kong: _____

55A. **(LO 1)** Explain *purchasing power parity theory*.

TABLE 11.12

Location	Big Mac Price		Actual Exchange Rate		
Toronto	2.50	Canadian dollars			
Shanghai	10.00	yuan	1 yuan	=	$0.20 Canadian
Singapore	3.50	Singapore dollars	1 Singapore $	=	$0.75 Canadian
Hong Kong	20.00	Hong Kong dollars	1 Hong Kong $	=	$0.15 Canadian

MACROECONOMIC
POLICY REVISITED

WHAT'S AHEAD...

In this chapter, we return to the topics of fiscal and monetary policy having "opened up" the economy to the effects of international trade and financial flows, which we discussed in the last two chapters. We shall see that changes in fiscal and monetary policy can affect both the interest rate and the exchange rate. In addition, we will see how changes in these two key economic variables will have a feed-back effect on the level of GDP and employment. We will also look at what is known as supply-side economics and see how these ideas might fit into fiscal and monetary policy making. Finally, we will look at the call for a fixed Canadian dollar and briefly explore why economists fear deflation.

┌ A Question of Relevance... ─

These are indeed confusing times that we live in. One wonders what the world will learn from the 2008–2010 recession which was the most severe financial crisis since the Great Depression of the 1930s. Could governments around the world have done more to help put economies back on the road to recovery? Is deflation a serious threat in today's economic environment? The significance of these questions can hardly be overemphasized.

Canada is one of the most open economies in the world. Our exports make up a high percentage of the national GDP, and imports from the rest of the world are a high percentage of total consumption spending. Foreigners buy and sell stock on the Toronto Stock Exchange and invest directly in Canada, while Canadians do the same in the rest of the world. Therefore, to truly understand all of the broad aspects of Canada's economy, we need to go back and look at the effectiveness of economic policy in an open economy.

12.1   FISCAL POLICY IN AN OPEN ECONOMY

Now that we have investigated international finance in Chapter 11, we can move forward with a more thorough examination of the effectiveness of fiscal policy.

LO1 Understand the impact of a change in interest rates and exchange rates on the effectiveness of fiscal policy through the crowding-out effect.

In Chapter 7, we learned that a recessionary gap can be reduced—even eliminated—by an increase in aggregate demand. This can be achieved using expansionary fiscal policy in one of two ways. The first is through a cut in taxes, which would translate into an increase in aggregate spending. The second way is an increased in government spending. We learned in Chapter 7 that an increase in spending will be more effective than a decrease in taxes of the same magnitude simply because a portion of the higher disposable income resulting from lower taxes will be saved rather than spent on increased consumption, whereas all of the increase in government spending will translate into a multiplied increase in GDP. This is one of the reasons that expansionary fiscal policy usually takes the form of increased government spending. Another reason is simply that, for political reasons, most governments prefer to increase spending rather than reduce taxes.

The use of expansionary fiscal policy raises an interesting question. Where does government get the funds to increase its spending? It could, of course, increase taxes but this would depress aggregate demand, which would be counter-productive. The conventional answer to the question is to fund stimulus spending by borrowing money from the general public. Government accomplishes this by selling new, interest-paying bonds on the open market.

Let us examine this effect in detail. Expansionary fiscal policy will increase aggregate demand and, as we can see in **Figure 12.1A**, the result is a rise in both the level of income, from Y_1 to Y_3, and the price level, from P_1 to P_2.

If prices had remained constant at P_1, real GDP would have risen to Y_2. However, since prices have risen to P_2, GDP in fact only increases to Y_3. In other words, higher prices have dampened down spending somewhat (there is a movement up the AD curve). Why should this be? You will recall from Chapter 5 that there are three reasons a higher price level reduces the aggregate quantity demanded. The first of these is caused by the real-balance effect, which reduces consumer spending. The second is the foreign-trade effect—what results when higher-priced domestic products become less competitive on world markets. The third is the interest-rate effect, which lies behind the **crowding-out effect**.

You may recall from Chapter 9 that an increase in the price level will raise the transactions demand for money. Assuming no increase in the money supply, this increase in the demand for money will tend to push up interest rates as seen in **12.1B**. This, in turn, will reduce the level of private investment spending. That is to say, expansionary fiscal policy can lead to the crowding out of investment spending as illustrated in **Figure 12.1C**.

crowding-out effect: the idea that when a government borrows to finance a deficit, it crowds out private investment because it causes interest rates to rise.

We know from both Chapters 5 and 6 that an increase in government spending—aimed at closing a recessionary gap—will increase the level of national income by an amount determined by the multiplier. However, we have just seen that the crowding out of investment spending offsets some of this increase in national income, resulting in a multiplier that is smaller than it appeared at first glance. Let us be clear that we are not saying fiscal policy is ineffective because of the crowding-out effect. What we are saying is that the crowding-out effect reduces the size of the expenditures multiplier when expansionary fiscal policy is applied.

FIGURE 12.1   **Effect of an Increase in Government Spending**

Expansionary fiscal policy implies an increase in aggregate demand, shown as a shift from AD_1 to AD_2. If the price level remains constant at P_1, GDP would increase from Y_1 to Y_2. However, the price level increases to P_2, and as a result, money demand and interest rates increase as shown in Figure B. Then, the higher interest rate reduces the level of investment spending, as seen in Figure C. The lower investment spending, in turn, reduces the aggregate quantity demanded (a movement along AD_2) in Figure A and thereby reduces real GDP to Y_3.

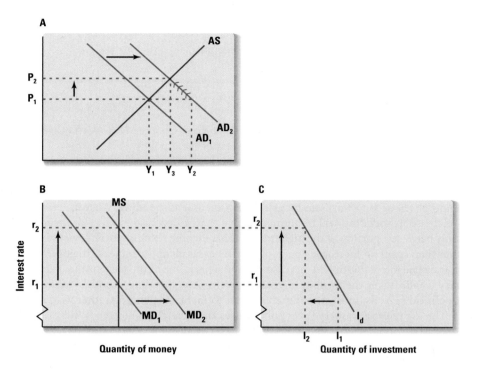

There is another reason increased government spending may not have such a big impact on the economy: net exports will also be affected by crowding out. We saw in Chapter 11 that higher interest rates will pull money into the country as foreign money managers buy Canadian dollars in order to make deposits in Canadian financial institutions. The effect of this inflow of foreign currencies is to increase the demand for the Canadian dollar and cause it to appreciate. This higher exchange rate will, of course, reduce the level of Canadian exports and encourage imports, so that we now see net exports also being crowded out as a result of expansionary fiscal policy.

In summary, expansionary fiscal policy means that the level of aggregate demand is increased through higher government spending and the result is a rise in both the level of national income

(▶) ADDED DIMENSION   Was the Crowding-out Effect Present in 2009–2010?

It is interesting to note that the experience of the North American economies in response to fiscal-policy-stimulus spending in 2009 does not fit the standard analysis of the crowding-out effect. Despite the application of stimulus packages by both the Canadian and U.S. governments, interest rates showed no tendency to rise and, in fact, remained very low. Why was this? One high profile economist, Paul Krugman, puts forward the following explanation.

The recession of 2008–2010 created a worldwide excess of savings; both businesses and consumers put spending plans on hold in the face of the uncertainty created by a near collapse in the financial system. Given this, the standard analysis that more government borrowing would lead to a rise in the interest rate simply did not apply. Even in the face of very low interest rates, the excess of savings persisted because the demand for new loans was so weak. The result was that governments were able to fund expansionary spending through the creation of budget deficits (enabled with borrowed funds) without pushing up interest rates. It appears that the economy was in a state of persistent excess liquidity where the desire to hold cash was so strong that interest rates were held down to low levels.

and the price level. However, the increase in national income will be somewhat muted by the crowding-out effect caused by:

- higher interest rates pushing down investment spending
- the appreciation of the Canadian dollar pushing down net exports

Let us expand a bit on how a government finances a deficit through borrowing. A government borrows money by issuing new government bonds that are bought by banks, insurance companies, corporations, and the general public; money moves from the lenders to government. What the public might have otherwise spent is instead being spent by government, so there is no change in the money supply.

However, very occasionally those bonds might be bought by the central bank rather than by the general public. Here, government, in a sense, lends to itself. This means that the money paid by the central bank does result in an increase in the money supply. Further, since the central bank is not a "spending agent" it does not in any sense reduce its own spending to compensate for the resulting increase in spending by government. As we mentioned in Chapter 7, this method of borrowing is called monetizing the debt and is highly inflationary, and for this reason it is seldom done by responsible governments.

 SELF-TEST

1. a) Suppose that GDP in Newland is $800 billion and government increases spending by $25 billion. If the multiplier equals 4, what is the new level of GDP?

b) Suppose that as a result of the increase in GDP the price level in Newland also rises, causing the demand for money to increase by $40 billion. Given the following graph of the money market and investment demand, by how much will investment fall?

c) Given the same value of the multiplier, what will be the new level of GDP?

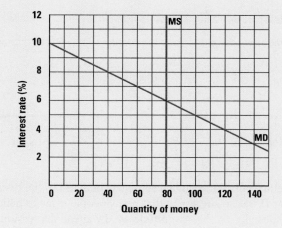

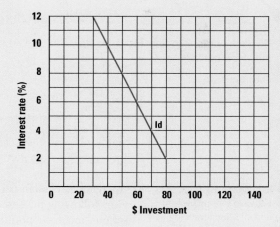

12.2 MONETARY POLICY IN AN OPEN ECONOMY

We learned in Chapter 9 that a central bank can either expand or contract an economy's money supply and thereby push interest rates down or up. When, for example the central bank buys T-bills from a member of the public, whether from a corporation, bank, or individual, a "swap" takes place. A T-bill that was being held outside of the central bank (that is, was in circulation)

L02 Understand how the effectiveness of monetary policy is enhanced under a flexible exchange rate.

moves to the central bank, and money that was held by the central bank moves to the general public and is then in circulation. In short, the economy's money supply has expanded, and this additional money will push interest rates down. And, of course, the lower interest rates will stimulate additional investment spending which increases aggregate demand and the level of national income. This is expansionary monetary policy.

How does the fact that we are now discussing an open economy affect this process? If the open economy has a flexible exchange rate, then expansionary monetary policy has an even larger effect on national income. This is because the lower interest rates will result in lower international demand for the Canadian dollar, and this will push the exchange rate lower. The lower exchange rate will stimulate exports and more exports means higher aggregate demand and, thus, a larger increase in national income. This is why many economists consider the combination of monetary policy and flexible exchange rates to be a power policy weapon that central banks possess.

Let us now consider the use of monetary policy *in cooperation* with fiscal policy. The above analysis of the crowding-out effect resulting from expansionary fiscal policy was based on the assumption that the higher level of income will push up interest rates, since the money supply was implicitly assumed to remain unchanged.

However, if government were to apply expansionary fiscal policy and the central bank expanded the money supply at the same time, then the crowding-out effect could be neutralized. The increase in the money supply would accommodate the increased money demand that results from expansionary fiscal policy. This means that interest rates remain the same and, as a result, there will be no crowding out of either investment spending or exports. This makes fiscal policy more effective than it is when not supported by an expansion in the money supply. In fact, this is the type of policy that, as we saw in Chapter 9, the Bank of Canada presently uses. By targeting interest rates it automatically accommodates changes in the money demand by adjusting the money supply.

✔ SELF-TEST

2. Given the graphs in Self-Test 1 for Newland, should its central bank increase or decrease the money supply to avoid crowding out? How much?

12.3 FISCAL AND MONETARTY POLICY IN THE POST-WAR WONDER YEARS

 L03 Explain the trade-off between unemployment and inflation levels implied by the Phillips Curve.

Applying Keynesian fiscal and monetary policy to regulate aggregate demand in the twenty-five years following the end of World War II was so successful that many people came to believe that serious macroeconomic trouble—especially of the magnitude of the great depression of the 1930s—was a thing of the past. Throughout the 1950s and 1960s, there were only minor and brief exceptions to modest inflation, benign unemployment, and robust growth.

There was however one glitch that was somewhat troubling. This was the fact that achieving the twin goals of complete full employment and stable prices appeared to be elusive. In 1958, British economist A.W. Phillips confirmed this suspicion with a time-series analysis of unemployment and inflation rates (actually, yearly changes in wage rates) for the British economy for the previous 100 years. He discovered that there were very few years of both low unemployment and low inflation rates. In fact, it seemed that when unemployment was low, inflation was above normal. At another time, the opposite might be true. In other words, there appeared to be a trade-off between the low unemployment and low inflation. **Table 12.1** is a simple table of hypothetical data that illustrates this idea.

TABLE 12.1	The Trade-off between Unemployment and Inflation
Unemployment Rate	**Inflation Rate**
4%	12%
6	8
8	5
10	3
12	2

Not only are low unemployment rates associated with high inflation and high unemployment with low inflation, but the cost of trying to achieve either of these goals also becomes more and more expensive as the respective rates fall. In other words, to reduce unemployment by 2 percentage points when the economy is suffering 12 percent unemployment "costs" society only a 1 percentage point increase in inflation—from 2 percent to 3 percent. But to reduce unemployment by a similar 2 percentage points when the economy is close to full employment, say, from 6 percent to 4 percent, "costs" the country 4 percentage points in inflation. The **Phillips curve** is illustrated in **Figure 12.2**.

The relationship between unemployment and inflation on the graph reveals a downward-sloping curve that illustrates a particular relationship between inflation and unemployment. As inflation rates fall, unemployment rates rise. However, it does not plot as a straight line but as a parabola; lower inflation rates are associated with increasingly higher unemployment rates.

Although the idea seemed like a fresh breakthrough at the time, in hindsight, the Phillips curve does nothing more than confirm the shape of the aggregate supply curve we introduced back in Chapter 5. You can validate this in your own mind by picturing what would happen as aggregate demand increases and we move up on the AS curve. Here, we can see that it would result in both higher GDP (lower unemployment) and higher prices (inflation). Additionally, as you move closer to full-employment GDP, the increase in the price level is greater than the increase in GDP.

What all this boils down to, in terms of fiscal and monetary policy, is that the best that policy makers can do is achieve a delicate balance between full employment and stable prices without ever completely attaining either goal. For instance, they might be able to help the economy achieve a modest amount of inflation combined with a not-too-high level of unemployment. However, any attempt to reduce inflation further would likely provoke unacceptably high rates of unemployment. Similarly, expansionary policy designed to reduce unemployment would cause acceleration in inflation rates. Policy makers indeed seemed caught between "a rock and a hard place." Nonetheless, this uneasy balance of using fiscal and monetary policy to maintain an acceptable level of employment and stable prices carried the day for some time.

Phillips curve: a curve that illustrates the inverse relationship between unemployment and inflation rates.

FIGURE 12.2	The Phillips Curve

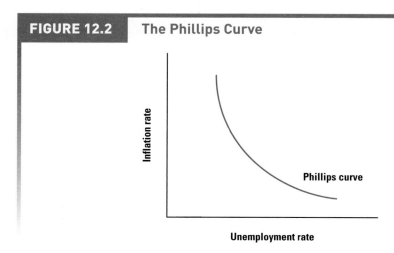

The top of the curve illustrates the fact that high inflation rates are associated with low unemployment rates. As we move down the curve, lower inflation rates are matched with increasingly higher unemployment rates.

SELF-TEST

3. The following data are for the very volatile economy of Mobile. Given that the labour force remained a constant 320 million, calculate the unemployment and inflation rates for each of the years 2006–11. From the data collected, draw a Phillips curve:

Year	Price Index	Unemployment (in millions)
2006	120	
2007	122.4	38.4
2008	126.1	25.6
2009	133.7	19.2
2010	147.1	14.4
2011	170.6	9.6

12.4 THE ARGUMENT OF THE SUPPLY-SIDERS

L04 Understand what is meant by the term *supply-side economics.*

stagflation: the simultaneous occurrence of high inflation and unemployment.

In the fall of 1973, OPEC (the Organization of Petroleum Exporting Countries)—which at the time controlled a very large percentage of the world's oil exports—imposed dramatic increases in the price of oil on the world. Within two years, the results of this shock to the world's economic systems included rising levels of both unemployment and inflation, a state of affairs that came to be known as **stagflation**. The prevailing macroeconomic theory of the day was badly shaken, since the standard Keynesian analysis at the time indicated that an economy might suffer high unemployment rates, or high inflation rates, but not both at the same time. The prolonged period of increases in both was a serious blow to the orthodox view. Economists began to scramble for explanations and this laid the groundwork for the rise of a new school of economic thought—the supply-siders.

There is only one explanation for stagflation: a decrease in the aggregate supply, as shown in **Figure 12.3**.

The 1973 increase in the price of imported oil caused a decrease in the short-run aggregate supply, as seen by the shift from AS_1 to AS_2, in **Figure 12.3**. The result of this was to increase the price level in Canada, from P_1 to P_2, and cause unemployment to rise, as is seen by the drop in real GDP from Y_1 to Y_2.

Inflation and unemployment rates remained high in Canada throughout the 1970s and early 1980s, peaking in 1982, when inflation hit 10.8 percent and unemployment was 11 percent. What was most alarming about stagflation when it first appeared was the fact that no one, including economists, was able to explain it or offer a cure. That's because the majority of economists were wedded to the idea that economic events could only be explained in terms of changes in aggregate demand. Although economists recognized the existence of aggregate supply, it was thought to be a very passive ingredient in the economy. After all, firms would never produce unless there was a demand for their products. If demand increased, firms would meet the increased demand by producing more; if demand decreased, firms would react by producing less. What more needs to be said about supply?

Unfortunately, this blind spot meant that most economists in the 1970s were unable to correctly diagnose the problem of stagflation and, worse, offered the wrong sort of remedies. This can be seen in **Figure 12.4**.

FIGURE 12.3	The Cause of Stagflation

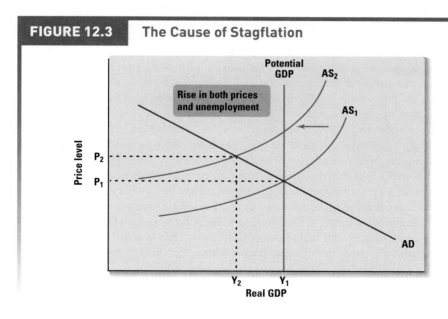

An increase in the price of imported resources (such as oil in 1973) will decrease aggregate supply, causing it to shift left as seen by AS_1 to AS_2. The result will be a higher price level, P_1 to P_2, and a lower level of real GDP, Y_1 to Y_2.

Neither expansionary fiscal policy nor expansionary monetary policy is able to cure the simultaneous problems of high unemployment and inflation. Such policies will increase aggregate demand, as shown by the rightward shift in the aggregate demand curve, from AD_1 to AD_2 in **Figure 12.4**. This will increase real GDP and, therefore, reduce unemployment. Unfortunately, it will also have the effect of pushing up prices, from P_1 to P_2.

Contractionary fiscal or monetary policy is no better. It will cause a decrease in aggregate demand, from AD_1 to AD_3, which will, indeed, reduce prices from P_1 to P_3. However, it will also cause an increase in unemployment, since GDP will fall.

In fact, the only way to boost production and employment and reduce prices at the same time is through policies designed to increase aggregate supply. We learned in Chapter 5 that one of the fundamental ways to do this is through the economy achieving an increase in productivity.

FIGURE 12.4	Aggregate Demand and Stagflation

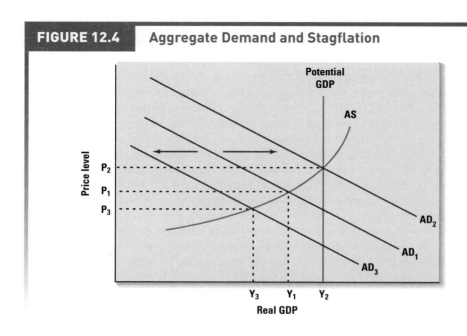

The economy is in a stagflationary situation with a high price level, P_1 (inflation), and a low level of real GDP, Y_1 (high unemployment). Expansionary policy, either fiscal or monetary, will shift the aggregate demand curve from the present AD_1 to AD_2. The result will be a higher level of GDP, Y_2, but unfortunately, this will cause even higher prices, P_2. Alternatively, government could use contractionary policy to curb inflation. This will result in a leftward shift in aggregate demand from the current AD_1 to AD_3. This will cut prices to P_3 but with the unfortunate result of reducing real GDP to Y_3, thus causing even higher unemployment.

Because of the failure of aggregate demand policies to cure stagflation in theory and in practice, emerging supply-side economists were highly critical of the old policies and called for a new direction in economic policy. They argued that the large government budgets that were the legacy of active Keynesian management of aggregate demand had, in the long run, stifled investment and international competitiveness. In the period following the outbreak of the OPEC-induced stagflation, these supply-side economists felt that attention must be refocused from the regulation of demand to the supply side of the equation.

It soon became evident that these supply-siders had revived the early twentieth-century neoclassic view that aggregate supply was not simply a passive element responding to changes in aggregate demand, but was itself a prime mover of economic activity. The supply-siders' view of the stagflation of the 1970s was straightforward and transparent. It had been triggered, they believed, by the dramatic increases in the price of imported oil but was rooted in sluggish rates of productivity growth. The combination of these two factors caused a decrease in aggregate supply, which is graphically illustrated as a shift of the AS curve to the left, and caused both higher unemployment (lower national income) and higher prices (inflation). They believed that the cure was equally straightforward: an increase in aggregate supply. This is shown in **Figure 12.5**.

FIGURE 12.5   Increasing Aggregate Supply to Fight Stagflation

Assume that the economy is at a price level of P_1 and a GDP level of Y_1. An increase in aggregate supply will shift the aggregate supply curve from AS_1 to AS_2. The result will be a lower price level, P_2 as well as a higher level of GDP, Y_2, the latter implying a lower unemployment rate.

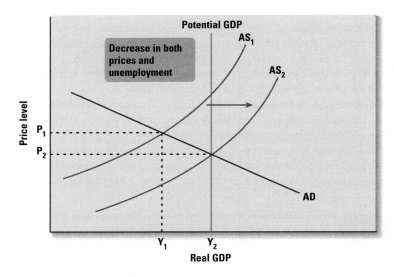

An increase in aggregate supply shifts the aggregate supply curve from AS_1 to AS_2. This results in a reduction in the price level, from P_1 to P_2, and thus in inflation as well as an increase in GDP from Y_1 to Y_2, which will result in reduced unemployment.

Furthermore, the supply-siders also believed that it was modern governments that had stifled initiative, and thus productivity growth, through high levels of taxation and excessive levels of government regulation and bureaucracy. Starting in 1981, this argument caught the attention of a number of new governments around the world, including the Brian Mulroney government in Canada, the Ronald Reagan government in the United States, and the Margaret Thatcher government in the United Kingdom.

Let us now turn to the nuts and bolts of the supply-side school of thought by asking what policies might increase aggregate supply and stimulate the production of goods and services. One of the first policies was to privatize many functions of government; it was thought that exposing these functions to the competition of the market would improve their efficiency. It was during this time, for example, that Air Canada and Canadian National [Railways] ceased to be Crown corporations and were privatized.

A second supply-side policy was the deregulation of industry, which also aimed to use the competitive market to increase efficiency. Deregulation of the airline industry in the United States is a dramatic example of this; it resulted in some long-established airlines going broke and new airlines successfully entering the industry. Most would argue that this has proved beneficial because it has resulted in lower airfares and increased consumer choice on the most popular routes. (On other, less traveled routes, higher fares resulted.) Canada also partially, but not completely, deregulated its airline, telephone, and trucking industries.

A third supply-side policy was the contracting-out of specific government services in the name of reducing the costs of these services (and the costs of running government). An example of this was Canada Post contracting out its retailing function to firms that put this service into local drugstores and convenience shops.

The fourth, and the most significant plank in the supply-siders' platform was the cutting of tax rates on business profits and on individual incomes. The rationale was to increase incentives for people to work more, save more, and invest more. The result, it was believed, would lead to an increase in aggregate supply. If income tax rates were cut, many workers would work longer hours, since high marginal tax rates tend to deter people from working long hours. Additionally, many unemployed workers would seek employment with more enthusiasm, while some homemakers and retired people would be tempted to return to the labour force. The argument was made that these results would be further enhanced if the social security net of welfare payments, unemployment coverage, and lifetime disability income were restructured to aid only those in real need, ceasing to provide what was seen by some as an easy income for those who did not deserve it. Furthermore, total savings would increase, since a cut in personal taxes would increase disposable income. Likewise, a cut in corporate taxes would provide increased profits for firms, who would then plough them back into the business in the form of new investment.

In short, advocates of the supply-side position saw this new approach as a necessary action to undo forty years of interventionist polices that, they believed, had sapped the economy of its vigor and its ability to grow, prosper, and adjust to change.

In summary, the four major policies of supply-side proponents were as follows:

- the privatization of Crown corporations
- the deregulation of regulated industries
- the contracting-out of many government services
- the reduction of tax rates

The promised benefits were very attractive: greater competition, more work effort, increased investment spending, and greater willingness to accept risk. The result was believed to be higher economic growth—creating jobs, lowering unemployment, increasing output, and easing inflation. However, there was in all this an unavoidable side effect. In advocating lower tax rates, supply-siders left themselves open to the accusation that like Keynesians, they too were proposing big government deficits as a way of curing stagflation. Surely, this would totally go against their fundamental principle of a balanced budget?

It was at this point (the late 1970s) that California economist Arthur Laffer came forward and made the intriguing argument that a cut in tax rates in North America would not decrease government's tax revenues but would actually increase them. Was Laffer being opportunistic in offering a convenient argument to rescue a weak spot in the supply-side argument, or had he, in fact, discovered something important?

The Laffer Curve

The essentials of Laffer's argument are contained in **Figure 12.6**. The curve (henceforth known as the **Laffer curve**) shows the amount of tax revenue received by government at various tax rates.

With a zero tax rate, tax revenue would, of course, be zero. At the other extreme, with a tax rate of 100 percent, presumably no one would work, and tax revenue would again be zero.

Laffer curve: the graphical representation of the idea that in terms of tax revenue, there is an optimal tax rate; above or below this rate, tax revenue would be lower.

FIGURE 12.6   The Laffer Curve

If the economy is at point *a* on the Laffer curve, then a drop in tax rates will cause an increase in tax revenues, pushing the economy to position *b*.

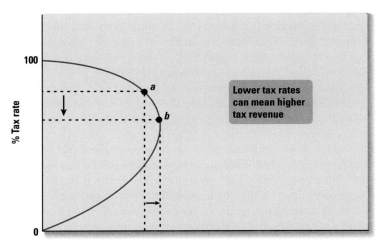

Lower tax rates can mean higher tax revenue

Between these extremes, there is a particular relationship between the tax rate and tax revenue. Over the years of Keynesian-type interventionism, supply-siders felt that tax rates had been pushed higher and higher so that many countries found themselves at a point represented by *a* in **Figure 12.6**. What was needed, argued Laffer, was a massive cut in tax rates that would increase incentives so that production, and therefore income, would increase so much that tax revenues would actually go up. This result is indicated by a movement from point *a* to *b* on the Laffer curve. So, although tax rates are lower, tax revenues are higher.

If Laffer's argument were correct, then a government could, figuratively speaking, have its cake and eat it, too. Appropriate tax cuts could increase work, savings, and investment and slash both unemployment and inflation. And on top of this, government's budget deficit would also be reduced. It sounded persuasive and the promised results were intoxicating. (Knowledge of this curve, legend has it, first bubbled up into social consciousness as a result of Laffer drawing it, on a napkin at a Hollywood restaurant, for President-elect Ronald Reagan.)

Unfortunately, the debate that started out mostly about economics slopped over into a debate about social policy generally, as many advocates of the new supply-side argument also pushed vigorously for massive cuts to social programs (while leaving the military budget untouched), and for curtailing the power of trade unions (in the name of increased competition in the labour markets). Needless to say, this led to a backlash, both inside and outside of the economics profession.

Outside the economics profession, this backlash quickly became very political. Within the discipline of economics the dispute centred on two aspects of the supply-side philosophy. First, the stimulative effect of tax cuts was questioned. A number of economists doubted that tax cuts would indeed increase the amount of work effort in the economy. Many of them criticized the supply-side argument on the grounds that a tax cut was likely to have a bigger impact on spending than on work effort and productivity. The average person in receipt of a higher disposable income is likely to choose more leisure time rather than work more hours to obtain an even bigger income. In economic terms, this means that the substitution effect of a pay raise will likely exceed the income effect of such an increase. Similarly, firms with higher after-tax profits are just as likely to pay higher dividends as they are to reinvest the increased earnings their companies. In short, the criticism of many economists was not that tax cuts do not provide incentives to people, but that the effect on spending and aggregate demand will be greater than the effect on the supply side. If these criticisms were correct then the heart of the supply-side argument would be severely compromised. It would mean that aggregate demand would rise more than aggregate supply, and not only would GDP increase but so would the price level.

The second criticism was a head-on challenge of Laffer's argument that tax cuts would increase tax revenues. More and more economists rose to say that they simply rejected this proposition out of hand.

Finally, there is one more obvious point that we need to mention here in reference to the thrust of the supply-side position. All of the proposed elements in the policy—privatization, deregulation, contracting out, and cutting taxes—are one-shot programs of action. Once all government functions are privatized, all industries are deregulated, all government services have been contracted out, and taxes have been cut to the point that they cannot be cut anymore, then there is no more powder in the cannon. If these actions did not put the economy on new course of high employment and low inflation—permanently—then what is next?

Looking back now, with nearly 30 years of hindsight, how might we evaluate the supply-side argument? Two points seem uncontested. First, there is clearly at least one glaring error. There has simply been no concrete evidence to support Laffer's argument that tax cuts can increase a government's tax revenue.

Second, it must be recognized that the direct impact of the oil price shocks of the 1970s must have been on aggregate supply and that, graphically, this impact must have been a shift of the AS curve to the left. To try to understand what was happening and to then design polices to counteract the effects using only demand-side policies would have been ineffective. Thus, it must be said that the supply-siders made a contribution to the debate on macro-economic policy.

So, how did we escape the trap of stagflation? The answer seems to be threefold. First, privatization, deregulation, and contracting out—along with the effects of a rather sharp recession in 1981–1983—did breathe more competition into the market place, and this aided productivity increases. Probably more significant, oil prices began to fall in 1981 and did not bottom out until 1999. This is not a small point and needs to be emphasized—oil prices were at historic lows during most of the 1990s (in real terms), and this gave aggregate supply an enormous boost over a sustained period. Third, the North American central banks shifted their priorities, and it is to those priorities that we now turn.

 ## SELF-TEST

4. Shown here are several different average tax rates (ATR) associated with various levels of GDP. Calculate the total tax revenue at each level of GDP, and indicate the tax rate that would maximize government's tax revenue.

ATR	GDP	Tax Revenue
0.30	$2000	_____
0.35	1900	_____
0.40	1700	_____
0.45	1500	_____
0.50	1300	_____
0.55	1100	_____

5. Supply-side economists say that a cut in tax rates will lead to an increase in real GDP. Keynesians agree with this, but for different reasons. In what ways do they differ?

12.5 EXCHANGE RATES REVISITED

L05 Show that Canada has been successful in maintaining the internal but not the external value of the Canadian dollar and why some people call for a fixed exchange rate.

We saw in Chapter 9 that over the last twenty years or so, the Bank of Canada has embarked on a new approach to monetary policy with its anti-inflationary program. Its stated goal is now to "preserve the internal and external value of the currency." Specifically, the bank operates a target range for inflation of between 1 percent and 3 percent per year.

The success of the Bank in staying within this range over the past two decades has been remarkable. Inflation rates have stayed under 3 percent every year between 1992 and 2011. This is in stark contrast to the inflationary and turbulent decades that preceded the early 1990s. In addition, unemployment in Canada went down during this period, and the growth of GDP was among the best in of the G8 nations. Good growth, falling unemployment and low inflation—an enviable record.

However, as we look back over this period, we note that the intent of the Bank of Canada's monetary policy was to preserve the external value of the Canadian currency (the exchange rate) as well. So what did happen to the Canadian–U.S. dollar exchange rate during this two-decade period? In the first half of the twenty-year period, the Canadian dollar dropped from $0.85 to 0.64 U.S. In the second half it rose from that all-time low of $0.64 to over par. This could hardly be called "preserving the external value" of the Canadian currency.

It would seem that the experience of the last two decades suggests Canada can enjoy low inflation and robust growth, and even low interest rates, but not in combination with steady, predictable exchange rates. In fact, the Canadian exchange rate has gone through rather dramatic swings both up and down.

Now, there are advantages to having a flexible exchange rate. Foremost is its tendency to stabilize fluctuations in trade. In other words, if the demand for Canadian products is falling, it will lead to a fall in the Canadian dollar, which, in turn, makes Canadian products cheaper for foreign buyers. In other words, the lower Canadian dollar cushions what otherwise might have been a more damaging fall in exports. However, as we saw in Chapter 11, there are a number of disadvantages associated with flexible exchange rates, especially an exchange rate that, like Canada's, has fluctuated so wildly over the last two decades. This has led a number of economists to propose that a small country, such as Canada, would do better to adopt a fixed exchange system, with the Canadian dollar fixed to that of its largest trading partner, the United States.

As we saw in Chapter 11, fixing Canada's exchange rate to the U.S. dollar would essentially let American monetary conditions set Canadian interest rates and would give Canada a long-term inflation rate equal to that in the United States. However, they argue that since the American business cycle drives the Canadian business cycle anyway, Canadian monetary independence is, in fact, often overstated in importance and elusive.

And what would be the advantage of a fixed-exchange rate? Again, we saw in Chapter 11 that it would increase certainty and thus boost trade between the nations. It would also lead to macro-economic stability and encourage investment in plants and equipment and in human capital. Such investment has been undermined by large swings in the Canada–U.S. exchange rate. For example, following the 12–14 percent fall in the exchange rate in 1998, many, mostly young, highly skilled Canadians migrated to the United States, where wages, measured in U.S. dollars, were much higher. If these people do not return to Canada, it will prove to be a serious loss to Canada over the next forty years.

There is a further advantage to a fixed exchange rate: it would make fiscal policy far more powerful. This is because with both interest rates and exchange rates fixed, there would be no crowding out of either investment or net exports, so expansionary fiscal policy would not be dampened down.

There is another alternative to switching to a fixed exchange rate, and that is to enter a common currency union. This means that instead of fixing the value of the Canadian dollar to that of the U.S. dollar (or, indeed, totally adopting the U.S. dollar as some have suggested), Canada, the United States, and possibly some Central American countries would adopt a common currency. This is what the majority of European countries did starting in 1999 with the introduction of the euro. Over a dozen local currencies were phased out when the euro was adopted. Today, 327 million Europeans in 17 countries use it daily and a couple of dozen smaller countries have fixed their currency value to the euro. And what has changed over the 12 plus years of use in these countries? The list of benefits is impressive.

First, corporate and government bonds now sell at a lower interest rate because of the credible claim that the European Central Bank will keep inflation low. It is interesting to note that this bank has the preservation of the internal value of the currency as its sole goal and makes no attempt to establish a target range for the euro against other currencies. Second, a common currency (or a fixed exchange rate) removes the uncertainty of doing business within the whole community and lowers the transactions cost of engaging in economic exchange or investment. Third, the areas within the European community that were depressed and lagging now have greater access to credit. As a result, the growth rate in these areas has increased. Fourth, the enlarged area of the common currency allows for greater specialization in banking that better fits the varied needs of business. Fifth, in the first few year's of the Euro's experience, the value of trade within the community is up 5 percent to 10 percent, physical investment is up 5 percent and foreign portfolio investment is up 20 percent.

Against that, it should be added that with a common currency union such as the European Union, interest rates and, indeed, monetary policy is determined by a central bank, the European Central Bank and not by individual member countries. This means a lack of autonomy for those countries. It also has serious implications if one member country, such as Greece, is suffering a serious recession and wants interest rates lowered while another country, such as Germany, is worried about inflation and pushing for higher interest rates. One size does not always fit all.

An intriguing question is whether the price of the most commonly purchased goods has began to converge in Europe, as the purchasing power parity theory from Chapter 11 would predict. In other words, with a common currency, does a Big Mac now cost the same wherever you travel in Europe? No, it doesn't, and that is true for all services like restaurant meals, haircuts, hotel rooms, and so on, which cannot be transported. In these cases, local labour costs tend to determine prices, and these do vary from country to country. But in the case of easily transportable products, such as cars, it does appear to be the case that prices are becoming roughly similar.

In summary, the case for Canada's central bank focusing on the internal value of the currency only and fixing the Canadian dollar to the U.S. dollar is stronger than most of us would probably have first believed.

SELF-TEST

6. Name two major benefits of fixed exchange rates.

12.6   THE FEAR OF DEFLATION

Stagflation was a new economic phenomenon when it struck most major economies in the mid-1970s. Another worrisome economic occurrence that many feel that we in North America will soon be suffering is deflation. Apart from a single year in the early 1950s, Canada has not suffered from falling prices since the early years of the Great Depression.

Why are a number of economists worried about **deflation**, and why is it a problem anyway? Part of the reason is the dramatic similarities between what has been happening in the United States

LO6 Understand why economists are concerned about the possibility of deflation.

deflation: a decrease in the overall price level.

in recent years and events in Japan in the 1990s. In Japan, both the real estate market and the stock market were rocked by bubble bursts, and Japanese policy stimulus proved inadequate. The result has been twenty years of growth that fluctuated between −4 percent and +2 percent along with persistent deflation. One cannot help but ask if the United States (and, by extension, Canada) is headed down the same path?

Deflation and very sluggish growth go together. There are two primary reasons for this. The first is that deflation causes a reduction in both consumer and investment spending because when prices are falling, people sometimes put off purchases in order to take advantage of the lower prices in the future. In short, economic growth is reduced because aggregate demand is dampened by deflation. The second reason is the effects of deflation on the real interest rate. In a situation where the inflation rate is 2 percent, a nominal rate of 6 percent is needed to ensure a real rate of 4 percent, which we will assume satisfies both lenders and borrowers. In contrast, consider the effects of deflation. If prices are falling at a rate of four percent, then those who have money to lend can gain a real rate of interest of 4 percent by doing nothing more than puttiung their money in a steel box under the bed. Therefore, they will not be willing to lend. Once this situation grips an economy, short-term interest rates will drop to zero, but they can go no lower. There is no such thing as a negative nominal interest rate, and nothing can be done to correct this situation. In short, deflation freezes credit markets, and this has a depressing effect on real output.

So, what causes deflation? History teaches us that a society can become vulnerable when it experiences a sudden collapse in the price of an asset whose bubble has expanded out of control—examples include Dutch tulip bulb prices in 1637, Britain's South Sea bubble in 1720, the Wall Street crash in 1929, or Japan's stock-market and real-estate-price bubbles of the 1990s. The shock of a significant bubble bursting can create so much fear in people that they simply cut their spending down to the absolute bare minimum. This fall in aggregate demand results in dramatic cuts in production, massive layoffs, cancelled investment plans, and general economic collapse. If a government is able to marshal a massive counter-action quickly, deflation might be forestalled and then reversed. This is what happened in the United States after the Black Monday of October 19, 1987, when the Dow Jones average fell by 508 points—a drop of over 22 percent and one of the largest one-day stock market declines in history. The U.S. Federal Reserve quickly and dramatically reduced interest rates by pumping money into the economy. The market turned around and actually ended "up" for the year; the economy was spared a dance with deflation.

However, some suggest that the problems of deflation—especially with rates below 5 percent—are often overstated. It is certainly likely that if deflation were 20 percent a year, many consumers and firms would delay their purchases. After all, a 20-percent saving is a significant amount. But are buyers really going to wait a year to buy products if the deflation rate is a mere 2 percent per year? It is more probably the case that at low rates of deflation of 1 or 2 percent, especially if the rate is stable, businesses (including banks) and consumers will build these rates into their expectations. After all, buyers and seller have no difficulty doing this with inflation rates of 1 or 2 percent.

 SELF-TEST

7. What is the difference between stagflation and deflation? What is similar under both of these circumstances?

STUDY GUIDE

Review

CHAPTER SUMMARY

Following the discussion of international markets in Chapter 11, this chapter takes a second look at fiscal and monetary policy.

12.1a Governments finance deficit spending by borrowing.
- But the expansionary effect is reduced because of the *crowding-out effect*.
- This happens because prices increase causing the transactions demand for money to increase.
- This causes interest rates to increase, further causing investment spending, and therefore GDP, to fall.

12.1b Higher interest rates caused by expansionary fiscal policy will encourage more foreign financial investment, thus increasing the exchange rate and crowding out net exports.

12.1c A government could also finance a budget deficit by issuing loans directly to the central bank. This is seldom done because the result causes an increase in the money supply and is therefore highly inflationary.

12.2 Monetary policy's effectiveness is enhanced when we take into account international financial flows. An increase in money supply reduces interest rates and this lowers the exchange rate. The result is a rise in both investment spending and in exports.

12.3 Fiscal and monetary policy can push unemployment or inflation down by either increasing or decreasing aggregate demand. However, since it cannot push aggregate demand both ways at the same time, lower unemployment is usually associated with higher inflation, and vice versa. This relationship between unemployment and inflation is illustrated by the *Phillips curve*.

12.4a Traditional fiscal and monetary policy is aimed at the level of aggregate demand. The supply-side school of thought argues that the phenomenon of stagflation in the 1970s highlighted the need to consider policies aimed at aggregate supply as well. These policies include:
- privatization of Crown corporations
- deregulation of private industry
- contracting-out of government services
- the reduction of tax rates

12.4b A concern of supply-siders was that a reduction in tax rates by lowering government tax revenues would cause budget deficits. Economist Arthur Laffer suggested that a lowering of tax rates would actually increase tax revenues because they increase incentives. His ideas are encompassed in the *Laffer curve*.

12.4c The ideas of supply-siders were challenged because critics suggested that:
- the amount of work and investment would not increase; only spending would rise
- contrary to Laffer's views, tax cuts would not increase tax revenues
- supply-siders' policies can only be implemented once; if they fail, there are no alternatives

12.5a In the years following stagflation, monetary policy makers shifted their goal to one of preserving the internal and external value of the currency, that is, maintaining internal price stability and a stable exchange rate. Canada was successful in curbing inflation; however, the exchange rate fluctuated greatly. Some suggested the introduction of a fixed exchange rate for Canada, which makes fiscal policy more effective because there is no crowding-out of exports.

Practise and learn online with Connect, where you can find the Answered Questions and the Unanswered Problems for all chapters of this textbook's Study Guide section.

12.5b There are many benefits for countries entering a common currency union.

- Corporate and government bonds are sold at a lower interest rate.
- Uncertainty is reduced and transaction costs are lowered.
- Depressed areas have easier access to credit.
- It increases specialization in banking.
- It increases the volume of trade.

The argument against a common currency union is that member countries give up autonomy and no longer can maintain an independent monetary policy.

12.6 Some economists fear that the financial crisis of 2007–2010 set the stage for the economy to slip into a period of prolonged deflation. Sluggish economic growth is associated with deflation.

- Consumption and investment spending are reduced because people postpone spending decisions hoping for lower future prices.
- Credit markets become less effective because it would require a negative nominal interest rate to encourage savings and investment; a negative interest rate is impossible.

NEW GLOSSARY TERMS AND KEY EQUATIONS

crowding-out effect 395	Laffer curve 403	stagflation 400
deflation 407	Phillips curve 399	

STUDY TIPS

You will probably find that the first three sections of this chapter contain material similar to Chapter 7 (fiscal policy) and Chapter 9 (monetary policy). Although this is true, Chapters 7 and 9 looked at the effects of policy in a closed economy—one in which it is assumed there is no international trade. Since Canada is a very open economy in which international trade is vitally important, it is necessary look at fiscal and monetary policy again after presenting the chapters on international trade (Chapter 10) and finance (Chapter 11). In addition, we need to examine the effects when both types of policies interact.

The discussion of stagflation and the rise of supply-side economics is, of course, presented in retrospect of actual events. To those of us who lived through them, the turbulent 1970s and 1980s seemed much more confusing than they do now. For an embarrassingly long period macroeconomics was very difficult to teach because demand-side theory could not explain what was happening and the importance of aggregate supply was not yet developed.

We very much hope that as you read this chapter, you will not be hearing about how large the rate of deflation has just become. If you are, then our fears will have been confirmed, and that will not be of any comfort to us.

Answered Questions

These questions can also be found online on Connect.

Indicate whether the following statements are true or false:

1. **(LO 1) T or F**   The most common way for government to fund expansionary fiscal policy is by borrowing from the general public.

2. **(LO 2) T or F**   Monetary policy cannot be used effectively when a country has a fixed exchange rate.

3. **(LO 1) T or F**   Expansionary fiscal policy may crowd out both private investment and export spending.

4. **(LO 3) T or F**   Aggregate demand policies are effective in curing the problems of stagflation.

5. **(LO 3) T or F**   The Phillips curve is based on the relationship between tax rates and the amount of tax revenue.

6. **(LO 4) T or F**   One of the major criticisms of the supply-side emphasis on tax cuts as a way to stimulate the economy is that such cuts affect aggregate demand more than they do aggregate supply.

7. **(LO 4) T or F**   The Laffer curve relates income levels with unemployment rates.

8. **(LO 4) T or F**   The rise of supply-side economics is rooted in the stagflation of the 1970s.

9. **(LO 5) T or F**   The Canadian dollar has not fallen below $0.80 U.S. for over twenty years.

10. **(LO 6) T or F**   Deflation means that the rate of inflation is falling.

Basic (Questions 11–24)

11. **(LO 1, 2)** All of the following, except one, would cause the aggregate demand curve to shift to the right. Which is the exception?
    a) An increase in taxes
    b) An increase in government spending on goods and services
    c) An increase in the money supply
    d) A decrease in the exchange rate

12. **(LO 1)** What is the crowding-out effect?
    a) The idea that when a government borrows to finance a deficit, it crowds out private investment because it causes interest rates to fall
    b) The idea that when a government borrows to finance a deficit, it crowds out private investment because it causes interest rates to rise
    c) The idea that fiscal policy crowds out economic growth
    d) The idea that balanced budgets crowd out economic growth

13. **(LO 3)** Stagflation is the simultaneous occurrence of both
    a) A recession and deflation
    b) A recession and inflation
    c) Inflation and rapid growth in GDP
    d) Recession and rapid growth in GDP

14. **(LO 5)** What characterized the economic conditions in Canada from 1990–2008?
    a) Low inflation and steady economic growth
    b) Stagflation
    c) Rising levels of unemployment but low inflation
    d) Low unemployment and high inflation

15. **(LO 4)** What is the name of the curve shown in Figure 12.7?
    a) Phillips curve
    b) Aggregate supply curve
    c) Laffer curve
    d) Production possibilities curve

FIGURE 12.7

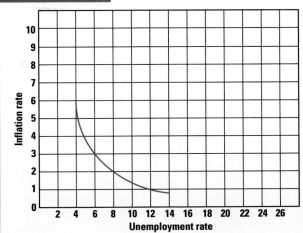

16. **(LO 5)** Which one of the following represents one of the basic problems illustrated by the Phillips curve?
    a) That the inflation rate tends to decrease as the economy moves closer to full employment
    b) That the inflation rate tends to increase as the economy moves closer to full employment
    c) That the unemployment rate tends to decrease as the economy moves toward price stability
    d) That high levels of unemployment tend to accompany high rates of inflation

17. **(LO 1, 2)** Which of the following would neutralize the crowding-out effect?
    a) An increase in tax rates
    b) An increase in the money supply
    c) An increase in money demand
    d) A decrease in the money supply

18. **(LO 4)** According to supply-siders, what is one of the keys to curbing stagflation?
    a) An increase in the money supply and a cut in government spending
    b) A decrease in the money supply and an increase in government spending.
    c) An increase in aggregate demand
    d) Convincing people to buy domestic rather than foreign-produced goods
    e) A cut in tax rates

19. **(LO 5)** During the last two decades, Canada has experienced all of the following, except one. Which is the exception?
    a) Robust economic growth
    b) A steady predictable exchange rate
    c) Low inflation rates
    d) Low interest rates

20. **(LO 6)** Which one of the following is true about deflation?
    a) It is associated with stagflation.
    b) It occurs whenever an inflationary gap gets large enough.
    c) It precedes periods of high investment.
    d) It is a period of decreases in the general price level.

21. **(LO 4)** Graphically, what is necessary for an economy to escape the grips of stagflation?
    a) Shift the AD curve to the right
    b) Shift the AD curve to the left
    c) Shift the AS curve to the right
    d) Shift the AS curve to the left

22. **(LO 4, 5)** Stagflation in North American economies during the 1970s was triggered by what event?
    a) OPEC-induced oil price increases
    b) A far too rapid increase in the money supply in both of the countries
    c) The Vietnam war
    d) Excessive government budget deficits

23. **(LO 6)** In the 1990s, Japan experienced all of the following, except one. Which is the exception?
    a) A decline in the real estate market
    b) A decline in the stock market
    c) An increase in inflation rates
    d) Low or negative economic growth rates

24. **(LO 4)** All of the following, except one, were policies supported by the supply-siders. Which is the exception?
    a) Privatization of Canada's crown corporations
    b) Contracting out of government services
    c) Government closing down labour retraining centres
    d) Deregulation of government involvement in the economy
    e) Reducing taxes

Intermediate (Problems 25–32)

25. **(LO 1)** What does "monetizing the debt" involve?
    a) Government selling bonds to the general public
    b) Government selling bonds to the Bank of Canada
    c) The Bank of Canada selling bonds to government
    d) The Bank of Canada selling bonds to the general public

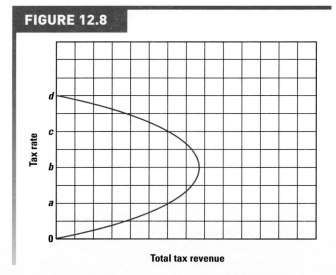

FIGURE 12.8

Tax rate (vertical axis, with levels marked d, c, b, a, 0)

Total tax revenue (horizontal axis)

26. **(LO 4)** Refer to **Figure 12.8** to answer this question. According to supply-side economists, at what level were tax rates in Canada in the 1980s?
    a) At some level like 0a
    b) At some level like 0b
    c) At some level like 0c
    d) At 0d

27. **(LO 1, 2)** Suppose that government wishes to affect the level of aggregate demand in the economy. All of the following, except one, are consistent policy measures. Which is the exception?
    a) A tax increase and an increase in money supply
    b) A tax reduction and an increase in money supply
    c) An increase in government spending and an increase in money supply
    d) A decrease in government spending and a decrease in money supply

28. **(LO 5)** If Canadian policy-makers wish to maintain the value of the dollar relative to the U.S. dollar, what should they do?
    a) Keep the money supply constant
    b) Continually adjust the money supply to keep interest rates in line with American rates
    c) Increase the money supply whenever the U.S. dollar starts to appreciate against the Canadian dollar
    d) Purchase American dollars

29. **(LO 2)** What is the most serious criticism of anti-inflationary monetary policy?
    a) Monetary policy is probably ineffective in fighting inflation.

b) Overemphasis on controlling inflation comes at the expense of the equally valid goals of low unemployment and economic growth.
c) Maintaining internal price stability means losing control of the exchange rate.
d) It leads to interest rates being far too low.

30. **(LO 2)** An increase in government spending can result in crowding-out. Which of the following is a correct statement of the process?
a) It leads to a decrease in savings, which leads to a decrease in investment spending.
b) It leads to an increase in money supply, which pushes interest rates up and causes a decrease in investment spending.
c) It causes bond prices to increase, which pushes interest rates up and leads to a decrease in investment spending.
d) It increases the price level and the demand for money, which causes interest rates to increase and investment spending to decrease.
e) It leads to an increase in GDP and in savings, which increases investment spending.

31. **(LO 5)** What effect does expansionary monetary policy have on the interest rate and the (flexible) exchange rate?
a) The interest rate will fall, and exchange rate will rise.
b) The interest rate will fall, and exchange rate will fall.
c) The interest rate will rise, and exchange rate will rise.
d) The interest rate will rise, and exchange rate will fall.

32. **(LO 5)** Why, according to some economists, should Canada adopt the U.S. dollar as its currency?
a) Because it would maximize foreign long-term investment in Canada
b) Because it would enhance the Bank of Canada's monetary policy
c) Because it would eliminate the need for active fiscal policy
d) Because it would eliminate inflation

Advanced (Problems 33–35)

33. **(LO 1, 2)** If counter-cyclical fiscal policy causes crowding-out, which of the following statements is correct?
a) Crowding-out increases the effectiveness of fiscal policy by pushing up interest rates and reducing investment spending.
b) Crowding-out reduces the effectiveness of fiscal policy by pushing up interest rates and reducing investment spending.
c) Crowding-out reduces the effectiveness of fiscal policy by lowering interest rates and reducing investment spending.
d) Crowding-out enhances the effectiveness of fiscal policy by lowering interest rates and increasing investment spending.
e) Crowding-out reduces money demand and thereby reduces the effectiveness of fiscal policy.

34. **(LO 5)** Why would Canadian monetary policy be ineffective if we fixed the value of our dollar to that of the U.S. dollar?
a) Expanding the money supply in Canada would crowd out investment spending.
b) Contracting the money supply in Canada would crowd out investment spending.
c) Expanding the money supply in Canada would cause a rise in interests rates and an outflow of Canadian dollars and thereby frustrate the money expansion.
d) Expanding the money supply in Canada would cause a fall in interests rates and an outflow of Canadian dollars and thereby frustrate the money expansion.

35. **(LO 6)** All of the following statements about deflation, except one, are true. Which is the exception?
a) It is characterized by interest rates at zero or near zero.
b) Apart from one year, it has not occurred in Canada since the Great Depression.
c) It means that a return on idle money is possible.
d) It encourages consumers to postpone major purchases.
e) It encourages large-scale investment in the economy.

Parallel Problems

ANSWERED PROBLEMS

36A. **(LO 1, 2, 4)** **Key Problem** The economy of Copland
is in equilibrium but is suffering from a recessionary
gap of $10 billion. Its aggregate demand and supply
curves are shown in **Figure 12.9**.

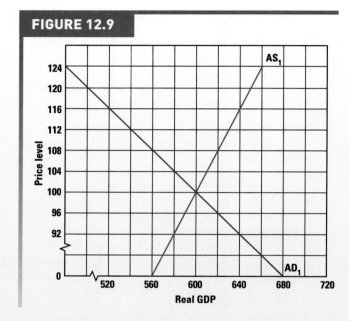

FIGURE 12.9

a) Draw in the potential GDP curve, and label it.
Both demand-side and supply-side economists in
Copland have been advising government to reduce
taxes in order to cure the recession. Independent
economic research has determined that for every
1 percent change in taxes, aggregate demand
changes by $20 billion.
b) Assuming that government decides to cut taxes
by 6 percent, and that aggregate supply is
unaffected, draw in and label the new curve,
AD₂, in **Figure 12.9**.
c) At the new equilibrium, by how much has real
GDP and the price level changed?
Change in real GDP: (+/−) $ _____
Change in price level: (+/−) _____

Independent economic research has also determined
that every 1-percent cut in tax rates in Copland
will increase aggregate supply by $5 billion
because it stimulates productivity.

d) For the same six percent cut in taxes, draw in and
label the new aggregate supply curve, AS₂, and the
new potential GDP curve 2, in **Figure 12.9**.
e) Assuming that aggregate demand did not change, by
how much would real GDP and the price level change?
Change in real GDP: (+/−) $ _____
Change in price level: (+/−) _____
f) Finally, assuming that the change in tax rates
affects both aggregate demand and aggregate
supply, add together the changes in b) and d).
Total change in real GDP: $ _____
Total change in price level: (+/−) _____
g) Is Copland's economy now at full employment?
If there is a gap, what type is it, and how much?
Type of gap: _____ of $ _____

Basic (Problems 37A–41A)

37A. **(LO 1, 2, 3, 4, 6)** Match each item in the left-hand
column with a related idea or event in the right-hand
column by placing a letter in each blank.

A. bubble bursts	1. Keynesians	_____
B. demand management	2. OPEC-induced oil price increases	_____
C. tax cuts as a stimulus to aggregate supply	3. Phillips curve	_____
D. stagflation	4. deflation	_____
E. trade-off	5. supply-siders	_____

38A. **(LO 1)** In the queendom of Frankland, GDP is
currently $500 million. Production in Frankland is
unaffected by changes in tax rates until the rate hits
35 percent. Thereafter, for each 5-percent increase
in the tax rate, GDP drops by $40 million.
a) Complete **Table 12.2** for the government of
Frankland.
b) In **Figure 12.10**, graph Frankland's tax revenue curve.
c) At what tax rate will the tax revenue be maximized?
What will be the amount of tax revenue?
Percentage tax rate: _____
Tax revenue: $ _____

39A. **(LO 2)** The nominal GDP of Etruria is $1500 billion.
Next year, the growth of nominal GDP is expected to
be 2.4 percent. If the transactions demand in Etruria
is 10 percent of nominal GDP, by how much must the
money supply be increased in order to avoid crowding-
out? Answer: _____

TABLE 12.2

% Tax Rate	GDP	Tax Revenue
0	$500	_____
5	_____	_____
10	_____	_____
15	_____	_____
20	_____	_____
25	_____	_____
30	_____	_____
35	_____	_____
40	_____	_____
45	_____	_____
50	_____	_____
55	_____	_____
60	_____	_____
65	_____	_____
70	_____	_____

FIGURE 12.10

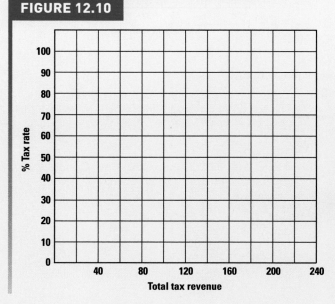

40A. **(LO 2)** If the money supply increases, what effect will it have on the following variables?

Interest rate _____ Investment _____
Exchange rate _____ Net exports _____

Intermediate (Problems 41A–46A)

41A. **(LO 1, 3)** The data in **Table 12.3** show Haydn's aggregate demand and aggregate supply. In this economy, the natural rate of unemployment is 6 percent, and for each $10 of recessionary gap, cyclical unemployment is 1 percent.

Suppose the economy of Haydn is in equilibrium and experiencing a recessionary gap of $60 and inflation of 1 percent.

TABLE 12.3

Price Index	Aggregate Quantity Demanded	Aggregate Quantity Supplied
110	860	740
115	840	760
120	820	780
125	800	800
130	780	820
135	760	840
140	740	860

a) What is the price index, equilibrium GDP, potential GDP and the unemployment rate?
Price index: _____
Equilibrium GDP: _____
Potential GDP: _____
Unemployment rate: _____
b) In the following year, AD increases by 40. What are the new unemployment and inflation rates?
Unemployment rate _____
Inflation rate _____
c) Sketch a Phillips curve from your answers in a) and b) in **Figure 12.11**.

FIGURE 12.11

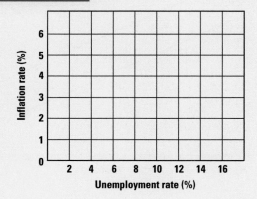

42A. **(LO 2)**

   a) Suppose that GDP in Rutland is $400 billion and the government increases spending by $16 billion. If the multiplier equals 3, what is the new level of GDP? Answer: $_____

   b) Suppose that as a result of the increase in GDP the price level in Newland also rises, causing the demand for money to increase by $10 billion. Given the graph of the money market, **Figure 12.12**, and investment demand **Figure 12.13**, by how much will investment fall? Answer: $_____

   c) Given the same value of the multiplier, what will be the new level of GDP? Answer: $_____

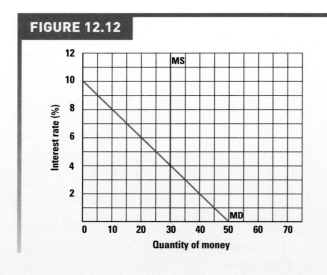

FIGURE 12.12

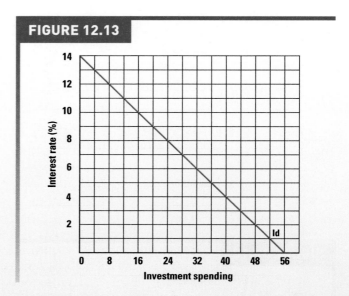

FIGURE 12.13

43A. **(LO 5)** Assume that **Figure 12.14** is referring to the Japanese economy in the 1990s. Describe in words what actually occurred during those years.

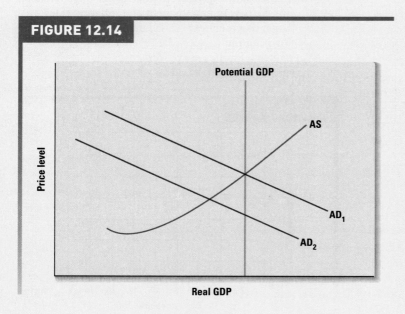

FIGURE 12.14

44A. **(LO 1, 2)** Using AD/AS curves, on the graphs below, illustrate a small (in A), a larger (in B), and a very large (in C) increase in the price level, resulting from expansionary fiscal (or monetary) policy.

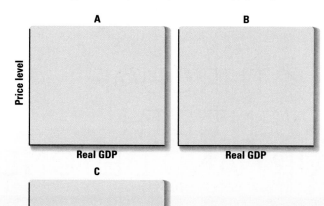

45A. **(LO 3)** What is the *Phillips curve*?

46A. **(LO 6)** Why will deflation lead to a drop in consumer spending and investment?

Advanced (Problems 47A–49A)

47A. **(LO 3)** The following data in **Table 12.4** is for the economy of Hyaku.
   a) Given that the labour force remained a constant 120 million, calculate the unemployment and inflation rates for each of the years 2006–2011.
   b) From the data collected, draw a Phillips curve.

48A. **(LO 4)** What are the causes of stagflation? How can stagflation be cured?

49A. **(LO 4)** According to supply-siders, a reduction in tax rates will increase work, saving, and investment. Explain why.

50A. **(LO 5)** Are the prices of products in different countries that use a common currency (like Europe) the same or different? Explain your answer.

TABLE 12.4

Year	Price Index	Inflation Rate (%)	Unemployment (in millions)	Unemployment Rate (%)
2006	100			
2007	102		12.0	
2008	105.1		9.6	
2009	110.4		7.2	
2010	119.2		6.0	
2011	133.5		4.8	

A WALK THROUGH THE TWENTIETH CENTURY AND BEYOND

LEARNING OBJECTIVES

At the end of this chapter, you should be able to...

LO1 understand why neoclassicists believe the economy will automatically achieve full-employment equilibrium.

LO2 understand why Keynesian economics challenged accepted beliefs about curing economic depression and maintaining prosperity.

LO3 understand the evolution of the welfare state and the rise of supply-side economics.

LO4 understand the significant economic changes that occurred in Canada and around the world at the end of the twentieth century.

LO5 understand the cause of the 2007–2010 financial crisis and its economic consequences.

WHAT'S AHEAD...

This chapter examines the evolution of economic theory and the use of economic policy with a look at specific periods of the twentieth and early twenty-first centuries. We begin by looking at the classical world of Say's Law in the context of the first years of the 1900s. We then move to World War I and its aftermath, which saw the evolution of neoclassical thought and the belief that economies are capable of self-correction. Keynesian economics emerged with the Great Depression and prevailed until the 1970s. Then, we look at the stagflation of the 1970s and the rise of supply-side economics. We then look at Canada at the turn of the twenty-first century and, finally, at the financial crisis and the ensuing economic recession that began in 2008.

A Question of Relevance...

Imagine that you are looking for an entry-level job as a graphic artist. After three months of job searching, you have gotten nowhere—not a single interview, let alone a job offer. What went wrong? Do you think that the cause of your problem is personal because you do not have the right qualifications, or perhaps are asking for too high a wage? Or is it the fault of businesses for their unwillingness to create enough jobs? Or is it, instead, a problem to be laid at the doorstep of government for not pursuing policies that would ensure that the economy created enough jobs?

We want to do two main things in this chapter. First, using the Canadian experience, we want to examine how contemporary events and economic theory are interrelated. We will look at five significant periods in the twentieth century, each of which had a profound influence on economic policy-making and on the evolution of economic theory. At the same time, we will look at how these same economic theories, and the thinking they generated, later helped shape some of the major events of the twentieth century.

The second thing we want to do is further examine a question that we have touched on throughout this text and that has claimed the attention of political commentators, economists, and many others for over two centuries:

What is the appropriate role of government in ensuring a successful economy?

In answering this question, we will discover that there are two widely contrasting views on the subject. Let us now turn to the first of our five periods.

13.1 CANADA AT THE START OF THE TWENTIETH CENTURY AND IN THE AFTERMATH OF WORLD WAR I

At the beginning of the twentieth century, Canada stood at the threshold of a new era, one filled with the promise of growth and prosperity. A major source of that confidence was the Canadian Pacific Railway, which had linked eastern and western Canada. More especially, the railway opened up the vast lands of the prairies and new immigrants were pouring in. All this led Prime Minister Wilfrid Laurier to declare: "A new star has risen upon the horizon. And it is to that star that every immigrant…now turns his gaze." The "Canadian miracle," as it was called, led to the construction of more railways in the west (the Canadian Northern, the Grand Trunk, and the National Continental), to a huge increase in wheat production and wheat exports, and to the birth of two new provinces, Alberta and Saskatchewan, in 1905. Fuelled by British and American investment, the economy of this "new star" boomed. Rapid growth in the demand for Canadian products combined with low transportation costs—especially declining ocean-freight rates—caused incomes, jobs, and immigration all to increase. Perhaps the most significant statistic was that in the first twenty years of the twentieth century, Canada's population grew from just over five million to almost nine million.

L01 Understand why neo-classicists believe the economy will automatically achieve full-employment equilibrium.

Classical Economics and Say's Law

As Canada was prospering, so, too, was the rest of the world. The new century was alive with promise, and this was echoed in the ideas of economists. Despite some earlier gloomy predictions, capitalism was alive, well, and flourishing. Although there was a certain amount of government intervention for the purpose of nation building, this was a period in which the laissez-faire approach was dominant. Economists, policymakers, and, indeed, most of the public believed that a government that governed least governed best. Furthermore, the prevailing belief was that those who earned above-average incomes deserved them because they must somehow be better than other people; otherwise, they would not have earned those high incomes. Similarly, the majority believed that the poor suffered from some failing of character or were unwilling to work hard enough to avoid poverty. In short, some people probably took on responsibility for many things for which they were not responsible.

However, a laissez-faire economy also meant an unplanned economy, and this was a source of disquiet for some. They wondered if it was possible that such lack of planning might result in an economy producing more than people would be willing and able to consume. They wondered if capitalism was likely to experience periodic bouts of overproduction. And wouldn't such over-production, and the resulting increase in inventories, lead to firms reducing output and laying off workers? In short, isn't capitalism prone to recessions?

These questions were not new. Almost a century before, the loud and clear voice of David Ricardo, one of the giants of the classical school, had answered no to each of them. Ricardo's answers relied on what is known as **Say's Law**, which states that *supply creates its own demand.* What this means is that:

> - **The act of production (supply) requires the use of factors of production, which must be paid.**
> - **Such payments are incomes to those who supply the factors, and these incomes are subsequently spent.**
> - **This spending automatically creates enough demand to buy the supply.**

Say's Law: the proposition that "supply creates its own demand," that is, production (supply) creates sufficient income and, thus, spending (demand) to purchase the production (attributed to French economist Jean-Baptiste Say).

This is actually a verbal description of the simple circular flow of income that we looked at in Chapter 3. Supply creates income, and this income creates enough demand to purchase the supply. If supply increases, then income and (it was assumed) demand increase by an equal amount. Furthermore, if supply decreased, incomes and demand would also fall. That is, supply is active and demand is the passive result.

With Ricardo's endorsement of Say's Law, the prevailing view of the classical economists was that it ensured that all that was produced would be bought. In short, equilibrium (the equality of supply and demand) in the economy was both automatic and normal.

This last statement does need some qualification. It was conceded that, if demand patterns changed, then temporary surpluses and shortages of specific goods were possible. For example, if demand changed so that a shortage of beaver-pelt hats and a surplus of cloth hats occurred, then there would be unemployment among those who made cloth hats and an increase in the demand for labour to make beaver-pelt hats. This would lead to wage rates and prices in the cloth industry quickly falling while those in the beaver-hat industry would rise. That is, a surplus in one industry is accompanied by a shortage in another industry, but there is a normal adjustment between the two. Thus, we can again state the conclusion of the majority of classical economists of the nineteenth century:

> **Equilibrium occurs automatically and is the normal state of affairs in a market economy.**

This optimistic view was shared by most economists in the first years of the twentieth century. This sense of confidence was, however, shaken by "the war to end all wars"—World War I.

World War I and Later

In 1914, Canada entered World War I as one of the Dominions of the United Kingdom. As a result of the enormous contribution Canada made to the Allied war effort, when the war ended four years later Canada was a far more confident nation with a more independent frame of mind. Furthermore, relatively cheap credit combined with a pent-up demand for consumer goods that had been in limited supply fuelled an immediate postwar boom during which prices rose.

Despite the boom, the transition to a peacetime economy proved difficult because the bubble of pent-up consumer demand burst. This led to a rapid contraction of the economy and a drop in prices. Returning soldiers, as well as workers who had been forced to make big sacrifices for the war effort, found that the promised rewards

Library and Archives Canada.

World War I poster encouraging Canadian citizens to support the war effort.

of victory were elusive. A widespread and bitter strike broke out in Winnipeg, followed later by strikes in Halifax and Vancouver. Particularly hard hit were the Prairies and the Maritimes, as the price of wheat, for example, fell by 60 percent. By December 1923, unemployment had reached 17 percent and many workers were forced to roam the country in search of work—a taste of what was to come less than a decade later.

Then, slowly, the Canadian economy improved, in tandem with a worldwide economic recovery. Fuelled by American investment (which surpassed that of Britain for the first time in 1921), Ontario, in particular, experienced a boom in industrial investment. Quebec saw a dramatic increase in the development of hydroelectric power, while the West enjoyed a recovery in world prices of grains and other resources. By the mid-1920s, the production of newsprint became the country's second-largest industry, next to agriculture. It seemed like the long-awaited time of plenty had arrived, and Canadians were determined to make the most of it.

Neoclassical Economists and Aggregate Demand and Supply

Neoclassical economists of the time could rejoice in the recovery taking place and remained as confident as Ricardo that market economies could recover from dislocations, even those caused by world wars. In short, they *believed that market economies were self-adjusting.* In fact, they went even further, and with the addition of three specific propositions, they built an argument that concluded that prolonged recessions were an impossibility in a market economy.

We examined the first of these propositions in Chapter 5. In terms of aggregate supply and demand analysis, neoclassical economists believed that any temporary overproduction (surpluses) or underproduction (shortages) would disappear through price changes. That is, flexible prices would ensure that the quantities demanded and supplied in the product market would be equal. Surpluses cause prices to drop; shortages cause prices to increase. This flexibility means that any change in aggregate demand will translate into a change in the price level but not a change in real GDP. This is illustrated in **Figure 13.1**.

If prices are truly flexible, then aggregate supply would be determined by resource availability, productivity, and the current state of technology. This is to say, the current price level for goods and services, or any change in that price level, would have no long-term affect on aggregate supply. Thus, an increase in demand, from AD₁ to AD₂ in **Figure 13.1**, would increase the price

---

FIGURE 13.1	**A Change in Demand in the Neoclassical Model**

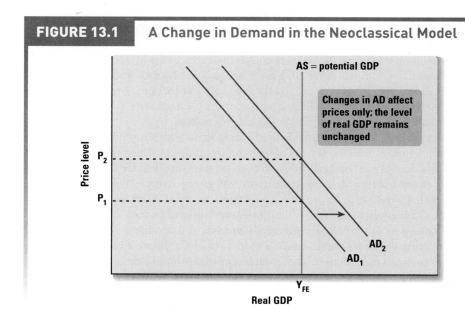

An increase in aggregate demand will cause a rightward shift in the aggregate demand curve from AD₁ to AD₂. The effect will be an increase in the price level from P₁ to P₂, but the level of real GDP will remain unchanged at Y_FE.

level and consequently wage levels, but it would not change aggregate supply. Similarly, a decrease in aggregate demand would decrease the price level and the wage level but would not change aggregate supply. In short, since they believed that prices and wages adjust rapidly to changes in aggregate demand, neoclassicists make no distinction between the long run and the short run. Another way of looking at this is to recognize that there is only one supply curve, which is synonymous with potential GDP. Of course, any change in resources, productivity, or technology would change aggregate supply, and this would shift the AS curve to the left, or to the right. However, it would always be vertical. In short:

> In the neoclassical model, the level of real GDP is unaffected by changes in aggregate demand.

The significance of this is that the economy can never produce below its potential GDP level, since this can only occur if the prevailing price level is above the equilibrium price level. But if this were to ever happen, then the resulting surplus of goods would simply cause the price level to drop, and as it does so, buyers would increase their spending until the economy is back at its normal full-employment level.

 SELF-TEST

1. Why did the neoclassical economists feel that the aggregate supply curve is vertical at the full-employment level of GDP?

Theory of Loanable Funds

To understand the neoclassicists' second proposition, we need to return to Ricardo's support of Say's Law. His argument also contained the proposition that any funds that were saved would automatically be invested, that is, spent but in a form other than consumption. Recall that Ricardo wrote in the context of the early nineteenth century, where most savers were profit-earning business owners who were quite willing to turn their savings into investment with an eye toward even greater profits in the future. However, by the early twentieth century, the incomes of a large percentage of working people had risen sufficiently so that savers (householders) and investors (businesses) had become different groups with different motivations.

This led some to ask how we could be certain that savings and investment would be equal in a modern market economy. Surely, their equality could come about only by coincidence! Not so, replied the neoclassical economists. After all, buyers and sellers of goods and services are different groups with different motivations, and yet they are still able to "come together." And what brings them together? A commonly agreed-upon price of the product. And what is the price of savings, or as they called them, loanable funds? The rate of interest.

Figure 13.2 shows the demand for loanable funds (from firms wishing to finance investment) and the supply of such funds (from the savings of household and firms). There is only one interest rate, r_E, at which the quantity of loanable funds demanded and supplied are equal. The rate of interest, therefore, equates savings and investment and will change automatically to ensure that the two are equal. What would happen, for instance, if firms, worried about the future, decide to reduce their demand for investment, that is, the investment demand curve shifted to the left? Would that likely cause a recession? No, according to neoclassical economists. This is because the ensuing surplus of loanable funds would cause a reduction in the interest rate. This, in turn, would induce firms to invest more. Lower interest rates, therefore, would help prevent a recession.

| FIGURE 13.2 | The Market for Loanable Funds |

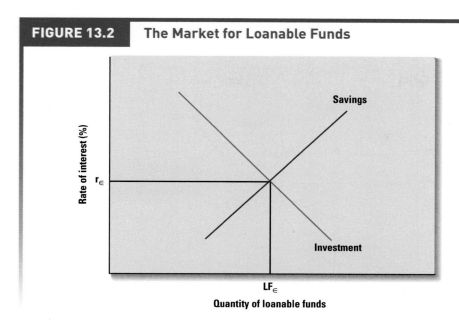

The savings function is upward sloping, illustrating the fact that a higher rate of interest will encourage people to save more. Conversely, a higher rate of interest will discourage firms from borrowing in order to invest. Therefore, the investment curve is downward sloping. There can only be one interest rate, r_ϵ, at which savings and investment are equal.

✓ **SELF-TEST**

2. According to neoclassical economists, what two things could cause a decrease in interest rates?

The Supply of Labour and the Demand for Labour

The third and final proposition of neoclassical theory in support of the idea that an economy is self-adjusting was the claim that any unemployment that might exist in the economy is temporary. This conclusion was arrived at by applying supply-and-demand analysis to the labour market. It was reasoned that there is only one equilibrium wage level at which the quantity supplied and the quantity demanded for labour are equal. Once this rate is achieved, there would be no surplus or shortage of labour, that is, no unemployment. Then, how can the fact that unemployment exists be explained? As **Figure 13.3** illustrates, unemployment can occur only if the prevailing wage rate is above the equilibrium wage rate.

At wage rate W_2, the number of workers demanded and therefore employed is quantity a. The number of workers who would like a job at this rate, however, is quantity b. The distance ab, then, represents the quantity of unemployed labour, those people who would like jobs but are unable to obtain them. We can see that unemployment is a result of the prevailing wage rate being above equilibrium. However, such unemployment cannot continue indefinitely. Competition for jobs among the employed and the unemployed will force wage rates down and, in doing so, will induce firms to hire more workers. Flexible wage rates, therefore, ensure full employment. This means that if there are unemployed workers, then they must be voluntarily unemployed because if they were willing to offer their services at a lower wage, they would be able to obtain a job. If, instead, they are holding out for a better wage, they must be doing so voluntarily.

In summary, neoclassicists built their view of how the macroeconomy works on four pillars:

- the validity of Say's Law
- the flexibility of prices
- the flexibility of interest rates
- the flexibility of wages

FIGURE 13.3   A Surplus of Labour

If the wage level is above equilibrium, there will be a surplus of labour. At wage level W₂ the number of workers demanded by firms, quantity *a*, would be less than at equilibrium. Conversely, the number of workers seeking jobs would be higher, quantity *b*. The distance *ab* therefore represents the surplus of labour, that is, unemployed labour.

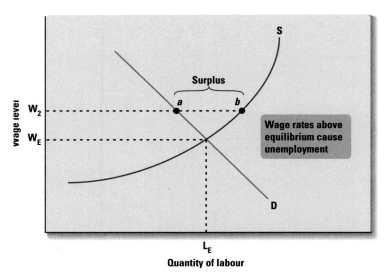

Quantity of labour

Given these four factors, neoclassical economists were convinced that serious or long-lasting recessions were an impossibility. Flexible prices, flexible wages, and flexible interest rates would all ensure that the macroeconomic market would quickly return to its normal equilibrium, and further, this equilibrium was at full employment, or what we could also call potential GDP. It seemed so simple and so logical. If the economy was starting to fall into a recession, then the resulting drop in the price level would encourage buyers to spend more; a drop in wages would induce firms to hire more people; and lower interest rates would entice firms to invest more. As a result, the recession would be averted. This view remained the prevailing view of most economists until the Great Depression of the 1930s.

✓ SELF-TEST

3. The accompanying table shows the labour demand and supply in a hypothetical economy.

   a) What is the equilibrium wage rate, and how many workers would be employed?

   b) Suppose that the wage rate increases to $8.50. How many workers are employed? How many are unemployed?

   c) How many of the unemployed are workers who have lost their jobs? Why is this figure less than the total number of unemployed?

Quantity of Labour Demanded (in millions)	Wage Rate ($)	Quantity of Labour Supplied (in millions)
12.8	6.00	11.0
12.4	6.50	11.5
12.0	7.00	12.0
11.6	7.50	12.5
11.2	8.00	13.0
10.8	8.50	13.5
10.4	9.00	14.0
10.0	9.50	14.5

13.2 THE GREAT DEPRESSION AND THE RISE OF KEYNESIANISM

L02 Understand why Keynesian economics challenged accepted beliefs about curing economic depression and maintaining prosperity.

The Depression

In the fall of 1929, Wall Street's stock market crashed, and over the next three years the American economy experienced such a severe depression that many observers at the time felt that it signalled the death throes of capitalism itself. Production in the United States dropped by 42 percent between 1929 and 1933, 85 000 businesses failed, 5000 banks closed their doors. and unemployment increased from 3 to 25 percent. The American experience spread quickly to Canada and was soon repeated in economies around the world. Clearly, something had gone wrong with the market economies.

Economic historians now recognize that the buoyant American economy of the 1920s was mainly built on hopes and dreams that lacked a solid foundation in reality. Firms and individuals overextended their credit limits in the hopes of making a "fast and furious" fortune, not through hard work, improved productivity, and innovation but by playing the stock market. Yet, the stock market bubble burst in a dramatic way, and people were left to wonder how the problem might be cured. To the neoclassical economists of the day the answer was clear and obvious: the economy should be left alone to cure itself. They felt that prices would soon drop, which would encourage people to buy more, and this would stimulate production; that interest rates would soon fall, thus stimulating investment; and that wage rates would soon drop, encouraging firms to increase hiring.

Thousands of unemployed men from British Columbia, Alberta, and Saskatchewan climbed aboard freight trains in an on-to-Ottawa protest against conditions in depression-era job camps in 1935.

The Canadian experience in these early years of the Great Depression can be used to show how right and how wrong neoclassicists were. Between 1929 and 1933, prices in Canada did drop by 23 percent. But production continued to fall. Wage rates also dropped by approximately 20 percent, but unemployment continued to hover around the 20-percent mark. Interest rates dropped to 2 percent, but gross investment remained low, and in 1933, net investment actually became negative.

It would be difficult to overstate the fear and pain experienced by Canadians during these dark years. The beginnings of a social security net was in place, but this was hardly enough to cushion the fall into unemployment and poverty—no unemployment insurance, a very limited pension plan, very limited and localized welfare payments (with the exception of a national war-widows benefits plan), no baby bonus cheques, no subsidized medical plan, and no subsidized housing.

▶ ADDED DIMENSION   Too Much or Too Little?

This extract from *Canada's Illustrated Heritage Series* neatly sums up the times: "The strange and terrifying thing about the depression was that there was too much of almost everything. Too much food. In Prince Edward Island, potatoes were left rotting in the ground, and on the prairies wheat was burned because it was not worth shipping. Too many houses. There were vacant houses on every street and you could rent a good-sized one for $10 a month. Too many automobiles. Factories could turn out 400 000 a year but only 40 000 were bought in 1932. Too many men for the jobs that needed doing. There was too much of everything, in fact, except jobs and money."

The freight trains that pulled into many Canadian cities carried dozens of men riding the empty boxcars in search of a new place that might have some work. The problem was that the trains leaving that same city heading in the other direction had just as many unemployed souls hoping that the next stop might offer something better. And it was not just the unemployed who were suffering. Those still working often faced the prospect of pay cuts, which they were in no position to argue about because they might be laid off next. And those in business faced falling sales and meagre profits.

Through all this there was a nagging question that continued to go unanswered: why wasn't the economy adjusting in the way neoclassicists thought it would? It took Keynes and his General Theory to finally provide some answers.

The Keynesian Response to Neoclassicists

In the previous chapters, we already looked at many of the ideas of Keynes on how the macro-economy works. Nonetheless, let us do an overview. Keynes disagreed with neoclassical economists as to how the economy adjusts if production exceeds total spending and a recessionary gap threatens. Where neoclassicists saw prices falling, Keynes saw prices that were "sticky" and would fall only slowly, if at all. Neoclassicists and Keynes saw the flexibility of prices so differently because each built their models on different assumptions. Neoclassicists assumed perfect competition in both the product and the labour markets. Keynes, however, argued that the product market was dominated by large oligopoly firms with the power to set their own prices and wages, and this meant that the forces of competition were weaker than was envisioned by the neoclassicists. Furthermore, Keynesians later argued that there is a more simple, practical way to explain why prices are inflexible downward: for a firm to change prices is both time-consuming and expensive. This is because existing labels, catalogues, advertisements, inventory valuations, and billing codes all have to be changed in order to institute a price adjustment.

Given this, what was the economy's response to a decrease in demand? The Keynesian answer was that firms would cut back on production and lay people off. This increases the level of unemployment but does not lead to much downward pressure on wages because they, too, are "sticky downward." The reason for sticky wages, Keynes argued, was the existence of trade unions, which had the power to resist wage cuts once labour contracts had been signed. In addition, even non-union workers would resist the idea of wages that fluctuate along with the employer's fortunes, since in the modern world most wages are fixed in the short run and are reviewed only periodically (often once a year). In short:

> Keynes saw the adjustment process in terms of a fall in production and employment, rather than a fall in prices and wages.

To emphasize the contrast between the neoclassical and Keynesian viewpoints, we can use a metaphor. Suppose there are two firms, Classical Cookies and Keynesian Kandies, both of whom face a downturn in business. The manager of Classical Cookies calls a meeting of her staff and informs them that she has some good news and some bad news: "Despite the 20 percent reduction in orders this month, you'll be pleased to learn that we are proposing no layoffs. You will all keep your jobs. Unfortunately, we have no choice in the circumstances but to reduce your pay by 20 percent. We will, however, maintain production levels, but it does mean—please note, sales department—that in order to do so, we will be cutting prices by 20 percent starting tomorrow."

Meanwhile, over at Keynesian Kandies, a very similar meeting is taking place between its manager and staff and here there is also both good and bad news: "Despite the 20 percent reduction in orders this month, you'll be pleased to learn that we are not proposing any pay cuts for our staff. Unfortunately, we have no choice in the circumstances but to lay off 20 percent of you, starting tomorrow. We will, however, maintain present prices, but it does mean—please note, production department—that production levels will be cut by 20 percent."

Keynes also disagreed with neoclassicists about the way in which the equality of savings and investment in the economy is brought about. To Keynes, this occurs as a result of a painful adjustment of production and income and not by changes in the interest rate, as suggested by neoclassicists. If savings are greater than investment, the value of total production must be greater than aggregate expenditures. This will lead to a cut in production, income, and savings until once more savings and investment are equal. In contrast, according to neoclassicists, a surplus of savings would simply lead to a fall in interest rates. which would increase investment until savings and investment were again equal. Keynes believed that changes in the interest rate have very little effect on the level of total savings, which are, instead, determined by the level of income. Finally, Keynes believed, as we saw in Chapter 8, that interest rates are determined by the demand and supply of money and not by the interaction of total savings and investment demand in the economy.

If, as Keynes believed, prices, wages, and interest rates do not adjust quickly, if at all, to a decrease in aggregate demand, then an economy can fall into a recession and remain there indefinitely. In these situations, only active government intervention will get the economy on the road to recovery. This point is illustrated in **Figure 13.4**.

Let us begin with the economy at full-employment-equilibrium income, Y_{FE}, with a price level of P_1. As the recession worsens, aggregate demand decreases from AD_1 to AD_2. If the price level is sticky downward and remains at P_1—and if wages exhibit the same resistance to falling—then the economy could get stuck at b with a GDP level of Y_1. But we know that prices and wages in the Great Depression did fall some. However, if wages do not fall enough, then the intersection of AS and AD_2 at point c is an equilibrium that could persist indefinitely. What we have just described is, of course, the recessionary-gap situation that we looked at in Chapters 7 and 12.

Since Keynes reasoned that sticky wages prevent aggregate supply from shifting to the right and achieving full-employment GDP at point d, then the only way out of such a recessionary trap was for aggregate demand to increase, enabling the economy to return to a. If the combination of fear, uncertainty, high unemployment, and excess plant capacity mean that neither households nor businesses are likely to increase their spending—and if exports do not go up—then the only way to increase aggregate demand is through increased government spending.

In a sense, Keynes put Say's Law on its head by proposing that demand creates its own supply. The engine of change for Keynes was aggregate demand. If people are willing to spend, firms will be happy to produce. Therefore, anything that cuts spending will simply worsen a recession.

FIGURE 13.4   **A Recessionary Gap with Sticky Wages and Prices**

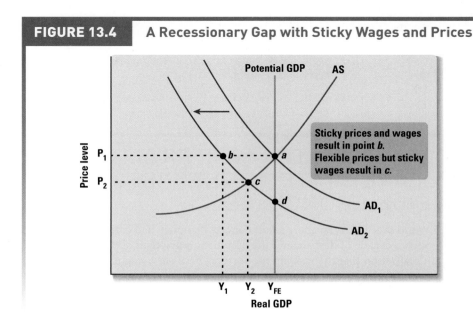

Originally, the economy is at full-employment equilibrium, as illustrated by point *a*. If aggregate demand decreases, then we have a shift from AD_1 to AD_2. If prices remain at (or near) P_1 and wages do not fall much either, then the economy could get stuck at point *b* and income level Y_1. If prices fall to P_2 but wages remain sticky downward, then equilibrium at point *c* and GDP at level Y_2 could become a permanent state of affairs. Point *d* occurs only if wages are completely flexible, which would shift the AS curve to the right.

In other words, instead of cutting back during a recession, people should spend more. Yet, this seemed to go against common sense. It would mean, for instance, that firms working well below capacity and in danger of being forced out of business should start to spend more on investment. Alternatively, it implied that governments should cut tax rates or increase their own level of spending at a time when they were already facing big budget deficits as a result of falling tax revenues. You can see why Keynes was regarded a heretic. He was suggesting that people should spend more when times are bad, and less when times are good. Of course, as we have seen in earlier chapters, there is a lot more to the basic expenditure theory than this, but:

> **Spending and aggregate demand lie at the heart of Keynesian analysis.**

So, how did governments initially react to Keynes' ideas? In most cases, the reaction was negative. It is true that the Canadian government did spend more to provide some limited relief for many of its impoverished citizens. For example, in 1932 government established work camps that were run by military officers under the control of the Department of National Defence. However, this was as much to stem the possibility of violent protests as to aid the unemployed. Wearing army fatigues, those in the work camps, mostly young men, worked on roads, bridges, historic sites, and so on. They received food, clothing, lodging, and 20 cents a day. Needless to say, the camps were not too popular.

There was also some direct relief in the form of money or vouchers, but the amounts were small. In rural Quebec, for instance, a family of five received a food allowance of $3.25 per week. Despite the small amounts, government was often criticized for its generosity. In a 1934 article, for instance, *Maclean's* magazine complained that total spending of all governments—municipal, provincial, and federal—had reached the incredible figure of $1 billion! Despite all this, the Canadian government did not spend a fraction of what would have been needed to pull the economy out of the depression. Furthermore, most governments of the time regarded Keynes as a radical who had dangerous ideas about the economy. The Depression persisted through the 1930s and the validation of his theory had to await the arrival of an event even more traumatic than the Great Depression: World War II.

✓ SELF-TEST

4. Explain why Keynes felt that the level of savings is not affected greatly by changes in interest rates.

5. According to Keynesian theory, will an increase in aggregate demand cause an increase in real GDP, nominal GDP, or both?

13.3 POST–WORLD WAR II: FROM THE WELFARE STATE TO THE RISE OF SUPPLY-SIDE ECONOMICS

 LO3 Understand the evolution of the welfare state and the rise of the supply-side economics.

Canadians entered World War II in a far more sombre mood than they had entered World War I. They had lived through a decade of despair, and the optimistic patriotism of the earlier age had given way to a grim realization that the task ahead, however necessary, might not yield a quick and easy victory.

War meant mobilization on all fronts. The Canadian government, like other governments around the world, suddenly opened the spout, and out flowed massive government spending on

| FIGURE 13.5 | Return to Full Employment |

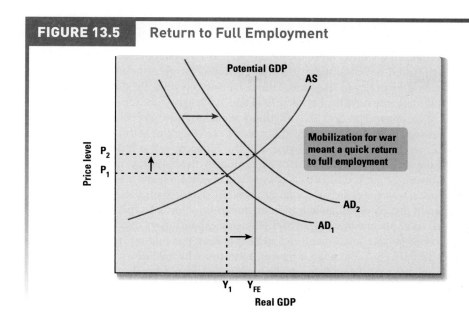

The increased government spending on the war effort greatly increased aggregate demand, as illustrated by the shift of the aggregate demand curve from AD_1 to AD_2. In addition, the price level increased from P_1 to P_2.

military goods, all in the name of defending democracy. Economies responded very quickly to this dramatic increase in aggregate demand. In Canada, the war quickly converted a surplus of labour into a shortage. By 1941, the unemployment rate had fallen from the double-digit rates of the 1930s to 4.1 percent, and by 1944, it was down to 1.2 percent. Factories that had been standing idle for years were now humming, turning out Bren guns, military aircraft, tanks, and ships. GDP grew by double digits—14.1 percent in 1940 and a whopping 18.6 percent by 1942. In addition, as Keynesian theory would suggest, such increases were accompanied by inflation: from the deflation of 0.9 percent in 1939, prices rose by 4 percent in 1940 and 6.3 percent in 1941. This is illustrated in **Figure 13.5**.

The increased aggregate demand resulting from massive military spending is illustrated as a rightward shift in the aggregate demand curve from AD_1 to AD_2. This led to an increase in real GDP from Y_1 to Y_{FE} as well as an increase in the price level from P_1 to P_2.

The depression was over, and massive increases in government spending had ended it. This fact resulted in a growing recognition that Keynes was probably right about how macroeconomy works.

Keynesian Economics in the Postwar Years

Following World War II, there was a widespread sentiment among politicians, a growing number of economists, and a majority of the population that the experience of the Great Depression should never be allowed to happen again. Prime Minister Mackenzie King, who had led Canada in wartime, was re-elected in 1945, partly on the strength of his "New Social Order," which promised social and economic policies designed to prevent a recurrence of the economic woes of the 1930s. The cautious beginnings of Keynesian countercyclical policies, which had started in 1940 with the introduction of an unemployment scheme, were augmented by a system of family allowances that, combined with the Old Age Pension Plan, laid the foundation of the welfare state. In addition, measures were introduced to promote home building, to provide work for demobilized war veterans, and to increase aid to health care.

Such measures were not unique to Canada. In fact, governments around the world passed legislation that could be described as "full-employment acts." It was becoming accepted ideology that governments had a responsibility to actively ensure that the economic goals of full employment and stable prices were maintained. The doctrine of laissez-faire was replaced by the ideology of interventionism, dressed in the clothes of Keynesian economics. This represents a fundamental shift in the perception of government's role in the economy.

For the 25 years following World War II, the ideas of Keynes reigned supreme in most countries in Europe and North America. Economies were now "managed" by governments using counter-cyclical fiscal and monetary policy to "fine-tune" them. During this time, the Canadian economy entered a period of remarkable stability. Between 1945 and 1970, except for four years, the unemployment rate was never above 6 percent and inflation was consistently held below 5 percent. The trick, it seemed, was to steer the ship of state at a steady pace while not getting too close to the banks of inflation or to the reefs of unemployment. If the economy was a little sluggish and in danger of falling into a recession, then a dose of expansionary fiscal and/or monetary injection was called for. If, however, it looked like the economy was overheating and a period of inflation threatened, the solution was a measure of contractionary fiscal and/or monetary policy.

It became apparent that economic stabilization might be even more effective if the two policies operated in tandem. After all, one of the drawbacks of using expansionary fiscal policy is the fact that it crowds out both private investment and net exports by pushing up interest rates. This makes fiscal policy less effective. But what if interest rates could be held down in the face of the increased demand for money? Then the crowding-out effect would be eliminated. And how could this be achieved? Simply by increasing money supply. This combination of fiscal and monetary policies produced a very powerful mixture and was used often in Canada. Occasionally, however, a conflict of policies occurred, as in the late 1950s when government wanted to pursue expansionary fiscal policy, while the Bank of Canada was intent on using contractionary monetary policy. Fortunately, such instances have been rare.

In summary, the quarter century following the end of World War II was a period of comparative prosperity for Canada, in which the size of the public sector grew significantly and people accepted the idea that government policy should be used to stabilize the economy. The growing income levels of this period caused the bad memories of the Great Depression to fade and gave rise to a new generation who were confident that all things could be accomplished and many things should be.

The Rise of Supply-Side Economics

By the early 1970s, the certainties of the postwar era had started to fade. The United States devalued its currency by abandoning a fixed gold price around the same time that its defeat in Vietnam seemed inevitable. The countries that would later be called the Asian Tigers were beginning to challenge established industries in both Canada and the United States. And in Canada, despite strong exports of prairie wheat to the Soviet Union, and British Columbian and Albertan coal to Japan, total exports began to falter. This was also the time when three million baby boomers began entering the labour market.

Then, in 1973, the Organization of Petroleum Exporting Countries (OPEC), dominated by the Arab states and angered by the falling value of the dollars that its members received for their oil and by the West's support of Israel during the Yom Kippur War, decided to reduce its exports of oil. The result was a quadrupling of prices in less than 16 months. The shock was felt around the world. The Liberal government of Pierre Trudeau tried to insulate Canada from this shock by providing subsidies for eastern Canadian oil imports, financed by a special tax on western Canadian oil exports to the United States. This created intense antagonism in the West and seriously intensified regional tensions in Canada.

The main problem facing the Canadian government, as well as other governments around the world, was how to deal with the OPEC-induced stagflation. With the increase in both inflation rates and unemployment rates, Canadian policymakers faced a dilemma they had never experienced before. Unemployment rose from a low of 4.1 percent in 1967 to over 7 percent by the mid-1970s. Worse still, inflation reached double digits and stood at 12.6 percent in 1974. Feeling that the latter was the more serious of the two problems, the Trudeau government introduced wage and price controls in October 1975, whereby the newly created Anti-Inflation Board could roll back price and wage increases it felt were excessive. However, despite the best of intentions, this was a little like trying to control inflation by declaring it illegal!

In another attempt to protect Canadians from the ravages of inflation, government tied the wages it paid, government pensions benefits, and welfare payments to a rising consumer price index. Furthermore, it also indexed tax exemptions to that same price index, which guaranteed that tax revenue would not rise as fast as government spending. These measures laid the groundwork for the huge budget deficits that followed in the late 1970s and 1980s.

We learned in Chapter 12 that trying to cure stagflation through traditional fiscal and monetary policies is impossible. In that same chapter, we looked at the rise of supply-side economics.

Let us quickly summarize that discussion. Supply-siders believe that the Keynesian approach to macroeconomic policy puts far too much emphasis on curing economic problems solely through manipulating aggregate demand, an approach that became known as *demand management*. They go on to argue that the only cure offered by the Keynesian interventionists was to throw more money at the problem. whatever the problem might be. In the period following the OPEC-induced stagflation, these supply-side economists felt that attention must be focused on the underlying malaise crippling North America's economies: falling rates of productivity. Supply-siders argued that it is only through increased productivity that a country can lay the foundation for dealing with both inflation and unemployment.

Like the neoclassicists earlier in the century, supply-side economists believed that the aggregate supply was not simply a passive element that responded to changes in aggregate demand but was itself a prime mover of economic activity. Their diagnosis of the stagflation of the 1970s was straightforward. It was caused by the high price of imported oil and further accentuated by declining productivity rates. Both these factors caused a decrease in aggregate supply. Similarly, they felt that the cure was equally straightforward: an increase in aggregate supply. This is shown in **Figure 13.6**.

An increase in aggregate supply shifts the aggregate supply curve from AS_1 to AS_2. This results in a reduction in the price level from P_1 to P_2 and an increase in GDP from Y_1 to Y_2, which will result in reduced unemployment. Supply-siders believed that modern governments had stifled initiative and productivity through high levels of taxation and government bureaucracy. At different times in the 1980s, this argument caught the attention of a number of governments around the world, including the Brian Mulroney government in Canada, the Ronald Reagan government in the United States, and the Margaret Thatcher government in the United Kingdom.

FIGURE 13.6   **Increasing Aggregate Supply to Fight Stagflation**

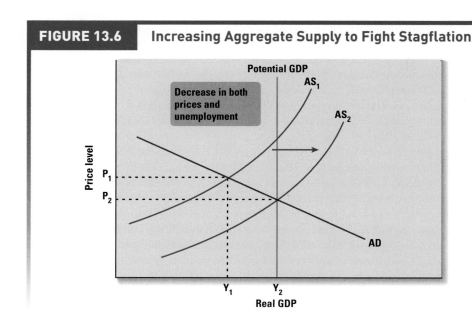

Assume that the economy is at a price level of P_1 and a GDP level of Y_1. An increase in aggregate supply will shift the aggregate supply curve from AS_1 to AS_2. The result will be a lower price level, P_2, as well as a higher level of GDP, Y_2, the latter implying a lower unemployment rate.

In short, advocates of the supply-side position saw the above policies as necessary steps to undo 40 years of interventionist polices that, they believed, had sapped the economy of its vigour and ability to grow, prosper, and adjust to change. In summary, the four major policies of supply-side proponents are:

- the privatization of Crown corporations
- the deregulation of industry
- the contracting-out of government services
- the reduction of tax rates

✓ SELF-TEST

6. Describe what will happen to real GDP, the unemployment rate and the price level as a result of a massive increase in military spending.

7. If fiscal and monetary policy are used in tandem to address a recessionary gap, which of the two is made more effective? Why is this?

13.4 CANADA AT THE TURN OF THE TWENTY-FIRST CENTURY: GOOD TIMES WITH UNCERTAINTY

 L04 Understand the significant economic changes that occurred in Canada and around the world at the end of the twentieth century.

The decade of the 1990s may well go down in history as one of the most significant of the twentieth century. It began with the collapse of the Soviet Union and, with it, the birth of over a dozen new nations—a well-spring of hope and some anxious expectations. This was the time when China began seriously experimenting with the market system, and the world witnessed the enormous success of the Asian Tigers. All of this seemed to clearly say that the market system was likely to reign supreme forever.

For Canada, the decade began with a brief but sharp recession that affected Ontario and Quebec more than it did Western Canada or the Maritimes. Once again, as with the much more serious recession of the early 1980s, some economists felt that this was a recession induced by the very tight monetary policy of the Bank of Canada, which seemed almost obsessed with holding inflation rates below 2 percent. For this reason, then-governor of the Bank of Canada John Crow was not a popular man with many Canadians. One of the first things that a new Liberal government did when it came to power in 1993 was to take advantage of the fact that Crow's first term as governor had just expired and replace him with Gordon Thiessen. Many thought this might signal a new direction for monetary policy. As events transpired, the change of governors did not produce any change in policy, as the Bank of Canada remained fixated on fighting inflation. The anti-inflationary policy was maintained under the tenures of David Dodge (2001–2008) and Mark Carney (2008 to the present).

On the fiscal side of policy, the big issue of the day was the federal government's budget deficits. The federal government had been running budget deficits for nearly twenty years straight, and these deficits were increasing year by year. The reasons for these huge deficits were at least three-fold. First was government's own attempt to shield Canadians from the effects of the inflationary 1970s. Second was unusually high interest rates in the early 1980s, which raised the interest payments on the public debt. Third was the simple fact that government was significantly larger than it had been twenty years earlier. All this led to a growing chorus of political commentators, joined by some economists, who called for reduced deficits, or even balanced budgets, regardless of the costs of achieving this. Then-finance minister Paul Martin responded by instituting massive cuts in federal government transfers to the provinces, in the form of cuts to health and education spending. By the fiscal year 1997–1998, the federal government's budget showed a modest surplus, followed by larger surpluses in the ensuing years.

From Deficit to Surplus and Back ($billion)

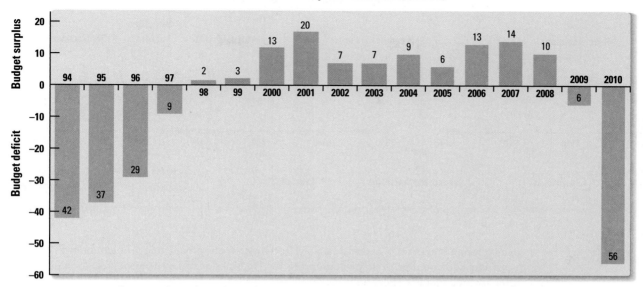

Source: Department of Finance Canada. Annual Financial Report of the Government of Canada, 2009–2010. Reproduced with the permission of the Minister of Public Works and Government Services, 2011

Despite a high level of exports, the Canadian dollar declined in value with respect to the U.S. dollar for most of the decade and fell to historic lows in the early twenty-first century. A long-term downward trend in commodity prices and an economic crisis in Asia certainly contributed to this. Perhaps more significant was the fact that long-term foreign investment into Canada slowed considerably in the mid-to-late 1990s. The reasons for this included political uncertainty about Quebec and a growing international perception that Canada had a restrictive business environment and high taxes. The external value of the loonie began a remarkable turnaround in the first half of 2003 and then experienced a gradual appreciation until it hit par with the American dollar in September 2007. Again, part of the reason for these changes was the fact that the American dollar lost value compared with most currencies in the world, not just the Canadian dollar. But we must also note that Canadian exports remained high and world commodity prices rose substantially. These two forces led to large Balance of Payments surpluses in the Canadian accounts.

The Fall and Rise of the Loonie

One thing that our brief overview of the last 100-plus years shows is that the economic goals that Canadians are concerned with are a reflection of the times they live in and are very much subject to change. At the beginning of the last century, the problems of nation building and economic growth were at centre stage. By the 1920s, there was growing concern that the benefits of economic growth were not always shared equitably among people. The 1930s understandably put full employment at the top of everyone's list of economic goals. The postwar period saw the balancing of the twin goals of full employment and stable prices. In the 1970s, Canadian concerns went in two very different directions. First, there was increasing anxiety about stagflation, and second, there was an increasing worry over resource depletion and environmental degradation. In the 1980s, bigger government deficits and debt became the major issue for many. This worry continued into the 1990s and then faded, to be replaced by alarm over the depreciating Canadian dollar. Then, a quiet kind of optimism settled in, only to be scattered by the financial crisis that we will discuss immediately below.

There is a clear message in all this: what is seen as the most important goal today is unlikely to be as important tomorrow. Problems arise and then get dealt with, only to be replaced with some new problem that attracts people's concern and attention. That is why the study of economic

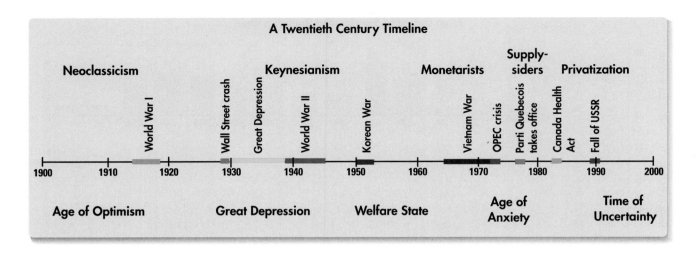

principles must remain broad and flexible. Too much focus on any one problem or any one issue is myopic and could prove to be counterproductive, since a student's perspective for a lifetime is often formed in a few short months.

13.5   THE FINANCIAL CRISIS OF 2007–2010

L05 Understand the cause of the 2007–2010 financial crisis and its economic consequences.

The trigger that caused the financial and economic crisis of 2007–2010 was a bursting of the real-estate-price bubble in the United States. Just how huge this bubble became before the crash can be measured in various ways. For example, between 1997 and 2006, the price of what was defined as a "typical American house" increased by more than 120 percent. Not only that, but during the two decades ending in 2001, the national median home price in the United States was three times the median household income, but by 2006, this had risen to 4.6 times. In short, in just five years the medium price of a house, expressed in terms of the medium income of U.S. households, rose over 50 percent. So, what caused this bubble, and why did it get so big?

A major underlying reason was that in the years preceding the escalation in house prices, interest rates were moderate or low and credit was very easy to obtain. This was because there was a large and steady flow of money into the United States from China and the oil exporting nations of OPEC—particularly Saudi Arabia. These nations were running huge balance of payments surpluses with the United States, returning a significant amount of the dollars that they had earned on their exports to the United States by buying U.S. bonds and T-bills. The result was that the United States became awash in liquidity and the return on things such as savings began a long, steady decline. Standard macroeconomic theory might well have predicted that a general inflation would soon follow. However, the upward pressure on prices became specifically focused on the housing market rather than generally on consumer goods and services.

As the easy credit conditions began to fuel an increase in house prices, existing home owners experienced an increase in their home equity. With interest rates so low, many of these home owners refinanced their houses to take advantage of very low mortgage rates. In addition, as we shall see, it encouraged new prospective home owners to enter the market fearing that prices might rise even further.

Furthermore, the rise in house prices led to a booming house construction market. Jobs were created by this increase in aggregate demand, growth rates were high, the Consumer Price Index reported low inflation (house prices are not part of the index) and the good times extended to a large percentage of the population.

Then, something really quite phenomenal occurred—the idea that house prices could only go up and never fall began to grip the entire nation. We will label this idea Blunder #1, the first of three blunders that we will examine.

Easy credit, low interest rates, good growth, low inflation, rising incomes, and the intoxicating illusion of house prices continuing to rise all led to what the *Economist* magazine came to call "the biggest bubble in history."

Next came some fascinating innovations in the financial securities market that greatly increased investor interest in the housing market. In the late 1990s, a giant pool of money had begun to accumulate in the world and was huge almost beyond belief. In fact, it was estimated that the size of this pool had reached $70 trillion by 2006! Yet, the supply of relatively safe, income-generating investments for this money lagged far behind. Furthermore, the yields on U.S. T-bills were so low that money managers were anxious to find new ways to place the funds they managed. Investment banks on Wall Street answered this demand by creating new types of financial securities known as **derivatives**. They were so named because their value was *derived* from the holding of house mortgages on which home owners made monthly repayments as well as on the house prices themselves. In effect, Wall Street connected the giant pool of money that was floating around the world to the mortgage market in the United States. This created a supply chain of new mortgage money. The players in this new financial security game were the mortgage brokers offering mortgage loans to new home buyers, the small banks that funded the these brokers, and the giant **investment banks** and **hedge funds** that supported the small banks by buying the completed mortgages from the small banks.

The investment banks and hedge funds that promoted these new securities argued that the practice of spreading both the location and the degree of risk of each mortgage across a wide spectrum of thousands of securities reduced the overall risk of default. In the years leading up to the crash, security-credit-rating agencies gave these new securities high marks—what is called a triple-A rating. As a result, these new securities paid a higher rate of return than old-fashioned T-Bills or bank savings accounts. Where money managers now put their clients' money thus came to be a "no-brainer."

There was a point of hesitancy when it appeared the flow of traditional mortgages could not keep pace with the demand created by these new derivatives. This small problem was soon overcome by simply lowering the lending standards necessary for people to take out a new mortgage. Here, one might well ask a question: Weren't the institutions that issued the mortgages regulated by government to ensure that minimal qualification standards for a new mortgage were maintained and thereby the risks of default controlled? The short answer to this question in the United States was: "Not any more." Why not? The answer is simply that most players in the game felt that there was no need for regulation.

As we saw earlier in the chapter, U.S. government policy from the early 1980s on emphasized broad, economy-wide deregulation in the belief that it would lead to long-term increases in business activity and more economic growth. This ideology had been challenged from time to time, especially when the London-based hedge fund Long Term Capital Management (LCTM) began its spectacular failure in the summer of 1998. Enormously successful at first, the managers of this fund had turned an initial $5 billion into $1 trillion and earned annualized returns for its investors of over 40 percent for several years running. Then, in 1998, it lost billions in less than four months following the Russian financial crisis and teetered on the verge of failure, thus becoming a prominent example of the risk potential in the hedge fund industry where derivatives were the security of choice. This led to a massive bailout by other major financial institutions, organized and supervised by the Federal Reserve Board. The fund escaped outright failure but was, nonetheless, closed in early 2000 and became the first-high profile casualty of many that would follow. This experience caused the tide to begin to turn in favour of the regulation of the derivatives market. But Federal Reserve Board Chairman Alan Greenspan argued that the LTCM example was simply an aberration and not likely to be repeated. His view held sway, and the derivatives markets remained unregulated.

This illustrates Blunder #2 in the lead-up to the financial crisis of 2007–2010: an almost blind belief in the ideology that unregulated markets are always preferable to even the most basic forms of government regulation.

derivative: a financial instrument whose value is derived from some other fixed-return asset.

investment bank: a financial institution that assists corporations and governments in raising money by acting as their agent in selling new bonds to the public.

hedge fund: an unregulated investment fund that is open only to a limited range of investors who pay a performance fee to the fund's managers.

sub-prime mortgage:
a mortgage made to a borrower with a low credit rating that carries a higher interest rate than that charged to a conventional borrower.

The next question is: "Just how low did the approval standards go?" The answer here leads us to a term that rose to the surface in 2003—the **sub-prime mortgage**. It is defined as the making of a loan to a borrower who has a lower credit rating than conventional borrowers. The income level, employment history, and credit rating needed to get a mortgage were now "below prime." At the time that the bubble burst, there were 25 million of these sub-prime mortgages in the United States. Furthermore, approximately 80 percent of U.S. mortgages issued to sub-prime borrowers were adjustable-rate mortgages. This means that a very low interest rate was charged the borrower in the first two years of the life of the mortgage, then adjusted to a higher rate for the rest of its life.

Let us take one documented case as an example of what this all means. In California, in 2004, a person with an unconfirmed income of $20 000 (from what was, it turns out, part-time work) was given a $400 000 mortgage with nothing down and an artificially low interest rate that would adjust upward in two years. After two years, the monthly payments on the mortgage would rise from $1000 to nearly $3000. However, the person taking out the mortgage was told not to worry about being able to afford the higher payments because, if necessary, he could always sell the house at a higher price than he paid for it.

This story sounds almost unbelievable, but there seem to be *millions* of similar ones.

Let us pause a moment and do a simple contrast of how people in the United States previously bought houses. In the "old days" of the twentieth century, a family would save for a certain period and then put 20 percent of the purchase price of a house down and get a mortgage for the other 80 percent from the local bank at a fixed interest rate. This same bank would hold the mortgage until it was paid off (it was not uncommon for the bank manager and the borrower to know each other personally). In most cases, the mortgage would be amortized over 20 or 25 years.

Beginning in the twenty-first century, local banks and mortgage brokers started giving sub-prime loans to people who put little or nothing down, whether or not they had any savings or a good credit history. To make the monthly payments even more affordable, the amortization period was often extended to 35 or even 50 years. These mortgages were then sold to one of the investment banks. These banks would bundle thousands of these mortgages into a financial security that would then be sold to buyers all over the world. As we mentioned above, these bonds received a triple-A credit rating and paid a good rate of return.

Then came the final step in this incredible story. A major insurance company began to issue insurance against any possible default on these financial securities. Rather quickly, the business of selling this insurance against default turned out to be bigger than the whole traditional banking industry had been before the turn of the century. Between 2004 and 2007, $2.8 trillion worth of sub-prime mortgages were written and insured, and the same practice spread to credit debt, student loans, and auto loans.

All the building blocks of the biggest financial crisis in history were now in place.

Let us now pause, step back for a moment, and look more closely at the circumstances under which each of the players in this story was operating. The brokers who gave these mortgages were never at any personal risk because they simply earned a commission on the number and dollar volume of loans they wrote. They had no incentive to wonder if the person across the desk could afford to repay the loan. The issuing broker or local bank also assumed no risk because they would sell the mortgage to a big investment bank. These banks would package many individual mortgages into a financial security and sell it to foreign banks, insurance companies, and mutual funds around the world. Thus, they, too, were off the hook in terms of any risk of loss. The agencies that rated the creditworthiness of these financial securities were never at risk and gave them a high rating because they wanted more business from the investment banks packaging the securities. The buyers of these securities would hedge the risk by buying an insurance policy and thus felt that they were off the hook in terms of any significant risk. In short, the inherent risks in all these loads was chopped up, disguised, and passed on so many times that the ultimate holder of the securities had no idea what was going on. And what of the people who originally took out the mortgages? They were told not to worry because they could always sell their new houses later at a higher price, so they too were lulled into believing that they were off the hook in terms of risk.

All this brings us to Blunder #3: no one was expected to take any responsibility for the way in which trillions of dollars were being handled.

What a wonderful world! Easy credit. Poorer people who had never owned a house were now in the market. Enormous commissions were being made at so many levels. The supply of riskless bonds that paid good interest seemed endless.

Common sense told sober minds that this was all a house of cards built on a totally faulty foundation—the most obvious of which was the fact that housing prices could not go up at incredible rates forever. However, the bright young math whizzes from prestigious business schools were confident that the ultimate power of the market was just being realized and that risk aversion had become a simple matter of finding the right formula for the mix of mortgages in the derivative.

The inevitable collapse began in 2007, but it was 2008 that was the really bad year for declines in house prices. Fifteen banks failed, including Washington Mutual (WaMu)—the biggest failure in U.S. history. Later, Congressional investigations revealed that fraud and grossly irresponsible policies were rampant at this bank—and, it appeared, at many others as well. And 2008 was also a bad year for the stock market. By March 6, 2009, the Dow Jones had dropped 54 percent to 6469 from its peak of 14 164 on October 9, 2007. This was the year that mortgage foreclosures reached 2.3 million, with even higher numbers expected in the years to follow. In 2008, over 9 percent of all mortgages were in default or delinquent, and this would grow to over 14 percent in the next year. It was revealed that 80 percent of the mortgages purchased by one of the investment banks for repackaging were "defective" even in terms of their own (not so strict) standards—missing documents, income and employment reports that were never verified, and so forth. A number of "solid" investment banks soon started to go under. Lehman Brothers was liquidated, Bear Sterns went on the block at fire sale prices. Goldman Sachs and Morgan Stanley were forced to become traditional depository banks as the age of investment banking faded.

All this also spread to Europe, where Iceland proved to be the hardest hit—its entire banking system collapsed. The governments of Europe purchased $1.5 trillion worth of bank stocks to keep the banking system afloat.

Perhaps the single-most symbolic event of the post-crash era was that of a pale-faced Alan Greenspan standing before the TV cameras saying that he was wrong about the derivative market being able to regulate itself.

Let us emphasize here that Canada escaped most of the chaos of this period. The reason why is not complicated and is rooted in the fact that the Canadian government's regulations did not allow Canadian banks to make sub-prime loans or use derivatives to try to spread risks.

SELF-TEST

8. What were the three blunders behind the financial crisis in the United States?

From Financial Crisis to Economic Recession

In Chapter 5, we saw that there is a very strong link between the confidence level of businesses and consumers, and the spending plans of those two sectors. This elusive confidence, which Keynes termed "animal high spirits," rapidly faded as a result of the financial crisis. What followed, not surprisingly, was that the industrial nations of Europe and North America fell into recession—either one by one, or in some cases at the same time. By the first quarter of 2008, nine countries of the 34 members of the Office of Economic Cooperation and Development (OECD), including Canada, Ireland, and the United States were experiencing negative growth. By the fourth quarter of that year, all but one member country was in a recession. (The exception, curiously, was the

| TABLE 13.1 | % Quarterly Change in GDP | | | | | | | | | | | | | |
Country	Q1 07	Q2 07	Q3 07	Q4 07	Q1 08	Q2 08	Q3 08	Q4 08	Q1 09	Q2 09	Q3 09	Q4 09	Q1 10	Q2 10	Q3 10
Canada	0.6	0.8	0.6	0.5	−0.2	0	0.1	−0.8	−1.8	−0.7	0.2	1.2	1.4	0.6	0.3
France	0.8	0.5	0.6	0.2	0.5	−0.6	−0.3	−1.5	−1.5	0.2	0.2	0.6	0.2	0.6	0.3
Germany	0.5	0.3	0.7	0.3	1.4	−0.7	−0.5	−2.2	−3.4	0.5	0.7	0.3	0.6	2.3	0.7
Greece	1.9	0.5	0.7	0.7	0.2	0.3	−0.2	−0.4	−1.1	−0.4	−0.7	−1.1	−0.6	−1.7	−1.3
Iceland	0	6.7	3.7	−5.1	1.8	−0.8	2.4	−3.6	−2.4	−0.8	−4.2	−0.3	−2.6	−0.3	1.2
Ireland	5.5	−1.2	−1	3.5	−2.5	−1.9	−0.5	−4.5	−2.5	−0.3	−0.6	−2.3	2.1	−1	0.5
Italy	0.2	0.1	0.2	−0.4	0.4	−0.7	−1.1	−2	−2.9	−0.3	0.4	−0.1	0.4	0.5	0.3
Japan	0.9	0.5	−0.1	0.5	0.3	−0.7	−1.2	−3.1	−5.4	2.7	−0.3	1.4	1.7	0.7	1.1
Spain	0.9	0.8	0.8	0.6	0.5	0	−0.8	−1.1	−1.6	−1.1	−0.3	−0.2	0.1	0.3	0
U.K.	1	0.6	0.5	0.3	0.5	−0.3	−0.9	−2.1	−2.2	−0.8	−0.3	0.5	0.3	1.1	0.7
U.S.	0.2	0.8	0.6	0.7	0.2	0.1	−1	−1.7	−1.2	−0.2	0.4	1.2	0.9	0.4	0.6

Source: Based on data from *Economic Outlook No 87—June 2010* under *OECD Economic Outlook* under *Economic Projections* from OECD.Stat Extracts, http://stats.oecd.org accessed on date, May 3, 2011.

Slovak Republic, which did not suffer negative growth until two quarters later, but was then hit harder than any other country: a drop of 7.6% in a single quarter.) **Table 13.1** gives growth data for some selected countries.

With most countries falling into recession, their policy pronouncements contained a common theme: the desire to ensure that there would be no repeat of the Great Depression of the 1930s. The mechanism to prevent such a recurrence was obvious and straightforward: fiscal stimulus became the agreed-upon panacea. It came as a surprise to many that the name John Maynard Keynes was being bandied about in the corridors of power from Washington to Ottawa to Beijing. Unusually, there was near-consensus among economists as to what should be done, and important figures, such as Joseph Stiglitz, Paul Krugman and Greg Mankiw, were all advocating strong action by central governments. Although expansionary monetary policy was a possible option for some countries, for the majority of countries, this was out of the question, as their interest rates were already at historically low levels. By November of 2008, economists at the International Monetary fund (IMF) and the United Nations (UN), and political leaders, such as U.S. President Barak Obama and British Prime Minister Gordon Brown, were calling for a coordinated international approach to stimulating the world economy through expanded government spending. The UN, in fact, suggested that countries should spend at least 2 percent of their GDP on programs to help kick-start their economies. Following their lead, in February 2009, the United States passed a stimulus bill amounting to almost $800 billion. The Chinese government followed suit with its own fiscal package amounting to $586 billion. Not to be left out, the European Union immediately announced plans to inject 30 billion euros and suggested that member countries should each add 1.2 percent of their GDPs (a total of 170 billion euros) into their own stimulus packages.

Canada put together its own expansionary fiscal program (The Canada Action Plan) in early 2009, and by the end of that year what proved to be the largest (compared with the size of the GDP) increase in government spending among the G20 nations was funding hundreds of new labour intensive projects across the country. This active fiscal policy was very much in keeping with the "Pittsburgh Consensus" reached by the G20 nations' meeting in September 2009, which called for quality job creation through fiscal stimulus.

✓ SELF-TEST

9. Why were most of the stimulus efforts by governments in the 2008–2010 recession focused on fiscal policy rather than on monetary policy?

By June 2010, the OECD reported that as a result of these stimulative policies, there were clear signs that the majority of nations were coming out of recession and recording positive growth rates again. In fact, by the second quarter of 2010, only 6 out of the 34 member nations were still suffering negative growth. The United States and Canada, in fact, had only experienced three consecutive quarters of negative growth, and both were in positive territory by the fourth quarter of 2009. The IMF also credited these stimulus packages with helping nations to rapidly recover. However, they cautioned governments to avoid complacency and not to abandon their expansionary policies too quickly.

There is another aspect of this financial crisis, and the stimulative response that followed, that we need to look at. As early as the summer of 2009, a number of economists and governments had became very concerned about the rising budget deficits that had resulted from the fiscal stimulus packages. In truth, many had been concerned from the outset and were not totally convinced of the effectiveness of the standard Keynesian medicine. What followed was a clear division between the neoclassical school and the Keynesian school—though neither side necessarily used those titles. Interestingly, it was the North American governments that were advocating a continuation of the stimulus packages, whereas most European governments were urging a retrenchment. Their arguments and counter-arguments were nothing more than a rehash of the debate that has simmered (and sometimes raged) in economics for two centuries and that we have tried to keep in focus, not only in this chapter but throughout the text generally.

To clarify some of the issues, let us look at some data. Firstly, it must be said that government budget deficits are an inevitable consequence of recessions: falling GDPs necessarily cause both a drop in tax revenues and a rise in transfer payments (higher Employment Insurance and welfare payments). On top of this, of course, the increased fiscal spending that is part of the recovery package will further increase the deficits. **Table 13.2** gives data for certain selected countries.

TABLE 13.2	% General Government Deficit/Surplus % GDP				
Country	2006	2007	2008	2009	2010 (Estimate)
Canada	1.6	1.6	0.1	−5.1	−3.4
France	−2.3	−2.7	−3.3	−7.6	−7.8
Germany	−1.6	0.2	0	−3.3	−5.4
Greece	−3.8	−5.4	−7.7	−13.5	−8.1
Iceland	6.3	5.4	−13.5	−9.1	−6.4
Ireland	3.0	0.1	−7.3	−14.3	−11.7
Italy	−3.3	−1.5	−2.7	−5.2	−5.2
Japan	−1.6	−2.4	−2.1	−7.2	−7.6
Spain	2.0	1.9	−4.1	−11.2	−9.4
U.K.	−2.7	−2.7	−4.9	−11.3	−11.5
U.S.	−2.2	−2.8	−6.5	−11.0	−10.7

Source: Based on data from *Economic Outlook No 87—June 2010* under *OECD Economic Outlook* under *Economic Projections* from OECD.Stat Extracts, http://stats.oecd.org accessed on date, May 3, 2011.

Perhaps inevitably, the call for "fiscal restraint" came mostly from those countries, such as Ireland and Japan, that had been hit hard by the recession, or other countries, such as Greece, France, and the United Kingdom, that went into the recession with already-sizable deficits. In terms of our look at economic goals in Chapter 1, the clear choice was whether the priority for countries was to "balance the budget and let the economy fall where it may" (the neoclassical position) or "balance the economy and let the budget fall where it may" (the Keynesian position). Europe chose the former, and Canada and the United States chose the latter. (This despite a great deal of pressure in the United States to take action on annual deficits approaching $1.5 trillion—the size of the whole Canadian economy!)

A number of arguments were brought forward to support the idea that the stimulus packages should be abandoned in favour of policy aimed at reducing deficits. It was suggested that the idea of deliberately running up deficits to cure recessions may well have worked during the 1930s (although it was never really tried), but the situation these days is vastly different; at the beginning of the Great Depression, governments did not have huge deficits, and the sizes of their national debts were comparatively small. For example, in 1929, the national debt of the United States was only 16.5 percent of GDP; in 2009, it was just below 100 percent.

A second argument put forward in rejecting Keynesian theory is that it tends to overemphasize government spending; it should instead be focused on aggregate demand. What this means is that expansionary fiscal policy will have little effect if the increased spending is entirely offset by a reduction in consumer and business spending. In other words, it is suggested that the value of the multiplier is far smaller than Keynesians claim. For instance, noted American economist Robert Barro recently suggested that the value of the multiplier is close to zero—far from the 1.5 that he says the American administration assumed when making their budget projections.

Finally—and probably the pivotal point of the neoclassical criticism—is that although fiscal stimulus packages may work in the short term, they may well harm the economy in the long term. Behind this suggestion is the idea that the major target of policy should be to provide a stable framework for growth, and this growth depends on consumer and business confidence. The huge deficits and debts that governments are running threaten to destroy that confidence, and by allowing politicians to "recklessly overspend" citizens begin to lose faith in the legitimacy of the political system.

As a result of these criticisms of the recovery programs a number of European countries reversed course and began to introduce restraint programs—higher taxes and cuts to government services. In the summer of 2010, for instance, the newly formed coalition government in the United Kingdom introduced a series of austerity measures to cut their ballooning deficit. These included a pay freeze on many public sector employees earning more than £21 000 (approximately $34 000), a freeze on child-benefit payments, an increase in the VAT (sales tax) by 2.5 percent (to 20 percent), an increase in the capital gains tax from 18 percent to 28 percent, and, most controversially of all, an increase in the cap on annual student tuition fees from £3000 ($4800) to £9000 ($14 400). Needless to say, these announcements were greeted with protests and demonstrations. In France and Spain, the most vexatious point of the governments' restraint programs was their plan to raise the early retirement age from 60 to 62 years (and the regular retirement age from 65 to 67 years), which caused violent demonstrations on the streets of Paris and Madrid.

If the aim of these restraint programs was to restore the confidence of the people, it is difficult to see how the threat of higher taxes, reduced benefits, and a loss of government services and jobs would exactly do that. (Economist Paul Krugman suggested that the U.K. budget would cost 490 000 jobs in the public sector). Only time will tell whether the North American approach or the European approach will be more successful.

In bringing this chapter, and this textbook, to an end, it is important to remind ourselves that although Keynes certainly did advocated stimulative government spending in the face of a recession, he also advocated the balancing of government budgets *over the life of the business cycle*. This, of course, means running budget surpluses when the economy is in a healthy growth phase. This is something that governments the world over have conveniently ignored all too often.

Review

CHAPTER SUMMARY

This chapter used five significant periods in Canada's history to illustrate the interaction between contemporary events and the development of macroeconomic theory. In the process, it discussed the role of government in a modern capitalist economy. The chapter ended with a brief look into the future.

13.1 At the turn of the last century, Say's Law and the philosophy of laissez-faire prevailed. In the years following World War I, *neoclassicists* were convinced that full-employment equilibrium was automatic because of:
- the flexibility of prices
- the flexibility of interest rates
- the flexibility of wages

13.2 The Great Depression led to the development of *Keynesian economics*, which argued that:
- the economy could get trapped in a long-term depression
- the solution was an increase in aggregate demand

13.3 Keynesian economic policies prevailed in the quarter century following World War II, which proved to be the longest period of relative stability in the macro-economy of the century. Yet, by the early 1970s, stagflation led to the rise of supply-side economics.

13.4 The twenty-year period surrounding the beginning of the twenty-first century saw the Bank of Canada maintain a strict, anti-inflationary monetary policy while the Government's budget shifted from deficits in the first seven years to surpluses in the next eleven and then a return to deficits.

13.5 The collapse of the housing market in the United States in 2008 was a result of unregulated and reckless actions by mortgage brokers, local banks, investment banks, insurance companies and security rating agencies. The result was a serious recession that drove up unemployment rates in the United States, which persisted for several years. Canada's unemployment rate turned back down, after two years of increasing, because of the federal government's expansionary policy.

NEW GLOSSARY TERMS

derivative 435	investment bank 435	sub-prime mortgage 436
hedge fund 435	Say's Law 420	

STUDY TIPS

1. It is important to realize that the different schools of thought examined in this chapter are products of their times: neoclassical theory is rooted in an era of buoyant growth and low unemployment; Keynesian theory was the product of the depression years, when unemployment was, by far, the most serious economic issue; and supply-side economics came into existence when mainstream economics could not offer any clear solutions to the problem of stagflation.

2. It would be a mistake to leave this chapter with the idea that every economist, past or present, belongs exclusively to one or another of these schools of thought. The different schools are starkly delineated here in order to clarify their contrasting viewpoints. In reality, few economists give their total allegiance to any one school.

Practise and learn online with Connect, where you can find the Answered Questions and the Unanswered Problems for all chapters of this textbook's Study Guide section.

3. In a similar vein, the different schools of economic thought are often characterized in political terms, with the Keynesians leaning left on the political spectrum and the other schools leaning to the right. But, as usual, all generalizations can be misleading (including this one). It is possible to be a Keynesian and also to be concerned about the size of the national debt or to be a neoclassicist and still have compassion for the underprivileged, and so on.

4. The final decade of the twentieth century and first few years of the new one illustrate how much can change in a relative short time. The Soviet Union collapsed, the Asian Tigers flexed their economic muscle and China's evolution in to a market economy became apparent. The Canadian government's tendency to run budget deficits was reversed, and the exchange rate bounced around over a wide range. It was this period that clearly illustrates how the economic "issue of the day" can quickly change.

5. The years 2007-2010 will be a historical reference point for a very long time. A financial crisis that was purely human-made shocked many of the world's economies into economic recession. Canada was hurt much less badly than the United States because it continued to regulate its banking industry, whereas the ideology of de-regulation was widely embraced in the United States.

Answered Questions

These questions can also be found online on Connect.

Indicate whether the following statements are true or false:

1. **(LO 1) T or F**   Say's Law suggests that supply creates its own demand.

2. **(LO 1) T or F**   According to neoclassical theory, the aggregate supply curve is horizontal at the prevailing price level.

3. **(LO 1) T or F**   According to neoclassical theory, an increase in the level of saving will cause the rate of interest to fall.

4. **(LO 2) T or F**   According to Keynesian theory, a change in aggregate demand might have little or no effect on the price level.

5. **(LO 1) T or F**   Neoclassical economists believe that market economies can achieve full employment through self-adjustment.

6. **(LO 3) T or F**   Aggregate demand policies are effective in curing the problems of stagflation.

7. **(LO 3) T or F**   The Phillips curve is based on the stable relationship between tax rates and the amount of tax revenue.

8. **(LO 3) T or F**   One of the major criticisms of the supply-side emphasis on using tax cuts to stimulate the economy is that such cuts affect aggregate demand more than aggregate supply.

9. **(LO 5) T or F**   Sub-prime mortgages and derivatives are associated with stagflation.

10. **(LO 4) T or F**   The external value of the Canadian dollar has been remarkably stable for several decades.

Basic (Questions 11–24)

11. **(LO 1)**   Which of the following is a statement of Say's Law?
    a) Demand creates its own supply.
    b) Supply creates its own demand.
    c) The costs of production decrease as output increases.
    d) The costs of production increase as output increases.

12. **(LO 1)**   Which school of thought believed that long-run equilibrium occurs automatically and is the normal state of affairs in a market economy?
    a) Keynesians
    b) Neoclassicists
    c) Supply-siders
    d) Symbolic analysts

13. **(LO 2)**   What do Keynesians believe?
    a) Saving depends on the level of the interest rate.
    b) Saving depends on the level of income.
    c) Investment is stable.
    d) Government policies should be neutral.

14. **(LO 1)**   What ensures the equality of savings and investment, according to neoclassical theory?
    a) Flexible prices
    b) Flexible interest rates
    c) Flexible wages
    d) Say's Law

15. **(LO 2)** When did the Great Depression occur?
    a) At the beginning of the twentieth century
    b) In the seven years following World War I
    c) During the decade of the 1930s
    d) In the five years following World War II

16. **(LO 3)** What characterized the decade of the 1970s in Canada?
    a) Prosperity and strong economic growth
    b) Stagflation
    c) Economic recovery from the 1960s depression
    d) Low unemployment and high inflation

17. **(LO 2)** A major shift in perceptions about the role of government occurred during which of the following periods in history?
    a) Immediately following World War II
    b) In the middle of the Great Depression
    c) Just prior to World War I
    d) In the 1990s

18. **(LO 4)** Which one of the following best describes the federal government's annual budgets for the last twenty years?
    a) There were budget surplus in the early period, then budget deficits for a number of years, followed by two years of surpluses.
    b) There were budget deficits in the early period, then budget surpluses for a number of years, followed by two years of deficits.
    c) There were budget deficits for all of the years.
    d) There were budget surpluses for all of the years.

19. **(LO 2)** According to Keynes, what determines interest rates?
    a) The level of saving
    b) The level of investment
    c) The velocity of money
    d) Both saving and investment
    e) The interaction of the demand and supply of money

20. **(LO 2)** All of the following, except one, are pillars on which neoclassical theory is built. Which is the exception?
    a) The flexibility of production
    b) The validity of Say's Law
    c) The flexibility of prices
    d) The flexibility of interest rates
    e) The flexibility of wages

21. **(LO 3)** According to supply-siders, what is one of the keys to curbing stagflation?
    a) Increasing the money supply and cutting government spending
    b) Using income policies to increase productivity
    c) Shifting the AD curve to the right

d) Convincing people to buy domestic rather than foreign-produced goods
    e) Lowering taxes

Refer to the following five statements to answer questions 22 and 23.

1. Housing prices will always rise.
2. Unregulated markets are preferable to markets that are regulated.
3. The risks inherent in granting sub-prime mortgages can never be hedged.
4. The collapse of Long Term Capital Management's hedge fund was a precursor to the future.
5. No one was responsible for the hundreds of billions of dollars that were being loaned out.

22. **(LO 5)** The chapter identifies three blunders during the several years leading up to the financial crisis of 2007–2010. Which three of these statements reflect those blunders?
    a) 1, 3 and 4
    b) 2, 3, and 5
    c) 1, 2 and 5
    d) 3, 4, and 5

23. **(LO 5)** Which name is most closely associated with the idea that unregulated markets are preferable (statement #2)?
    a) Arthur Laffer
    b) John M. Keynes
    c) Mark Carney
    d) Alan Greenspan

24. **(LO 2)** What characterized the decades of the 1950s and 1960s?
    a) Low growth and high unemployment
    b) Low unemployment and high inflation
    c) Stagflation
    d) Economic stability with reasonably low unemployment and inflation

Intermediate (Questions 25–30)

25. **(LO 1)** Which of the following do neoclassical economists believe?
    a) That, in equilibrium, the leakage of savings from the circular flow would always be matched by an equal amount of investment
    b) That if savings exceed investment, the interest rate will fall
    c) That surplus output would lead to a fall in prices
    d) All of the above

26. **(LO 4)** Which of the following best explains the ups and downs of the Canadian dollar in the last several years?
   a) They are caused by changes in productivity and wage rates within Canada
   b) They are the result of differences in inflation rates in Canada compared to those in the United States
   c) They are the result of changes in commodity prices and long-term investment by Canadians to foreign nations
   d) They are the result of changes in commodity prices and long-term investment by foreigners into Canada

27. **(LO 5)** With which of the following terms are derivatives, hedge funds, sub-prime mortgages, and Fannie Mae all associated?
   a) The Great Depression
   b) The post–World War II economic boom period
   c) The financial crisis of 2007–2010
   d) The stagflation years of the 1970s

28. **(LO 1)** According to neoclassical economists, what would happen if total spending was less than total output?
   a) Product prices would rise, but wage rates would fall.
   b) Product prices would fall, but wage rates would rise.
   c) Nominal GDP would rise, but real GDP would remain constant.
   d) Both product prices and wage rates would fall.
   e) Both product prices and wage rates would rise.

Refer to **Figure 13.7** to answer questions 29 and 30.

29. **(LO 1)** According to neoclassicists, which of the following is true?
   a) The horizontal axes of both graphs A and B show nominal GDP.
   b) It is not possible for an economy to be at Y_2 in graph B.
   c) The shift from AD_3 to AD_4 is caused by an increase in the price level.
   d) Graph A illustrates that changes in aggregate demand have no effect on the price level.
   e) Graph B illustrates a Laffer-curve-type trade-off.

30. **(LO 2)** According to Keynesians, which of the following is true?
   a) The horizontal axes of graphs A and B show nominal GDP.
   b) The shift from AD_3 to AD_4 illustrates what should have happened in the 1930s but did not.
   c) Graph B illustrates a Phillips-curve-type trade-off.
   d) A shift from AD_1 to AD_2 is the result of contractionary fiscal and monetary policy.

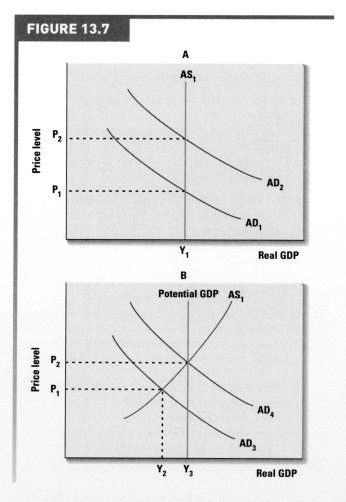

FIGURE 13.7

e) The economy is always automatically at income level Y_1.

Advanced (Questions 31–35)

31. **(LO 1, 2)** What is the essential difference between Keynesian and neoclassical views of macroeconomy?
   a) The Keynesian view is that the economy is capable of automatically adjusting to economic changes because of the flexibility of wages, prices, and interest rates, while the neoclassical view is that the economy could get stuck in a recessionary gap because of their inflexibility.
   b) The neoclassical view is that the economy can automatically adjust to economic changes because of the flexibility of wages, prices, and interest rates, while the Keynesian view is that the economy could get stuck in a recessionary gap because of their inflexibility.

c) While both views agree on the automatic adjustment ability of the economy, the Keynesian view sees wages as flexible, but the neoclassical view does not.
d) While both views agree on the automatic adjustment ability of the economy, the neoclassical view sees wages as flexible, but the Keynesians do not.

32. **(LO 3)** What was the supply-side diagnosis of stagflation?
a) It was triggered by the high price of imported oil and accentuated by declining productivity rates.
b) It was triggered by the stock market crash and accentuated by the high price of imported oil.
c) It was triggered by the stock market crash and accentuated by declining productivity rates.
d) It was triggered by the stock market crash and accentuated by the high price of imported oil.

33. **(LO 5)** All of the following, except one, does not explain why Canada survived the financial crisis so much better than did the United States.
a) Canada's banking regulations limit the amount of risk that Canadian banks could take.

b) Canada's Financial Consumer Agency restricted sub-prime lending.
c) Canadians were generally in favour of regulation of the banking system.
d) House prices in Canada did not increase.

34. **(LO 4)** What would be the most reliable sign that the new economy is a phenomenon of real historical significance?
a) Rising real GDP
b) Falling unemployment
c) Low inflation
d) Rising productivity over a sustained period of time

35. **(LO 1)** How is a historical look at the macroeconomy of Canada beneficial?
a) It assures us that the real issues of the day do not change.
b) It enables us to realize that the views of economists about the issues of the day are very similar over time.
c) It helps us to identify the relationship between economic events and changes in macroeconomic theory.
d) It establishes the unchanging nature of macroeconomic theory.

Parallel Problems

ANSWERED PROBLEMS

36A. **(LO 1, 2, 3)** Key Problem The economy of Copland is in equilibrium but is suffering from a recessionary gap of $10 billion. Its aggregate demand and supply curves are shown in Figure 13.8.
a) Draw in the potential GDP curve, and label it GDP$_1$. Both demand-side and supply-side economists in Copland have been advising government to reduce taxes in order to cure the recession. Independent economic research has determined that for every one percent change in taxes, aggregate demand changes by $20 billion.
b) Assuming that government decides to cut taxes by 6 percent, and that aggregate supply is unaffected, draw in and label the new curve, AD$_2$, in Figure 13.8.
c) At the new equilibrium, by how much have real GDP and the price level changed?
Change in real GDP: (+/−) $ _____
Change in price level: (+/−) _____
Independent economic research has also determined that every 1 percent cut in tax rates in Copland will increase aggregate supply by $5 billion because it stimulates productivity.

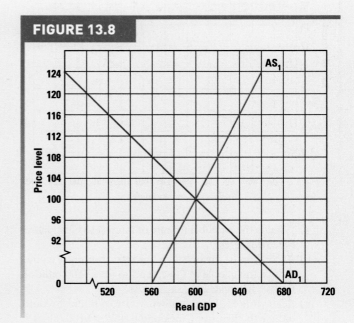
FIGURE 13.8

d) For the same 6-percent cut in taxes, draw in and label the new aggregate supply curve, AS_2 and the new potential GDP curve 2, in **Figure 13.8**.

e) Assuming that aggregate demand did not change, by how much would real GDP and the price level change?
Change in real GDP: (+/−) $ _____
Change in price level: (+/−) _____

f) Assuming that the change in tax rates affects both aggregate demand and aggregate supply, add together the changes in b) and d).
Total change in real GDP: $ _____
Total change in price level: (+/−) _____

g) Is Copland's economy now at full employment? If there is a gap, what type is it, and how much?
Type of gap: _____ of $ _____

Basic (Problems 37A–40A)

37A. **(LO 1)** **Figure 13.9** shows the savings and investment of loanable funds for the highly classical economy of Gluckland.

FIGURE 13.9

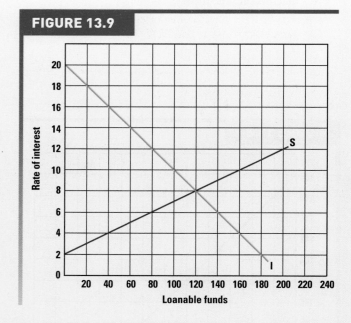

a) What is the equilibrium rate of interest in Gluckland?
Rate of interest: _____ %.

b) According to the graph, what rate of interest would induce the people of Gluckland to save $100 billion?
Rate of interest: _____ %.

c) According to the graph, what rate of interest would induce the firms of Gluckland to invest $100 billion?
Rate of interest: _____ %.

d) What change in savings would reduce the interest rate to 6 percent from its present equilibrium, and how much would savings and investment be as a result?
Change in savings: $ _____ ;
new level of savings/investment $ _____ .

e) Starting at the original equilibrium in **Figure 13.9**, what change in investment would reduce the interest rate to 6 percent, and how much would savings and investment be as a result?
Change in investment: $ _____ ;
new level of savings/investment $ _____ .

38A. **(LO 1, 2, 3)** Match each item in the left-hand column with a related idea or event in the right-hand column by placing a letter in each blank.

A. laissez-faire   1. Keynesians   _____

B. demand management   2. OPEC-induced oil price increases   _____

C. tax cuts as a stimulus to aggregate supply   3. supply-siders   _____

D. stagflation   4. neoclassicists   _____

39A. **(LO 1)** What is Say's Law?

40A. **(LO 1, 4)** In what way were economic conditions in the first decade of the twenty-first century similar to those in the 1920s?

Intermediate (Problems 41A–43A)

41A. **(LO 2)** Assume that **Figure 13.10** refers to the 1930s. Describe in words what actually occurred that enabled the economy to return to full-employment equilibrium.

FIGURE 13.10

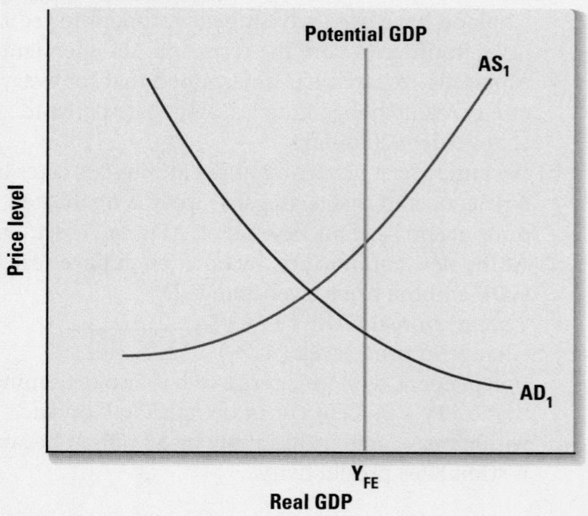

42A. **(LO 5)** Why have many argued that Canada's "Action Plan" of fiscal stimulus in 2009–2010 was a success?

43A. **(LO 1)** Why is unemployment voluntary, according to neoclassical theory?

Advanced (Problems 44A–47A)

44A. **(LO 1, 2)** Figure 13.11 shows the aggregate demand for the economy of Bachland. Its potential GDP is $350. According to neoclassical theory:

a) If the price level is 110, is the economy of Bachland currently in equilibrium? If not, what might happen?

_____

_____ .

b) If, instead, the economy of Bachland were in equilibrium, what would happen to GDP and the price level if aggregate demand were to increase by $50?

_____

_____ .

According to Keynesian theory:

c) If the present price level is 110 and the economy of Bachland is in equilibrium, what is the level of real GDP?

_____

_____ .

d) If the economy of Bachland were in equilibrium at a price of 110 and a GDP of 250, what would happen to GDP and the price level if aggregate demand were to increase by $50?

_____

_____ .

45A. **(LO 2)** If you were a Keynesian, how would you explain the effect of an increase in savings on the economy? What if you were a neoclassicist?

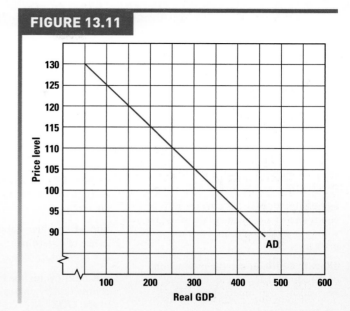

FIGURE 13.11

46A. **(LO 2)** Explain the circumstances in which economic policy might increase real GDP without affecting the price level.

47A. **(LO 2)** How do Keynesians see the economy adjusting to a reduction in aggregate demand?

48A. **(LO 5)** Why was Canada the first of the G20 nations to recover from the recession of 2008–2010?

49A. **(LO 5)** What three arguments were brought forward to support the idea that the stimulus packages of 2009–2010 should be abandoned in favour of policy aimed at reducing deficits?

GLOSSARY

A

aggregate demand: the total quantity of goods and services that consumers, businesses, government, and those living outside the country would buy at various price levels.

aggregate expenditures: total spending in the economy, divided into the four components: C, I, G, and (X–IM).

aggregate supply: the total quantity of goods and services that sellers would be willing and able to produce at various price levels.

allocative efficiency: the production of the combination of products that best satisfies consumers' demands.

arbitrage: the process of buying a commodity in one market where the price is low and immediately selling it in a second market where the price is higher.

asset demand for money: the desire of people to use money as a store of wealth, that is, to hold money as an asset.

assets: the part of a company's balance sheet that represents what it owns or what is owed to it.

automatic stabilizers: provisions of tax laws and government spending programs that automatically take spending out of the economy when it is booming and put spending in when it is slowing down.

autonomous spending (expenditures): the portion of total spending that is independent of the level of income.

B

balanced budget: net tax revenues equal government spending on goods and services.

balanced-budget fiscal policy: the belief that a government's budget should be balanced each budget period.

balance of payments: an accounting of a country's international transactions that involves the payment and receipts of foreign currencies.

balance of trade: the value of a country's export of goods and services less the value of its imports.

bank rate: the rate of interest that the Bank of Canada charges a commercial bank for a loan; the rate of interest payable by the commercial banks on loans from the Bank of Canada.

budget deficit: government spending on goods and services in excess of net tax revenues.

budget surplus: net tax revenue in excess of government spending on goods and services.

business cycle: the expansionary and contractionary phases in the growth rate of real GDP.

C

capital: the human-made resource that is used to produce other products.

capital account: a subcategory of the balance of payments that reflects changes in ownership of assets associated with foreign investment.

ceteris paribus: other things being equal, or other things remaining the same.

change in demand: a change in the quantities demanded at every price, caused by a change in the determinants of demand.

change in supply: a change in the quantities supplied at every price, caused by a change in the determinants of supply.

change in the quantity demanded: the change in quantity that results from a price change. It is illustrated by a movement along a demand curve.

change in the quantity supplied: the change in the amounts that will be produced as a result of a price change. This is shown as a movement along a supply curve.

commodity money: a type of money that can also usefully function as a commodity.

comparative advantage: the advantage that comes from producing something at a lower opportunity cost than others are able to do.

complementary products: products that tend to be purchased jointly and for which demand is therefore related.

consumer goods and services: products that are used by consumers to satisfy their wants and needs.

consumer price index: a measurement of the average level of prices of the goods and services that a typical Canadian family consumes.

consumption: the expenditure by households on goods and services.

consumption function: the relationship between income and consumption.

contractionary monetary policy: a policy in which the amount of money in the economy is decreased and credit becomes harder and more expensive to obtain.

cost-push inflation: inflation caused by an increase in the costs of production or in profit levels, affecting the supply side.

countercyclical fiscal policy: deliberate adjustments in the level of government spending and taxation in order to close recessionary or inflationary gaps.

crowding-out effect: the idea that government borrowing to finance a deficit crowds out private investment because it causes interest rates to rise.

currency appreciation: a rise in the exchange rate of one currency for another.

currency depreciation: the fall in the exchange rate of one currency for another.

currency-exchange controls: government-imposed restrictions limiting the amount of foreign currencies that can be obtained.

current account: a subcategory of the balance of payments that shows the income or expenditures related to exports and imports.

cyclical unemployment: occurs as a result of the recessionary phase of the business cycle.

cyclically balanced budget fiscal policy: the use of countercyclical fiscal policy to balance the budget over the life of the business cycle.

deflation: a decrease in the overall price level.

demand: the quantities that consumers are willing and able to buy per period of time at various prices.

demand deposit: money deposited in a chequing account, which is available on demand.

demand-pull inflation: inflation that occurs when total demand for goods and services exceeds the economy's capacity to produce those goods.

demand schedule: a table showing the various quantities demanded per period of time at different prices.

derivative: a financial instrument whose value is derived from some other fixed-return asset.

devaluation: the refixing by government of an exchange rate at a lower level.

direct investment: the purchase of real assets or of more than 50% of a company's equity.

dirty float: an exchange rate that is not officially fixed by government but is managed by the central bank's ongoing intervention in the market.

discouraged worker: an individual who wants work but is no longer actively seeking it because of the belief that no opportunities exist.

disposable income: the personal after-tax income of households.

dis-saving: spending on consumption in excess of income.

E

economic growth: an increase in an economy's real GDP per capita or an increase in the economy's capacity to produce.

employed: those who are in the labour force and hold paid employment.

enterprise: the human resource that innovates and takes risks.

equation of exchange: a formula that states that the quantity of money times the velocity of money is equal to nominal GDP (price times real GDP).

equilibrium: a state of balance of equal forces.

equilibrium price: the price at which the quantity demanded equals the quantity supplied such that there is neither a surplus nor a shortage.

equilibrium quantity: the quantity that prevails at the equilibrium price.

excess reserves: reserves in excess of what the bank wants to hold as its target reserves.

exchange rate: the rate at which one currency is exchanged for another.

expansionary monetary policy: a policy that aims to increase the amount of money in the economy and make credit cheaper and more easily available.

expenditure equilibrium: the income at which the value of production and aggregate expenditures are equal.

exports: goods and services that are sold to other countries and create an injection into the circular flow of income.

F

factor market: the market for the factors of production.

factors of production: physical or virtual entities that can be used to produce goods and services.

fiat money: anything that is declared as money by government order.

financial intermediaries: financial institutions, such as banks, that act as agents between borrowers and lenders.

fiscal policy: government's approach toward its own spending and taxation.

fixed exchange rate: a currency exchange rate pegged by government and therefore prevented from rising or falling.

flexible exchange rate: a currency exchange rate determined by the market forces of supply and demand and not interfered with by government action.

foreign factor income: income (such as wages, interest, or dividends) that nationals receive from providing their services to another country.

foreign-trade effect: the effect that a change in prices has upon exports and imports.

fractional reserve system: a banking system whereby banks keep only a small fraction of their total deposits on reserve in the form of cash.

frictional unemployment: that part of total unemployment caused by the fact that it takes time for people to find their first job or to move between jobs.

full employment: frictional and structural unemployment exist, but cyclical unemployment is zero.

G

GDP deflator: a measure of the price level of goods included in the GDP, calculated by dividing the nominal GDP by the real GDP and multiplying by 100.

GDP gap: the difference between potential GDP and actual GDP (real or nominal).

government spending: purchases of goods and services by government.

gross domestic product (GDP): the value of all final goods and services produced in an economy in a certain period.

gross investment: the total value of all new capital goods, both replacement and additional capital.

gross national product (GNP): the total market value of all final goods and services produced by the citizens of a country, regardless of the location of production.

hedge fund: an unregulated investment fund that is open only to a limited range of investors who pay a performance fee to the fund's managers.

human capital: the accumulated skills and knowledge of human beings.

I

imports: goods and services that are bought from other countries and constitute a leakage from the circular flow of income.

income: the earnings of factors of production expressed as an amount per period of time.

income effect: the effect that a price change has on real income and therefore on the quantity demanded of a product.

induced spending: the portion of spending that depends on the level of income.

inferior products: products for which demands will decrease as a result of an increase in income and will increase as a result of a decrease in income.

inflation: a persistent rise in the general level of prices.

inflationary gap: the difference between actual real GDP and potential real GDP when the economy is temporarily producing an output above full employment.

injection: any spending flow that is not dependent on the current level of income.

inputs: physical or virtual entities that can be used to produce goods or services.

interest: the payment made and the income received for the use of capital.

interest rate: the annual rate at which payment is made for the use of money (or borrowed funds); a percentage of the borrowed amount.

interest-rate effect: the effect that a change in prices, and therefore interest rates, has upon investment; for example, higher prices cause higher interest rates, which leads to lower investment.

investment: spending on new capital goods.

investment bank: a financial institution that assists corporations and governments in raising money by acting as their agent in selling new bonds to the public.

L

labour: human physical and mental effort that can be used to produce goods and services.

labour force: members of the working-age population, both employed or unemployed.

labour productivity: a measure of the amount of output produced per unit of labour input in a specific period.

Laffer curve: the graphical representation of the idea that in terms of tax revenue there is an optimal tax rate; above or below this rate, tax revenue would be lower.

land: any natural resource that can be used to produce goods and services.

law of increasing costs: as an economy's production level of any particular item increases, its *per-unit* cost of production rises.

leakage: income received within the circular flow that does not flow directly back.

liabilities: the part of a company's balance sheet that represents what it owes.

M

M1: currency in circulation plus demand deposits.

M2: M1 plus all notice and personal term deposits.

M3: M2 plus nonpersonal term deposits known as *certificates of deposit*.

macroeconomic equilibrium: a situation in which aggregate demand equals aggregate supply.

macroeconomics: the study of how the major components of an economy interact; it includes the topics of unemployment, inflation, interest rate policy, and the spending and taxation policies of government.

marginal leakage rate: the ratio of change in leakages that results from a change in income.

marginal propensity to consume: the ratio of the change in consumption corresponding to the change in income.

marginal propensity to expend: the ratio of the change in expenditures that results from a change in income.

marginal propensity to import: the ratio of the change in imports that results from a change in national income.

marginal propensity to save: the ratio of the change in savings corresponding to the change in income.

marginal tax rate: the ratio of the change in taxation that results from a change in income.

market: a mechanism that brings buyers and sellers together and assists them in negotiating the exchange of products.

market demand: the total demand for a product by all consumers.

market supply: the total supply of a product offered by all producers.

medium of exchange: something that is accepted as payment for goods and services.

microeconomics: the study of the outcomes of decisions by people and firms; it focuses on the supply and demand of goods, the costs of production, and market structures.

monetarism: an economic school of thought that believes that cyclical fluctuations of GDP and inflation are usually caused by changes in money supply.

monetary policy: policy designed to change the money supply, credit availability, and interest rates.

monetizing the debt: when government borrows from the central bank to finance increased spending.

money: any medium of exchange that is widely accepted; anything that is widely accepted as a medium of exchange and therefore can be used to buy goods or to settle debts.

money multiplier: the increase in total deposits that would occur in the whole banking system as a result of a new deposit in a single bank.

multiplier: the effect on income of a change in autonomous spending, such as I, G, X, or autonomous C.

N

national debt: the sum of the federal government's budget deficits less surpluses.

national income equilibrium: that level of income where total leakages from the circular flow equal total injections.

national income (Y): total earnings of all the factors of production in a certain period.

natural rate of unemployment: the unemployment rate at full employment.

near-banks: financial institutions, such as credit unions or trust companies, that share many of the functions of commercial banks but are not defined as banks under the *Bank Act* (they are also known as *nonbank financial intermediaries*).

net domestic income: incomes earned in Canada (equals the sum of wages, profits, interest, farm, and self-employed income).

net exports: total exports minus total imports of goods and services which can be written as (X–IM) or as X_N.

net investment: the addition to the capital stock during a year (equals gross investment less depreciation).

net national product (NNP): gross national product less capital consumption (or depreciation).

net tax revenue: total tax revenues minus government transfer payments; total tax revenue received by government less transfer payments.

net worth: the total assets less total liabilities of a company (also called *equity*).

nominal GDP: the value of GDP in terms of prices prevailing at the time of measurement.

nominal income: the present dollar value of a person's income.

nominal wage: the present day value of a current wage.

normal products: products for which demand will increase as a result of an increase in income and will decrease as a result of a decrease in income.

normative statement: a statement of opinion or belief that cannot be verified.

notice deposit: money deposited in a savings account which is available only after notice is given.

O

official settlements account: a subcategory of the balance of payments that shows the change in a country's official foreign exchange reserves.

Okun's law: the observation that for every 1 percent of cyclical unemployment, an economy's GDP would be 2.5 percent below its potential.

open-market operations: the buying and selling of securities by the Bank of Canada in the open (to the public) market.

opportunity cost: the value of the next-best alternative that is given up as a result of making a particular choice.

output costs: (of inflation) costs of loss of output resulting from inflation.

overnight interest rate: the interest rate that commercial banks charge one another on overnight loans.

P

participation rate: the percentage of those in the working-age population who are actually in the labour force.

personal income: income paid to individuals before the deduction of personal income taxes.

Phillips curve: a curve that illustrates the inverse relationship between unemployment and inflation rates.

portfolio investment: the purchase of bonds or of shares representing less than 50 percent ownership.

positive statement: a statement of fact that can be verified.

potential GDP: the total amount that an economy is capable of producing when all of its resources are being fully utilized.

procyclical: action by government that tends to push the economy in the same direction that it is leaning in.

product market: the market for consumer goods and services.

production possibilities curve: a graphical representation of the various combinations of maximum output that can be produced from the available resources and technology.

productive efficiency: the production of an output at the lowest possible average cost.

profit: the income received from the activity of enterprise.

protectionism: the economic policy of protecting domestic producers by restricting the importation of foreign products.

portfolio investment: the purchase of shares or bonds representing less than 50 percent ownership.

purchasing power parity theory: a theory suggesting that exchange rates will change so as to equate the purchasing power of each country's currency.

Q

quota: a limit imposed on the production or sale of a product.

R

real-balances effect: the effect that a change in the value of real balances has on consumption spending.

real GDP: the value of GDP measured in terms of prices prevailing in a given base year.

real income: the purchasing power of income; that is, nominal income divided by the price level.

real interest rate: the rate of interest measured in constant dollars.

real wage: the amount of goods and services that an employee can buy for a given amount of nominal wage.

recession: a period when the economy is producing below its potential and has had two consecutive quarters of negative growth.

recessionary gap: the difference between actual real GDP and potential real GDP when the economy is producing below its potential.

redistributive cost: (of inflation) costs that are shifted from one group in society to another group by inflation.

rent: the payment made and the income received for the use of land.

resources (or factors of production or inputs): physical or virtual entities that can be used to produce goods and services.

S

saving: the portion of income that is not spent on consumption.

saving function: the relationship between income and saving.

Say's Law: the proposition that "supply creates its own demand"; that is, production (supply) creates sufficient income and thus spending (demand) to purchase the production (attributed to French economist Jean-Baptiste Say.)

shortage: at the prevailing price, the quantity supplied is smaller than the quantity demanded.

spread: the difference between the rate of interest a bank charges borrowers and the rate it pays savers.

stagflation: the simultaneous occurrence of high inflation and unemployment.

store of wealth: the function of money that allows people to hold and accumulate wealth.

structural unemployment: the part of total unemployment that results from a mismatch in the skills or location between jobs available and people looking for work.

sub-prime mortgage: a mortgage made to a borrower with a low credit rating that carries a higher interest rate than that charged to a conventional borrower.

subsidy: a payment by government for the purpose of increasing some particular activity or increasing the output of a particular good.

substitute products: any products for which demand varies directly with a change in the price of a similar product.

substitution effect: the substitution of one product for another as a result of a change in their relative prices.

supply: the quantities that producers are willing and able to sell per period of time at various prices.

supply schedule: a table showing the various quantities supplied per period of time at different prices.

surplus: at the prevailing price, the quantity demanded is smaller than the quantity supplied.

T

target for the overnight rate: the Bank of Canada's key policy interest rate; it is the midpoint of the Bank's 50-basis-point operating band.

target reserve ratio: the portion of deposits that a bank wants to hold in cash.

tariff: a tax (or duty) levied on imports.

technology: a method of production; the way in which resources are combined to produce goods and services.

terms of trade: the average price of a country's exports compared with the price of its imports.

transactions demand for money: the desire of people to hold money as a medium of exchange, that is, to effect transactions.

transfer payments: one-way transactions in which payment is made by the government, but no good or service flows back in return.

transmission process: the Keynesian view of how changes in money affect (transmit to) the real variables in the economy.

U

unemployed: those who are in the labour force and are actively seeking employment, but do not hold paid employment.

unemployment: the number of persons 15 years old and over who are actively seeking work but are not employed.

unemployment rate: the percentage of those in the labour force who do not hold paid employment.

unit of account: the function of money that allows us to determine easily the relative value of goods.

unplanned investment: the amount of unintended investment by firms in the form of a buildup or rundown of inventories, that is, the difference between production (Y) and aggregate expenditure (AE).

V

value of production: the total receipts of all producers.

velocity of money (or circulation): the number of times per year that the average unit of currency is spent (or turns over) buying final goods or services.

voluntary export restriction (VER): an agreement by an exporting country to restrict the amount of its exports to another country.

W

wages: the payment made and the income received for the use of labour.

wealth effect: the direct effect of a change in wealth on consumption spending.

working-age population: in Canada, the total population, excluding those under 15 years of age, those in the armed forces, and residents of aboriginal reserves or the territories.

INDEX

TOP TEN LISTS

World's Most Visited Countries

Rank	Country	Annual Number of Arrivals (in millions per year)
1	France	74.2
2	United States	54.9
3	Spain	52.2
4	China	50.9
5	Italy	43.2
6	United Kingdom	28.0
7	Turkey	25.5
8	Germany	24.2
9	Malaysia	23.6
10	Mexico	21.5

Source: UN World Tourist Organization June 2010

World's Best-Selling Global Brands

Rank	Brand	Brand Value ($ billions)
1	Coca-Cola (U.S.)	70.5
2	IBM (U.S.)	64.7
3	Microsoft (U.S.)	60.9
4	Google (U.S.)	43.6
5	General Electric (U.S.)	42.8
6	McDonalds (U.S.)	33.6
7	Intel (U.S.)	32.0
8	Nokia (Finland)	29.5
9	Disney (U.S.)	28.7
10	HP (U.S.)	26.9

Source: Interbrand's Annual Rankings, 2010

World's Cleanest Countries

Rank	Country	Environmental Performance Index (EPI)
1	Iceland	93.5
2	Switzerland	89.1
3	Costa Rica	86.4
4	Sweden	86.0
5	Norway	81.1
6	Mauritius	80.6
7	France	78.2
8	Austria	78.1
9	Cuba	78.1
10	Columbia	76.8

Source: Columbia/Yale EPI Index